THE COMPLEAT BASEBALL ADVOCATE 1994

By
David Srinivasan
Douglas Byron
Evan Rentschler
Todd Willoughby

CBPS Publishing, Grass Lake, MI 1994

Copyright 1994 CBPS Publishing

Cover art copyright 1994 by Graphic Concepts Unlimited

First Edition: February 1994
Printed in the United States of America

ISBN #:0-9635768-1-X

Contents

Introduction 1

Player Essays

    Catcher 7

    First Base 21

    Second Base 39

    Third Base 55

    Outfield 85

    Starting Pitchers 131

    Relief Pitchers 185

Team Essays

    AL East 219

    AL Central 240

    AL West 261

    NL East 275

    NL Central 295

    NL West 313

Index 327

Introduction

First off, a quick plug for **STATS, Inc.**

Except for our rating system, every number you read in this book (with noted exceptions) came from STATS. We would personally like to thank Ross Schaufelberger and the crew out in Lincolnwood, Illinois for the fabulous help they've given us over the last two years. These guys produce all manner of books and statistical data for all four major sports in the U.S. But we don't hold that against them as their first love is baseball and they do an incredible job of baseball data gathering and dissemination. For information about any of STATS' great products (or for information on how to join their scoring network), please call them at **1-800-637-8287** or **1-708-676-3322**.

You can also write the STATS gang at:
**STATS, Inc.
7366 N Lincoln Ave.
Lincolnwood IL
60646-1708**

In addition, we'd also like to thank Howard Bossen and the staff of Graphic Concepts Unlimited; Pat Lamb, Kirsten Dahlquist, Jerry Jenkins and everyone at Publishers' Distribution Service; Associate Business Professor Curt Cremeans and Mark Childs of Jackson Community College; Denise Green and the staff at Thomson-Shore Printers; Proofer and occasional idea guru David Weinstock; and all our families and friends who put up with our garbage during the "Advocate Grind" period from September 1993 - January 1994.

Player Ratings for 1994:

The Advocate's player-rating system is all new for 1994. During this past year, I thought about a system that wasn't arbitrary like the '93 Advocate rankings. After looking at the ranking systems in other annuals out there, I'm convinced that we have the best and most easily understood rankings around.

The system is the latest permutation of one I've been playing with for a year. Hopefully it will make sense after reading this section.

I designed the system after making several assumptions.

The first assumption is that half a baseball team's job is to score runs. The other half is to prevent runs through pitching and defense. A team that does a good job of scoring more runs than it allows (through any combination of good pitching, defense and offense) will win. Just picture a system where half the responsibility is the defensive unit's (including the pitcher), and the other half belongs to the nine guys in the batting order.

Our system gives each player a point total for his accomplishments on defense, at bat and on the mound. The basic idea behind the system is that a "perfect player" should get 100 points. It adjusts for the fact that glovemen at key defensive positions (e.g. shortstop and catcher) like Cal Ripken and Ron Karkovice don't ever have Babe Ruth-like offensive seasons because of the physical demands made by the positions they play. It does so by giving them vastly more defensive value (which, by the way, is the way it should be) than positions like left field and first base. In addition, the system cannot be maxed out. It is possible for a player to be worth over 100 points, but it'd be awfully hard, as you'll see.

On offense and pitching, the system adjusts itself depending on how many runs are being scored during the year in question.

A player would earn 100 points for his bat if he had this line during the 1992 season:

AB	H	2B	3B	HR	BB	B.A.	OBP	SL%
600	216	41	11	47	132	.360	.475	.700

Notice how there's no RBI and run-scored totals here? There aren't any in the system.

Runs and RBI are very context oriented. If you put Cecil Fielder in the Marlins' cleanup hole with their poor ability to score runs, he may have only 85-90 RBI because there's no one on base to drive in. But in Tiger Stadium, with table-setters like Tony Phillips, Lou Whitaker and Travis Fryman, he's a potential RBI champ.

Here's a line that's pretty similar to the 100-pointer there.

AB	H	2B	3B	HR	BB	B.A.	OBP	SL%
579	210	40	6	49	109	.363	.464	.706

This season took place a little while ago when offense was easier to come by. It checks in at 88.4 points.

It's Lou Gehrig's 1934 season. If the Iron Horse can't break 100 points, then you know this system is pretty harsh. I haven't done a whole lot of checking, but my bet is that there hasn't been a 100-point season since Babe

Ruth hung up his spikes. Not even Ted Williams or Mickey Mantle could break 100 points.

Enough of that, let's take a thorough look at the system.

First off, three more assumptions.

1) In order for a system to be really accurate, it has to look at a player's season in the context in which he played. A hitter having a great year in a season where pitchers are dominant is more valuable than a player having a comparable season during a hitter's year. E.G., Mark McGwire's 49-homer rookie season should be rated down somewhat because 1987 was one of the greatest offensive seasons in recent memory. It should not be compared directly to a great season in the AL in 1992, where many fewer homers were hit and many fewer runs scored (the league had a 4.46 ERA in 1987, 3.94 in 1992). You also can't compare Barry Bonds' 1993 season directly to the averages of the NL in 1930 (when the Dodgers' 4.03 ERA led the league, Philly had a 6.71 ERA, and six *teams* hit over .300!).

Because each season is unique, you have to figure out the context, i.e. how many runs were being scored during the season in question, and compare the player to that context.

2) All things being equal, there is no real difference between an NL hitter and an AL hitter. It's true that a No. 8 hitter in an NL lineup will sometimes have tons of unintentional walks (which an AL hitter won't get), but it's rare for a No. 8 hitter to be of much value (except for players like Kevin Stocker on the Phillies' power-house roster). The people we're really looking at are guys like Fred McGriff, Derek Bell and Mike Greenwell anyway. What I'm saying is that AL hitters and NL hitters should *usually* be directly compared.

3) Because of this, I can (with some adjustments for expansion, etc.) use the AL averages for run production to examine NL hitters, i.e. AL hitters and NL hitters are comparable ... and a .300 average with 20 HR in the NL is the same as a .300 average with 20 HR in the AL. If you don't believe this, then explain why Fred McGriff performs at the same level in the NL as he did in the AL. His performance is almost identical because the two leagues have extremely similar talent pools and a player of his ability will do great in either league.

OK, I've argued that, why bother to use only AL averages? Well, it's because the lack of a DH in the NL really drives down run production. NL ERAs and runs-scored go down between 0.33 and 0.5 runs per-team per-game compared to the AL every year.

Tony Gwynn doesn't find it any harder to single or homer in the NL than he would in the AL, it's just that Doc Gooden hits in the NL; in the AL, someone like Mickey Tettleton or Julio Franco would hit instead. This is what drives down NL runs-scored: replacing a solid hitter with a guy who hits .140.

We either have to acknowledge this primary difference, or we have to assume that every NL hitter is vastly superior to the AL. Of course, anyone knowledgeable will tell you this is bunk.

In 1992, the NL ERA was 3.50 and the AL was 3.94 (the AL ERA was 12.6 percent higher). In 1993, the NL ERA was 4.04, the AL's was 4.32 (the AL's was 6.9 percent higher).

What happened?

Quite simple: Colorado and Florida. Two major things happened with expansion.

1) The talent pools in both leagues were depleted by expansion (more so in the NL).

2) More importantly, Colorado has the most explosive offensive ballpark the National League has seen since the Phillies played in the Baker Bowl. The league hits over .300 at Mile-High and it turns poor-to-average hitters into stars. If it wasn't for this park, Charlie Hayes and Dante Bichette would have been nothing last year (And no Mr. Galarraga, I'm not forgetting you, you're not exactly Stan Musial either).

So for the 1993 season, I adjusted the NL run-production to account for expansion.

Our system measures how many runs a player created (using Bill James' runs-created method), and determines how many runs he was better than a "replacement-level player" (RLP). An RLP is a guy who's 15 percent below the AL average in runs-created per out.

Runs-created is an extremely accurate formula that determines how many runs a batter put on the board single-handedly. For more info on runs-created, go to your library and check out an old Bill James' *Baseball Abstract* (they were published annually until 1987). These books are eyesight to the blind.

Our system doles out points according to how many runs-created a player was better than an RLP.

Let's take a look at a player, say Ken Griffey, Jr.

In 1993, Junior had 180 hits (H), 359 total bases (TB), 96 walks (W), 17 steals (SB) and 9 caught stealing (CS) in 582 at-bats (AB).

The formula for runs-created is:

$$\frac{(H+W-CS) * (TB + 0.55 * SB)}{AB + W}$$

According to the formula, Junior created 145.1 runs, an incredibly high total (this is Hank Aaron, Willie Mays territory).

To determine runs-created per out, we look at Junior's outs made which is basically his at-bats minus his hits plus his caught stealing.

582 AB - 180 H + 9 CS = 411 outs.

Junior created 145.1 runs and used 411 outs. His RCPO was .353 (145.1/411). Last year, the AL replacement-level runs-created per out was .167 (the AL's RCPO was .192).

Subtract Junior's RCPO from the RLP's. ... .353 - .167 = .186

Multiply by his outs.

.186 * 411 = 76.45.

Basically, Junior was 76.5 runs better than a replacement level player.

According to the Advocate system, a player must be 145 runs better than replacement level to earn 100 offensive points, so we divide Junior's 76.5 runs by 1.45 to get his unadjusted offensive rating of 52.8.

The system may seem a little confusing at first, but when defense and pitching are added to the mix, the Advocate Rating System gives us a sensible and easy-to-understand the valuation of all three elements.

To get a player's TOTAL RATING, we average his offensive ratings for 1992 and 1993, adjust for the park he plays in (which in Colorado's case will cause the player to plummet) and add his defensive points.

We'll talk more about that later, first here's an unadjusted list of the offensive-points leaders from 1993:

1	Barry Bonds	71.7
	John Olerud	66.2
	Frank Thomas	56.1
	Ken Griffey, Jr.	52.8
5	Paul Molitor	42.9
	Andres Galarraga	40.6
	Juan Gonzalez	40.2
	Rafael Palmiero	38.0
	Robby Alomar	37.4
10	Lenny Dykstra	36.5
	Chris Hoiles	35.4
	Gregg Jefferies	34.1
	Rickey Henderson	33.8
	Albert Belle	32.8
15	Mike Piazza	31.8
	John Kruk	31.8
	Mo Vaughn	31.2
	Tony Gwynn	31.0
	Fred McGriff	30.7
20	Jeff Bagwell	30.3
	Tim Salmon	28.4
	Mark Grace	28.2
	Travis Fryman	27.8
	Kenny Lofton	26.6
25	Rick Wilkins	26.5
	Mike Stanley	26.3
	Kevin Mitchell	26.3
	Carlos Baerga	25.8
	Harold Baines	24.9
30	Mike Greenwell	23.9
	Charlie Hayes	23.4
	Tony Phillips	22.9
	Paul O'Neill	22.6
	Tim Raines	21.9
35	Matt Williams	21.9
	Darren Daulton	21.8
	Jay Buhner	21.7
	Mickey Tettleton	21.2
	Robby Thompson	20.8
40	Dave Justice	20.4
	Danny Tartabull	20.4
	Alan Trammell	20.4
	Dante Bichette	20.3
	Jeff Blauser	20.0

You can see that the fact that RBI and runs-scored aren't in the system doesn't affect rankings very much.

Guys like Cecil (who checks in at a respectable, but certainly not awesome 18.5 points) who are solid hitters, but blemish their strengths with one or two flaws (in Fielder's case, he can't hit for average and doesn't hit many doubles or triples), don't get super-high rankings.

Given the fact that Galarraga is really a bum (he'll be smoked when park effects are adjusted for), our list of the top-10 hitters has all the 1993 offensive MVP candidates. It also did a great job of showing who deserved each league's award.

John Olerud was the best offensive player in the AL last year. His Runs+RBI wasn't as good as Molitor's (Olerud had 223 R+RBI, Molitor 232), but for most of the season Olerud hit in the less-desirable five hole, while Molitor hit in the uber-desirable three hole.

What would Olerud have done in Fielder's batting slot in Detroit? We can't really say, but this system equalizes players by looking only at the elements of offense that they themselves control.

My guess is that Olerud would've had more RBI than Cecil and would've had around 150 runs scored. I am sure that Olerud would have improved the Tiger offense by 50-60 runs.

Think about it, Olerud hit .363 with 114 walks and 80 extra-base hits (154.8 runs created). Cecil hit .267 with 90 walks and 53 extra-base hits (97.1 runs created). Not only did Cecil have fewer walks and less power, but he used 421 outs to Olerud's 353. That means that Olerud handed 68 extra outs to the rest of his teammates instead of using them up. If I had to explain the phenomenon of this beautiful young player, I'd say he put 58 more runs on the board than Fielder, and then handed almost three whole games worth of extra chances for his teammates to plate more runs. That, my friends, is the real-world difference between a 66-point superstar and a 19-point guy who bats cleanup for the best run-scoring team on the planet.

People who don't live in Michigan invariably point to Cecil's clutch ability to drive in runs. Well, most people in the Michigan area think ole Cecil went into the tank in the second half of the season. ... that he should have had 160-170 RBI with the number of opportunities he had.

One last bloody point before I bury this argument: Cecil hit .292 with runners in scoring position, Johnny O. hit .371.

Pitching and Defense: You know the old saying, "Pitching and defense wins ballgames." Well, as we've discussed earlier, we've given 50 percent of all value to hitting, 33.33 percent to pitching and 16.67 percent to defense. So how do we do that? Well, it's a bit complicated and I'll give a full explanation in the 1995 edition, but just think of it this way: The values given to pitching and defense are educated guesses. The stuff about offense equaling pitching+defense is quantifiable. It's just that this book is going to be under 400 pages if it takes every fiber in my being to make it so. ... If we were to give you a treatise on this quantification, it would take a good 80+ pages.

Our pitching system basically measures ERA and runs-created by each pitcher and averages the two values (ERA is sort of a clutch-pitching indicator). Since the range of ERAs is much lower than that of runs-created for hitters (think about any pitcher that allowed runs like John Olerud created 'em last year. ... Think he would have gotten 200 innings?). Since no pitcher allows zero runs and no pitcher allows more than 6.5 runs over a full season, there's less variance. In English: a pitcher with a 2.00 ERA is going to be worth a ton, a pitcher with a 5.00 ERA is going to be worth doo-doo, but a hitter who creates seven runs a game (e.g. Paul Molitor) would not be obscenely worse than a hitter who created 10 per game (e.g. John Olerud), even though the run-differential for all players is three runs per game. Basically understand that Greg Maddux's performance in its context was close to being as rare as Barry Bonds' performance in its context. Within the next two years or so, you'll be able to directly compare the value of a pitcher to a hitter using our system.

On defense, what we measure is a player's zone-rating – how often he makes an out when a ball is hit into the area where he fields. STATS keeps track of all this stuff. What we did was assign a run value to each ball not caught and gave each fielder a credit or a debit for his runs-saved (you can see each individual player's defensive runs-saved in the player-ratings pages at the beginning of each position chapter. In all cases, a player gets credit for being 15 percent below league-average at his position. Basically this gives an average player value rather than making him worth exactly zero. Look guys, I'm making it harder than it is. Craig Biggio saved his team 22 runs on defense last year and has created 27 more runs (on average each year) than the NL average from 1992-93. We add 27 to 22 (getting 49) and divide by 1.45 to get his Advocate Player Rating of 33.8 points.

Any questions? Write Doug or myself. I really apologize, guys, but the Winter of 1993-94 has been a heckuva busy time for all of us here at the Advocate. Last year we promised our readers much greater depth in our book. Next year we promise much greater explanations of our methods. We owe you that much. Enjoy the 500-600 more players and the new team essays. They've been a bear to write, but we think you'll enjoy them.

Team Essay stuff: ... The team essays this year are completely new, too. Each essay starts with a discussion of last year's season and continues with a discussion of the team's depth chart for this year (as of early January). Then we take a brief look at the farm team and the management. We add up all the Advocate Rating System values at each position and that gives the total player value which determines the team's value for 1994. Just about everything in the section is self-explanatory. We give letter grades (A-F, plus various arcane grades) for bench, farm, management, etc. A lot of these things are not quantifiable, so they get intuitive and subjective grades.

Any questions? Please write. We'd love to hear from ya.

— David Srinivasan

David Srinivasan
4205 Southport 2A
Okemos MI 48864
(517) 347-0754

Douglas Byron
6455 Birch View
Saginaw MI 48609

CATCHERS – *RANKINGS*

	Player	Total	Avg. Off.	Def. Points
1	Chris Hoiles	44.6	26.0	18.6
2	Darren Daulton	32.5	27.5	5.1
3	Rick Wilkins	31.5	14.7	16.7
4	Mike Macfarlane	24.3	6.3	18.0
5	Ron Karkovice	23.3	-0.2	23.5
6	Chad Kreuter	23.2	7.1	16.2
7	Mike Piazza	21.4	16.4	5.0
8	Ivan Rodriguez	20.9	2.2	18.7
9	Mike Stanley	20.7	16.4	4.3
10	Mickey Tettleton	19.8	21.4	-1.6
11	Dave Valle	19.2	0.6	18.7
12	Kirt Manwaring	16.4	-0.9	17.3
13	Terry Steinbach	14.1	10.0	4.1
14	Don Slaught	12.8	12.4	0.4
15	Scott Hemond	3.7	2.0	1.7
16	Erik Pappas	2.9	-0.1	3.0
17	Joe Oliver	2.7	-2.6	5.3
18	Tom Pagnozzi	2.6	-2.2	4.8
19	Junior Ortiz	2.1	-7.8	9.9
20	Matt Nokes	1.7	1.9	-0.2
21	Eddie Taubensee	-0.9	-1.9	0.9
22	Benny Santiago	-1.0	-5.8	4.8
23	Dave Nilsson	-1.5	-0.4	-1.2
24	Greg Myers	-2.6	-2.3	-0.3
25	Joe Girardi	-2.8	-3.7	0.9

CATCHERS – *PROSPECTS*

Short-range

1. Carlos Delgado
2. Javy Lopez
3. Derek Parks
4. Scott Hatteberg
5. Jason Moler
6. Matt Walbeck
7. Mike Lieberthal
8. Mike Durant
9. Eric Helfand
10. Jorge Fabregas

Long-range

1. Charles Johnson
2. Jorge Posada
3. Marcus Jensen
4. Ryan Luzinski
5. James Bonnici
6. Tom Wilson
7. Mark Skeels

Sleepers

1. Rich Rowland
2. Todd Pratt
3. Randy Knorr
4. Brian Johnson
5. Tim McIntosh

CATCHERS – *ESSAYS*

SANDY ALOMAR — INDIANS

AB	R	H	2B	3B	HR	RBI	BB	K	SB	CS	AVG
215	24	58	7	1	6	32	11	28	3	1	.270

Get this. In March of '93 he strained his back *driving* to spring training. Next year, he'll blow out his rotator cuff clearing his throat. He looks like he's back to where he was in 1990 as a hitter, but we're giving up frail catchers for Lent.

BRAD AUSMUS — PADRES

AAA – Colorado Springs

AB	R	H	2B	3B	HR	RBI	BB	K	SB	CS	AVG
241	31	65	10	4	2	33	27	41	10	6	.270

AB	R	H	2B	3B	HR	RBI	BB	K	SB	CS	AVG
160	18	41	8	1	5	12	6	28	2	0	.256

Ausmus, 25, logged decent stats while splitting time between Colorado Springs and San Diego. The fly in his ointment was a 28/6 K/W ratio. He just doesn't look like a hitter.

The Padres love him, so expect to see lots more of him this year, but don't expect him to be above average with the bat.

DAMON BERRYHILL — ???

AB	R	H	2B	3B	HR	RBI	BB	K	SB	CS	AVG
335	24	82	18	2	8	43	21	64	0	0	.245

He's just not a championship caliber player. He plays adequate defense, but he's a poor hitter. Anyone who watched him during the post-season understands why we call him "Damon Rally-kill."

JAMES BONNICI — MARINERS

A – Riverside

AB	R	H	2B	3B	HR	RBI	BB	K	SB	CS	AVG
375	69	115	21	1	9	58	58	72	0	0	.307

James, 22, will probably start the season in Double-A. The California League is a notorious hitters' league, but Bonnici still doesn't look too bad.

With Dan Wilson and the scrubfest that personifies the Mariner depth chart at catcher, it doesn't take a genius to see there's no Yogi Berra in the pack. Someone has to step forward and claim the job eventually, why not Bonnici?

PAT BORDERS — BLUE JAYS

AB	R	H	2B	3B	HR	RBI	BB	K	SB	CS	AVG
488	38	124	30	0	9	55	20	66	2	2	.254

Borders can handle a pitching staff pretty well and is still one of the best in the league at blocking balls in the dirt. He allowed only six passed balls last season. But, his bat has been slipping the last few years and Carlos Delgado is waiting in the wings. Borders could become a backup sooner than he expected.

DARREN DAULTON — PHILLIES

AB	R	H	2B	3B	HR	RBI	BB	K	SB	CS	AVG
510	90	131	35	4	24	105	117	111	5	0	.257

Darren can't hit lefties. Apart from that, there's little we can tell the average fan that they don't already know. He's a fine player and is the best catcher in the league.

BRIAN DEAK — ???

AAA – Calgary

AB	R	H	2B	3B	HR	RBI	BB	K	SB	CS	AVG
235	43	58	12	0	11	41	41	65	5	1	.247

He's a replacement-level bat who can catch. Brian's 26 years old, so he could move up the food chain a bit, but don't put much faith in him.

CARLOS DELGADO — BLUE JAYS

AA – Knoxville

AB	R	H	2B	3B	HR	RBI	BB	K	SB	CS	AVG
468	91	142	28	0	25	102	102	98	10	3	.303

Doug: Delgado was 16 years old when he signed a contract with the Blue Jays in 1988. He has spent the last four years punishing minor-league pitching, belting 79 home runs.

He's now 22 and will probably spend a good part of the season in Syracuse. It's arguable he doesn't need the extra season in the minors and any more time spent there is only detracting from a brilliant big-league career. But folks, a Griffey, Jr. comes along only once a generation.

If the Toronto player development guys have their heads together in 1995, Carlos will be installed as the starter. And Borders, you ask? He'll be given a dust rag to keep his World Series MVP Trophy polished and a hardy, "thanks-for-being-there" handshake.

Dave: I heartily disagree with the notion that this Puerto Rican beauty should spend most of the season in the minors.

Delgado may not be a gem defensively, but offensively he has nothing to prove. Southern League coaches said Delgado was the best hitter there in 1993. It's inexplicable how Alex Gonzalez won No. 1 prospect honors over him.

Toronto should bring Carlos up and let him earn his rookie salary by smashing AL pitching. He's adequate defensively and with good coaching he could become solid very quickly. This is a kid who improved his BB/K from 59/91 in 1992 to 102/98 in 1993, after all. He's talented, very bright and a hard worker.

This is a kid who's so strong he had a checked-swing, opposite-field homer. The opposing manager had the bat confiscated after the dinger. ... If you look at Delgado's build, you'll realize that the ump should have confiscated Delgado's upper-body instead.

MIKE DURANT — TWINS
AA – Nashville

AB	R	H	2B	3B	HR	RBI	BB	K	SB	CS	AVG
437	58	106	23	1	8	57	44	68	16	4	.243

Mike's one of those rare catchers who's solid behind the plate, has a little line-drive power and good base-stealing speed.

He's 24 and working his way up through the Twins' organization. He still needs a year or two in Triple-A to improve his batting average, though.

JORGE FABREGAS — ANGELS
AA – Midland

AB	R	H	2B	3B	HR	RBI	BB	K	SB	CS	AVG
409	63	118	26	3	6	56	31	60	1	1	.289

STATS, Inc. has him listed at third. ... We don't understand why *Baseball America* and STATS, Inc. can't be in agreement on that (they both get their information from Howe Sportsdata, after all).

Fabregas is 24 and doesn't look like anything special. He superficially looks good, but Midland is a place where bad hitters look decent and decent hitters look great.

The Angels are stacked depth-wise, so look at Jorge as meat until he does a lot better.

JOHN FLAHERTY — RED SOX
AAA – Pawtucket

AB	R	H	2B	3B	HR	RBI	BB	K	SB	CS	AVG
365	29	99	22	0	6	35	26	41	0	2	.271

With Pena gone, it looks like the job will fall to Flaherty. He's got a Karkovice-like arm and can call a good game.

He hasn't done much at the plate, but after Pena he'll look like Ted Williams no matter what he does. He's 26 and his hitting has been improving, but don't expect much more than .250-.260 this year.

JOE GIRARDI — ROCKIES

AB	R	H	2B	3B	HR	RBI	BB	K	SB	CS	AVG
310	35	90	14	5	3	31	24	41	6	6	.290

He went on the DL in early June with a hand injury and didn't make it back until August. It didn't affect his hitting too much – Girardi turned in his best offensive season. The move to the thin air suits him, so barring injury, Girardi could smack 50-60 RBI this year. He's a bad ballplayer, but a good rotisserie draft.

JERRY GOFF — PIRATES
AAA – Buffalo

AB	R	H	2B	3B	HR	RBI	BB	K	SB	CS	AVG
362	52	91	27	3	14	69	55	82	1	1	.251

Goff could get some time spelling Slaught this year for Pittsburgh, but at 30, he's not what you would call a hot prospect.

He has some power and takes a few walks, but he definitely has problems in the field. Hence, he doesn't see it very often.

BRIAN HARPER — ? ? ?

AB	R	H	2B	3B	HR	RBI	BB	K	SB	CS	AVG
530	52	161	26	1	12	73	29	29	1	3	.304

Harper remains a fine grab for his offensive production, but he's a porous backstop. In '93, his 18 passed balls were the most in the AL and his 10 errors and 4.50 catcher's ERA were less than impressive. The Twins agree with this assessment as they didn't meet his free-agent demands.

Regardless, he can still hit. Whether he's worth anything to you or not depends entirely on your fantasy league.

Bill Haselman											Mariners
AB	R	H	2B	3B	HR	RBI	BB	K	SB	CS	AVG.
137	21	35	8	0	5	16	12	19	2	1	.255

Hasselman's a pretty good No. 2 or No. 3 catcher. He wears the gear and actually squats behind the plate, but he's as adept at catching as Yogi Berra is at haiku.

What saves him is his bat. Haselman isn't going to win the batting title, or lead the league in walks, but he can hit a few homers and come in and catch in a pinch.

Scott Hatteberg											Red Sox
AA – New Britain											
AB	R	H	2B	3B	HR	RBI	BB	K	SB	CS	AVG.
227	35	63	10	2	7	28	42	38	1	3	.278

Scott didn't get the ML PT we thought he might, but his bat still looks impressive. He slugged .432 and hit 7 HR in a park that virtually eliminates power from your game. Adjust for park effects and he slugged close to .500.

In addition, he's an excellent fielder and should get the chance to battle Flaherty for the job. The Sox being the Sox, this may not happen, but he's earned the shot nonetheless.

Eric Helfand											Athletics
AA – Huntsville											
AB	R	H	2B	3B	HR	RBI	BB	K	SB	CS	AVG.
302	38	69	15	2	10	48	43	78	1	1	.228

After toiling away in Double-A obscurity for the last two years, Helfand was inexplicably brought up to the bigs. He's 25 and kind of looks like a young Tettleton.

Scott Hemond											Athletics
AB	R	H	2B	3B	HR	RBI	BB	K	SB	CS	AVG.
215	31	55	16	0	6	26	32	55	14	5	.256

Hemond had been hanging around Oakland since 1989 doing almost nothing, and getting paid too much to do it. He showed signs of being a solid hitter in '93. But at 28, it was probably a career year. Still, he's a good backup if he can continue to hit like that.

Carlos Hernandez											Dodgers
AB	R	H	2B	3B	HR	RBI	BB	K	SB	CS	AVG.
99	6	25	5	0	2	7	2	11	0	0	.253

At 27, Hernandez probably won't improve much. He's an adequate backup who's shown modest bat skills and can call a decent game.

Of course he'll find it even more difficult to grow if Mike Piazza continues to blot out the sun as he did in '93.

Kevin Higgins											Padres
AB	R	H	2B	3B	HR	RBI	BB	K	SB	CS	AVG.
181	17	40	4	1	0	13	16	17	0	1	.221

The poop on Higgins is that he has no pop but the potential for major-league plate discipline. Of course, the point may be moot since he's 27 and behind Brad Ausmus.

Chris Hoiles											Orioles
AB	R	H	2B	3B	HR	RBI	BB	K	SB	CS	AVG.
419	80	130	28	0	29	82	69	94	1	1	.310

You can't say enough about Chris in '93, he just went ballistic. He's been improving his numbers season by season and we told you he'd be a great pickup. But his 29 HR and .585 slugging percentage were still surprising.

Hoiles was far and away the most productive catcher in the game last year. Piazza was the only one to come close, but since he was just a rookie, Hoiles gets the current nod for classiest act. Defensively, he's well above average. His biggest weakness was his caught-stealing percentage, but he improved that from 20 percent to an excellent 41 percent between '92 and '93.

Plain and simple, he's the man.

Todd Hundley											Mets
AB	R	H	2B	3B	HR	RBI	BB	K	SB	CS	AVG.
417	40	95	17	2	11	53	23	62	1	1	.228

It was a frustrating season for the young Hundley. He struggled at the plate all season long, his clubhouse was a war zone and he was generally lost in the shadows when Mike Piazza was anointed as the best young catcher in the National League.

We still believe in Hundley. He is honing his skills behind the dish and he can handle a pitching staff. If he would just relax at the plate and work the count a little more, he would hit much better.

Until he starts getting more production out of his trips to the plate though, Hundley will continue to be a platoon catcher.

MARCUS JENSEN — GIANTS
A – Clinton

AB	R	H	2B	3B	HR	RBI	BB	K	SB	CS	AVG.
324	53	85	24	2	11	56	66	98	1	2	.262

He's young, 21, and hungry.

Good power and atypical plate discipline make him very attractive. It's possible that Kirt Manwaring might have company in a couple of seasons.

Of course, we know all about Manwaring's defense, but the kid's got a good rep too. His ETA is somewhere between late 1994 and early 1996.

BRIAN JOHNSON — PADRES
AAA – Las Vegas

AB	R	H	2B	3B	HR	RBI	BB	K	SB	CS	AVG.
416	58	141	35	6	10	71	41	53	0	0	.339

Even though he hit well (very well for a catcher, actually), he's getting too old (26) to be considered a serious prospect. While starter Brad Ausmus doesn't have Johnson's bat, the catcher's job is still Brad's to lose.

CHARLES JOHNSON — MARLINS
A – Kane County

AB	R	H	2B	3B	HR	RBI	BB	K	SB	CS	AVG.
488	74	134	29	5	19	94	62	111	9	1	.275

Johnson, 22, would have been promoted to Double-A last year, but Florida didn't have a Double-A team (they'll get one this year).

Johnson was voted the No. 1 prospect in the Midwest League. He has a powerful throwing arm – he threw out 47 percent of enemy base stealers – and is very smooth in other facets of his defensive game.

He's also shortened his once long and inelegant swing, cutting his strikeouts and allowing him to put together a nice offensive game.

If things go well, look for Johnson to get an audition with Florida by season's end. Santiago's contract ends after this year and the Marlins are hoping that Charles will be their starting catcher in 1995.

RON KARKOVICE — WHITE SOX

AB	R	H	2B	3B	HR	RBI	BB	K	SB	CS	AVG.
403	60	92	17	1	20	54	29	126	2	2	.228

Kark had a feast or famine season in '93.

Given 403 at-bats, he belted 38 extra-base hits. On the other hand, he hit .228 and reached base at a torpid .287 clip, both one point off his career averages. His K/W ratio of 4.35/1 is awful (the AL average was 1.62/1).

His defense continues to be excellent and this combined with his power makes him one of the best catchers in the game.

RANDY KNORR — BLUE JAYS
AAA – Syracuse

AB	R	H	2B	3B	HR	RBI	BB	K	SB	CS	AVG.
228	27	62	13	1	11	27	17	38	1	0	.272

AB	R	H	2B	3B	HR	RBI	BB	K	SB	CS	AVG.
101	11	25	3	2	4	20	9	29	0	0	.248

He's not a bad hitter and could improve if given time. Unfortunately, when Delgado makes it to the show, Knorr will look like he's standing still in comparison.

CHAD KREUTER — TIGERS

AB	R	H	2B	3B	HR	RBI	BB	K	SB	CS	AVG.
374	59	107	23	3	15	51	49	92	2	1	.286

The Tigers began 1993 looking for a way to use Kreuter's defense without losing Mickey Tettleton's bat. This was partly accomplished by moving Mickey all over the field, but Kreuter did a lot to relieve the situation by hitting .431 and slugging .765 in April. After that, the job was his.

Kreuter improved his hitting significantly and played a big part in the Tigers early surge. He's not a Tettleton-type slugger, but he showed line-drive pop and got some walks.

The Tigers like the way he handles pitchers and cuts down basestealers (44 percent CS).

Even with Tettleton out of the way, he'll have to keep hitting to keep the starting job because he's got power-hitting Rich Rowland breathing down his neck.

Chad's a solid player, but it's improbable that he'll become a star. His offensive production probably peaked last year.

TIM LAKER — EXPOS

AB	R	H	2B	3B	HR	RBI	BB	K	SB	CS	AVG.
86	3	17	2	1	0	7	2	16	2	0	.198

Laker needs to take a large step forward, or he'll be nothing. He's decent defensively, but was absolutely blah with the bat at Triple-A Ottawa (.230 with 4 HRs in 204 at-bats).

Laker is still young enough (24) to develop more, but right now, he's got little to offer.

TOM LAMPKIN — ? ? ?

AB	R	H	2B	3B	HR	RBI	BB	K	SB	CS	AVG
162	22	32	8	0	4	25	20	26	7	3	.198

This guy is so miserable with the lumber that he must burst into tears when asked to pick up a bat. His lifetime average is just a tad off the Mendoza line, while his on-base and slugging hug the Belliard line.

Somehow we don't think his catching ability is enough to merit his presence on a major-league roster. The Brewers must agree, since they cut him loose after the season.

MIKE LAVALLIERE — WHITE SOX

AB	R	H	2B	3B	HR	RBI	BB	K	SB	CS	AVG
102	6	26	2	0	0	8	4	14	0	1	.255

He's 33 and still calls a good game. Mike probably won't see many more at-bats in '94 than he did this year. His K/W deteriorated tremendously last year. It could be his greatly lowered playing time. Just as likely: He could be losing it. Avoid him.

MIKE LIEBERTHAL — PHILLIES

AAA – Scranton/Wilkes Barre

AB	R	H	2B	3B	HR	RBI	BB	K	SB	CS	AVG
382	35	100	17	0	7	40	24	32	2	0	.262

At 6-0, 180, he's considered too frail to be a starting catcher in the big leagues. He definitely has the defensive tools, but his bat and physique are holding him back. He didn't have a bad year for a kid in Triple-A, but his stock has fallen so low that he was supplanted by Jason Moler on the Phillies depth chart.

Still, Mike's only 22. He can make great improvements in his game and there is such a thing as a weight room. There's no reason why he can't lift weights and bulk up enough to make the Phills take him seriously again.

DOUG LINDSEY — WHITE SOX

AAA – Scranton/Wilkes Barre

AB	R	H	2B	3B	HR	RBI	BB	K	SB	CS	AVG
121	9	21	4	1	2	7	5	24	0	0	.174

If we didn't know better, we'd say the Sox were stealing all the crappy backup catchers in the majors for themselves. But then, there's the Angels (who have raised this "skill" to art-form levels).

Doug must have a decent arm and call a good game 'cause his bat suggests he's a zero.

JAVY LOPEZ — BRAVES

AAA – Richmond

AB	R	H	2B	3B	HR	RBI	BB	K	SB	CS	AVG
380	56	116	23	2	17	74	12	53	1	6	.305

Dave: On this team, a "steady," non-throwing, non-hitting catcher (you're welcome, Damon and Greg) is as important as a Slim-Fast shake is to John Kruk's girlish figure.

When you realize this and factor in Lopez, a fine bat and glove, rotting on the pine in 1993 for no reason, you can see why the Braves were doomed to lose somewhere down the road. At several positions (centerfield, catcher, and for the first half, third and first), the Braves were subpar.

The Braves had several supremely talented kids who should've been given a chance early. If the Braves had more faith in players like Lopez, who hit .375 in his minuscule playing time, then maybe they would have gotten some RBI out of the catcher slot in the playoffs and made it to the World Series.

The Braves suffered from "Baseball Hubris" in 1993; they made the mistake of believing their own hype. They beat Bonds' Giants and won 104 games, but someone forgot to tell them that any team can win a short series and that it's hard to score if you always have cancer bats at the plate with runners on.

Javy's an All-Star caliber performer and just has to do what he did in the minors, plus take a few more walks, to be a star. The Braves can win 104+ games this year, but we certainly weren't impressed with the way their kids were used in 1993.

RYAN LUZINSKI — DODGERS

A – Yakima

AB	R	H	2B	3B	HR	RBI	BB	K	SB	CS	AVG
237	32	61	10	3	4	46	41	44	6	1	.257

He's considered more of an offensive player than a true catcher at this point. The Dodgers have stressed defense and have even demoted him to make an impression on him. He's a couple of years away, but he's 20 and has a lot of potential.

MIKE MACFARLANE — ROYALS

AB	R	H	2B	3B	HR	RBI	BB	K	SB	CS	AVG
388	55	106	27	0	20	67	40	83	2	5	.273

Despite hitting .293 with runners in scoring position, Macfarlane drove in a mere 39 runs in 269 at-bats in the cleanup spot. Still, he hits very well for a catcher, and would be beneficial to any club. He's 30 now, so he is a good candidate for lower production in 1994.

KIRT MANWARING										GIANTS
AB	R	H	2B	3B	HR	RBI	BB	K	SB	CS	AVG.
432	48	119	15	1	5	49	41	76	1	3	.275

Kirt was a pleasant surprise in his second full season, batting .275 and reaching base at a sturdy .345 clip. For those of you who don't know Mr. Manwaring, these are pretty durn good numbers.

As usual, Kirt's defense was lovely. Consider his offense a bonus. Because he's 28, '93 smells like a career year to us. Expect him to return to Terra Firma.

BRENT MAYNE										ROYALS
AB	R	H	2B	3B	HR	RBI	BB	K	SB	CS	AVG.
205	22	52	9	1	2	22	18	31	3	2	.254

Before we judge Mayne on his offensive ineptitude, consider this: The Royals only gave him 436 at-bats in the minors before making him Macfarlane's backup in '89.

That said, let's judge him on his offensive ineptitude! Seriously, there is a chance Mayne can bring his bat around. Granted, he hasn't shown much in pro ball yet, but he did hit .350 for Cal State Fullerton before he was drafted. It's not fair to say he's washed up at 26 based on a cursory glance at his stat sheet. Give him until the end of this season to prove he doesn't deserve a job.

TIM MCINTOSH										EXPOS
AAA – Ottawa										
AB	R	H	2B	3B	HR	RBI	BB	K	SB	CS	AVG.
106	15	31	7	1	6	21	10	22	1	0	.292

McIntosh, 29, has been bouncing around between the majors and the minors for years now. He still has a good bat, but he's not going to get more than 100-150 at-bats.

JASON MOLER										PHILLIES
A – Clearwater										
AB	R	H	2B	3B	HR	RBI	BB	K	SB	CS	AVG.
350	59	101	17	2	15	64	46	40	5	7	.289

In his first year of pro ball, Moler, 24, managed to displace Mike Lieberthal as the Phillies top catching prospect. No small feat.

He's already a fine hitter and probably could be ready for major-league action by mid-to-late season. The only question is his throwing. He threw out 46 percent of enemy base-runners, but he throws with a strange motion which could spur injury.

Because Lieberthal will start at Triple-A this year, Moler will spend most of 1994 in Double-A. Some scouts eventually see him as a first baseman (because of the combination of his bat and throwing), but we'll wait and see how he shakes out by letting him play.

GREG MYERS										ANGELS
AB	R	H	2B	3B	HR	RBI	BB	K	SB	CS	AVG.
290	27	74	10	0	7	40	17	47	3	3	.255

He could hit somewhat better this year, but the bottom line is that he can't field and he's hard-pressed to hit well.

BOB NATAL										MARLINS
AB	R	H	2B	3B	HR	RBI	BB	K	SB	CS	AVG.
117	3	25	4	1	1	6	6	22	1	0	.214

A solid hitter – he should be much better than he was for Florida last year. He is too old and unestablished (28) to really be considered in the running for a starting job. He's a good candidate for a No. 2 or No. 3 job.

DAVE NILSSON										BREWERS
AB	R	H	2B	3B	HR	RBI	BB	K	SB	CS	AVG.
296	35	76	10	2	7	40	37	36	3	6	.257

Nilsson, 24, showed some serious growth as a player in 1993. Sure the league played at a higher offensive level, but Nilsson displayed greater patience and a better average. In his favor is the dramatic improvement he made after the All-Star break with a .377 on-base and a .404 slugging.

Nilsson has a solid chance to develop into a good hitter, but he needs to jam it in gear to have any chance of becoming the superstar that his minor-league numbers indicated he could become.

MATT NOKES										YANKEES
AB	R	H	2B	3B	HR	RBI	BB	K	SB	CS	AVG.
217	25	54	8	0	10	35	16	31	0	0	.249

Last year was more of the same for Nokes. Here's a quicky chart for your edification:

	1993	Last 5 years
BA	.249	.248
OBP	.303	.302
SLG%	.424	.420

What we expect from Nokes this year is pretty obvious: mediocre average, poor plate skills and modest pop.

That sucking sound you're hearing is Nokes' at-bats being gobbled up by Mike Stanley, the bench catchers and Yankee DH candidates.

CHARLIE O'BRIEN — BRAVES

AB	R	H	2B	3B	HR	RBI	BB	K	SB	CS	AVG.
188	15	48	11	0	4	23	14	14	1	1	.255

Yes, he's still alive. He's doing the same things he's done for the last few years ... not hitting, not scoring and not driving 'em in. He'll play bad ball and teach Javy at the big-league level.

JOE OLIVER — REDS

AB	R	H	2B	3B	HR	RBI	BB	K	SB	CS	AVG.
482	40	115	28	0	14	75	27	91	0	0	.239

Oliver had a really inconsistent year at the plate. As a matter of fact, he's had a really inconsistent career at the plate.

He's a prognosticator's nightmare: when he's hot, he's hot, etc. He does have decent power and is solid defensively, but he'll never lead the charge for your rotisse-pennant.

GREG OLSON — METS

AB	R	H	2B	3B	HR	RBI	BB	K	SB	CS	AVG.
262	23	59	10	0	4	24	29	27	1	0	.225

We look at his release and think he was probably 18 months from professional extinction anyway. He doesn't stay healthy and he's old and creaky. If and when he catches on with another team, he'll be a No. 2 or No. 3 catcher.

JUNIOR ORTIZ — INDIANS

AB	R	H	2B	3B	HR	RBI	BB	K	SB	CS	AVG.
249	19	55	13	0	0	20	11	26	1	0	.221

Ortiz threw out 45 percent of the runners trying to steal on him last season, but that's the only positive thing about his package. One peek at his age, 34, and batting line is enough to tell you to story on Ortiz.

JOHN ORTON — ANGELS

AB	R	H	2B	3B	HR	RBI	BB	K	SB	CS	AVG.
95	5	18	5	0	1	4	7	24	1	2	.189

Rafael Belliard in a chest protector.

JAYHAWK OWENS — ROCKIES

AAA – Colorado Springs

AB	R	H	2B	3B	HR	RBI	BB	K	SB	CS	AVG.
174	24	54	11	3	6	43	21	56	5	3	.310

Owens had a breakthrough season in Colorado Springs last year, hitting .310 and slugging .511. He hadn't shown much before that though. The jury is still out on his hitting. In normal circumstances, his numbers would be massively deflated because of the difference between the PCL and the NL, but he's going to Colorado. On top of that, he fans so much, he makes Rob Deer look like Tony Gwynn.

TOM PAGNOZZI — CARDINALS

AB	R	H	2B	3B	HR	RBI	BB	K	SB	CS	AVG.
330	31	85	15	1	7	41	19	30	1	0	.258

He can't hit anymore and his arm may be gone. Any value he provides is his ability to call and catch pitches.

ERIK PAPPAS — CARDINALS

AB	R	H	2B	3B	HR	RBI	BB	K	SB	CS	AVG.
228	25	63	12	0	1	28	35	35	1	3	.276

Originally Cubs property, they just played him to death in the minors. Pappas has plated 873 games in nine years of bush-league ball.

He should have been called up in '89 after he put up a fantastic season in Double-A Charlotte, but it didn't happen. Pappas, 28, can contribute if the Cardinals are smart enough to use him.

DEREK PARKS — TWINS

AAA – Portland

AB	R	H	2B	3B	HR	RBI	BB	K	SB	CS	AVG.
363	63	113	23	1	17	71	48	57	0	0	.311

Derek, 25, was the Twins' first round pick in 1986 and 1993 was his breakthrough year. Minnesota was a bit sour on him after years of subpar hitting, but that's been turned around.

With Harper gone, Parks will battle ex-Cub prospect Matt Walbeck for the job. They're both unproven hitters coming off good years and both have excellent defensive reputations.

TONY PENA											? ? ?
AB	R	H	2B	3B	HR	RBI	BB	K	SB	CS	AVG.
304	20	55	11	0	4	19	25	46	1	3	.181

Boston had enough of Pena after his "blistering" year at the plate last year ... and who hasn't? He may hang on with a team desperate for defense, but he isn't good at that either.

He likes to slap pitchers in the face after they pitch a good game, presumably because they'll never need to smack him back.

With any luck, he'll spare respectable baseball fans the slap stick and join Madonna's next Girlie Show Tour. ... He should be able to do 150 squat thrusts without being seen.

GENO PETRALLI											RANGERS
AB	R	H	2B	3B	HR	RBI	BB	K	SB	CS	AVG.
133	16	32	5	0	1	13	22	17	2	0	.241

The decline continues. Geno's saving grace was his defense – which could have made him useful as a backup to Rodriguez. That seems to be gone, along with any hope of PT.

MIKE PIAZZA											DODGERS
AB	R	H	2B	3B	HR	RBI	BB	K	SB	CS	AVG.
547	81	174	24	2	35	112	46	86	3	4	.318

The phrase "Wow!" comes to mind when discussing Piazza's season. He set records for Dodger rookies with his homers and RBI and was only one of a handful of NL catchers ever to hit 35+ HR, hit over .300 and drive in 100+ runs in a season.

The glove work currently plays silent partner to his rather raucous offense, but with his work ethic, don't be surprised if he becomes Gold-Glove caliber in a year or two.

After '93, you might think Piazza would develop a bit of the swelled ego. Think again. Early in the season he was quoted as saying, "I've still got a lot to learn and a lot to work on. I think playing catcher keeps you from getting a big head." Yeah. If anything, he taught the position a few lessons.

Mike could continue to hit over .300 as he did this year, but considering his exceptional season; the fact it was an expansion year; and the demands of catching, one has to expect an across the board drop in production. But he's determined to kick your butt any way he can – a very un-Dodger-like quality – and that's half the stuff you need to earn $10 million a year.

JORGE POSADA											YANKEES
A – Prince William											
AB	R	H	2B	3B	HR	RBI	BB	K	SB	CS	AVG.
410	71	106	27	2	17	61	67	90	17	5	.259

Jorge looks like the real deal. He's young, 22, and powerful for his size (6-0, 167). He can draw the walk and he even steals bases.

He got a trial in Double-A Albany at the end of the year and hit well despite a power drought (likely caused by late-season fatigue).

Posada is one of the most complete packages you'll see in a catcher, so go get him.

TODD PRATT											PHILLIES
AB	R	H	2B	3B	HR	RBI	BB	K	SB	CS	AVG.
87	8	25	6	0	5	13	5	19	0	0	.287

The Phillies are terrified of Pratt's glove. He isn't that bad, but his terrific bat is his strong suit.

If Daulton got hurt, Todd could replace his offense with ease. It hasn't been determined if Pratt could perform at this level for a full season, though.

TOM PRINCE											PIRATES
AB	R	H	2B	3B	HR	RBI	BB	K	SB	CS	AVG.
179	14	35	14	0	2	24	13	38	1	1	.196

Prince finally got a chance to post some major league AB's last year, and, true to form, he reeked. But the Bucs have never expected him to hit and neither should you.

He's a defensive specialist who is useful only in giving the real catchers a rest. Unless he spends the off-season in Lourdes, he'll spend this season giving Slaught relief.

JEFF REED											GIANTS
AB	R	H	2B	3B	HR	RBI	BB	K	SB	CS	AVG.
119	10	31	3	0	6	12	16	22	0	1	.261

This Cincinnati cast-off performed admirably as a backup backstop for the Gigantes. While his BA was an average .261, the guy does know how to take a walk and he showed some power.

Reed should be around a few more years and, while he's not much use to fantasy players, Giant fans should be happy their team has a reliable journeyman to spell Manwaring.

IVAN RODRIGUEZ											RANGERS
AB	R	H	2B	3B	HR	RBI	BB	K	SB	CS	AVG.
473	56	129	28	4	10	66	29	70	8	7	.273

Reputation may have helped Young Man Pudge grab his second-consecutive Gold Glove last year. He had more errors and passed balls than we'd like, but he caught 44 percent of his base stealers and he handled the pitchers well.

He picked up his offense to compensate, raising his slugging to .412 and knocking in 66 runs. The weight training clearly helped.

Rodriguez, 22, will own the Gold Glove for years to come – count on it. He's a workhorse and will do nothing but improve at the plate.

RICH ROWLAND											TIGERS
AAA – Toledo											
AB	R	H	2B	3B	HR	RBI	BB	K	SB	CS	AVG.
325	58	87	24	2	21	59	51	72	1	6	.268

Rowland's time has come. He's a 27-year-old slugger who's been languishing in the Tigers' system for too long.

He slugged .548 in Triple-A last year and has all the tools to make it in the majors. He takes his walks, has a good defensive reputation, and wreaks havoc on base stealers (although he also reaps what he sows).

We've been saying that he should get a shot for a couple years now. With Tettleton either gone or occupied elsewhere this year, Rowland should get the chance to backup Kreuter and challenge for the starting spot.

BENITO SANTIAGO											MARLINS
AB	R	H	2B	3B	HR	RBI	BB	K	SB	CS	AVG.
469	49	108	19	6	13	50	37	88	10	7	.230

Plays the percentages like the coach who goes for it on 4th-and-20 in the first quarter.

He doesn't reach base; doesn't hit for that much power; doesn't catch or throw well and can't handle the staff well. He does have a nice earring and drives good fast cars, though.

SCOTT SERVAIS											ASTROS
AB	R	H	2B	3B	HR	RBI	BB	K	SB	CS	AVG.
258	24	63	11	0	11	32	22	45	0	0	.244

Servais bulked up in the weight room in the off-season and added decent power to his previously inept offensive game. He also added mental muscle and doubled his walk total.

He's not even close to Mike Piazza, but he isn't going to be signing off on Damon Berryhill's paychecks either. But he is the perfect right-handed hitting platoon catcher. He hit .297 with a .522 slugging versus lefties.

With the glove, he still wasn't throwing runners out enough, but he's extremely sure-handed and the staff had a 3.28 ERA when he was behind the plate. He's 27, so he could do even better this year.

MARK SKEELS											MARLINS
A – High Desert											
AB	R	H	2B	3B	HR	RBI	BB	K	SB	CS	AVG.
300	48	83	16	4	6	56	69	62	3	1	.277

Skeels is a bit old at 24, but he looks like someone who could easily become a No. 2 catcher behind Johnson in the next year or two. It sure looks like he has a bit of offensive skill; the jury's out on his defense, however.

DON SLAUGHT											PIRATES
AB	R	H	2B	3B	HR	RBI	BB	K	SB	CS	AVG.
377	34	113	19	2	10	55	29	56	2	1	.300

Don's the oldest and most productive of Pittsburgh's aging backstops. He was forced to catch more innings last year after LaValliere's release and he held up well under the strain. Still, he's 35 and can use the rest.

Slaught is the front-runner for the starting role in Pittsburgh – with Goff and Prince providing adequate relief. That said, expect Slaught's ABs to decrease this year.

TIM SPEHR											EXPOS
AB	R	H	2B	3B	HR	RBI	BB	K	SB	CS	AVG.
87	14	20	6	0	2	10	6	20	2	0	.230

Spehr's strength is supposed to be defense, but he hasn't done much with the glove. The man is not a good hitter, but he's somewhat competent against lefties.

He's 27, so he's at his peak.

MIKE STANLEY											YANKEES
AB	R	H	2B	3B	HR	RBI	BB	K	SB	CS	AVG.
423	70	129	17	1	26	84	57	85	1	1	.305

We warned you last year – given enough at-bats – that Stanley could be a very productive hitter. To be perfectly truthful, we never expected him to take us this seriously.

Mike not only hit over .300 for the first

The Compleat Baseball Advocate – 17

time since his 30 at-bat inaugural season, he also belted 26 HRs, over half his career total.

Stanley has a history of brutalizing pitchers when he's ahead in the count. Fourteen of his homers and 43 of his 84 RBI came in the 94 at-bats where he got ahead of the pitcher.

The only thing anchoring him to the planet was his rather average plate discipline. This resulted in a roller-coaster season where he hit .378 with 9 HR and 27 RBIs for July followed immediately by a diabolical August with a .194 BA and a 400-point drop in his slugging.

Because Mike's 31, '93 shouldn't necessarily be held aloft as a litmus test for things to come. He'll probably be expensive in fantasy drafts and you have to adjust accordingly.

TERRY STEINBACH — ATHLETICS

AB	R	H	2B	3B	HR	RBI	BB	K	SB	CS	AVG
389	47	111	19	1	10	43	25	65	3	3	.285

In a year that saw the A's tumble from their usual perch atop the AL West, Steinbach was a rock in an ocean of doubt and discord.

He hit lefties and righties with equal facility and added some pop. He flashed a solid arm and displayed his usual canniness behind the plate.

A reversion to his normal 3/1 K/W ratio from 1992's unprecedented 58/45 left his on-base at a modest .333, and an early exit due to injury marred his season. His hand is recovering well, so he should be strong in '94.

EDDIE TAUBENSEE — ASTROS

AB	R	H	2B	3B	HR	RBI	BB	K	SB	CS	AVG
288	26	72	11	1	9	42	21	44	1	0	.250

Eddie has an adequate glove and last year actually hit righties enough to give the Astros a good platoon combination with Servais. Given his age, 25, he still can improve. His arm is supposed to be ungodly, but we're still waiting to see him gun down even 31 percent of enemy runners.

MICKEY TETTLETON — TIGERS

AB	R	H	2B	3B	HR	RBI	BB	K	SB	CS	AVG
522	79	128	25	4	32	110	109	139	3	7	.245

Tettleton, 33, ceased being a catcher and became a utility slugger early in the season. By May 1, Sparky had penciled him in at first, catcher, left field and right field. None of this seemed to affect his excellent offense.

He's the rare hitter who can hit 30+ HRs, draw 100+ walks and drive in 100+ runs. His .245 average may seem low, but it is more than offset by a .372 OBP.

His ability to produce at several positions has been invaluable to the Tigers and the fans love him. But the club sees him as the sacrifice they have to make for a good pitcher. If the Tigers dump him, they may face a debacle similar to the one the O's wrought when they sent the Mick to Detroit for Jeff M. Robinson.

RON TINGLEY — MARLINS

AB	R	H	2B	3B	HR	RBI	BB	K	SB	CS	AVG
90	7	18	7	0	0	12	9	22	1	2	.200

He *can* throw, he can't call a game and he can't hit. He's just another scrub behind the plate for the Marlins.

CHRIS TURNER — ANGELS

AB	R	H	2B	3B	HR	RBI	BB	K	SB	CS	AVG
75	9	21	5	0	1	13	9	16	1	1	.276

Chris, 25, has a decent rep with the glove and looks like he'll have a good OBP (compared to the Angels' gang of idiots, anyway). The Angels love him and want to platoon him this year. They'll start him full-time in '95.

DAVE VALLE — BOSTON

AB	R	H	2B	3B	HR	RBI	BB	K	SB	CS	AVG
423	48	109	19	0	13	63	48	56	1	0	.258

Last year we erred in saying he was washed up. His K/W ratio really deteriorated in 1992 and other indicators suggested that his career was on the wane. Instead, he had one of his best seasons with the bat and the glove.

The thing is, he's 33; he's had a 10-year-career; and he's been worked pretty hard. Something's gotta give within the next two years ... our guess is that it'll be Dave's body.

MATT WALBECK — TWINS

AAA – Iowa

AB	R	H	2B	3B	HR	RBI	BB	K	SB	CS	AVG
331	31	93	18	2	6	43	18	47	1	2	.281

He's young at 24 and has hit for decent average and power in the minors. He's also solid behind the plate. Matthew Lovick Walbeck looks like he'll compete with Derek Parks for the starting job. They're pretty similar players and it's anyone's guess who'll win.

ERIC WEDGE — ROCKIES

AAA – Colorado Springs

AB	R	H	2B	3B	HR	RBI	BB	K	SB	CS	AVG.
90	17	24	6	0	3	13	16	22	0	0	.267

He seems to have recovered from the elbow surgery that sidelined him for a good chunk of the year. Only time will tell how much he will be affected behind the plate, but from all indications, he doesn't seem to have suffered with the bat (he had a solid season in the AFL).

RICK WILKINS — CUBS

AB	R	H	2B	3B	HR	RBI	BB	K	SB	CS	AVG.
446	78	135	23	1	30	73	50	99	2	1	.303

The Cubs have to be credited with the way they used Wilkins last year. They knew he couldn't hit lefties too well and limited him to just 67 at-bats against them. This was responsible, in large part, to his .303 average.

He shouldn't hit .300 again though, not with a 50/99 W/K ratio. Hey, let's not get too skeptical. He's 27 and with his hitting and knack for throwing out base stealers, he's one of the best in the biz.

DAN WILSON — MARINERS

AAA – Indianapolis

AB	R	H	2B	3B	HR	RBI	BB	K	SB	CS	AVG.
191	18	50	11	1	1	17	19	31	1	0	.262

The baseball gods smiled on Wilson in the off-season and sent him to Seattle. With Valle gone, Dan will get a shot at starting, despite the fact he's never been able to hit a lick.

He's got lots of skills defensively (he can't throw, however), but he's never shown much ability at the plate and doesn't look like he ever will. None of Seattle's other benchers look better, though, and Dan should be able to slide into the vacancy. Talent is no substitute for being in the right place at the right time.

TOM WILSON — YANKEES

A – Greensboro

AB	R	H	2B	3B	HR	RBI	BB	K	SB	CS	AVG.
394	55	98	20	1	10	63	91	112	2	5	.249

He's a little old, 23, to be driving out of A-ball in a Lotus, but he showed some power and plate savvy that might turn some heads.

He doesn't look as explosive as Posada, but he may be a decent player. Posada's still the better prospect by far.

First Base – *Rankings*

	Player	Total	Avg. Off.	Def. Runs Saved
1	Frank Thomas	53.8	57.7	-5.6
2	John Olerud	47.1	41.3	8.3
3	Fred McGriff	38.0	38.0	3.9
4	Jeff Bagwell	36.0	36.9	9.7
5	John Kruk	35.0	35.0	3.4
6	Rafael Palmeiro	34.3	31.0	4.9
7	Mark Grace	30.0	30.0	6.6
8	Mark McGwire	28.5	28.7	-0.3
9	Gregg Jefferies	23.5	23.5	-0.4
10	Will Clark	22.3	22.3	-1.1
11	Don Mattingly	21.1	16.6	6.6
12	Wally Joyner	18.2	11.7	9.4
13	Eddie Murray	15.8	15.8	3.3
14	Mo Vaughn	14.8	14.2	0.8
15	Cecil Fielder	14.6	17.0	-3.4
16	Andres Galarraga	14.6	14.6	1.8
17	Hal Morris	13.5	13.5	3.3
18	Kent Hrbek	12.0	9.6	3.5
19	Jim Leyritz	12.0	10.1	2.8
20	Paul Sorrento	10.4	10.9	-0.8
21	Tino Martinez	9.5	7.4	3.0
22	Randy Milligan	9.5	8.4	1.5
23	Phil Clark	8.8	8.8	2.3
24	Sid Bream	5.3	5.3	1.5
25	Dave Magadan	4.8	4.9	-0.1

First Base – *Prospects*

Short-range	Long-range	Sleepers
1 Clifford Floyd	1 D.J. Boston	1 Dave McCarty
2 Ryan Klesko	2 Ryan McGuire	2 Tino Martinez
3 Roberto Petagine	3 Chris Weinke	3 Tim Costo
4 Dmitri Young	4 Omar Garcia	4 Brain Hunter
5 Rich Aude	5 Brian DuBose	5 J.T. Snow
6 Jamie Dismuke	6 Alan Burke	6 Greg Colbrunn
7 Gene Schall		7 Phil Clark
8 J.R. Phillips		8 Sam Horn
9 Matt Franco		9 Bob Hamelin
10 T.R. Lewis		10 Tim Hyers
11 Marco Armas		11 Alan Zinter
		12 Paul Carey
		13 Drew Denson

First Base – *Essays*

MIKE ALDRETE — ATHLETICS

AB	R	H	2B	3B	HR	RBI	BB	K	SB	CS	AVG.
255	40	68	13	1	10	33	34	45	1	1	.267

Journeyman Aldrete was a pleasant surprise for the A's in the wake of Mark McGwire's season-ending injury.

Aldrete, who at 33 is unlikely to catch on with a team for 255 at-bats, used his time well. He displayed his customarily solid K/W ratio and slugged 24 extra-base hits in his tenure (10 of them homers).

The power was very unexpected seein' as how Aldrete only has 27 homers in a seven year career. Not unexpected was his inability to hit lefties.

Even pending McGwire's full recovery in '94, the A's would be wise to hang onto Aldrete. While the electric company is likely to cut-off his power in '94, Aldrete should scatter some hits and play utility defense between first and left field.

MARCOS ARMAS — ATHLETICS

AAA – Tacoma

AB	R	H	2B	3B	HR	RBI	BB	K	SB	CS	AVG.
434	69	126	27	8	15	89	35	113	4	0	.290

Armas showed that Double-A Huntsville was no fluke by duplicating in Triple-A Tacoma what he'd done the year before.

His power remained intact and his batting average was a solid .290. While he stole fewer bases in Tacoma, he did up his triples to eight.

On the flipside, he showed no improvement in his ability to draw the walk. Excellent numbers notwithstanding, this may have been what kept him locked in Triple-A and earned him only a 15-game stint in Oakland.

Armas was designated for minor league assignment over the winter, but look for him in the spring. At 25, he's ready to earn a job.

RICH AUDE — PIRATES

AA – Carolina

AB	R	H	2B	3B	HR	RBI	BB	K	SB	CS	AVG.
422	66	122	25	3	18	73	50	79	8	4	.289

Aude, 22, wasn't highly regarded by the Pirates prior to '93, so he went gonzo on a weight-training program and had an impressive year at the plate. Last year, he slugged .491, over 100 points higher than the Southern League average. In addition, his plate discipline improved tremendously.

He's three years younger than current Pirate first baseman Kevin Young and is at least his equal as a hitter. Rich's problem is that he has a weak defensive reputation, so the Bucs must decide which way they want to go.

Of course, a good glove at first is like a toothpick on your Swiss Army knife: Both have their uses, but who the heck knows when they'll come in handy?

JEFF BAGWELL — ASTROS

AB	R	H	2B	3B	HR	RBI	BB	K	SB	CS	AVG.
535	76	171	37	4	20	88	62	73	13	4	.320

Mr. Bagwell pushed his game up a significant notch in '94. In 1992, he hit .263 against right-handed pitching. In 1993, he pushed the average up to .320 versus righties, the same as his overall average.

According to *Baseball Weekly*, Bagwell used to spend all his spare time watching good hitters on ESPN games and copying their stances. He stopped doing that and he feels that contributed to his success.

It is well-nigh impossible to overstate how hard it is to hit like Bagwell does, given the fact he eats his home cookin' at the 'Dome. If it wasn't for a broken pinky, courtesy of Ben Rivera's wild fastball, Bagwell would have had an excellent shot at 100 RBI.

In addition to his bat, his defense continues to be brilliant. In short, Bagwell is a renaissance first baseman, as adept at squelching rallies with his glove as he as at igniting them with the lumber. He is definitely on the short list of 1994 MVP candidates.

DON BARBARA — BREWERS

AAA – New Orleans

AB	R	H	2B	3B	HR	RBI	BB	K	SB	CS	AVG.
255	34	75	10	1	4	38	42	38	1	3	.294

Barbara, 25, is three years younger than Jaha but he lacks the power of the older man. Excellent plate discipline is nice, but you've got to slug if you're going to play the corners.

Barbara could play a backup role, but he won't see much playing time.

SKEETER BARNES											TIGERS
AB	R	H	2B	3B	HR	RBI	BB	K	SB	CS	AVG.
160	24	45	8	1	2	27	11	19	5	5	.281

Barnes is one of several Tiger fielders who can be listed at almost any position. He's got a dependable glove and can fill in wherever needed. He's primarily becoming a good pinch-hit specialist, however.

He provided several key hits for the Tigers and batted .315 with runners in scoring position (STATS, Inc.).

Skeeter's a good role player, but at 37, he'll never be more than that.

TODD BENZINGER											GIANTS
AB	R	H	2B	3B	HR	RBI	BB	K	SB	CS	AVG.
177	25	51	7	2	6	26	13	35	0	0	.288

Benzinger did fine filling in between Gold-Glove appearances by teammate Will Clark.

His history is one of unexceptional consistency. He doesn't hit better in any given month, which makes him a valuable utility-man year round.

Todd seems to be the kind of player who thrives on being a back-up, no matter what he says to the contrary. His best seasons are the ones where he's logged around 200 at-bats. Nonetheless, it looks like he's the only one around to fill McGriff's shoes and the starting job will be his this year, pending miraculous strides by shaky prospect J.R. Phillips

Evan: My two enduring memories of Benzinger are his making the final out in game four of the 1990 World Series and his crying two months into '91 about the Reds letting him go in favor of the younger and better-hitting Hal Morris.

At 31, Benzie had better reconcile himself to the fact that his passion to play can't make him more than second fiddle to a Stradivarius.

FRANK BOLICK											EXPOS
AB	R	H	2B	3B	HR	RBI	BB	K	SB	CS	AVG.
213	25	45	13	0	4	24	23	37	1	0	.211

Bolick came to the Expos from the Mariners organization with a reputation as an extremely solid hitter who could play first and third. ... In 1993, he managed to undo that reputation, while his rival, Sean Berry, put up some impressive numbers.

Frank really is a pretty good hitter and he could do much better, but it's not like there's much competition for a job in Montreal: there's only Cliff Floyd, Oreste Marerro, John VanderWal and Sean Berry to name a few.

Frank needs to do some real damage in the Spring to get a decent job. He certainly is capable, but he's also quite capable of being lost in the shuffle.

D.J. BOSTON											BLUE JAYS
A – Hagerstown											
AB	R	H	2B	3B	HR	RBI	BB	K	SB	CS	AVG.
464	76	146	35	4	13	92	54	77	31	11	.315

Daryl's brother was named the fifth-best prospect in the Sally League last year and looks to have a bright future ahead of him. The 6-foot-7 first baseman hit .315 with a .489 slugging average and 31 steals for Hagerstown. He's only 22 and he's got the goods.

Although the Blue Jays are well stocked with first base prospects and Joe Carter is about as displaceable as the Queen Elizabeth II, Boston has enough potential to crack someone's lineup in two or three years. D.J. is one to watch.

SID BREAM											ASTROS
AB	R	H	2B	3B	HR	RBI	BB	K	SB	CS	AVG.
277	33	72	14	1	9	35	31	43	4	2	.260

Bream isn't a bad player, but he's just about done. He can still work a pitcher for the walk, or beat you with a single or the occasional dinger, but he's fighting the best young first baseman in the league in Jeff Bagwell – and one of the best hitting prospects in the league in Roberto Petagine. He's just a backup and that's it.

ROD BREWER											CARDINALS
AB	R	H	2B	3B	HR	RBI	BB	K	SB	CS	AVG.
147	15	42	8	0	2	20	17	26	1	0	.286

He could hit 15 homers if he had a full-time job, but at the ripe old age of 28, that's about as big a deal as one of those drive-through death-burger value meals. On the positive side, he has shown some knowledge of the strike zone. Unless he undergoes a position change though, he'll probably be a bench warmer in '94. There are worse utility men in the league.

RICO BROGNA											TIGERS

AAA – Toledo

AB	R	H	2B	3B	HR	RBI	BB	K	SB	CS	AVG.
483	55	132	30	3	11	59	31	94	7	4	.273

Rico, 24, was a highly touted slugger who zipped through the Tiger's system in the last few years. He got a tryout in the bigs in '92, but Sparky didn't like him and essentially gave him the major-league-career-ending kiss-off.

He's stagnated ever since and it's beginning to look doubtful that he'll ever make it.

ALAN BURKE											PHILLIES

A – Spartanburg

AB	R	H	2B	3B	HR	RBI	BB	K	SB	CS	AVG.
481	62	135	29	0	17	96	49	92	1	1	.281

Burke is 23 and solidly behind Gene Schall on the Phillies first-base depth chart. Burke has decent power and walks a bit, but he'll have to improve his game for him to be more than bench/backup material.

FRANCISCO CABRERA											BRAVES

AB	R	H	2B	3B	HR	RBI	BB	K	SB	CS	AVG.
83	8	20	3	0	4	11	8	21	0	0	.241

Still remains a fine hitter, but he has two weaknesses: 1) He has poor plate discipline; 2) He's not the manager, so he can never increase his playing time.

PAUL CAREY											ORIOLES

AAA – Rochester

AB	R	H	2B	3B	HR	RBI	BB	K	SB	CS	AVG.
325	63	101	20	4	12	50	65	92	0	0	.311

If Baltimore and Rochester were farther apart, Paul would've racked up enough frequent-flyer miles last year for a free trip to Rio. The Orioles brought him up and sent him down three times while David Segui was earning the full-time job.

Carey batted .311 during his stints at Rochester, .318 against right-handers. At 26, he's not a super-prospect, but he's got plate discipline, the ability to hit for average and good power to all fields.

He could've pushed Segui for the starting slot, but he's got his work cut out for him now that Rafael's come to Camden.

PHIL CLARK											PADRES

AB	R	H	2B	3B	HR	RBI	BB	K	SB	CS	AVG.
240	33	75	17	0	9	33	8	31	2	0	.313

Clark seems to have lived up to the promise of his minor league numbers, namely good average and light power.

He seemed to be destined for a starting role with Detroit as he methodically worked his way through their farm system (and we do mean methodically, since the Tigers have a way of imprisoning their prospects in their inferior farm chain).

Besides the Tigers' penchant for overcautious player development, Clark hit a snag (which was about all he could hit) when he reached Triple-A Toledo. He checked in around 1990 and finally turned in his room key two and a half years later.

In yet another brilliant Motor City moment, the Tigers let Clark go after only a 23-game stint in the bigs.

Now, we're not saying Clark was going to hit anywhere near the .407 he did in those 54 at-bats, but does it make sense to develop a player for seven years and then dump him after a month of honest work? This is the equivalent of paying to educate a lawyer and then trading him to another firm after two or three court dates. The Tigers must have enjoyed paying (read: "over-paying") Dan Gladden one million smackers to do the job Phil could have done for one-fifth the money.

Meanwhile, Clark performed more than adequately in San Diego (formerly home to big brother Jerald) and should continue to succeed there as long as his salary doesn't exceed $5.00 an hour.

Clark is 26, can play four positions and hits like he wants a job. Check him in the Spring and draft accordingly.

WILL CLARK											RANGERS

AB	R	H	2B	3B	HR	RBI	BB	K	SB	CS	AVG.
491	82	139	27	2	14	73	63	68	2	2	.283

At 30, Clark seems to be settling into a pleasant groove of a .280 BA, 15-20 homers and 80-90 RBI. This isn't to say that he won't have several more great seasons, but his stats have stabilized at this level.

Will has lost some speed, and he seemed a little less intense (spelled h-u-n-g-r-y) after Bonds assumed the mantle of team savior for the Giants. This could be an optical illusion, but Clark doesn't seem to glare pitchers into the mound the way he used to.

It'll be interesting to see how the move and the surrounding controversy affect his attitude. All the talk about him invading Palmeiro's turf is pretty silly; Rafael and the Rangers were clearly not going to come to terms by the time Clark showed up. Otherwise, they wouldn't have been talking to him in the first place. Still, that kind of talk can distract a lesser ballplayer.

Controversies aside, Clark will continue to provide golden defense and the ability to will himself to hit in close and late situations.

GREG COLBRUNN — MARLINS

AB	R	H	2B	3B	HR	RBI	BB	K	SB	CS	AVG
153	15	39	9	0	4	23	6	33	4	2	.255

If Greg is healthy, he can be a fine power hitter. Last year he missed two months after surgery on his right elbow. In addition, he has two players to supplant in Jeff Conine and Orestes Destrade, but he has enough power to beat the competition. The only question one has is if Colbrunn can stay healthy. His past track record is very poor and in recent times he's done nothing to dispel this. He needs to get 450 at-bats before he can make a name for himself and the Marlins are saying he may not be ready by the spring. When he comes back, the Marlins will either have him backup Destrade, or play full-time at Triple-A.

TIM COSTO — REDS

AAA – Indianapolis

AB	R	H	2B	3B	HR	RBI	BB	K	SB	CS	AVG
362	49	118	30	2	11	57	22	60	3	2	.326

Costo literally exploded in Triple-A last year. He led International League first basemen with his .326 average, and though his homers fell from 28 to 11, 30 doubles pushed his slugging up to .511.

We figured he would raise his average by about 20 points last year; he raised it 80 points. He could be a little more patient at the plate, but other than that, he's ready.

Since Milligan is gone and Morris is a chronic doofus, Costo should get some serious PT with the Reds this year.

DREW DENSON — WHITE SOX

AAA – Nashville

AB	R	H	2B	3B	HR	RBI	BB	K	SB	CS	AVG
513	82	144	36	0	24	103	46	98	0	0	.281

He's a little old to be breaking into the bigtime, but the White sox usually keep a couple of guys like Denson around to fill the gaps.

He hit extremely well in Triple-A Nashville and was hit by a pitch a phenomenal 23 times!

Drew's problem is that he's a talented first baseman in a Sox uniform who's impossibly overmatched by Big Frank (otherwise known as "Chris Cron-itis"). With George Bell gone and Warren Newson getting older, Drew has a chance to squeeze in 200 ABs in the majors.

ORESTES DESTRADE — MARLINS

AB	R	H	2B	3B	HR	RBI	BB	K	SB	CS	AVG
569	61	145	20	3	20	87	58	130	0	2	.255

According to STATS, Inc., he hit .301 with a .570 slugging percentage in August, which probably saved his season and his job.

While superficially, he had a good season, let's tear it up a bit. ... He hit .255, hardly impressive for the position; his 43 extra-base hits doesn't put him anywhere near a league-leading total. Then you take a look at the 17 double-play grounders he hit and the fact that he drew a mediocre 58 walks.

The end result is a .406 slugging percentage and a .324 on-base average. Let's put it this way, the NL had a .327 OBP and a .399 SLG: At best he's an average hitter for the league. If you adjust for the fact that Florida appears to be a hitter's park and that first base is a position where you stack your hitters, then he's actually a well-below-average hitter.

He's OK with the glove and could hit better in 1994, but there about 20 first basemen we'd look at first.

JAMIE DISMUKE — REDS

AA – Chattanooga

AB	R	H	2B	3B	HR	RBI	BB	K	SB	CS	AVG
497	69	152	22	1	20	91	48	60	4	2	.306

Jamie, 24, is a fine young slugger who's steadily climbing the ranks in Cinci's system.

He combines power and discipline and looks like a pretty nice prospect, although his age may soon take him out of that category. He can hit, but he's got to get in line behind Tim Costo for the job in Riverfront.

BRIAN DuBOSE — TIGERS

A – Lakeland

AB	R	H	2B	3B	HR	RBI	BB	K	SB	CS	AVG
448	74	140	27	11	8	68	49	97	18	18	.313

DuBose, 23, is an excellent line-drive hitter and isn't afraid of walks. He slugged .475 last year and looks like he's ready to move up a level or two.

He's got enough speed to stretch some singles to doubles, but once he's stopped at first somebody ought to anchor him there. He doesn't help anybody by getting caught stealing 18 times. Considering that part of the game isn't essential for a first baseman, it would behoove him to give it up.

CECIL FIELDER — TIGERS

AB	R	H	2B	3B	HR	RBI	BB	K	SB	CS	AVG
573	80	153	23	0	30	117	90	125	0	1	.267

As you may or may not know, we're from the Detroit area and we took a lot of flak last year for not cooing over the 'Sultan of Squat.' But big contracts and declining stats have a way of spoiling the strongest of love affairs and we've felt somewhat vindicated.

Since his phenomenal '90 season, his numbers have decreased to slightly-better-than-average. The weight thing, once a hot topic, is now a dead issue. He's just too damn big and he gets bigger and slower every year. It doesn't take a master statistician to see that there probably is some correlation here.

Defenders of the faith will point out that Cecil improved his plate discipline last year and brought his batting average up to .267, his highest in three years. That's true, compare his 181 K's in 1990 to 125 in 1993, but we'll be more impressed when he hits .280, gets 110+ walks and steals 15 bases. He's being paid big bucks for power, not OBP.

His 117 RBI are certainly respectable, but look who's setting him up:

Phillips .... .443 OBP
Whitaker .... .412 OBP
Fryman .... .379 OBP

Tiger watchers will tell you that most of those RBI came in the early innings with little on the line. Cecil had a lousy year in the clutch, hitting .214 and slugging .334 in close and late situations (STATS, Inc.).

He also had terrible slumps in two crucial stretches of the season last year; in May, when the Tigers were trying to protect their division lead against three contenders, and in September, when Cecil went AWOL while Detroit was trying to stay in the race. The team just couldn't count on him when they needed him.

When the announcer at the All-Star Game doesn't know how to pronounce your name, it's got to tell you something.

Fielder's numbers are decent, but we're talking about a guy who, at one time, aspired to be league-MVP. If he wants to return to that kind of season, he needs to bear down and lose some weight. We're not sure he can.

CLIFFORD FLOYD — EXPOS

AA – Harrisburg

AB	R	H	2B	3B	HR	RBI	BB	K	SB	CS	AVG
380	82	125	17	4	26	101	54	71	31	10	.329

He's the man! His stats at Triple-A Ottawa aren't exactly hearkening back to images of Jimmie Foxx, but as soon as you note the .417 OBP and the .600 slugging percentage at Double-A Harrisburg (26 HR in 380 ABs?!), you realize the kind of ability this phenomenal young hitter has. Also, he has good speed and the tools of a good defensive player.

Because of the Expos' wealth of young outfielders, he's seen as a first baseman and his skills are reportedly not so hot right now. It wouldn't surprise us if he were to win the job in the spring and win the Rookie of the Year award. His performance in the minors is similar to that of your average superstar.

MATT FRANCO — CUBS

AA – Orlando

AB	R	H	2B	3B	HR	RBI	BB	K	SB	CS	AVG
237	31	75	20	1	7	37	29	30	3	6	.316

Although he is only 24, Franco has already spent seven years in the minor leagues. Logically, he was moved along slowly as a youngster, but saw both Double-A and Triple-A action last year. Franco has a nice bat, and could hit in the .260-.270 range with a little power and some walks in the majors if given a shot. He has Grace to displace though. Check in on him from time to time next season.

ANDRES GALARRAGA											ROCKIES
AB	R	H	2B	3B	HR	RBI	BB	K	SB	CS	AVG.
470	71	174	35	4	22	98	24	73	2	4	.370

What a difference a ballpark makes!

A career .267 hitter going into the season, Galarraga became overwhelmed by the Mile-high atmosphere and had delusions of being Joe Jackson. He actually took a .400 average into July before literally falling out of the clouds. Whereas Olerud's challenge of the sacred Ted Williams barrier was legitimate, Galarraga's had the credibility of an Amy Fisher Movie of the Week.

Galarraga does not rank among the top first basemen in the NL, and doesn't deserve to. But fans, be prepared to hear about the "MVP-calibre" Galarraga from all kinds of pre-season media sources. A bit of advice to my brethren (the fans, not the media sources), a solid .350 hitter walks more than 24 times in a season. Stick Thomas, McGriff or Olerud into Galarraga's park (granting that Galarraga was hurt last year), and you'll see a lot more production than 71 runs and 98 RBI.

He'll probably hit over .300 this year, but he can give his thanks to his ballpark, not to his new-found ability to hit like an immortal. A fine rotisserie player, Galarraga is nothing special in real-life terms.

OMAR GARCIA											METS
A – St. Lucie											
AB	R	H	2B	3B	HR	RBI	BB	K	SB	CS	AVG.
485	73	156	17	7	3	76	57	47	25	8	.322

He's a good-looking prospect who has shown an ability to hit for average and get on base for two seasons now. He isn't the prototypical slugger, but he does have good speed. Garcia, 22, is a few years away, but he should make it to the show sooner or later. With the departure of Eddie Murray, it could be sooner.

MARK GRACE											CUBS
AB	R	H	2B	3B	HR	RBI	BB	K	SB	CS	AVG.
594	86	193	39	4	14	98	71	32	8	4	.325

Grace pumped up the power a bit in '93 with his 14 dingers. Nine of them were hit on the road, so yes, folks, the power surge was real. Even if it wasn't for real, though, Grace is still the prototypical No. 3 hitter, and the definition of consistency.

It is not often when an out is wasted in a Grace at-bat. He is a contact hitter who rarely strikes out, collects more than 180 hits a year and complements these hits with a fair amount of walks. He can advance runners with his bat, and when he's on base, he can advance himself with savvy baserunning. Top it all off with Gold-Glove calibre defensive work, and the package that Grace offers a team looks a hell of a lot better than most of the legislation being passed by Congress.

Grace has established his level of play for the past five years. He won't be remembered as the best first baseman in the Windy City during this decade, but in this case, second-best don't look too bad.

BOB HAMELIN											ROYALS
AAA – Omaha											
AB	R	H	2B	3B	HR	RBI	BB	K	SB	CS	AVG.
479	77	124	19	3	29	84	82	94	8	3	.259

If he's finally healthy, he's as ready as he'll ever be. Hamelin, 26, has shown the Royals all he needs to at Triple-A Omaha, hitting 29 homers there in '93. He can be a Hrbek-type hitter and find some at-bats at DH, but he's gotta come up now if he's to have a decent career. If Hamelin doesn't find a job in the spring, his career is in dire straits.

SAM HORN											YANKEES
AAA – Charlotte											
AB	R	H	2B	3B	HR	RBI	BB	K	SB	CS	AVG.
402	62	108	17	1	38	96	60	131	1	0	.269

"Big Sam Horn" caught on with the Indians last year and spent most of the season rockin' the free world in Charlotte. The Tribe called up this International League bully in September, and with 38 homers on the season, he deserved it. The big question floating around at the end of '93 was what took them so long?

Horn isn't washed up yet. At 30, he should have a few more seasons left in him. The Indians may have canned him (as so many teams have) but the Yankees rose to the challenge.

They need to remember that he is a pure slugger, with the strikeouts and abysmal batting average to prove it. Still, there's no reason why he can't hit 20 dingers if given the playing time. It's doubtful that he'll get it with Mattingly at first and Tartabull as full-time DH, but we'd bat Sam before Nokes or Maas.

Kent Hrbek — Twins

AB	R	H	2B	3B	HR	RBI	BB	K	SB	CS	AVG.
392	60	95	11	1	25	83	71	57	0	0	.242

Even though Hrbek's average was a little low, he had an impressive comeback last year. You may recall that he missed much of '92 with dislocated shoulders (both).

His power returned and he was good for 25 dingers and a .467 slugging percentage. And his .995 fielding percentage shows he's still got the good glove.

But injury is becoming more common for Kent. He was out for a while with a strained muscle in his right side last season, and at 34, he can probably expect more of the same in the future. And with Maksudian and McCarty around, competition is growing for his job.

Hrbek may be seeing more time at DH soon, and that may help him avoid injury. Regardless, look for his ABs to drop.

Brian Hunter — Pirates

AB	R	H	2B	3B	HR	RBI	BB	K	SB	CS	AVG.
80	4	11	3	1	0	8	2	15	0	0	.138

Hunter's karma is similar to that of Frankie Cabrera's. In fact, one would think they are almost clones as hitters. Hunter has excellent power, but has yet to show an ability to work the count in his favor, which means his batting average could move up and down line like a sine wave.

He's 26 and should still have his best years ahead of him, but the clock's ticking: He has to displace Rich Aude and Kevin Young.

Tim Hyers — Padres

AA – Knoxville

AB	R	H	2B	3B	HR	RBI	BB	K	SB	CS	AVG.
487	72	149	26	3	3	61	53	51	12	3	.306

Hyers, 22, has a nice, easy line-drive swing and impressive discipline at the plate. He was stuck behind Olerud in the organization's depth chart, but the Padres grabbed him in the Rule V draft.

If he can excel at Triple-A, then he could get some PT in the majors this year. Chances are, he's rookie insurance against the possibility that prospect Dave Staton fails at first.

John Jaha — Brewers

AB	R	H	2B	3B	HR	RBI	BB	K	SB	CS	AVG.
515	78	136	21	0	19	70	51	109	13	9	.264

Jaha has turned out to be close to the hitter we predicted last year.

His power came into line in '93 and he finished the last two months of the year with very good numbers, overcoming a slump which Brewer management feared had sapped his confidence at the plate.

Jaha showed some ineffectiveness against lefties, but not so much that he can't bat against them. Curiously, he was able to draw the walk more consistently against lefties.

Jaha has the job in Milwaukee unless the next Fred McGriff is skulking in the Brewers system. It's not unreasonable to project him for 20-25 homers and 80-90 RBI in '94.

Gregg Jefferies — Cardinals

AB	R	H	2B	3B	HR	RBI	BB	K	SB	CS	AVG.
544	89	186	24	3	16	83	62	32	46	9	.342

You could almost hear a collective groan in the Kansas City area the day the Herk-ster traded Jefferies to his I-80 rivals for 28-year-old Felix Jose. Well, Jefferies settled in at Busch Stadium, keying the Cardinal offense with a .342 average, while Jose struggled to break the .250 mark.

Jefferies' stock has risen dramatically, especially since he juiced up his running game and started taking a few more walks. At the ripe old age of 26, Jefferies has become the undisputed leader of the Cardinal offense, and one of the most exciting players in the National League. He is a threat to win the batting title in the NL, and he should contend for the MVP for the next few seasons.

Wally Joyner — Royals

AB	R	H	2B	3B	HR	RBI	BB	K	SB	CS	AVG.
497	83	145	36	3	15	65	66	67	5	9	.292

Even though at 32 Joyner's hitting will probably start slowing down, he isn't ready for the scrap heap yet. He can still hit for a decent average and draw a healthy amount of walks. He flashed some power in '93, but don't expect 15 home runs to become a trend in spacious Kauffman Stadium.

Although he is not in the same class as Thomas and McGriff, Joyner can contribute to the Royals offense for a few more years with his clutch hitting and ability to score runs. His defense is also of value (as valuable as first base defense can be, of course).

The only thing there is for the Royals not to like about Joyner is his salary. He was paid over $4 million for his '93 season.

Ricky Jordan — Phillies

AB	R	H	2B	3B	HR	RBI	BB	K	SB	CS	AVG.
159	21	46	4	1	5	18	8	32	0	0	.289

Over the last four years, Jordan has settled into his natural role as a reserve and done a fine job. Ricky was a starter for the Phillies in the early going, but with the arrival of John Kruk, he was pushed to the bench. He isn't an exceptional hitter, but he's a fine replacement-level player and there's no reason why he shouldn't continue to perform well.

Eric Karros — Dodgers

AB	R	H	2B	3B	HR	RBI	BB	K	SB	CS	AVG.
619	74	153	27	2	23	80	34	82	0	1	.247

Karros had an adequate year in Chavez Ravine. He kept the power from '92 and drove in a predictable 80 RBI.

His weaknesses continued to be his average and a marked lack of discipline, drawing only 34 BB in 619 ABs (shades of Ruben Sierra)!

While we didn't really have the heart to cross him up last year, after the performances of the '93 Rookies of the Year it's pretty obvious that Karros was the nominal winner in a weak class.

Karros' really socks it to lefties and really stinks against right-handers (.223 BA). He faded after the All-Star break, indicating that perhaps the number of games he played (158) wore on him.

Eric should continue in the vein he's traveled thus far. The Dodgers have really played up the fact that that they've grown the last two Rookies of the Year and have built their offense around them as a result.

Fantasy leagues which weigh on-base and batting average heavily will want to be wary of this player. While his average should rise, we wouldn't want to bet that it won't head toward the equator unexpectedly.

Ryan Klesko — Braves

AAA – Richmond

AB	R	H	2B	3B	HR	RBI	BB	K	SB	CS	AVG.
343	59	94	14	2	22	74	47	69	4	3	.274

He's a helluva good young hitter who should draw some walks and hit for adequate average. Ryan, 23, also has legitimate 30-homer potential this year. It's not much of a stretch to say that 20+ homers is a given if Klesko's healthy and gets the at-bats.

Klesko was being given time in the outfield, so his role on the team is still in question. It's possible that either Gant or McGriff could be traded, so he'd take their position in left or first base, respectively. It's also possible that both players will be retained, and Klesko will be a pine-time player, or Triple-A fodder. He could be a star, though.

John Kruk — Phillies

AB	R	H	2B	3B	HR	RBI	BB	K	SB	CS	AVG.
535	100	169	33	5	14	85	111	87	6	2	.316

Our prediction in last year's Advocate was not exactly the most accurate. We predicted a decline for Kruk without really adjusting for expansion. Kruk's performance actually declined relative to the league, but with the huge increase in offense in 1993, his unadjusted numbers are much better. That would be fine, but every hitter's numbers improved, it's just that Kruk's didn't improve as much as everyone else's.

For 1994, we make the same prediction we did last year: expect him to be very good, one of the best in the league even, but expect him to decline.

T.R. Lewis — Orioles

AA – Bowie

AB	R	H	2B	3B	HR	RBI	BB	K	SB	CS	AVG.
480	73	146	26	2	5	64	36	80	22	8	.304

Lewis is a decent line-drive hitter with good speed. He has an excellent swing, but clearly needs to improve his plate discipline.

A shoulder injury has prevented him from throwing and kept him at first, but he can play third when healthy. At 23, he's a young and fine prospect.

John Lindeman — Astros

AAA – Tucson

AB	R	H	2B	3B	HR	RBI	BB	K	SB	CS	AVG
390	72	141	28	7	12	88	41	68	5	0	.362

How long has this guy been around? He's been bouncing around from organization to organization for eight years. Last year he had a fine season at Triple-A Tucson.

Lindeman looks like he could do an adequate job off the bench, but it's doubtful he'll do much more with Jeff Bagwell and Roberto Petagine around.

Kevin Maas — Yankees

AB	R	H	2B	3B	HR	RBI	BB	K	SB	CS	AVG
151	20	31	4	0	9	25	24	32	1	1	.205

Maas seems to have given up hope of ever finding a job. And since the Yanks have imprisoned him in DH limbo for the last few years, it's unlikely that he'll ever hook up with another organization. The Yanks have added insult to injury with the recent signing of the nomadic Big Sam Horn.

New York has committed an unpardonable sin, keeping a talented player in developmental hell until he's too old to do anybody any good. We recommend that Maas find a good lawyer and bring suit.

Mike Maksudian — Twins

AAA – Portland

AB	R	H	2B	3B	HR	RBI	BB	K	SB	CS	AVG
264	57	83	16	7	10	49	45	51	5	1	.314

Maksudian saw a little time with the Twins last year when Larkin went on the DL, but he wasn't there long (11 days, 12 AB).

He's always had good plate discipline and his numbers at Portland look good (.314 avg., .542 SLG). You should know that the Pacific Coast League is a hitter's paradise, however (.291 avg., .436 SLG).

He could come up and fill Hrbek's shoes adequately, though probably not with the same power. He may get a shot in the near future, although Dave McCarty is first in line. It all depends on what Dave and his therapist accomplish in the off-season.

Oreste Marrero — Expos

AA – Harrisburg

AB	R	H	2B	3B	HR	RBI	BB	K	SB	CS	AVG
255	39	85	18	1	10	49	22	46	3	3	.333

Marrero bummed around the Brewers organization for six years before doing anything remotely competent.

Marrero's half-season at Harrisburg looks impressive (as do his major-league equivalencies), but his plate-discipline and past history don't prove he has the talent necessary to hit .300 consistently. Our guess is that Marrero has decent power, but probably is a .260-.270 hitter. He's in the same boat as the other pack of Expo first basemen: He needs to kick some booty in the Spring, or he'll be in Ottawa.

Domingo Martinez — Blue Jays

AAA – Syracuse

AB	R	H	2B	3B	HR	RBI	BB	K	SB	CS	AVG
465	50	127	24	2	24	79	31	115	4	5	.273

Martinez signed with the Jays when he was 17 and he certainly has filled out for them, averaging 21 HR at Triple-A Syracuse over the last three seasons. He's shown solid power and good defense in the minors, but he hurts his chances by striking out way too much.

Domingo's 26 this year and stuck behind Olerud at first and Sprague at third. The Jays might consider getting some value in trade for this prospect, as he's losing the prospect label.

Tino Martinez — Mariners

AB	R	H	2B	3B	HR	RBI	BB	K	SB	CS	AVG
408	48	108	25	1	17	60	45	56	0	3	.265

Tino's season went up in flames when he tore up his left knee on the turf at Kansas City. He missed over 50 games and also missed a shot at hitting 25 homers.

Tino has proven he can hit at the major-league level. He can control the strike zone, hit for power and has an adequate batting average. In addition, his glove is quite good. He's just a solid all-around performer. If the knee is OK, he could really surprise us in '94.

Don Mattingly — Yankees

AB	R	H	2B	3B	HR	RBI	BB	K	SB	CS	AVG
530	78	154	27	2	17	86	61	42	0	0	.291

Last year we pegged Mattingly to hit close to .300 with line-drive pop. He obliged us by batting .291 with 17 homers and 27 doubles. Kudos to Don for justifying our faith in him.

His 61 walks were a return to old form and he remained one of the toughest batters in the league to strike out.

It's almost redundant to remark on his Gold Glove but, being the classy kind of guy he is, it's always a pleasure to write good things about him.

Mattingly had minor hand surgery after the season and seems to be recovering nicely.

Evan: I'm especially glad that Mattingly has made such recuperative strides in recent years. I remember reading a heart-breaking article in *The National* chronicling his shoddy treatment by Yankee management and the back problems which plagued his '90 season.

At the time, the prospect of his leaving baseball seemed frighteningly eminent, and literally brought a tear to my eye.

Thank the maker that his determination and spirit gave him the strength to stay in baseball and be an exemplar.

DAVE McCARTY — TWINS
AAA – Portland

AB	R	H	2B	3B	HR	RBI	BB	K	SB	CS	AVG.
143	42	55	11	0	8	31	27	25	5	2	.385

AB	R	H	2B	3B	HR	RBI	BB	K	SB	CS	AVG.
350	36	75	15	2	2	21	19	80	2	6	.214

McCarty, 24, has a legendary temper and tosses helmets around like a loon, which is why he was demoted at mid-season. Given his 80 Ks last year, he had plenty of opportunities to act like that. He's also getting a reputation as an insensitive, arrogant idiot, which is why many of the Twins don't like him.

They do like his defense, however, and they aren't sure whether to use him at first or in right field. With Hrbek's frequent ailments, odds are he'll stay at first.

He hit like gangbusters early in the season, but virtually disappeared in August and September. His minor-league career suggests that he has much better plate discipline and hitting ability than he showed last year.

Dave's still a hot prospect. If he has half a brain, he'll realize that the tantrums are about all that stand between him and a starting role.

FRED McGRIFF — BRAVES

AB	R	H	2B	3B	HR	RBI	BB	K	SB	CS	AVG
557	111	162	29	2	37	101	76	106	5	3	.291

Another year, another 30 homers. Over the last five years, Fred's averaged 35 homers and 98 RBI. So with expansion, he hit two more HR than usual and drove in three extra runs.

He saved his best for the stretch drive, hitting .310 and slugging .612 for Atlanta.

The only question about him, is what is Atlanta going to do with him. He could be traded, or he could be Ryan Klesko's worst nightmare. Wherever he goes, he'll hit 30-40 homers and drive in 100 runs.

RYAN McGUIRE — RED SOX
A – Fort Lauderdale

AB	R	H	2B	3B	HR	RBI	BB	K	SB	CS	AVG.
213	23	69	12	2	4	38	27	34	2	4	.324

McGuire, 22, is a fantastic defensive first baseman drafted out of UCLA. He throws a 96 MPH fastball, and in case you're wondering, he's a lefty, which helps explain why he isn't playing third.

He hits for average, has good discipline, and led the NCAA Division I in homers last year. We're not saying Big Mo should be hearing footsteps just yet, but this McGuire kid is for real.

MARK McGWIRE — ATHLETICS

AB	R	H	2B	3B	HR	RBI	BB	K	SB	CS	AVG.
84	16	28	6	0	9	24	21	19	0	1	.333

Mark may be the single-biggest home run threat in the major leagues and that includes his drastically shortened '93 season.

Note that McGwire has hit over 30 HR in five of six full seasons and has hit over 40 HR twice. Only his 22 homer season in '91 keeps him out of Fred McGriff territory. In fact, since he and McGriff began full-fledged major league PT in '87, McGwire's only two home runs behind the man who's lauded as the most consistent power threat in the bigs.

Even more noteworthy, he hit nine dingers in 27 games last year! That's a .726 slugging percentage with a home-run frequency of one for every 9.33 AB. Consider that home run titleists Juan Gonzalez and Barry Bonds had AB/HR ratios of 11.6 and 11.7 respectively.

Factor in Mark's ability to draw the walk and you'll be faced with one of the most potent offensive threats in the majors. When was the last time you met a ML batter with a career BA of .249 and a career OBP of .359?!

The oddity doesn't end there. McGwire hits as many homers in the Coliseum as he does on the road. Only former "Bash Brother" Jose Canseco can even approach him in Oakland.

Look for McGwire to return to health in '94 (reports are that his foot is fully recovered and he's hitting the weights) and try to avoid being struck by one of the 30-35 balls that he'll boost out of AL parks.

BRENT MILLER										ORIOLES
AA – Bowie										
AB	R	H	2B	3B	HR	RBI	BB	K	SB	CS	AVG.
404	35	104	13	0	11	66	19	41	6	1	.257

Miller doesn't look like he's going anywhere soon. His batting average and slugging aren't what you'd expect of a first baseman, and his plate discipline is lousy.

He's only 23 and can afford a few more formative years.

RANDY MILLIGAN										CUBS
AB	R	H	2B	3B	HR	RBI	BB	K	SB	CS	AVG.
261	37	84	18	1	6	36	60	53	0	2	.299

In 1987, Randy Milligan was 26 years old and Mets property. That year, he led the International League in average (.326), runs (99), RBI (103), and walks (91). Two years prior to that, Milligan hit .309 with 13 homers in the Texas League. If the Mets had done the right thing and brought him to the major leagues when he was 24 or 25, Milligan's career might have turned out like Mike Greenwell's. But the Mets, and later the Pirates, missed the boat and let him languish an extra two seasons in the minors. Time he could have spent pillaging National League pitching.

The Orioles deserve a hand for realizing Milligan's value back in 1989. Honestly, he's not as valuable as Brian Barnes, but the Expos could afford to trade from strength. Milligan is a viable option should Cliff Floyd falter.

HAL MORRIS										REDS
AB	R	H	2B	3B	HR	RBI	BB	K	SB	CS	AVG.
379	48	120	18	0	7	49	34	51	2	2	.317

Todd: In a spring training game against the Indians, Morris charged the mound and found El Bandito Jose Mesa waiting. El Bandito gave him a good whoopin' and Hal missed the first third of the season recovering from surgery on a separated shoulder. The incident highlighted the Reds' lack of a legitimate enforcer to protect the team's superstars.

Hal came back in June and posted respectable numbers, a considerable improvement over his dismal '92 season. In '93, he sprayed quite a few singles, but his slugging was down and it looks like he's lost some power.

All that may be irrelevant, anyway.

This is the second year in a row Morris has been bothered by injury. What kind of moron charges the mound in spring training, especially when he's trying to come back from a dismal, injury-filled season? Morris is a wild card and I would prefer a little more dependability (intelligence?) on my team.

Or maybe I'm just underestimating how important fighting has become to the game.

EDDIE MURRAY										INDIANS
AB	R	H	2B	3B	HR	RBI	BB	K	SB	CS	AVG.
610	77	174	28	1	27	100	40	61	2	2	.285

His game is still slowly declining, it's just taking a lot longer than anyone thought it would. But anyone capable of turning in the kind of season he did, surrounded by a media feeding-frenzy and a total lack of decorum deserves every penny of his salary, and Jeff Torborg's and Al Harazin's.

TROY NEEL										ATHLETICS
AB	R	H	2B	3B	HR	RBI	BB	K	SB	CS	AVG.
427	59	124	21	0	19	63	49	101	3	5	.290

Neel lived up to our expectations and in some respects exceeded them.

We pegged him as a good hitter and he proved that he was. But he really made the jump to the bigs like he'd been there before.

The A's are very pleased and probably wondering why he was in Tacoma for the last three years. If anything, Neel, rather than third baseman Paquette is the bat that the A's should be applauding.

JOHN OLERUD										BLUE JAYS
AB	R	H	2B	3B	HR	RBI	BB	K	SB	CS	AVG.
551	109	200	54	2	24	107	114	65	0	2	.363

There was no easy way to get Olerud out in '93. He hit the living tar out of the ball, to all fields, in every park, all season long. He was lauded everywhere he went for his natural swing, and for a time, there were whispers of Ted Williams' .406 mark. It was not meant to be, but hats off to a fantastic season anyway.

What's so intriguing about Olerud is that he is only 25 years old, with plenty of time for improvement. Not that there's a whole lot of room in his game for refinement, though. The season he turned in last year was intimidating enough. But to think that he might even get better is enough to make pitchers around the league call in sick when slated to pitch against the Blue Jays.

Olerud may never again have the statistically astounding season he had in '93, but that isn't to say that he won't become a perennial All-Star. He should have no problem hitting .300 again, and you can expect close to 100 walks and 100 runs scored. But the jury is still out as to whether he can maintain his newfound power.

RAFAEL PALMEIRO											ORIOLES
AB	R	H	2B	3B	HR	RBI	BB	K	SB	CS	AVG.
597	124	176	40	2	37	105	73	85	22	3	.295

After a subpar '92 season, Palmeiro regained his old form, plus added new dimensions to his game that no one expected. And we all know how the Rangers repaid him.

He raised his average to .295 and his slugging to a career-high .554, which was largely due to his 37 HRs (his previous best was 26 in '91). He also broke 100 RBI for the first time. Rafael absolutely crushed right-handers, hitting 35 HRs and slugging .621 (STATS, Inc.).

But his running game was even more unbelievable. He led the league in runs-scored with 124 and his 22 steals came out of nowhere.

Combine these numbers with his exceptional fielding skill and you've got one solid package.

How, then, can the Rangers let him go in favor of a 30-year-old ex-superstar who's numbers have been steadily declining? Is Clark somehow a better buy? This will be one of the bigger stories in the game this year and they'll have the opportunity to settle the issue mano-a-mano.

Odds are that Palmeiro will be vindicated, but you can't shake those flashbacks from that Canseco-Sierra fiasco.

GERALD PERRY											CARDINALS
AB	R	H	2B	3B	HR	RBI	BB	K	SB	CS	AVG.
98	21	33	5	0	4	16	18	23	1	1	.337

He did really well as a pinch-hitter last year, but his career is almost over and he'll never be more than a spare part.

ROBERTO PETAGINE											ASTROS
AA – Jackson											
AB	R	H	2B	3B	HR	RBI	BB	K	SB	CS	AVG.
437	73	146	36	2	15	90	84	89	6	5	.334

This 23-year-old takes his plate discipline seriously: "I'm not going to swing at a bad pitch. I'd rather walk," or so he said in *B.A.*

Wrap him up, we'll take him home.

It's a sad story, because the Astros already have the best all-around first baseman in the league in Mr. Bagwell.

Still, Petagine is the reigning Texas League MVP and batting-title winner. He's also the league's No. 4 prospect. If we were the Astros, we'd make room for him on the roster. He'd be the second-best hitter on the team and he's got enough youth to challenge Bagwell for best-hitter honors.

If he gets a job, look for him to hit .300 with power and walk numbers very similar to Bagwell's rookie season.

J.R. PHILLIPS											GIANTS
AAA – Phoenix											
AB	R	H	2B	3B	HR	RBI	BB	K	SB	CS	AVG.
506	80	133	35	2	27	94	53	127	7	5	.263

He's 24 and seems to have above-average power potential. His .263 BA and .336 on-base are extrememly disturbing for the notoriously hitter-friendly PCL.

Now that Will Clark is gone, he has a much improved shot at the job in the spring. However, unless he improves his average, and thus his on-base percentage, the proven Benzinger will be much more viable.

GREG PIRKL											MARINERS
AAA – Calgary											
AB	R	H	2B	3B	HR	RBI	BB	K	SB	CS	AVG.
445	67	137	24	1	21	94	13	50	3	3	.308

A 23-year-old with no concept of the strike zone, but good power. He looks like he'll hit some homers, but his ability to hit for average will be forever in doubt until he learns to swing at and hit strike three and stop swinging at ball four.

His role will be determined by what happens to Tino. If Tino's healthy, Pirkl will either back-up first and DH. Otherwise, he could get a shot at the full-time job.

CLYDE POUGH — INDIANS
A – Kinston

AB	R	H	2B	3B	HR	RBI	BB	K	SB	CS	AVG
418	66	113	18	1	13	57	59	95	8	3	.270

Anyone who has flipped through a Baseball America probably knows him as "Pork Chop" Pough. We here at the Advocate know him as "24 years old and still in Single-A" Pough. He's not much of a prospect; we just thought you'd enjoy the nickname.

HOWARD PRAGER — CARDINALS
AAA – Louisville

AB	R	H	2B	3B	HR	RBI	BB	K	SB	CS	AVG
209	27	55	17	0	4	28	24	37	0	0	.263

Prager has a good eye at the plate and a history of success in the minors. But he's 27 this season and playing behind one of the best hitting first basemen in the NL. His only hope of serious playing time is via a trade.

CHRIS PRITCHETT — ANGELS
AA – Midland

AB	R	H	2B	3B	HR	RBI	BB	K	SB	CS	AVG
464	61	143	30	6	2	66	61	72	3	7	.308

Pritchett, 24, probably will start the season at Triple-A. He looks like a guy who would hit .260-.275 with enough walks to put him in the .320-.340 OBP range if he made the big club. Midland is a hitter's paradise, so you need to take his numbers with a carton of salt.

He can develop power, but right now he has none. His best shot right now is as a reserve.

GENE SCHALL — PHILLIES
AA – Reading

AB	R	H	2B	3B	HR	RBI	BB	K	SB	CS	AVG
285	51	93	12	4	15	60	24	56	2	1	.326

Gene led Phillies minor-leaguers with 19 dingers last year. Schall, 24, is a pretty good power hitter (.554 slugging percentage at Reading) who needs to improve his plate discipline to move it up to the major-league level (he was quite overmatched at Triple-A). Right now, he's blocked by Ricky Jordan and (*of course*) John Kruk. He's considered semi-weak with the glove (an experiment in left failed horribly) and has little foot-speed. Still, it's not inconceivable that he could get some PT with the big club by mid-season.

DAVID SEGUI — ORIOLES

AB	R	H	2B	3B	HR	RBI	BB	K	SB	CS	AVG
450	54	123	27	0	10	60	58	53	2	1	.273

Plain and simple, Segui is in there for his defense. It isn't that he has no punch at all; his offensive numbers were right around league averages. But compared to other first base hitting talent around the league, he's about as intimidating as Michael Bolton.

To be fair, '93 was the first year that the O's let him stay all season and he did improve his stats considerably. He showed a little power last year, slugging .400 with 27 doubles and 10 homers. He has hitting potential, but he isn't showing it yet. Defensively, his zone rating was marginal, but he has a great rep.

Still, he's a guppy in a very big ocean. Hence, he'll battle Paul Carey for the right to sing back up for Rafael Palmeiro.

BUBBA SMITH — REDS
A – Winston-Salem

AB	R	H	2B	3B	HR	RBI	BB	K	SB	CS	AVG
342	55	103	16	0	27	81	35	109	2	0	.301

Yeah, that's right... Bubba Smith.

Bubba bounced all over the minors last year and even got a tryout in Double-A, which was less than impressive. He looked good in Winston-Salem, though, slugging .585 with 27 HR and 81 RBI, all in 342 ABs.

But he's 24 and getting a little old to break out of Single-A. His .219 average in 137 ABs at Double-A last year doesn't bode well.

J.T. SNOW — ANGELS

AB	R	H	2B	3B	HR	RBI	BB	K	SB	CS	AVG
419	60	101	18	2	16	57	55	88	3	0	.241

Snow destroyed his season by hitting six homers and slugging .687 in April. He tried to become a slugger and became a slug instead.

Disgusted by his poor showing after April, the Angels sent Snow to Vancouver in July and he hit .340 with a .617 SLG there.

He came back in late August and hit .297 with 4 homers in September (STATS, inc.).

J.T. is at exactly the same point he was last year: He's got great glove potential (scouts in spring training 1993 said he looked better than Mattingly *and* Keith Hernandez in their primes!) and the kind of line-drive bat that should yield an average in the .270-.290 range with up to 20 homers.

PAUL SORRENTO											INDIANS
AB	R	H	2B	3B	HR	RBI	BB	K	SB	CS	AVG.
463	75	119	26	1	18	65	58	121	3	1	.257

Sorrento can be a dangerous hitter. He generates plenty of bat speed and he has hit 18 homers the past two seasons. However, he's coming off a season that saw him strike out 121 times. That's an awful lot of outs to give away without putting the ball in play, Paul.

He homered 14 times in the first half, and only 4 times in the second. This does not bode well for a 28-year-old whose batting eye is getting worse, not better. Paul better show the Indians something special in spring training. If he doesn't get his act going, he might see some bench time.

DAVE STATON											PADRES
A – Rancho Cucamonga											
AB	R	H	2B	3B	HR	RBI	BB	K	SB	CS	AVG.
221	37	70	21	0	18	58	30	52	0	0	.317
AB	R	H	2B	3B	HR	RBI	BB	K	SB	CS	AVG.
42	7	11	3	0	5	9	3	12	0	0	.262

Staton, 26, is a formidable power-threat and has his act together in the on-base department.

Rotator-cuff surgery forced a lengthy demotion to Rancho Cucamonga (where he drove pitchers cuckoo with 21 doubles and 18 home runs), but he surfaced in Triple-A Las Vegas and then San Diego for 42 promising at-bats. The shoulder injury seems to have spared his hitting while rendering his fielding questionable.

Staton is by no means a complete package, but with Fred McGriff's unexpected departure and the Padres' movement toward the "Young and the Check-less" he's slated to begin '94 as the Pads' first baseman.

FRANK THOMAS											WHITE SOX
AB	R	H	2B	3B	HR	RBI	BB	K	SB	CS	AVG.
549	106	174	36	0	41	128	112	54	4	2	.317

Because Thomas is 26, it seems strange that so many people use the word "finally" when discussing his winning AL MVP honors. In truth, the award leaves a slightly sour tinge in the mouth as Blue Jay John Olerud deserved it more than Thomas. (As for Olerud's finishing behind teammate Paul Molitor, it takes all kinds to swell the ranks and heads of the Baseball Writers' Association).

Perhaps this year's balloting was an altruistic attempt to save face for Thomas' shameful vote-getting in recent years. He has amassed the most potent batting stats in recent memory, but really fellas, do you honestly think he was a unanimous choice?

This is not to diminish Thomas's achievements one whit. He was the only major leaguer aside from Bonds and Olerud to post 100+ runs scored, RBI and walks this year. Rather elite company.

To go a step further, he is the career leader among active players in both on-base and slugging percentages and is third in BA at .321 behind noted average-fiends Wade Boggs and Tony Gwynn. While Juan Gonzalez has more raw power and Griffey Jr. has more upward mobility, Thomas is undoubtedly the best all-around hitter in the game.

The only dilemma facing the authors of the Advocate is which of us gets to ask for his hand in marriage.

JOHN TOALE											MARLINS
A – High Desert											
AB	R	H	2B	3B	HR	RBI	BB	K	SB	CS	AVG.
517	108	148	30	3	28	125	84	101	1	3	.286

He's 29, so don't get any delusions of grandeur for him. Take the starch out of his numbers and he's really nothing. Chalk him up as a big-time N.P. (non-prospect).

PAUL TORRES											CUBS
A – Daytona											
AB	R	H	2B	3B	HR	RBI	BB	K	SB	CS	AVG.
353	63	98	17	5	13	43	52	94	5	4	.278

He's got good power, but this 23 year-old has spent four seasons in Single-A ball trying to prove to the Cubs that he can hit well on a consistent basis. He also strikes out a lot, so don't put much stock in him unless he makes a dramatic turn around next season.

MO VAUGHN											RED SOX
AB	R	H	2B	3B	HR	RBI	BB	K	SB	CS	AVG.
539	86	160	34	1	29	101	79	130	4	3	.297

The Red Sox finally got around to giving Vaughn a full shot last year and, as we predicted, he kicked butt. Mo took it up several notches, shedded that nasty 'P' word (potential) and proved he is a legitimate slugger.

Still competing for the position in April, he got off to a fast start, hitting .412 and slugging .735. Despite this, the Sox earned Mo's wrath by sitting him against lefties (In retrospect, this was ridiculous since he ended up with a .268 average against southpaws and hit 12 HR off them in 164 AB!). The Sox gradually caught on and gave Mo the job full time.

All he did between '92 and '93 was raise his average 63 points to .297 and his slugging 125 points to .525. He broke 500 ABs and 100 RBI for the first time in his career.

Mo has good plate discipline, but he's prone to strikeouts. Given his track record and work ethic, he's likely cut down on his Ks. The question now is whether he can take it to the next level and hit 35+ HR and 120+ RBI. He's young, capable and he excels in Fenway, so it's definitely possible.

JOHN VANDERWAL											EXPOS
AB	R	H	2B	3B	HR	RBI	BB	K	SB	CS	AVG.
215	374	50	7	4	5	30	27	30	6	3	.233

VanderWal had shown in his minor-league career that he could be a decent line-drive hitter. His performance in the majors, however, indicates that it's time for the Expos to look at other options. If he can drive up his average, he would be a pretty solid hitter, if he can't he'll be just another guy thrown on the discard pile. He's 28 and he better fire his bullets if he's got any left in the gun.

GUILLERMO VELASQUEZ											PADRES
AAA – Las Vegas											
AB	R	H	2B	3B	HR	RBI	BB	K	SB	CS	AVG.
129	23	43	6	1	5	24	10	19	0	0	.333
AB	R	H	2B	3B	HR	RBI	BB	K	SB	CS	AVG.
143	7	30	2	0	3	20	13	35	0	0	.210

He spreads his power around, draws an occasional walk and the Padres seemed high enough on him this year to liberate McGriff.

He didn't show very well in his '93 showcase as a Padre, but we know how the ownership loves a cheap date. Keep an eye open when he shows in the spring. He'll have to be phenomenal to best Dave Staton.

JOE VITIELLO											ROYALS
AA – Memphis											
AB	R	H	2B	3B	HR	RBI	BB	K	SB	CS	AVG.
413	62	119	25	2	15	66	57	95	2	0	.288

The Royals really like what they've seen from Vitiello the past two seasons. He has shown good power, decent plate discipline and a willingness to take on a leadership role. He's 24 and should be able to improve the home run totals as he matures, and he can play in outfield as well as first base.

Vitiello is behind Joyner in the Royal depth chart, but he's a full season away from the majors anyway. If he hits well in Omaha this year, look for the Royals to perform the "salary dump" ritual dance during the winter of '94, with Joyner as the sacraficial lamb.

DERRICK WHITE											EXPOS
AB	R	H	2B	3B	HR	RBI	BB	K	SB	CS	AVG.
49	14	18	1	0	2	12	5	17	2	0	.224

The word "reach" immediately comes to mind when his name comes up. The Expos reached into their system, pulled up a 24-year-old non-prospect and installed him at first, when Greg Colbrunn was hurt. Apart from cranking a pair of homers he did very little. After a quick perusal of his minor-league career, it's pretty apparent that doing "very little" is about all he'll do if he gets a job.

CHRIS WEINKE											BLUE JAYS
A – Dunedin											
AB	R	H	2B	3B	HR	RBI	BB	K	SB	CS	AVG.
476	68	135	16	2	17	98	66	78	8	6	.284

He has shown good power and a good eye at the plate for the past two seasons, so there's a chance this 21-year-old second round draft pick could really shine in '94. After Gonzalez and Silva, he's about as good a prospect as there is in the Blue Jay system.

But his position is manned by the reigning AL batting champ and is getting crowded in the minors. He'll see two more years in the minors at the very least.

DMITRI YOUNG											CARDINALS
A – St. Petersburg											
AB	R	H	2B	3B	HR	RBI	BB	K	SB	CS	AVG.
270	31	85	13	3	5	43	24	28	3	4	.315

Young took a step backward last season. His hitting suffered after a promotion to Double-A Arkansas, he displayed questionable defense and was switched to first base. He was shut down late in the season due to shoulder soreness. Even with all that bad news, he should still be considered a hot commodity.

This former No. 1 draft pick is only 20 years old. Despite his setbacks, he was good enough to earn status as the No. 5 prospect in the Florida State League, according to *Baseball America*. And yes, his '92 performance is a true representation of his ability. He can hit for average and power from both sides of the plate and he has already developed a good eye at the plate. Look for him to once again dominate minor league pitching and regain his top prospect status.

Kevin Young											Pirates
AB	R	H	2B	3B	HR	RBI	BB	K	SB	CS	AVG
449	38	106	24	3	6	47	36	82	2	2	.236

It was a pretty rotten rookie season for the Young-ster. Lousy plate discipline, low average, no power.

He's got a great glove, though, which explains what he's doing in the bigs. He made only 3 errors in 1,056.2 defensive innings. But you don't even see shortstops survive hitting like that and he'll have to turn it around if he wants to keep the cushy job.

Young has never hit for power, but at least he had some control of the strike zone at Triple-A and could hit for average. He can still hit like that, but he needs to fight off Aude. Maybe he needs to talk to McGriff or Grace about translating that minor-league talent to the game played in the NL. ... We have to wonder if his defense isn't being wasted at first. He was so good last year, maybe he should've stayed at third.

Alan Zinter											Mets
AA – Birmingham											
AB	R	H	2B	3B	HR	RBI	BB	K	SB	CS	AVG
432	68	113	24	4	24	87	90	105	1	0	.262

At first glance, Zinter's '93 stats look really impressive. But he was 25 years old last year in his third year in Double-A, beating up on younger, less experienced pitchers.

With the departure of Eddie Murray, his chances of making the show are considerably better. However, he will have to prove his worth, over and above abusing pitchers in the Arizona Fall League.

SECOND BASE – *RANKINGS*

	Player	Total	Avg. Off.	Def. Runs Saved
1	Ryne Sandberg	36.6	21.6	21.6
2	Craig Biggio	33.7	18.7	21.8
3	Carlos Baerga	31.1	27.2	5.6
4	Robby Thompson	29.2	16.6	18.3
5	Robby Alomar	28.8	32.5	-5.3
6	Lou Whitaker	24.3	19.2	7.5
7	Delino DeShields	23.8	13.7	14.6
8	Scott Fletcher	11.9	3.6	12.2
9	Bip Roberts	11.8	9.4	3.6
10	Pat Kelly	10.6	-1.9	18.1
11	Geronimo Pena	9.6	5.7	5.5
12	Luis Alicea	9.5	3.2	9.1
13	Jeff Gardner	7.6	-3.4	15.8
14	Jeff Kent	6.2	3.4	4.1
15	Chuck Knoblauch	5.8	6.7	-1.2
16	Bret Barberie	4.9	-3.9	12.7
17	Damion Easley	4.5	1.9	3.7
18	Torey Lovullo	4.0	-2.2	9.1
19	Chico Walker	3.4	1.5	2.6
20	Jody Reed	3.2	-4.8	11.5
21	Tim Teufel	2.8	-0.2	4.3
22	Mariano Duncan	2.4	1.3	1.7
23	Mark Lemke	1.8	-7.4	13.3
24	Harold Reynolds	1.4	-5.5	9.9
25	Juan Bell	1.1	-4.5	8.1

SECOND BASE – *PROSPECTS*

Short-range	Long-range	Sleepers
1 Michael Tucker	1 Arquimedez Pozo	1 Roberto Mejia
2 Quilvio Veras	2 Kevin Jordan	2 Bret Barberie
3 Darrel Deak	3 Jason Hardtke	3 Kevin Flora
4 James Mouton	4 Tony Graffagnino	4 Tim Naehring
5 Jim Crowley	5 Bob Juday	5 Bret Boone
6 Ruben Santana	6 Jose Vidro	6 Torey Lovullo
7 Miguel Flores	7 Carlton Fleming	7 Luis Lopez
8 Mike Hardge	8 Kevin Sefcik	8 Billy Hall
		9 Norberto Martin
		10 Brad Tyler

Second Base – *Essays*

LUIS ALICEA — CARDINALS

AB	R	H	2B	3B	HR	RBI	BB	K	SB	CS	AVG.
362	50	101	19	3	3	46	47	54	11	1	.279

He shared second base with Geronimo Pena last year, taking over the position when Pena broke his toe in July. Both have excellent range, but Alicea is a better fielder than Pena, and offers a similar, more refined, package at the plate. Playing time is the key to Alicea's worth, though.

Do you platoon two switch-hitting second basemen? There's no reason why you should. So what we have in St. Louis is a choice between Alicea and Pena as the starter. The winner gets the position and the lead-off spot in the lineup. The loser gets a plane ticket and a new home. As Ross Perot would say, "Fair and square; plain and simple; easy as pie."

ROBERTO ALOMAR — BLUE JAYS

AB	R	H	2B	3B	HR	RBI	BB	K	SB	CS	AVG.
589	109	192	35	6	17	93	80	67	55	17	.326

He hit only .241 against lefties last year, and he only hit .259 in May, but that's just nit-picking. The rest of his season was simply outstanding across the board.

Alomar hit .309 with runners in scoring position, stole a career-best 55 bases, hit a career-high 17 homers and contended for the AL batting title with two of his teammates. His '93 season might have been overlooked in the aftermath of the most explosive offensive year in recent memory. But rest assured, his accomplishments were noticed.

His range factor and zone rating for last season were both uncharacteristically low. The same discrepancy was noticed in Ken Griffey's stats. Just watch them play, and you'll come to the same conclusion as we have. Alomar and Griffey are the class of their respective positions.

All speculation aside, Alomar's career is careening down the track to Cooperstown at 125 MPH. He has the broad-based talent to go into the Hall of Fame with 3,000 hits, an MVP award, several Gold Gloves and the reputation as his generation's greatest second baseman.

RICH AMARAL — MARINERS

AB	R	H	2B	3B	HR	RBI	BB	K	SB	CS	AVG.
489	64	133	27	1	2	51	39	75	19	11	.290

He was such a pleasant surprise in the spring of '93, that Lou Piniella was able to demote his least-favorite Mariner, Bret Boone, to Triple-A and start the season with the then 31-year-old rookie at second base.

Richie held up his end of the bargain, getting on base at a .348 clip and hitting an amazing .354 in the lead-off slot (credit STATS, Inc.).

Also, he played solid defense. He was shunted between second, third and short and did at least a competent job at each position. He looks like an excellent backup infielder.

ALEX ARIAS — MARLINS

AB	R	H	2B	3B	HR	RBI	BB	K	SB	CS	AVG.
249	27	67	5	1	2	20	27	18	1	1	.269

Showed he was a decent batsman by putting together a .269 season with an excellent 27/18 BB/K ratio. Arias has decent range, but was rather lackluster on the D.P. He's a good player, but we like Bret Barberie better.

CARLOS BAERGA — INDIANS

AB	R	H	2B	3B	HR	RBI	BB	K	SB	CS	AVG.
624	105	200	28	6	21	114	34	68	15	4	.321

How effective was Baerga at the plate last year? He reached 200 hits for the second straight season. But more impressively, he hit .341 with runners in scoring position. That kind of production out of a second baseman is a Godsend. Put Lofton ahead of him, and Albert Belle behind him, and you're going to score a lot of runs.

But as potent as Baerga was at the plate, he was just as effective in the field. Without a doubt, Baerga has the best range in the major leagues at his position and he's pretty smooth around the bag, too.

With Knoblauch and DeShields falling off the pace, Baerga and Alomar have emerged as the two best second basemen in baseball. It's almost impossible to say right now who is the better of the two, but who cares? It's just a pleasure to watch them play.

Bret Barberie — Marlins

AB	R	H	2B	3B	HR	RBI	BB	K	SB	CS	AVG
375	45	104	16	2	5	33	33	58	2	4	.277

A solid bat with a fine glove, Barberie has the potential to really shine this year. Bret's season was torn apart by injuries to his non-throwing shoulder and his left knee. In all, he missed over 60 games.

As it is, he can hit for average with a high number of walks and a smidge of power. He also has very good range and is pretty excellent on the double-play pivot. He just has fine skills and could really surprise you this year.

Craig Biggio — Astros

AB	R	H	2B	3B	HR	RBI	BB	K	SB	CS	AVG
610	98	175	41	5	21	64	77	93	15	17	.287

While Craig Biggio fell on his face on the basepaths, he really came into his own in two areas: defense and power.

Craig's zone-rating was well above-average and he looked much better on the double-play this year. As for his power, he had over 60 percent more extra-base hits than in 1992.

Craig is 28 this year, so that was probably his peak season. His terrible baserunning has to be somewhat of a concern, but it's doubtful he's lost his speed at this early an age. Look for the power to drop, but expect his steals and OBP to increase this year.

Bret Boone — Reds

AB	R	H	2B	3B	HR	RBI	BB	K	SB	CS	AVG
271	31	68	12	2	12	38	17	52	2	3	.251

With his long swing and myriad other "faults," Mr. Third Generation MLB'er moved into Lou Piniella's doghouse, coming out long enough to get 271 at-bats and his walking papers.

There's no doubt that Boone will punch out 100 times unless he shortens his swing, but he is also a good bet to hit 15-20 HR this year if given a full-time job. The jury's still out on his defense. Last year he had a low range-factor, but turned quite a few double-plays behind the Mariners ground-ball prone staff. The bottom line is Erik Hanson is a fine pitcher and Bret Boone is a pretty good young player (25). Bobby Ayala could be very good, but Dan Wilson hasn't shown much yet. The Reds beat the Mariners with a hose on this trade.

Rafael Bournigal — Dodgers

AAA – Albuquerque

AB	R	H	2B	3B	HR	RBI	BB	K	SB	CS	AVG
465	75	129	25	0	4	55	29	18	3	5	.277

He's 28, a light hitter and saw about two pitches per plate appearance in the majors. Write him off.

Jeff Branson — Reds

AB	R	H	2B	3B	HR	RBI	BB	K	SB	CS	AVG
381	40	92	15	1	3	22	19	73	4	1	.241

Branson's a utility infielder who doesn't look like he'll ever find a permanent home. His glove is more than adequate, but the Reds have a jumble of middle infielders and Branson needs to perform at the plate to rise above the crowd.

As it is, Schottzie 02 still draws more walks than he does and probably has more power.

Miguel Cairo — Dodgers

A – Vero Beach

AB	R	H	2B	3B	HR	RBI	BB	K	SB	CS	AVG
343	49	108	10	1	1	23	26	22	23	16	.315

Miguel's a young hitter, 20, with good bat control and some speed. Good tools, but no signs of power yet.

He's at least a couple of years away from making an impact. The Dodgers probably have an eye on him, as he'd make a good bargaining chip when contract talks with DeShields come up.

Casey Candaele — Reds

AB	R	H	2B	3B	HR	RBI	BB	K	SB	CS	AVG
121	18	29	8	0	1	7	10	14	2	3	.240

He lost his job with the Astros because of the league's salary structure and a subpar season with the lumber. Casey's still a decent player, but he's nothing that you'd want to trot out 90 times a year or something. He'll do fine on the Reds bench.

Ramon Caraballo — Braves

AB	R	H	2B	3B	HR	RBI	BB	K	SB	CS	AVG
470	73	128	25	9	3	41	30	81	20	14	.272

He flat-out cannot hit. Ramon may develop this ability in the future, but at 25, it's doubtful.

It's highly improbable that he can field better than Lemke, let alone hit .250 with a .330+ OBP. He's a pseudo-prospect at best.

JOEY CORA											WHITE SOX
AB	R	H	2B	3B	HR	RBI	BB	K	SB	CS	AVG.
579	95	155	15	13	2	51	67	63	20	8	.268

Joey had his first full-season in his six-year career and it was generally unremarkable.

Aside from 20 stolen bases and a league-leading 19 sacrifice hits he didn't add much to the Sox batting order.

He doesn't have exceptional range, but he can generally make the play in the hole. Craig Grebeck is a better fielder, but he may be even more lackluster with the timber than Cora.

JIM CROWLEY											RED SOX
AA – New Britain											
AB	R	H	2B	3B	HR	RBI	BB	K	SB	CS	AVG.
369	49	89	19	1	11	51	59	95	3	7	.241

Crowley, 24, started off last season like gangbusters, but faded toward the end. He should start at Triple-A in '94 and will likely improve his numbers in Pawtucket after spending a year in the hitter's mausoleum known as Beehive Stadium.

DARREL DEAK											CARDINALS
AA – Arkansas											
AB	R	H	2B	3B	HR	RBI	BB	K	SB	CS	AVG.
414	63	100	22	1	19	73	58	103	4	8	.242

Two solid seasons have elevated Deak to prospect status in the Cardinals organization. He's averaged 17 homers and 76 RBI over the past two years in both Single and Double-A.

With 58 walks in '93 it's hard to say Deak is a hacker at the plate, but you have to be concerned with the amount of strikeouts he racked up. He definitely needs to lay off the junk and pick his pitches with more scrutiny. The next two seasons will tell if Deak has what it takes to work major league pitching.

DELINO DESHIELDS											DODGERS
AB	R	H	2B	3B	HR	RBI	BB	K	SB	CS	AVG.
481	75	142	17	7	2	29	72	64	43	10	.295

With all the minor-league pitching and outfield depth the Expos have, it was really crazy of them to trade Delino. He was arguably the most valuable player on the team. He doesn't have Walker's power or Grissom's speed, but he's one of the top infielders in the game and he's not the most replaceable player on the field or in the locker room.

Delino's season was rudely interrupted by chicken pox and torn ligaments in his thumb. He missed about 40 games, but still had his finest all-around season.

On offense, he set career-bests with his .295 average, .389 OBP and his 81 percent stolen-base rate. On defense, he really improved his range and double-play rate, making himself one of the better defensive second basemen in the league.

Right now, the only facet of Delino's game that is lacking is his power. He's a fantastic athlete and is incredibly motivated. The Expos performed a salary dump and the joke will probably be on them.

Evan: From the Dodgers' perspective, they made out like bandits in the deal for Delino. While Pedro Martinez was lauded as their best pitcher last year, he spent most of his innings in long relief. The arrival of prospects like Jose Parra, Rick Gorecki and Ben VanRyn should render his departure a dim memory by the end of next year.

DeShields value is tenfold. He fills a gap in the Dodger infield which had only recently been jury-rigged by the acquisition of excellent-glove/declining bat Jody Reed. Delino brings a glove, a bat, excellent speed and a vow to improve the play of Jose Offerman.

BILL DORAN											BREWERS
AB	R	H	2B	3B	HR	RBI	BB	K	SB	CS	AVG.
60	7	13	4	0	0	6	6	3	1	0	.217

Doran didn't play much at all, and when he did he really showed his age. (Note to STATS, Inc.: Don't you guys think he's a little old to be called Billy?)

Doran doesn't have much time left, but he's always been a classy guy with a slick glove. It's possible that he'll call it quits before the '94 season starts.

If he doesn't, chalk it up to just another old-timer trying to hang on to the dream.

MARIANO DUNCAN											PHILLIES
AB	R	H	2B	3B	HR	RBI	BB	K	SB	CS	AVG.
496	68	140	26	4	11	73	12	88	6	5	.282

Duncan has been very consistent over the last few years. You know you'll get some power and a decent average, but you also know you'll get no on-base ability and indifferent defense. He's been grinding these seasons out since '89 and he'll probably do more of the same in '94. The only thing he's lost over the years is his once-electrifying speed.

RAY DURHAM — WHITE SOX
AA – Birmingham

AB	R	H	2B	3B	HR	RBI	BB	K	SB	CS	AVG.
528	83	143	22	10	3	37	42	100	39	25	.271

He's a developing hitter, 22, who's got some good extra-base pop.

His big problems are judgment problems concerning plate discipline and stealing bases.

Ray's got a way to go, but nobody in Chicago has their name tattooed on second.

DAMION EASLEY — ANGELS

AB	R	H	2B	3B	HR	RBI	BB	K	SB	CS	AVG.
230	.33	72	13	2	2	22	28	35	6	6	.313

Damion spent much of last year hobbled by mysterious shin splints. When he did play, he hit for a nice average and displayed a newfound ability to draw the walks. The results were an extremely impressive .392 OBP in about half a season's worth of work.

In the off-season, the Angels were still trying to figure out what was causing Easley's problems. It'll be something to watch for in the Spring. He apparently has made a significant stride forward as a hitter. If he can stay healthy, he'll loom large in the Angels' plans.

PAUL FARIES — GIANTS
AAA – Phoenix

AB	R	H	2B	3B	HR	RBI	BB	K	SB	CS	AVG.
327	56	99	14	5	2	32	22	30	18	11	.303

Succeeded in lowering his career stats yet again. If the Giants are lucky, the Paul Fairy will lift him off their roster and leave a nice shiny quarter under the bench.

CARLTON FLEMING — YANKEES
A – Prince William

AB	R	H	2B	3B	HR	RBI	BB	K	SB	CS	AVG.
442	72	132	14	2	0	25	80	23	21	10	.299

He has no power, but had an unprecedented 80/23 BB/W in A-ball Prince William.

Fleming is an unknown quantity, but he's 22-years-old (two years younger than Kevin Jordan) and with plate discipline like his he can only mature into a fine hitter. If he's got a glove, he'll be moving up in the world in '94.

SCOTT FLETCHER — RED SOX

AB	R	H	2B	3B	HR	RBI	BB	K	SB	CS	AVG.
480	81	137	31	5	5	45	37	35	16	3	.285

Fletcher, the journeyman, turned up his offense a bit and proved to be a solid acquisition for the Sox last year. He raised his average, hit a career-high 31 doubles, and showed surprising speed. To top it off, his 5.38 range factor was the third highest in AL.

Scott's been consistent throughout his career, he will be again this year. If Tim Naehring stays healthy, though, he will give him some competition for the starting job.

KEVIN FLORA — ANGELS
AAA – Vancouver

AB	R	H	2B	3B	HR	RBI	BB	K	SB	CS	AVG.
94	17	31	2	0	1	12	10	20	6	2	.330

Kevin's season effectively ended when his wife and nephew tragically died in a car accident on April 22, 1993.

He's 25 and still on the 40-man roster. The Angels still view him as a prospect because he's a fine hitter and seems like a team player.

We just hope he can get his life in order after this trauma. ... Whether he can succeed as a ballplayer is a secondary concern.

MIGUEL FLORES — INDIANS
AA – Canton-Akron

AB	R	H	2B	3B	HR	RBI	BB	K	SB	CS	AVG.
435	73	127	20	5	3	54	59	39	36	9	.292

He's stuck behind Baerga for the useful part of his Indians career. Flores, 23, is a speed-driven player with excellent command of the strike zone.

Cleveland has another two seasons to decide what they're going to do with him and a lot of things can happen in that span. But there's a good chance that if Flores makes it to the show, it will be with another team.

TOM FOLEY — PIRATES

AB	R	H	2B	3B	HR	RBI	BB	K	SB	CS	AVG.
194	18	49	11	1	3	22	11	26	0	0	.253

Foley provides a solid glove to backup Garcia and Young when needed. He picked up his numbers a little last year, but he's never had much punch.

His career, though long and less-than-illustrious, is about over.

JEFF FRYE — RANGERS
Missed 1993 season due to injury.

Frye missed the whole season after tearing an anterior-cruciate ligament (you know right where that is) in his right knee while jogging. One of those injuries that management loves.

He worked hard in rehab and played winter ball, where he seriously injured his wrist. Texas is still high on him, but the wrist will keep him from battling for the starting job.

MIKE GALLEGO — YANKEES

AB	R	H	2B	3B	HR	RBI	BB	K	SB	CS	AVG
403	63	114	20	1	10	54	50	65	3	2	.283

Gallego has proven to be a pretty smooth acquisition for the Yankees, who seem to be running a retirement community in their infield with the likes of Mikey, Wade Boggs and Spike Owen on the roster.

Gallego's career took a sort of fluky turn his last year with the A's. Apparently someone gave him some power for his birthday since he has hit 25 of his 36 career home runs since turning 30.

Gallego picks it like "Duelling Banjoes" at second with fabulous range and zone ratings.

He outhit the much younger Pat Kelly by quite a bit, so although management didn't start him at second, they made sure to get him some PT at third and short whenever possible.

Even though Mike will probably fall off the wagon and resume his inferior status with the bat, he'll see quality time as a utility man.

CARLOS GARCIA — PIRATES

AB	R	H	2B	3B	HR	RBI	BB	K	SB	CS	AVG
546	77	147	25	5	12	47	31	67	18	11	.269

Garcia surprised everyone by hitting .269 last year, which should tell you nobody expected very much. The thing is he hits so much better than Lind ever did, nobody in Pittsburgh cares if his average isn't stellar. Carlos hit 12 HR last year; Lind hit eight HR in six years in Pittsburgh. His defensive ability is light-years below Lind's (and most everybody else's), but that may be overlooked somewhat with Bell anchoring the middle infield.

Garcia has never had much use for walks and he doesn't show much sign of improving as a hitter. Hopefully, Pittsburgh will soon realize that there better players out there who can handle the pivot and hit. We hate to say it, but until then, he's the man.

JEFF GARDNER — PADRES

AB	R	H	2B	3B	HR	RBI	BB	K	SB	CS	AVG
404	53	106	21	7	1	24	45	69	2	6	.262

He's a great fielder with exceptional range. Defines mediocre when he's at the plate.

BRENT GATES — ATHLETICS

AB	R	H	2B	3B	HR	RBI	BB	K	SB	CS	AVG
535	64	155	29	2	7	69	56	75	7	3	.290

Apparently the A's heeded our warning about not shelving Gates. He not only exceeded our expectations by making it to the A's a year early, he spent a combined 24 games in Double-A and Triple-A enroute.

This kid looks like a keeper. His power isn't exceptional, but second base doesn't exactly have a reputation for producing Ruthian sluggers.

Gates showed a lot of patience for a youngster, taking almost four pitches per plate appearance. Bizarrely, he hit for better average when he was behind in the count than when he got ahead of the pitcher! Thirty-one of his RBI came after the pitcher had two strikes on him. Go figure.

His defense was just about the worst in the AL. His year was somewhat like that of California 1B J.T Snow, except that he was a much more polished hitter. All in all he adds up to a pretty little package with the lumber; let's see what he can do with the glove.

TONY GRAFFAGNINO — BRAVES
A – Durham

AB	R	H	2B	3B	HR	RBI	BB	K	SB	CS	AVG
459	78	126	30	5	15	69	45	78	24	11	.275

This is a pretty nice looking 22-year-old. Durham is a pretty neutral park in a pitcher's league, so his offensive numbers were a fair measure of his ability.

In addition, *B.A.* identified him as the top defensive infield prospect in the organization, so he's well regarded with the leather.

He'll start 1994 in Double-A Greenville, but with some solid play, he should graduate to Richmond by season's end. If he's on schedule, he'll be challenging for Lemke's job as a 23-year-old in the spring of '95.

BILLY HALL — RED SOX
AA – Wichita

AB	R	H	2B	3B	HR	RBI	BB	K	SB	CS	AVG.
486	80	131	27	7	4	46	37	88	29	19	.270

Billy lost some of his speed in the transition from A-ball to Double-A, but retained his lousy habit of getting caught about 40 percent of the time.

Hall's not a bad prospect, but he really hit an impasse in Wichita (while still a Padre). He'll have to prove he can get over this hurdle and improve his stealing habits. A guy who gets caught that much hurts his team and Lord knows the Sox can't afford to give up runs.

MIKE HARDGE — EXPOS
AA – Harrisburg

AB	R	H	2B	3B	HR	RBI	BB	K	SB	CS	AVG.
386	70	94	14	10	6	35	37	97	27	8	.244

He's 22 and the Expos figure he'll eventually replace DeShields. ... We guess the fact that Delino finished second in Rookie of the Year balloting by age 21 doesn't figure into this. ... Anyway, Hardge looks nice. He knows he needs to work the strike zone and was quoted in *B.W.* as saying he's working on it.

As we all know, we can't lick a problem until we accept we have one. When you hear a player saying, "I'm not doing this and I need to be," they're half way there. If he can improve that K/W, his average will improve and he'll be a solid hitter. The jury's out on his defense, but he could get Lansing's old job as infield rover this year if Lansing wins the starting second-base job.

JASON HARDTKE — PADRES
A – Rancho Cucamonga

AB	R	H	2B	3B	HR	RBI	BB	K	SB	CS	AVG.
523	98	167	38	7	11	85	61	54	7	8	.319

He's three years younger than Billy Hall and looks like a better hitter. He doesn't have Hall's speed, but he should be in San Diego while Hall sits on Boston's bench.

LENNY HARRIS — DODGERS

AB	R	H	2B	3B	HR	RBI	BB	K	SB	CS	AVG.
160	20	38	6	1	2	11	15	15	3	1	.238

He was really ineffective this year. He'll probably improve next year, but how much is enough to make him worth something? The arrival of DeShields and the Dodgers' apparent commitment to 3B Dave Hansen is leaving Lenny fewer positions to fill.

DAVE HOWARD — ROYALS
AAA – Omaha

AB	R	H	2B	3B	HR	RBI	BB	K	SB	CS	AVG.
157	15	40	8	2	0	18	7	20	3	1	.255

Howard will end up as an organizational player if he doesn't retire first. It's hard to foresee him earning a roster spot in '94 unless a real big-leaguer gets injured.

KEVIN JORDAN — YANKEES
AA – Albany

AB	R	H	2B	3B	HR	RBI	BB	K	SB	CS	AVG.
513	87	145	33	4	16	87	41	53	8	4	.283

The 24-year-old Jordan looked great in Double-A Albany last year. He's got remarkable power for a second baseman and he does all the little things, such as getting on base and scoring runs.

Jordan will battle for his position in the spring, but there's no reason why the Yanks shouldn't try him out instead of dinosaurs like Gallego and lesser players like Pat Kelly.

Jordan was ranked No. 8 in the Eastern League by *Baseball America*.

BOB JUDAY — RED SOX
A – Lynchburg

AB	R	H	2B	3B	HR	RBI	BB	K	SB	CS	AVG.
354	67	105	15	1	4	32	83	58	5	5	.297

Bob's showing a lot of promise at the plate.

He's got some power, but his calling card is his remarkable plate discipline. He tallied 83 walks and a .430 OBP in Lynchburg, which is excellent at 22. He's solid in the field as well.

PAT KELLY — YANKEES

AB	R	H	2B	3B	HR	RBI	BB	K	SB	CS	AVG.
406	49	111	24	1	7	51	24	68	14	11	.273

He complemented Gallego very nicely as a fielder, improving immensely over last year's glovework. With these two in a platoon, defense isn't much of a problem.

He had an adequate year with the bat and hit righties and lefties about the same. As usual, his K/W ratio left much to be desired.

He's young so he might even get a little better. Even if he doesn't, his glove seems to have found a job.

JEFF KENT — METS

AB	R	H	2B	3B	HR	RBI	BB	K	SB	CS	AVG
496	65	134	24	0	21	80	30	88	4	4	.270

He needs some polish on his strike zone, but he has shown an ability to hit for power and that should keep him in the lineup. His defensive stats stunk, but he's been shifted around the infield throughout his minor league career, so there's little wonder why.

CHUCH KNOBLAUCH — TWINS

AB	R	H	2B	3B	HR	RBI	BB	K	SB	CS	AVG
602	82	167	27	4	2	41	65	44	29	11	.277

Knoblauch had a really inconsistent year and his production suffered. But then, most of the Twins can say that. His numbers weren't bad, but his reputation made everyone look for a breakthrough year.

His defense isn't coming along as expected, but his .354 OBP and 29 stolen bases still add to the offense. And though '93 wasn't what everyone expected, there weren't any warning signs to scare you away. His plate discipline is good and he managed to cut down on his K's. Maybe the All-Star projections should be postponed, but he looks he'll be a consistent .280+ hitter with some speed.

BRIAN KOELLING — REDS
AA – Chattanooga

AB	R	H	2B	3B	HR	RBI	BB	K	SB	CS	AVG
430	64	119	17	6	4	47	32	105	34	13	.277

Koelling, 25, is a decent hitter, though certainly not outstanding. His BA is above average and he has good speed, but he has little power and terrible plate discipline.

He can play in the field and could fill Branson's backup role. Cinci has a ton of these guys, though, so he's on a long waiting list.

MARK LEMKE — BRAVES

AB	R	H	2B	3B	HR	RBI	BB	K	SB	CS	AVG
493	52	124	19	2	7	49	65	50	1	2	.252

Lemke had a much more consistent season with the glove: flashing his typically high range with a much improved double-play rate.

Lemke's bat is nothing really special, but at least he draws some walks and keeps his OBP respectable. He's nothing great, but with his glove and grit, he's certainly a championship caliber player.

JOSE LIND — ROYALS

AB	R	H	2B	3B	HR	RBI	BB	K	SB	CS	AVG
431	33	107	13	2	0	37	13	36	3	2	.248

So what did you expect? A .300 average and 100 runs scored?

The Royals are waiting with bated breath for the emergence of Mike Tucker. Until that time, Lind can fail to produce as well as the next guy and have a decent glove.

LUIS LOPEZ — PADRES
AAA – Las Vegas

AB	R	H	2B	3B	HR	RBI	BB	K	SB	CS	AVG
491	52	150	36	6	6	58	27	62	8	0	.305

Lopez doesn't look like an exceptional hitter and his defense probably isn't better than Jeff Gardner's. He's 23, though, so watch for him in the spring.

TOREY LOVULLO — ANGELS

AB	R	H	2B	3B	HR	RBI	BB	K	SB	CS	AVG
367	42	92	20	0	6	30	36	49	7	6	.251

Lovullo was thrust into a full-time role when Damion Easley went down in June with his shin-splint problem.

Lovullo's bat carried him for the first two months of the season, but he slumped and ended up with mediocre numbers. On defense, Lovullo really shined.

If given a similar shot in 1994, Torey would probably show more with the lumber. He's had a good minor-league career and has more power and plate discipline than he showed last year. Because he's only 28, it's really doubtful that those skills have deserted him.

ANTHONY MANAHAN — MARINERS
AAA – Calgary

AB	R	H	2B	3B	HR	RBI	BB	K	SB	CS	AVG
451	70	136	31	4	3	62	38	48	19	4	.302

Manahan played third at Calgary and short in the Arizona Fall League. The Mariners may be seriously considering this guy for a job, but with his numbers, he'd be a .240-.255 hitting joke. He's 25 and, given his performance in the PCL, he'd have no power, no walks and little average.

His glove better be like Bill Mazeroski's if he's gonna hit like that. But, from what we've heard, Robby Alomar isn't exactly quaking in his cleats.

But a final disclaimer: AFL managers love this guy and he may have moved his game up with his fall stint. Watch carefully in spring, but be very skeptical.

NORBERTO MARTIN — WHITE SOX
AAA – Nashville

AB	R	H	2B	3B	HR	RBI	BB	K	SB	CS	AVG.
580	87	179	21	6	9	74	26	59	31	5	.309

He's a little old to be attempting entry into the majors. He's had as average a career as possible in his nine minor league seasons so expect almost nothing out of him.

JEFF MCKNIGHT — METS

AB	R	H	2B	3B	HR	RBI	BB	K	SB	CS	AVG.
164	19	42	3	1	2	13	13	31	0	0	.256

He's the best athlete to come out of South Side High School in Bee Branch, Arkansas. Not too distinguishing? Neither is his hitting.

ROBERTO MEJIA — ROCKIES
AAA – Colorado Springs

AB	R	H	2B	3B	HR	RBI	BB	K	SB	CS	AVG.
291	51	87	15	2	14	48	18	56	12	5	.299

The Dodgers signed him when he was 16 years old and the Rockies chose him in the second round of the expansion draft after only two years as a pro. That gives you an idea of how talented this 22-year-old youngster is. He bypassed Double-A altogether and, flexed his muscles for Colorado Springs in '93. Though his home park had quite a bit to do with the power surge, his bat is for real.

Scouts say Mejia's glove-work is of major-league calibre right now, even if his bat isn't. If Colorado can wait for his plate discipline to come around, Mejia should break through in '94 or '95 and pay some serious dividends.

CHARLIE MONTOYO — EXPOS
A – Ottawa

AB	R	H	2B	3B	HR	RBI	BB	K	SB	CS	AVG.
319	43	89	18	2	1	43	71	37	0	9	.279

He's a typical career minor-leaguer: great control of the strike zone, but no power or speed. He's sort of like an Amaral type, but Hardge and Lansing are solid performers and the only way Montoyo will get PT is if the injury big hits Montreal hard this year.

MICKEY MORANDINI — PHILLIES

AB	R	H	2B	3B	HR	RBI	BB	K	SB	CS	AVG.
425	57	105	19	9	3	33	34	73	13	2	.247

An average fielder and a poor hitter. He's got good base-running judgment, but can't do anything else that well.

JAMES MOUTON — ASTROS
AAA – Tucson

AB	R	H	2B	3B	HR	RBI	BB	K	SB	CS	AVG.
546	126	172	42	12	16	92	72	82	40	18	.315

At first glance, he appears to be a one-man wrecking-crew with the bat. His glove at second is abysmal.

If you take the air out of his PCL-inflated stats, he's a pretty good hitter, but at the .250-.270 level with about half the power.

He did quite excellent work in the AFL, but he also made a bunch of throwing errors. What the Astros should do is stick him in the outfield and let him play rover for 100 games, or trade someone (most probably Finley).

ORLANDO MUNOZ — ANGELS
A – Palm Springs

AB	R	H	2B	3B	HR	RBI	BB	K	SB	CS	AVG.
237	38	64	8	3	0	24	47	25	23	14	.270

What is he? According to *B.A.*, he played second at Palm Springs; he then played third at Double-A Midland. STATS, Inc. split the difference and said he's a shortstop.

It doesn't matter, Munoz is 23 and he looks like he's got enough plate discipline to make his game work at any level. He'll probably see Triple-A this summer and might have a shot at the bench come fall. He's not a star, but he looks like a good replacement-level player.

TIM NAEHRING — RED SOX

AB	R	H	2B	3B	HR	RBI	BB	K	SB	CS	AVG.
127	14	42	10	0	1	17	10	26	1	0	.331

Tim could be an awesome hitter if he could stay healthy. He's been in the league for four years and hasn't lasted long enough to get 200 ABs once. He's had back problems and had surgery last year to repair a torn muscle in his right shoulder. But his rehab assignment in Pawtucket suggests he may be ready to play. He hit .331 and slugged .433 in 55 games.

We know he's a great hitter, but we're getting tired of waiting for him to prove it.

JOHN PATTERSON										GIANTS
AB	R	H	2B	3B	HR	RBI	BB	K	SB	CS	AVG
16	1	3	0	0	1	2	0	5	0	1	.188

Saw mostly pinch-hitting duty in '93 and sure didn't make much of it. Yet another 27-year-old wannabe floating around the majors for no apparent reason.

GERONIMO PENA										CARDINALS
AB	R	H	2B	3B	HR	RBI	BB	K	SB	CS	AVG
254	34	65	19	2	5	30	25	71	13	5	.256

He missed most of July and all of August with a broken toe, but he had fallen out of Torre's favor before that with some shoddy defensive work. The book on his fielding is that he has excellent range, but his glove was forged from the hardest pit iron in the land.

His offensive skills revolve around speed; he once stole 80 bases in the minors. But he certainly hasn't shown much in the way of plate discipline. He has the tools, he just needs to use them.

TONY PHILLIPS										TIGERS
AB	R	H	2B	3B	HR	RBI	BB	K	SB	CS	AVG
566	113	177	27	0	7	57	132	102	16	11	.313

Phillips is the spark that makes the Tigers go; it's impossible to overstate his value. His versatility allows Sparky to try any cock-eyed lineup he can dream up, knowing Tony can fill the gap anywhere he's needed.

This shuffling hurts his defense a little, but it doesn't affect him at the plate. He led the major leagues in walks last year and reached base more often than any other lead-off hitter.

He's a workhorse and at 35, you wonder when he's going to slow down. But our advice is never to bet against Tony the Tiger.

ARQUIMEDEZ POZO										MARINERS
A – Riverside										
AB	R	H	2B	3B	HR	RBI	BB	K	SB	CS	AVG
515	98	176	44	6	13	83	56	56	10	10	.342

Whoooo! This kid's 20 and he looks unbelievably good. ... Like Montreal's Jose Vidro, Pozo is compared to Carlos Baerga. Like Baerga, he has good defensive range and, importantly, he has better plate discipline than Baerga did at the same age.

OK, how about some accountability: Pozo was named the No. 4 prospect in the California League by *B.A.* Can anyone explain this? We'd put him at No. 1, end of story.

He'll start at Double-A, but if he hits well enough, you may see him in the bigs before the season ends. Don't count on it, but he's got enough talent to be Seattle's starter by '95.

RANDY READY										EXPOS
AB	R	H	2B	3B	HR	RBI	BB	K	SB	CS	AVG
134	22	34	8	1	1	10	23	8	2	1	.254

He's still the same player he always was, possessing those great on-base skills, but his power is waning as he hits the mid-30s. He's really one of baseball's good guys and you have to hope he'll get a shot at managing in a few years. Something tells us he'd know how to handle mega-prospects that don't initially live up to their potential, but don't ask us why (look at his career numbers in the minors).

JODY REED										DODGERS
AB	R	H	2B	3B	HR	RBI	BB	K	SB	CS	AVG
445	48	123	21	2	2	31	38	40	1	3	.276

Continued to be hellacious with the mitt, but his hitting has gone into a tailspin. Not only did his line-drive power go under, but he completely lost any notion of drawing a walk.

Reed was gutsy enough to turn down a three-year, $8 million deal from the Dodgers, figuring he was worth enough to push negotiations further. L.A. responded by acquiring Delino DeShields and waving bye-bye to the still gutsy, and newly unemployed Reed. It's doubtful that he'll see an offer as sweet as the Dodgers' from anyone else he solicits.

RICH RENTERIA										MARLINS
AB	R	H	2B	3B	HR	RBI	BB	K	SB	CS	AVG
263	27	67	9	2	2	30	21	31	0	2	.255

A 32-year-old stopgap who can hit righties OK, but doesn't really field well. He's suitable for a platoon arrangement, but Bret Barberie and Alex Arias are much better players.

HAROLD REYNOLDS										ORIOLES
AB	R	H	2B	3B	HR	RBI	BB	K	SB	CS	AVG
485	64	122	20	4	4	47	66	47	12	11	.252

Unfortunately, the O's didn't heed our advice last year and nail Harold's foot to first. He doesn't add much to the offense in the first place and 11 CS just adds salt to the wound.

His defense is still above-average, though, and he led AL second basemen with 111 DPs.

Harold's stats have been consistent the last four years and he gets the job done. He just needs to admit he's lost a step or ten.

BILLY RIPKEN — RANGERS

AB	R	H	2B	3B	HR	RBI	BB	K	SB	CS	AVG.
132	12	25	4	0	0	11	11	19	0	2	.189

Ripken has absolutely no hitting ability, his defense is declining and he keeps a second home on the DL.

Really, he's never been much more than Cal's brother and that doesn't count for much outside Baltimore.

BIP ROBERTS — REDS

AB	R	H	2B	3B	HR	RBI	BB	K	SB	CS	AVG.
292	46	70	13	10	1	18	36	46	26	6	.240

Roberts was bothered by a thumb injury all year, which really hurt his production and muddled the Reds' infield situation. So does the arrival of Bret Boone.

But Bip finally got to concentrate on one position and his defense improved as a result.

If he's healthy this year, the position should be his to lose. He's proven himself to be a consistent hitter and still has impressive speed. He also avoids those nasty little temper tantrums that tend to limit your playing time.

Bip will be back and so will his .280+ BA.

RICO ROSSY — ROYALS

AB	R	H	2B	3B	HR	RBI	BB	K	SB	CS	AVG.
86	10	19	4	0	2	12	9	11	0	0	.221

His name has a nice ring to it and probably looks neat on the back of a jersey, but otherwise, Rossy has no business being in the bigs.

JUAN SAMUEL — REDS

AB	R	H	2B	3B	HR	RBI	BB	K	SB	CS	AVG.
261	31	60	10	4	4	26	23	53	9	7	.230

Samuel worked the most innings at second for the Reds last year, but only because of the injury to Bip Roberts. With the arrival of Bret Boone, we guarantee it won't happen again.

Juan's been bouncing around the league the last few years and he just happened to land on the right team.

At 33, he still gets a ton of K's and he's light-years away from his 72 SB season in '84. Unless the Reds cut him and he gets lucky again, he won't see the field very often this year.

RYNE SANDBERG — CUBS

AB	R	H	2B	3B	HR	RBI	BB	K	SB	CS	AVG.
456	67	141	20	0	9	45	37	62	9	2	.309

His broken hand might explain his power outage last year. He missed all of April and suffered from a lack of run production, but Sandberg still hit .309 on the season, .326 after the All-Star break and .282 with runners in scoring position. And his work in the field was as solid as it ever was.

He's been showing the brat pack how it's done at second for the last four years and now they've surpassed him in ability. But Ryne is far from washed up; he should rebound in '94.

RUBEN SANTANA — MARINERS

AA – Jacksonville

AB	R	H	2B	3B	HR	RBI	BB	K	SB	CS	AVG.
499	79	150	21	2	21	84	38	101	13	8	.301

At 6-2, 175, the 24-year-old Santana may be too large for the position, but he can pick it a little at second. And he sure as heck has enough of a bat for the position, even if his plate discipline is atrocious.

He looks like he'll get a good shot at a job in the spring, but his long-term future is in grave danger because of Arquimedez Pozo.

STEVE SCARSONE — GIANTS

AB	R	H	2B	3B	HR	RBI	BB	K	SB	CS	AVG.
103	16	26	9	0	2	15	4	32	0	1	.252

He had a 8/1 K/W ratio this year. You'd better be Robbie Alomar and have a glove the size of Cecil Fielder if you're gonna "not hit" like that and survive in the bigs.

KEVIN SEFCIK — PHILLIES

A – Batavia

AB	R	H	2B	3B	HR	RBI	BB	K	SB	CS	AVG.
281	49	84	24	4	2	28	27	22	20	7	.299

Consider him a 23-year-old infield rover, kind of like Mike Lansing of the Phils. He's a lot like Lansing, very good speed, great hustle, but otherwise average tools.

These kinds of players get major league jobs and hold onto them. He's probably 12-to-18 months away from a shot at the show.

MIKE SHARPERSON											DODGERS
AB	R	H	2B	3B	HR	RBI	BB	K	SB	CS	AVG.
90	13	23	4	0	2	10	5	17	2	0	.256

Mike saw almost no PT and didn't even come close to 1992's apparent swan song. The Dodgers' neglect seems to have caused him to lose faith in himself as a hitter.

Thirty-two is a funny age. He's young enough to keep going for several more productive years and old enough to be deader than a doornail. Let's hope for the former.

TERRY SHUMPERT											ROYALS
AAA – Omaha											
AB	R	H	2B	3B	HR	RBI	BB	K	SB	CS	AVG.
413	70	124	29	1	14	59	41	62	36	8	.300

The glove is decent, but he's known in our social circles as Terry Slumpert (AKA "Chumpert"). Put a bat in his hands and you get a blank expression and a wasted plate appearance in return. Could his Triple-A numbers be for real? Only the shadow knows.

LUIS SOJO											BLUE JAYS
AAA – Syracuse											
AB	R	H	2B	3B	HR	RBI	BB	K	SB	CS	AVG.
142	17	31	7	2	1	12	8	12	2	1	.218

What he's shown in the majors is really not what he's capable of. In the minors, Sojo has been a contact hitter with a decent average. But the name of the game is playing time, and Sojo will get very little.

BILL SPIERS											BREWERS
AB	R	H	2B	3B	HR	RBI	BB	K	SB	CS	AVG.
340	43	81	8	4	2	36	29	51	9	8	.238

He didn't return at all well after having lost '92 to injury. Let's just say that what Spiers and platoon-mate Doran did with the bat this year was a lot closer to the Jose Lind end of the spectrum than it was to Carlos Baerga.

Bill was a decent hitter not long ago, so he may still be suffering from lingering injuries. The Brewers took a chance and re-signed him for '94, but another year like this and they'll be passing out blindfolds in the Brewer dugout.

ANDY STANKIEWICZ											ASTROS
AAA – Columbus											
AB	R	H	2B	3B	HR	RBI	BB	K	SB	CS	AVG.
331	45	80	12	5	0	32	29	46	12	8	.242

Evan: Stankie was one of my pet Rotisserie projects in '93. As you may have surmised, it failed miserably.

I still think that he has a chance to contribute as he did in '92, but to be shipped to Siberia after 400 fairly productive at-bats as he was, can bruise the tender, leaf-green psyche of a sensitive sapling like Andy.

Sorry Andy, but I just can't afford you this time around. Good luck, keep in touch and be sure the return address on the envelope is marked Tucson, just to be on the safe side.

DOUG STRANGE											RANGERS
AB	R	H	2B	3B	HR	RBI	BB	K	SB	CS	AVG.
484	58	124	29	0	7	60	43	69	6	4	.256

Doug got his first shot at being a full-time starter last year at 29, which is a little too late.

Defensively, he's average and he's never had much of a bat. He should be a backup and if Texas can find anybody else, he will be.

TIM TEUFEL											PADRES
AB	R	H	2B	3B	HR	RBI	BB	K	SB	CS	AVG.
200	26	50	11	2	7	31	27	39	2	2	.250

Teufel's nice, boring stats may have saved his job after two seasons of complete doodoo. He proved once again that he has absolutely no business batting against right-handers, but at his age, who really cares.

Basically, Tim's another guy who we've probably seen the last of. If it's not this year, it'll be the next.

ROBBY THOMPSON											GIANTS
AB	R	H	2B	3B	HR	RBI	BB	K	SB	CS	AVG.
494	85	154	30	2	19	65	45	97	10	4	.312

Robby's year was pretty comparable to what he did in '91, as he hit a career high 19 homers. His '93 definitely gets the edge, though. He scored and drove in a lot more runs, he hit for 40 more points better average and had significantly higher on-base and slugging percentages.

Thompson has had a nicely productive tenure with the Giants and his career is far from over as he showed this year. His glovework combines with his bat to place him nice and high on the list of major-league second basemen. The Giants were wise to place his re-signing atop their winter agenda.

Mike Tucker — Royals

AA – Memphis

AB	R	H	2B	3B	HR	RBI	BB	K	SB	CS	AVG
244	38	68	7	4	9	35	42	51	12	5	.279

There's no question about this 23-year-old's ability to hit. He has the potential to hit .300 in the majors with line-drive power and a healthy on-base percentage.

He moved to second from his natural shortstop position because of questionable defense, but scouts say he has the smarts, and more than enough athletic ability, to earn a roster spot at either position in the future. He's a season or two away, but his bat will be the major determinant as to when he gets the call.

Brad Tyler — Orioles

AA – Bowie

AB	R	H	2B	3B	HR	RBI	BB	K	SB	CS	AVG
437	85	103	23	17	10	44	84	89	24	11	.236

Tyler, 25, has a nice combination of speed and power. His average suffered last year in a pitcher's league, but he made the most of his hits and scored a lot of runs.

He still has some lessons to learn, though, like patience at the plate and judgment on the basepaths. He's still a year or two away.

Quilvio Veras — Mets

AA – Binghamton

AB	R	H	2B	3B	HR	RBI	BB	K	SB	CS	AVG
444	87	136	19	7	2	51	91	62	52	23	.306

A 23-year-old middle infielder from the Dominican Republic, Veras has what it takes to be one of the better leadoff hitters in the National League in two or three years. He led the Eastern League in walks (91) and on-base percentage (.430) and finished second in stolen bases (52). With the potential to become a .300 hitter in the show, Veras fits the leadoff mold as well as anyone in the minors right now. If things break right for Veras, he'll spend the first half of '94 in Triple-A and the second half in New York.

Jose Vidro — Expos

A – Burlington

AB	R	H	2B	3B	HR	RBI	BB	K	SB	CS	AVG
287	39	69	19	0	2	34	28	54	3	2	.240

The scouts love this 19-year-old and compare him to Carlos Baerga. As you can see, there's little to really to go on. At 18, Baerga was doing pretty well in the Sally League (he hit for better average and more power than Vidro, but had worse K/W data). At 19, Carlos was hitting .270 with 12 dingers in the Double-A Texas League.

What this means, is that Vidro is going to have to improve a lot over the next year or two. The thing is, he doesn't have a Robby Alomar in front of him, like Baerga did. If he can push his game up, he'll start for the el cheapo Expos.

Chico Walker — Cubs

AB	R	H	2B	3B	HR	RBI	BB	K	SB	CS	AVG
213	18	48	7	1	5	19	14	29	7	0	.225

He's had one hell of a career ... in the minors. Sadly, no team was willing to give him a chance to develop at the major-league level. The Cubs, in their infinite wisdom, gave up on him twice. He's 35 this season, so the clock has just about run out on him.

Lou Whitaker — Tigers

AB	R	H	2B	3B	HR	RBI	BB	K	SB	CS	AVG
383	72	111	32	1	9	67	78	46	3	3	.290

You have to love a player like Sweet Lou. You keep expecting a drop-off from a 37-year-old infielder; Lou just keeps rolling on.

His line-drive power and ability to draw walks make him an excellent No. 2 hitter behind Phillips. He does whatever it takes to move the runner.

He can still match his defensive skills with any second baseman in the league and his offensive skills with most first basemen.

The only thing you should question is his future playing time. It's been decreasing the last few years, and with Sparky's endless shuffling of the lineup, you can expect the same next year.

Chris Wimmer — Giants

A – San Jose

AB	R	H	2B	3B	HR	RBI	BB	K	SB	CS	AVG
493	76	130	21	4	3	53	42	72	49	12	.264

Great speed and no power, the age-old story at second.

At 23, Wimmer's getting old for an A-baller, so he'd better catch a highball out of there. He can hit some, but he doesn't look exceptional.

Eric Yelding — Cubs

AB	R	H	2B	3B	HR	RBI	BB	K	SB	CS	AVG.
108	14	22	5	1	1	10	11	22	3	2	.204

He used to at least have excellent speed. But his lame bat should force him into retirement within a year or so.

Eric Young — Rockies

AB	R	H	2B	3B	HR	RBI	BB	K	SB	CS	AVG.
490	82	132	16	8	3	42	63	41	42	19	.269

He's not really impressive with the lumber, but he does have the tools of an adequate lead-off hitter. Besides, it seems all you've got to do in Colorado to be successful is get on base and wait for someone to hit a double up the gap. Young can do that, steal a few bases and, while he's at it, keep the position warm and cozy for Roberto Mejia.

THIRD BASE – *RANKINGS*

	Player	Total	Avg. Off.	Def. Runs Saved
1	Robin Ventura	30.1	20.2	14.4
2	Matt Williams	25.7	12.9	18.5
3	Wade Boggs	21.8	5.8	23.1
4	Terry Pendleton	18.8	11.5	10.6
5	Gary Sheffield	18.4	29.7	-16.3
6	Dave Hollins	16.6	18.3	-2.4
7	Ken Caminiti	16.2	11.1	7.4
8	Tim Hullett	15.9	2.6	19.2
9	Steve Buechele	12.6	4.3	12.0
10	Jeff King	11.9	2.3	14.0
11	Mike Lansing	11.5	1.8	14.1
12	Charlie Hayes	11.2	6.9	6.1
13	Dean Palmer	9.4	9.7	-0.4
14	B.J. Surhoff	8.1	-0.5	12.4
15	Rene Gonzales	7.9	2.1	8.4
16	Sean Berry	7.1	5.0	3.1
17	Todd Zeile	6.9	9.2	-3.4
18	Leo Gomez	6.8	3.3	5.1
19	Chris Sabo	5.7	1.6	6.0
20	Kevin Seitzer	5.3	5.3	-0.1
21	Jim Thome	5.2	1.9	4.8
22	Mike Blowers	5.0	4.1	1.3
22	Dave Magadan	5.0	2.0	4.3
24	Mike Pagliarulo	4.9	2.1	4.0
25	Scott Livingstone	4.3	1.3	4.3

THIRD BASE – *PROSPECTS*

Short-range

1. Phil Nevin
2. Butch Huskey
3. Shane Andrews
4. Russ Davis
5. David Bell
6. Jose Oliva
7. Scott Stahoviak
8. Jeff Cirillo
9. Mike Busch
10. George Williams
11. Luis Ortiz
12. Howard Battle
13. Joe Randa

Long-range

1. Brad Fullmer
2. Preston Wilson
3. Jason Giambi
4. Julio Bruno
5. Ken Bonifay
6. Dominic Therrien
7. Tim Forkner

Sleepers

1. Jim Thome
2. Willie Greene
3. Leo Gomez
4. Tim Costo
5. Russ McGinnis
6. Jeff Manto
7. Stan Royer

THIRD BASE – *ESSAYS*

SHANE ANDREWS — EXPOS
AA – Harrisburg

AB	R	H	2B	3B	HR	RBI	BB	K	SB	CS	AVG
442	77	115	29	1	18	70	64	118	10	6	.260

Shane, 22, did what we asked him to do in last year's Advocate: drive up the average and cut down on the K's while keeping the power.

With the trade of DeShields, there is a hole in the infield and there's a job waiting to be won. If Andrews can impress in the spring, he could be with the big club to open the season. If not, he'll be in Ottawa with a solid chance to play big-league ball by mid-summer.

He still needs to improve his game, but he's not too far from having the requisite skills of a quality starter in the majors.

KIM BATISTE — PHILLIES

AB	R	H	2B	3B	HR	RBI	BB	K	SB	CS	AVG
156	14	44	7	1	5	29	3	29	0	1	.282

He has terrible plate discipline, but hit for good average and solid power. Kim's "clutch defense" in Playoffs notwithstanding, Batiste is a decent fielder (especially when compared to Hollins last year).

Batiste absolutely smashed lefties: He had a .349 BA and hit four of his five homers in 43 anti-southpaw at-bats. He posted a .698 SLG against 'em (credit STATS).

He must drive up his ridiculous 29/3 K/W ratio, or one will have to conclude that the .282 average was a fluke.

HOWARD BATTLE — BLUE JAYS
AA – Knoxville

AB	R	H	2B	3B	HR	RBI	BB	K	SB	CS	AVG
521	66	145	21	5	7	70	45	94	12	9	.278

It'll be at least another two years before we'll see Battle in a Blue Jays lineup. But he's only 22 and his career won't really suffer from the delay. He needs to cut the strikeouts by at least 20 percent before he can be considered a grade-A prospect, but he could do it in Syracuse. Check in with us in a year, and we'll let you know how bright his future is.

DAVID BELL — INDIANS
AA – Canton-Akron

AB	R	H	2B	3B	HR	RBI	BB	K	SB	CS	AVG
483	69	141	20	2	9	60	43	54	3	4	.292

A couple of things stand out about this lad. First, he had a breakthrough season, hitting .292 with a .350 on-base, at the age of 21. He was the youngest player in the Eastern League. That's a pretty advanced brand of ball for such a puppy. Bell has plenty of time to hone his skills and develop some power, but it appears his work at the plate is already sharp.

Second, he has an excellent pedigree. As the son of Buddy Bell, and the grandson of Gus Bell, David should join Bret Boone in the third-generation MLB'er within the next few years. Can he displace Thome, though?

SEAN BERRY — EXPOS

AB	R	H	2B	3B	HR	RBI	BB	K	SB	CS	AVG
299	50	78	15	2	14	49	41	70	12	2	.261

Sean bounced back from a poor start in April and May (.190 BA, one extra-base hit) and finished up with a respectable season.

He provided adequate glove work and a potent bat at third base: something the Expos haven't seen since 1990, when Tim Wallach was still good. This is not to say that Sean Berry is a star (he's 28 this year), but he'll be a fine player until Shane Andrews is ready, or Wil Cordero is permanently switched to third.

MIKE BLOWERS — MARINERS

AB	R	H	2B	3B	HR	RBI	BB	K	SB	CS	AVG
379	55	106	23	3	15	57	44	98	1	5	.280

Basically, he was the American League Sean Berry. He came into a situation where there was great flux (because of the Edgar Martinez injury) and provided about as good a backup play as you could dream up.

Blower's defense is adequate and his bat more than made up for his minor deficiencies in the field.

Blowers demolished left-handed pitching, hitting .357 off them with 10 homers in 154 at-bats! He slugged .669 off them and tallied 34 of his 57 RBI (credit STATS, Inc.).

The problem is that he only hit .280, so you can imagine how easily righties handled him (.227 BA, 74 K's in 225 at-bats).

His future is a little cloudy, despite his good works. A healthy Edgar Martinez is one of the best hitters in the AL and he'll drive Mike to the bench and leave the meter running.

Wade Boggs — Yankees

AB	R	H	2B	3B	HR	RBI	BB	K	SB	CS	AVG
560	83	169	26	1	2	59	74	49	0	1	.302

At 36, Boggs' slugging may have permanently dropped below .400. And while he rebounded from 1992's aberrant .259 BA, he has cut his doubles in half while also lowering his walks.

Still, Boggsie has little to apologize for. Five batting titles and six on-base crowns mark him as a solid candidate for the Hall.

He continued to be a solid third baseman with a zone rating far above-average.

He should contribute significantly to the Yanks for the next couple of years (or at least until Russ Davis matures), but he's certainly not the force that aging counterparts Molitor and Winfield are.

Ken Bonifay — Pirates

A – Salem

AB	R	H	2B	3B	HR	RBI	BB	K	SB	CS	AVG
361	59	100	19	1	18	60	42	63	12	2	.277

Bonifay slugged an impressive .485 last year in Salem, but then, everybody punished the ball in Salem last year. The park effect adjustment there was 138 percent for runs and 201 percent for homers! Take Bonifay's power numbers with a block of salt.

Still, his season last year should earn him an upgrade at least to Double-A. He has good discipline and some speed, but he's 23 and needs to make the move soon.

Mike Brumley — Angels

AAA – Tucson

AB	R	H	2B	3B	HR	RBI	BB	K	SB	CS	AVG
346	65	122	25	8	0	46	44	71	24	11	.353

He's 31, so he's not a prospect. He has never been able to stick in the show. He needs to keep his solid on-base ability and show some sparkle with the glove.

Julio Bruno — Padres

AA – Wichita

AB	R	H	2B	3B	HR	RBI	BB	K	SB	CS	AVG
246	34	70	17	1	3	24	11	46	3	5	.285

Bruno's pretty young at 21 years old and accompanied by the usual plate discipline shortcomings.

He doesn't have much power, but can stretch the extra base. According to Baseball America, the Padres see him as a Terry Pendleton-type who could develop a home run stroke.

Bruno's not a great prospect but his youth and the fact that his stiffest competition is Archi Cianfrocco work in his favor.

Steve Buechele — Cubs

AB	R	H	2B	3B	HR	RBI	BB	K	SB	CS	AVG
460	53	125	27	2	15	65	48	87	1	1	.272

The Cubs got some production out of his bat, but they shouldn't depend on it too much longer. Buechele took an inordinate amount of time getting the rust off his bat last year and was hitting just .234 at the break. He had a strong second half though and probably saved his job for another season. The Cubs have Craig Worthington in Iowa for insurance and there's a few good-looking prospects lower down, so Buechele might be on his way out the door in '94 or '95. Ya dig?

Mike Busch — Dodgers

AAA – Albuquerque

AB	R	H	2B	3B	HR	RBI	BB	K	SB	CS	AVG
431	87	122	32	4	22	70	53	89	1	2	.283

He's got very good power and he draws a walk. The Dodgers aren't happy with his glove, but they're less happy with Wallach.

The lone sticking point may be Dave Hansen, who needs to have a good spring to keep his job.

Ken Caminiti — Astros

AB	R	H	2B	3B	HR	RBI	BB	K	SB	CS	AVG
543	75	142	31	0	13	75	49	88	8	5	.262

Caminiti is a fine glove tempered with an adequate bat. He's solid on the double-play, has good range and makes a lot of fine hustle plays. The thing is, our 1993 prediction was dead on. His high ranking in the book has everything to do with his fine defense and his fine 1992 season, and little to do with his lackluster 1993.

The man lost 50 points off his slugging average and 30 off his on-base in a year while everyone else was going berserk, so the end result was that he was unimpressive.

He's a decent player, but it's doubtful, at age 31, he's going to duplicate his 1992 feats.

Pedro Castellano — Rockies

AAA – Colorado Springs

AB	R	H	2B	3B	HR	RBI	BB	K	SB	CS	AVG.
304	61	95	21	2	12	60	36	63	3	5	.313

This Venezuelan prospect signed with the Cubs when he was 18 and put in four years of growth in their system. Then the Rockies took him in the third round of the expansion draft. There may be a good reason why the Cubs left him unprotected, but he looks fine from here.

He's got an idea of what the strike zone is, and he should develop a little more power as he fills out (he's only 24). He can play short as well, so if his bat improves, a move to the middle of the infield might be in order.

Archi Cianfrocco — Padres

AB	R	H	2B	3B	HR	RBI	BB	K	SB	CS	AVG.
296	30	72	11	2	12	48	17	69	2	0	.243

Cianfrocco, 27, slugged much better than could have been reasonably expected, but his measly 17 walks led to a Belliardesque .287 on-base percentage.

He finished the year strongly (a loose use of the term) for the Padres, so they may overlook his shortcomings.

At best, he's a slightly below average fielder with 15-20 HR potential. A more likely scenario is that he'll hit fewer homers and strike out more in '94. It's fair to say the Padres are kidding themselves if they see him as a viable, long-term alternative to Sheffield.

Jeff Cirillo — Brewers

AA – El Paso

AB	R	H	2B	3B	HR	RBI	BB	K	SB	CS	AVG.
249	53	85	16	2	9	41	26	37	2	3	.341

Cirillo, 24, has decent power and a great B.A. His plate discipline is one problem which he should try to correct to retain the average.

Jeff will get an invite to Spring Training and, while he probably won't win a job, he may impress the Brewers enough to be considered competition for Surhoff and Seitzer.

Scott Cooper — Red Sox

AB	R	H	2B	3B	HR	RBI	BB	K	SB	CS	AVG.
526	67	147	29	3	9	63	58	81	5	2	.279

Cooper faced a tough task filling in after the Boggs defection and he quickly won over Sox fans by hitting .350 in April and .280 in May. He cooled off after that, but if you're going to get hot before a wary crowd, early is the time to do it. The Sox should be grateful if only because he helped calm the inevitable uproar that follows Boston handing over yet another star to the Yanks.

Cooper isn't the fielder that Boggsie once was, but no one expected him to be. He's a consistent, patient hitter with decent line-drive power. He'll continue to hit over .270 with 10+ HR.

Adell Davenport — Giants

AA – Shreveport

AB	R	H	2B	3B	HR	RBI	BB	K	SB	CS	AVG.
370	43	97	21	0	15	62	29	73	4	2	.262

Davenport, 26, showed good power, but his best moments were after his demotion to Double-A Shreveport. He's getting on in years and needs to prove he can do it at Phoenix before the Giants would even consider giving him a shot at Williams' job.

Even then, he probably wouldn't be good enough to really give Matt D. a fight.

Russ Davis — Yankees

AAA – Columbus

AB	R	H	2B	3B	HR	RBI	BB	K	SB	CS	AVG.
424	63	108	24	1	26	83	40	117	1	1	.255

Big power with a small average. Davis is in much the same position that Hensley Meulens was several years ago. The big difference is, Wade Boggs wasn't covering third when Bam-Bam was arriving.

Davis has a great arm, but managers question his overall defense. If his glove doesn't improve, the Yanks may opt for the less potent bat and slicker glove of Boggs.

Davis was the No. 7 prospect in the International League according to *Baseball America*. This doesn't mean he couldn't spend another season in Columbus. He's 24, so the Yanks want to move on him quickly.

Chris Donnels — Astros

AB	R	H	2B	3B	HR	RBI	BB	K	SB	CS	AVG.
179	18	46	14	2	2	24	19	33	2	0	.257

A decent stop-gap player with good offensive skills (some ability to hit for average, decent line-drive power, and good plate-discipline), but with a middling-to-poor glove.

His breadth of skills is not that different from a Blowers, or a Berry: pretty good, but probably not enough to make him a full-time third baseman for more than a couple of years. He's 28, so he really isn't going to do anything incredible.

ALVARO ESPINOZA											INDIANS
AB	R	H	2B	3B	HR	RBI	BB	K	SB	CS	AVG.
263	34	73	15	0	4	27	8	36	2	2	.278

With the emergence of Jim Thome, Espinoza should get squeezed out of the Indian's young infield in a heartbeat. He is still under contract for '94, but half a million dollars is a lot of money to pay for a bit player, though.

TIM FORKNER											ASTROS
A – Auburn											
AB	R	H	2B	3B	HR	RBI	BB	K	SB	CS	AVG.
267	32	76	14	9	0	39	38	29	3	3	.285

Forkner's 21. He played in the New York-Penn League, which is short-season A-Ball, so we're not probably not talking super talent here. What he can do, though is play solid ball in mid- to high-level A-Ball and possibly (not probably) make it to Double-A to finish out the season. This guy looks like a project, so don't go great guns after him.

TRAVIS FRYMAN											TIGERS
AB	R	H	2B	3B	HR	RBI	BB	K	SB	CS	AVG.
607	96	182	37	5	22	97	77	128	9	4	.300

Todd: Maybe you were looking for Fryman under shortstops, but according to Sparky, this move is permanent.

Travis began his career as a third baseman and the move should be good for him, provided Sparky keeps his word. For whatever reason, Trav hit .331 while playing third last year and .275 while at short.

The Tigers have invested a lot in Fryman and last year was the explosion they've been waiting for. He finally learned how to take walks, raised his average 32 points and his slugging 70 points.

He's only 25 and in four years he's proven that he's consistently good for 20+ HR and 90+ RBI, as well as solid fielding.

In my opinion, his move to third represents a changing of the guard in the AL.

Consider this: The Tigers and Yankees met for the last series of their respective seasons. In the second game, Boggs went 3-for-4 to raise his average to .302 while Fryman went 0-for-5 to drop his to .300. Before the finale, Boggs told Showalter he was done for the season so he could protect his stats; when Sparky asked Fryman if he wanted to do the same it was out of the question. He ended up going 1-for-4 for a .2998 (.300) average.

Travis has a reputation as a workhorse who loves the game and will do anything it takes to improve. Boggs is too busy watching his statistics and the babes outside the clubhouse. I'll take Fryman over Boggs, or anybody else at third, anyday.

BRAD FULLMER											EXPOS
No Professional Experience											

Fullmer, 19, is considered a young George Brett clone. He's a defensive liability, though, so he'll only go as far as his bat will take him.

The Expos consider him to be a talent on a par with Clifford Floyd. If that's the case, then Fullmer could be in the show within two years. He'll probably start his career at Burlington in the Class-A Midwest League, but if he's as good as the Expos think, it's possible that he'll be at Double-A by season's end.

GARY GAETTI											ROYALS
AB	R	H	2B	3B	HR	RBI	BB	K	SB	CS	AVG.
331	40	81	20	1	14	50	21	87	1	3	.245

Apparently, the Angels thought Gaetti was washed up when they released him in June. Who could blame them? Up to that point, Gaetti was hitting .180 and didn't really have a job anyway.

The Royals signed him June 19, planted him at third ,and as luck would have it, Gaetti hit 18 doubles and 14 homers for them in the second half. The book on Gaetti hasn't changed much over the years. If he makes contact, he can drive the ball. But his bat has slowed considerably and his K's are rising.

If the Royals use him wisely next year (sparingly off the bench), they may be able to coax one more decent season out of him. If not, they're setting themselves and Gaetti up for failure.

Jason Giambi — Athletics
A – Modesto

AB	R	H	2B	3B	HR	RBI	BB	K	SB	CS	AVG
313	72	91	16	2	12	60	73	47	2	3	.291

Good pop and phenomenal K/W ratio.

He's another A's prospect who's getting older (23), so they should act as they did with Brent Gates and accelerate his progress.

He looks a helluva lot better than Paquette if his power can hold up to ML pitching. The A's have nothing to lose by watching his response to the pressures of the show.

Leo Gomez — Orioles

AB	R	H	2B	3B	HR	RBI	BB	K	SB	CS	AVG
244	30	48	7	0	10	25	32	60	0	1	.197

Just when we thought Gomez was going to have a breakthrough year, he came down with a nagging case of tendinitis in the left wrist.

The injury killed his bat speed and forced him to miss most of the season. If he can stay healthy this year, however, we still stand by him. The O's have plenty of guys competing for the position, especially with the arrival of Sabo, but Leo's power, discipline, age and defensive ability make him the best one for the job. He'll hit .250+ with 15+ HR and .270+ with 25+ HR is not out of the question.

Rene Gonzales — ???

AB	R	H	2B	3B	HR	RBI	BB	K	SB	CS	AVG
335	34	84	17	0	2	31	49	45	5	5	.251

Rene, 32, has a sweet glove. He also has a decent OBP, but hit for little power and didn't drive in or score many runs. He also didn't help himself with a .200 BA in 75 September ABs.

Rene's role is in jeopardy depending on what happens with Easley, Eduardo Perez and Luis Polonia. If Polonia is not signed, then it's quite possible that Eduardo will move to left. That leaves Easley and Gonzales to fight over the position. If Polonia is signed, Gonzales will be lucky to get 335 at-bats again. As of now, he's got nothing.

Rob Grable — Phillies
A – Clearwater

AB	R	H	2B	3B	HR	RBI	BB	K	SB	CS	AVG
351	60	110	27	5	5	55	49	72	16	9	.313

Rob's 24 and a former Tiger farmhand. He doesn't look great, but he could possibly be a backup third baseman by the end of the year.

Willie Greene — Reds
AAA – Indianapolis

AB	R	H	2B	3B	HR	RBI	BB	K	SB	CS	AVG
341	62	91	19	0	22	58	51	83	2	4	.267

Cinci was working Greene in at short last year, but he's viewed as their third baseman of the future. He'll have the job, sooner or later.

He has excellent bat speed, which powered him to a .516 SL% in the American Association last year. Plus, he's not afraid of the base on balls. His reputation in the field isn't great, but he has all the tools at the plate.

Willie's only 22 and ready to contribute now, today. Given the chance, he'd easily be good for 20+ HR and 70+ RBI ... now that the goggle-headed goof has gotten out of the way.

Kelly Gruber — Blue Jays

AB	R	H	2B	3B	HR	RBI	BB	K	SB	CS	AVG
65	10	18	3	0	3	9	2	11	0	0	.277

He's got one last chance.

He's an incredible athlete and because of that the Jays will give him another try. But he'll have to make it out of Triple-A and challenge Sprague. Sprague's not a great player, but he could easily fend off Gruber.

Chip Hale — Twins

AB	R	H	2B	3B	HR	RBI	BB	K	SB	CS	AVG
186	25	62	6	1	3	27	18	17	2	1	.333

Don't be fooled by Hale's .333 batting aberration; he's a .260-.280 hitter at best. But the Pagliarulo trade left the Twins with a hole at third, and Hale will be competing with Terry Jorgensen for the spot. Tom Kelly definitely likes to switch the lineups around, so Hale may end up in a platoon situation. He can also back up second and DH, so he'll end up with more ABs next year. He's competent and gets his walks, but he's 29 and no great shakes, at the plate or in the field.

Dave Hansen — Yankees

AB	R	H	2B	3B	HR	RBI	BB	K	SB	CS	AVG
105	13	38	3	0	4	30	21	13	0	1	.362

Hansen really had an impressive year, but note that it came in only 105 at-bats.

His BA, on-base and slugging were far above previous tries, and he showed poise drawing 21 BB to 13 K's.

Interestingly, his best outings were against Giant aces John Burkett and Bill Swift. He did not bat against lefties at all, so Tommy must know something we don't.

Last year was an insanely short trial, but it's a good bet that young Hansen is the third baseman to knock dinosaur Tim Wallach back to Jurassic Park.

Charlie Hayes										Rockies
AB	R	H	2B	3B	HR	RBI	BB	K	SB	CS	AVG.
573	89	175	45	2	25	98	43	82	11	6	.305

The phenomenon of hitting in Colorado in a nutshell. He can duel it out with Galarraga and Bichette for the "Ballpark Helps Me the Most" award.

In '93, he set career highs in average, on-base, slugging, doubles, homers, runs, RBI, stolen bases and walks. Like all Rockies, the vomit-inducing thing is he could duplicate '93 season with ease.

Phil Hiatt										Royals
AB	R	H	2B	3B	HR	RBI	BB	K	SB	CS	AVG.
238	30	52	12	1	7	36	16	82	6	3	.218

Phil's a free-swinger who doesn't have a clue as to the location of the strike zone. We're talking about a guy who, in '92, collected a mere 25 walks and struck out 157 times. He was out of his league in the field too, committing 16 errors in 557 defensive innings. Granted, he's young, but a Rob Deer clone doesn't exactly fit in with the Royals image or stadium.

Dave Hollins										Phillies
AB	R	H	2B	3B	HR	RBI	BB	K	SB	CS	AVG.
543	104	148	30	4	18	93	85	109	2	3	.273

He made strides with his defense in '92 and undid all his progress with a poor '93. His .788 zone rating and his .914 fielding percentage both indicated that his head was elsewhere.

It's not as if Dave had any distractions last year, however. With the surgery on his hand after breaking his hamate bone, Hollins was expected to miss six-to-eight weeks. He came back in less than three (and even played on it for a couple of weeks before realizing the injury)! The man is psychotically intense and there were many articles about how the Phils were terrified that Hollins and Danny Jackson would have bad days in the same game.

In addition, much has been made of his inability to hit righties. Because he switch hits and hits lefties so well, there has been talk of a permanent switch to hitting right-handed. This would make a great deal of sense as history has shown that the platoon difference is usually lower for hitters who swing from one side of the plate. There have been very few Mantles and Roses, but the majors are littered with Williamses, Musials, DiMaggios, Aarons and Mayses.

Currently, Dave is a fine rotisserie pick, but in real life, his glove work negates a good deal of his offensive value.

Tim Hulett										Orioles
AB	R	H	2B	3B	HR	RBI	BB	K	SB	CS	AVG.
260	40	78	15	0	2	23	23	56	1	2	.300

Last year, Hulett had the best season in his inconsistent hitting career. He's never hit anything close to .300, though, and it probably won't happen again. His glove was excellent, parking him in the neighborhood of Wade Boggs, defensively.

If Gomez or Sabo is healthy, Hulett will be contending for the backup slot, but he won't get enough ABs to register in your league.

Butch Huskey										Mets
AA – Binghamton										
AB	R	H	2B	3B	HR	RBI	BB	K	SB	CS	AVG.
526	72	132	23	1	25	98	48	102	11	2	.251

He got a cup of coffee at Shea last year, but he's not in the Met's plans for '94. They want to see if he can grow a few more inches (in height, not girth) at Triple-A. His frame is pretty intimidating at 6-3, 240, and there were some concerns that he may become too heavy. Rest assured, however, even the Mets can hear him pounding at the door. If he keeps the power turned on in Norfolk, this 22-year-old should see some major-league PT in '95.

Howard Johnson										Rockies
AB	R	H	2B	3B	HR	RBI	BB	K	SB	CS	AVG.
235	32	56	8	2	7	26	43	43	6	4	.238

His career has been derailed the last two seasons by injury, so it's not wise to bet on his health. Since his move to Colorado, though, people have been going bonkers. Can you say Galarraga?

TERRY JORGENSEN											TWINS
AB	R	H	2B	3B	HR	RBI	BB	K	SB	CS	AVG.
152	15	34	7	0	1	12	10	21	1	0	.224

Jorgensen's stint with the Twins was disappointing last year, which put him out of the picture by the time Pagliarulo was traded. His four years in Triple-A suggest that he's a better hitter than that, though, and he should get a chance to battle Chip Hale for third. He's two years younger, has more power and a quicker glove, so he's got a shot.

Given the opportunity, he could hit .260+ with 10+ homers.

JEFF KING											PIRATES
AB	R	H	2B	3B	HR	RBI	BB	K	SB	CS	AVG.
611	82	180	35	3	9	98	59	54	8	6	.295

Will the real Jeff King please stand up?

After a typically slow start, Jeff reinvented himself. He hit .362 and slugged .514 in June, stayed hot after that, and wound up hitting .295 and slugging. .406. This from a career .230 hitter. No, these aren't superstar numbers, but they're a world of improvement.

Unfortunately, the honeymoon probably won't last. He's just been too inconsistent in the past and he'll have to repeat these numbers before we'll tell you he's anything more than a .250-.260 hitter. Defensively, he's among the best in the league. And you can expect 10+ HR from him, but his hits and run production won't be this high again.

COREY KAPANO											CUBS
AA – Orlando											
AB	R	H	2B	3B	HR	RBI	BB	K	SB	CS	AVG.
263	44	67	12	1	8	35	22	58	17	4	.255

His '93 season was a big disappointment. But this 24-year-old led the Carolina League in batting average, slugging average and on-base average in 1992, so it might be worth your time to check in on him once in a while. He isn't going anywhere in the near future.

KEITH LOCKHART											CARDINALS
AAA – Louisville											
AB	R	H	2B	3B	HR	RBI	BB	K	SB	CS	AVG.
467	66	140	24	3	13	68	60	43	3	3	.300

See Russ McGinnis.

MIKE LANSING											EXPOS
AB	R	H	2B	3B	HR	RBI	BB	K	SB	CS	AVG.
491	64	141	29	1	3	45	46	56	23	5	.287

With his explosive offense early in the year, many observers were wondering if Mike Lansing was the next Mike Schmidt or something. He was definitely "or something," but still, he was a pretty darn nice little "or something."

Mike displayed a fine glove at second and short, good speed and a solid ability to hit for average and reach base.

With the trade of DeShields, it's possible that Lansing will move to second. Either that, or Lansing will play shortstop and Wil Cordero will shift to second.

Lansing is 26, no spring chicken, so the best thing would be to let him play one position and use him to set the table at the No. 1 or No. 2 hole in the batting order.

SCOTT LIVINGSTONE											TIGERS
AB	R	H	2B	3B	HR	RBI	BB	K	SB	CS	AVG.
304	39	89	10	2	2	39	19	32	1	3	.293

Livingstone has been quietly providing solid defense and dependable hitting for the Tigers for three years now. Although he's had his chances, he's never quite proven that he can be a consistent starter for them.

His problem is that the Tigers have better hitters they can play at third, but he's too good a hitter to let go. Now, with Fryman taking over third, and the Tigers desperate for pitching, he's been mentioned as potential trade-bait so its possible that he may be elsewhere next year.

Livingstone will never be a star at the position, but he could start regularly if he picked up with the right team. With the Tigers, he'll never be more than a backup and pinch-hitter.

DAVE MAGADAN											MARLINS
AB	R	H	2B	3B	HR	RBI	BB	K	SB	CS	AVG.
455	49	124	23	0	5	50	80	63	2	1	.273

What a curious thing it is to trade back for a player using the player you acquired. Doesn't this send a signal to each team?: "Thanks for letting us use your player, but we don't think he's that good."

The Marlins traded Magadan to Seattle essentially for reliever Jeff Darwin. In the off-season, the two were traded for each other again. This has to be the weirdest baseball trade since the Cubs traded Dickie Noles to Detroit for a player-to-be-named later (the PTBNL was named Dickie Noles) in 1987.

Dave has fine on-base skills, no power and he showed a surprisingly decent glove. With Gary Sheffield's lousy defensive year, there's talk of moving Sheff to the outfield. As things stand in the off-season, this looks to be reality. Pencil Magadan in as the starter at third.

JEFF MANTO											PHILLIES
AAA – Scranton/Wilkes-Barre											
AB	R	H	2B	3B	HR	RBI	BB	K	SB	CS	AVG.
388	62	112	30	1	17	88	55	58	4	1	.289

Jeff is pretty close to professional extinction. He's a solid hitter, but he's always been the kind of guy who's easy to ignore 'cause of his defense. Now, he's 29 and you can dump him in the Potomac 'cause he's a little on the old side. Still, he had a .379 OBP and a .503 SLG at Triple-A and there aren't that many backups at third with that kind of lumber.

CARLOS MARTINEZ											INDIANS
AB	R	H	2B	3B	HR	RBI	BB	K	SB	CS	AVG.
262	26	64	10	0	5	31	20	29	1	1	.244

His career has come and gone in the minor leagues. Even if he gets a job in the spring, he wouldn't see much playing time.

EDGAR MARTINEZ											MARINERS
AB	R	H	2B	3B	HR	RBI	BB	K	SB	CS	AVG.
135	20	32	7	0	4	13	28	19	0	0	.237

Edgar had problems with his hamstrings all season and was an almost complete non-factor in the Mariners' attempt to contend in '93. A healthy Martinez is the best-hitting third baseman in the league. With the probable move of Sheffield to left field, Martinez could be the best-hitting third baseman in the game. If he's OK in the spring, then he'll be beautiful in the summer.

RUSS MCGINNIS											ROYALS
AAA – Omaha											
AB	R	H	2B	3B	HR	RBI	BB	K	SB	CS	AVG.
275	53	80	20	2	16	54	42	44	1	0	.291

If the A's had brought him up in '89, when he was 26, he might have had a decent career. But they weren't willing to take a chance with him because of his poor fielding. Alas, McGinnis is 31 years old now and still beating up on inexperienced, young pitchers. Nine years is a lot of time to spend in the minors, especially when all you have to show for the effort is 13 big league at-bats.

The Royals shouldn't give up on him though. Plate discipline is one of the best indicators of a good hitter, and McGinnis still has an excellent eye at the plate. He could be used as an occasional DH or pinch hitter and create more runs than David Howard and Chico Lind combined. Warren Newson-type potential.

KEITH MILLER											ROYALS
AB	R	H	2B	3B	HR	RBI	BB	K	SB	CS	AVG.
108	9	18	3	0	0	3	8	19	3	1	.167

Miller is mediocre with the bat and just plain rotten in the field. Even if he's healthy, he doesn't help a team enough to justify a full-time role.

PHIL NEVIN											ASTROS
AAA – Tucson											
AB	R	H	2B	3B	HR	RBI	BB	K	SB	CS	AVG.
448	67	128	21	3	10	93	52	99	8	1	.286

Considered the classiest college hitter in the 1992 draft, Nevin wowed the Astros in the spring of 1993 and started the season at Triple-A. He wasn't too impressive at first, but finished the season in a flurry, raising his BA 50 points in the season's second half.

Nevin doesn't have a great glove, so he's got to overcome that. But if he can put it together this year, he'll push Caminiti.

Drayton McLane appears to be a cantankerous, strange owner. Replacing a player like Caminiti with a young gun would cut his payroll drastically while helping sever ties with the previous Astro ownership.

Right now, Nevin is not an impressive hitter. If he can show the standard growth a good college hitter demonstrates in his second pro year, he could explode at Triple-A. For Phil Nevin, 1994 is the season of truth.

JOSE OLIVA											BRAVES
AAA – Richmond											
AB	R	H	2B	3B	HR	RBI	BB	K	SB	CS	AVG.
412	63	97	20	6	21	65	35	134	1	5	.235

A smooth fielder, Oliva was voted the best defensive third baseman in the International

League last year. Jose's problem is obvious: He needs to work the strike zone. He has major-league power right now, but he needs to drive up his average.

Oliva is only 23. He can spend a good portion of the year at Richmond polishing his bat and could see some time at third in the bigs. The thing is, Chipper Jones and Ryan Klesko need PT, too. If there's a trade, or some kind of roster movement, the logjam will clear and space will be available. Until that time, think of Jose as finest quality Triple-A dead wood.

LUIS ORTIZ — RED SOX

AAA – Pawtucket

AB	R	H	2B	3B	HR	RBI	BB	K	SB	CS	AVG.
402	45	118	28	1	18	81	13	74	1	1	.294

Ortiz is a young slugger considered to be a mega-hitting prospect. He has excellent power (slugged .502 in the International League), but he doesn't seem to have heard about walks.

He's only 24 and has time to learn. He is injury-prone, though, and is plagued by hamstring problems.

MIKE PAGLIARULO — JAPAN

AB	R	H	2B	3B	HR	RBI	BB	K	SB	CS	AVG.
370	55	112	25	4	9	44	26	49	6	6	.303

Pags was having the best season of his career ... so the Twins traded him for Erik Schullstrom.

He did the job for the O's, hitting .325 and slugging .556 in 117 ABs. But with Gomez back, Mike packed his bags and hopped a slow boat to Japan. Don't draft him.

DEAN PALMER — RANGERS

AB	R	H	2B	3B	HR	RBI	BB	K	SB	CS	AVG.
519	86	127	31	2	33	96	53	154	11	10	.245

Palmer still doesn't hit for average, but raising your slugging 83 points to .503 with 33 HR and 96 RBI goes a long way to make up for it.

He gets the job done with his rocket arm and he's quietly moving his offensive stats up to par with the league leaders at third.

He looks like he'll be able to sustain the power and his average is improving year by year. He needs to cut down on the K's though, especially with runners in scoring position (41 in 140 AB). Plus, he should have a permanent red-light when he's on first.

Still, he's a hard-worker and he was able to shake that 'fades-late-in-the-season' rep last year. There's no reason why he can't repeat, if not improve, his numbers this year.

CRAIG PAQUETTE — ATHLETICS

AAA – Tacoma

AB	R	H	2B	3B	HR	RBI	BB	K	SB	CS	AVG.
183	29	49	8	0	8	29	14	54	3	3	.268

Craig, 25, really hurt the A's more than he helped them last year, despite his 20 doubles and 12 major-league HR.

A .219 BA and a nearly 8/1 K/W ratio make him a real pain in the order.

It's no secret that Paquette's always been this type of hitter, so why did the desperate A's give him almost 400 AB when reserve Jerry Browne was riding the pine?

Browne didn't have a spectacular year himself, but we always pick the guy who gets on base over the K-chump with a little pop.

TERRY PENDLETON — BRAVES

AB	R	H	2B	3B	HR	RBI	BB	K	SB	CS	AVG.
633	81	172	33	1	17	84	36	97	5	1	.272

Pendleton stunk last year.

If you adjust his numbers to account for stat inflation at Fulton County, then you see this guy was nothing. His first half was disastrous and he saved his bacon by hitting .288 with 12 second-half HRs.

His glove is still OK, but he's 33, quite overweight and his K/W ratio, 1.79 from 1989-1992, skyrocketed to 2.69 in '93. All his indicators are way down.

He was sweet in 1991-92, but he's much more of a gamble in 1994.

EDUARDO PEREZ — ANGELS

AAA – Vancouver

AB	R	H	2B	3B	HR	RBI	BB	K	SB	CS	AVG.
363	66	111	23	6	12	70	28	83	21	7	.306

AB	R	H	2B	3B	HR	RBI	BB	K	SB	CS	AVG.
180	16	45	6	2	4	30	9	39	5	4	.250

The jury is still out on what the Angels want to do with Eduardo. He's shown decent tools at third despite his inexperience (he's 24), yet the Angels are talking about a switch to left field if Polonia isn't signed.

Currently, he doesn't look like much of a hitter. He has some power and will hit .260-.270, but he has poor plate discipline and that'll hamper his progress. The Angels really like his desire and work ethic, but he has a long way to go to match his father. Still, he's young enough to do it.

Joe Randa — Royals
AA – Memphis

AB	R	H	2B	3B	HR	RBI	BB	K	SB	CS	AVG.
505	74	149	31	5	11	72	39	64	8	7	.295

At 24, he's a whiz with the leather, and, unlike Hiatt, makes consistent contact. The Royals will probably want him to prove his readiness in Triple-A for a full season, but they could very well deal Hiatt before the beginning of the '95 season if Randa is ripe.

Stan Royer — Cardinals
AAA – Loisville

AB	R	H	2B	3B	HR	RBI	BB	K	SB	CS	AVG.
368	46	103	19	0	16	54	33	74	2	0	.280

Royer has displayed good power the last few years in Louisville. As an added bonus, he has learned to be a little more patient at the plate. In his sporadic appearances in the bigs over the last three years, Royer has yet to look overmatched. He's a smooth fielder and entering his peak performance years, so the Cards had better get serious about playing him if they want to contend in the NL Central.

Chris Sabo — Orioles

AB	R	H	2B	3B	HR	RBI	BB	K	SB	CS	AVG.
552	86	143	33	2	21	82	43	105	6	4	.259

When you think of Sabo you should be seeing legions of flashing, yellow caution signs. His defense has declined to well below mediocrity, his K's have sky-rocketed, he's beginning to be injury-prone and he's tiring and slumping late in the season.

Sabo's 32 and falling apart fast, which led to his battle off-season battle with the Reds. It was pretty clear he wasn't going to stay in Cincinnati. We were tipped off by his quote in *B.W.*, "As far as I'm concerned, I'm not a Red anymore."

Them's fightin' words and intuitive guys like us can read between the lines and see that he wasn't happy. He was fishing for $4+ million/year and the Orioles were the only ones that nibbled.

Kevin Seitzer — Brewers

AB	R	H	2B	3B	HR	RBI	BB	K	SB	CS	AVG.
417	45	112	16	2	11	57	44	48	7	7	.269

Seitzer's season was one of those little quirks that we've seen before with guys like Dave Magadan (who was shuttled between Florida and Seattle) and Rickey Henderson (who left for Toronto only to end up re-signing with Oakland after the season.

Seitzer began '93 in Oakland, leaving Milwaukee to make room for converted catcher Surhoff at third.

After about half a year in Oaktown, where he played adequately at best, he was shipped to make way for rookie Craig Paquette. Where'd he end up? You guessed it ... Milwaukee. He proceeded to play his butt off upon his return (batting .290 with seven homers in his 47 games) and was eventually re-signed by the Brewers after the season.

Surhoff had a great year with the glove, but Seitzer's resurgence with the bat may mean less innings for B.J. The Brewers can't afford not to take a chance on someone who hit as well as Seitzer did this year.

Gary Sheffield — Marlins

AB	R	H	2B	3B	HR	RBI	BB	K	SB	CS	AVG.
494	67	145	20	5	20	73	47	64	17	5	.294

If the Marlins are to be believed, he's changing his name to "Gary Leffield."

Gary took two giant steps backward in 1993. His previously solid glove turned to stone, and he fielded a "Butch Hobson-ian" .899. In addition, his triple-crown threat numbers of 1992, descended to a more mortal plane in '93. While a .294 average and 20 homers inspires respect, it doesn't hold the terror of a .330, 33 homer performance.

But hey, the kid's 25 and he's been through a lot of stuff in his short career. We're not sure if you remember this, but Gary was named the third baseman on the Padres 25th anniversary "dream team" the day he was traded to the Marlins. How'd you like to be harvesting them apples?

Gary's still one of the best hitters in the league and the position switch may allow him to put up more 1992-type seasons. Don't automatically pencil him in at third.

ED SPRAGUE											BLUE JAYS
AB	R	H	2B	3B	HR	RBI	BB	K	SB	CS	AVG.
546	50	142	31	1	12	73	32	85	1	0	.260

The Blue Jays can get away with not having a stud hitter at third because the rest of their batting order is as loaded as Ted Kennedy on Saturday night. That's not to say that sprague didn't contribute in '93. He did hit a few homers in the bottom of the batting order, and that's about all anyone should expect out of Sprague.

Sprague isn't spectacular in the field, but he's not the worst fielding third baseman in the league. We're giving our cancer-mitt award for Dean Palmer at third this year.

Offensively, he's reaching his peak performance years and might hit 20 HR or more, but it's unlikely his strike zone will improve. Neither will his baserunning.

JIM THOME											INDIANS

AAA – Charlotte

AB	R	H	2B	3B	HR	RBI	BB	K	SB	CS	AVG.
410	85	136	21	4	25	102	76	94	1	3	.332

Even though his home ballpark in Charlotte was responsible for a 35 percent increase in home runs last year, Thome's display of power was for real. If he's not the starting third baseman on Opening Day, there's something very wrong in Cleveland.

Although he is only 23 years old, Thome has all-star potential in the major leagues. He could hit easily hit .300 in '94 and should contend for the batting title within the next three or four years. Stir 15-20 dingers into the mix and Thome makes Cleveland's young lineup even more dangerous.

SCOTT STAHOVIAK											TWINS

AA – Nashville

AB	R	H	2B	3B	HR	RBI	BB	K	SB	CS	AVG.
331	40	90	25	1	12	56	56	95	10	2	.272

Scott's a young prospect who suddenly found a degree of line-drive power last year. His speed and defense make him a candidate to sneak onto the roster this year, but he'll more than likely be trying to prove he can keep the power and lose the K's in Triple-A.

B.J. SURHOFF											BREWERS
AB	R	H	2B	3B	HR	RBI	BB	K	SB	CS	AVG.
552	66	151	38	3	7	79	36	47	12	9	.274

He played left and right as well as third for the Brouhas, so Surhoff made himself useful with the glove.

With the bat he was pretty unimpressive. He set a career high in doubles with 38, but his on-base lingered painfully close to his career .315 and the move from catcher didn't improve his base-stealing stats as management had hoped.

B.J. has never been especially effective with the timber and at 29 it isn't likely that he'll experience some miraculous renaissance. Look for the same old plugger in '94.

DOMINIC THERRIEN											BRAVES

A – Durham

AB	R	H	2B	3B	HR	RBI	BB	K	SB	CS	AVG.
387	53	116	26	3	6	55	34	49	10	7	.300

Therrien is 22 and will probably start the season in Double-A Greenville.

Because of his youth, he could be up and challenging for a job in a year or so. Of course his problem is that he's just another cog in the Atlanta minor-league machine and he could get lost in the shuffle. Still, he's not a bad hitter and he's not strikeout prone. If he can work his plate discipline a bit, he could become a pretty impressive hitter.

JEFF TREADWAY											INDIANS
AB	R	H	2B	3B	HR	RBI	BB	K	SB	CS	AVG.
221	25	67	14	1	2	27	14	21	1	1	.303

He showed that he can still hit alright, but Thome would run circles around him in Cleveland. If he gets the playing time, Treadway would be OK at the bottom of the order, but he's nowhere near the top echelon of third basemen, and he's heading downhill.

ROBIN VENTURA											WHITE SOX
AB	R	H	2B	3B	HR	RBI	BB	K	SB	CS	AVG.
554	85	145	27	1	22	94	105	82	1	6	.262

First off, let's address the insane voting in the Associated Press position polls which left Ventura about seventh on the list. Seventh?!

While his average dropped 20 points from '92, Ventura returned to his '91 form in terms of homers, on-base and slugging (22, .379 and

.433 respectively). Remember, '91 was the year that all the baseball publications picked him as the AL third baseman of the future. Apparently, the AP has the memory of a flea.

He drew 105 walks and had an awesome zone rating at third. He hit equally well against left- and right-handers, a true sign of ability with the bat.

If the AP guys would actually take Terry Pendleton's stats for '93 (-66 points in on-base, -25 points in slugging, 70 fewer walks and an inferior zone rating) over Ventura's, then they're crazier than the Manson Family on mescaline. Pendleton had over 100 more at-bats than Ventura so his stats are even more of a drain on the Braves order. Ventura is 26, Pendleton is 33, case closed.

Ventura is probably the best combination of bat and glove at third in the AL. He slugs it out with NL counterpart Matt Williams and comes in a close second for best in the majors.

TIM WALLACH											DODGERS
AB	R	H	2B	3B	HR	RBI	BB	K	SB	CS	AVG.
477	42	106	19	1	12	62	32	70	0	2	.222

This guy has had it. He can't hit for power or average and his glove has gone south.

'Nuff said.

GEORGE WILLIAMS											ATHLETICS
AA – Huntsville											
AB	R	H	2B	3B	HR	RBI	BB	K	SB	CS	AVG.
434	80	128	26	2	14	77	67	66	6	3	.295

Williams, 25, is another feasible alternative to Paquette at third. He's got power, discipline and he scores runs.

Between him and Giambi, someone has to push Paquette this spring. Let's hope the A's aren't so blind to Craig's faults that they ignore the superior talent on the farm.

MATT WILLIAMS											GIANTS
AB	R	H	2B	3B	HR	RBI	BB	K	SB	CS	AVG.
579	105	170	33	4	38	110	27	80	1	3	.294

Matt looked like an early lock for the home-run title but was beaten by a month-long stint on the DL.

Too bad. Matt D. had a great year with the bat, hitting nearly 40 dingers and more than 40 points above his career .251 BA. He still can't draw the walk, but he lowered his K's and his average more than compensated.

He was a wizard with the glove, probably the best in the NL. He's right in the meat and potato years of his career so reservedly expect more solid play in '94.

PRESTON WILSON											METS
R – Kingsport											
AB	R	H	2B	3B	HR	RBI	BB	K	SB	CS	AVG.
259	44	60	9	0	16	48	24	75	6	2	.232

Preston didn't post monster numbers in his first full season of pro ball, as many expected. But who needs eye-popping stats when you're the adopted son of former Met Mookie Wilson and you have the best bat speed in the minors. Scouts say Wilson's power is an 8 on a scale of 2-8. They also say he is the best high-school hitter to come out of the draft since Gary Sheffield. The comparison is valid.

He's raw right now and the Mets don't want to push him. He's only 19 years old, though. Look for him to start the season in A-ball and spend two or three more years in the minors learning to hit the curve. The switch to third base will continue, but there's talk of a move into left field. If he develops the way we think he will, he could pocket the Rookie of the Year award in '96 or '97 and become one of the most dangerous hitters in the NL. We'll be tracking him like coon hounds.

TRACY WOODSON											CARDINALS
AB	R	H	2B	3B	HR	RBI	BB	K	SB	CS	AVG.
77	4	16	2	0	0	2	1	14	0	0	.208

He's like the Vice President of the United States. His job is to wait around until the guy in charge assumes room temperature (i.e. pushing up daisies).

TODD ZEILE											CARDINALS
AB	R	H	2B	3B	HR	RBI	BB	K	SB	CS	AVG.
571	82	158	36	1	17	103	70	76	5	4	.277

Zeile came out of the gate slowly last year, hitting .261 with 3 home runs in the first half. Thoughts of last season's demotion probably crept into Zeile's thoughts. Joe Torre stuck with him, though, and Zeile rewarded the Cards by hitting 14 homers after the break.

Regardless of the streaky nature of his hitting, Zeile seems to have finally broken through at the major-league level. The Cardinals can expect the same kind of production out of him for the next three or four years.

SHORTSTOP – *RANKINGS*

	Player	Total	Avg. Off.	Def. Runs Saved
1	Ozzie Smith	37.1	10.0	43.7
2	Jeff Blauser	26.8	19.3	19.5
3	Barry Larkin	24.9	29.3	6.8
4	Travis Fryman	24.0	18.5	7.1
5	Omar Vizquel	20.8	-5.8	38.5
6	Ozzie Guillen	19.4	-2.3	31.3
7	Alan Trammell	16.8	11.0	8.4
8	John Valentin	14.7	5.5	13.1
9	Rey Sanchez	14.5	-6.9	27.9
10	Tony Fernandez	14.0	4.9	8.1
11	Cal Ripken	13.7	3.1	15.3
12	Greg Gagne	12.6	-3.4	23.1
13	Jay Bell	11.5	20.1	-3.4
14	Manuel Lee	9.2	-3.7	18.6
15	Mike Gallego	8.3	4.7	5.2
16	Jose Vizcaino	7.9	8.0	19.4
17	Tim Bogar	7.6	-3.3	14.3
18	Pat Listach	6.1	2.2	5.7
19	Kevin Stocker	4.9	6.5	0.7
20	Jose Offerman	4.3	-2.9	9.0
21	Mario Diaz	3.1	-1.2	6.3
22	Mike Bordick	3.0	2.1	1.2
23	Gary DiSarcina	2.5	-12.2	21.3
24	Vinny Castilla	0.2	-8.2	8.4
25	Walt Weiss	0.1	-11.0	11.1

SHORTSTOP – PROSPECTS

Short-range

1. Chipper Jones
2. Alex Gonzalez
3. Benji Gil
4. Calvin Reese
5. Jason Bates
6. Orlando Miller
7. Kurt Abbott

Long-range

1. Edgardo Alfonzo
2. Kevin Orie
3. Alex Rodriguez
4. Glenn Williams
5. Derek Jeter
6. Juan Castro
7. Mike Neal
8. Sean Drinkwater
9. Chad Fonville
10. Fausto Cruz
11. Brian Rupp
12. Edgar Renteria

Sleepers

1. Mark Lewis
2. John Valentin

SHORTSTOPS – *ESSAYS*

KURT ABBOTT — MARLINS

AAA – Tacoma
AB	R	H	2B	3B	HR	RBI	BB	K	SB	CS	AVG.
480	75	153	36	11	12	79	33	123	19	9	.319

Not a very hot prospect. He showed some power in Tacoma last year, but his K/W was just terrible, both in Triple-A and Oakland.

Kurt, 25, has some speed on his side, but not enough to merit wasting ABs. He wasn't going to replace McGwire, so the move to Florida should raise his stock slightly.

MANNY ALEXANDER — ORIOLES

AAA – Rochester
AB	R	H	2B	3B	HR	RBI	BB	K	SB	CS	AVG.
471	55	115	23	8	6	51	22	60	19	7	.244

Todd: Alexander's a 23-year-old shortstop with a great arm, no bat and a lousy job.

As long as he's in the O's organization, he gets to wait forever for Ripken to miss a few games. Then, when Cal finally heads into the sunset, Manny gets to replace the biggest thing to hit Baltimore since Johnny U. (for ultra-baseball-geeks like Dave and Doug, he was a pitcher for the Colts).

EDGARDO ALFONZO — METS

A – St. Lucie
AB	R	H	2B	3B	HR	RBI	BB	K	SB	CS	AVG.
494	75	145	18	3	11	86	57	51	26	16	.294

Alfonzo, 20, was signed out of his native Venezuela as a free-agent back in '91, but last year was his first full season of ball. This kid was born to play the game. Scouts rave about his natural instincts and it's certainly hard to find fault with the work he's put in at the plate. To top things off, *B.A.* ranked him as the No. 4 prospect in the Mets' system.

As soon as Edgardo's body catches up with his ability to play, he should develop more power. It's not hard to imagine this kid earning another batting title or two in the minors, either. Keep in mind, he won the NY-P League crown in '92 with a .356 average.

The Mets could let Alfonzo skip Double-A and send him to Norfolk this season, so his stats might suffer. But the advanced play would be good for him. The Mets need a harvest from their system soon, even if it's just to get their marshmallows out of the media bonfire.

KEVIN BAEZ — METS

AB	R	H	2B	3B	HR	RBI	BB	K	SB	CS	AVG.
126	10	23	9	0	0	7	13	17	0	0	.183

He is very inconsistent in the field and an absolute disaster at the plate. Any PT given to Baez should be considered a waste.

TIM BARKER — EXPOS

AA – Harrisburg
AB	R	H	2B	3B	HR	RBI	BB	K	SB	CS	AVG.
185	40	57	10	1	4	16	30	32	7	4	.308

Barker, 26, wasn't that impressive at Triple-A (.228 average, but a .340 OBP), but he looks like a possibility for the bench. There's little chance he's going to break into the starting lineup of the Expos, though.

JASON BATES — ROCKIES

AAA – Colorado Springs
AB	R	H	2B	3B	HR	RBI	BB	K	SB	CS	AVG.
449	76	120	21	2	13	62	45	99	9	8	.267

Drafted out of Arizona by the Rockies in the organization's first amateur draft in '92. In his first two pro seasons, Bates, 23, hasn't been overmatched at the plate. The power he displayed at Colorado Springs shouldn't be trusted. There's some question whether he can become anything more than a Mike Lansing-type backup. But he can at least get on the basepaths, and he shows a lot of hustle when he gets there.

Besides, he made the jump from Single-A to the PCL with relative ease, even if his strikeouts increased. He may need another year of seasoning, but he could see major-league action by the end of '94 if his hitting remains true to form.

JAY BELL — PIRATES

AB	R	H	2B	3B	HR	RBI	BB	K	SB	CS	AVG.
604	102	187	32	9	9	51	77	122	16	10	.310

With Lind gone, the Pirates hoped Bell could anchor the middle infield; we suppose 11 errors in 1,349 innings and one Gold Glove is good enough. Add in his improvement with the stick and you've got one stellar season.

The biggest difference in his hitting last year was that he learned to watch a few pitches, drive the right ones and take more walks. If he can keep that up his offensive stats should remain high. He's always been a consistent hitter, but consistent in the .250-.270 range. More than likely, he'll come in around .280-.290 this year.

Defensively, he has excellent range and can turn the double play. In '93, he cemented himself among the best in the majors.

JUAN BELL											BREWERS
AB	R	H	2B	3B	HR	RBI	BB	K	SB	CS	AVG.
351	47	80	12	3	5	36	41	76	6	7	.228

Bell doesn't have much going for him. How often do you look at a 26-year-old player who already has five years of MLB experience and see mediocrity.

Juan has proved unequivocably that he cannot hit at the major league level. He's proved it in both leagues. He's struck more times Cliff Clavin at a singles' bar and he's just as attractive.

Bell is an excellent second baseman and a mediocre shortstop. Listach is in no danger, but light-hitting second baseman Spiers could lose time to the shining glove of Bell.

RAFAEL BELLIARD											BRAVES
AB	R	H	2B	3B	HR	RBI	BB	K	SB	CS	AVG.
79	6	18	5	0	0	6	4	13	0	0	.228

With the renaissance of Jeff Blauser, Rafael got only 127.1 innings at shortstop. He played with aplomb, displaying admirable range and solid pivot work. This is a nice change from '92, when he was rather lackluster.

In addition, his hitting was impressive, too. He hit .228 and slugged a career-high .291, only 386 points off Bonds' league-leading mark. If you add up his 1992 and 1993 slugging percentages he's just one point below Fred McGriff's excellent career .531 SL%.

He combines a fine glove with a bat that makes Samantha Fox look like Jimmie Foxx.

FREDDIE BENAVIDES											ROCKIES
AB	R	H	2B	3B	HR	RBI	BB	K	SB	CS	AVG.
213	20	61	10	3	3	26	6	27	3	2	.286

He missed May and June of '93 with a bum knee, but it seems that the Rockies didn't miss much. His ballpark raised his average quite a bit in the limited playing time he saw, but his offensive numbers were anemic at best.

Benavides played shaky defense when he was healthy and right now it appears he really doesn't have the tools to hold down a regular job in the majors. It might take the Rockies another year to find this out, but they have a huge need for a shortstop who can field and hit. Benavides and Castilla are bench bait.

MIKE BENJAMIN											GIANTS
AB	R	H	2B	3B	HR	RBI	BB	K	SB	CS	AVG.
146	22	29	7	0	4	16	9	23	0	0	.199

Mikey continued his ignominious career with the bat. Word has it that he's very proud of his bat collection. Unlike teammates Bonds and Williams, his bats aren't scuffed and marred by contact with those nasty baseballs.

Jokes aside, Mike hit extremely well with runners in scoring position (.294 BA, .385 OBP. and .500 SL%), so perhaps he's readying himself to be productive as a pinch-hitter.

JEFF BLAUSER											BRAVES
AB	R	H	2B	3B	HR	RBI	BB	K	SB	CS	AVG.
597	110	182	29	2	15	73	85	109	16	6	.306

Blauser detonated on the league at age 27 last year. He showed massive improvement in the field and took charge at the plate, keying the top of the order when the Braves diaper-wearing center-field platoon was too busy crying into its milk bottles to bother reaching base. Blauser's key improvement was his .312 average against righties. He didn't hit for much power against them, but he had an excellent .410 OBP.

It's hard to see Jeff bettering his '93 performance, but if he hits in the .270 range with his power, walks and glove, he'll be an All-Star. He was the best everyday shortstop in the NL in '93 and as long as Larkin keeps missing 50+ games a year, he appears to have a lock on the title.

TIM BOGAR											METS
AAA – Tidewater											
AB	R	H	2B	3B	HR	RBI	BB	K	SB	CS	AVG.
481	54	134	32	1	5	38	14	65	7	7	.279

The Bogar-man's only career distinction is having played all nine positions in one game for Tidewater in '91. Although he's a defensive wonder, he's no great shakes at the plate and undeserving of that precious commodity known as PT.

MIKE BORDICK											ATHLETICS
AB	R	H	2B	3B	HR	RBI	BB	K	SB	CS	AVG.
546	60	136	21	2	3	48	60	58	10	10	.249

He remained average with glove and proved our predictions accurate by hitting .249 with a measly .311 SL%. As lukewarm a player as he is, he's still better than some the A's could replace him with.

VINNY CASTILLA											ROCKIES
AB	R	H	2B	3B	HR	RBI	BB	K	SB	CS	AVG.
337	36	86	9	7	9	30	13	45	2	5	.255

Castilla stepped into the starting role when Benavides went on the DL, turning in 337 extremely uneventful at-bats. He had a suspect glove coming into the season, but seemed to have dispelled some of those fears by providing solid defense. There's not much depth at shortstop in the Rockies' system, and if they have to rely upon bit players like Castilla to solidify the middle of the infield, it'll be another long season in Denver.

JUAN CASTRO											DODGERS
AA – San Antonio											
AB	R	H	2B	3B	HR	RBI	BB	K	SB	CS	AVG.
424	55	117	23	8	7	41	30	40	12	11	.276

At 22, he's a pretty nice prospect with the bat, able to keep his K's down and flash some extra-base speed. Castro's defense is an unknown, but he's gotta be solid if he's moving this fast through the organization.

If he continues to hit, the Dodgers should probably try him out at second. Offerman is doing well enough that short should be safe. Of course, a little friendly competition might help Jose get his head back in the game.

ANDUJAR CEDENO											ASTROS
AB	R	H	2B	3B	HR	RBI	BB	K	SB	CS	AVG.
505	69	143	24	4	11	56	48	97	9	7	.283

Young 'uns can really come into their own in a single season and this young 'un kicked the league squarely in its hinder. ... It's still safe to say Cedeno's glove work is terrible, but his bat now emits sounds from the old Burt Ward "Batman" show: Pow! Biff! Poom!

Incredibly impressive was his improved plate-discipline. He cut his strikeout rate by nearly 70 percent and walked 50 percent more, moving from 5.07 K/W to 2.02 K/W!

He has the arm and he's improving his error-rate. The only question is can he use his decent footspeed to improve his weak range and run the bases well. If he can do that, then he'll be a star.

DOMINGO CEDENO											BLUE JAYS
AAA – Syracuse											
AB	R	H	2B	3B	HR	RBI	BB	K	SB	CS	AVG.
382	58	103	16	10	2	28	33	67	15	10	.272

He finally started hitting like a man who wants a job. At 25, it's too little, too late. Alex Gonzalez is on the scene now, and should take care of all the playing time at shortstop. Andujar's brother will either ride the pine as a backup or try to learn to hit in Syracuse.

ROYCE CLAYTON											GIANTS
AB	R	H	2B	3B	HR	RBI	BB	K	SB	CS	AVG.
549	54	155	21	5	6	70	38	91	11	10	.282

He seems to have shaken competitors Uribe and Benjamin for the time being, but Clayton still has a ways to go.

The .282 BA is surprising, but the almost 91/38 K/W is not. The Giants seem to be sold on him, probably because he's young, but don't be surprised if he finds himself being pushed by a better fielder in Spring Training.

We don't question his talent, just his hunger to improve as a player.

WILFRED CORDERO											EXPOS
AB	R	H	2B	3B	HR	RBI	BB	K	SB	CS	AVG.
475	56	118	32	2	10	58	34	60	12	3	.248

Wilfredo is a lot like Andujar Cedeno. He has great ability (but needs to harness it), decent speed, a strong throwing arm and is a pretty quick study.

Given his youth, his ability to make good contact and an above-average penchant (for someone of his age and talent) for taking walks, he should become a fine hitter within a year or so. Given his general build and future, he has a chance to be the next Cal Ripken.

ROD CORREIA											ANGELS
AB	R	H	2B	3B	HR	RBI	BB	K	SB	CS	AVG.
128	12	34	5	0	0	9	6	20	2	4	.266

A rookie who must say lots of nice things about pitchers' mothers while batting: he was nailed four times in 128 at-bats.

Correia isn't really much more than a career minor leaguer who came up when Easley went down in late June. He has fine defensive skills, but he's an inadequate hitter if he hits like he did last year and he was probably hitting way over his head. If the Angels infield is healthy, he's a backup at best.

CRAIG COUNSELL — ROCKIES
A – Central Valley

AB	R	H	2B	3B	HR	RBI	BB	K	SB	CS	AVG
471	79	132	26	3	5	59	95	68	14	8	.280

Counsell's K/W ratio is indicative of someone who could rise quickly if given the opportunity. On the other hand, at 23, he's a little old to be cutting teeth in the California League. See where the Rockies are playing Counsell in '94 and judge the Rockies' plans for him accordingly.

TRIPP CROMER — CARDINALS
AAA – Louisville

AB	R	H	2B	3B	HR	RBI	BB	K	SB	CS	AVG
309	39	85	8	4	11	33	15	60	1	3	.275

Although his fielding has improved over time in the minors, his discipline has always stunk. He looks like a waste of time for a team that must replace an icon within a few years.

FAUSTO CRUZ — ATHLETICS
AA – Huntsville

AB	R	H	2B	3B	HR	RBI	BB	K	SB	CS	AVG
251	45	84	15	2	3	31	20	42	2	4	.335

Cruz, 22, is really being rushed by the A's

He moved from A-ball to Triple-A in the space of the year, and while Double-A Huntsville agreed with him, he was pooped by the time he reached Tacoma.

Cruz is known for his glove and he's got potential with the bat. Considering Mike Bordick is his biggest roadblock, Cruz could be up by late '94 or early '95.

MARIO DIAZ — RANGERS

AB	R	H	2B	3B	HR	RBI	BB	K	SB	CS	AVG
205	24	56	10	1	2	24	8	13	1	0	.273

Diaz is a career backup guy who got some serious PT last year due to injuries and general confusion in the dugout. At 32, his time has never come but has gone. Texas has better shortstops to look at; you should too.

GARY DISARCINA — ANGELS

AB	R	H	2B	3B	HR	RBI	BB	K	SB	CS	AVG
416	44	99	20	1	3	45	15	38	5	7	.238

He continues to display a positively stellar glove along with a David Howard bat. He still has a slim chance of becoming more competent as a hitter, but right now, he's just another semi-young glove wizard with a bat in intensive care.

GLENN DISARCINA — WHITE SOX
A – Sarasota

AB	R	H	2B	3B	HR	RBI	BB	K	SB	CS	AVG
477	73	135	29	5	4	47	33	77	11	5	.283

He's a decent run-scorer without many exceptional qualities. There's no way he's good enough to move Guillen.

SEAN DRINKWATER — PADRES
A – Rancho Cucamonga

AB	R	H	2B	3B	HR	RBI	BB	K	SB	CS	AVG
486	69	131	29	1	10	84	35	78	2	0	.270

Good power and strong RBI capability. He may not have the average of a major leaguer but his power is really strong for his position.

He's not a pup at 23 so the Pads might look at him the spring.

SHAWON DUNSTON — CUBS

AB	R	H	2B	3B	HR	RBI	BB	K	SB	CS	AVG
10	3	4	2	0	0	2	0	1	0	0	.400

After missing almost two complete seasons, Shawon's career is in jeopardy. He's reportedly ready to begin working out in earnest for the first time in two seasons, and the Cubs are still determined to bring him back from the dead.

Even if he's healthy, remember that Dunston is now 31 years old. He probably will never regain the stroke he once had, so don't expect too much from him.

FELIX FERMIN — MARINERS

AB	R	H	2B	3B	HR	RBI	BB	K	SB	CS	AVG
480	48	126	16	2	2	45	24	14	4	5	.263

With the trade to Seattle, Felix will probably have a career for two more years. He should keep the bench warm, though.

Tony Ferandez — ? ? ?

AB	R	H	2B	3B	HR	RBI	BB	K	SB	CS	AVG.
526	65	147	23	11	5	64	56	45	21	10	.279

He sure turned on the after-burners for the Blue Jays. Of course, they had liberated him from the New York Zoo, and he was just expressing his appreciation.

There's something about the Jays that turns mediocre players near the end of their careers into useful and productive hitters. Fernandez will be OK, but it looks like he won't be in Toronto. With their refusal to give arbitration to both Alfredo Griffin and Fernandez, it looks like the Jays will use bench depth and Alex Gonzalez at short this year.

Chad Fonville — Giants
A – Clinton

AB	R	H	2B	3B	HR	RBI	BB	K	SB	CS	AVG.
447	80	137	16	10	1	44	40	48	52	16	.306

Chad, 23, has a good eye and great to awesome speed. He couldn't beat his way out of a wet paper bag, but power is a bonus when you've got wheels.

Fonville could be up by age 25, right about the time the Giants will be looking for someone to replace Clayton and Shipley.

Greg Gagne — Royals

AB	R	H	2B	3B	HR	RBI	BB	K	SB	CS	AVG.
540	66	151	32	3	10	57	33	93	10	12	.280

Even though he's becoming overmatched at the plate as he ages, it's hard to argue over what he can contribute to a team. He provides excellent defense up the middle, saving more than his fair share of runs in the process.

It's just that the Royals' screaming need last season was good hitters, not good fielders. He would be much more valuable to a club like the Blue Jays, a team that can afford to hide his bat in the bottom of the order. The Royals cannot.

Benji Gil — Rangers
AA – Tulsa

AB	R	H	2B	3B	HR	RBI	BB	K	SB	CS	AVG.
342	45	94	9	1	17	59	35	89	20	12	.275

Gil was the No. 5 prospect in the Texas League last year for good reason. He's got good range, an excellent glove, some speed and he's vastly improved his power.

If the Rangers were smart, they'd give Benji a shot and hand the rest of their shortstops nickel-plated walkers as they boot them out the door. Benji is 21 and easily has the best stick of the bunch, even without the home-run power.

The time is right and they have nothing to lose so you should expect to see him soon.

Chris Gomez — Tigers

AB	R	H	2B	3B	HR	RBI	BB	K	SB	CS	AVG.
128	11	32	7	1	0	11	9	17	2	2	.250

It's been a long time since the Tigers were without a solid bat at short. Sparky has proclaimed Gomez the starter, and since he fits that description, the time has come.

Chris came to the Tigers with a sterling reputation as a fielder so he should be solid there. He's never done much at the plate, though, and will probably hit in the .240-.260 range with little power.

Alex Gonzalez — Blue Jays
AA – Knoxville

AB	R	H	2B	3B	HR	RBI	BB	K	SB	CS	AVG.
561	93	162	29	7	16	69	39	110	38	13	.289

Gonzalez, 21, was named the numero-uno prospect in the Southern League last year by Baseball America, and there's good reason why. Scouts say he has everything you would look for in a young shortstop, soft hands, range, accurate arm, durability, an ability to hit for average with some power, a good build ... stop me if your salivary glands can't take it anymore.

Seriously, the only negative he has is that he piles up a lot of K's, but with 162 hits, you can't really say he's a hacker. The Jays will give him every opportunity to win the job in spring. In fact, they're counting on him. Alex won't disappoint.

Brian Grebeck — Angels
AA – Midland

AB	R	H	2B	3B	HR	RBI	BB	K	SB	CS	AVG.
405	65	119	20	4	5	54	64	81	6	1	.294

He's not a very viable candidate to replace DiSarcina. In the majors, he'd have a pretty good OBP in the .320-.340 range, but he does little else, and it's doubtful that he can turn the DP or range about the infield like his major-league competition.

CRAIG GREBECK — WHITE SOX

AB	R	H	2B	3B	HR	RBI	BB	K	SB	CS	AVG.
190	25	43	5	0	1	12	26	26	1	2	.226

Craig didn't help himself at all this year. After his trial last season, necessitated by an injury to starter Ozzie Guillen, we thought Grebeck was ready to provide the bat that was lacking at short.

Unfortunately, he headed south for spring training and just kept going. He showed a complete inability to hit the fastball or curve. He kills junkballers, but mostly guys like Matt Young and dinosaurs like Frank Tanana.

It's too bad, but without a bat, there's no way short of a steam shovel that Grebeck can push the obnoxious Guillen off short.

ALFREDO GRIFFIN — BLUE JAYS

AB	R	H	2B	3B	HR	RBI	BB	K	SB	CS	AVG.
95	15	20	3	0	0	3	3	13	0	0	.211

There's got to be some longevity record Griffin is hanging around to break. There's no other reason why we should see him in '94.

OZZIE GUILLEN — WHITE SOX

AB	R	H	2B	3B	HR	RBI	BB	K	SB	CS	AVG.
457	44	128	23	4	50	50	10	41	5	4	.280

He's easily one of the best-fielding shortstops in the game. His zone rating is about 75 points higher than the norm, which means that any ball hit within 5 miles of him is destined to find its way into Frank Thomas's mitt.

On the other hand, Guillen has a mouth big enough to house the Sears Tower ... sideways! He is an annoying hot dog who would benefit from studying the composure of fellow middlemen such as Alomar and Guillen idol Ozzie Smith.

Smith may turn his somersaults after great plays, but can hit the ball a helluva lot better. Rumor has it that Guillen has been taking BP with watermelons and is trying to work his way down to grapefruits. At this rate, Gallagher has a better chance of getting on-base.

RICKY GUTIERREZ — PADRES

AB	R	H	2B	3B	HR	RBI	BB	K	SB	CS	AVG.
438	76	110	10	5	5	26	50	97	4	3	.251

Ricky performed fairly well in his debut. He scored a lot of runs and showed some marginal pop. He struck out too much, but he did walk 50 times. He's young enough to improve in this category.

He'll never be a strong hitter, but he showed that he could field, which means that the El Cheapo Padres will try anything to make this young, inexpensive player succeed.

JOSE HERNANDEZ — CUBS

AA – Orlando

AB	R	H	2B	3B	HR	RBI	BB	K	SB	CS	AVG.
263	42	80	8	3	8	33	20	60	8	4	.304

He's 24 and probably best known as one of the three players named Hernandez involved in trades with the Indians. This Hernandez went to the Cubs for Heathcliff Slocumb.

He has a lot of minor-league miles on his odometer, so he doesn't look like much of a prospect. But if there's a team in the majors in need of backup shortstop meat, it's Cubbies.

DENNY HOCKING — TWINS

AA – Nashville

AB	R	H	2B	3B	HR	RBI	BB	K	SB	CS	AVG.
409	54	109	9	4	8	50	34	66	15	5	.267

Hocking, 24, broke his foot before spring training or he may have beaten Pat Meares out for the starting spot with the Twins. Instead, he spent his time getting his game together at Double-A. Denny has great potential as a hitter and very good speed. He could be a major league success story this year if everything breaks right.

RAY HOLBERT — PADRES

AA – Wichita

AB	R	H	2B	3B	HR	RBI	BB	K	SB	CS	AVG.
388	56	101	13	5	5	48	54	87	30	17	.260

Ray's average and walks were down from last year but he really drove his RBI up in a big way. He has good speed but it's negated by the fact that he gets caught so much.

At 23, he's a decent prospect, but like SEan Drinkwater, he's no uber-prospect.

DEREK JETER — YANKEES

A – Greensboro

AB	R	H	2B	3B	HR	RBI	BB	K	SB	CS	AVG.
515	58	152	14	11	5	71	58	95	18	9	.295

Derek looks a lot like a poor man's Chipper Jones. He's got marginal power which should develop and a combination of plate discipline and speed which will get him the stolen bases.

Jeter, 22, was ranked No. 2 in the Sally League by *B.A.*. Despite his 57 errors, scouts think he has very good glove potential.

CHIPPER JONES											BRAVES
AB	R	H	2B	3B	HR	RBI	BB	K	SB	CS	AVG.
536	97	174	31	12	13	89	57	70	23	7	.325

Dave: A Mets scout claimed in *"Baseball America"* that Alex Gonzalez is the best prospect in the minors, but we'd take Chipper in a heart beat. Gonzalez is more consistent with the leather, but Chipper has better all-around defensive tools and is probably better than Jeff Blauser as a hitter.

The Braves aren't sure what to do with him as he's extremely error prone. Some feel he should play short in the majors, but others are considering him at third or second.

Personally, I'd look at him as the future at short until he proves incapable of handling the position. Regardless of where he plays, he'll be the best hitter at that position. He could be an All-Star as early as this year.

TIM JONES											CARDINALS
AAA – Louisville											
AB	R	H	2B	3B	HR	RBI	BB	K	SB	CS	AVG.
408	72	118	22	10	5	46	44	67	13	8	.289

He's not going to replace Ozzie. Heck, at 31 he's almost ready to retire himself.

KEITH KESSINGER											REDS
AA – Chattanooga											
AB	R	H	2B	3B	HR	RBI	BB	K	SB	CS	AVG.
161	24	50	9	0	3	28	24	18	0	3	.311

Kessinger has decent plate discipline, but he's an inconsistent hitter. Last year was his best at the plate (also hit .283 in 120 AB at Indianapolis) and he has a good fielding reputation, but he won't be pushing Larkin out anytime soon.

He may be called on to fill in if Larkin is injured again this year, but at 27 it's probably too late for him to find a more permanent role in the bigs.

BARRY LARKIN											REDS
AB	R	H	2B	3B	HR	RBI	BB	K	SB	CS	AVG.
384	57	121	20	3	8	51	51	33	14	1	.315

Larkin was bothered all year by torn ligaments in his left thumb which finally ended his season in August. This kept him from reaching the bleachers as often as he's accustomed to, but he still hit .315, cut down on his K's, and improved his OBP to .393.

Injuries are beginning to be an annual problem and they have hurt his defense, but he continues to improve his hitting. He was eclipsed somewhat last year by Blauser and Bell, but he remains among the best shortstops in the game. His .445 SL% and .933 SB% at short should make rotisse-owners drool.

MANUEL LEE											RANGERS
AB	R	H	2B	3B	HR	RBI	BB	K	SB	CS	AVG.
205	31	45	3	1	1	12	22	39	2	4	.220

After being pushed out of Toronto, Lee was hoping to find a permanent spot in Texas. Injuries early in the season (pulled rib-cage muscle and jammed thumb) prevented him from making an impact and he ended up competing with Diaz and Shave for time. They're all the same player, decent field and no bat. Lee loses in the age category, so he'll probably be backing up the middle infield this year.

MARK LEWIS											INDIANS
AAA – Charlotte											
AB	R	H	2B	3B	HR	RBI	BB	K	SB	CS	AVG.
507	93	144	30	4	17	67	34	76	9	5	.284

The Indians thought he could use another season in Triple-A to hone his fielding skills, so Lewis spent most of his time last season punishing minor-league pitching. There were favorable reports about his glove coming from the scouts, and it is expected that Lewis will open the '94 season in the new stadium as the Indian's new-improved starting shortstop. He probably won't make a big impact his first model year, but he could turn in solid numbers batting behind Baerga and Belle.

Although many pre-season sources, including the Advocate, were clamoring for the insertion of Lewis into the lineup, the Indians did the right thing. They said, "This is our ball club and our player. We know him better than you and we think he needs another year of work." The Indians are a pretty classy ball club, and you have to respect the way they've drafted and developed talent over the last five years. Their approach with Lewis should pay off this year.

NELSON LIRIANO — ROCKIES

AB	R	H	2B	3B	HR	RBI	BB	K	SB	CS	AVG.
151	28	46	6	3	2	15	18	22	6	4	.305

He resurfaced with the Rockies last year and turned in some pretty good numbers off the bench. If used sparingly against right-handers, he might be of some use to a team looking for a pinch-hitter.

PAT LISTACH — BREWERS

AB	R	H	2B	3B	HR	RBI	BB	K	SB	CS	AVG.
356	50	87	15	1	3	30	37	70	18	9	.244

Listach didn't follow up his Rookie of the Year performance in very stellar fashion, but neither did he turn in the worst sophomore slump ever seen. He had a merely mediocre year. His slugging seemed improved as he pounded out more homers and similar doubles in 200 less at-bats than '92.

The only thing that lowered his SL% was the drop in triples, attributable to the early season injury which robbed him of the speed he'd shown the year before.

Chances are the increase in doubles was due to the fact that he couldn't stretch two or three of them into triples.

Look for a full recovery in '94. Pat should even his average to about .275 and give the Brewers about 50-60 SB with a strong presence in the field.

CHRIS MARTIN — EXPOS
AA – Harrisburg

AB	R	H	2B	3B	HR	RBI	BB	K	SB	CS	AVG.
395	68	116	23	1	7	54	40	48	16	6	.294

Martin can do a little of everything and that makes him a good utility infield type. He's 26 and he's spent three-consecutive years at Double-A, so don't get too excited about him.

RAMON MARTINEZ — MARLINS
A – High Desert

AB	R	H	2B	3B	HR	RBI	BB	K	SB	CS	AVG.
412	73	109	10	6	2	46	49	79	46	11	..265

Martinez is 24, but the Marlins are viewing him as the second base partner of future shortstop Edgar Renteria. We think it's pretty doubtful that they'll be together long as Renteria is six years Martinez's junior. Martinez has some tools, but he's a year away from non-prospect status. In many ways, he's like a poor-man's Darryl Whitmore: he has some tools, but his lack of youth is a minus.

PAT MEARES — TWINS

AB	R	H	2B	3B	HR	RBI	BB	K	SB	CS	AVG.
346	33	87	14	3	0	33	7	52	4	5	.251

Meares, 25, rose above the Twins' crowd of shortstops to claim the starting spot last year. Basically, he was the cream of a lousy crop.

He's a better-than-average fielder with no bat, which describes all his competition. His age is all that sets him apart. He may remain the regular in '94, but who really cares?

ORLANDO MILLER — ASTROS
AAA – Tucson

AB	R	H	2B	3B	HR	RBI	BB	K	SB	CS	AVG.
471	86	143	29	16	16	89	20	95	2	4	.304

Orlando Miller, 25, is a head-case with a OK bat. He's got terrible plate discipline and this doesn't bode well if he's supposed to jump from Triple-A to the majors. He's considered to be a decent glove, but remember, a coach was quoted in *Baseball America* as saying, "He's a manager's nightmare."

There's little reason, other than possible injuries or total disgust with Cedeno's glove, to believe that he'll earn a full-time job.

MIKE MORDECAI — BRAVES
AAA – Richmond

AB	R	H	2B	3B	HR	RBI	BB	K	SB	CS	AVG.
205	29	55	8	1	2	14	14	33	10	2	.268

This guy is 26 and he's really no prospect, but he hit really well in the AFL and he could win a job as a bench jockey for the big club in the spring. He's described as a hustler and a gamer. Avoid him unless he gets really hot (a la Mike Lansing in the first weeks of the 1993 season), then you can trade him to some fool before he realizes Mordecai's really a chump.

TITO NAVARRO — METS
AAA – Norfolk

AB	R	H	2B	3B	HR	RBI	BB	K	SB	CS	AVG.
273	35	77	11	1	0	16	33	39	19	3	.282

It was an agonizingly slow recovery from April '92 shoulder surgery, but Navarro finally reported to Norfolk physically sound. There might have been questions about his throwing, but his skills at the plate and on the basepaths didn't suffer from the long layoff.

Navarro has great discipline at the plate. That alone should be worth something to the team that had, by a large margin, the worst on-base average in the majors. He'll go into spring with a good chance of winning the starting job at shortstop and the leadoff spot in the batting order. Watch him in the spring and if he can throw the ball to first, put your money down on this 23-year-old dark horse.

MIKE NEAL											INDIANS

A – Watertown

AB	R	H	2B	3B	HR	RBI	BB	K	SB	CS	AVG.
234	47	68	15	3	4	43	55	45	7	1	.291

Neal, 22, was taken in the 16th round of the '93 draft out of Louisiana State where he had played a variety of positions. Baseball America rated him as the best fielder of Cleveland's '93 draft crop. He was very selective at Watertown in his first pro season, and if it continues, he should progress rather quickly. Versatility may be the key to him eventually earning a job in the big leagues.

JOSE OFFERMAN											DODGERS

AB	R	H	2B	3B	HR	RBI	BB	K	SB	CS	AVG.
590	77	159	21	6	1	62	71	75	30	13	.269

Remember all those stories you've read about what an awful fielder Offerman is? Well they're not accurate.

Offerman's problem is not his glove, it's the cloud which sometimes forms over his brain during routine plays.

His zone rating is quite good, so he's picking the balls hit his way. He just forgets what to do with it once it's in his glove.

Teammates complained of Jose's neglectful coverage of second and third to back-up throws as well as some stupid misplays on force-outs. On the other hand, he turned the DP much better than expected, somewhere just below the lofty heights of Ozzies Smith and Guillen.

He wasn't too bad with the lumber, and his plate-discipline was mighty impressive. If Jose can bring his mind down out of the stratosphere long enough to play nine innings in the hole, he'll turn himself into one of the best shortstops in the game.

JOSE OQUENDO											CARDINALS

AB	R	H	2B	3B	HR	RBI	BB	K	SB	CS	AVG.
73	7	15	0	0	0	4	12	8	0	0	.205

Briefly, Oquendo is 30 years old and entering the decline phase of his career. He has not produced one productive season in his tenure in the bigs. He can pinch-hit somewhere, but it's doubtful he'll ever see significant playing time again.

KEVIN ORIE											CUBS

A – Peoria

AB	R	H	2B	3B	HR	RBI	BB	K	SB	CS	AVG.
238	28	64	17	1	7	45	21	51	3	5	.269

The Cubs took Orie with a first-round sandwich pick out of Indiana University. He showed an ability to make contact in short-season Peoria, so he should start climbing the ladder this season. He's built like Ripken, (6-4, 205), and he may be their best hope of filling the position from within. He's a couple of years away, but Kevin could become a .280-.290 hitter.

SPIKE OWEN											YANKEES

AB	R	H	2B	3B	HR	RBI	BB	K	SB	CS	AVG.
334	41	78	16	2	2	20	29	30	3	2	.234

Owen displayed waning skills in '93. He's never been a great hitter, but he flashed his typically adequate glove. His stock as a veteran back-up is diminishing as he gets older (see Dickie Schofield), so the Yanks trade of Andy Stankiewicz makes very little sense.

JEFF REBOULET											TWINS

AB	R	H	2B	3B	HR	RBI	BB	K	SB	CS	AVG.
240	33	62	8	0	1	15	35	37	5	5	.258

At 30, Reboulet is trying to finally secure himself in the majors. That's wonderful, but let him do it on someone else's staff. He's a decent fielder with a quiet bat who will be a reliable utility backup for the Twins. Period.

CALVIN REESE											REDS

AA – Chattanooga

AB	R	H	2B	3B	HR	RBI	BB	K	SB	CS	AVG.
345	35	73	17	4	3	37	23	77	8	5	.212

Reese, 21, had his season essentially demolished when his girlfriend was killed in and accident during Spring Training.

He's a smooth, graceful infielder with great athleticism. He has more stick than he showed last year and the Reds are supposedly looking at him at second. But what about Bret Boone?

Edgar Renteria — Marlins

A – Kane County

AB	R	H	2B	3B	HR	RBI	BB	K	SB	CS	AVG
384	40	78	8	0	1	35	35	94	7	8	.203

One of those "world-of-potential" types. Renteria is only 18! Right now he's about a wash with Sally Jessy Raphael as a hitter, but he has good defensive tools and since he's already 6-1, 172, he could sprout some muscle and turn himself into a good hitter.

Rotisserie owners with courageous blood coursing through their veins might want to gamble on him now, but it would probably be prudent to sit and wait a year or two.

Cal Ripken — Orioles

AB	R	H	2B	3B	HR	RBI	BB	K	SB	CS	AVG
641	87	165	26	3	24	90	65	58	1	4	.257

Defensively, Ripken is deteriorating rapidly. He doesn't have the great range anymore and his errors are on the rise, although he can still turn the DP with the best of them.

Offensively, he still produces better than your average shortstop, but his '91 MVP season is long past. He's settled into what looks to be the normal hitting-level for his career.

In his thirteen seasons, Cal has hit below .265 eight times, .282 twice and over .300 three times. This doesn't mean he hasn't had a great career, or that his production is lousy now; but it does mean that what you see is what you will get from here on out.

Everyone knows that Ripken has a great work ethic and that he loves the game. He'll be able to sustain these numbers, but the downward trend in defense will also continue. But that won't affect his ABs very much. He's so close to Gehrig, Oates would play him with a broken throwing arm and a wooden leg.

Luis Rivera — Red Sox

AB	R	H	2B	3B	HR	RBI	BB	K	SB	CS	AVG
130	13	27	8	1	1	7	11	36	1	2	.208

Luis is done, kaput, finis. He consistently adds less than nothing to the offense and there are other gloves around to play backup to Fletcher and Valentin.

Maybe the Sox will let him hang around and clutter the clubhouse, but they'd be better off adding younger blood to the roster.

Alex Rodriguez — Mariners

No Professional Experience

The No. 1 pick in last year's amateur draft. Alex is considered to be one of the great high-school infielders of all time. He has great defensive potential, but many scouts think he may grow too much to play at short.

Rodriguez, 18, is considered a great batting prospect, but right now he can't hit the breaking ball. He's a long-range pick, but he could end up being a superstar.

Brian Rupp — Cardinals

A – Savannah

AB	R	H	2B	3B	HR	RBI	BB	K	SB	CS	AVG
472	80	151	31	7	4	81	48	70	3	2	.320

Drafted out of a small college in the 43rd round of the '92 draft, Rupp, 22, impressed the Cardinals brass with a pretty good stick in his first full season. His bat wasn't the only thing that made an impression. On June 24, he was hit in the face with a pitch and suffered a broken nose. It could have been worse, as the ball hit near Rupp's eye. He recovered quickly, and on July 16, his first game back, he doubled and went 2-for-4.

Brian has quite an imposing frame (6-4, 190 lbs.) for a middle infielder, so a switch to a less demanding position might be in order. But this draft-and-follow pick should definitely be followed.

Rey Sanchez — Cubs

AB	R	H	2B	3B	HR	RBI	BB	K	SB	CS	AVG
344	35	97	11	2	0	28	15	22	1	1	.282

He's a "Punch and Judy" hitter who probably wouldn't have a job right now if the middle of the Cubs infield had been healthier the last two years. He can hold the position for a while with his glove, but his bat certainly isn't the answer to Chicago's offensive woes.

Duckie Schofield — Blue Jays

AB	R	H	2B	3B	HR	RBI	BB	K	SB	CS	AVG
110	11	21	1	2	0	5	16	25	3	0	.191

He shouldn't be considered a starter anymore, his hitting has fallen way too far off the mark. He could be a useful spare part, though, and should find himself a spot in someone's clubhouse.

TOMMY SHIELDS											CUBS
AAA – Iowa											
AB	R	H	2B	3B	HR	RBI	BB	K	SB	CS	AVG.
314	48	90	16	1	9	48	26	46	10	6	.287

The Cubs signed him as a minor-league free agent in December of '92, and he tried to help the club in June when they needed him. But he couldn't produce and it was back to the minors for Tommy. His bat isn't much better than Sanchez's and he's three years older. Tommy's 29 and his career is about on the.

CRAIG SHIPLEY											PADRES
AB	R	H	2B	3B	HR	RBI	BB	K	SB	CS	AVG.
230	25	54	9	0	4	22	10	31	12	3	.235

He's pretty old, and Gutierrez looks good enough to severely limit his playing time.

Craig is about seven years older than his competitor, so he'll have to take a demotion to hourly wage to convince the money-grubbing Padres to give him a job.

OZZIE SMITH											CARDINALS
AB	R	H	2B	3B	HR	RBI	BB	K	SB	CS	AVG.
545	75	157	22	6	1	53	43	18	21	8	.288

He struck out a grand total of 18 times in almost 600 plate appearances last season. He can still make contact, that's for sure. He can keep going at his current level of production for one or two more years, but anything longer would just be prolonging the inevitable. Regardless of his health, the time is coming soon when he will be more valuable to the Cardinals in the front office than on the field.

Just remember to get out and see him at a ballpark near you before he retires. Celebrate your icons before they're gone, folks.

Dave: One thing about the Oz: his defensive line is about as impressive as anyone's in the game. ... still! His zone ratings blow Jay Bell's away. Ozzie's problem is that his pitching staff is way better than Bell's, so his total chances are lower (more strikeouts and fewer balls hit to short). His bat is slowly fading, but Ozzie works hard in the off-season to stay in shape. He could be around for some time still.

KURT STILLWELL											REDS
AB	R	H	2B	3B	HR	RBI	BB	K	SB	CS	AVG.
182	11	42	6	2	1	14	15	33	6	3	.231

He's hanging onto his major-league career by the tips of his finger nails. He's about as close to extinction as one can be and still have a pulse. In actuality, he's not that bad, it's just that no one has faith in him. Except the Reds, and they don't have much room for him.

KEVIN STOCKER											PHILLIES
AB	R	H	2B	3B	HR	RBI	BB	K	SB	CS	AVG.
259	46	84	12	3	2	31	30	43	5	0	.324

He really surprised everyone with the bat at the major-league level. Given his minor-league performance, it's pretty unrealistic to think he'll hit a consistent .300. Somewhere between .250-.280 is much more like it.

His glove is solid major-league average: a nice improvement over the monkey crew the Phillies have had over there in recent memory. If he can draw his walks, get his steals, and hit .260 to .270, he'll be one of the better shortstops in the game.

DICKIE THON											? ? ?
AB	R	H	2B	3B	HR	RBI	BB	K	SB	CS	AVG.
245	23	66	10	1	1	33	22	39	6	5	.269

He's probably one of the better back-ups the Brewers could have had for the injured Listach, even at his age. Dickie's always had a solid glove, and, despite the migration of his power, he doesn't really hurt too badly at the plate. The Brewers let him go, but someone's sure to pick him up.

ALAN TRAMMELL											TIGERS
AB	R	H	2B	3B	HR	RBI	BB	K	SB	CS	AVG.
401	72	132	25	3	12	60	38	38	12	8	.329

Trammell stayed relatively healthy last year and delivered his best season since '87.

But now that he's finally shaken Fryman out of short, Chris Gomez will step in and take the job. There's still a lot of quality innings left in Alan, but he simply can't play everyday. Say what you will about Sparky's constant lineup juggling, this is one case where it's worked.

Alan's been fighting injuries for some time and Sparky's made sure that he's gotten the time he needs to rest and recuperate.

He'll probably need more time each year, so you can expect his ABs to decrease. His production has got to drop off at some point as well. He's had to be an ironman to accomplish what he has, but age and injuries have to catch up eventually. He'll probably return to earth next year and hit in the .270-.290 range with around 320 ABs.

JOSE VALENTIN — BREWERS
AAA – New Orleans

AB	R	H	2B	3B	HR	RBI	BB	K	SB	CS	AVG
389	56	96	22	5	9	53	47	87	9	10	.247

Jose, 24, looks like a promising young hitter. He's a switchie who drives the ball pretty well. He's also young, he's got decent speed, and he can draw a walk.

Valentin has the usual drawbacks of a pup hitter in that he strikes out too much and his average is sub-par. But these are areas in which noticeable improvement is most likely to occur at his age.

All things considered, it isn't likely that Jose can push Listach out of short this year, but there's no reason that the Brews shouldn't try him out at second in order to replace the cast of cripples presently in residence. Look for him in the spring.

JOHN VALENTIN — RED SOX

AB	R	H	2B	3B	HR	RBI	BB	K	SB	CS	AVG
468	50	130	40	3	11	66	49	77	3	4	.278

Valentin had a rough time in the field last year and his 20 errors were a bit out of character. Much of this was due to a broken finger on his throwing hand, though, and he still has good range and reputation.

The hand slowed him down at the plate as well; he hit .243 before the All-Star break and .313 once the finger had time to heal. Had he been healthy, it may have been a breakthrough season. Valentin's a consistent hitter with a little pop. You can count on him to hit .260+ with 10+ HRs; a .290+ season with 15-20 HR is possible.

RANDY VELARDE — YANKEES

AB	R	H	2B	3B	HR	RBI	BB	K	SB	CS	AVG
226	28	68	13	2	7	24	18	39	2	2	.301

Another utility guy who didn't hurt the Yanks one jot. His bat was solid and he provided versatile defensive skills.

While no one wants a team full of Velardes (except the Angels and Mets apparently), one or two isn't a bad idea. He has a good chance of being Dan Pasqua without the 20 dingers.

JOSE VIZCAINO — CUBS

AB	R	H	2B	3B	HR	RBI	BB	K	SB	CS	AVG
551	74	158	19	4	4	54	46	71	12	9	.287

He can play most of the infield spots, so he's a useful spare part. But his offensive package includes a decent average and little else. If Dunston can get over his back troubles, Jose will probably fight over backup duties with Sanchez and get some starts at third. However, his bat's nothing to get excited about.

OMAR VIZQUEL — INDIANS

AB	R	H	2B	3B	HR	RBI	BB	K	SB	CS	AVG
560	68	143	14	2	2	31	50	71	12	14	.255

Last year we said he was a .250-.270 hitter, not a .290 hitter. Indeed, he hit .255 last year. In case you're wondering, his Gold Glove was deserved because his defense is just beautiful.

He has great range, turns the DP with the best of them and doesn't make that many errors. We'll continue the motif of referring to last year's edition by saying, *"Please Stop Trying To Steal*, Omar, your baserunning stinks!" The Mariners will rue the day they salary-dumped him. Fermin is not even close to a replacement.

WALT WEISS — ROCKIES

AB	R	H	2B	3B	HR	RBI	BB	K	SB	CS	AVG
500	50	133	14	2	1	39	79	73	7	3	.266

He drew a magnificent 79 walks and posted a very un-Weiss-like .367 OBP. Of course, one has to realize that Weiss jumped ship from the Oakland Mausoleum to sunny, hitter-friendly Florida and this was a tonic to his offense.

In addition, the warm clime helped push his fielding back to his solid pre-injury levels.

He'll never be a star, but he's a pretty good player if he can stay healthy and continue to put together seasons like this. He could have a .400 OBP in Colorado.

GLENN WILLIAMS — BRAVES
No Professional Experience

Dave: If you're a complete, total loser whose life revolves around fantasy baseball (which means your name is David Srinivasan), here's one of about 10 players you should be following with bated breath.

The Braves coughed up $800,000 for this Aussie kid. The thing is, he's 16 and he's already 6-foot-2, 175, and the Braves consider him to be another Chipper Jones.

In addition, Glenn's dad is a baseball nut who played on the Australian national team and therefore, the kid has been around baseball his entire life.

He may outgrow the position and become a third baseman by the time he's 20, but he has a chance to be playing in the Sally League at age 16 (he turns 17 on July 18!).

Our rotisserie league allows you to hold over minor-leaguers indefinitely without penalty from year-to-year. You damn right I'll try to draft him!

BRANDON WILSON — WHITE SOX

AA – Birmingham

AB	R	H	2B	3B	HR	RBI	BB	K	SB	CS	AVG.
500	76	135	19	5	2	48	52	77	43	10	.270

Another no-pop, good-wheels prospect at short. There's nothing about Wilson, 25, that makes him worth more than Guillen's glove, and he's probably not worth training as a second baseman.

TONY WOMACK — PIRATES

AA – Carolina

AB	R	H	2B	3B	HR	RBI	BB	K	SB	CS	AVG.
247	41	75	7	2	0	23	17	34	21	6	.304

He's a speedy, sure-handed, 25-year-old shortstop who can hit. There are a lot of teams who need a guy like this; Pittsburgh isn't one of them so he won't be going anywhere soon.

EDDIE ZOSKY — BLUE JAYS

AAA – Syracuse

AB	R	H	2B	3B	HR	RBI	BB	K	SB	CS	AVG.
93	9	20	5	0	0	8	1	20	0	1	.215

He underwent arthroscopic surgery in mid-March to remove bone chips from his throwing shoulder. By the time he made it back, the Jays had already traded for Fernandez, and he spent the remainder of his season stinking up Syracuse. Who knows, he could win a spot on the bench in spring training, but he sure as hell won't stand in the way of Alex Gonzalez.

LEFT FIELD – *RANKINGS*

	Player	Total	Avg. Off.	Def. Runs Saved
1	Barry Bonds	77.5	71.8	8.2
2	Rickey Henderson	42.2	33.8	12.3
3	Juan Gonzalez	34.9	33.6	2.0
4	Albert Belle	27.9	26.5	2.0
5	Tim Raines	24.1	21.7	3.6
6	Tony Phillips	23.5	19.9	5.3
7	Kevin Mitchell	21.0	17.9	4.5
8	Greg Vaughn	20.2	12.5	11.2
9	Brady Anderson	18.1	17.6	0.7
10	Ron Gant	15.8	11.8	5.9
11	Luis Gonzalez	13.1	8.7	6.4
12	Bernard Gilkey	12.6	18.0	-7.8
13	Dion James	10.1	10.0	0.2
14	Pete Incaviglia	9.4	9.2	0.3
15	Randy Velarde	8.7	7.4	2.0

CENTER FIELD – *RANKINGS*

	Player	Total	Avg. Off.	Def. Runs Saved
1	Kenny Lofton	42.5	21.9	29.9
2	Lenny Dykstra	40.4	25.7	21.2
3	Ken Griffey, Jr.	39.1	43.3	-6.1
4	Marquis Grissom	29.4	18.4	15.9
5	Lance Johnson	28.3	9.3	27.5
6	Brett Butler	27.0	16.4	15.3
7	Chad Curtis	24.7	4.1	29.8
8	Devon White	23.7	8.2	22.4
9	Kirby Puckett	23.5	25.9	-3.4
10	Andy Van Slyke	20.2	26.4	-9.0
11	Shane Mack	21.9	16.9	7.3
12	Bernie Williams	15.8	4.1	16.9
13	Steve Finley	14.7	10.6	5.9
15	Roberto Kelly	11.4	10.3	1.6
15	Deion Sanders	11.4	6.6	6.9

RIGHT FIELD – *RANKINGS*

	Player	Total	Avg. Off.	Def. Runs Saved
1	Tony Gwynn	34.2	23.8	15.1
2	Larry Walker	32.4	23.4	12.9
3	Tim Salmon	25.3	12.9	18.0
4	David Justice	20.8	15.8	7.2
5	Orlando Merced	19.2	12.6	9.6
6	Rob Deer	18.6	6.4	17.7
7	Bobby Bonilla	18.3	16.3	3.0
8	Paul O'Neill	17.8	14.4	4.9
9	Reggie Sanders	15.8	9.9	8.6
10	Jim Eisenreich	15.2	5.2	14.4
11	Darryl Hamilton	14.1	13.4	1.1
12	Willie McGee	13.4	7.2	9.0
13	Ellis Burks	11.1	7.5	5.2
14	Joe Carter	10.8	12.7	-2.7
15	Jay Buhner	9.8	15.2	-7.8

OUTFIELD – PROSPECTS

Short-range

1. Manny Ramirez
2. Jeffrey Hammonds
3. Rondell White
4. Marc Newfield
5. Roger Cedeno
6. Melvin Nieves
7. Ray McDavid
8. Rich Becker
9. Midre Cummings
10. Brian Hunter
11. Todd Hollandsworth
12. Tony Tarasco
13. Stanton Cameron
14. Danny Bautista
15. Curtis Pride
16. Willie Canate
17. Greg Blosser
18. Nigel Wilson
19. Darryl Whitmore

Long-range

1. Johnny Damon
2. Chad Mottola
3. Karim Garcia
4. Richard Hidalgo
5. Ruben Rivera
6. Alex Ochoa
7. Calvin Murray
8. Curtis Goodwin
9. Bob Abreu
10. Anthony Byrd
11. Damon Hollins
12. Andre King
13. Matt Lawton
14. Jose Malave
15. Buck McNabb
16. Vince Moore
17. Chris Schwab
18. Matt Luke
19. Trey Beamon

Sleepers

1. Eric Anthony
2. Bernardo Brito
3. Geronimo Berroa
4. Stan Javier
5. Ray Lankford
6. Billy Masse
7. Karl Rhodes
8. Ryan Thompson

OUTFIELD – *ESSAYS*

BOB ABREU — ASTROS
A – Osceola

AB	R	H	2B	3B	HR	RBI	BB	K	SB	CS	AVG
474	62	134	21	17	5	55	51	90	10	14	.283

Osceola is a slight pitcher's park which increases triples by 20 percent and slices homers in half. What that means is this 20-year-old kid can hit ... he can hit triples ... and pretty soon he'll be cranking homers.

He's one of the top prospects in the Astros farm system and he's one of the better young hitters in the minors. But he needs to work the strike zone more and use his speed more effectively to go to the head of the class.

MOISES ALOU — EXPOS

AB	R	H	2B	3B	HR	RBI	BB	K	SB	CS	AVG
482	70	138	29	6	18	85	38	53	17	6	.286

He may be a bit overmatched when he runs into center field and his relative inability to draw a walk keeps his OBP down, but that's about it. The man can play some ball.

One can only hope that those absolutely gruesome late-season leg injuries don't take away too much of his solid speed. It's just too bad that the Expos have so many good outfielders. A couple of these guys are gonna grab some bench and they don't deserve to. Something tells us that Felipe's son won't be seeing that bench, but he's just too good to just chalk it up to nepotism.

RUBEN AMARO — INDIANS
AAA – Scranton/Wilkes-Barre

AB	R	H	2B	3B	HR	RBI	BB	K	SB	CS	AVG
412	76	120	30	5	9	37	31	44	25	4	.291

Kind of a poor-man's Kenny Lofton. He hits for some average, a bit of power and can steal some bases without getting caught. He's a fine top-of-the-order reserve who could take over the starter's role if injuries hit.

BRADY ANDERSON — ORIOLES

AB	R	H	2B	3B	HR	RBI	BB	K	SB	CS	AVG
560	87	147	36	8	13	66	82	99	24	12	.263

Warning you about Brady last year made us look like geniuses (which we are, eh...).

It wasn't so much that he stank last year; his stats fell slightly, but not to disaster levels. Rather, the league just exploded past him.

At 30, Anderson is a couple years past his peak and he's not going to improve much in the future. The league, however, is full of hot-hitting youngsters who are passing him by.

He still provides a solid bat and glove for the O's. But as a rotisse-owner, you'd be better off avoiding Brady's pricey salary and using your dough to buy more promising talent around the league.

GARRET ANDERSON — ANGELS
AAA – Vancouver

AB	R	H	2B	3B	HR	RBI	BB	K	SB	CS	AVG
467	57	137	34	4	4	71	31	95	3	4	.293

A raw, but talented player. Anderson, 22, is an OK hitter who is so young, he could become an excellent one by the time he's 24. If you're willing to sit on him for a year, he's your man, but he has little power now and he has no speed.

WILLIE ANSLEY — ASTROS
AAA – Tucson

AB	R	H	2B	3B	HR	RBI	BB	K	SB	CS	AVG
382	71	100	20	7	5	61	79	93	22	9	.262

If you follow the Astros, or the minors, carefully then this guy's name should ring a bell. He was a first-rounder many moons ago and is only now raising his head above water.

Ansley is 24 now, so it's improbable that he'll be much, but he still could demonstrate some of the power he showed in high school and force his way into a job.

ERIC ANTHONY — MARINERS

AB	R	H	2B	3B	HR	RBI	BB	K	SB	CS	AVG
486	70	121	19	4	15	66	49	88	3	5	.249

There's no doubt that Eric is a fine athlete. He displayed fine defense in 1993, overcoming his massive deficiencies in previous years.

The thing is, when is he going to hit .270? His K/W ratio has been steadily improving over the last few years and this is indicative of a player whose average and power should be increasing, not stagnating.

Our guess is that 1994 should be a breakthrough year. He's 26, so he should be squeezing out his best seasons now. In addition, he hit .163 with no homers in September (STATS, Inc.). He should be physically mature, it's now time for him to meld that athleticism with his experience and intelligence and move his game to the next level.

The only question is, can he show this growth while adjusting to a new league? He's a solid player for 1994, but he's also a question mark.

BILLY ASHLEY — DODGERS

AAA – Albuquerque

AB	R	H	2B	3B	HR	RBI	BB	K	SB	CS	AVG.
482	88	143	31	4	26	100	35	143	6	4	.297

Ashley has been a favorite son of the Dodger organization for years. He's only 23 and he's been in their farm system since 1988.

Last year his long-awaited power surge arrived and L.A. thought they had a monster on their hands. In terms of hitting, we're inclined to be doubtful, but in terms of striking out we can only agree whole-heartedly.

Ashley had a 143/35 K/W in Triple-A Albuquerque last year. This is in the PCL no less. The fact that he had an 11/2 ratio in his 37 major league at-bats was seen as a vast improvement.

Ashley's young, but there's nothing about him that signifies his being anything more than another Steve Balboni or Pete Incaviglia.

DANNY BAUTISTA — TIGERS

AA – London

AB	R	H	2B	3B	HR	RBI	BB	K	SB	CS	AVG.
424	55	121	21	1	6	48	32	69	28	12	.285

AB	R	H	2B	3B	HR	RBI	BB	K	SB	CS	AVG.
61	6	19	3	0	1	9	1	10	3	1	.311

Bautista was the Tigers' experiment late in the season and they were pretty impressed.

He was the fastest baserunner in the Eastern League last year and had the best arm. His raw ability reminds Sparky of Sammy Sosa, which isn't a bad comparison. Critics are complaining about what a free-swinger he is, but, at 22, he's nothing like Sosa or even guys like Nelson Simmons who were in the Tigers chain a few years back.

He, along with Jose Lima and Rudy Pemberton, are part of what Detroit hopes is a new way of doing things: getting good Hispanics on the team.

KEVIN BASS — ASTROS

AB	R	H	2B	3B	HR	RBI	BB	K	SB	CS	AVG.
229	31	65	18	0	3	37	26	31	7	1	.284

He gets on-base well against right-handers and has some pop against lefties. This makes him a versatile pinch-hitter/fifth outfielder.

TREY BEAMON — PIRATES

A – Augusta

AB	R	H	2B	3B	HR	RBI	BB	K	SB	CS	AVG.
373	64	101	18	6	0	45	48	60	19	6	.271

Trey was the No. 4 prospect in the South Atlantic League last year. He has a good line-drive stroke and decent discipline, although he needs to develop more power. He's a speedster and looks like a center fielder.

Beamon's still a couple of years away, but he's only 20.

RICH BECKER — TWINS

AA – Nashville

AB	R	H	2B	3B	HR	RBI	BB	K	SB	CS	AVG.
516	93	148	25	7	15	66	94	117	29	7	.287

Becker, 22, is a scrapper outfielder with some power, good speed and excellent plate discipline. He strikes out a lot, but 94 walks go a long way to offset that weakness.

In the field, he has a great arm and range. He's been compared to Dykstra for his all-out, psycho defensive style, but it actually looks like he may have a more consistent career.

DEREK BELL — PADRES

AB	R	H	2B	3B	HR	RBI	BB	K	SB	CS	AVG.
542	73	142	19	1	21	72	23	122	26	5	.262

Bell showed that he may yet live up to the hoopla afforded him by the Blue Jays before they traded him to the Padres (not to mention our picking him as the No. 1 sleeper in left field last year).

Derek drove the ball well and stole bases at an impressive clip. All in all, he was one of the few bright spots in San Diego's Waterloo of a season. His speed made him a very good center fielder and he even played some OK defense at third in the wake of Gary Sheffield's sudden departure.

He needs to work the zone to be a complete hitter, but that's his only glaring flaw. Look for this exciting player to be on All-Star ballots for the next few years.

ALBERT BELLE — INDIANS

AB	R	H	2B	3B	HR	RBI	BB	K	SB	CS	AVG
594	93	172	36	3	38	129	76	96	23	12	.290

Belle, despite his head-case reputation, was a solidifying influence on a team that watched their season end before it even started. He led the league in RBI, beating out Frank Thomas on the final day of the season, and hit 38 round-trippers to complement his .290 batting average. In fact, 1993 was the career year we predicted for Belle in the first edition of the Advocate.

Belle did give us a few surprises, though. We said that he probably didn't have the capability to draw more than 50 walks and he was terrible in the field. Well, not only did Belle take 76 free passes for a career-best .370 on-base average, but he put in a decent season in left field. He displayed reasonable range, fielded at a .986 clip and recorded 16 outfield assists. Not a bad refinement of his game, eh?

Speaking of fines, on May 19, Hipolito Pichardo challenged him with an inside pitch, and Belle ran out to the mound to give the Royal's pitcher some destructive criticism. Belle said of the incident, "I guess I'll be making my yearly visit to Dr. Brown's office." You see, Belle hasn't totally shrugged off his combative ways. But as long as he's an offensive powerhouse, the Indians probably don't mind his frequent visits to the principal's office.

Belle should continue to produce at the levels he has established over the past two seasons, balancing out somewhere in the middle. If the Indians knock out the White Sox in the AL Central this year, Albert Jojuan (Joey) Belle will be a big reason why.

GEORGE BELL — WHITE SOX

AB	R	H	2B	3B	HR	RBI	BB	K	SB	CS	AVG
410	36	89	17	2	13	64	13	49	1	1	.217

Bell's season was a shambles. He only hit above .230 for one month all year and he couldn't get on base short of being beaned.

Interestingly he turns 34, which seems to be the magic number this year.

Bell's got enough talent that he may get over this hurdle, but he's not a good risk. It's doubtful that we'll ever see him in a White Sox uniform again.

YAMIL BENITEZ — EXPOS

A – Burlington

AB	R	H	2B	3B	HR	RBI	BB	K	SB	CS	AVG
411	70	112	21	5	15	61	29	99	18	7	.273

Benitez isn't quite in the Cliff Floyd- or Rondell White-class of player, but at 21, he's still a pretty good little hitter. He has no concept of the strike zone, but given the budget-conscious nature of the Expos, he could take a job from someone on the big club in two or three years.

GERONIMO BERROA — MARLINS

AAA – Edmonton

AB	R	H	2B	3B	HR	RBI	BB	K	SB	CS	AVG
327	64	107	33	4	16	68	36	71	1	2	.327

The man's a hitter, plain and simple. He's not going to draw 100 walks and have a .400 OBP, but he can hack in the .270-.280 range with enough power to slug in the .450-.500 range. He's 29, so he's not going to get the chances that a Whitmore or a Nigel Wilson will get, but he could do the job if he got one.

DANTE BICHETTE — ROCKIES

AB	R	H	2B	3B	HR	RBI	BB	K	SB	CS	AVG
538	93	167	43	5	21	89	28	99	14	8	.310

Bichette's home runs were all legitimate. Of the 21 balls he put out of the park, only 11 came in Denver. He had the capability to hit 20 homers in the show even before he was traded to the Rockies.

Minor-league outfielders playing in Colorado Springs have for years complained that the velocity of baseballs hit into the outfield in Colorado was far greater than in other ballparks. This effect results in an ungodly amount of balls reaching the gaps before fielders can get to them.

This is how the thin air of Colorado aids Bichette's hitting the most. With a line-drive swing and good speed, Bichette hit 29 of his 43 doubles and all 5 of his triples at home. Look for this trend to continue in Colorado. But remember that his '93 stats do not reflect his true ability. He strikes out too much to be considered a threat to the upper echelon of outfielders.

Lance Blankenship — Athletics

AB	R	H	2B	3B	HR	RBI	BB	K	SB	CS	AVG
252	43	48	8	1	2	23	67	64	13	5	.190

Blankenship's primary value is as a utility fielder with the ability to play CF, 2B and LF with adeptness.

As a batsman, he's a six-figure number in the debit column. He supplies about as much power as a AAA battery and he has an annoying tendency to draw more walks than he gets hits. In an A's line-up which needs RBI hitters rather than potential run-scorers, this is death.

Blankenship should get some playing time because of his glove, but fantasy leaguers should not be taken in.

Greg Blosser — Red Sox

AAA - Pawtucket

AB	R	H	2B	3B	HR	RBI	BB	K	SB	CS	AVG
478	66	109	22	2	23	66	58	139	3	3	.228

Boston's first-round pick in '89, Blosser has awesome power and a decent arm. But he was K-prone last year at Pawtucket so the Sox sent him to the Mesa Seguaros in the AFL to work on making contact.

While visiting the Scottsdale Scorpions, Greg chased down a foul ball and slammed kisser-first into the concrete left-field wall. He caught the ball, but he also lost two teeth and received four stitches in his chin.

He has a fine bat and as soon as he can improve his strike zone, he'll be ready for a shot. Until then, you won't be seeing his smiling face in Boston. Then again, he may not be smiling even if he gets there.

Barry Bonds — Giants

AB	R	H	2B	3B	HR	RBI	BB	K	SB	CS	AVG
539	129	181	38	4	46	123	126	79	29	12	.336

He repeated 1992's feat of leading the league in OBP and SLG, and topped it by tying Juan Gonzalez for the home run crown with 46 as well as leading in RBI with 123. Just when you thought the Barry Bonds show couldn't get any more spectacular, it did.

There seems little doubt that Barry was the best player in baseball last year and he should continue to produce at this level for years to come. An improvement on this year's achievements is doubtful, but we're not crazy enough to rule it out.

If anything, the next plateau Bonds should strive for is maturity, the maturity to accept his talent and the mixture of criticism and adulation it inspires in fans and the press.

He shuts himself away in his home, craving peace in a way which shames Greta Garbo.

Nobody would deny him this peace, but baseball is a sport desperate for heroes it can use as a draw. When the best player does his impression of a hermit, it's the sport which ultimately loses out.

Michael Jordan. a retired athlete, still makes more in endorsements than possibly the entire fraternity of active baseball players. Average basketball players, the equivalents of Jeff Blausers and Dave Martinezes, routinely receive shoe contracts.

Mature and meet the public Barry. Be the Jordan of baseball, or at least the Charles Barkley. You don't have to be a role model, you just have to be the best at what you do.

Bobby Bonilla — Mets

AB	R	H	2B	3B	HR	RBI	BB	K	SB	CS	AVG
502	81	133	21	3	34	87	72	96	3	3	.265

On the field, Bonilla put in a solid season. After an injury-plagued '92, he rebounded to hit 34 dingers and post a career-best .522 slugging percentage. It seems "Bobby Bo's" bat is back.

Unfortunately, so is the street-gang mentality he displayed when he threatened New York writer Bob Klapisch in the Mets' clubhouse April 10. Taking off his shirt and modeling his sculptured bod, Bonilla told Klapisch, "I will hurt you," in an attempt to pick a fight with the reporter. ESPN cameras recorded the event, thankfully, and we were able to witness first-hand Bonilla's tactful approach to a book that offended him. Such a classy guy belongs in New York.

However, we at the Advocate aren't taking chances. We've all enrolled in a jujitsu class in case Mr. Bonilla wishes to take us on that tour of the Bronx he offered Klapisch.

Daryl Boston — Rockies

AB	R	H	2B	3B	HR	RBI	BB	K	SB	CS	AVG
291	46	76	15	1	14	40	26	57	1	6	.261

Boston is 31 this season, which means that his hitting should start falling off soon. He's never had a full-time job in the show and will continue that trend in '94. But as long as he's a Rockie, there's no reason to expect any serious power outage. He'll contribute mainly as a utility outfielder for a couple more seasons.

DARREN BRAGG — MARINERS
AA – Jacksonville

AB	R	H	2B	3B	HR	RBI	BB	K	SB	CS	AVG
451	74	119	26	3	11	46	81	82	19	11	.264

Bragg, 24, looks like a pretty good hitter – not too different from Mickey Brantley, or Greg Litton (in his 1993 incarnation). If he can improve a bit, he'd be a fine possible replacement if injuries hit, or if Marc Newfield isn't ready for the big leagues.

GREG BRILEY — MARLINS

AB	R	H	2B	3B	HR	RBI	BB	K	SB	CS	AVG
170	17	33	6	0	3	12	12	42	6	2	.194

He probably hasn't lost his ability, but Pee-Wee needs to get his act together. One more season like last year and his career will be over. With some PT, he could steal some bases and hit for a bit of power, but the Marlins are stacked in the outfield.

BERNARDO BRITO — TWINS
AAA – Portland

AB	R	H	2B	3B	HR	RBI	BB	K	SB	CS	AVG
319	64	108	18	3	20	72	26	65	0	2	.339

Bernardo turned in his fifth straight 20+ HR season while languishing in Portland last year. He has great power, but the Twins have inexplicably wasted the prime years of his career. He should have been in the majors long ago, but now that he's 30, he can't be considered much of a prospect.

HUBIE BROOKS — ROYALS

AB	R	H	2B	3B	HR	RBI	BB	K	SB	CS	AVG
168	14	48	12	0	1	24	11	27	0	1	.286

The warranty has long since expired on this outfielder's career. Anyone combing through the junkyard looking for spare parts deserves the ultimate breakdowns that will result.

SCOTT BROSIUS — ATHLETICS

AB	R	H	2B	3B	HR	RBI	BB	K	SB	CS	AVG
213	26	53	10	1	6	25	14	37	6	0	.249

It may rhyme with atrocious, but he's really only mediocre. He's not much at reaching base, but he showed some pop. He's adequate enough to get some cheap PT on a weakened A's squad.

JARVIS BROWN — BRAVES
AAA – Las Vegas

AB	R	H	2B	3B	HR	RBI	BB	K	SB	CS	AVG
402	74	124	27	9	3	47	41	55	225		.308

A former journeyman in the Twins' farm system, Jarvis was snapped up as a cheap lead-off man by, you guessed it, those fiscally conscientious Padres.

While he didn't exactly spark the top of the order as hoped, he was good enough that the Pads were going to keep him as a back-up for the somewhat injury-prone Derek Bell.

But Jarvis is lucky, the team won't put him into their new program, where players are found lucrative jobs as fast food managers and gas station attendants to survive in the off-season. This is because the Braves rescued him and will pay him handsomely to take Frank Cabrera's well-worn spot on the bench.

JERRY BROWNE — ATHLETICS

AB	R	H	2B	3B	HR	RBI	BB	K	SB	CS	AVG
260	27	65	13	0	2	19	22	17	4	0	.250

Browne wasn't much to write home about this year, but he did the little things like drawing walks and performing solidly in the field.

Although he seems ancient, you may have noticed he's only 28. He used to crank some doubles and score quite a few runs, so this might be the time to pick him up for a buck or two, fantasy leaguers.

We're not guaranteeing a career year, but the A's are desperate enough to bestow significant PT on anyone who shows an inclination to get on base (see Lance Blankenship).

TOM BRUNANSKY — ???

AB	R	H	2B	3B	HR	RBI	BB	K	SB	CS	AVG
224	20	41	7	3	6	29	25	59	3	4	.183

The Red Sox appear to have dropped Bruno at exactly the right time, as he severely injured his credibility as a hitter in Milwaukee. We predicted last year that his days in baseball were numbered and they're heading exponentially toward zero even as you read.

See who he's with in the spring, but he is a very, very, very bad risk.

DAMON BUFORD — ORIOLES

AAA – Rochester

AB	R	H	2B	3B	HR	RBI	BB	K	SB	CS	AVG.
116	24	33	6	1	1	4	7	16	10	2	.284

AB	R	H	2B	3B	HR	RBI	BB	K	SB	CS	AVG.
79	18	18	5	0	2	9	9	19	2	2	.228

Buford's a young speedster with a decent bat who could find himself getting some serious innings in center very soon. He doesn't have much power, but he's not afraid of walks and is an excellent baserunner (his SB percentage is perennially around 80 percent).

Devereaux's lock on center is not as strong as it once was; Buford should get some time.

JAY BUHNER — MARINERS

AB	R	H	2B	3B	HR	RBI	BB	K	SB	CS	AVG.
563	91	153	28	3	27	98	100	144	2	5	.272

Had a pretty impressive season. He was just a smidge away from driving in 100 runs and was pretty close to scoring 100 times. In addition, Mr. Buhner also showed a massive improvement in K/W ratio.

Jay's greatest strength, his fearsome throwing arm (voted best in the AL by *"Baseball America"*), compensates for his lack of range. Buhner has always had the reputation of being a fine defensive player, but like his Gold Glove teammate in center, he is way below-average at turning balls hit to him into outs.

His last three years have been pretty similar, so there's no real reason to expect him to anything other than hit in the .240-.270 range with, let's say, 27 homers. Also, he'll probably steal two or three bases and be nailed twice as many times as he's successful. Stay on first, Jay, as a baserunner, *you stink!*

SCOTT BULLETT — PIRATES

AAA – Buffalo

AB	R	H	2B	3B	HR	RBI	BB	K	SB	CS	AVG.
408	62	117	13	6	1	30	39	67	28	17	.287

Scott looked good in his tryout with Pirates last ear and he figures to get some time with the club in '94.

He's a solid hitter who's developed discipline in the last few years. He's a consistently rotten baserunner, though, and the Pirates should cure him of that.

Bullett's 25 and not exactly a hot prospect, but he'll provide solid backup this year.

ELLIS BURKS — ROCKIES

AB	R	H	2B	3B	HR	RBI	BB	K	SB	CS	AVG.
499	75	137	24	4	17	74	60	97	6	9	.275

Burks really saved his bacon with last year's performance as a White Sox. He symbolized his return by homering in his first at-bat against the Red Sox, the team which gave up on him after a couple of inferior seasons.

Aside from a continued decline in base-stealing ability (which sadly appears to be permanent), Burks returned to prime form in terms of power and run-scoring ability.

As in the past, he showed facility as a batsman against both lefties and righties, making him a valuable weapon in the middle of the line-up (he wreaked havoc in the six-hole and wasn't too shabby hitting fifth).

Burks had us worried in recent years (especially 1992s injury-plagued campaign which cost him his job in Boston) so we're more than happy to see a talented player back on track and wish him continued success. The Sox' loss is the Rockies gain. Watch him rock Mile-High this year.

CARLOS BURGUILLOS — TIGERS

A – Fayetteville

AB	R	H	2B	3B	HR	RBI	BB	K	SB	CS	AVG.
240	45	70	11	6	3	40	30	26	13	6	.292

Carlos, 22, is a young hitter with excellent plate discipline, but not much power. He gets a lot of walks and that helped him to a .366 OBP last year.

He's getting a reputation as code name: Double-O Rally Kill, though, after grounding into 12 double plays in 240 ABs. But that won't happen every year.

Burguillos is a good prospect.

JEROMY BURNITZ — METS

AAA – Norfolk

AB	R	H	2B	3B	HR	RBI	BB	K	SB	CS	AVG.
255	33	58	15	3	8	44	25	53	10	7	.227

Jeromy's 25 and there's no questioning his makeup. That's one of the things the Mets fell in love with. Likewise, there's no question about his potential to hit the long ball. He was a 30-30 man in '91 while playing for Double-A Williamsport, and his .475 slugging percentage in the show last year is probably a true representation of his ability.

What is in question here is his ability to make consistent contact at the major league level. His batting average over the last three seasons has been within spitting distance of the Mendoza line. An awfully high percentage of his hits were for extra bases. Now that fact is nothing to complain about, but it does paint the picture of a free-swinger.

BRETT BUTLER											DODGERS
AB	R	H	2B	3B	HR	RBI	BB	K	SB	CS	AVG.
607	80	181	21	10	1	42	86	69	39	19	.298

Whatever power source Butler uses to keep motoring along should be marketed for mass consumption.

The season which most compares to this one is 1983, when he was 27!

He continues to get on base as well as lead-off hitters in their prime and he busted NL pitchers for 10 triples this year.

We noted a decline in defense last year, but this wasn't evident in '93 as his zone rating was 20+ points higher than league standard.

As we also mentioned last year, his base-stealing is just good enough to avoid a negative effect on the Dodgers. At his age, this won't change. With luck and the absence of injury he'll reach 500 career SB in '94.

ROB BUTLER											BLUE JAYS
AAA – Syracuse											
AB	R	H	2B	3B	HR	RBI	BB	K	SB	CS	AVG.
208	30	59	11	2	1	14	15	29	7	5	.284

Butler is a native of the Toronto area, so that alone should be enough to warrant some playing time. But he does have a decent reputation at the plate after hitting .358 at Dunedin in '92. And he didn't seem over-matched in his 48 at-bat trial with Toronto last year.

He is a contact hitter with speed. The consensus is that he could become a Brett-Butler type leadoff hitter. He needs to develop better judgement on the basepaths, but at 24, what do you expect?

Rob could make the roster in the spring. He is slated to battle Willie Canate for left field since Rickey Henderson wasn't re-signed.

ANTHONY BYRD											TWINS
A - Fort Wayne											
AB	R	H	2B	3B	HR	RBI	BB	K	SB	CS	AVG.
479	84	140	19	10	16	79	58	78	24	11	.292

Byrd's a 22-year-old slugger who's been compared to Kirby Puckett. While those are mighty big shoes to fill, he looks like he can handle it.

He figures to be in Double-A next year and you'll definitely be hearing more about him.

IVAN CALDERON											WHITE SOX
AB	R	H	2B	3B	HR	RBI	BB	K	SB	CS	AVG.
239	26	50	10	2	1	22	21	33	4	2	.209

Calderon's career is in a shambles. After leaving Chicago for Montreal in 1991 he seemed to be on top of his game.

Things took a turn for the worse in '92 when injuries drastically shortened his season, and he was shipped to Boston to begin this year. Suffice it to say that you won't have to scrutinize his numbers to see that he's a pale shade of his former self.

The only halfway happy note is that he's back in Chicago where he enjoyed the cream of his career. Unless it has a remarkably rejuvenating effect you can bet Calderon will be on a bullet train out of the majors.

STANTON CAMERON											PIRATES
AA – Bowie											
AB	R	H	2B	3B	HR	RBI	BB	K	SB	CS	AVG.
384	65	106	27	1	21	64	84	103	6	7	.276

Cameron, 24, was one of Baltimore's top prospects until he came to the Pirates in the Lonnie Smith trade.

He's a proven slugger who's feasted on Single- and Double-A pitching; he's slugged over .500 three out of the last four years. Plus, he takes a ton of walks.

The Pirates have a lot of outfield prospects, though, and Stanton will have at least a year in Triple-A. Hopefully it will give him time to break his nasty habit of trying to steal second. Nonetheless, he's a real comer.

WILLIE CANATE											BLUE JAYS
AB	R	H	2B	3B	HR	RBI	BB	K	SB	CS	AVG.
47	12	10	0	0	1	3	6	15	1	1	.213

Willie is a 22-year-old taken in the Rule V draft from Cleveland. In 1992, he hit .316 with a .388 OBP, a .445 slugging and 25 steals in high A-Ball. He'll probably need a year to 18 months in Double-A and Triple-A, but he's really a nice-looking player.

Jose Canseco — Rangers

AB	R	H	2B	3B	HR	RBI	BB	K	SB	CS	AVG
231	30	59	14	1	10	46	16	62	6	6	.255

Jose, El Dolto Grande, reached new heights in lunacy during his infamous week in May.

We'll cut him a break and admit that head-butting Carlos Martinez's flyball over the right field wall for a homer on the 26th wasn't necessarily due to stupidity as much as lack of coordination. But his season-ending elbow injury on the 29th was moronic. He pitched one inning and gave up three walks, then two hits and three runs in a 15-1 loss to Boston.

But more importantly, according to scouts quoted in *BW*, he threw about 100 pitches warming up in the 'pen. He underwent ligament transplant surgery (the Tommy John procedure) and his career may be in jeopardy.

He may return and be able to put up big numbers again, but you certainly have to question his staying power. Even if he's healthy, you still have to worry about the courts and the tabloids bringing him down. His attitude, and now his injury, make him a serious risk.

Chuck Carr — Marlins

AB	R	H	2B	3B	HR	RBI	BB	K	SB	CS	AVG
551	75	147	19	2	4	41	49	74	58	22	.267

Played much better than he had a right to, but so what. ... He's still a one-dimensional offensive player and a merely average fielder.

His 75 runs scored is a very modest total for a No. 1 hitter and his power is minimal.

Rotisserie owners need someone like him to give them the steals, but his real-life skills are pretty mediocre.

Mark Carreon — Giants

AB	R	H	2B	3B	HR	RBI	BB	K	SB	CS	AVG
150	22	49	9	1	7	33	13	16	1	0	.327

What got into this guy in '93?

We've always prided ourselves as staunch defenders of this homer threat with a solid glove, but his numbers were simply ridiculous. He improved his BA by nearly 100 points in one year and retaught himself plate discipline to boot.

It's either a fluke or something in the San Francisco jet stream. Expect a change in air currents to return Carreon to Earth.

Joe Carter — Blue Jays

AB	R	H	2B	3B	HR	RBI	BB	K	SB	CS	AVG
603	92	153	33	5	33	121	47	113	8	3	.254

There isn't anything original left to say about Joe Carter. What he did last season is exactly what he's been doing for years: Hitting in the cleanup spot of a good offensive team and driving in 100+ runs. He still can't draw a lot of walks, but that isn't what he's paid to do batting fourth. His job is to drive in runners, and he feels he can't do that if he's not swinging.

Carter came to the plate with runners in scoring position an incredible 209 times last year. That's how he collected 121 RBI. But he did not rank in the top ten in runs created primarily because of his low average and inability to get on base regularly. He's a one-dimensional hitter in a three-dimensional lineup, but he flourishes in his role.

He's still a good bet to produce a ton of RBI, even though he will be 34 next season. With the likes of Molitor and Alomar ahead of him in the batting order, he should get plenty of opportunities to drive them in. He's slipping in the field, though, and a permanent move to DH could be in order.

Roger Cedeno — Dodgers

AA – San Antonio

AB	R	H	2B	3B	HR	RBI	BB	K	SB	CS	AVG
465	70	134	13	8	4	30	45	90	28	20	.288

Amazingly, Cedeno found himself in Triple-A Albuquerque at the age of 18 and doing well to boot.

Admittedly, most of his season was spent in Double-A San Antonio, but he performed above any reasonable expectation.

His slugging was understandably low (he'll have to grow into power), but his average and eye were well in place.

His base-stealing was off track (considering he went 40-for-49 in '92), but that should correct itself by next year.

The Dodgers aren't rushing him, they probably just want to push the envelope and watch his response. They had to be impressed. Cedeno is definitely one of the best prospects in baseball.

WES CHAMBERLAIN											PHILLIES
AB	R	H	2B	3B	HR	RBI	BB	K	SB	CS	AVG.
284	34	80	20	2	12	45	17	51	2	1	.282

He's not exactly Stan Musial against right-handers, but he burns lefties like a pyromaniac with a gas-station credit card.

He's a hacker who should never get a first pitch strike. If his K/W data doesn't tell you that, then maybe this will: He hit .462 with a .795 slugging percentage on the first pitch.

In his current role, he's fine. One has to wonder if he'd keep slugging around .500 if he had to face righties full time.

JERALD CLARK											ROCKIES
AB	R	H	2B	3B	HR	RBI	BB	K	SB	CS	AVG.
478	65	135	26	6	13	67	20	60	9	6	.282

He enjoyed the best offensive season of his career. However, aside from the moon, Colorado is probably the best place in the universe in which to hit. If you adjust for the park effect, you see very little actual improvement in his hitting. As long as he calls the Mile-High city home, though, his stats should look very much the same as they did in '93.

TIM CLARK											MARLINS
A – High Desert											
AB	R	H	2B	3B	HR	RBI	BB	K	SB	CS	AVG.
510	109	185	42	10	17	126	56	65	2	5	.363

Clark is 25 and it's improbable that he's a real prospect. His statistics look beautiful at first, but remember this is the California League and High Desert is an extreme hitter's park. If you adjust for his age, the league and the park, there's little to be impressed about. Let someone else be wowed into drafting him.

TONY CLARK											TIGERS
A – Lakeland											
AB	R	H	2B	3B	HR	RBI	BB	K	SB	CS	AVG.
117	14	31	4	1	1	22	18	32	0	1	.265

Clark, 21, was the second pick overall in the 1990 draft and the Tigers have waited impatiently while Tony's pursued a college basketball career at the U of Arizona. Family problems and injuries have further delayed any return on their investment. Clark now appears ready to devote himself to baseball full-time, and the Tiges are encouraged by his recent hitting at Lakeland.

But his 6-foot-8 frame provides an enormous strike zone and he just hasn't had much experience in the game. He was drafted high even though he'd only played 35 games in high school, and any number of distractions have kept him away from the diamond for the last three years.

Basically, he looks like another of Detroit's hard-luck stories.

ALEX COLE											ROCKIES
AB	R	H	2B	3B	HR	RBI	BB	K	SB	CS	AVG.
348	50	89	9	4	0	24	43	58	30	13	.256

Cole is an extreme groundball hitter who uses his legs as his main offensive weapons. He's got a decent eye at the plate and will take his fair share of walks. That, coupled with his speed should be enough to build a career on. But he hasn't shown enough at the plate yet to warrant a full-time job. And at 28, he shouldn't show any appreciable improvement.

VINCE COLEMAN											METS
AB	R	H	2B	3B	HR	RBI	BB	K	SB	CS	AVG.
373	64	104	14	8	2	25	21	58	38	13	.279

Doug: Vinny "Boom Boom" Coleman was not the cause of the clubhouse calamity in New York last year. He was just a very serious symptom. There were plenty of people to point the finger at. Bobby Bonilla's confrontation with New York writer Dave Klapisch over the book "The Worst Team Money Could Buy" comes immediately to mind. "I will hurt you," Bobby told him. Bret Saberhagen and his squirt gun full of bleach is another candidate for blame. However, the true fault lies with those responsible for managing the team, from Jeff Torborg and Dallas Green all the way down to the clubhouse caterer. But instead of accepting the responsibility of turning the team into a Barnum and Bailey nightmare, the Mets front office will simply clean house over the winter and stick to their no-comment story. What a joke!

But let's not gloss over what Coleman did. When he tossed that M-100 firecracker in the direction of that little girl, Coleman embarrassed himself, his team, his family and the game of baseball as a whole. In all probability, he didn't intend to hurt anybody. But the fact that it took him an entire week before he would even comment on the act (in a press conference with a sobbing wife next to him) tells you a lot about his character ... or lack thereof. Where was his concern for that little girl during that week of silence? Did he try to contact her or her parents? No, he didn't. So we're not buying the penitent family-man act.

Coleman should count his blessings. He had a lucrative major-league career, and is probably set for life. He has a supportive wife. And he has children who haven't been scarred for life by an arrogant sports figure. There are probably a few teams around that would pick him up as a spare part, but a good number of fans believe Major League Baseball has no room in it for injury ridden, mediocre ballplayer/explosive experts. Coleman copped a misdemeanor plea in hopes of keeping his baseball career alive. But the time to get out of the game is now, Vince.

JEFF CONINE — MARLINS

AB	R	H	2B	3B	HR	RBI	BB	K	SB	CS	AVG.
595	75	174	24	3	12	79	52	135	2	2	.292

He had a pretty good overall season, but surprisingly, considering his past, he didn't hit for much power and he struck out quite a bit.

Conine is a fine athlete and a pretty stellar first baseman, but his defense left quite a bit to be desired. He's really a much better player than Destrade and he should really have a chance to beat him out at first and let a good hitting kid (or someone like Geronimo Berroa) get a shot at left. The Marlins have a weak offense and getting rid of dead wood should be a priority.

MARTIN CORDOVA — TWINS

AA – Nashville

AB	R	H	2B	3B	HR	RBI	BB	K	SB	CS	AVG.
508	83	127	30	5	19	77	64	153	10	5	.250

Cordova, 24, is a young slugger who had a tremendous season in '92, slugging .589 with 28 homers in Single-A. His numbers fell off last year in Nashville, but the Twins still like his stick.

He takes his share of walks, but 153 K's are something to be concerned about. He should get at least another year or two in Double or Triple-A to work on making contact.

HENRY COTTO — MARLINS

AB	R	H	2B	3B	HR	RBI	BB	K	SB	CS	AVG.
240	25	60	8	0	5	21	5	40	16	5	.250

He can run, he can throw, and he punches out eight times for every time he walks. His hitting ability is as stable as John Hinckley with a riot shotgun. He's fine off the bench, but if you start him, you can write off the season by mid-May.

MIDRE CUMMINGS — PIRATES

AA – Carolina

AB	R	H	2B	3B	HR	RBI	BB	K	SB	CS	AVG.
237	33	70	17	2	6	26	14	23	5	3	.295

AAA – Buffalo

AB	R	H	2B	3B	HR	RBI	BB	K	SB	CS	AVG.
232	36	64	12	1	9	21	22	45	5	1	.276

Cummings is a fine athlete who's torn up the Rookie and Single-A leagues since 1990 and moved up through the ranks last year.

He's 22 and an excellent prospect. He strikes out a lot, but has good power when he makes contact. His steals were down last year from 23 and 28 the previous two years, but he should be good for 20+ in the bigs.

Midre looks like he's ready to go now, but the Pirates have found a guy they like in Al Martin. The job appears to be Martin's in left, but Cummings could, and should, push him.

CHAD CURTIS — ANGELS

AB	R	H	2B	3B	HR	RBI	BB	K	SB	CS	AVG.
583	94	166	25	3	6	59	70	89	48	24	.285

His power went south and his SB percentage was poor, but he's a lot better than Carr.

For one thing, he's got better plate discipline and this makes him likely to continue to hit in the .270-.300 range. In addition, he probably will regain his power this year.

He's a vacuum cleaner in center and could really surprise us this year or next with a .300 average and 15-20 homers.

MILT CUYLER — TIGERS

AB	R	H	2B	3B	HR	RBI	BB	K	SB	CS	AVG.
249	46	53	11	7	0	19	19	53	13	2	.213

Cuyler's a speedburner, but that doesn't mean diddley if he can't get on base. He's had problems with his knees the last two years, so the speed may be in jeopardy anyway.

The Tigers have invested a lot of time and energy in Cuyler and have been frustrated by his injuries, abysmal hitting, refusal to take a walk, and perpetual "rookie" base-running mistakes.

The signing of big-money free agent Eric Davis suggests that Cuyler's now in a put-up-or-shut-up situation. The better money's on the shut-up side.

JACK DAUGHERTY											REDS
AB	R	H	2B	3B	HR	RBI	BB	K	SB	CS	AVG
62	7	14	2	0	2	9	11	15	0	0	.226

Daugherty turned in one good season in 1990 with Texas; the rest of his six-year career has looked like this line, fairly pathetic.

He's hung on for a few years as a mediocre backup and, at 33, that ride is about over.

CHILI DAVIS											ANGELS
AB	R	H	2B	3B	HR	RBI	BB	K	SB	CS	AVG
573	74	139	32	0	27	112	71	135	4	1	.243

Not a bad season, but not terribly impressive, either. Yeah, he's a full-time DH, but we don't have a dedicated DH section and this is the most appropriate section to place him in.

He's 34 and his average sank big time last year. Our guess is that he could probably hit 20+ homers again, but the chances of him driving 100+ runs is very low. He really was just taking advantage of Tim Salmon's excellent season, he wasn't displaying any great ability as a hitter himself.

Don't spend much on him as he is probably a year or two away from completely losing his ability and his job. Heck, he could run out of steam this year.

ERIC DAVIS											TIGERS
AB	R	H	2B	3B	HR	RBI	BB	K	SB	CS	AVG
451	71	107	18	1	20	68	55	106	35	7	.237

Trading for Davis at the end of August last year wasn't enough to keep the Tigers in the pennant race, but it was still one of the best moves they've made in a while.

The move should be beneficial for both sides. Davis seemed comfortable enough; his numbers for five weeks as a Tiger:

AB	R	H	2B	3B	HR	RBI	BB	K	SB	CS	AVG
75	14	19	1	1	6	15	14	18	2	2	.253

That's a .533 slugging percentage as well. The Tigers need speed and Eric's seems to have returned along with his power (he led the NL in stolen base percentage the last two years). Davis' biggest problem, besides Marge Schott and L.A. in general, has always been injuries. Sparky has both the will and the spare outfielders to rest him enough to keep him healthy.

Plus the Tigers are tired of waiting for Cuyler to learn the fundamentals of the game and stay healthy, so Davis has the job.

It's too late for Davis to cash in on that MVP-type potential he once had, but his new home will help him turn in a few more exceptional seasons. Look for a .275+ average, 25+ HR and 30+ steals next year.

ANDRE DAWSON											RED SOX
AB	R	H	2B	3B	HR	RBI	BB	K	SB	CS	AVG
461	44	126	29	1	13	67	17	49	2	1	.273

Last year, Dawson underwent arthroscopic surgery on his left knee for the fourth time in his career. They pieced him back together in May and he went on to hit .310 after the All-Star break. It looks as if his knees are going to keep him out of the field from now on, but nothing is going to keep him from the plate.

And as long as he remains a threat, why not? His power dropped last year, but he's still a consistent hitter. Hopefully, he can stay consistent and avoid any Winfield-esque slumps when they start counting down to his 3,000th hit in a few years.

ROB DEER											JAPAN
AB	R	H	2B	3B	HR	RBI	BB	K	SB	CS	AVG
466	66	98	17	1	21	55	58	169	5	2	.210

When the Sox acquired Deer from the Tigers in August, it was truly a testament to Boston's desperation for power-hitting. After all, he's led the league in K's four years out of his 10-year career.

On the other hand, he's always gotten more than enough walks to justify his existence and his .323 career-OBP isn't bad for a pure slugger. And he gave Boston what they wanted, hitting seven homers in just over a month.

It wasn't enough for the Sox to keep him around, however, and Rob will be whiffin' in Nippon this year.

Mike Devereaux — Orioles

AB	R	H	2B	3B	HR	RBI	BB	K	SB	CS	AVG
527	72	132	31	3	14	75	43	99	3	3	.250

Devereaux joined teammate Brady Anderson by following his flash-in-the-pan '92 season with a swift return to earth.

He simply doesn't have the staying power the others guys do, as evidenced by his horrible late-season slump last year.

Forget what ESPN told you about this guy. He's 31 and he's not going to get any better.

Alex Diaz — Brewers

AB	R	H	2B	3B	HR	RBI	BB	K	SB	CS	AVG
69	9	16	2	0	0	1	0	0	5	3	.319

He's a 25-year-old switch-hitter with decent average who has yet to draw a walk in the majors. He's young, but there's no commodity on no-hit/good-field outfielders. His best asset is eye-opening stolen-base potential.

Also, the Brewers only have about five prospects worth mentioning and none of them happens to be an outfielder, meaning Diaz will be given every possible opportunity to prove himself in the spring.

D.J. Dozier — Padres

AAA – Louisville

AB	R	H	2B	3B	HR	RBI	BB	K	SB	CS	AVG
139	24	32	10	1	6	15	18	43	0	4	.230

Dozier, 28, has decent power and improved plate discipline. He's far too old to be a prospect, but many teams could find work for him now that he's plateaued at solidity.

Rob Ducey — Rangers

AAA – Oklahoma City

AB	R	H	2B	3B	HR	RBI	BB	K	SB	CS	AVG
389	68	118	17	10	17	56	46	97	17	9	.303

Rob's 29, been around forever and can still hit. If we managed the Rangers, we'd take the job from Dave Hulse and hand it to him.

Lenny Dykstra — Phillies

AB	R	H	2B	3B	HR	RBI	BB	K	SB	CS	AVG
637	143	194	44	6	19	66	129	64	37	12	.305

Lead-off King: Rickey or Lenny?

Lenny has averaged 121 games played and 83 runs scored per year over the last five seasons. Rickey Henderson has averaged 134 games and 105 runs over the same stretch. That works out to 127.5 runs per 162 games for Rickey and 111.6 per 162 for Dykstra.

Rickey has 1,586 career runs scored, a mere 910 more than Lenny. Rickey has scored 100+ runs 11 times (and he led the league with 89 during the strike-shortened 1981 season). Lenny has scored 100+ runs twice.

In addition, despite playing most of his career in Oakland, the most extreme pitcher's park in baseball, Rickey kicks Dykstra's butt in career OBP (.406 to .373) and slugging percentage (.443 to .421).

We do think that Lenny can continue to score 100+ runs, but Rickey has already done enough to get into the Hall of Fame and he's still going strong.

The MVP Fight: Bonds vs. The Dude

The BBWAA MVP voters who picked Dykstra over Bonds were probably etherized. There is no way to rationalize voting for Dykstra. *Period.* As our ratings show, Bonds had one of the greatest seasons in the last 40 years. Dykstra had what would've been an MVP-caliber season in a non-expansion year, but his season was more a function of his staying healthy and the incredible lineup behind him, as opposed to his own incredible performance.

Take Rickey's 1985 season. He scored 146 runs and whipped Dykstra's butt in almost every category despite having 90 fewer ABs.

In short, Dykstra had the best lead-off season in the majors last year, but he needs to do this for a couple more years before he passes Rickey. And with Bonds' current level of play being where it is, there's no way Dykstra is even on the same planet.

Jim Edmonds — Angels

AAA – Vancouver

AB	R	H	2B	3B	HR	RBI	BB	K	SB	CS	AVG
356	59	112	28	4	9	74	41	81	6	8	.315

He doesn't look like a good hitter, merely an adequate one. He could slug .400+ and hit around .270-.280 if given a job and things work out well.

Since he's 24, he could improve enough to become a viable option in left field, thus allowing the Angels the luxury of giving Eduardo Perez a full trial at third. His fate lies with Luis Polonia's.

Given Jackie Autry's absolute mania for salary cutting, it was virtually guaranteed that

Polonia would be gone. Because of this, Edmonds will have a chance in the spring of procuring a job.

JIM EISENREICH — PHILLIES

AB	R	H	2B	3B	HR	RBI	BB	K	SB	CS	AVG.
362	51	115	17	4	7	54	26	36	5	0	.318

Jim had a solid season, but it wasn't exceptional. He doesn't have good power and, though he doesn't strike out often, he tempers this by walking even more infrequently.

What he does is provide a superb glove in right and a pretty good bat. In his current platoon job, he looks pretty good.

CARL EVERETT — MARLINS

A – High Desert

AB	R	H	2B	3B	HR	RBI	BB	K	SB	CS	AVG.
253	48	73	12	6	10	52	22	73	24	9	.289

AAA – Edmonton

AB	R	H	2B	3B	HR	RBI	BB	K	SB	CS	AVG.
136	28	42	13	4	6	16	19	45	12	1	.309

A little old at 24 to be a top-notch prospect, but he's a thoroughbred. He has a great arm, great power, very good speed and outfield range and no plate discipline. He was the No. 2 prospect in the Callie League this year and is probably ready for a big-league trial now. It's possible he could take Carr's starting job from him, but that'll be determined in the spring.

RIKKERT FANEYTE — GIANTS

AAA – Phoenix

AB	R	H	2B	3B	HR	RBI	BB	K	SB	CS	AVG.
426	71	133	23	2	11	71	40	72	15	9	.312

Because he's getting too old (25-years-old) to be a top prospect, the Giants jumped Faneyte from A-ball to Triple-A and then the majors over the course of the last two seasons.

He's a moderately talented hitter with some speed, but he doesn't reek of uber-prospect-hood. While he performed well, Giant coaches felt that he was sometimes overwhelmed by the higher minor-league levels.

Faneyte has been a leftfielder for most of his career, but it seems unlikely that the Giants will require him in that capacity for obvious reasons.

Perhaps he's being groomed as a viable alternative to the McGee/Carreon/Mercedes platoon in right, in which case he'll be interesting to follow in the spring.

MONTY FARISS — MARLINS

AAA – Edmonton

AB	R	H	2B	3B	HR	RBI	BB	K	SB	CS	AVG.
254	32	65	11	4	6	37	43	74	1	5	.256

Pity poor Mr. Fariss. He had a good chance to impress at Triple-A and played mediocrely while the younger Marlin prospects were going psycho. He probably is a decent hitter, but he's now buried behind several younger players. Unless the injury bug hits big, Fariss' best shot at a major-league job is as a reserve.

MIKE FELDER — ASTROS

AB	R	H	2B	3B	HR	RBI	BB	K	SB	CS	AVG.
342	31	72	7	5	1	20	22	34	15	9	.211

Mike Felder needs to get his act together and put together another season like 1992. His 1993 was a joke. The only thing he did right was to get hurt in mid-August to keep his embarrassing stats to a minimum. Even at his best, he's merely decent, so the Mariners let him slide over to some other team. ... Chances are he'll ride the pine anyway.

STEVE FINLEY — ASTROS

AB	R	H	2B	3B	HR	RBI	BB	K	SB	CS	AVG.
545	69	145	15	13	8	44	28	65	19	6	.266

After we lauded his growth as a player last year, Finley slipped back to his mediocre ways. He was hurt early and his OBP slipped back to subparsville when he rediscovered that you won't reach base if you don't take walks. The end result is a season not much different than Chuck Carr's (if Carr only stole about 20 bases a year). Finley can bounce back, but he'll have to draw 50+ walks to be of much offensive help to the Astros.

LOU FRAZIER — EXPOS

AB	R	H	2B	3B	HR	RBI	BB	K	SB	CS	AVG.
189	27	54	7	1	1	16	16	24	17	2	.286

In the minors Frazier, 29, looked like a low-average, high-walk (95 in 477 Double-A ABs) speedster with no power. He didn't draw too many bases-on-balls for Montreal, but he looks like an adequate lead-off type bench player. It'll take about six major injuries before this guy gets a starting job.

Ron Gant											Braves
AB	R	H	2B	3B	HR	RBI	BB	K	SB	CS	AVG.
606	113	166	27	4	36	117	67	117	26	9	.274

Ronnie caught a lot of deserved flak for his lousy hitting in the playoffs, but his '93 season was a nice rebound from his disappointing '92. Gant set career-bests in runs-scored, RBI, homers and games-played and played solid defense in left.

As this is being written, Gant is on the trading block. All we can ask is why the hell are idiots like Deion Sanders being protected at Gant's expense?

Deion is 60 percent sizzle, 25 percent bull dumplings and only 15 percent steak. Gant, on the other hand, is the consummate quiet, classy guy: He's too busy scoring and driving in 100 runs to act like an elephant's butt for the benefit of the national media.

Karim Garcia											Dodgers
A – Bakersfield											
AB	R	H	2B	3B	HR	RBI	BB	K	SB	CS	AVG.
460	61	111	20	9	19	54	37	109	5	3	.241

He's 18 and very good for his age. Frankly, he's the best long-term prospect who isn't named Roger Cedeno on the Dodger farm.

His power was very precocious and he had an unusually high number of triples for someone who doesn't steal bases.

Garcia could easily be up by the age of 20 or 21, which brands him a future All-Star in all likelihood.

Phil Geisler											Phillies
A – Clearwater											
AB	R	H	2B	3B	HR	RBI	BB	K	SB	CS	AVG.
344	72	105	23	4	15	62	29	70	4	5	.305
AA – Reading											
AB	R	H	2B	3B	HR	RBI	BB	K	SB	CS	AVG.
178	25	48	14	1	3	14	17	50	4	2	.270

His stock really rose in the AFL. He's 24 years old, so he's not mega-star material, but he looks pretty good. Good defense and a decent lefty bat.

Steve Gibralter											Reds
AA – Chattanooga											
AB	R	H	2B	3B	HR	RBI	BB	K	SB	CS	AVG.
477	65	113	25	3	11	47	20	108	7	12	.237

Gibralter, 21, had a lousy year in Double-A last year, but his hitting in Single-A suggests that he's better than this line shows.

The Reds like him, but he obviously has some things he needs to work on before he's ready. His judgment on the basepaths is horrid and he has little plate discipline.

Steve's still a pup, though, and he has time to improve.

Kirk Gibson											Tigers
AB	R	H	2B	3B	HR	RBI	BB	K	SB	CS	AVG.
403	62	105	18	6	13	62	44	87	15	6	.261

Gibson made a heck of a return to baseball last year and the Tigers got their peanuts' worth. He provided decent defense and a surprisingly solid bat.

But his season last year pretty much followed the trend of his last five years. He came out on fire, hitting .407 in April, and .328 in July after resting at the All-Star break. He then steadily declined and finished each half poorly; he hit .191 and .168 in June and September, respectively (STATS, Inc.). This is generally the mark of a man on his last leg.

Give him credit for a great comeback, but with many new arrivals in the Tigers' outfield, there probably won't be much room for Gibson this year.

Bernard Gilkey											Cardinals
AB	R	H	2B	3B	HR	RBI	BB	K	SB	CS	AVG.
557	99	170	40	5	16	70	56	66	15	10	.305

Prior to the '93 season, Gilkey's highest home run total, including his seasons in the minors, was seven. That makes his 16 homers totally inexplicable. He's got good speed, so 40 doubles is perfectly acceptable. But if you expect more than 10 home runs out of him in '94, you'll be disappointed.

Despite last years fielding stats, Gilkey is a pretty solid fielder with a rocket launcher for an arm. The area he really needs work on is his base-running. For the second straight season, Gilkey was nailed in 40 percent of his steal attempts. Joe Torre should consider a fine for every time he leaves first base without permission. But Gilkey is a high-average hitter with a decent eye at the plate. As long as he can get on base and score runs, his lead-off spot in St. Louis should be safe.

DAN GLADDEN										JAPAN
AB	R	H	2B	3B	HR	RBI	BB	K	SB	CS	AVG.
356	52	95	16	2	13	56	21	50	8	5	.267

The Tigers were originally hoping Gladden could give them some speed on the bases when they signed him in '92. That hope was quickly forgotten, but he surprised them with some newfound power. Dingers will keep you on the payroll in Detroit for a while, but not forever. So Dan will join ex-teammate Rob Deer in Japan this year.

JUAN GONZALEZ										RANGERS
AB	R	H	2B	3B	HR	RBI	BB	K	SB	CS	AVG.
536	105	166	33	1	46	118	37	99	4	1	.310

After a breakthrough year in '92, Gonzalez firmly established himself as one of the big boys in '93. You know that he led the league with 46 HR and .632 slugging percentage, but you may not have noticed that he raised his batting average 50 points to .310. He's become a more than just a slugger. Imagine what he could do if he took some walks.

Juan's not a rookie anymore and 24 is a great age to start blowing the rest of the league away. Only Bonds and Ken, Jr., come close to his offensive stats in the outfield.

We told you last year that it's crazy to expect 40+ HRs a year until he's more established; well, you can start expecting 40+.

He racked up great stats the last two years in Arlington Stadium, which was a tad stingy. The new stadium, rumored to be designed for Juan anyway, promises to boost his numbers even more next year.

He's already posting MVP-type numbers and doesn't show any sign of slowing down.

LUIS GONZALEZ										ASTROS
AB	R	H	2B	3B	HR	RBI	BB	K	SB	CS	AVG.
540	82	162	34	3	15	72	47	83	20	9	.300

He's just a smooth little player.

Gonzalez hits for good average; has pretty solid power; and an acceptable K/W ratio. In addition, he's a good fielder and a lefty who can hit lefties.

He's 26 and at his peak, so this may be the year he hits 20-25 homers.

CURT GOODWIN										ORIOLES
A – Frederick										
AB	R	H	2B	3B	HR	RBI	BB	K	SB	CS	AVG.
555	98	156	15	10	2	42	52	90	61	15	.281

Goodwin's a 21-year-old speed burner who's been compared to Lofton... Kenny had 61 steals last year. Curt was the No. 1 prospect in the Carolina League ... and he had 61 steals last year. He doesn't have much power and he doesn't take many walks ... but he had 61 steals last year. Keep an ear out for him; you may hear him before you see him.

MIKE GREENWELL										RED SOX
AB	R	H	2B	3B	HR	RBI	BB	K	SB	CS	AVG.
540	77	170	38	6	13	72	54	46	5	4	.315

As usual, injuries played a role in Greenwell's season last year. This time, however, he was able to play through them and find some of his old power.

He'd been declining ever since his outstanding '87 season and that killed the projections of certain stardom. But he proved in '93 that he's not quite ready for the Scud depot.

Last season should be considered an example of what he's capable of and not necessarily what you should expect every year. The fact that he is injury-prone is a big concern and his age suggests that he may not be able to play through his injuries in the future.

You can't take anything away from his performance last year; he was among the most productive left fielders in the majors. But the overall trend in his career has been downhill and that could easily return.

RUSTY GREER										RANGERS
AA – Tulsa										
AB	R	H	2B	3B	HR	RBI	BB	K	SB	CS	AVG.
474	76	138	25	6	15	59	53	79	10	5	.291

Todd: Rosie, I mean Rusty, is a patient hitter who can provide a little pop to the lineup. He slugged .474 last year in the Texas League, which wasn't known for its kindness to hitters. On the other hand, Tulsa's park was fairly generous, so take that last comment with a grain of salt.

Greer isn't exactly tearing up the diamond, but the Rangers are thin in center. He's 25 and could use a year in Triple-A. You may see him in Arlington sooner than that.

Ken Griffey, Jr. — Mariners

AB	R	H	2B	3B	HR	RBI	BB	K	SB	CS	AVG
582	113	180	38	3	45	109	96	91	17	9	.309

OK. It appears that he has lost some of the speed that gave him 35-40 steal potential.

If you look at pictures of him as a rook and pictures now, you'll see his legs are now much more thickly muscled. He now has a power hitter's legs.

But apart from that, he's pretty damn flawless on offense.

Last year, we talked about the stars of the 1950s and their explosions at age 23. Well, Junior went berserk with the bat and he was only 23.

The comparisons were not looney and we have to look at Junior as a Frank Robinson/Mickey Mantle/Hank Aaron-type hitter. He looks to have 35-40 homer power – with a possible high range in the 50s; a solid average in the .300s; and it looks like he'll draw 70-100 walks. This combination makes him one of the two or three best hitters in the AL and one of the top five hitters in the game. He's as good an MVP candidate as you can find.

Dave: On defense, his zone ratings are always distressingly low, yet he wins Gold Glove after Gold Glove. My gut-level reaction is that there may be some flaw in the system that doesn't adjust for the unique dimensions of the King Dome.

It's also possible Junior is extremely overrated, but I've been watching him since he was a rook and he looks pretty fabulous to me.

Hey, he's fooled Gold Glove voters for four straight years. Thing is, the Gold Glove has oft-times been a joke award, with the best defensive player at each position often not getting his due.

Marquis Grissom — Expos

AB	R	H	2B	3B	HR	RBI	BB	K	SB	CS	AVG
630	104	188	27	2	19	95	52	76	53	10	.298

As we predicted last year, Grissom pushed his game up a notch and hit close to 20 HR, with big boosts in RBI and runs-scored. He also won his first Gold Glove, although his zone ratings over the past two years indicate he's just a good (not exceptional) fielder.

We think of him as a faster Moises Alou, a fine all-around talent, but not one of the best players in the game. He's an All-Star, but his power isn't great, and he doesn't draw enough walks to push his OBP way above average.

He's 27 this year, so he could push his game even higher. If he does that, then he could be an MVP candidate.

Chris Gwynn — Royals

AB	R	H	2B	3B	HR	RBI	BB	K	SB	CS	AVG
287	36	86	14	4	1	25	24	34	0	1	.300

All but 17 of Gwynn's at-bats last year came against right-handers. That's how he managed a .300 average and a .354 OBP. He can help a team from the left side of the plate. But if it weren't for the platoon differential, and the fact that his managers noticed and employed it, Gwynn wouldn't have a job. Since he has a .179 average against lefties over the past five years, it's safe to say a full-time role isn't in the cards for Gwynn..

Tony Gwynn — Padres

AB	R	H	2B	3B	HR	RBI	BB	K	SB	CS	AVG
489	70	175	41	3	7	59	36	19	14	1	.358

After two sub-par years, Gwynn really turned it on in 1993. He recorded a career high with 41 doubles and his .358 BA was the second highest of his career. If not for the shame of Andres Galarraga's Mile High-aided batting crown, Gwynn would have won his fifth title.

Gwynn helped spark the top of the Padre order, hitting .348 in the two-spot and almost .400 in third. He was very egalitarian at the plate, destroying both righties and lefties with slashing doubles and stinging groundballs.

Gwynn more than anyone was shocked by the financial decisions the Padres levied on the team. As a career Padre he was hurt that ownership would tank the season by dealing integral cogs such as Sheffield and McGriff.

Being the consummate professional, he responded by turning in one of the best years of a career which speaks for itself. Thank goodness he's one Padre that's safe from the blaze.

Darryl Hamilton — Brewers

AB	R	H	2B	3B	HR	RBI	BB	K	SB	CS	AVG
520	74	161	21	1	9	48	45	62	21	13	.310

Hamilton's a fairly valuable outfielder who is getting too old to learn that many new tricks.

He hits for good average (.297 for his career) and he steals some bases (although this dropped significantly from 1992's unprecedented 41).

He's mainly a rightfielder, but he can play center and left with the best of them. He's no Jesse Barfield, but his arm is pretty good.

Hamilton's at-bats versus lefthanders are pretty much wasted, but his hitting versus righties more than makes up for it. In 338 at-bats versus righthanders he slugged .459 and got on-base at a .394 clip.

On a really good team, Hamilton would only be a reasonably talented player, but on the Brewers he's a superstar. Look for more of the same in '94.

JEFFREY HAMMONDS — ORIOLES

AAA – Rochester

AB	R	H	2B	3B	HR	RBI	BB	K	SB	CS	AVG.
151	25	47	9	1	5	23	5	27	6	3	.311

AB	R	H	2B	3B	HR	RBI	BB	K	SB	CS	AVG.
105	10	32	8	0	3	19	2	16	4	0	.305

When Hammonds was drafted by the O's, he was considered a line-drive power hitter. That may have changed after an impressive year split between the majors and Triple-A. He showed exceptional power in both leagues, slugging .467 and .483, respectively.

He's not without weaknesses, though. He has an average arm and lousy plate discipline. He also had surgery on a herniated disc in the off-season and although he's supposedly recovered, this may slow him down next year.

But he's only 23 and has plenty of time to learn and heal. He may be hitting 20+ HR and stealing 50 bases in a couple years.

SHAWN HARE — TIGERS

AAA – Toledo

AB	R	H	2B	3B	HR	RBI	BB	K	SB	CS	AVG.
470	81	124	29	3	20	76	34	90	8	4	.264

Hare's always been a pretty good hitter. His average fell last year but he slugged .466 in the International League.

But he got passed on the depth chart last year by Danny Bautista because he lacks speed. With the team he puts on the field, Sparky needs speed. At 27, Hare is getting too old to break out of the doghouse and beat out guys like Davis and Bautista.

BILLY HATCHER — RED SOX

AB	R	H	2B	3B	HR	RBI	BB	K	SB	CS	AVG.
508	71	146	24	3	9	57	28	46	14	7	.287

Hatcher pulled a season out of thin air last year and probably saved his career. We think he did just to spite us after we told you he was worthless.

Even after raising his average 38 points and his slugging 72 points to .400, he's still average. Which means that for most of his career, mediocrity was an unattainable dream.

Be not deceived. He slumped hard late in the season, hitting .227 and .192 in August and September, respectively. He's 33 and his stamina isn't going to get any better.

DAVE HENDERSON — ATHLETICS

AB	R	H	2B	3B	HR	RBI	BB	K	SB	CS	AVG.
382	37	84	19	0	20	53	32	113	0	3	.220

Hendu returned in reduced form after injuries destroyed his '92 season.

His playing time was reduced because the A's obviously don't trust him when saddled with the wear and tear of a full season.

While his power was intact, his BA was abominable and he drew even fewer walks than he usually does.

Henderson may persevere for a season or two, but the A's will continue to reduce his at-bats as long as he stays this prone to injury.

RICKEY HENDERSON — ATHLETICS

AB	R	H	2B	3B	HR	RBI	BB	K	SB	CS	AVG.
481	114	139	22	2	21	59	120	65	53	8	.289

Rickey had another productive season, cementing his reputation as the best lead-off man in the show. He misplaced his power somewhere between the Bay Area and the Great White North, but the Jays can't complain. They got Rickey to get on base and score runs, which he did admirably.

While his other stats in Toronto were weak, his OBP was still a solid if un-Rickey-like .356. He stole 22 bases in 203 plate appearances and was caught only twice.

While he didn't make the impact Molitor and Olerud did, he did earn his pay. You've gotta admire (and resent) a team like the Jays which has money and isn't afraid to buy what or whom it takes to win a World Series.

There's method to their madness. The Jays will receive two first-round draft picks as compensation for losing him. Though they lose prospects in trades, they restock their system in the draft.

At the time of the trade, the Blue Jays already had the second-most potent offense in American League next to the Tigers. If they had a weakness, it was pitching. So what does Gillick do? He trades the organization's most advanced pitching prospect for three months of the best leadoff hitter in baseball. Where does that trade help Toronto in '94 or '95? It doesn't and that could end up burning them.

JOSE HERRERA — ATHLETICS
A – Hagerstown

AB	R	H	2B	3B	HR	RBI	BB	K	SB	CS	AVG
388	60	123	22	5	5	42	26	63	36	20	.317

Jose, 21, was the best batting prospect in the SAL according to managers. He's a skinny kid, but he's got a great arm.

He slumped at the end of the season and many questioned his stamina. More likely it was the 20 times he was caught stealing (56 attempts). That would wear anybody out.

RICHARD HIDALGO — ASTROS
A – Ashville

AB	R	H	2B	3B	HR	RBI	BB	K	SB	CS	AVG
403	49	109	23	3	10	55	30	76	21	13	.270

Richard has poor base-running judgment, has little concept of the strike zone and is only playing ball at the Sally League level. Those are his weaknesses.

Here are his two strengths: He's 18 and he can hit pretty well.

He will at least start the season in high A-Ball and could conceivably be at Double-A. It's possible that he could be ready for the majors by the end of this year. More realistic is to assume that he's two years away, but if he can continue to hit at this level as he goes through the farm system, he could be a superstar by the time he's 25.

Bob Abreu is a pretty impressive player, but Hidalgo's potential is significantly greater.

BOB HIGGINSON — TIGERS
AA – London

AB	R	H	2B	3B	HR	RBI	BB	K	SB	CS	AVG
224	25	69	15	4	4	35	19	37	3	4	.308

Higginson, 23, is a solid hitter and a comer in the Tigers organization. He didn't get many walks last year, but his history suggests he has better plate discipline. He has a few guys in line ahead of him, but he should be in Triple-A next year.

GLENALLEN HILL — CUBS

AB	R	H	2B	3B	HR	RBI	BB	K	SB	CS	AVG
261	33	69	14	2	15	47	17	71	8	3	.264

He was a spare part with the Indians and apparently developed a bad attitude. The Indians swapped pouting outfielders when they acquired Candy Maldonado from the Cubs. The trade seemed to agree with Hill, as he hit 10 home runs in only 87 at-bats in Wrigley.

He still acts like taking a walk is against the law, but the Cubbies were impressed with the power he displayed and plan to start him in left field in '94. With the advantage of hitting in Wrigley, he should be able to knock 20+ out of the park given 500 at-bats.

TODD HOLLANDSWORTH — DODGERS
AA – San Antonio

AB	R	H	2B	3B	HR	RBI	BB	K	SB	CS	AVG
474	57	119	24	9	17	63	29	101	23	12	.251

According to Peter Gammons in *B.A.*, scouts said that Hollandsworth was the best prospect in the AFL.

He reached Double-A San Antonio by age 20, so he must be doing something right. Mostly that something is spank the ball and then show off his speed.

Of course he has no plate discipline, but who does at that age.

He's commonly compared to Kirk Gibson and Andy Van Slyke for his tools and attitude.

DAMON HOLLINS — BRAVES
R – Danville

AB	R	H	2B	3B	HR	RBI	BB	K	SB	CS	AVG
240	37	77	15	2	7	51	19	30	10	2	.321

Hollins, 20, is considered a wee bit better than Andre King, his probable 1994 teammate somewhere in the A-Ball bowels of the Braves farm system.

Hollins has an exceptional throwing arm, good power and is a solid all-around athlete.

He is probably three years away, but make sure you watch out for him, he has the tools necessary to accelerate the timetable.

Tyrone Horne — Expos

A – West Palm Beach

AB	R	H	2B	3B	HR	RBI	BB	K	SB	CS	AVG
288	43	85	19	2	10	44	40	72	11	10	.295

AA – Harrisburg

AB	R	H	2B	3B	HR	RBI	BB	K	SB	CS	AVG
128	22	46	8	1	4	22	22	37	3	2	.359

Horne, 23, will at least see Triple-A by season's end. As you can see, he can hit a little, but his Double-A ability has yet to be proven because his 37/22 K/W ratio is not the kind of thing that Stan Musial (or any other .330+ hitter) would ever show.

Dwayne Hosey — Padres

AAA – Phoenix

AB	R	H	2B	3B	HR	RBI	BB	K	SB	CS	AVG
455	70	133	40	4	16	85	66	129	16	10	.292

At 27, he's not young, but he could probably duplicate his minor league numbers on the major league level.

He should join the Padre outfield platoon, but don't expect much PT.

Thomas Howard — Reds

AB	R	H	2B	3B	HR	RBI	BB	K	SB	CS	AVG
319	48	81	15	3	7	36	24	63	10	7	.254

At 29, he's the youngest and most versatile of the Reds' corps of aging, journeyman, backup outfielders ... which certainly isn't saying much.

But Thomas can provide a solid glove anywhere in the outfield and come up with an occasional extra-base hit. Don't be confused, though. He's nothing more than a backup and you'll have to be as desperate as the Reds before you draft him.

Dann Howitt — Mariners

AAA – Calgary

AB	R	H	2B	3B	HR	RBI	BB	K	SB	CS	AVG
333	57	93	20	1	21	77	39	67	7	5	.279

He looks like a solid hitter off the bench but he's 30 years old and has minimal defensive value, so the chance of him blossoming into a full-timer of great value is basically nil.

But he can start 50 games and deliver 8-15 homers with enough at-bats.

Keith Hughes — Reds

AAA – Indianapolis

AB	R	H	2B	3B	HR	RBI	BB	K	SB	CS	AVG
283	55	81	28	4	13	42	41	61	5	0	.286

Hughes is 30 and with his sixth organization in seven years. He's a younger incarnation of Jack Daugherty and only a club like the Reds could end up with both these guys.

Troy Hughes — Braves

AA – Greenville

AB	R	H	2B	3B	HR	RBI	BB	K	SB	CS	AVG
383	49	102	20	4	14	58	44	67	7	3	.266

Hughes is 23 and plays right field. He's a solid little player who provides a good arm and nice defense. At 6-4, 215, he's well put together. He'll start at Triple-A this year and with some luck (or injuries), he could win a reserve role by mid- to late-season.

David Hulse — Rangers

AB	R	H	2B	3B	HR	RBI	BB	K	SB	CS	AVG
407	71	118	9	10	1	29	26	57	29	9	.290

Hulse landed the starting role last year and consistent with our prediction, Elvis will be elected president in '96. Place your bets now.

He's still not the greatest hitter in the world, though, and he's average defensively.

In a word, he's adequate and the Rangers just don't have anybody to displace him. His speed is a nice plus for rotisse-owners, but his slugging and OBP aren't going to win any championships for you.

Brian Hunter — Astros

AA – Jackson

AB	R	H	2B	3B	HR	RBI	BB	K	SB	CS	AVG
523	84	154	22	5	10	52	34	85	35	18	.294

The No. 2 prospect in the Texas League behind pitching phenom Ben Van Ryn. Hunter, 23, plays excellent defense, has a good arm and pretty amazing speed. The Astros are going to seriously consider him for a job sometime this season.

At the risk of sounding like parrots, he needs to work on his plate discipline and base-running judgment. Super runners like Rickey and Lofton don't get nailed 18 times a year when they steal only 35 bases.

Pete Incaviglia — Phillies

AB	R	H	2B	3B	HR	RBI	BB	K	SB	CS	AVG
368	60	101	16	3	24	89	21	82	1	1	.274

We'll probably take a lot of flak for this, but here it is: His defense isn't that bad! Sure it's not average, but it's so barely below-average that for all practical purposes, it is average. Does that make sense? Well just think of him as having an average glove in left.

His K's dropped about 30 percent last year, but with expansion and the fact that he's 30, we don't know how much stock to put in this.

Our best guess is that he'll slug .450-.500 if he gets the playing time. It's remains to be seen whether he'll get enough quality at-bats to chalk up 89 RBI again, though.

Bo Jackson — ? ? ?

AB	R	H	2B	3B	HR	RBI	BB	K	SB	CS	AVG
439	63	108	16	4	25	68	25	146	27	6	.246

Bo knows comebacks. Or so the media would have us think.

In actuality, Jackson had a pretty decent year for a guy with a prosthetic hip and pretty rotten year for your average ballplayer.

16 homers aside, Bo had a juicy (and typical) 106/23 K/W ratio. He also batted .232. So he basically showed that he can strike out and not hit for average as well as he ever did.

Gene Lamont, especially cognizant of the effect Bo's press could have on the team, was careful to de-emphasize Bo's contribution in comparison to the rest of the roster.

Imagine being Ventura or Thomas and having the press ignore your 4-for-4 hitfest to ask you about Bo's throw to the cut-off man.

As heartwarming as Bo's return may be, it would be foolish to think that he'll ever be more than a role player who'd be hard-pressed to beat Sid Bream in a footrace.

Darrin Jackson — Mets

AB	R	H	2B	3B	HR	RBI	BB	K	SB	CS	AVG
263	19	55	9	0	6	26	10	75	0	2	.209

Jackson is a terrific fielder. In fact, he's one of the best fielders in the National League. But the outs he saves with his glove are not worth the outs he gives away with his bat. Jackson can look up the definition of "all-around player" in the dictionary and it will read, "Not you!"

Dion James — ?????

AB	R	H	2B	3B	HR	RBI	BB	K	SB	CS	AVG
343	62	114	21	2	7	36	31	31	0	0	.332

Dion didn't hurt the Yanks at all this year. We predicted that he might not see 250 at-bats. Well he did, and he kept driving until he reached 343.

He's a safe bet at the plate. He's a groundball hitter who can draw the walk very well and he showed his best power since '87 when he was with Atlanta.

Dion's defense is still below average in left, and he flat-out stunk in the few innings he spelled Bernie Williams in center. He's a pretty darn good pinch-hitter, so perhaps his team should relieve the stress in the dugout by hiding his glove from him.

Barring injury, Dion should perform at around his current level while tending to move back to the neighborhood of his career numbers (.289 BA, .366 OBP and .396 SLG).

Stan Javier — Athletics

AB	R	H	2B	3B	HR	RBI	BB	K	SB	CS	AVG
237	33	69	10	4	3	28	27	33	12	2	.291

Stan rebounded from an absolutely horrendous first half to post a season that was much better than Luis Polonia's.

Given his age and past performance, it's probably a bit much to expect him to continue to perform at this level, but many teams could do worse than to give a player with such nice on-base and base-running skills a job.

Lance Johnson — White Sox

AB	R	H	2B	3B	HR	RBI	BB	K	SB	CS	AVG
540	75	168	18	14	0	47	36	33	35	7	.311

Johnson helped his cause by hitting for a good enough average to drive his OBP up to a respectable .354.

He also did the usual in leading the league in triples (as he has for the two previous years) and proving his value as a base-stealer.

He never hurts his team with the glove and '93 was no exception. As long as he can track down long flies and stretch doubles into triples he'll be a fixture in Comiskey II.

CHRIS JONES — ROCKIES

AB	R	H	2B	3B	HR	RBI	BB	K	SB	CS	AVG
209	29	57	11	4	6	31	10	48	9	4	.273

He needs someone to sit down with him and teach him a little bit about the strike zone. While they're at it, they can explain to him why he has no future in the majors.

MOTOR-BOAT JONES — REDS

A – Winston-Salem

AB	R	H	2B	3B	HR	RBI	BB	K	SB	CS	AVG
330	58	99	21	4	19	69	30	47	8	4	.300

At age 25, Jones has finally found some power. He slugged .561 and hit over .270 for the first time in his career. At the same time, he dropped from 37 steals in '92 to 11 in '93 (he got three in 89 ABs in Double-A).

He's a player in transition and needs some time in Double-A, but the improvements he made last year are the ones you want to see.

BRIAN JORDAN — CARDINALS

AB	R	H	2B	3B	HR	RBI	BB	K	SB	CS	AVG
223	33	69	10	6	10	44	12	35	6	6	.309

He's a great athlete just entering into his peak performance years. But due to the fact that, until just last year, baseball was only a part-time job to him, he's still going to need about three more coats of Turtle Wax before he can be considered a star player.

FELIX JOSE — ROYALS

AB	R	H	2B	3B	HR	RBI	BB	K	SB	CS	AVG
499	64	126	24	3	6	43	36	95	31	13	.253

Herk Robinson must've been accidentally injected with elephant tranquilizers the day he traded Gregg Jefferies to the Cards for Jose. After all, Jefferies is three years younger and, at the time of the trade, a better hitter than Felix will ever be. The Herk-ster strikes again.

Jose's stock took a dramatic hit in '93. He suffered from a mysterious shoulder ailment that prevented him from swinging from the right side all season and his defense went right out the window. Kauffman Stadium is likely to rob him of any power he might have left, regardless of whether or not he can switch, and his on-base skills are horrid to begin with. Herk better get used to the sound of chains rattling, because he'll be haunted by this boner of a trade for years to come.

DAVID JUSTICE — BRAVES

AB	R	H	2B	3B	HR	RBI	BB	K	SB	CS	AVG
585	90	158	15	4	40	120	78	90	3	5	.270

Dave: I managed to cover my keister last year by saying he could still hit 30-35 homers, despite his inability to stay healthy. Well, he stayed healthy and drove in 120 runs. According to various stories on TV and in the papers, Davey's marriage with Halle Berry was what got his head on straight.

He's 28 now, so chances are 1993 was his peak year. Still, he could belt 30+ dingers and drive in 100 runs 'til he's 35, so that gives him five to seven more years of star-caliber performance. Not only that, but he actually looked pretty smooth in right.

Now if we could just clone Halle and get her to marry Deion. ...

MIKE KELLY — BRAVES

AAA – Richmond

AB	R	H	2B	3B	HR	RBI	BB	K	SB	CS	AVG
424	63	103	13	1	19	58	36	109	11	7	.243

Mike, 24, showed some growth and a bit of decay as he moved from Double-A to Triple-A in 1993. He cut his strikeouts and raised his average a bit, but lowered his walks, power and did not use his speed effectively.

Still, Kelly has as much raw power as Klesko and has the tools to be a decent center fielder, or an excellent left fielder. If he can continue to cut his K's down, then Kelly will make himself a viable outfield candidate towards the end of the season.

ROBERTO KELLY — REDS

AB	R	H	2B	3B	HR	RBI	BB	K	SB	CS	AVG
320	44	102	17	3	9	35	17	43	21	5	.319

Roberto suffered through a slow start in April last year and decided to change his name to Bobby for luck. He broke his slump and hit .335 through the next two months, but a separated shoulder ended his season in July ... so he's Roberto, again.

We like "Rock" better, but whatever.

We were predicting a breakthrough year for Kelly and it looks like he was almost there. He slugged .474 in just over half the season and was on his way to 15-20 homers, 30+ steals and a .300+ average.

If his shoulder is healthy in the spring, expect him to pick up where he left off.

Andre King — Braves

R – Danville

AB	R	H	2B	3B	HR	RBI	BB	K	SB	CS	AVG
223	41	69	10	6	0	18	36	40	15	5	.309

King is 20 this year and should play a full season in A-Ball. He has great speed –B.A. rated him the third best base-runner coming out of high school in last year's draft – and is considered the top defensive outfielder in the Braves system.

He has not adjusted to a wooden bat yet, but has shown good discipline and an ability to make solid contact. He's a long-term prospect, probably three years away. But with his youth and ability (considered the second-best high school athlete in the draft), he could be in the majors by mid-1995.

Wayne Kirby — Indians

AB	R	H	2B	3B	HR	RBI	BB	K	SB	CS	AVG
458	71	123	19	5	6	60	37	58	17	5	.269

This 30-year-old benchwarmer saw his career come and go in the minors. The Indians really have no need for this ancient brave. But they'll be hard pressed to find anybody desperate enough to take him off their hands.

Ray Lankford — Cardinals

AB	R	H	2B	3B	HR	RBI	BB	K	SB	CS	AVG
407	64	97	17	3	7	45	81	111	14	14	.238

Lankford suffered from a strained shoulder early in the season and never really got into his groove. In June, he went on the DL with a sore wrist. Brian Jordan took over his position in the interim and did an admirable job. It put a scare into Lankford, and he was unable to do anything about it.

Lankford saw his average drop 55 points and his slugging percentage plummet 134 points. Rest assured, Lankford should regain his '92 form, albeit without all the power. He is still a steady fielder, which will give him the edge over Jordan in the spring.

A word of advice for Joe Torre, though. Nail this guy's foot to the bag whenever he gets on base. Throughout his career, he's been dead meat in almost half of his steal attempts.

Gene Larkin — Twins

AB	R	H	2B	3B	HR	RBI	BB	K	SB	CS	AVG
144	17	38	7	1	1	19	21	16	0	1	.264

Larkin lost most of the season to a strained left achilles tendon. Ouch.

He's in the twilight of his career and injuries are beginning to make him miss it. He's never been much of a hitter anyway, and the Twins are running out of places to play him. If he's lucky he'll be a backup this year.

Matt Lawton — Twins

A – Fort Wayne

AB	R	H	2B	3B	HR	RBI	BB	K	SB	CS	AVG
340	50	97	21	3	9	38	65	43	23	15	.285

Matt, 22, has line-drive power and some speed, but apparently not as much as he thinks. He walks a lot and sported a .410 OBP in '93.

He should be working on his base-running in Double-A next year.

Derek Lee — Twins

AAA – Portland

AB	R	H	2B	3B	HR	RBI	BB	K	SB	CS	AVG
381	79	120	30	7	10	80	60	51	16	5	.315

Lee knocked the ball all over a tough pitcher's park in Portland last year. He hit .315 and slugged .509; Portland's park effect for hits and homers is 85 percent and doubles is 89 percent. It's pretty safe to say he can hit.

Derek's got all the skills: power, speed and he takes a ton of walks.

He's 27 and his time is now. The Twins would be fools to let him rot in Triple-A, but they've done it before with Bernardo Brito.

Darren Lewis — Giants

AB	R	H	2B	3B	HR	RBI	BB	K	SB	CS	AVG
522	84	132	17	7	2	48	30	40	46	15	.253

Like the song says, he remained the same.

Everyone's heard of Darren's glove since he now holds the record for consecutive errorless attempts.

By the same token, no one hears about his bat because it is almost non-existent. As much as his fielding aids the Giant cause, you've got to imagine that his .299 OBP. and .308 SL%. in the leadoff spot detracted radically from their line-up's ability to score runs.

Lewis opened up his running game, stealing 46 bases this year. Imagine what he could do if he got to first more often.

Because of his age, he should be having his peak season within the next couple of years.

GREG LITTON											MARINERS
AB	R	H	2B	3B	HR	RBI	BB	K	SB	CS	AVG.
174	25	52	17	0	3	25	18	30	0	1	.299

For years he was a cheesy role player for the Giants. All it took for him to actually acquire value was a trip north; a switch to the Junior Circuit and a less demanding defensive role. He's OK as long as he doesn't play up the middle.

Litton's got some power and it looks like he'll finally take a walk if you'll give it to him. This makes him a pretty good hitter.

KENNY LOFTON											INDIANS
AB	R	H	2B	3B	HR	RBI	BB	K	SB	CS	AVG.
569	116	185	28	8	1	42	81	83	70	14	.325

As a leadoff hitter, Lofton is one of the best in the league. If it weren't for three Blue Jay hitters, Lofton would have won the batting title last year. Only 37 of his 185 hits were for extra bases, but that doesn't matter much. He offsets his inability to hit for power with an excellent eye at the plate and the ability to steal second base with impunity.

At 27, Lofton is a little old to be considered a mega-star, but the package he offers the Indians looks pretty darn attractive in the short run. Look for him to continue hitting for a high average and stealing 50+ bases for the next few years.

TONY LONGMIRE											PHILLIES
AAA – Scranton/Wilkes-Barre											
AB	R	H	2B	3B	HR	RBI	BB	K	SB	CS	AVG.
447	63	136	36	4	6	67	41	71	12	4	.304

Not a super prospect, but this 25-year-old kid can hit a little. The only question is whether he can make enough of an impact to replace one of the pretty good outfielders on the Phillies. If he gets a shot and makes the most of it, he'll hit in the .290 range with some line-drive power.

TERRELL LOWERY											RANGERS
AA – Tulsa											
AB	R	H	2B	3B	HR	RBI	BB	K	SB	CS	AVG.
258	29	62	5	1	3	14	28	50	10	12	.240

Lowery, 23, is a great athlete who played hoops for Loyola Marymount. He has excellent speed, although you wouldn't know it from his stealing percentage. His judgment on the basepaths definitely needs improvement.

He has good plate discipline for a youngster, however, and plays excellent defense anywhere in the outfield.

MATT LUKE											YANKEES
A – Greensboro											
AB	R	H	2B	3B	HR	RBI	BB	K	SB	CS	AVG.
549	83	157	37	5	21	91	47	79	11	3	.286

Matt, 23, has good power and the ability to both score and drive in runs.

There's really no place to put him in the Yankee outfield so it's be nice if he found his way onto another team.

SCOTT LYDY											ATHLETICS
AAA – Tacoma											
AB	R	H	2B	3B	HR	RBI	BB	K	SB	CS	AVG.
341	70	100	22	6	9	41	50	67	12	4	.293

The A's heeded our call and brought this aging, 25-year-old prospect up for a bit in '93.

His performance was not brilliant, but he's still got a shot at developing into a major league hitter. The A's seem perfectly happy giving their young farmers a shot (e.g. Troy Neel, Brent Gates and Craig Paquette).

With most of Oakland's outfield prospects a year or two away and Rickey Henderson being the only lock position-wise, Lydy's chances of getting a serious look in the spring are vastly improved.

SHANE MACK											TWINS
AB	R	H	2B	3B	HR	RBI	BB	K	SB	CS	AVG.
503	66	139	30	4	10	61	41	76	15	5	.276

Mack had a lot of trouble with injuries last year. A separated shoulder kept him out of spring training and a strained tendon in his left arm put him on the DL in May. His numbers really suffered as a result.

The Twins showed their great confidence in Shane by signing him to a one-year deal. He's probably worth more than that since he hit .300+ and slugged .460+ in the three previous seasons. But the Twins have some young sluggers who are ready to step into the outfield, so he may have to prove himself again.

That shouldn't be a problem. He's been a consistent hitter with power for some time and if he stays healthy, he should be able to return to form.

Jose Malave — Red Sox

A – Lynchburg

AB	R	H	2B	3B	HR	RBI	BB	K	SB	CS	AVG
312	42	94	27	1	8	54	36	54	2	3	.301

Malave was the No. 9 prospect in the Carolina League last year, due primarily to an impressive year at the plate. He's a good hitter with a little power and discipline.

But he has a reputation as a poor fielder and had his season cut short by a broken hand last year. He's a couple years away, but the Sox are pretty high on him.

Candy Maldonado — Indians

AB	R	H	2B	3B	HR	RBI	BB	K	SB	CS	AVG
221	19	46	7	0	8	35	24	58	0	1	.208

Candy endured one of the worst seasons of his career last season and was shipped off to Cleveland for Glenallen Hill in August. While he might be able to rebound in '94, he'll have to steal PT from Manny Ramirez, one of the best outfield prospects in baseball. If he's lucky, he could start the season in right while Ramirez gets some seasoning in Charlotte.

Al Martin — Pirates

AB	R	H	2B	3B	HR	RBI	BB	K	SB	CS	AVG
480	85	135	26	8	18	64	42	122	16	9	.281

Martin spent a lot of time filling in for the injured Andy Van Slyke in center last year, but he figures to be a regular in left.

It took a while for him to adjust to major league pitching but he seemed to get comfortable around June, when he hit .287 and slugged .519. He finished out the season hitting .308 and slugging .549 after the All-Star break with 12 homers in the last two months.

He was inconsistent, but he showed definite improvement in his rookie season. Martin's history suggests that he'll be a consistent .275+ hitter with good power. He's a bit of a free swinger and could afford to take more walks, but he's pretty solid otherwise.

Dave Martinez — Giants

AB	R	H	2B	3B	HR	RBI	BB	K	SB	CS	AVG
241	28	58	12	1	5	27	27	39	6	3	.241

We're not sure how or why Martinez ended up in a Giant uniform. He continued his decline as a batter and his ability as a fielder was rendered moot by the presence of Darren Lewis.

The Giants also experimented with him in the lead-off spot where he had a pathetic .300 OBP. Between him and Lewis, it's a miracle the Giants ever drew first blood in a game.

Martinez's value is as a back-up right-fielder who should hit around sixth or seventh in the order. Anything else is a waste of major league at-bats.

Billy Masse — Yankees

AAA – Columbus

AB	R	H	2B	3B	HR	RBI	BB	K	SB	CS	AVG
402	81	127	35	3	19	91	82	68	17	7	.316

He really has a lot going for him, everything except his age (27), as a matter of fact.

He can hit for average, draw a lot more walks than K's and can really belt the ball.

He's better than the Gerald Williamses and Dion Jameses of recent years, so the Yanks will probably ignore him and let him rot. It's a shame, because he's been ready to hit at the major-league level for the last two years.

Derrick May — Cubs

AB	R	H	2B	3B	HR	RBI	BB	K	SB	CS	AVG
465	62	137	25	2	10	77	31	41	10	3	.295

His defense is subpar, and he is too impatient at the plate. Otherwise, May has shown solid improvement in his hitting over the past two seasons. Since he's only 25, he should continue to get better. We're not talking MVP numbers here, but he should develop a little more power and become a serviceable fielder.

Chad McConnell — Phillies

A – Clearwater

AB	R	H	2B	3B	HR	RBI	BB	K	SB	CS	AVG
300	43	72	17	3	6	37	51	98	9	5	.240

Chad was a fantastic hitter in college, even playing for the 1992 Olympic team.

He has decent discipline and hits to all fields. In addition, he's a fine fielder. He uppercuts too much and needs to get his game in gear. He has the potential to be an impact hitter, but he's 23 and hasn't shown much yet.

Ray McDavid — Padres

AA – Wichita

AB	R	H	2B	3B	HR	RBI	BB	K	SB	CS	AVG
441	65	119	18	5	11	55	70	104	33	17	.270

Ray is another member of the new breed of speedy power hitters in the Ron Gant mode.

He fell back a little last year, both in terms of slugging and using his head on the basepaths. This wasn't unexpected considering he was making the transition from A-ball to Double-A where the stakes are a little higher these days.

Ray's not known for his arm, which will be a liability in Jack Murphy.

McDavid shouldn't spend much time in Triple-A, unless he does especially poorly there. He may even get a chance to win a job in the Spring. Regardless, the Padres can't afford to keep a talented 22-year-old like Ray cooling his heels on the farm.

JASON McFARLIN — GIANTS
A – San Jose

AB	R	H	2B	3B	HR	RBI	BB	K	SB	CS	AVG
395	71	123	20	4	7	53	29	67	49	10	.311

He had to be demoted to A-ball before he'd perform and he didn't burn up the world there.

At 24, Jason's an OK prospect, but he' a little old to be spending seasons in A-ball.

WILLIE McGEE — GIANTS

AB	R	H	2B	3B	HR	RBI	BB	K	SB	CS	AVG
475	53	143	28	1	4	46	38	67	10	9	.301

Willie can still get on base with a few walks and a nice average, but he's past the point where he can be a truly threatening hitter and a full-time player.

MARK McLEMORE — ORIOLES

AB	R	H	2B	3B	HR	RBI	BB	K	SB	CS	AVG
581	81	165	27	5	4	72	64	92	21	15	.284

The Orioles exiled several guys last year to free up space for McLemore in right. He rewarded them by increasing his offensive production from zip to mediocre and now it looks like they're going to ace Reynolds and move McLemore back to second.

Mark did improve at the plate quite a bit last year, took more walks, raised his average 40 points and slugged over .300 for the first time since '88. Still no big deal for a right fielder, but the move to second may make him a bit more attractive to rotisse-owners.

The question is whether he can maintain these numbers. History is not on his side. He's never hit over .250 before '93 and he probably won't next year.

WILLIAM McMILLON — MARLINS
A – Elmira

AB	R	H	2B	3B	HR	RBI	BB	K	SB	CS	AVG
227	38	69	14	2	6	35	30	44	5	4	.304

Depending on how he does in the spring, McMillon, 22, should make it to one of the high-level A-Ball clubs to start '94. At this level, solid play does not guarantee one prospect status, so he has to establish himself before we know where he checks in. In addition, he's going to be battling the outfield depth chart of the Marlins and, if you read this section thoroughly, you know that the Marlins are well-stocked.

BUCK McNABB — ASTROS
A – Osceola

AB	R	H	2B	3B	HR	RBI	BB	K	SB	CS	AVG
487	69	139	15	7	1	35	52	66	28	15	.285

McNabb is 21 and will probably be in Double-A this year. He's not as impressive as Hidalgo or Abreu, but he's still not a bad player now, and he's extremely young. We'll get a fairer estimate of his power in the more neutral environment of the Texas League.

JEFF McNEELY — RED SOX
AAA – Pawtucket

AB	R	H	2B	3B	HR	RBI	BB	K	SB	CS	AVG
498	65	130	14	3	2	35	43	102	40	7	.261

McNeely's a young speedster with very little stick. He'd be more valuable if he took more walks, but his .322 OBA is already higher than his .313 slugging percentage. And considering Pawtucket's HR park effect is 210 percent, those two dingers were gifts.

He's 24 and has time to improve at the plate. Billy Hatcher will need help in center and McNeely's speed and defense make him a viable candidate to compete for the job. He may get some PT this year, but don't expect Ken, Jr., to start looking over his shoulder.

BRIAN McRAE — ROYALS

AB	R	H	2B	3B	HR	RBI	BB	K	SB	CS	AVG
627	78	177	28	9	12	69	37	105	23	14	.282

What Hal got out of his son Brian last year is about his true level of ability. It's doubtful the young McRae will ever surpass the .340 on-base barrier, but a .290 BA wouldn't be out of the question. The only thing that seemed out of line with his career trends was his 12 HR. He's fighting the park on that issue, and in the end, it's going to be a losing battle.

He can become a solid fielder with a little work. The same goes for his baserunning. McRae is only 26 this year, so improvements in both of these areas is likely. He really needs to cut down on the K's, though, if he wants to hold on to his position for any length of time.

KEVIN MCREYNOLDS											METS
AB	R	H	2B	3B	HR	RBI	BB	K	SB	CS	AVG.
351	44	86	22	4	11	42	37	56	2	2	.245

He still looks good in the field, but his offense has been slipping the last three seasons. He's 34 this year, so the chances that he will regain his 1990 form are about as good as Rush Limbaugh's chances of joining the National Organization of Women.

ORLANDO MERCED											PIRATES
AB	R	H	2B	3B	HR	RBI	BB	K	SB	CS	AVG.
447	68	140	26	4	8	70	77	64	3	3	.313

Jim Leyland was impressed with Orlando's focus last year after he religiously watched tapes of opposing pitchers to learn their patterns. Merced's diligence paid off and earned him the starting job in right.

His biggest problem in the past has been his impotence against lefties, but he improved on his .193 career-average against them last year with a .297 average.

In short, he's a solid fielder who's recognized his deficiencies at the plate and worked hard to overcome them. Next year will tell a lot about how much he's actually improved, but his plate discipline and work ethic suggest he can remain productive.

The Pirates are talking about moving him to first permanently, which seems crazy considering the Young/Aude/Hunter pile-up that already exists there. If they're smart, they'll let him have another year in right to consolidate his gains without added distractions.

LUIS MERCEDES											GIANTS
AAA – Phoenix											
AB	R	H	2B	3B	HR	RBI	BB	K	SB	CS	AVG.
244	28	71	5	3	0	15	36	30	14	6	.291

Luis fought and lost in the battle for playing time as an Oriole, so the Giants saw fit to pick him up.

He was a non-productive acquisition who showed little in Triple-A and less in S.F.

Despite decent plate discipline he's a lousy baserunner who costs his team runs with foolish mental errors.

MARK MERCHANT											REDS
AA – Chattanooga											
AB	R	H	2B	3B	HR	RBI	BB	K	SB	CS	AVG.
336	56	101	16	0	17	61	50	79	3	5	.301

See Motor-Boat Jones, they're basically the same guy.

MATT MIESKE											BREWERS
AAA – New Orleans											
AB	R	H	2B	3B	HR	RBI	BB	K	SB	CS	AVG.
219	36	57	14	2	8	22	27	46	6	4	.260

He's still waiting for the Brewers to give him a full trial. Until they do he's just treading water in New Orleans. From Milwaukee's perspective, he'll have to stay healthy if they're going to give him at-bats.

Mieske has the ability to hit in a major league line-up, especially the talent-hungry Brewers. Considering their diminishing list of prospects he should get his break in '94.

KEVIN MITCHELL											REDS
AB	R	H	2B	3B	HR	RBI	BB	K	SB	CS	AVG.
323	56	110	21	3	19	64	25	48	1	0	.341

Kevin missed lots of games last year with hamstring and rotator-cuff injuries, but still managed to put up his best numbers since '89.

He slugged .601; .745 against lefties with eight HR in 94 ABs. He proved he still has the power the Reds need in the outfield.

His shoulder (rotator cuff) is supposed to be ready in the spring, but you should be concerned that injuries are consistently limiting his ABs. He's at that age (32) where injuries suddenly claim a lot of careers.

But he's a heck of a hitter and he'll continue to produce as long as he's healthy.

RAUL MONDESI											DODGERS
AAA – Albuquerque											
AB	R	H	2B	3B	HR	RBI	BB	K	SB	CS	AVG.
425	65	119	22	7	12	65	18	85	13	10	.280

This 23-year-old youngster developed some line-drive power in Albuquerque but he has some serious trouble with his K/W ratio.

The Dodgers consider Mondesi one of their top prospects but their faith may be misplaced. In his favor are his rather impressive numbers in his L.A. debut. It's not often that a guy hits better in the NL than in the PCL.

We'll be convinced by more of the same. Look for improvements in walks and B.A. as indicators that Raul is what Lasorda claims he is. This will be a good season to watch as it will probably be his first full workout.

RAY MONTGOMERY — ASTROS
AA – Jackson

AB	R	H	2B	3B	HR	RBI	BB	K	SB	CS	AVG.
338	50	95	16	3	10	59	36	54	12	6	.281

Montgomery, 24, might be considered a prospect, but the Astros are well-stocked with kids who can hit and play the outfield. Right now, he shouldn't be considered much more than a possible role-player off the bench. If he were to slide into a starting role, he'd probably slide right out of it soon enough.

KERWIN MOORE — ATHLETICS
A – High Desert

AB	R	H	2B	3B	HR	RBI	BB	K	SB	CS	AVG.
510	120	137	20	9	6	52	114	95	71	16	.269

Moore, 23, was acquired from the Marlins in trade for 25-year-old shortstop Kurt Abbott.

This was a good trade for the A's. Abbott, as we state in his essay, isn't that hot and Moore's speed blows his out of the water.

Oakland gives up some power with Moore, but he showed a phenomenal ability to draw walks. If he can lower his K's and keep his BA up he'll make the A's look really good.

MIKE MOORE — DODGERS
A – Bakersfield

AB	R	H	2B	3B	HR	RBI	BB	K	SB	CS	AVG.
403	61	116	25	1	13	58	29	103	23	10	.288

A former UCLA wide receiver, Moore, 23, is reputed to have the best arm in the Cali League. He has a decent bat, but he's K-prone.

A shoulder injury in July ended his season, so the Dodgers will want to give him more time to flaunt his goods.

VINCE MOORE — PADRES
A – Durham

AB	R	H	2B	3B	HR	RBI	BB	K	SB	CS	AVG.
319	53	93	14	1	14	64	29	93	21	8	.292

Vince, 22, arrived in San Diego along with Donnie Elliott and Mel Nieves by way of the trade for McGriff.

Like his fellow tradees, Moore is a talented young player with a lot to offer the Pads.

Scouts consider him an Alex Ochoa (Baltimore OF prospect) clone with more power and less of an arm. He's a switch-hitter with good speed and a penchant for whiffing.

He was also ranked the No. 5 prospect in the Carolina League.

GARY MOTA — ASTROS
AA – Jackson

AB	R	H	2B	3B	HR	RBI	BB	K	SB	CS	AVG.
90	7	13	2	0	3	8	2	25	1	1	.144

Gary is 23.

We touted him last year, but two games into the season, he ruptured a tendon sheath in his left wrist and was basically finished.

He played poorly in the AFL this winter, but the wrist was OK. Apparently, he was just rusty. In 1992, Mota hit .291 with 23 homers and 22 steals in the Sally League.

He'll probably start at Double-A, but he could be in Houston by September or earlier if he's healthy.

CHAD MOTTOLA — REDS
A – Winston-Salem

AB	R	H	2B	3B	HR	RBI	BB	K	SB	CS	AVG.
493	76	138	25	3	21	91	62	109	13	7	.280

Mottola, 22, is considered a Tim Salmon/Dale Murphy-esque package, with Murphy's modesty. He has a rifle arm, good power, and can run a little.

He was the No. 6 prospect in the Carolina League last year and has a reputation as a heck of a hustler (as in hard worker). He tired late in the season, though, and needs to work on his stamina.

PEDRO MUNOZ — TWINS

AB	R	H	2B	3B	HR	RBI	BB	K	SB	CS	AVG.
326	34	76	11	1	13	38	25	97	1	2	.233

Pedro started off hot enough last year, hitting .306 and slugging .571 in April. But he was knocked out for most of July with torn cartilage in his left knee, and that pretty much destroyed his season. He hit .122 after his return in July and August, and never got settled bouncing around between left and right.

He still managed to hit 13 HR despite his injury, which is a good indication he should continue improving his power when he's healthy. He's a right fielder by trade and that's where he's at his best. If he's healthy next year, he should have a home in right and be able to get back to his .275+, 15+ HR form.

CALVIN MURRAY — GIANTS
A – San Jose

AB	R	H	2B	3B	HR	RBI	BB	K	SB	CS	AVG.
345	61	97	24	1	9	42	40	63	42	10	.281

Calvin's young and he's got explosive base-stealing skills. He was voted the No. 10 prospect in the Callie League.

He wasn't doing a darn thing at Double-A so he was demoted to A-ball San Jose where he caught fire and ran amok on the basepaths. he was rewarded by a short stint in Triple-A at the end of the year.

GLENN MURRAY — EXPOS
AA – Harrisburg

AB	R	H	2B	3B	HR	RBI	BB	K	SB	CS	AVG.
475	82	120	21	4	26	96	56	111	16	7	.253

Murray, 23, stayed at Double-A, while Floyd, Pride and White jumped to the majors. He's a solid player with very nice power and a few walks, but he's decidedly below them in ability. Realistically, he's probably going to rot at Triple-A in this organization.

MARC NEWFIELD — MARINERS
AA – Jacksonville

AB	R	H	2B	3B	HR	RBI	BB	K	SB	CS	AVG.
336	48	103	18	0	19	51	33	35	1	1	.307

Had a .374 OBP and a .530 SL% at Double-A Jacksonville.

Newfield, 22, is one of the best young hitters in the minors. He has good power; very good control of the strike zone and the ability to hit for average. He lacks speed, but this kid appears to be one or two years away from being the perfect cleanup hitter behind Junior.

Fantasy owners should try to get him: He's a fine hitter and Piniella says the job in left is his to lose. By '95, he could be a monster.

WARREN NEWSON — WHITE SOX
AAA – Nashville

AB	R	H	2B	3B	HR	RBI	BB	K	SB	CS	AVG.
176	40	60	8	2	4	21	38	38	5	2	.341

Newson got a measly 40 ABs as a White Sox and spent 61 games in Nashville. He proved, once again, that he can hit through Triple-A pitchers like they're wet Kleenex and he's still effective on the ML level.

We think he can contribute in an expanded role, but he probably won't get a chance from the White Sox. How many more times can we write this essay? Somebody please get a clue.

MELVIN NIEVES — PADRES
AAA – Richmond

AB	R	H	2B	3B	HR	RBI	BB	K	SB	CS	AVG.
273	38	76	10	3	10	36	25	84	4	3	.278

AAA – Las Vegas

AB	R	H	2B	3B	HR	RBI	BB	K	SB	CS	AVG.
159	31	49	10	1	7	24	18	42	2	2	.308

Many were puzzled when the Padres took Nieves instead of pushing for blue-chippers like Chipper Jones and Javy Lopez. It's quite possible that they did exactly the right thing.

Nieves looks like he could be as potent a hitting threat as either of the aforementioned and he's just as young as they are.

His offensive numbers look similar to years past and of course the PCL helped account for a rise in BA and walks.

With the outfield glut in Atlanta (starters Gant, Sanders and Justice as well as prospects Tony Tarasco and Mike Kelly) this move is the best thing that could have happened to Mel. It's likely that the Padres have themselves an All-Star in this kid.

OTIS NIXON — RED SOX

AB	R	H	2B	3B	HR	RBI	BB	K	SB	CS	AVG.
461	77	124	12	3	1	24	61	63	47	13	.269

Otis continues to display his fine glove and a decent ability to reach base, but his lack of power gives him limited value. Can you believe the Braves could have traded him even up for Rafael Palmiero in May or June? Can you believe they refused to do it?

The Braves move in mysterious ways. Perhaps that's why they can't win the big games.

Deion was given the starting job in center, making Otis expendable. It's sad because the Red Sox need a power hitter. Their OBP is not great, but it's not a tremendous weakness. A bat to support Maurice Vaughn, on the other hand, is something the Sox need pretty dearly.

TROY O'LEARY — BREWERS
AAA – New Orleans

AB	R	H	2B	3B	HR	RBI	BB	K	SB	CS	AVG
388	65	106	32	1	7	59	43	61	6	3	.273

O'Leary hit very well in a short trial with the Brewers, drawing some walks and showing a nice B.A.

Early comparisons to Luis Polonia are not misplaced, as long as he can show that '92 Double-A El Paso numbers weren't a fluke.

PAUL O'NEILL — YANKEES

AB	R	H	2B	3B	HR	RBI	BB	K	SB	CS	AVG
498	71	155	34	1	20	75	44	69	2	4	.311

We were cautious enough last year not to rule out a good year for Paulie, so he obliged us by batting over .300 and slugging over .500 (both career firsts).

He really turned it on in the first half and had a tremendous June, batting .343 with a .608 SL%. He didn't leave many wondering who'd gotten the better end of the O'Neill for Roberto Kelly trade, at least in the short term.

O'Neill remained sharp with the mitt and seems to enjoy popping balls off and over Yankee Stadium's right field wall. You'll be safe if you bet on him to put up solid numbers rather than the eye-catchers of '93.

SHERMAN OBANDO — ORIOLES

AB	R	H	2B	3B	HR	RBI	BB	K	SB	CS	AVG
92	8	25	2	0	3	15	4	26	0	0	.272

Obando was obtained essentially as a backup to the Martinez/McLemore/Mercedes logjam in right field. Those guys are all out of the way, but now he has deal with the newest phenom, Alex Ochoa.

Sherman can hit, but not as well as Ochoa. He can field, but not as well as Ochoa. He does have more experience in the bigs, which may be win him the spot ... at least for '94.

ALEX OCHOA — ORIOLES
A – Frederick

AB	R	H	2B	3B	HR	RBI	BB	K	SB	CS	AVG
532	84	147	29	5	13	90	46	67	34	13	.276

Ochoa has a cannon arm, one of the best in minors. He's no slouch offensively, either, as he slugged .423 while stealing 34 bases.

He was the No. 2 prospect in the Carolina League (Baltimore seems to have cornered the market down there). A shortstop in high school, he's considered a great athlete, and at 22, he's a mega-prospect. He will start the year on the O's 40-man roster and has an excellent chance to stay on it for a long time.

JOE ORSULAK — METS

AB	R	H	2B	3B	HR	RBI	BB	K	SB	CS	AVG
409	59	116	15	4	8	35	28	25	5	4	.284

He makes plenty of contact and should continue to hit in the .280 range and play steady defense. Orsulak can play either right or left field, and as long as he can get on base a little, he should be able to help somebody in '94 coming off the bench.

ORLANDO PALMEIRO — ANGELS
AA – Midland

AB	R	H	2B	3B	HR	RBI	BB	K	SB	CS	AVG
535	85	163	19	5	0	64	42	35	18	14	.305

Dave: He's somehow related to Rafael (cousin?), but I forget how. The only thing he has in common with his relation is the surname. He looks like a non-hitter in a position where you have to whack if you're going to get a job.

Orlando's 25 and he'll be in Triple-A. He could see some bench time this year, but really that's the only role he's suited for.

DAN PASQUA — WHITE SOX

AB	R	H	2B	3B	HR	RBI	BB	K	SB	CS	AVG
176	22	36	10	1	5	20	26	51	2	2	.205

He's a useful utility fielder but he's really starting to deteriorate. Look for a quiet exit in the next few years

DAN PELTIER — RANGERS

AB	R	H	2B	3B	HR	RBI	BB	K	SB	CS	AVG
160	23	43	7	1	1	17	20	27	0	4	.269

Peltier did an adequate job replacing the Bonehead last year, although neither he nor Gary Redus will make anyone forget about Canseco's bat. Dan's been a good minor-league hitter with some line-drive power and a high OBP, but he hasn't shown much at the major league level.

His status next year depends solely on Canseco's elbow. If Jose's healthy, Peltier will provide solid backup. If not, he has the edge over the ancient Redus for the starting role.

Rudy Pemberton — Tigers

AA – London

AB	R	H	2B	3B	HR	RBI	BB	K	SB	CS	AVG
471	70	130	22	4	15	67	24	80	14	12	.276

Pemberton's from the Dominican Republic, which, given his name, is a kooky homeland.

He has poor discipline and, at 24, he may be a tad on the old side, but he has some power and still looks pretty good.

William Pennyfeather — Pirates

AAA – Buffalo

AB	R	H	2B	3B	HR	RBI	BB	K	SB	CS	AVG
457	54	114	18	3	14	41	18	92	10	12	.249

Pennyfeather, at one time, looked like he could be the heir to Van Slyke. Now he's 26, become a terrible baserunner and done nothing to correct his discipline problem.

He's got younger, better players coming up behind him and his lukewarm prospect days are over.

Phil Plantier — Padres

AB	R	H	2B	3B	HR	RBI	BB	K	SB	CS	AVG
462	67	111	20	1	34	100	61	124	4	5	.240

There were rumblings of what Plantier could do in 1991, when he hit .331 with 11 homers in 148 at-bats for the Red Sox.

Displeased with his lack of progress in '92 (the Red Sox are reknowned for their lack of patience ... see Ellis Burks and Mo Vaughn) and they traded him to San Diego for talented, but anonymous middle reliever Jose Melendez (who pitched all of 16 ML innings in '93).

Needless to say, Plantier turned 24, exploded under that California sun and walloped 34 dingers with 100 RBI. As much as we berate the Pads for trading away young gems like McGriff and Sheffield they seem to have an uncanny knack of replacing them with Plantiers, Nieveses and Bells.

Plantier was our No. 1 sleeper pick in right field last year, and you just wonder what Dead Sox management was sniffing. As great as it was to finally see the Sox give Mo Vaughn his due and watch him blossom, Plantier probably had the larger impact of the two.

The power has arrived. If Phil's B.A. of '91 returns, Boston fans will be lining up from Beantown to Nova Scotia to kick Lou Gorman squarely in the keister.

Luis Polonia — Yankees

AB	R	H	2B	3B	HR	RBI	BB	K	SB	CS	AVG
576	75	156	17	6	1	32	48	53	55	24	.271

Chances are he will bounce back to the .300 level and he'll have to: He's inadequate as a .271 hitter. Luis is fast, but his base-running game is of marginal value. He hits for average, but his ability to draw walks is below average and his "power" is horrid. In addition, he's not a very good fielder.

He can be a very good player, but at his '93 level, Luis Polonia is a poor left fielder.

Scott Pose — Marlins

AAA – Edmonton

AB	R	H	2B	3B	HR	RBI	BB	K	SB	CS	AVG
398	61	113	8	6	0	27	42	36	19	9	.284

Pose is now 27 and it looks like his chance is over. With Conine, Nigel Wilson, Everett, Whitmore, Carr, et al, there appears little reason for a guy like him to get a shot. He was a mess early in the season and rallied to do quite well at Edmonton, but his stats pale when compared to his Triple-A teammates. He'd be a decent lead-off guy as long as he doesn't try to pull anything, but he'll be living out of a minor-league suitcase this year.

Curtis Pride — Expos

AA – Harrisburg

AB	R	H	2B	3B	HR	RBI	BB	K	SB	CS	AVG
180	51	64	6	3	15	39	12	36	21	6	.356

AAA – Ottawa

AB	R	H	2B	3B	HR	RBI	BB	K	SB	CS	AVG
262	55	79	11	4	6	22	34	61	29	12	.302

Curtis, 25, has great speed, great talent and great heart. Much has been made about the fact that he suffers from 95 percent deafness, but we're talking about a fine player here. He appears to be extremely mature, intelligent and he seems like a really nice person.

His K/W data isn't the greatest, but other than that and his age, there doesn't seem to be much that could keep him from being a fine player if he gets a full shot.

Kirby Puckett — Twins

AB	R	H	2B	3B	HR	RBI	BB	K	SB	CS	AVG
622	89	184	39	3	22	89	47	93	8	6	.296

Everybody's talking about what a cruddy year Kirby had last year. There must be an awful lot of outfielders hitting .310 and 35 HR out there. Sure, his numbers were well below his '88 mega-season, but whose weren't? He hit 20 HRs for the first time in five years and slugged a more-than-respectable .474. That's good enough to keep him among the most productive outfielders in the game.

His game has dropped a level and he no longer leads the league in many categories. His range has also diminished and he played 47 games in right after the All-Star Break. But he's still a solid, consistent performer.

If your team needs an outfielder to blow away the rest of the league, he's probably not your guy. But if you have other guys going gangbusters and you need someone you can count on for a positive contribution, Kirby'll get the job done for you.

CARLOS QUINTANA											RED SOX
AB	R	H	2B	3B	HR	RBI	BB	K	SB	CS	AVG.
303	31	74	5	0	1	19	31	52	1	0	.244

The word is that Quintana's on a mission to win back the starting job at first. We suggest he keep up his outfield skills or he may end up living in a mission.

You can understand his problem; the Sox have a number of guys they can stick in right, but only Mo Vaughn at first. Only Mo Vaughn?! Forget it.

Mo's 26 and he's improved his numbers to the threshold of superstar level; Quintana's 28 and coming off a season in which he dropped 51 points off his average and 141 off his slugging. It just isn't going to happen.

However, you shouldn't ridicule somebody for not hitting as well as Mo, few people do. Carlos is a better hitter than he showed last year and should be able to find some time in right and backing up first.

TIM RAINES											WHITE SOX
AB	R	H	2B	3B	HR	RBI	BB	K	SB	CS	AVG.
415	75	127	16	4	16	54	64	35	21	7	.306

Raines is still pouring it on. Despite dropping off significantly in stolen bases (33 to 35 years old is often the range his type of player falters), he managed to hit over .300 for the first time in five seasons and crack an impressive 16 HR.

A look at his recent career shows diminishing skills. He walks less, scores fewer runs and is losing footspeed (which hasn't affected his defense drastically). However, he remains one of the most canny batters in the AL with the ability to switch hit and kill pitchers when he's behind in the count.

Raines will be instrumental in the white Sox bid to rule the AL Central in '94.

MANNY RAMIREZ											INDIANS
AA – Canton-Akron											
AB	R	H	2B	3B	HR	RBI	BB	K	SB	CS	AVG.
344	67	117	32	0	17	79	45	68	2	2	.340

Ramirez was named *Baseball America*'s Minor League Player of the Year for good reason. He has ripped apart every league he has visited in his three professional seasons. He has yet to hit below .278 or slug less than .502. At 22, he is a superstar in waiting.

The Indians may opt to send him to Triple-A Charlotte for a full season, but it would be a waste of time. So what if he needs a little polish in the field, his bat is ready right now. If the Indians are serious about contending, they'll break in their new star outfielder and their new stadium in the same season.

KEVIN REIMER											???
AB	R	H	2B	3B	HR	RBI	BB	K	SB	CS	AVG.
437	53	109	22	1	13	60	30	72	5	4	.249

He didn't have a great year, even for him. His power is leaking and he doesn't walk.

Reimer did OK playing left and right, but any time he has to play defense it shaves 20-30 points off his batting average.

Reimer's still good for 15 dingers and possibly 20, but his stock is dropping.

KARL RHODES											CUBS
AAA – Omaha											
AB	R	H	2B	3B	HR	RBI	BB	K	SB	CS	AVG.
365	81	116	31	2	23	64	38	60	10	5	.318

The thing to remember about Rhodes is that he had been playing pro ball since he was 18, way back in 1986, and had yet to hit anywhere near like he did in 1993. He homered 31 times between Omaha, Iowa and the majors. His previous high in dingers was 4 in 520 at-bats in the Southern League. Consider the park he played in most, Omaha, was home to a 35 percent home run advantage in '93.

But fear not, Karl Rhodes fans, he's only 25 years old. He's small, 5-7, 170 lbs., but he has excellent speed and a super arm. He impressed the Cubs with his selectivity at the plate in Iowa, so even if his power drops a great deal, which seems quite possible, he could show enough in the spring to win a job.

RUBEN RIVERA — YANKEES
A – Oneonta

AB	R	H	2B	3B	HR	RBI	BB	K	SB	CS	AVG
199	45	55	7	6	13	47	32	66	11	5	.276

Ruben's a 20-year-old who hit as many homers as he did doubles and triples combined. Good arm, good speed, good bat.

He was the No. 1 prospect in the New York-Penn League on the basis of his athleticism alone. Rivera's a Grade-A prospect so draft away, dudes.

KEVIN ROBERSON — CUBS
AAA – Iowa

AB	R	H	2B	3B	HR	RBI	BB	K	SB	CS	AVG
263	48	80	20	1	16	50	19	66	3	2	.304

He's a tall, lanky dude with enough power to hit 30 home runs in Wrigley. Roberson has a little speed and a decent arm, and the Cubs are looking for him to win a job in the spring. But when looking at Roberson, one must consider three negatives.

First, he is 26 years old. While he's not ready for adult diapers just yet, Roberson is a little old to become a top-flight major-leaguer. Second, he isn't selective enough at the plate. He has to hit the breaking pitch, and, as a result, chases way too many bad pitches. It's entirely possible that he will whiff over 100 times in '94. Finally, he had back surgery in '92. While he has apparently recovered from the ailment, one cannot help but wonder if it will flare up again.

Roberson is worth a long look. He has the tools to become a solid big-league ballplayer, but only if he can improve his eye at the plate.

HENRY RODRIGUEZ — DODGERS
AAA – Albuquerque

AB	R	H	2B	3B	HR	RBI	BB	K	SB	CS	AVG
179	26	53	13	5	4	30	14	37	1	2	.296

AB	R	H	2B	3B	HR	RBI	BB	K	SB	CS	AVG
176	20	39	10	0	8	23	11	39	1	0	.222

Rodriguez has good pop but poor on-base skills. A perfect example of how inflated PCL stats can make a mediocre player look like Willie Mays. He's also 26, so don't talk yourself into thinking he'll develop much more.

TIM SALMON — ANGELS

AB	R	H	2B	3B	HR	RBI	BB	K	SB	CS	AVG
515	93	146	35	1	31	95	82	135	5	6	.283

He missed the end of the season when he fractured his finger trying to snag a sinking liner in right. If it hadn't been for this hustle play, Salmon would have driven in and scored 100 runs and gotten the 150+ strikeouts we predicted he'd get.

Tim performed exactly as advertised and showed he's a true tools player (if one can leave speed out of this), he's got a fine arm, excellent range and a killer bat. If he can repeat 1993, he'll be the best right fielder in the game.

DEION SANDERS — BRAVES

AB	R	H	2B	3B	HR	RBI	BB	K	SB	CS	AVG
272	42	75	18	6	6	28	16	42	19	7	.274

What is there to say about Deion Sanders that you don't already know? People either love him or hate him, but we're curious as to how anyone could think he's more than an idiot-savant.

When it comes to dealing with human beings, he has the decorum a dog with the runs would show to Mom's Persian rug. Put him in the field and you'll see some pretty amazing stuff: Sometimes it's excellence and other times it's so bad it's mind-numbing.

It's just our opinion, but we're weird. ... We like Braves like Ron Gant, John Smoltz and Fred McGriff: They're the guys that do the butt kicking and let Deion take care of rubbing their opponents' faces in the dirt.

REGGIE SANDERS — REDS

AB	R	H	2B	3B	HR	RBI	BB	K	SB	CS	AVG
496	90	136	16	4	20	83	51	118	27	10	.274

Sanders is a solid ballplayer for the Reds but it doesn't look like he's going to be the superstar many predicted.

He picked up 8 HR between '92 and '93, but also dropped 10 doubles, 2 triples and his slugging fell slightly to .444. His batting average isn't all that impressive, but he supplements it with a fair amount of walks.

He has good range in right and is a consistent contributor in every phase of the game.

Some people expected more from him, but there are worse things than being a solid, everyday player.

TRACY SANDERS — PADRES
AA – Wichita

AB	R	H	2B	3B	HR	RBI	BB	K	SB	CS	AVG
266	44	86	13	4	13	47	34	67	6	5	.323

Sanders improved vastly from Double-A Canton-Akron to Double-A Wichita last year. We don't know what happened, but we liked it.

In the space of a few hundred at-bats he went from being a non-prospect to a pretty damn good, 24-year-old player.

Hope the Padres noticed. When a guy detonates like this it usually means he figured out some flaw in his game and has corrected it.

MACKEY SASSER — MARLINS

AB	R	H	2B	3B	HR	RBI	BB	K	SB	CS	AVG
188	18	41	10	2	1	21	15	30	1	0	.218

He's simply inadequate.

STEVE SAX — WHITE SOX

AB	R	H	2B	3B	HR	RBI	BB	K	SB	CS	AVG
119	20	28	5	0	1	8	8	6	7	3	.235

Sax has really sunk low. His defense has diminished to the point that he was reduced to spelling Raines in left and garnering a few lousy DH at-bats.

There seems to be a group of moderately talented players like Sax who have hit the wall in their mid-thirties (guys like Pasqua and Calderon just to name a couple of White Sox).

If he's smart he'll leave the game with his good memories intact. A couple more seasons of this will only hurt his reputation.

CHRIS SCHWAB — EXPOS
R – Expos

AB	R	H	2B	3B	HR	RBI	BB	K	SB	CS	AVG
218	21	48	12	1	0	20	22	53	0	2	.220

Believe it or not, Schwab, 19, is considered to have the most power of any kid taken in the 1993 draft. Schwab was the No. 18 pick in the first round. He has shown nothing as yet (and his defense is considered pretty atrocious), but just be aware of him.

RUBEN SIERRA — ATHLETICS

AB	R	H	2B	3B	HR	RBI	BB	K	SB	CS	AVG
630	77	147	23	5	22	101	52	97	25	5	.233

Ruben had an up-and-down season. He responded to last year's critics by hitting the weights in the off-season. Rather than helping, the regimen seems to have hurt his hitting while not significantly improving his power.

Couple this with the fact that he's swinging in the Coliseum and Ruben is in trouble.

Two pluses were that he drove in 101 runs and stole a by-far career high 25 bases. This doesn't excuse his BA and OBP, which hurt all the more because of his continued streak of 600+ at-bat seasons. The last thing the A's need is a drain like this in the three spot, especially when he hits about .185 for the last two months of the year.

Sierra is in his prime and should recover, but it is terribly disappointing to see a player of his caliber stumble so badly in what could have been a career year. The Roberto Clemente comparisons may have to be abandoned.

MIKE SIMMS — PADRES
AAA – Las Vegas

AB	R	H	2B	3B	HR	RBI	BB	K	SB	CS	AVG
414	74	111	25	2	24	80	67	114	1	1	.268

A possibility for bench time at the major-league level, Simms is 27 and could do some damage if given a decent role. He's nothing special – and could be a major bust – but he does have some power.

BENJI SIMONTON — GIANTS
A – Clinton

AB	R	H	2B	3B	HR	RBI	BB	K	SB	CS	AVG
310	52	79	18	4	12	49	40	112	8	7	.255

Benji's a 21-year-old with exciting power and the ability to walk a little. He shows poor judgment on the basepaths but should improve rapidly.

Observers say his power potential is incredible, similar to that of Kevin Mitchell.

DWIGHT SMITH — CUBS

AB	R	H	2B	3B	HR	RBI	BB	K	SB	CS	AVG
310	51	93	17	5	11	35	25	51	8	6	.300

Yes, the bat is for real. But at 30, Smith has probably seen his best years pass by him in the minors. If he can avoid the eventual onslaught of injuries, he can produce a couple of seasons that are comparable to '93. The problem is that his defense is so subpar that he doesn't warrant the playing time in the NL. He needs to set up residence in an AL park and spend the rest of his days as a DH.

CORY SNYDER   DODGERS
AB	R	H	2B	3B	HR	RBI	BB	K	SB	CS	AVG
516	61	137	33	1	11	56	47	147	4	1	.266

Cory had a good Snyder-type year with the bat and played some decent defense. Unfortunately he's a role-player when what the Dodgers need are full-time heroes.

Expect Cory to roll along while the rest of the team limps.

SAMMY SOSA   CUBS
AB	R	H	2B	3B	HR	RBI	BB	K	SB	CS	AVG
598	92	156	25	5	33	93	38	135	36	11	.261

Sosa finally emerged last year as the powerful, young hitter the Cubs thought he would become. He slugged .485 and joined the exclusive 30-30 club. At the tender age of 25, it seems the sky's the limit for Sammy.

But there's good reason to temper our expectations of him. First, he lacks the strike zone of a solid hitter. Last year, he struck out 135 times (countering with a scant 38 walks) and he hit a measly .187 when behind in the count. And he wasn't exactly the "go-to" guy in the clutch either. He only hit .213 with runners in scoring position.

Second, most of Sosa's power is a result of Wrigley Field's friendliness to right-handed hitters. Righties hit the ball out of the park with 62 percent more frequency than lefties and all but 10 of Sosa's HRs came at home.

Sosa made a name for himself in '93. But he isn't a good bet to repeat his performance unless he can learn to make better contact at the plate and stop turning so many plate appearances into outs.

SHANE SPENCER   YANKEES
A – Greensboro
AB	R	H	2B	3B	HR	RBI	BB	K	SB	CS	AVG
431	89	116	35	2	12	80	52	62	14	2	.269

He's a good all-around hitter who is big in the runs department. His power should really develop in the next couple of years.

By the time he's ready to come up, Tartabull or O'Neill might be ready to make room for him. His age, separates him from the other good Yankee OF prospects all of whom are too old to break in at present.

DARRYL STRAWBERRY   DODGERS
AB	R	H	2B	3B	HR	RBI	BB	K	SB	CS	AVG
100	12	14	2	0	5	12	16	19	1	0	.140

Plagued by injuries and his penchant for foot-in-mouth disease, Strawberry looked more like a Straw Dog this year.

The biggest mistake we made on him last year was thinking that he was less injury-prone than pal Eric Davis. Well ... it seemed logical at the time.

As usual, when Darryl doesn't have anything to do (e.g. play baseball) he opens his trap and lets fly with some sleekly insensitive soundbite. This year's doozy was his off-color remarks concerning the Malibu brushfires which cost many people their homes. He tried to play it off as a gag and of course sounded completely insincere.

The Dodgers are baffled and Darryl's got to be a little confused himself. Even if he's injury-free in '94, his brain may be too mushy to produce the solid seasons of his past.

The Dodgers aren't taking chances. While they're allowing him to workout with the team, they made sure they waived him first.

ERICK STRICKLAND   MARLINS
A – Elmira
AB	R	H	2B	3B	HR	RBI	BB	K	SB	CS	AVG
213	30	56	12	3	4	36	35	32	8	4	.263

Strickland's a project. He's a strapping 6-3, 195 with a great athlete's body. Problem is, he's a hoops player for Nebraska and is considering playing football for them too. According to Baseball America, expect him to rot at Elmira (NY-P League) until he decides if baseball's for him.

MARK SWEENEY   ANGELS
A – Palm Springs
AB	R	H	2B	3B	HR	RBI	BB	K	SB	CS	AVG
245	41	87	18	3	3	47	42	29	9	6	.355

AA – Midland
AB	R	H	2B	3B	HR	RBI	BB	K	SB	CS	AVG
188	41	67	13	2	9	32	27	22	1	1	.356

Sweeney, 24, should at least reach Triple-A this year if he can continue to hit like he did at

Midland. You need to take a lot of starch out of those numbers, but it certainly looks like Mr. Sweeney can hit a little.

TONY TARASCO — BRAVES
AAA – Richmond
AB	R	H	2B	3B	HR	RBI	BB	K	SB	CS	AVG
370	73	122	15	7	15	53	36	54	19	11	.330

A year ago at this time, we were going through the Braves organization trying to identify prospects and we wrote Tarasco off because there were so many quality outfielders ahead of him in terms of ability.

The Braves were extremely high on him and now it's easy to see why. All Tarasco did at the Triple-A level was improve his power by 40 percent, and improve his K/W ratio by 208 percent, over 1992.

Basically, Tarasco projects to hit like Deion Sanders, the differences being that Deion has much better base-running judgment, and much more significantly, Tony's three years younger (23).

With Otis gone and Gant's status in jeopardy, it's possible that Tarasco could get a lot of PT in right or left. If he does, he should demonstrate some pretty good power and, given the friendliness of Fulton County, he could hit close to, maybe even over .300.

DANNY TARTABULL — YANKEES
AB	R	H	2B	3B	HR	RBI	BB	K	SB	CS	AVG
513	87	128	33	2	31	102	92	156	0	0	.250

Danny had another solid year.

It's a sure bet that New York fans will find something to groan about, but Tartabull continues to grind out these seasons routinely.

He had over 100 RBI for the fourth time in the last seven years and he's got a great eye at the plate. The Yanks learned their lesson and began to DH him regularly to save wear and tear on his injury-prone body. As a result he played in 138 games.

He's a rare combination of power and discipline. For some reason he had more trouble hitting lefties last year (typically he's more effective against them), but he compensated by drawing walks in those plate appearances.

New Yorkers beware! If you continue to predict Tartabull's failure you may spawn a self-fulfilling prophecy which the Yanks can ill afford.

JESUS TAVAREZ — MARLINS
A – High Desert
AB	R	H	2B	3B	HR	RBI	BB	K	SB	CS	AVG
444	104	130	21	8	7	71	57	66	47	14	.293

Like his thoroughbred former stablemate, Kerwin Moore, Tavarez is 23. He's not as highly regarded and is lower on the Marlins depth-chart. But since their skills are pretty similar and they are the same age, it's possible Tavarez could surpass him in ability this year.

SAM TAYLOR — PHILLIES
AA – Reading
AB	R	H	2B	3B	HR	RBI	BB	K	SB	CS	AVG
173	31	48	12	0	5	27	30	24	9	3	.277

Taylor, 25, is not a non-pareil prospect, but he might be someone for the Phillies bench. His numbers at Triple-A (.241, 6 HR, 4 SB) aren't the greatest, but he could move his game up this year. He's still reasonably young and very experienced.

RYAN THOMPSON — METS
AB	R	H	2B	3B	HR	RBI	BB	K	SB	CS	AVG
288	34	72	19	2	11	26	19	81	2	7	.259

Thompson has the tools to become a pretty solid major leaguer. He's plenty fast, plays good defense and has the potential to hit 20 home runs. But his career has been slowed by injuries. He seems to pull a hamstring every five minutes. He's never been able put his speed to good use on the basepaths and he has the strikeout numbers of a Rob Deer wannabe. It's hard to predict stardom for this 25-year-old, but it's quite possible that he could turn in a few solid seasons.

MILT THOMPSON — PHILLIES
AB	R	H	2B	3B	HR	RBI	BB	K	SB	CS	AVG
340	42	89	14	2	4	44	40	57	9	2	.262

Milt's a good defender with good on-base skills. He's losing his speed as his eight double-play grounders in 340 AB show. He picks his spots well and doesn't get caught stealing.

He's no spring chicken, so he could lose his ability quickly. But if Milt plays like he did in 1993, then he's a solid player.

Lee Tinsley — Mariners

AAA – Calgary

AB	R	H	2B	3B	HR	RBI	BB	K	SB	CS	AVG
450	94	136	25	18	10	63	50	98	34	11	.302

It seems like Seattle has had this type of player popping out of their system for eons.

Tinsley, 25, ain't half bad. He's got decent power and speed, but his average is going to drop big time if he gets significant playing time in the AL (or in the NL for that matter).

You could see his average drop 60 points or more. Right now, he's probably not considered more than a bench-jock. It'll take some injuries or a poor performance in the spring by Marc Newfield for his opportunity to arrive.

Brian Turang — Mariners

AAA – Calgary

AB	R	H	2B	3B	HR	RBI	BB	K	SB	CS	AVG
423	84	137	20	11	8	54	40	48	24	8	.324

He's 27, so if he gets a shot, he'll probably play as well as he's capable of playing. He's not that bad a player, but his fancy Triple-A stats aren't that impressive once you take the air out of them. He's probably a .270 hitter who'd be hard-pressed to slug over .400.

Andy Van Slyke — Pirates

AB	R	H	2B	3B	HR	RBI	BB	K	SB	CS	AVG
323	42	100	13	4	8	50	24	40	11	2	.310

Andy was tearing up the league when a Van Slyke-type injury, a full-speed collision with the centerfield wall, derailed his season in June. He hit .360 and slugged .571 in May and was on his way to another killer season before the collision.

He hit .308 against lefties and seems to have permanently buried his rep as a patsy for southpaws. The newest knock in the rumor mill is that he's injury prone. He is 33 now and he's been on the DL twice in the last five years, so there is some cause for concern, especially for rotisse-owners. But Andy's injuries come because he's hustling his butt off and it's hard to fault a player for that.

Another thing to remember is that he's an intelligent, dedicated ballplayer, and should be able to make some concessions to his age. Keeping his .300+ bat and Gold Glove healthy for a whole season is more important to the team than one out in one game.

He should recognize that and make the adjustments necessary to remain an All-Star-calibre player.

Greg Vaughn — Brewers

AB	R	H	2B	3B	HR	RBI	BB	K	SB	CS	AVG
569	97	152	28	2	30	97	89	118	10	7	.267

What a year for Vaughn. He's 28 and he smelled blood. He pounded 30 HR and came close to both scoring and driving in 100 runs. He continued to bemuse fans by trying to steal bases, but he was less damaging in this respect than in the past.

Vaughn really gets a lot of his offensive improvement from his slaughter of left-handed pitching. He's also grown to fit the cleanup role very nicely.

To say he's a good fielder is a radical understatement. The MLB zone rating for left field is .818 and Vaughn was light years beyond this at .873.

Last year we ranked Greg eleventh at left field. The improvement in his bat coupled with his glove almost certainly moves him into an elite circle comprised of names like Bonds, Gant and Henderson.

Larry Walker — Expos

AB	R	H	2B	3B	HR	RBI	BB	K	SB	CS	AVG
490	85	130	24	5	22	86	80	76	29	7	.265

Close to being a player without weakness.

Batting: He didn't hit for average in 1993, but he has in the past (and will probably do so again); he draws walks and doesn't strike out; he has nice power; and is a fine base-runner.

Let's talk about his defense: there's the excellent zone rating; the superb throwing arm and the consecutive Gold Gloves.

He's 27 now, so if Bonds has an off year, he is a fine MVP candidate. All he has to do is play 150+ games and achieve the peak performance that the average 27-year-old displays.

Turner Ward — Brewers

AB	R	H	2B	3B	HR	RBI	BB	K	SB	CS	AVG
167	20	32	4	2	4	28	23	26	3	3	.192

After hitting .192 last year, Ward had used up his chances in an organization crawling with outfield prospects, so he moved on.

MIKE WARNER — BRAVES

A – Durham

AB	R	H	2B	3B	HR	RBI	BB	K	SB	CS	AVG.
263	55	84	18	4	5	32	50	45	29	12	.319

Warner is 23 and is probably going to be in Double-A this year. It's pretty obvious he has good plate discipline, some speed and line-drive pop. In most other organizations that would put him near the top of the class. In Atlanta, he can check in at No. 10 or No. 11 on the outfield prospect list. If he can show sustained growth over the next year or so, he might force his way into Atlanta's plans.

DEVON WHITE — BLUE JAYS

AB	R	H	2B	3B	HR	RBI	BB	K	SB	CS	AVG.
598	116	163	42	6	15	52	57	127	34	4	.273

White is one of the best defensive outfielders in the game and that alone would justify his PT. But he adds an ability to hit for average and power. The K's are a little alarming, but he'll get by as long as he's in the Jays' batting order and scoring 100 runs a season. Still, one can't help but wonder what kind of hitter he'd be if he weren't in Toronto.

JIMMY WHITE — ASTROS

A – Osceola

AB	R	H	2B	3B	HR	RBI	BB	K	SB	CS	AVG.
447	80	123	9	12	7	37	54	120	24	17	.275

White is 21 and, like Buck McNabb, is a prospect ranked lower than Richard Hidalgo and Bob Abreu.

Still, he can hit a little and he's going to be in Triple-A by age 23 unless he gets hurt or has statistics that smell like Pepe LePew.

RONDELL WHITE — EXPOS

AA – Harrisburg

AB	R	H	2B	3B	HR	RBI	BB	K	SB	CS	AVG.
372	72	122	16	10	12	52	22	72	21	6	.328

AAA – Ottawa

AB	R	H	2B	3B	HR	RBI	BB	K	SB	CS	AVG.
150	28	57	8	2	7	32	12	20	10	1	.380

Rondell, 22, had a terrible K/W ratio at Double-A, but after three similar minor-league seasons, he looks like he can be one of those rare hitters who can post a .300 average while being a hacker.

His strike zone will improve with experience. But he's beautiful right now because his base-running has really improved and it looks like his power has moved into the 20-25 homer range with double-figures in triples.

We said last year that he was a must-grab minor-leaguer. In 1994, it's even more imperative: You must get him for fantasy team or card collection now because he's got the potential to be an All-Star.

MARK WHITEN — CARDINALS

AB	R	H	2B	3B	HR	RBI	BB	K	SB	CS	AVG.
562	81	142	13	4	25	99	58	110	15	8	.253

On September 6, Mark Whiten had 18 home runs in the books. At the end of September 7, he had 22, courtesy of a four-dinger performance against the Reds in the first game of a doubleheader. He hit three more the rest of the way and finished with a career-best 25 home runs on the season.

But Whiten fans should bask in the afterglow of his '93 season while they can because it probably won't get any better. His speed and defensive prowess (check out his arm!!!) are enough to guarantee his return as the starting right-fielder. And if a semblance of his power stroke returns it should be considered a bonus. Last year was his peak, but 15-20 HR and up to 20 steals is to be expected for 1994.

DARRELL WHITMORE — MARLINS

AAA – Edmonton

AB	R	H	2B	3B	HR	RBI	BB	K	SB	CS	AVG.
273	52	97	24	2	9	62	22	53	11	8	.355

The No. 1 prospect in the PCL. Scouts are just crazy about his fine tools and his attitude. We've got one thing to say: Hey, you morons, he's 25! Is the PCL so talent-starved that a 25-year-old is the league's top prospect?!

Sometimes the scouts, coaches and managers forget to take into account little things like the fact that Whitmore is just six months younger than the reigning AL MVP.

This age thing really takes a lot of wind out of his sails. He'll probably be a good player and he does have a shot at "Rookie of the Year" (provided he gets a job), but let's get real: He's got almost zero chance of getting into the Hall of Fame and he's gotta really turn it on at the major-league level to even be an All-Star.

He's got a terrible K/W ratio (he can't hit lefties and has problems with breaking stuff) and his base-running is currently abysmal. He does have good power and could hit for average (if his K/W doesn't tear him apart). Go ahead and draft him, but prepare for two things: 1) the distinct possibility that he'll be a stink-bomb; 2) the Marlins see him as needing more time in Triple-A next year. There's a good chance he'll be fine, but there's also the chance that he'll crumble under the extreme weight of his weaknesses.

P.S. for Rotisserie fans: Part of the reason the scouts love him is for his defense (good defensive range, cannon arm), so take that into account.

P.P.S. He suffered from tendinitis in the Mexican Winter League and was shut down. He should be OK for Spring Training.

BERNIE WILLIAMS — YANKEES

AB	R	H	2B	3B	HR	RBI	BB	K	SB	CS	AVG.
567	67	152	31	4	12	68	53	106	9	9	.268

He didn't exactly burst into full flower as we'd hoped, but he stayed productive under the pressure of his first full season.

He displayed developing plate discipline and slashing power. He also showed off his glove, which is the main reason the Yankees wanted him in the first place.

He's very poised for a 25-year-old. He could have his first 20 HR season this year or next.

NIGEL WILSON — MARLINS
AAA – Edmonton

AB	R	H	2B	3B	HR	RBI	BB	K	SB	CS	AVG.
370	66	108	26	7	17	68	25	108	8	3	.292

He doesn't have a good arm and the scouts aren't as high on him as they are on Darrell Whitmore. But Nigel's only 24 and is a decent prospect. He probably has 25-homer potential now, but he's fighting his K/W ratio. The jury is out on whether he'll be able to hit for average, but our guess is that he'll hit in the .230 - .260 range until he starts taking some walks.

It looks like his speed isn't as great as advertised, so look at him as a 15-steal guy at best. In addition, he was hurt late in the season and was shut down in the winter because of a quadriceps tear.

WILLIE WILSON — CUBS

AB	R	H	2B	3B	HR	RBI	BB	K	SB	CS	AVG.
221	29	57	11	3	1	11	11	40	7	2	.258

At 38, the chances of Wilson getting enough PT to pull his career out of it's nose-dive are nil. He could still help out with the youngsters, but his contributions on the field should be limited to coming out of the bullpen between innings to warm up the left fielder.

DAVE WINFIELD — TWINS

AB	R	H	2B	3B	HR	RBI	BB	K	SB	CS	AVG.
547	72	148	27	2	21	76	45	106	2	3	.271

Yet another year, yet another 20+ HRs and 70+ RBI.

Dave's pretty much done contributing in the field but he's still getting the job done at the plate. His numbers were down slightly last year, but we'll put his power up against any other 42-year-old in the league any day.

The Twins may want him to split DH duties with Hrbek and others, but he'll be around as long as he can swing the bat.

We have to mention that he had one of the most ill-timed slumps of the season last year. We got plenty tired of the endless 3,000-hit watch... 1-for-4... 0-for-5... 1-for-5. Ugh!

Still, it was a heck of an accomplishment and we were ecstatic when he made it.

JERRY WOLAK — WHITE SOX
AA – Birmingham

AB	R	H	2B	3B	HR	RBI	BB	K	SB	CS	AVG.
525	78	160	35	4	9	64	26	95	16	12	.305

Wolak's 23 and will probably see Triple-A this year. His plate discipline has always been a problem, as has his stolen-base percentage. That being said, Wolak has a career .293 average. Not an uber-prospect, but someone who could get some playing time and surprise.

MIKE WOLFF — ATHLETICS
A – Cedar Rapids

AB	R	H	2B	3B	HR	RBI	BB	K	SB	CS	AVG.
407	63	100	18	5	17	72	74	104	8	8	.246

Mike, 23, has exceptional power and a good eye. Like most A-ballers with these characteristics he's old enough to require the challenges of Double-A to truly test his ability.

Wolff's only a solid prospect, but he may get a look just because the A's are probably ready to give anybody an interview.

They want badly to get back atop their division. The Mike Wolffs of the world won't solve their problems, but they can be of value.

TED WOOD											EXPOS
AB	R	H	2B	3B	HR	RBI	BB	K	SB	CS	AVG.
231	39	59	11	4	1	21	38	54	12	2	.255

It appears that his move from the PCL to the International League knocked 50 points off his average and left him bereft of power. He looks like he has good base-running judgment and he can get on base a bit. But other than that, he's a 27-year-old piece of jetsam.

ROBIN YOUNT											BREWERS
AB	R	H	2B	3B	HR	RBI	BB	K	SB	CS	AVG.
454	62	117	25	3	8	51	44	93	9	2	.258

Yount continued the step-by-step decline he began in 1990. He's 38 and he's still better than 70 percent of the players out there.

He'll most likely retire within the next two years and is unlikely to receive the farewell of his gaudier peers Brett and Ryan. Class act that he is, he probably he prefers it that way.

BOB ZUPCIC											RED SOX
AB	R	H	2B	3B	HR	RBI	BB	K	SB	CS	AVG.
286	40	69	24	2	2	26	27	54	5	2	.241

Zupcic's an average utility outfielder who's been doing a decent job in the field the last couple years. Meanwhile, his offense has gone from bad to worse. Any other club probably would have given him a train ticket after his last season at the plate, but in Boston's outfield, anything can happen.

Whether he deserves it or not, he may win the starting role in right field by default. But don't pay any attention, he's a 27-year-old piece of flotsam.

STARTERS – *RANKINGS*

	Player	Pitcher Ranking
1	Greg Maddux	59.7
2	Kevin Appier	55.3
3	Randy Johnson	54.3
4	Jose Rijo	48.4
5	David Cone	47.4
6	Mark Langston	42.8
7	Roger Clemens	42.5
8	Juan Guzman	40.1
9	John Smoltz	39.4
10	Kevin Brown	37.5
11	Jack McDowell	37.3
11	Billy Swift	37.3
13	Curt Schilling	36.5
14	Jimmy Key	35.0
15	Pete Harnisch	32.5
16	Doug Drabek	32.2
16	Sid Fernandez	32.2
18	Denny Martinez	31.6
19	Cal Eldred	31.0
20	Tom Candiotti	30.7
21	Mike Mussina	30.3
22	Ben McDonald	29.8
23	Melido Perez	29.6
24	Tom Glavine	29.0
25	Danny Darwin	28.2
26	Ken Hill	27.8
27	Frank Viola	27.6
28	Steve Avery	27.3
28	Alex Fernandez	27.3
30	Andy Benes	26.5
31	Bosio	26.1
32	Mark Portugal	25.8
33	Chuck Finley	24.0
33	Mike Morgan	24.0
34	Dwight Gooden	22.8
35	Terry Mulholland	21.3
36	Bob Tewksbury	21.2
37	Jim Abbott	21.1

STARTERS – *PROSPECTS*

Short-range	Long-range	Sleepers
1 Steve Karsay	1 Jose Silva	1 Kevin Rogers
2 Salomon Torres	2 Terrell Wade	2 Pat Rapp
3 Scott Ruffcorn	3 LaTroy Hawkins	3 Arthur Rhodes
4 James Baldwin	4 Frankie Rodriguez	4 Allen Watson
5 Joey Eischen	5 Ty Hill	5 Ryan Bowen
6 Ben VanRyn	6 Jeff Granger	6 Jeff Juden
7 Alvin Morman	7 Rod Henderson	7 Sterling Hitchcock
8 Rick Helling	8 Ugueth Urbina	8 Sam Militello
9 Mark Hutton	9 Allan Benes	9 Chris Nabholz
10 John Burke	10 Brian Bevil	10 Pat Mahomes
11 Brian Barber	11 Jamie Arnold	11 Chris Hammond
12 Kurt Miller	12 John Carter	12 Tyler Green
13 Gabe White	13 John Dettmer	13 Hector Fajardo
14 Roger Salkeld	14 Kevin Gallaher	14 Alan Embree
15 Chris Looney	15 Jason Isringhausen	15 Willie Banks
16 Domingo Jean	16 Keith Heberling	16 David Nied
17 Miguel Jimenez	17 Chris Holt	17 Todd Van Poppel
18 Rick Krivda	18 Glen Dishman	18 David Weathers
19 Albie Lopez	19 Jim Pittsley	
20 Paul Spoljaric	20 Donnie Blair	

STARTING PITCHERS – *ESSAYS*

JIM ABBOTT							YANKEES
W	L	SV	ERA	IP	H	BB	K	Ratio
11	14	0	4.37	214	221	73	95	1.374

Jim took a big step backward in 1993.

As a matter of fact, his stats this year are eerily similar to his '90 season when he went 10-14 with a 4.51 ERA.

Abbott, who's never been a strikeout king, was especially weak this year, knocking out only 95 batters in 214 innings. At the same time, he walked 73 batters and allowed more than a hit an inning.

A large part of Abbott's problem was a marked lack of velocity. His pitches weren't as sharp and tended to hang over the plate. Texas Rangers players noted that Abbott wasn't hiding the ball well and was tipping batters as to what was coming.

These problems are very correctable. Abbott does not have a history of injury, so if arm fatigue is the problem, it's something he should snap out of. As for hiding the ball, this is something his pitching coach should have noticed before the other team did. Expect the quality Abbott to return in '94.

PAUL ABBOTT							INDIANS
AA – Canton-Akron							
W	L	SV	ERA	IP	H	BB	K	Ratio
4	5	0	4.06	75.1	71	28	86	1.314

Hey, Paul's strikeout numbers in Double-A look sweet, but he hasn't done anything at higher levels. He's 26 and could be a decent pitcher, but he's not an excellent candidate.

JEFF ALKIRE							CARDINALS
A – Savannah							
W	L	SV	ERA	IP	H	BB	K	Ratio
15	6	0	2.46	171.2	143	68	175	1.229

Alkire, 24, was a little old for the league he was in last year, but you can't argue with the numbers he put up. He's not a super prospect, but if he can put in a solid season and advance to Triple-A Louisville this year, he will improve his stock quite a bit.

TAVO ALVAREZ							EXPOS
AAA – Ottawa							
W	L	SV	ERA	IP	H	BB	K	Ratio
7	10	0	4.22	140.2	163	55	77	1.550

Alvarez, 22, started the 1993 season as the No. 1 pitching prospect in the system. He went on the Oprah Winfrey cheesecake 'n lard diet and pitched like Rosie O'Donnell against the AL All-Star team. He was put on an intensive weight-training program during the season, but really wasn't able to turn the year around (he wasn't losing weight, either). He's still a prospect, but he's been replaced by about 15 kids on the Expos depth chart. We're sure he's learned a lesson, but we'd also give him a year to get back to where he was in '92.

WILSON ALVAREZ							WHITE SOX
W	L	SV	ERA	IP	H	BB	K	Ratio
15	8	0	2.95	207.2	168	122	155	1.396

Wilson had the breakthrough season so many Sox fans hoped for, but so few faithfully predicted.

There were three phases to Alvarez' pitching performance last season.

The first part of the year he was unstoppable. He came out of his first seven starts with a 5-0 record, despite a horrendous 33/27 K/W ratio over this period. Frankly, Alvarez was more than a little blessed by the gods as he allowed 71 baserunners in his first 47 innings.

It caught up with him in the second phase: he went 3-8 to reach .500 by early August after a 1-2 July. At this point, he was optioned to Triple-A Nashville to work on his control. After being straightened out by pitching coach Rick Peterson and performing solidly in a minor league start, a rejuvenated Alvarez returned to spark the Sox stretch run.

His final eight starts netted him a 7-0 record and AL Player of the Month honors for September. During this stretch, Alvarez' fastball was clocked as high as 98 MPH!

Alvarez also pitched excellently to win Game Three of the ALCS, where he showcased his oft-excellent breaking ball.

BRIAN ANDERSON							ANGELS
AA – Midland							
W	L	SV	ERA	IP	H	BB	K	Ratio
0	1	0	3.38	10.2	16	0	9	1.263

A lefty taken with the No. 3 pick in 1993, Brian, 22, was drafted out of Wright State.

He doesn't have outstanding stuff, but his K/W in college was 98/6. He throws a fastball, curve, slider and change and will battle for a spot in the rotation in the spring. Brian could be a dandy, but since he's a finesse guy, it might take him longer to get settled in than someone with better stuff.

KEVIN APPIER								ROYALS
W	L	SV	ERA	IP	H	BB	K	Ratio
18	8	0	2.56	238.2	183	81	186	1.106

July 27, 1993: The Kansas City Royals lose 1-0 to the Texas Rangers.

Big Deal, right? Well that particular loss was a Kevin Appier one-hitter, in which the only hit he allowed was a game-winning home run to Rafael Palmiero. The Royals had nine hits that day and couldn't score a single run. That's the kind of thing Appier has to live with in Kansas City.

Appier's '93 season was almost identical to his '92 campaign save for the fact that he remained healthy for the final four games of '93 and picked up three more wins. He deserved more than just consideration for the Cy Young award, but McDowell put the award in his pocket the moment the White Sox clinched the AL West. Had the Royals not fallen out of the pennant race in August, Appier could well have been the recipient rather than "Black Jack."

But regardless of the size of his trophy case, Appier has become one of the most consistent pitchers in the AL, grinding out quality starts like Taiwan pumps out paper cocktail umbrellas. In fact, 28 of Appier's 34 starts were quality starts (82 percent).

From the end of May on, Appier was practically untouchable, posting a record of 13-4. In June and July, Appier started 11 games, 10 of which were quality starts. In the final two months of the season, Appier turned in 11 consecutive quality starts, including a stretch of 28.1 scoreless innings.

Appier is only 26 this season and, as long as he stays healthy, he should be considered a contender for the Cy Young.

The thought of him going free-agent must be giving Herk Robinson spasms. The Royals better start counting their pennies right now.

LUIS AQUINO								MARLINS
W	L	SV	ERA	IP	H	BB	K	Ratio
6	8	0	3.42	110.2	115	40	67	1.401

It appears that Aquino is back to normal. He wasn't on the DL in 1992, but his performance dropped across the board. The dramatic decrease in his K-rate was disturbing. His control hasn't come back, but this guy is a marginal fantasy pick anyway. He might provide some quality innings, but he's never had great stamina and he's not proven he can pitch enough innings to qualify for the ERA title.

JACK ARMSTRONG								RANGERS
W	L	SV	ERA	IP	H	BB	K	Ratio
9	17	0	4.49	196.1	210	78	118	1.467

He did look respectable early, posting a 3.62 ERA and a 30/11 K/W ratio in 32.1 April innings. Instead of building on that month though, the All-American Boy did the All-American half-gainer into the tank.

His major problem seems to be lefties. In the past he was merely cuffed about the ears by them. In '93, Jack was pasted by 'em. They hit .288 with a .373 OBP and slammed 22 HR for a .512 SLG off his sorry hide.

He's not *that* bad. But as Don Henley sang: "How *bad* do you want it?" ... Not bad enough.

JAMIE ARNOLD								BRAVES
A – Macon								
W	L	SV	ERA	IP	H	BB	K	Ratio
8	9	0	3.12	164	142	56	124	1.207

Dave: The Braves are so good they're almost sickening. But then again, I always respect/love organizations that stockpile talent, so I think the Braves are just fine, thanks.

Arnold, 20, was the Braves No. 1 pick in 1992. He has a fastball, curve and change. The heat checks in at 92 MPH already. His curve and change aren't great yet, but he occasionally impresses with them, so it's just a matter of honing his consistency. He'll probably start in the Carolina League (high A-ball) and will get a shot at Double-A if he performs.

RENE AROCHA								CARDINALS
W	L	SV	ERA	IP	H	BB	K	Ratio
11	8	0	3.78	188	197	31	96	1.213

Arocha looks like a solid, adequate pitcher. He throws about 80 different kinds of pitches, but nothing really distinguishes him from other competent hurlers. He may have a surprise year, but chances are he'll keep chugging along at his current level.

ANDY ASHBY								PADRES
W	L	SV	ERA	IP	H	BB	K	Ratio
3	10	1	6.80	123	168	56	77	1.821

Ashby didn't look that great this year. His Colorado numbers were understandably high, but his San Diego stats weren't exactly stellar.

Ashby has the ability to strike batters out, but he also throws some mistakes (he gave up 14 homers in his 69 Padre innings).

He may make a better long reliever than a starter (shorter innings with his strikeout capability), and Colorado did use him that way. If he continues to perform as he did in '93, the Padres may decide to make him a middle-man.

PEDRO ASTACIO								DODGERS
W	L	SV	ERA	IP	H	BB	K	Ratio
14	9	0	3.57	186.1	165	68	122	1.251

Pedro looked awfully good for a 23-year-old in his first full season.

His record and K/W ratio resemble those of a veteran pitcher, and his ERA wasn't too bad considering who he was pitching for.

The main concern for Astacio is his workload. Whith his physique, too many innings and he could blow out.

STEVE AVERY								BRAVES
W	L	SV	ERA	IP	H	BB	K	Ratio
18	6	0	2.94	223.1	216	43	125	1.160

Even though his ERA wasn't awesome (merely exceptional), it's impossible to find a hole in his season.

Avery allowed four runs in only one of his wins (8IP 4R 3ER 2BB 7K's). Compare that line to the average win by Gullickson or Moore. In addition, Avery allowed 0-2 earned runs in 21 of his 35 starts (in 10 starts he allowed no earned runs)!

He allowed 4+ runs in only six games (five runs once and six runs once).

Avery's one weakness remains his inability to get strikeouts. His exceptional control (1.73 W/9IP) may be part of the problem. Still, it wouldn't surprise us if he were to get 170+ K's this year. He could be the left-handed Greg Maddux.

JAMES BALDWIN								WHITE SOX
AA – Birmingham								
W	L	SV	ERA	IP	H	BB	K	Ratio
8	5	0	2.25	120	94	43	107	1.142
AAA – Nashville								
W	L	SV	ERA	IP	H	BB	K	Ratio
5	4	0	2.61	69	43	36	61	1.145

James is considered the best of the bunch as far as Sox pitching prospects are concerned.

He's got a great arm and can maintain velocity on his 90+ MPH fastball throughout the game. He's got a curve and change and is working on a cut fastball as his fourth pitch.

Ruffcorn may be more polished, but Baldwin will surely get a trial in '94.

WILLIE BANKS								CUBS
W	L	SV	ERA	IP	H	BB	K	Ratio
11	12	0	4.04	171.1	186	78	138	1.541

The Twins waited forever for this former No. 1 pick to explode and it never happened.

They made him a regular for the first time in '93 and his numbers weren't all that bad. The only Twin to keep his ERA below the league average, he was able to keep a lot of games close. But his modest success made him prime trade bait and they shipped him off to the Cubs for Walbeck and Stevens.

Willie averaged 7.3 K/9IP, but his 78 walks-allowed really hurt him. Obviously, he's letting too many guys on base, especially in the late innings. He's consistent enough and will get you a few wins, but it's time he started pitching up to his hype.

BRIAN BARBER								CARDINALS
AA – Arkansas								
W	L	SV	ERA	IP	H	BB	K	Ratio
9	8	0	4.02	143.1	154	56	126	1.456

His march through the minors has been a steady one, culminating in one appearance in Triple-A Louisville last year. The Cardinals have been very pleased with the 21-year-old, as he has shown good health, a willingness to learn and excellent work habits.

Brian's fastball is consistently clocked in the 90s, and he throws a curve and a change to complement it. Up until last year, Barber threw a slow curve, but his manager convinced him to junk it and develop the slider. Scouts say he sets up hitters well and goes after them aggressively.

Barber will start the season at Louisville. He's still quite young, so the Cardinals won't be in a hurry to promote him. But at his age, he has a high ceiling and a bright future.

Brian Barnes							Indians	
W	L	SV	ERA	IP	H	BB	K	Ratio
2	6	3	4.41	100	105	48	60	1.530

We're pretty firmly convinced that this guy needed a change of scenery. What we said last year still holds: Despite his small stature, this lefty has the curve and the moxie to make it work. Cleveland must have recognized that this guy has talent and will give him a chance to make the rotation. We think of him as a left-handed version of Tom Gordon.

Tim Belcher							? ? ?	
W	L	SV	ERA	IP	H	BB	K	Ratio
12	11	0	4.44	208.2	198	74	135	1.304

Belcher spent the majority of the season in the NL, so his ERA is worse than it seems. In fact, his ERA has been climbing the last three years, while his K's have been falling. His jump to the AL certainly isn't going to improve that situation.

For example, in 22 starts with Cinci, he had a 101/47 K/W ratio and averaged 6.6 K/9IP; in 11 starts with Chicago, he had a 34/27 ratio and averaged 4.2 K/9IP.

Whether it was the move or the number of innings, Belcher should see a reduced pitching role wherever he ends up.

Alanso Beltran							Blue Jays	
A – St. Catherines								
W	L	SV	ERA	IP	H	BB	K	Ratio
11	2	0	2.36	99	63	28	101	0.919

The 22-year-old Beltran was drafted in '92 and hasn't yet pitched in a full-season league. But what he has done in rookie ball has been impressive.

He gets a lot of strikeouts, averaging a little over one an inning last year, and is tight-fisted with the free pass, so he could make the jump to Double-A Knoxville this season and be included in Toronto's plans for '95.

Alan Benes							Cardinals	
A – Glens Falls								
W	L	SV	ERA	IP	H	BB	K	Ratio
0	4	0	3.65	37	39	14	29	1.432

Andy's baby brother was the first selection by the Cardinals in the '93 draft and signed late. By the time he pitched his first game for Glens Falls, his fastball was merely average and he was inconsistent with his breaking pitches. But St. Louis expects great things from the 22-year-old Benes. They believe his heater will pick up. They also think highly of his ability to challenge hitters and to throw his slider for strikes anytime in the count.

He'll probably start the season with full-season St. Petersburg. The Cardinals will go from there. If he's ready, they will not hesitate to promote him to Double-A.

Andy Benes							Padres	
W	L	SV	ERA	IP	H	BB	K	Ratio
15	15	0	3.78	230.2	200	86	179	1.240

By all rights, 1993 should have been The Year of the Benes.

We said last year that he's poised for greatness, and he remains poised, unable to break .500 ball and move into the elite.

He showed his usual fine control, allowing only a .232 BA to opposing hitters. His strikeouts rose slightly from past years and he really kept his hits down.

It wasn't until August and September that Andy really had problems. Until that point, he'd had an ERA well under 3.00.

To point up some of the troubles that haunt Padre pitchers, Andy was 1-3 with a 2.38 ERA for the month of June. He was also striking out almost a man an inning during this period. With this luck, Benes and John Smoltz must be brothers.

Despite all this, Benes welcomes the ace role, demanding the ball in starts against the Madduxes and Rijos.

Andy has pitched so well over the last few years that he's almost certain to break out in the next year. He seemed safe from the Padres fire sale, but a Mike Ricigliano cartoon in *Baseball Weekly* lampooned the situation by depicting a fan holding a sign which read "My clock radio for Andy Benes."

Scarier still, GM Randy Smith was talking serious trade with the Tigers by the end of the season. Other than Travis Fryman (whom they wouldn't trade on a triple-dog dare), whom do the Tiges have that would be anywhere close to Benes' value? Lay off the booze, Randy!

Joel Bennett — Red Sox

A – Lynchburg

W	L	SV	ERA	IP	H	BB	K	Ratio
7	12	0	3.83	181	151	67	221	1.204

Joel has a primo curve which helped him slice up over 200 batters in the Carolina League last year.

He gives up a few walks but the K's more than make up for it. How many guys do you know who can give up 67 walks and still have a 3.3 K/W?

Bennett's 24 and will make the move to Double-A (possibly Triple-A) this year. If he gets anything close to 200 K's, you'll probably see him in Fenway.

Jason Bere — White Sox

W	L	SV	ERA	IP	H	BB	K	Ratio
12	5	0	3.47	142.2	109	81	129	1.332

Considering his performance this year, we can only contritely make amends for not giving him a full essay in last year's tome.

After some shoddy pitching by Kirk McCaskill and some disastrous starts by Dave Stieb, the White Sox were ready to discard former greatness for future promise.

On May 27, Bere got his first chance ... to lose as a starter. Unfazed, he reeled off three straight wins.

Like teammate Wilson Alvarez, he displayed spotty control with occasionally dominating strikeout numbers. Also like Alvarez, he ended the '93 season with a streak of seven straight wins.

Even scarier than young gun Bere's season finale, is the possibility that White Sox prospects Scott Ruffcorn and James Baldwin may be better still.

Andres Berumen — Padres

A – High Desert

W	L	SV	ERA	IP	H	BB	K	Ratio
9	2	0	3.62	92	85	36	74	1.315

The Padres have brought Berumen along slowly and he's still learning his lessons.

He's got good control with good, but not overpowering K potential.

He was placed on the DL late in the season with a tired arm. He throws extremely hard at the age of 23.

Brian Bevil — Royals

A – Wilmington

W	L	SV	ERA	IP	H	BB	K	Ratio
7	1	0	2.30	74.1	46	23	61	0.928

Bevil, 21, already has an 88 MPH fastball and the Royals think it will top out in the 90s when his body matures. He also throws a decent curve and a changeup. His control is excellent, as his 2.7 career K/W ratio will testify. That kind of command with his pitches will buy him a quick flight to Omaha or parts better sometime in '94.

Bud Black — Giants

W	L	SV	ERA	IP	H	BB	K	Ratio
8	2	0	3.56	93.2	89	33	45	1.302

It doesn't seem that there's any conceivable way in which Bud Black could be good. But he was good last year.

Part of the explanation is that he does a pretty good job of keeping runners off the bases (he had a decent 1.3 ratio). When he does give up runs, it's typically due to his giving up the long ball (which he does well and often) and doing it with men on.

Black has a lifetime 3.75 ERA and a .500 record. Look for him to return to equilibrium.

Donnie Blair — Brewers

A – Beloit

W	L	SV	ERA	IP	H	BB	K	Ratio
9	6	0	3.40	135	130	11	126	1.044

He really shined in Beloit. His record and ERA were solid, but his K/W ratio says it all.

He's 21, so that means at least two more years of minor-league service before he'll be ready. The Brewers are looking forward to his arrival if his control remains this sharp.

Ron Blazier — Phillies

A – Clearwater

W	L	SV	ERA	IP	H	BB	K	Ratio
9	8	0	3.94	155.1	171	40	86	1.358

Ron's a 22-year-old who's at least two years away. He has an average fastball, a hard slurve and is considered to be very sound mechanically. He needs to up his K-rate and drop the hits-allowed.

Ben Blomdahl — Tigers

AA – London

W	L	SV	ERA	IP	H	BB	K	Ratio
6	6	0	3.71	116	108	42	72	1.293

AAA – Toledo

W	L	SV	ERA	IP	H	BB	K	Ratio
3	4	0	4.88	62.2	67	19	27	1.273

Ben is 23 and coming off a fairly mediocre season. He had a 15-7 combined record for Fayetteville and Lakeland in '92, but didn't show much last year.

Blomdahl has a good fastball and slider and he could bounce back. He's never been extremely impressive, though, so you'll want to wait and see.

Rod Bolton — White Sox

AAA – Nashville

W	L	SV	ERA	IP	H	BB	K	Ratio
10	1	1	2.88	115.2	108	37	75	1.254

W	L	SV	ERA	IP	H	BB	K	Ratio
2	6	0	7.44	42.1	55	16	17	1.677

If you saw Bolton pitch in Chicago last year you probably thought he stunk. And you wouldn't be wrong.

On the other hand, if you saw him pitch in Triple-A Nashville you would have broken your arm patting him on the back.

His 10-1 record and 2.88 ERA in the minors was proof that the hype over him wasn't exaggerated.

Bolton is just one cog in the White sox pitching machine. With hurlers like Ruffcorn, Baldwin and Bere hanging around, the competition should be pretty fierce. Chalk up Bolton's '93 failures to freshman jitters and figure he's pitched himself into top contention for a job on the staff.

Ricky Bones — Brewers

W	L	SV	ERA	IP	H	BB	K	Ratio
11	11	0	4.86	203.2	222	63	63	1.399

Although he scored double-figures in the win column for the first time, Ricky fell back as a pitcher, reconfirming himself as a project for the Brewers.

He had the same number of K's this year as in '92, but in more innings. He also walked as many men as he sat down. He gave up 28 HR, 41 doubles and 11 triples and his ERA was too close to 5.00 for Milwaukee's comfort.

Bones may be young, but he's been a pro for some time now. With his experience he should have been a lot better than this by age 25. He may still mature into a pitcher, but if it doesn't happen this year or the next, he's probably destined to be a never-was.

Chris Bosio — Mariners

W	L	SV	ERA	IP	H	BB	K	Ratio
9	9	1	3.45	164.1	138	59	119	1.201

Chris had a crazy up and down season with peaks like his no-hitter and valleys like his shoulder injury in Cleveland (when Jeff Treadway collided with him at first base).

Bosio contributed many fine performances and finished strong with a 1.61 ERA over his last seven starts. There still may be questions about the soundness of his shoulder, but as of now (late December), he looks good.

Denis Boucher — Expos

AAA – Ottawa

W	L	SV	ERA	IP	H	BB	K	Ratio
6	0	0	2.72	43	36	11	22	1.093

W	L	SV	ERA	IP	H	BB	K	Ratio
3	1	0	1.91	28.1	24	3	14	0.953

Last year he pitched at his peak, and apart from a massacre in the PCL, he did fine. He's a Bob Tewksbury type who'll live on the edge. He doesn't throw many groundballs (which was what was advertised when he was in the Blue Jays chain). But with an excellent defense behind him, and continued command of his breaking stuff, he could win 15-18 games. All he has to do is beat a couple of guys in mortal combat during the spring.

Ryan Bowen — Marlins

W	L	SV	ERA	IP	H	BB	K	Ratio
8	12	0	4.42	156.2	156	87	98	1.551

Unlike Armstrong, Bowen can keep the ball in the park while allowing a similar amount of baserunners. He's finally gotten some innings at the major-league level and he wasn't beaten senseless.

With his stuff, one should expect the K/W rate to get better (especially the K's). The question is, does he have what it takes to make it to the next level? He does have the ability, he just needs to hone it.

He's 26, so if he's going to do it, it should be in the next couple of years.

Marshall Boze — Brewers

A – Stockton

W	L	SV	ERA	IP	H	BB	K	Ratio
7	2	0	2.65	88.1	82	41	54	1.393

AA – El Paso

W	L	SV	ERA	IP	H	BB	K	Ratio
10	3	0	2.71	86.1	78	32	48	1.274

He finally jumped to Double-A El Paso. After showing nothing in his earlier years, the last two seasons have been revelatory.

He doesn't have overpowering pitches and his K-rate is alarmingly low. Boze throws in the mid-80s with a decent curve and a good change, and considering his record and ERA last year he's doing something right.

He won't be truly ready for a year or two, but watch the Brewers interest rise as their pitching stock plummets.

Doug Brocail — Padres

W	L	SV	ERA	IP	H	BB	K	Ratio
4	13	0	4.56	128.1	143	42	70	1.442

Considering how long San Diego has waited on Brocail, 27, you'd have thought he was something special.

He pitched poorly from the get-go and yet the Pads kept giving him starts, 24 in all. It was obvious that he was a late starter who wasn't catching on to major-league hitting.

The Padres may hold on to him next year, but there are plenty of pitchers who are at least three or four years younger who can pitch as ineptly as he does.

Chris Brock — Braves

A – Macon

W	L	SV	ERA	IP	H	BB	K	Ratio
7	5	0	2.70	80	61	33	92	1.175

Brock, 23, also went 5-2 in Durham with a 2.51 ERA and a 67/35 K/W ratio. He's a notch lower than the rest of the young guns in the Braves' system, but keep an eye on him.

Kevin Brown — Rangers

W	L	SV	ERA	IP	H	BB	K	Ratio
15	12	0	3.59	233	228	74	142	1.296

Brown's numbers slipped slightly last year, but then, he did lead the league with 21 wins in '92 so you can expect a little drop off.

Most disturbing was his increased walk-rate, and the fact that he drilled 15 batters last year, so you have to wonder a little bit about his control. But his walks are still well below his pre-'92 totals and his ratio and K's are respectable.

The hard sinker continues to keep the ball on the ground and avoid the big hits. The league only slugged .353 against him, .325 with runners in scoring position. Kevin gave up 0.54 HR/9IP, the second lowest average in the AL (STATS, Inc.).

Brown will keep going strong as long as the sinker does. He's 29, so that could be a while.

Tom Browning — Reds

W	L	SV	ERA	IP	H	BB	K	Ratio
7	7	0	4.74	114	159	20	53	1.570

Browning's performance has been declining for the last five years, and last season did nothing to change the trend.

Neither did a possession of marijuana charge. The goof, apparently struggling with a bout of Steve-Howe-itis, tried to drive on the median to beat a traffic jam, and got busted with a joint in his ashtray.

Then, his season was cut short on August 8 by a broken middle finger on his left hand. You may remember that he was on the DL for most of '92 as well.

Browning played long enough last season to show that his numbers are still in decline. His ERAs for the last five years: '89–3.39, '90–3.80, '91–4.18, '92–5.07, '93–4.74. Age and injuries are beginning to take their toll and his innings may be numbered.

Brownie's an extreme finesse pitcher and that is something you should be concerned about. His strikeout rate hasn't declined that much, but he's not the safest gamble for '94.

Duff Brumley — Rangers

A – St. Petersburg

W	L	SV	ERA	IP	H	BB	K	Ratio
5	1	0	0.64	56	26	13	67	0.696

AA – Arkansas

W	L	SV	ERA	IP	H	BB	K	Ratio
4	5	0	3.50	69.1	57	26	79	1.197

Brumley, 23, has a good, tight-breaking slider and an average fastball. He also holds the distinction of being Homer Simpson's favorite minor leaguer (don't worry if you don't get it, that just means you aren't a slave to pop culture like us).

St. Petersburg was a pitchers' park last year; the park effect was 89 percent for runs and 67 percent for homers. That helped Duff to his unbelievably low ERA. But he was still a man among boys in the FSL and the move to Double-A didn't hurt him much, either.

He has excellent control and deserves a shot in Triple-A immediately.

Greg Brummett								Twins
AAA – Phoenix								
W	L	SV	ERA	IP	H	BB	K	Ratio
7	7	0	3.70	107	114	27	84	1.318
W	L	SV	ERA	IP	H	BB	K	Ratio
4	4	0	5.08	72.2	82	28	30	1.514

After four years in San Francisco's farm system, Brummett came to the Twins in September as part of the Deshaies trade.

He averaged over 7 K/9IP last year in Triple-A, but the jump to majors, and then the mid-season trade, didn't suit him well.

He had excellent control and kept his hits-allowed down in Single-A; he should be able to do the same in the bigs once he has a chance to adjust.

He's still only 27 and with the departure of Willie Banks, he will get some serious action this season.

Melvin Bunch								Royals
A – Wilmington								
W	L	SV	ERA	IP	H	BB	K	Ratio
5	3	0	2.33	65.2	52	14	54	1.005

He was a 15th-rounder in the '92 draft, and this is probably the first time you've ever heard of him. But check out his season totals the (6-4, 2.12 ERA in 85 innings at Single-A Rockford) and you'll realize why he's in this book. He's 22 and a few years away, but so far, he's a nice looking prospect.

John Burke								Rockies
AAA – Colorado Springs								
W	L	SV	ERA	IP	H	BB	K	Ratio
3	2	0	3.14	48.2	44	23	38	1.377

His 1992 shoulder injury cost him a few MPH off his fastball, but he still throws in the low 90s. His managers point out that he's learning how to pitch, now that he won't be able to simply blow hitters away anymore. *Baseball America* named him the best prospect in the California League and managers agreed in a mid-season poll that he had the league's best breaking pitch.

Burke, 24, isn't far from the majors right now, but will have to improve his control before he takes the final step. He'll start out in Triple-A in '94, but an injury among the Rockies' staff could open the door.

John Burkett								Giants
W	L	SV	ERA	IP	H	BB	K	Ratio
22	7	0	3.65	231.2	224	40	145	1.140

John was much-toasted by fans this year, but because of his ERA and cheap wins (six), he looked like McDowell with fewer K's.

While this may not be bad, it isn't as good as the media professed.

What was great about Burkett was his control. Walking only 40 batters in 230 innings is no mean feat. He did give up 18 dingers, but this hurts him less than a pitcher who allows runners to roam the bases.

Because he's never displayed an ability to win like this, the probability of him repeating this year's performance is slim.

It's more likely that he'll win closer to 15 games than 20, which makes him about as valuable as he's been in the past.

Paul Byrd								Indians
AAA – Charlotte								
W	L	SV	ERA	IP	H	BB	K	Ratio
7	4	0	3.89	81	80	30	54	1.358

Paul was a sure bet to make it to the bigs in '93, but he didn't look sharp in the spring and started the season in the minors. While with Triple-A Charlotte, he suffered a strained something-or-other and spent nearly a month on the DL. Last year was his first taste of hard luck in pro ball. We'll see how he handles it.

He still has a chance of making it to the big leagues this year. Goodness knows the Indians need the arms. The control needs work, but he has decent movement on his breaking pitches.

Tom Candiotti								Dodgers
W	L	SV	ERA	IP	H	BB	K	Ratio
8	10	0	3.12	213.2	192	71	155	1.231

Candiotti had another tough season as a Dodger. While he had very good months, May through August, he's a summer pitcher who can't win a Cy Young because his knuckler gets stomped in cool weather.

Candiotti's present condition proves how difficult it is to live by the knuckleball. He has a 3.06 ERA over the last two seasons, but has a 19-25 record to show for it.

For fantasy owners, the book on Candiotti is knowing that he's completely dependent on his team for wins and he can deteriorate on you if you trade for him in early spring or fall.

RON CARIDAD								TWINS
A – Fort Wayne								
W	L	SV	ERA	IP	H	BB	K	Ratio
6	8	0	3.51	143.2	138	91	124	1.594

Caridad averaged 7.8 K/9IP in the Midwest League last year, which is excellent for a 22-year-old. It doesn't take a swami to tell he needs to work on his control, however. The walks are killing him.

DAN CARLSON								GIANTS
AAA – Phoenix								
W	L	SV	ERA	IP	H	BB	K	Ratio
5	6	0	6.56	70	79	32	48	1.586
AA – Shreveport								
W	L	SV	ERA	IP	H	BB	K	Ratio
7	4	0	2.24	100.1	86	26	81	1.119

After being racked up in Phoenix, he was demoted to Shreveport where he returned to the impressive form of his last two seasons.

He's 24 years old and the Giants won't be satisfied until he can prove himself in Triple-A, but once he does he should make it to the bigs and perform solidly.

JOHN CARTER								INDIANS
A – Columbus								
W	L	SV	ERA	IP	H	BB	K	Ratio
17	7	0	2.79	180.1	147	48	134	1.081

Obtained from the Pirates in '92 for Alex Cole, John is further evidence of the Indians' knack for evaluating talent. Not only can they draft and develop solid youngsters, but they can steal them from other teams as well.

Carter, 22, dominated the Sally League last year, leading the circuit in wins and placing in the top ten in ERA. He added a few MPH to the heater, so he's now throwing it in the low 90s with consistency. That is the primary reason for his emergence.

Carter is at least two years from the majors, but he is at the top of the long-range prospect pile in the Cleveland organization.

FRANK CASTILLO								CUBS
W	L	SV	ERA	IP	H	BB	K	Ratio
5	8	0	4.84	141.1	162	39	84	1.422

He really fell apart last year. The NL hit .293 and slugged .474 off him. But Castillo is only 25, so he should be able to turn it around this season. He still has his good control and if he can get the changup working, he'll be in good shape to win some ballgames.

SCOTT CHRISTMAN								WHITE SOX
R – White Sox								
W	L	SV	ERA	IP	H	BB	K	Ratio
0	0	1	0.00	11.1	3	4	15	.618

Scott's a big boy at 6-3, 190. He's a lefty with a high-80s fastball and was the No. 17 pick in the first round out of Oregon State.

Some scouts thought his arm was weak, which probably means he needs some seasoning to build his stamina. With the abundance of Sox pitching prospects, he'll get it.

MARK CLARK								INDIANS
W	L	SV	ERA	IP	H	BB	K	Ratio
7	5	0	4.28	109.1	119	25	57	1.320

He spent nearly a month and a half on the DL last season with a strained muscle in his back. That's not a good sign for Clark, who would be fighting for his baseball life if it weren't for the fact that the Indians are the most pitching-starved club in the majors.

Even though he is only 26, he might pitch himself off Cleveland's roster by June if Lopez, Tavarez, Ogea and/or Embree pan out.

CRAIG CLAYTON								MARINERS
No Professional Experience								

Converted from third base, Clayton went from marginal prospect to viable prospect because of his 93-MPH sinking blower and his ability to throw his slider for strikes.

He pitched for Cal State-Northridge and went 14-5 with a 2.25 ERA in 1991. He's compared by some to Trevor Hoffman.

ROGER CLEMENS								RED SOX
W	L	SV	ERA	IP	H	BB	K	Ratio
11	14	0	4.46	191.2	175	67	160	1.263

He experienced the unthinkable in '93: a losing season. But you may have already heard.

Roger's injuries, including a strained groin muscle, played a major role in his downfall. He started the season as the same old Roger; in April he was 3-1 with a 1.64 ERA. But after a 141-pitch shutout in Baltimore on May 11, there was already talk of tendinitis in his left elbow. Between his elbow and groin, he simply couldn't rear back and let loose. He struggled through May and finally went on the DL in June. In that time, his ERA soared.

His groin recovered and he came back in July. Going on another tear, in his first four starts, he went 2-1 with a 2.17 ERA.

His elbow started bothering him and he tried to pitch through it until September 25, when he was done for the year. During that period, he was 2-7 with an ERA over 7.00.

The point is, forget about last year's stats, they aren't representative. Sure, Roger's K-totals have been slipping slightly, but only slightly. Even in last year's debacle, he still averaged 7.5/9IP.

Incidently, the last time Roger's season was shortened by injury was 1985. He came back in '86 to win 24 games and the first of his three Cy Young Awards.

Roger's still the man.

DAVID CONE — ROYALS

W	L	SV	ERA	IP	H	BB	K	Ratio
11	14	0	3.33	254	205	114	191	1.256

If there's a pitcher in the American League with a legitimate beef about his own team, it's David Cone.

To understand Cone's 11-14 record, one only has to look at his run-support. The Royals offense gave him only 2.97 runs per nine innings to work with, the lowest support in the AL. He finished second only to Tom Candiotti for the worst support in the Major Leagues. Cone went 11-7 in his 23 quality starts.

He didn't exactly help himself out by allowing 114 bases-on-balls, but he has always been rather generous with the free pass. Besides, he pitched well enough to last at least six innings in 30 of his 34 starts. That, my friends, is the kind of consistency you look for in a starter.

Cone has to be considered the Royals' No. 2 starter behind Appier, but even as a second banana, he still ranks among the top Major League starting pitchers.

BRIAN CONROY — RED SOX

AAA – Pawtucket

W	L	SV	ERA	IP	H	BB	K	Ratio
5	7	0	5.86	106	126	40	64	1.566

Conroy was manhandled last year by International League hitters. He allowed a .288 batting average, including 24 HR's in 106 innings (over 2 HR/9IP).

He's looked better in the past, but he's been hanging around Pawtucket for three years now without showing any improvement.

Brian's 25 and the Red Sox still have time to wait on him, should they choose. They have better guys they should be looking at, but that doesn't mean a thing in Beantown.

JIM CONVERSE — MARINERS

AAA – Calgary

W	L	SV	ERA	IP	H	BB	K	Ratio
7	8	0	5.40	121.2	144	64	78	1.710

He's only 5-9, but he's a solid 180 pounds and throws 93-95 MPH on the fast gun. He has a curve and a change as well.

As the numbers show, he was clobbered at Triple-A. But that was the PCL and Calgary had a team ERA of 5.21. If you directly translate his performance to the AL, his equivalent ERA would be 4.48: Not great, but similar to what young power pitchers like Willie Banks and Chuck Finley were doing at that age.

He's 22, so he's got a lot of time to develop. All he needs to do is harness his control and he could be a solid contributor for the Mariners. All you need to do is wait on him.

STEVE COOKE — PIRATES

W	L	SV	ERA	IP	H	BB	K	Ratio
10	10	0	3.89	210.2	207	59	132	1.263

Cooke has never pitched anything close to 210 innings, but he fared well in his initiation.

He developed an impressive curveball to complement an excellent change, improved his control and cut down on his walks. His 2.24 K/W was respectable, even though his K-rate did fall slightly. You have to like any 24-year-old who throws 20 quality starts in his first full season in the majors.

Jim Leyland calls him the best pitching prospect the Pirates have ever developed. He may be right.

RHEAL CORMIER — CARDINALS

W	L	SV	ERA	IP	H	BB	K	Ratio
7	6	0	4.33	145.1	163	27	75	1.307

Cormier wasn't the "rheal ting" last year. His K/W ratio remained stellar at 2.78, but righties hit .310 with a .513 SL% against him. Lefties are shut down completely (.207 BA, .290 SLG). Rheal does his best cooking at home (15-7, 3.40 in St. Louis) and gets clobbered on the road (6-14, 4.58 ERA). This is one hombre that wasn't helped by expansion.

TIM CRABTREE — BLUE JAYS

AA – Knoxville

W	L	SV	ERA	IP	H	BB	K	Ratio
9	14	0	4.08	158.2	178	59	67	1.544

Crabtree, 24, was rocked last year in Knoxville and has yet to show command of the strike zone. He throws very hard, reaching the mid 90s and he junked his good curveball (umps never called it a strike) for a very nice slider. The Blue Jays are quite high on him and expect him to be in their rotation by 1995.

He also is distinguished by being a high school classmate of one of the members our rotisserie league, Brian Seidenstucker. It doesn't matter who Crabtree went to high school with, wait until he's getting more K's before you take him.

JOHN CUMMINGS — MARINERS

AA – Jacksonville

W	L	SV	ERA	IP	H	BB	K	Ratio
2	2	0	3.15	45.2	50	9	35	1.292

AAA – Calgary

W	L	SV	ERA	IP	H	BB	K	Ratio
3	4	0	4.13	65.1	69	22	45	1.393

He was beaten like a rented mule on "animal-mutilation day" in Seattle (6.02 ERA in 46.1 IP), but he's a pretty good lefty pitcher.

Cummings, 25, throws a good cutter fastball and has a solid curveball and change. Despite the quality of the pitches, he is considered to have more of a finesse pitcher's repertoire than a power pitcher's.

He looks like he handled the jump to Triple-A competition, so all he has to do is keep plugging away until he sticks. Right now, he looks better than Converse and probably a smidge below Mike Hampton.

JEFF D'AMICO — BREWERS

No Professional Experience

D'Amico's a huge high school pitcher (6-7, 240 lbs.) with 91 MPH cheese. He's impressive but raw. Wait a couple years to see how he develops.

MIKE D'ANDREA — BRAVES

A – Macon

W	L	SV	ERA	IP	H	BB	K	Ratio
8	7	0	4.03	136.1	129	55	156	1.350

D'Andrea is 24. There's nothing really outstanding about him except his strikeout rate and his decent control. But then again, a 2.84 K/W ratio is damn good and a 10.3 K/9IP rate is damn phenomenal. Give him a year, but remember his name.

RON DARLING — ATHLETICS

W	L	SV	ERA	IP	H	BB	K	Ratio
5	9	0	5.16	178	198	72	95	1.517

Ron set out to prove that his performance last year wasn't a fluke and ended up showing that 1990 (7-9) and 1991 (8-15) were the rule.

This sweetheart is toast for at least the rest of this century.

DANNY DARWIN — RED SOX

W	L	SV	ERA	IP	H	BB	K	Ratio
15	11	0	3.26	229.1	196	49	130	1.069

As we predicted, Darwin got a full shot in '93 and brought home 15 wins. He started out slow, going 0-4 in April, but turned his season around when he decided to try a shortened delivery in May. He went 5-0 with a 1.88 ERA for the month after making the switch.

Danny led the Sox staff with 34 starts and with an impressive 22 quality starts. His 9.73 baserunner/9IP average was the lowest in the AL (STATS, Inc.). Though his K's fell slightly last year, his 2.65 K/W ratio is still very respectable. And his 1.07 ratio is outstanding.

Darwin showed he could provide numerous quality innings for the Sox when they needed them. He's 38, but his control is excellent, so we see no reason why he can't get another 12-15 wins next year.

JAVIER DELAHOYA — MARLINS

AA – San Antonio

W	L	SV	ERA	IP	H	BB	K	Ratio
8	10	0	3.66	125.1	122	42	107	1.309

Good control and throws hard.

He's not a super-phenom, but he's posted good ERAs the last couple of years. We aren't sure how high Florida is on him for '94, but a good strikeout pitcher is always welcome.

JIM DESHAIES — GIANTS

W	L	SV	ERA	IP	H	BB	K	Ratio
13	15	0	4.39	184.1	183	57	85	1.302

Jim allowed 24 home runs and couldn't strike anybody out in Minnesota. He looked a little better in San Fran, but how much better is a 4.24 ERA than a 4.41. No matter which way you slice him he comes up mediocre.

JOHN DETTMER — RANGERS

A – Charlotte

W	L	SV	ERA	IP	H	BB	K	Ratio
16	3	0	2.15	163	132	33	128	1.012

John had an outstanding season in the FSL. He showed excellent control, had a 3.9 K/W and didn't let anybody on base. He has a great curve to follow up a mid-80s fastball.

John's already 24 years old, so if he starts hot in Double-A this year, he could be on the fast track to the majors.

LANCE DICKSON — CUBS

AA – Orlando

W	L	SV	ERA	IP	H	BB	K	Ratio
2	3	0	3.83	49.1	37	17	46	1.095

Although he has battled injury problems the past two seasons, Dickson, 24, is still young enough to put it back together again.

He made a lot of progress last year, refining his already quality curveball and becoming quite aggressive in challenging the hitters. New pitching coach Moe Drabowsky likes his makeup, so he'll get a shot in the spring. He could surprise a lot of people if he's healthy.

GLENN DISHMAN — PADRES

A – Spokane

W	L	SV	ERA	IP	H	BB	K	Ratio
6	3	0	2.20	77.2	59	13	79	0.927

Dishman looked great at Spokane and just awful in his two starts at Rancho Cucamonga. Because he's 23, the real Glenn is the one who was striking 79 guys in 77.2 innings.

Dishman should be up by the time he's 25 if he continues to progress.

JOHN DOHERTY — TIGERS

W	L	SV	ERA	IP	H	BB	K	Ratio
14	11	0	4.44	184.2	205	48	63	1.371

Doherty was one of several Tiger pitchers who enjoyed enormous run support (5.85 runs, 8th highest in AL). He didn't waste it and led the team with 14 wins.

You could say he was a little lucky. Out of his 31 starts, only 14 were quality and he won 12 (86 percent) of these. The average pitcher only wins around 60 percent of his quality starts. Without the generous run support, John would've finished somewhere around 10-14.

He definitely has problems with his control, especially in clutch situations. He got whacked with runners in scoring position, giving up a .324 BA and .547 slugging percentage (STATS, Inc.). His 20 walks in those situations didn't help much either.

Last season was his first as a full-time starter and, at 27, he still has time to improve his stamina and control. He may continue to be effective for the Tigers, but that doesn't mean he's a viable fantasy draft.

JOHN DOPSON — RED SOX

W	L	SV	ERA	IP	H	BB	K	Ratio
7	11	0	4.97	155.2	170	59	89	1.471

Last year, we told you to treat him like dirt unless he gives you reason to think otherwise. He's done nothing to change our opinion.

In fact, Dopson's proven beyond a shadow of a doubt that he cannot start for a full season. In the last two years, he's gone 13-9 before the All-Star break and 1-13 after.

The league just knocks him all over the ballpark. He only managed 9 quality starts out of 28, less than a third of his starts and that's unacceptable.

If the Sox decide to use him in long relief, we can talk. Otherwise, treat him like dirt.

DOUG DRABEK — ASTROS

W	L	SV	ERA	IP	H	BB	K	Ratio
9	18	0	3.79	237.2	242	60	157	1.273

This poor guy went 9-8 in his 22 quality starts. The rest of the rotation (Harnisch, Kile,

Portugal and Swindell) went 54-13 in their 85 quality starts (an .806 W/L percentage).

Luck like that would have netted him a 14-13 record: not exceptional, but possibly enough to have saved Art Howe's job.

Some of Drabek's indicators were low last year (e.g., much greater hits-allowed, worse performance on artificial turf), but he's done nothing to tarnish his reputation. He is capable of a 20-win season this year.

If pitchers ever earn the right to knock off selected members of their offense and bullpen, we'll be loaning our Glock to Drabek.

MATT DREWS — YANKEES
No Professional Experience

Drews was the Yanks No. 1 pick in '93 and is one impressive pitcher.

He's tall and rangy (6-8, 217) and will inevitably get a little more meat on his bones.

He throws in the 90s (as high as 96) and has a good curve and changeup. His primary weapon is that fastball, though, which has great movement.

Like the White Sox, the Yanks are loaded with prospects, so Drews will be given a chance to work on his skills.

STEVE DREYER — RANGERS
AAA – Oklahoma City

W	L	SV	ERA	IP	H	BB	K	Ratio
4	6	0	3.03	107	108	31	59	1.299

Dreyer's a young junkballer with decent control and little velocity. The Rangers considered him to be better than Kurt Miller; hence Miller's exit in the Cris Carpenter deal.

Personally, we think they're crazy, especially since Miller is three years younger. But Dreyer's only 24 and has already gotten a six-start tryout with the Rangers (3-3, 5.71 ERA).

Steve will probably get a chance to prove us wrong this year, but young guys who rely on pinpoint accuracy make us nervous.

JOEY EISCHEN — EXPOS
AA – Harrisburg

W	L	SV	ERA	IP	H	BB	K	Ratio
14	4	0	3.62	119	122	60	110	1.529

With a 92-94 MPH fastball, a low-80s curve and a good changeup, Eischen is considered to have the best stuff in Montreal's farm system.

The 'Spos consider him a potential No. 1 starter and the only thing this 24-year-old lefty has to do is start throwing more strikes – especially with the curve. If he can do that, he'll get a job with Montreal this year. The thing is, for the short term, the Expos are looking at him as bullpen help.

CAL ELDRED — BREWERS

W	L	SV	ERA	IP	H	BB	K	Ratio
16	16	0	4.01	258	232	91	180	1.252

Considering how many people were waiting for Cal to fall on his face after last year's fantastic debut, he didn't pitch all that badly.

He led the league in innings pitched and displayed surprising strikeout potential. On a better team his ERA would have been lower and his record better.

One indicator of the Brewers' desperation for pitching was that Cal threw 150 pitches on August 20. Think that might've had something to do with his late-season slump? *Madness!*

Expect Eldred to be the best pitcher on the Brewer staff (which isn't necessarily saying much) and to continue winning games. This guy has definite All-Star potential.

DONNIE ELLIOT — PADRES
AAA – Richmond

W	L	SV	ERA	IP	H	BB	K	Ratio
8	5	0	4.72	103	108	39	99	1.427

Donnie was part of the infamous McGriff CARE package that Atlanta was kind enough to ship to the "Dollar Tree of the N."

He has good hard stuff: slider and fastball. His problem is that he can't throw a consistent change, so the hitters are seeing two minor variations in velocity on his pitches.

His K-rate and control look adequate. It's probably just a matter of spending Spring and a few months in the minors adjusting.

We're afraid he'll be in the PCL if he doesn't make San Diego in the spring. He got rocked there in eight starts last year and that happens to the best of 'em in that band-box league.

ROBERT ELLIS — WHITE SOX
AA – Birmingham

W	L	SV	ERA	IP	H	BB	K	Ratio
6	3	0	3.10	81.1	68	21	77	1.094

Ellis isn't as highly regarded as comrades James Baldwin or Scott Ruffcorn, but he's still an important piece in the Sox' plans in the wake of Ruffin and Pierce leaving.

He's pretty polished, throwing a fastball, curve and changeup. All are considered good and he's known for his excellent control.

ALAN EMBREE — INDIANS
AA – Canton-Akron

W	L	SV	ERA	IP	H	BB	K	Ratio
0	2	0	7.00	18	19	8	12	1.500

Going into spring training last year, Alan was the highest rated hurler in the Cleveland's system and a favorite to win a starting job.

Elbow discomfort forced him to start the season in the minors and on the DL. He made four dismal starts in June, but the pain returned and Embree had season-ending surgery to repair a torn ligament in his left elbow.

He was expected to start throwing in late December or early January, but since he has been off for a full year, he probably won't see any game action until May. It's too early to tell how the surgery will affect his 90+ fastball. His offspeed stuff is acceptable, but won't sustain him if he loses substantial velocity. The best-case scenario would have Embree in good health playing for Charlotte and receiving a September call-up.

SCOTT ERICKSON — TWINS

W	L	SV	ERA	IP	H	BB	K	Ratio
8	19	0	5.19	218.2	266	71	116	1.541

Scott led the AL in several categories last year, including losses, runs- and hits-allowed.

He started the season on the DL with a strained stomach muscle and it was all downhill from there. He just got rocked all year. The league hit .305 off him and slugged .431. Lefties especially enjoyed his fare, hitting .342 and slugging .481. Bon Appetit!

The injury obviously knocked Erickson off his usual form and many of you will remember that he won 20 games only two years ago. You may be thinking that he'll be a decent gamble when he becomes available in your spring draft, which he will. But don't do it, those odds are way too long.

Even Tom Kelly thinks he's lost his stuff. Kelly was quoted in *Baseball Weekly* as saying, "He'll never (pitch like his 20-8 season in 1991 again). He threw 92 (MPH), just overpowered people. Now he's got to pitch."

Erickson's always let too many guys on base, even when he led the league in wins, and the chickens finally came home to roost in '93. Let him prove himself, if he can, on someone else's roster.

SCOTT EYRE — RANGERS
A – Charleston-SC

W	L	SV	ERA	IP	H	BB	K	Ratio
11	7	0	3.45	143.2	115	59	154	1.211

Scott's a 22-year-old lefty with an exceptional curve and good control. He's extremely skinny, though, so there is some concern about his stamina and ability to avoid injury.

He only averaged 5.5 innings per start last year, but tallied 9.7 K/9IP in those appearances. He's clearly ready to move out of Single-A and he may be able to fill out and gain some stamina in time.

HECTOR FAJARDO — RANGERS
R – Rangers

W	L	SV	ERA	IP	H	BB	K	Ratio
3	1	0	1.80	30	21	5	27	.867

Fajardo was plagued by injury last year and got a few innings in the Gulf Coast, Florida State and major leagues.

The injuries are a recurring problem, but he's probably got the best arm in the Rangers' farm system. He's got a hot fastball and the control to use it effectively.

Hector's only 23 and about half-a-season away from being ready for the bigs. You should be concerned about the injuries, but he's the kind of talent that's worth the gamble if he looks healthy in the spring.

JEFF FASSERO — EXPOS

W	L	SV	ERA	IP	H	BB	K	Ratio
12	5	1	2.29	149.2	119	54	140	1.156

It wasn't a surprise that Fassero was a fine pitcher, it was a surprise that he stepped into the rotation and kept his ERA at 2.29.

He delivered a pretty devastating combo. He averaged 8.4 K/9IP and was an extreme groundballer. Despite being a lefty, there was no platoon advantage. Neither lefties nor righties could hit him and he got stronger as the season wore on.

The end result was he ruled. If no one in your league has him, consider getting him.

ALEX FERNANDEZ							WHITE SOX
W	L	SV	ERA	IP	H	BB	K	Ratio
18	9	0	3.13	247.1	221	67	189	1.164

After '93, the word you'll find on the lips of most Sox fans is "finally." Long touted as the next great Sox pitcher, Alex delivered more than could have been imagined after two years of on-the-job training in the bigs.

Luckily for the White Sox, Alex went from mediocre to Cy Young-calibre in one year. His 18 wins were nine more than his previous high, and he logged an impressive 247.1 innings.

The season's length was a little much for the young 'un, though: His ERA rose almost a run in the second half – a previously missing element in his pitching form.

Importantly for the team's future, Fernandez relied less on the whims of the Chicago offense than did his colleague Jack McDowell. Fernandez had a 2.76 ERA in games he won and a 4.88 ERA in games which he lost. If you were to undertake a start-by-start analysis of Black Jack, you'd find there was a *positive correlation* between his quality starts and his losses!

SID FERNANDEZ							ORIOLES
W	L	SV	ERA	IP	H	BB	K	Ratio
5	6	0	2.93	119.2	82	36	81	.986

Despite losing a good part of his season to a knee injury, Fernandez was very effective last year. Of course, the Mets failed him horribly and his success wasn't reflected in his win-loss percentage. He received only 3.53 runs of support, almost a full run below the league average.

Fortunately, he's been released from his bondage and the Orioles will probably be more generous. In 10 years with the Mets, Fernandez posted an impressive overall ratio of 1.113. That will rise a bit in the American League, but Baltimore's offensive machine should provide more than enough support to give him 12+ wins.

CHUCK FINLEY							ANGELS
W	L	SV	ERA	IP	H	BB	K	Ratio
16	14	0	3.15	251.1	243	82	187	1.293

Chuck bounced back strongly from his poor '92 season, posting 16 wins and one of the league's best ERAs. For those of you in doubt, peruse these lines:

Date	IP	H	R	ER	BB	K	Game Score
4/22	9	2	0	0	2	10	91
6/26	9	3	0	0	0	7	88
7/11	9	6	2	2	2	9	74
8/24	8	2	2	2	3	10	81
9/22	9	4	1	0	4	5	78

You won't find any starts like these in Bob Walk's resume.

Finley had a Drabek-ian 13-9 record in his 25 quality starts, but he allowed 11 unearned runs in five of his quality losses, and that can be the difference between going 4-1 and 0-5. Finley allowed 20 unearned runs total.

Other ace caliber starters (Appier, Brown, Clemens, Cone, McDowell, McDonald, Eldred, Juan Guzman, Randy Johnson, Key, Langston and Mussina) averaged 6.23 unearned runs in an average of 215 innings. According to the Pythagorean formula, that would have caused a swing of two games. This would have put Finley at 18-12.

GAR FINNVOLD							RED SOX
AAA – Pawtucket							
W	L	SV	ERA	IP	H	BB	K	Ratio
5	9	0	3.77	136	128	51	123	1.316

Finnvold's one of those guys you really want to see in the bigs just so you can hear his name on SportsCenter. But that doesn't necessarily mean you want him on your team.

Gar throws a 90+ MPH heater and is considered a real student of pitching. At 26, he has yet to post a winning record, however, and isn't considered a top prospect.

DAVE FLEMING							MARINERS
W	L	SV	ERA	IP	H	BB	K	Ratio
12	5	0	4.36	167.2	189	67	75	1.527

Dave went 9-1 in his 14 quality starts. His record is over-inflated, but overall, Fleming pitched OK, especially since he was coming off an injury.

He struck out 5+ batters only three times in his 26 starts ... quite disturbing. But it is quite probable that his strikeout rate will rise in 1994. As long as he can continue to display his good control and mix his eephus-type 55-60 MPH curve unpredictably, he'll win some games with a good team behind him.

He's a decent second-echelon pitcher with upward potential.

RICK FORNEY							ORIOLES
A – Frederick							
W	L	SV	ERA	IP	H	BB	K	Ratio
14	8	0	2.78	165	156	64	175	1.333

Forney is 6-4, 210 and 22 years old. He has average velocity and a four-pitch arsenal which includes a splitter, a curve and a change. He has a propensity to put on fat, but he looks like he might be battling for a spot on the big club in '95.

JOHN FRASCATORE							CARDINALS
A – Springfield							
W	L	SV	ERA	IP	H	BB	K	Ratio
7	12	0	3.78	157.1	157	33	126	1.208

John's 24 years old and has spent his career since being drafted in 1991 in Single-A. But since he cut out weightlifting, which he was fanatical about in high school, he's picked up seven MPH on his fastball and has become a power-pitching prospect with good control.

He'll start the year at Double-A Arkansas, but he could be promoted to Triple-A by mid-season. Currently, though, he's a longshot.

JOHN FRITZ							ANGELS
AA – Midland							
W	L	SV	ERA	IP	H	BB	K	Ratio
9	5	0	3.61	129.2	125	42	85	1.288

Fritz is 25 and has been floating about California's organization since 1988. He's not a great prospect, but numbers like those in Midland (and his 4.07 ERA in 42 Triple-A innings) are indicative of a guy who can pitch in rough circumstances. This means he could succeed if he got a job.

KEVIN GALLAHER							ASTROS
A – Osceola							
W	L	SV	ERA	IP	H	BB	K	Ratio
7	7	0	3.80	135	132	57	93	1.400

Gallaher, 25, is 6-3, 190. In addition to his work in the FSL, he had a 2.63 ERA and 30 K's in 24 Double-A innings. He has a sinking fastball that hits the low 90s, a decent curve and is considered a quick study. He needs a changeup and is considered to be between half-a-year to a year away from a big-league job.

MARK GARDNER							ROYALS
W	L	SV	ERA	IP	H	BB	K	Ratio
4	6	0	6.19	91.2	92	36	54	1.396

Mark came over from the Montreal system in a package deal that included Tim Spehr going to the Expos. You might remember him from for a 1991 game in which he no-hit the Dodgers for nine innings, but gave up two hits in the tenth and lost.

Gardner didn't exactly have a smooth transition to the AL in '93. He began the season by giving up seven earned runs to the Twins. His next three starts were OK, but from the beginning of May until he went on the DL in July, Gardner went 2-4, while his ERA climbed a full run. After regaining his health, Gardner was assigned to Omaha where he finished the season.

Gardner's value has fallen considerably since 1990. Once considered a decent second-echelon starter, he is now just a spare part in the Kansas City rotation. He's 32 years old now and the strained shoulder he suffered in mid-season may be the harbinger of further health woes.

TOM GLAVINE							BRAVES
W	L	SV	ERA	IP	H	BB	K	Ratio
22	6	0	3.20	239.1	236	90	120	1.362

He was the lucky member of the Braves rotation. He had 28 quality starts and was 21-4 in them. In his eight other starts, he was just dreadful (1-2, 11.77 ERA in 32.1 IP), but he got bailed out with excellent run support. With average support, his record would have been closer to 19-10.

He started the season giving up 22 walks while fanning just seven. This probably scared the bejabbers out of a bunch of fans. His low K-rate is still a little bothersome, but his 113/68 K/W over his last 207.2 IP was pretty close to his career average.

This is not to demean his achievements, but he was definitely the No. 4 Braves starter in terms of last year's accomplishments and he was not really a Cy Young-caliber performer.

DWIGHT GOODEN							METS
W	L	SV	ERA	IP	H	BB	K	Ratio
12	15	0	3.45	208.2	188	61	149	1.193

Dwight looked a lot better in 1993. He obviously has lost some stuff, but his K-rate stabilized and his hits- and earned-runs-allowed totals dropped during a hitters' year. His team stank, so his won-lost record suffered, but he's still a good pitcher and he could still make it to the Hall of Fame if he can continue to nail down 12-15 wins a year.

Tom Gordon							Royals
W	L	SV	ERA	IP	H	BB	K	Ratio
12	6	1	3.58	155.2	125	77	143	1.298

Tom sat down this season and watched game films of himself from '89-'90 and regained control of his sharp-breaking curveball. When Hal McRae inserted him into the rotation in July, Gordon went 8-4, "flashing" the stuff that made him runner-up to Gregg Olson for the Rookie of the Year award.

Last year we had him at No. 4 on our sleeper list for right-handed starters. His '93 performance made us look psychic, but one had only to look at his career strikeout record to realize that he needed to make but a slight adjustment to excel. Gordon seemed to have turned the corner last year. Expect him to continue to improve on his gains next season.

Rick Gorecki							Dodgers
AA – San Antonio							
W	L	SV	ERA	IP	H	BB	K	Ratio
6	9	0	3.35	156	136	62	118	1.269

At 20 he's already got an average major league fastball and a curve compared to Blyleven's. This kid is pretty close to the very definition of a Grade-A starter.

Jeff Granger							Royals
A – Eugene							
W	L	SV	ERA	IP	H	BB	K	Ratio
3	3	0	3.00	36	28	10	56	1.056

Drafted out of Texas A&M in last year's amateur draft, Granger, 22, destroyed hitters in the Northwest League getting 14 punchouts per nine innings. This young lefty throws in the low 90s and scouts say he has three pitches that are ready for the show right now. There's no doubt about it folks, Granger has "the goods" to make it in the majors.

He got a brief tour of Kauffman Stadium and one inning's work as part of his contract, but he might need a full season in the minors just to get accustomed to the long season. But then again, Kansas City doesn't have a thing to lose by giving him a shot at the rotation in the spring.

Tyler Green							Phillies
AAA – Scranton/Wilkes-Barre							
W	L	SV	ERA	IP	H	BB	K	Ratio
6	10	0	3.95	118	102	43	87	1.229

Well, you've probably been hearing about this guy for ages now. He's still only 24 and he's pretty close to being ready to pitch for the Phillies. In the past, Green's problems have been his shoulder (probably due to his wild delivery), which has greatly hampered him in his three years as a Phillie, and a failed experiment as a closer (think starter 100 percent).

The Phillies brass swear up and down that his shoulder is 100 percent and all he has to do is get movement back on his 88-90 MPH fastball to be up with the big club.

He has an adequate changeup and, of course, there's his wicked knuckle-curve. If he can get major-league hitters to respect his heater, he'll carve 'em up with the change and the breaking-ball.

There are a lot of "ifs" and "ands" here, but Green has great ability.

Tommy Greene							Phillies
W	L	SV	ERA	IP	H	BB	K	Ratio
16	4	0	3.42	200	175	62	167	1.185

Mr. Greene bounced back hard in '93, pitching strongly in the spring and extending that into the regular season. The Advocate staff was extremely wary of him because of his injuries, but the vintage Tommy Greene heater (MIA in September '92) returned.

Greene was incredible during his first 10 starts, fashioning an 8-0 record and a 1.94 ERA. He was slowed in late July with a strain of his groin (Owww!), but came back late in the season and threw quality starts in four of his last six appearances.

He appears healthy. As long as he is, he'll win with his good stuff, excellent control and K-rate, and the incredible Phillies offense.

Jason Grimsley							Marlins
AAA – Charlotte							
W	L	SV	ERA	IP	H	BB	K	Ratio
6	6	0	3.39	135.1	138	49	102	1.382
W	L	SV	ERA	IP	H	BB	K	Ratio
3	4	0	5.31	42.1	52	20	27	1.701

Grimsley has always been plagued by a lack of control. That is, until last year.

He signed a minor-league contract with the Indians and was sent to Charlotte, where he spent most of the season. There, he averaged just a little over three walks per nine innings. The Indians were encouraged by the improvement and called him up in September, but Grimsley definitely didn't wow anybody in his six starts.

The improvement in Grimsley's control is illusory. He tossed 18 wild pitches in 135.1 innings while at Charlotte. Cleveland can expect the same wildness he has shown his entire career.

KEVIN GROSS — DODGERS

W	L	SV	ERA	IP	H	BB	K	Ratio
13	13	0	4.14	202.1	224	74	150	1.473

Gross's pitching line for 1993 is pretty much his average year. If you've seen one you've just about seen them all.

Gross will continue to find his way into the pitching rotation for the next several years, with someone else if not the Dodgers. Just don't expect more than he gave this year and everything should be all right.

EDDIE GUARDADO — TWINS

W	L	SV	ERA	IP	H	BB	K	Ratio
3	8	0	6.18	94.2	123	36	46	1.688

Despite appearances, Guardado is considered a fast worker who throws strikes. He has average pitches (fastball, slider, change), which is why his control is still good, but his K-rate is blech at the major league level.

But he made a big leap last year going from Double-A to the show. At 23, he has time to learn. He won't make a huge impact this year, but he's a scrapper and should improve.

BILL GULLICKSON — TIGERS

W	L	SV	ERA	IP	H	BB	K	Ratio
13	9	0	5.37	159.1	186	44	70	1.444

Detroit waited anxiously while Gullickson spent the first month of the season recovering from arthroscopy on his shoulder and knee.

He came back on May 10, but it took a lot longer than that for him to get going. He was, in fact, less than mediocre until August, when he went 6-0, keeping the Tigers in the race. But one month does not a season make.

Bill enjoyed a stunning 6.95 runs of support per game, which explains how he got 13 wins with a 5.37 ERA. If he'd pitched three more innings, he could've stolen the AL run-support crown from teammate Mike Moore.

The league slugged .496 off him; lefties alone slugged .554. He gave up 28 home runs, fourth highest in the league. He simply makes hitters salivate.

In *Baseball Weekly*, Gullickson was quoted, "If you look at my track record, I have had a bad game here and there." Yeah, and Stalin had his off-days, too.

Just like the rest of the Tiger staff, he may be a winner for them, but you don't want him.

JOSE GUZMAN — CUBS

W	L	SV	ERA	IP	H	BB	K	Ratio
12	10	0	4.34	191	188	74	163	1.372

More than five runs per game of support helped Guzman win 12 games despite the fact that his ERA was 4.34 and he allowed 25 home runs. He is ever-so-slightly better than a league average pitcher right now, but at 31, his skills will not get any better. In fact, they'll start deteriorating soon.

JUAN GUZMAN — BLUE JAYS

W	L	SV	ERA	IP	H	BB	K	Ratio
14	3	0	3.99	221	211	110	194	1.453

Guzman can certainly be overpowering, as evidenced by his 194 strikeouts in '93. But with 110 walks and 26 wild pitches, it's a miracle that the Jay's mascot, B.J. Bird, is still alive. Seriously, Guzman needs to draw a bead on the strike zone pretty soon if he's going to step into the role of ace in the Toronto rotation.

JOEY HAMILTON — PADRES

AAA – Las Vegas

W	L	SV	ERA	IP	H	BB	K	Ratio
3	2	0	4.40	47	49	22	33	1.511

The talented Hamilton was laid low by rotator-cuff tendinitis during the spring and lost the year to rehab.

When he's healthy he's got a good fastball, decent curve and excellent changeup. Joey's also had weight problems in the past, so a season of sitting around hasn't helped him much.

The Padres want him (*Baseball America* ranked him tops among San Diego prospects), so you should see him in the spring.

Chris Hammonds							Marlins
W	L	SV	ERA	IP	H	BB	K	Ratio
11	12	0	4.66	191	207	66	108	1.429

Hammond looks like he's one or two notches away from becoming a solid starter. His control is now above-average and his K-rate has improved every year. He has yet to demonstrate fully his fine ability to change speeds. That might be the final piece he fits into the puzzle this year. He's 28, so he's not going to be a perennial All-Star, but he could win 125 games before it's all over.

Mike Hamilton							Astros
AA – Jacksonville							
W	L	SV	ERA	IP	H	BB	K	Ratio
6	4	0	3.71	87.1	71	33	84	1.191

Hampton is 21 and a southpaw. This pup has a good fastball, a hard, tight-breaking curve (what them new-fangled folk call a gol-durn slider?!) and a decent changeup.

Hampton made the jump from Double-A to the majors last year and he pitched like his former Seattle teammates Converse and Cummings. That is to say, he pitched batting practice to the AL for 17 innings. Because of his youth, Double-A performance and control, we'd say for right now he's the best of the Mariner's three young guns.

This can change in the future (Converse has by far the best heat of the three), but chances are Hampton will be the best candidate for success this year. In other words, Houston got a nice young pitcher.

Chris Haney							Royals
W	L	SV	ERA	IP	H	BB	K	Ratio
9	9	0	6.02	124	141	53	65	1.565

Haney looked good pitching for Omaha early in the season. He went 6-1 and had a 2.27 ERA when he was called to the show. He was overmatched once he got up to the big time, though.

Chris allowed an opposition batting average of .282, a slugging average of .424, and let the enemy to got on base at a .356 clip.

Think about it. The entire AL looked like Will Clark when facing this guy.

His three starts in September were ghastly. He gave up 21 hits and 17 earned runs in only nine innings. Those three games caused his ERA to go from 4.78 to 6.02.

He's only 25 and, with a little luck and a lot of development, he could become a league-average pitcher in the future. His control started to come around in '93, and the fact that he's a lefty and relatively young will buy him a few more seasons to prove himself. But he should *not* be considered a super prospect.

Greg Hansell							Dodgers
AAA – Albuquerque							
W	L	SV	ERA	IP	H	BB	K	Ratio
5	10	0	6.93	101.1	131	60	60	1.885

Hansell was a disaster in Triple-A. He has a good fastball, but hasn't been able to work his breaking ball into the mix. How much of his problems were caused by Albuquerque's obscene favoring of hitters can only be guessed at. He's only 23, so he's still a prospect. He could be a part of L.A.'s future.

Erik Hanson							Reds
W	L	SV	ERA	IP	H	BB	K	Ratio
11	12	0	3.47	215	215	80	163	1.372

Erik started the season with a vengeance, reeling off 11 straight quality starts (22 QS overall). He credited some of his success to an improved changeup. He got a little weary and was hurt in the late going, but Hanson was one of the great comeback stories of the year.

He lost or got a no decision in 11 of his 22 quality starts; here's his line in those games:

W	L	ERA	IP	H	BB	K
0	3	2.51	71.2	70	18	69

With a 14-4 record in his decisions (an average performance for pitchers in their quality starts), he would have been 15-8. But there's often no justice. He even missed a shot at finishing at .500 for the year.

Insiders said that he relied too much on the curve, but if you had his curve, you'd rely on it too. He's a good bet to win 15+ games this year. He can win 20 if the Reds stay healthy.

Mike Harkey							Rockies
W	L	SV	ERA	IP	H	BB	K	Ratio
10	10	0	5.26	157.1	187	43	67	1.462

He's paid about as many dividends as a failed S&L. Although he sprained his surgically repaired knee in June and spent a couple weeks on the DL, the Cubs had to have been pleased that he held up as long as he did.

Don't let his 10 wins fool you. He was roughed up most of the season, but survived because his offense scored 5.43 runs a game to back him up. If his knee holds up this year, expect more of the same, because of Colorado's park.

PETE HARNISCH — ASTROS

W	L	SV	ERA	IP	H	BB	K	Ratio
16	9	0	2.96	217.2	171	79	185	1.149

Peter "Harnisch-ed" his fastball and hard slider last year, posting a killer season while the league's offense was climbing into the stratosphere.

He had a slump in the middle of the season, but threw four shutouts in his last 14 starts including these gems:

Date	IP	H	R	ER	BB	K	Game Score
7/10	9	1	0	0	3	10	92
8/14	9	3	0	0	3	12	90
9/17	9	1	0	0	1	7	91

In the '93 Advocate we told rotisserie owners, "(He) is real close to being a dominant starter. ...Trade for him before he duplicates (or surpasses) his 1991 season."

He performed as advertised and is solidly entrenched in the first echelon of NL starters.

GREG W. HARRIS — COLORADO

W	L	SV	ERA	IP	H	BB	K	Ratio
11	17	0	4.59	225.1	239	69	123	1.367

As many of you may know, Harris has an incredible curve – one of the best in the game. Greg was 10-9 with a 3.67 ERA in San Diego. He was 1-8 with a 6.50 ERA in Colorado. In addition his K/W ratio was 40/30 in Colorado! They say that a pitcher's curveball is much flatter at high altitude ... Need we say more? He's nothing until he's traded.

JAMES HARRIS — ANGELS

A – Boise

W	L	SV	ERA	IP	H	BB	K	Ratio
8	3	0	1.89	105	80	29	96	1.038

Harris is a 22-year-old kid who looks like he'll be a fast riser. At this level, the kid's gotta be a super-prospect for any word on him to get out. He's not garnered that label yet, but there are tons of kids who never do and end up starring in the bigs.

HILLY HATHAWAY — ANGELS

AAA – Vancouver

W	L	SV	ERA	IP	H	BB	K	Ratio
7	0	0	4.09	70.1	60	27	44	1.237

Vancouver is a pitchers' park compared to the rest of the PCL, but that's like being the friendliest axe-murderer on the cellblock.

What we're saying is that Hilly didn't look too bad. He's young, 24, and he throws a nice knuckle-curve. Thing is, he's been hurt a few times in the minors, and for us to call his speediest pitch a "fastball" would make us guilty of using ironic misnomer.

If he can adjust at the big-league level and display the incredible control he showed at Midland in 1992 (10 BB in 95.1 IP!), then he could do quite well. It may take him a bit of time to do so, so watch carefully in the spring.

GARY HAUGHT — ATHLETICS

A – Madison

W	L	SV	ERA	IP	H	BB	K	Ratio
7	1	0	2.58	83.2	62	29	75	1.088

For some reason he was haught, haught, haught in A-ball Madison but lost it when he moved to Modesto.

He had good K/W, a great record and ERA and Madison pitched him in relief to get a feel for his skills.

Modesto pitched him only in relief, and it really messed him up. Who knows whether it was him or the role? Either way, he's already 22, so we'll probably wait for him to produce in Double-A before we look at him as a serious candidate for a major-league staff.

RYAN HAWBLITZEL — ROCKIES

AAA – Colorado Springs

W	L	SV	ERA	IP	H	BB	K	Ratio
8	13	0	6.15	165.1	221	49	90	1.633

His control slipped a bit and his mediocre fastball wasn't getting by anyone in the PCL last year. Add the fact that Colorado Springs is a hitter's haven, and it pretty much explains Hawblitzel's year.

He has an excellent changeup and scouts think it would be even more effective if he added a few MPH on the old heater.

He threw a no-hitter for nine innings on July 27, but lost it 1-0 when he allowed two hits and a run in the tenth inning.

Hawblitzel is only 23, so he shouldn't be written off, but he'll have to prove he can handle pitching in Colorado Springs before he reaches Denver.

LaTroy Hawkins — Twins
A – Fort Wayne

W	L	SV	ERA	IP	H	BB	K	Ratio
15	5	0	2.06	157.1	110	41	179	.960

Wow! Hawkins simply blew away the Midwest League last year.

He has an 88 MPH fastball, a good curve, a decent slider and changeup and he clearly knows how to use them.

LaTroy is only 21 and has a 6-5, 195-pound frame, so he could develop more heat as he fills out. At this stage in his career, he's a mega-prospect.

Jimmy Haynes — Orioles
A – Frederick

W	L	SV	ERA	IP	H	BB	K	Ratio
12	8	0	3.03	172.1	139	61	174	1.161

Haynes, 21, is the most highly regarded of the Frederick Five, five Young Gun starters seen as the future of the O's. His heater checks in at 91 MPH. He has nice slow curve as well. This guy looks very nice.

Keith Heberling — Yankees
A – Greensboro

W	L	SV	ERA	IP	H	BB	K	Ratio
8	1	0	2.07	69.2	47	18	74	.933

Heberling was phenomenal in his A-ball starts, with an 11-2 record between Oneonta and Greensboro.

He's got great K-numbers and he showed darn good control. He looks even better because unlike most pitchers who throw this well, he's barely old enough to drink.

Heberling, 22, is a good long-term prospect who should lead the next wave of Yankee pitchers. When he gets to the bigs, veterans Sterling Hitchcock and Sam Militello will be able to school him in the basics.

Rick Helling — Rangers
AA – Tulsa

W	L	SV	ERA	IP	H	BB	K	Ratio
12	8	0	3.60	177.1	150	46	188	1.105

Helling, 23, has a decent fastball and a good hard slider, both of which helped him to the highest strikeout total in the Texas League since Sid Fernandez threw 209 in 1983. Not bad company!

He has excellent control, doesn't give up many hits and he's already torn up the Florida State and Texas leagues. He also has an excellent shot at making the starting rotation in Texas this year.

Daryl Henderson — Rangers
A – Charlotte

W	L	SV	ERA	IP	H	BB	K	Ratio
7	2	0	2.64	92	71	33	81	1.130

Daryl's a little unusual in that he pitches backwards, using the curveball to get strikes and the fastball as a tease. Whatever works!

Daryl is super-competitive and you can't argue with his success last year. He is a bit of a hot head and that may cause him problems, especially if hitters figure out his schtick.

But he's only 21 and will be moving up to Double-A this year.

Rod Henderson — Expos
A – West Palm Beach

W	L	SV	ERA	IP	H	BB	K	Ratio
12	7	0	2.90	143	110	44	127	1.077

The No. 1 prospect in the FSL, Henderson, 23, came back from a devastating car accident in 1992 and is now placed highly among the myriad of Expo pitching prospects.

Henderson throws in the 88-91 MPH range and mixes in an excellent slider that hits 85+ MPH. He also throws two other pitches for strikes, including a nice late-breaking curve. He threw harder before the accident, so it's possible he may regain some velocity.

He will probably start at Double-A, but could make the jump to the majors by year's end. He isn't as highly regarded as Eischen, but he looks pretty damn nice.

Rob Henkel — Red Sox
A – Lynchburg

W	L	SV	ERA	IP	H	BB	K	Ratio
8	7	0	4.29	113.1	120	27	96	1.297

Henkel had an excellent 3.6 K/W last year and showed a lot of stamina, completing seven out of his 18 starts.

He has decent control, but at this point, he's giving up too many hits. He's 23 and will probably start next year in Double-A.

Pat Hentgen							Blue Jays	
W	L	SV	ERA	IP	H	BB	K	Ratio
19	9	0	3.87	216.1	215	74	122	1.336

Early in the season, when the Blue Jays rotation suffered from lackluster performances, Hentgen stepped into the breach.

He didn't single-handedly carry the staff, but by the end of June he was 11-2, the best record of the lot. He got roughed up a little the rest of the way, but with 5.72 runs of support per game, he was still good enough to win 19 games for the world champs.

Gil Heredia							Expos	
W	L	SV	ERA	IP	H	BB	K	Ratio
4	2	2	3.92	57.1	66	14	40	1.395

Heredia's your typical off-speed, breaking-ball pitcher. He gives up tons of grounders – and many kilos of them scoot through holes in the infield.

He's 28 and he can be much better, but still, he could be much worse. With the wealth of pitching talent the 'Spos have, he could be one of those guys trapped in Ottawa all year.

Fernando Hernandez							Indians	
A – Rancho Cucamonga								
W	L	SV	ERA	IP	H	BB	K	Ratio
7	5	0	4.15	99.2	90	67	121	1.575

Hernandez was moved all over the lot last year, spending 51 kick-butt innings in Single-A Kinston, 7.2 gettin' butt kicked innings in Double-A Canton-Akron and finished off with a demotion to Rancho Cucamonga where his record was so-so and his K-rate was exceptional.

He'll be 23, so he should be right in line and spend most of '94 in Canton-Akron. He has a super-strong arm and his control isn't as bad as most youngsters who throw this hard. He's one of the better prospects out there.

Orel Hershiser							Dodgers	
W	L	SV	ERA	IP	H	BB	K	Ratio
12	14	0	3.59	215.2	201	72	141	1.266

It's doubtful that Hershiser will ever return to his 1988 form since he's never fully recovered from his shoulder surgery. In essence, he's a very good pitcher who's been rendered average by that incident.

He remains a pitcher that most teams would be happy to have pitch third or fourth. Teams such as the Brewers and Mets would be ecstatic to pitch him second in the rotation. Hershiser will never make a pitching staff the way a Clemens or Rijo does, but he is the glue that solidifies a decent rotation.

Greg Hibbard							Mariners	
W	L	SV	ERA	IP	H	BB	K	Ratio
15	11	0	3.96	191	209	47	82	1.340

Despite turning in a 15-win season, Hibbard should be considered a good candidate to flop in '94. His run support, which checked in at 4.76 runs per nine, played a huge role in his win total.

What, you think he won 15 games because of vastly improved stuff? Only half of his starts were quality performances. This is not surprising, since he averaged just a shade over six innings per start in '93, and surrendered a .446 slugging percentage.

He won't be of much use to the Mariners in a year or two, and they have some good young pitchers in their organization.

Ted Higuera							Brewers	
W	L	SV	ERA	IP	H	BB	K	Ratio
1	3	0	7.20	30	43	16	27	1.967

He's still got some strikes in him, but he should really be wearing a vendor's uniform if he's gonna hang around baseball stadiums.

Ken Hill							Expos	
W	L	SV	ERA	IP	H	BB	K	Ratio
9	7	0	3.23	183.2	163	74	90	1.377

What happened to those K's? Hill dropped from 6.2 K/9IP in 1992, to 4.4 in 1993. Possibly more significantly, his K/W dipped from 2/1 to 1.22/1.

He was on the DL with a strained groin (one of our personal favorite injuries) and five will get you 50, he was hurting all summer. In fact, his K/W after April was 67/62.

With the off-season to rest, Hill should come back strong in 1994. He's 28, so he shouldn't have lost anything off his excellent forkball, or his heat. As with many others, watch him carefully in the spring.

Ty Hill — Brewers

A – Stockton

W	L	SV	ERA	IP	H	BB	K	Ratio
1	3	1	4.50	66	43	60	65	1.561

You guessed it, Milwaukee found its thrill on Tyrone Hill.

He's got a good fastball and an excellent curve, but his key pitch is a circle change.

Despite an ugly ERA and poor control, Hill's strikeouts were right in line. He's pretty young at 22, so he has plenty of time to recover and make up the difference.

Hill's been hampered by tendinitis in the elbow and he missed much of last season with an ankle injury incurred in a basketball game.

The Brewers consider him a key prospect so expect him as soon he shows some mastery of the upper minor-league levels.

Eric Hillman — Mets

W	L	SV	ERA	IP	H	BB	K	Ratio
2	9	0	3.97	145	173	24	60	1.359

Hillman's a sinkerball specialist who gives up an enormous amount of hits. Sure the Mets have a porous infield, and a lot of those hits scooted through because of cruddy defense, but do you really need to find excuses to avoid this guy?!

Sterling Hitchcock — Yankees

AAA – Columbus

W	L	SV	ERA	IP	H	BB	K	Ratio
3	5	0	4.81	76.2	80	28	85	1.409
1	2	0	4.65	31	32	14	26	1.484

Between his Triple-A and major league innings, Hitchcock suffered a set-back season.

His strikeout totals remained devastating, but there was very little sign of his usual diminutive ERA.

While the condition is undoubtedly temporary and he remains one of the top prospects in baseball, it may have cost him some ground in the race for the rotation.

Chris Holt — Astros

A – Quad City

W	L	SV	ERA	IP	H	BB	K	Ratio
11	10	0	2.27	186.1	162	54	176	1.159

Holt's a 22-year-old kid with more than a modicum of pitching moxie. He'll be ticketed either for the Florida State League or Double-A Jackson this year. With his K-rate and control, it wouldn't be out of the question for him to get a trial with the Astros in the fall.

Mark Holzemer — Angels

AAA – Vancouver

W	L	SV	ERA	IP	H	BB	K	Ratio
9	6	0	4.82	145.2	158	70	80	1.565

Holzemer is kind of a wild-card. He's 24 (because he's an Angel, he's automatically a lefty) and has steadily climbed through the organization. His K/W ratio is nothing to get excited about, but the Angels are going to consider him for the rotation this year. We suspect his K/W will improve, but what he'll do in the majors is anyone's guess.

John Hope — Pirates

AA – Buffalo

W	L	SV	ERA	IP	H	BB	K	Ratio
9	4	0	4.37	111.1	123	29	66	1.365
0	2	0	4.03	38	47	8	8	1.447

Hope's been climbing up through the organization for a few years and it looks like the Pirates will give him a shot this season.

His tryout in the bigs last year was unremarkable, but the Pirates liked his effort in his seven starts.

John throws in the low 90s and gets plenty of K's, which is promising. But at 23, he still doesn't have good breaking stuff. You'll want to wait and see how he adjusts to the majors.

Rich Huisman — Astros

AAA – Phoenix

W	L	SV	ERA	IP	H	BB	K	Ratio
3	4	0	5.97	72.1	78	45	59	1.701

Huisman, 25, was someone we were reservedly high on last year. He's had a history of arm trouble (shoulder surgery last spring) and great success. He throws pretty hard and has a split-finger, a curve and a slider to complement the heat.

Rich had a terrible year in '93, but his career record is 38-20, with a 2.67 ERA and 543 strikeouts in 522 innings. He's a gamer, and, if he's healthy, he could be a stallion.

MARK HUTTON — YANKEES

AAA – Columbus

W	L	SV	ERA	IP	H	BB	K	Ratio
10	4	0	3.18	133	98	53	112	1.135

W	L	SV	ERA	IP	H	BB	K	Ratio
1	1	0	5.73	22	24	17	12	1.864

Of the young Yankee pitchers, Hutton, 24, has probably improved the most since last year.

He improved his slider and added a changeup to his 95 MPH fastball. It was enough to convince the Yanks to try him out with the mother club. His control should come into line given more seasoning.

Hutton is the first Aussie ever to start a MLB game. Let's hope there are more like him floating around the Great Barrier Reef.

BLAISE ILSLEY — CUBS

AAA – Iowa

W	L	SV	ERA	IP	H	BB	K	Ratio
12	7	4	3.94	134.2	147	32	78	1.329

Ilsley, 30, has been in the minors for nine seasons now. His stuff isn't very intimidating, and he gets hit hard. He's lost the prospect label and should be considered poison.

JASON ISRINGHAUSEN — METS

A – Pittsfield

W	L	SV	ERA	IP	H	BB	K	Ratio
7	4	0	3.29	90.1	68	28	104	1.063

His career certainly didn't get off to an asupicious beginning. After being drafted in the 44th round of the 1992 draft, he underwent surgery to remove bone chips in his elbow following his first season in the minors.

Undaunted, Isringhausen dominated the New York-Penn League, leading the circuit in strikeouts. This 21-year-old stands 6-3, and he has a loose, natural delivery that enables him to reach the mid-90s with his fastball. The Mets think that as he matures, he should be able to get a little more velocity on his heater. He also throws an above-average curveball that racks up a lot of strikeouts.

He'll probably be assigned to a full-season Single-A team coming out of spring training. The Mets will want to see if the can remain healthy. If he can, he will progress quickly.

DANNY JACKSON — PHILLIES

W	L	SV	ERA	IP	H	BB	K	Ratio
12	11	0	3.77	210.1	214	80	120	1.398

Jackson had a misleading season. He had 22 quality starts, two more than John Smoltz, but he finished only one game over .500. Jackson should have gone 16-8.

Jackson's hits-allowed rate continues to be kinda high, but he really improved his strike-out rate over 1992. With all his injuries, Jackson hasn't put that much mileage on his arm over the last few years. He's not a front-line pitcher, but as long as he's with the Phils, he's got a chance to win a lot of games.

KEVIN JARVIS — REDS

A – Winston-Salem

W	L	SV	ERA	IP	H	BB	K	Ratio
8	7	0	3.41	145	133	48	101	1.248

AA – Chattanooga

W	L	SV	ERA	IP	H	BB	K	Ratio
3	1	0	1.69	37.1	26	11	18	.991

Jarvis, 24, doesn't give up too many hits and gets his share of K's. His control needs improvement and that's kept him from boosting his win-loss percentage much over .500.

His tryout in Double-A last year seemed to give him new life; he'll get a chance to keep it going this year.

DOMINGO JEAN — ASTROS

AA – Albany

W	L	SV	ERA	IP	H	BB	K	Ratio
5	3	0	2.51	61	42	33	41	1.230

W	L	SV	ERA	IP	H	BB	K	Ratio
1	1	0	4.46	40.1	37	19	20	1.389

It was no surprise that the Yanks traded one of their young starters for a closer, it was only a question of who it would be.

After the trade, *Baseball America* rated him only the tenth best prospect on the Houston farm, citing his lack of pitches as their biggest concern. They further stated that in his present condition he was likely slated for relief work.

Apparently they missed his starts for New York, which were probably the deciding factor in the Astros picking him for trade. He's added a killer forkball to his already well-developed fastball and slider. Last time we checked, three good pitches is practically over-qualification for ML pitching.

MIGUEL JIMINEZ — ATHLETICS

W	L	SV	ERA	IP	H	BB	K	Ratio
1	0	0	4.00	27	27	16	13	1.593

Jimenez looks like he'll join colleagues Steve Karsay and Todd Van Poppel in the reconstruction of the A's staff.

He possesses a 92-95 MPH blower with great movement. He adds a hard slider and is working on a curve/change.

Jimenez attended Fordham, and was scheduled to join the FBI until the A's gave him a contract. We don't want to know what he's trained to do to base-stealers.

RANDY JOHNSON — MARINERS

W	L	SV	ERA	IP	H	BB	K	Ratio
19	8	1	3.24	255.1	185	99	308	1.112

He was on *Baseball Weekly's* 1994 potential breakthrough player list.

He already broke through last year! What is he going to do, go 27-3 with a 1.15 ERA?

Considering the jump in offense, his 1993 ERA is equivalent to a 2.95 ERA in 1992. Sure he could get better, but his performance level is about as impressive as any pitcher in the league, except Appier.

Johnson had 24 quality starts among his 35 appearances and even nailed down a save when Seattle's bullpen was ailing. And, for the first time in a full season, Randy walked less than 100 batters. He walked 99, but he's so tough to hit that his ratio (1.112) is Maddux or Clemens-like.

He also fired two of the most impressive starts of the season:

Date	IP	H	R	ER	BB	K	Game Score
5/16	9	1	0	0	3	14	96
9/21	9	3	0	0	1	11	91

Johnson was the second-best pitcher in the American League last year.

BOBBY JONES — METS

AAA – Norfolk

W	L	SV	ERA	IP	H	BB	K	Ratio
12	10	0	3.63	166	149	32	126	1.090

Bobby Jones is one of the top sleeper picks you'll find this year. He didn't pitch that well in the majors, but he has the potential to really be a gem within the next two years or so. He doesn't have exceptional stuff, but he throws four pitches for strikes and has excellent command. Go get 'em.

JEFF JUDEN — PHILLIES

AAA – Tucson

W	L	SV	ERA	IP	H	BB	K	Ratio
11	6	0	4.63	169	174	76	156	1.479

He's baaaack! The man Bill James once referred to as "Baby Huey" is again a viable prospect.

In the past, he worked too much on his breaking stuff – trying to finesse hitters. He topped this off by eating more donuts than a "Sweatin' to the Oldies" class on Fat Tuesday.

Last spring, he dropped his baby (Huey) fat, reported to camp in shape and threw almost as hard as he did when he was first signed (he's throwing in the 92-94 MPH range now).

With his trade from Houston to Philly, his role is in question. The Phils have a strong rotation and it might take him a few months to a year at Triple-A before something opens up.

But if things go right, Juden has forever junked his attempts to fit two men in a pair of Dockers and will stop pretending he's Charlie Leibrandt. That gives him some serious potential.

SCOTT KAMIENIECKI — YANKEES

W	L	SV	ERA	IP	H	BB	K	Ratio
10	7	1	4.08	154.1	163	59	72	1.439

Scott (we refuse to put ourselves out writing his last name) had a pretty mediocre year.

Couple this with his age and you have a guy who's gonna be bulldozed out of the starter role by the host of Yankee diaper dandies (apologies to Dick Vitale).

Scott, like several other Yankee starters, did some time in the 'pen last year (10 games) so he might have a chance of lasting for a year or two New York as a middle reliever.

SCOTT KARL — BREWERS

AA – El Paso

W	L	SV	ERA	IP	H	BB	K	Ratio
13	8	0	2.45	180	172	35	95	1.150

Karl's another Brewer pitching prospect who's got some actual talent.

Drafted out of University of Hawaii, Karl throws in the low 80s with a great change and a decent curve.

He's a control freak with a tendency to induce groundballs. May develop into a Jimmy Key type.

RYAN KARP — YANKEES

A – Greensboro

W	L	SV	ERA	IP	H	BB	K	Ratio
13	1	0	1.81	109.1	73	40	132	1.034

AA – Prince William

W	L	SV	ERA	IP	H	BB	K	Ratio
3	2	0	2.20	49	35	12	34	.959

Karp throws his heat in the low-90s and has a very good curve.

The Yankees know he can dominate the low minors, now they want to know if he's a top-notch prospect. This means he'll toil for at least a couple more years while they find out.

STEVE KARSAY — ATHLETICS

AA – Knoxville

W	L	SV	ERA	IP	H	BB	K	Ratio
8	4	0	3.38	104	98	32	100	1.250
0	0	0	4.04	49	49	16	33	1.327

Karsay was the excellent Blue Jays prospect who landed in Oakland via the Rickey Henderson trade.

His fastball averages around 92 MPH and peaks at 96-97. The beauty of his cheese was that it still showed up in later innings.

His curveball may be even more impressive. It's as impressive as Gregg Olson and Erik Hanson-type curves and when he throws it for strikes, watch out!

Karsay was ranked fourth among prospects in the Southern League by *Baseball America*. The A's only concern was some tendinitis he developed this season. He'll rebound and could eventually help the A's back atop the AL West. The Jays paid in more than money for this World Series ring.

KOREY KELING — ANGELS

A – Palm Springs

W	L	SV	ERA	IP	H	BB	K	Ratio
8	8	0	3.29	158.2	152	62	131	1.349

This guy is border-line/marginal/on-the-cusp, whatever you call some guy who's thumb-and-forefinger's distance from being thrown on the scrap heap. He's 25 and has to do some fast rising through the system. His performance at Palm Springs indicates he could survive at higher levels, but he has about 18 months to ensure he's a major-leaguer and not another Steve Fireovid.

JIMMY KEY — YANKEES

W	L	SV	ERA	IP	H	BB	K	Ratio
18	6	0	3.00	236.2	219	43	173	1.107

Key was simply one of the best pitchers in the AL last year, proving that a career of quality can overcome time. At an age when most pitchers are beginning to hit the wall, he was having a career year.

He showed the best control of his 10 seasons, and his 173 K's were a career high. His ERA was in the mid-2.00 range for much of the season and ended up at a very respectable three flat by the end.

Jimmy has always embodied solidity on the mound. He's not a power pitcher but he throws a lot of strikes with excellent control. Who would've expected him to be the better of the two pitchers Steinbrenner acquired over the winter of '93?

Key typically wins about 13-15 games a year, so there's no reason why he shouldn't perform at slightly below this level for the next few years. He's just young enough that he has a good chance at 200+ career wins.

DARRYL KILE — ASTROS

W	L	SV	ERA	IP	H	BB	K	Ratio
15	8	0	3.51	171.2	152	69	141	1.291

We said last year, "if he can throw strikes like he did in the second half, he could be one of the best in the league. He has low mileage on the arm and the type of pitches one needs to excel."

He cut his BB/9IP from 4.5 in 1992, to 3.6 in 1993 and improved his K/W ratio from a mediocre 1.43/1 to a very solid 2.04/1.

There's little else to say. If you've seen him when he's got good command of the curve, then you know why he threw a no-hitter last year. You also know why he's a threat to win 15-20 this year.

DARON KIRKREIT — INDIANS

A – Watertown

W	L	SV	ERA	IP	H	BB	K	Ratio
4	1	0	2.23	36.1	33	11	44	1.211

When it came time for the Indians to pick in the first round of the '93 amateur draft, they had little trouble choosing Daron Kirkreit. They wanted a durable, college pitcher that wasn't far removed from major-league action.

Kirkreit fits the bill perfectly, checking in at 6-6, 225 lbs and averaging 9.8 K/9 IP his last year in college.

Kirkreit, 21, used his hard sinking fastball and quality slider to chew up the NY-Penn League for seven late-season starts. He needs at least another full season of work on an off-speed pitch, but if things break well for Kirkreit and the Indians, he could be on the team charter to Cleveland in the spring of 1995 for the season opener.

RICK KRIVDA — ORIOLES

AA – Bowie

W	L	SV	ERA	IP	H	BB	K	Ratio
7	5	0	3.08	125.2	114	50	108	1.305

Krivda had the best curveball in the Eastern League last year, which helped him to an impressive 7.74 K/9IP.

He's not a power pitcher, but he has good control and doesn't give up too many hits. His 3.08 ERA last year was his highest ever; he usually comes in right around 3.00.

Rick's 24 and some time in Triple-A may still be in order. But he's a lefty and if Rhodes can't come back from his injury or he's traded, Krivda could get a shot.

MARK LANGSTON — ANGELS

W	L	SV	ERA	IP	H	BB	K	Ratio
16	11	0	3.20	256.1	220	85	196	1.190

He had an excellent year and his K-rate was quite stable despite the offensive increase in the AL. This makes him a safe '94 pick.

Mark made 23 quality starts, including 12 in his first 14 appearances. He went 14-4 in these starts with five no-decisions. From what we've seen among '93 starters, this is a pretty average record.

He wasn't unlucky or lucky, despite the fact he only got 3.54 runs of support per start. If you go through his starts, you'll see that his luck evened out. He lost some tough games, but he also got bailed out of some rotten performances that Ben Rivera wouldn't have signed for.

Langston started off like gangbusters, putting together a 9-1 record by June 19. He went 7-10 the rest of the way.

His real problems were due to a slump at the season's end. From September 3-23, Langston had a 6.68 ERA pasted on his forehead for 33.2 innings. This pushed his ERA from 2.65 to 3.22 and sent his hopes for a Cy Young or an ERA title into the chute.

He's still one of the best starters in the league, though, and should contend for the Cy in '94 if his offense is up to the task.

ANDY LARKIN — MARLINS

A – Elmira

W	L	SV	ERA	IP	H	BB	K	Ratio
5	7	0	2.97	88	74	23	89	1.102

Larkin, 20, throws a hard sinker and has a late-breaking curve that's considered unhittable at times. He's a rail-thin 6-4, 175, so you want him to add some pounds, but he's just a kid and the Marlins figure he's at least two years away. Keep an eye on him.

TIM LEARY — MARINERS

W	L	SV	ERA	IP	H	BB	K	Ratio
11	9	0	5.05	169.1	202	58	68	1.536

The true test of a contender is how many starts they give to 35-year-olds who deliver 13 quality starts in 33 appearances. If the Mariners are to move forward as a team, they have to have one or two of their kids take roles away from encrustations like Leary. If he gets 27 starts next year, the Mariners may not be in the hunt.

CHARLIE LEIBRANDT — RANGERS

W	L	SV	ERA	IP	H	BB	K	Ratio
9	10	0	4.55	150.1	169	45	89	1.716

Charlie's return to the AL started out rather well. In April and May he went 6-2 with a 2.52 ERA. But while Texas' management was congratulating themselves, the hitters were figuring him out. In June, they clubbed him for a 6.59 ERA. He should have quit there.

In August, he went down with tendinitis in the left shoulder. He came back, but landed on the DL again with the same injury. During this period, he went 0-3 with a 9.42 ERA.

His K/W still looks good and you can argue that he was going fine until the arm started hurting. But he really got knocked around last year. The league slugged .440, including 15 HRs and 40 doubles in 150.1 innings.

"Persistent tendonitis" is not a phrase you want to hear in connection with any 37-year-old pitcher. Talk to his doctor and get several second opinions before you consider him.

Mark Leiter — Tigers

W	L	SV	ERA	IP	H	BB	K	Ratio
6	6	0	4.72	106.2	111	44	70	1.453

The Tigers used Leiter as a starter more frequently as the season progressed. He was starting full-time when a sore right shoulder knocked him out in early August.

Most of Leiter's numbers were right at league averages, except for his 4.72 ERA. He gave up 10 home runs in 47 innings in Tiger Stadium, driving his ERA at home up to 4.98.

Considering Detroit's pitching glut, he'll probably get another shot at starting next year. If he can correct his problems at home and stay healthy, he could be a solid contributor.

Phil Leftwich — Angels

AAA – Vancouver

W	L	SV	ERA	IP	H	BB	K	Ratio
7	7	0	4.64	126	138	45	102	1.452

W	L	SV	ERA	IP	H	BB	K	Ratio
4	5	0	3.79	80.2	81	27	31	1.339

Last year, Paul Molitor said that because of Leftwich's name, he had practically beaten the Blue Jays before he took the mound.

Actually, Phil has a misnomer along the lines of Frank White (who, of course, was black), Bud Black (who, of course, is white) and Darryl Strawberry (who, of course, is a dingleberry): His name should be Rightwich.

He was doing absolutely awful in Triple-A, but according to *B.A.*, Matt Keough straightened him out and he went on a 5-1, 1.44 ERA run and was promoted.

Leftwich had eight quality starts in 12 appearances in the majors and is being penciled in as the No. 4 starter for the Angels rotation in '94. Well, at least that's what Buck Rodgers said in *B.A.*

Curt Leskanic — Rockies

AA – Wichita

W	L	SV	ERA	IP	H	BB	K	Ratio
3	2	0	3.45	44.1	37	17	42	1.218

He's 26, throws 93 MPH, and is a quirky, outgoing guy. Leskanic went 4-3, 4.47 in Colorado Springs, so there's a good chance he could be decent in Denver (the sequel to "Sleepless in Seattle"?). He might be a fine pickup for a weaker rotisserie team as he's got fine upward potential (stronger teams won't want to risk getting a Mile-High hurler, tho').

Jon Leiber — Pirates

A – Wilmington

W	L	SV	ERA	IP	H	BB	K	Ratio
9	3	0	2.67	114.2	125	9	89	1.169

AA – Carolina

W	L	SV	ERA	IP	H	BB	K	Ratio
4	2	0	3.97	34	39	10	28	1.441

Lieber was tearing up the Carolina League, so the Royals sent him up to Memphis and quickly traded him to the Pirates in the Belinda deal.

Jon's 24 and has pinpoint control and good motion on his 86 MPH fastball. He relies mostly on his slider and sinker. Those in the know say he needs a change.

But whatever he's got now was good enough for a phenomenal 9.9 K/W in Wilmington. He should get some time to prove he can throw the K's in Triple-A, but with the Pirates' starter situation, anything can happen.

Jose Lima — Tigers

AA – London

W	L	SV	ERA	IP	H	BB	K	Ratio
8	13	0	4.07	177	160	59	138	1.237

Lima was slowed by a case of the mumps in the beginning of his first season in Double-A last year and dropped 11 of his first 13 starts. He felt better in the second half, however, and won six out of his last eight.

His specialty is the circle change, which keeps his hits-allowed totals low and strikeouts high. He has a decent fastball as well, and isn't afraid to pitch inside.

Jose's 22 and his handlers say he is maturing well, both physically and mentally. He's considered a good prospect, despite the fact he's never had a winning record in four minor-league seasons.

Felipe Lira — Tigers

AA – London

W	L	SV	ERA	IP	H	BB	K	Ratio
10	4	0	3.38	152	157	39	122	1.289

AAA – Toledo

W	L	SV	ERA	IP	H	BB	K	Ratio
1	2	0	4.60	31.1	32	11	23	1.373

You have to like Lira's 3.1 K/W in London with 122 total K's, especially since he's only 22 years old. He has a sweet sinking fastball and excellent control.

His numbers dropped when he made the jump to Toledo, but he's adjusted well to each level as he's risen through the ranks. He'll get a shot to master Triple-A this year, but don't be surprised if he gets the call from Detroit midway through the season.

BRIAN LOONEY — EXPOS

A – West Palm Beach

W	L	SV	ERA	IP	H	BB	K	Ratio
4	6	0	3.14	106	108	29	109	1.292

AA – Harrisburg

W	L	SV	ERA	IP	H	BB	K	Ratio
3	2	0	2.38	56.2	36	17	76	0.935

Looney, 24, throws harder than Kirk Rueter, but is compared to him nonetheless. He has excellent control, changes speeds well and has an excellent K-rate. His Double-A performance was simply beautiful. If he can approximate that performance at the major-league level, then he's beautiful.

He broke his finger in a bar-room brawl during his stint in the AFL. He should be back to speed by spring training.

ALBIE LOPEZ — INDIANS

AA – Canton-Akron

W	L	SV	ERA	IP	H	BB	K	Ratio
9	4	0	3.11	110	79	47	80	1.145

Albie, 22, is a homely young pitcher with pretty ability. He throws hard and has several pitches, including decent breaking stuff. The Indians are looking at him as a possible rotation member in 1994. He made several starts at the big-league level, but was up and down. He could be a surprise this year because the only thing stopping him is his control.

LARRY LUEBBERS — CUBS

W	L	SV	ERA	IP	H	BB	K	Ratio
2	5	0	4.54	77.1	74	38	38	1.448

Luebbers is a finesse-type pitcher who has good action on his fastball, but little velocity. He's only 24 and the Reds thought his excellent mechanics would allow him to pick up some heat with time. He also uses a slider and changeup.

He doesn't mow anybody down; he just gets outs. Larry will be battling for a spot on the Cubs staff as the Reds traded him for Chuck McElroy.

GREG MADDUX — BRAVES

W	L	SV	ERA	IP	H	BB	K	Ratio
20	10	0	2.36	267	228	52	197	1.049

He had an absolutely incredible season. With decent luck, he could have finished with a 28-5 record!

Here's a 13-start sampler for you:

IP	H	BB	K	ERA
94.1	93	17	76	2.48

Guess what his record was in these starts. ... Give up? It was 0-7.

His hits-allowed rate in this stretch was pretty high, but how many people have ever had this kind of performance in their losses and no-decisions? With Clemens' relatively poor season, Maddux is now the best pitcher in the game.

MIKE MAGNANTE — ROYALS

AAA – Omaha

W	L	SV	ERA	IP	H	BB	K	Ratio
2	6	2	3.67	105.1	97	29	74	1.196

W	L	SV	ERA	IP	H	BB	K	Ratio
1	2	0	4.08	35.1	37	11	16	1.359

He doesn't overpower anyone and he doesn't have a lot of guile. But he does have a bachelor's degree in applied mathematics from UCLA. This is good, because in the baseball world, he's probably average at best.

JOE MAGRANE — ANGELS

W	L	SV	ERA	IP	H	BB	K	Ratio
11	12	0	4.66	164	175	58	62	1.421

Basically, Angels fans don't want to see Joe running out there and getting 30+ starts.

See Tim Leary.

PAT MAHOMES — TWINS

AAA – Portland

W	L	SV	ERA	IP	H	BB	K	Ratio
11	4	0	3.03	115.2	89	54	94	1.236

W	L	SV	ERA	IP	H	BB	K	Ratio
1	5	0	7.71	37.1	47	16	23	1.687

Mahomes, 23, has gotten a couple chances in the last two seasons to make an impression with the Twins, but his control collapses every time he gets the call.

Still, he was the No. 2 prospect in the PCL last year and everyone thinks he has the talent to make it. They love his stuff, but people are beginning to question the mental part of his game and his inner toughness. There's also some concern that he may have lost some velocity on his fastball.

That doesn't seem likely since he's only 23. There is a marked difference between his performance at Triple-A and the majors, however. You expect that in a young pitcher, but at some point, he has to start proving his worth.

Pat's got a lot of pressure on him this year. We're tempted to say he'll have a good year considering his minor-league career, but if the rumors about his attitude are true, he could easily be a huge bust.

DENNY MARTINEZ — INDIANS

W	L	SV	ERA	IP	H	BB	K	Ratio
15	9	0	3.85	224.2	211	64	138	1.224

There were a couple of stretches (April and August) where Denny was abysmal. If you remove those two months, he was 12-4 with a 3.17 ERA.

His K/W data and his average-allowed didn't rise inordinately. On the other hand, he allowed 27 homers after allowing only 12 the year before and for the first time he started getting lit up late in the game.

The thing is, it's hard to judge this individual at this time. He still fired 22 quality starts, and many aspects of his previously excellent game are intact. But then again, he's 39 and he's switching leagues. We would err on the side of caution and assume that at his age, there has been a loss of ability.

With the potent Cleveland team around him, though, he could quite well deliver the 12-15 wins asked of him.

PEDRO MARTINEZ — EXPOS

W	L	SV	ERA	IP	H	BB	K	Ratio
10	5	0	2.61	107	761	571	119	1.243

Pedro looked like the pitcher the Dodgers hoped he would be. He threw hard, he won a lot of games (albeit in long relief) and he's only 22. He was considered by many Dodger players to be the best pitcher on the staff.

So they traded him.

This seems unconscionable, unless you consider the other end of the trade... namely fleet-footed second baseman Delino DeShields.

Pedro might be good, or even great, but for how long? As hard as he throws, he happens to be built a lot like his brother (6-2, 155, to be exact). We all know the problems that the slender, elder Martinez has had with his arm.

The trade really doesn't make sense when the Expos say that they want Pedro as a starter. Considering the long line of prospects clogging their farm system it doesn't follow that they traded a fine, young 2B for a good pitcher with Purple Heart potential written all over him. We think L.A. stole one here.

RAMON MARTINEZ — DODGERS

W	L	SV	ERA	IP	H	BB	K	Ratio
10	12	0	3.44	211.2	202	104	127	1.446

The Dodgers seemed happy with Martinez's performance this year. Catcher Mike Piazza noticed increased velocity from Ramon and Lasorda concurred.

Of course, control flew right out the window as Ramon led the league with 104 walks in 211.2 innings. Since he allowed 202 hits he was left with a ratio of 1.446.

He'd better develop a 120 MPH beanball if he's gonna throw with that lack of accuracy.

DARRYL MAY — BRAVES

A – Macon

W	L	SV	ERA	IP	H	BB	K	Ratio
10	4	0	2.24	104.1	81	22	111	0.987

A – Durham

W	L	SV	ERA	IP	H	BB	K	Ratio
5	2	0	2.09	51.2	44	16	47	1.161

Darryl's a 22-year-old who's often compared to Tom Glavine. He doesn't have outstanding stuff, but has tons of moxie and changes speeds well. He'll probably need a year at Double-A before we can accurately place him among the Braves' prospects.

KIRK McCASKILL — ???

W	L	SV	ERA	IP	H	BB	K	Ratio
4	8	2	5.23	113.2	144	36	65	1.584

Kirk was toast by the midway point of the season and relegated to bullpen duty to make way for Bere and Ruffcorn.

In one way, Kirk's breakdown was partly responsible for the Sox' success in the West, forcing them to bring up pitchers who might not otherwise have surfaced until September.

Considering Kirk's performance in recent years (a far cry from his more productive seasons as an Angel) he'll be lucky indeed if he's hurling in the pros in 1994.

BEN McDONALD							ORIOLES
W	L	SV	ERA	IP	H	BB	K	Ratio
13	14	0	3.39	220.1	185	86	171	1.230

McDonald improved his game in every category last year, except won-lost percentage. Considering the O's offense was on the DL for most of the season, that's understandable.

Poor Ben just wasn't getting any help. Out of an impressive total of 20 quality starts, six ended up losses and three were no decisions. With decent luck, he would have been 16-10. Any pitcher with a 3.39 ERA averaging seven strikeouts a game deserves better.

His batting average allowed was only .228, good for fifth best in the AL. He's improved his ERA and strikeouts three years running and last year he cut his home-runs allowed in half. Even more importantly, he managed to stay healthy two years in a row.

He's a big gun who has proven he can pitch the innings and mow down the opposition. He's also one of about 15 guys in the AL who could lead the league in wins given decent run support.

JACK McDOWELL							WHITE SOX
W	L	SV	ERA	IP	H	BB	K	Ratio
22	10	0	3.37	256.2	261	69	158	1.286

It's never a popular task to dress-down the Cy Young winner (who remembers the year the obviously superior Clemens lost to the win-heavy Bob Welch?). So it is with heavy heart and sad pen that we discuss some of the strong points and many of the weak points in Black Jack's game.

No one can deny his competitiveness. He's a tall, lean yet imposing figure on the mound, who throws himself into every pitch. He's not an overwhelming power pitcher but he can sneak the ball past a lot of good batters. He also led right-handers with 13 pick-offs.

On the other hand (here we go), until '92 he'd had good years but never great ones. That year, he finally won 20 games and garnered some attention. Of his 34 starts last year, 21 were true quality starts and the rest were pretty much garbage. He routinely gives up anywhere from 4-6 runs and wins, leading the league this year in cheap wins with 10.

Peter Gammons, a big fan of McDowell as his ESPN commentary shows, cited Jack as the leader of the team, especially the pitching staff. Apparently pitching just well enough to win a quarter of the time and relying heavily on team offense are attributes of a good pitching role model. Gammons should've been pointing to the stunning season-ending finale by youngsters Alvarez and Bere as examples to follow.

Speaking of late-season, where was McDowell in the post-season? Oh yes, *Baseball America*'s Gerry Fraley points out that Jack was busy going 0-2 with a 10.00 ERA and a 2.300 ratio. Now that's a leadership performance for you. Alvarez, who was busy mowing down Blue Jay batters in his ALCS start, must not have been paying close enough attention. Word is that Jack was tipping his pitches during post-season and that's why the Jays socked his butt around the lot.

McDowell the person is another matter. He's not a big mouth, but he's not afraid to speak his mind.

In a Gammons' article McDowell is quoted as saying re: the Reinsdorf/Jordan retirement fiasco (which upstaged the Sox ALCS appearance) that, "Winning a world series is not a priority here."

Jack, among others, had enough class to invite veterans Terry Leach and Carlton Fisk into the locker room during post-season. The equally crass Sox management denied them entrance. Obviously they made the mistake of leaving their Scottie Pippen masks at home.

Evan: The Cy Young is a fragile award, and it irks us fans that the press traditionally weighs wins much more highly than categories which depend more on pitching expertise. When Bill Gullickson of the Tigers won 20 games in '91, there was actually talk of him as a candidate for the award. I'm sure the Sox fans would have swallowed that one.

Two pitchers were better than McDowell this year: Randy Johnson and Kevin Appier. If you leaf through this book and compare their stat lines in terms of ERA, ratio, K's and BA-allowed, the conclusion is inevitable that McDowell is gonna lose.

The back of the STATS, Inc. *Major League Handbook* says it all. Johnson allowed the fewest hits among AL pitchers as well as striking out the most men per nine innings. Appier led in least homers per nine innings, best average against right-handed batters and slugging allowed. This list continues.

Having said my piece, it's time to start gearing up for the Tigers' season. I'm sure this is Mike Moore's Cy Young year.

REY MENDOZA — MARLINS
A – Kane County

W	L	SV	ERA	IP	H	BB	K	Ratio
12	5	0	2.86	163.2	129	45	153	1.063

Rey is 23, so he's not top-flight, but Kane County is a fair ballpark, so his performance is a reasonable approximation of his ability against mid-level A-Ball competition. He should start the season in either high A, or Double-A. If he progresses quickly, he might be seen in the bigs by the end of the year. If not, he could get his chance in early 1995.

JOSE MESA — INDIANS

W	L	SV	ERA	IP	H	BB	K	Ratio
10	12	0	4.92	208.2	232	62	118	1.409

Mesa pitched 200 innings for the first time in his career last season, but considering the league hit .286 against him, the Indians could do without the help. There are about 150 pitchers in baseball right now who are better than Mesa, so cast your eye elsewhere.

SAM MITELLO — YANKEES
AAA – Columbus

W	L	SV	ERA	IP	H	BB	K	Ratio
1	3	0	5.73	33	36	20	39	1.697

Militello was tragically sidelined by a shoulder injury which put him out for the year. The weird part was that nobody could figure out what the source of his ailment was.

His curve, one of his strongest pitches, suffered most as he lost velocity, control and break. The Yanks are trusting that rest will cure his problems.

Militello appears to be making progress in rehab. There were no plans for him to work out strenuously this winter (i.e. no competitive starts) but he was slated to do some throwing to build his arm back up.

Sam was the Yanks' best short-term prospect and may be the best of the lot (including Brien Taylor). It'd be terrible if his shoulder caused him to be less than a fine hurler.

KURT MILLER — MARLINS
AAA – Edmonton

W	L	SV	ERA	IP	H	BB	K	Ratio
3	3	0	4.50	48	42	34	19	1.583

Miller, 21, has bounced around between Pittsburgh, Texas and Florida, but he's the goods. He has a fine fastball and an excellent curve that just needs to hit the strike zone occasionally.

His mechanics are considered beautiful, but the Rangers questioned his stamina and thought he wasn't developing fast enough.

The bottom line is this: The Rangers thought they were in the hunt last year and for a quick roll in the hay with long-reliever Cris Carpenter, they got rid of their best pitching prospect. If Miller has it in him, he'll prove this trade to be a major folly for Texas within two or three years. We're betting people – we're in rotisserie leagues – and our money's on the six-five kid with the golden arm.

NATE MINCHEY — RED SOX
AAA – Pawtucket

W	L	SV	ERA	IP	H	BB	K	Ratio
7	14	0	4.02	194.2	182	50	113	1.192

W	L	SV	ERA	IP	H	BB	K	Ratio
1	2	0	3.55	33	35	8	18	1.303

Minchey is yet another product of the Braves' farm system and looks like he could play a role in Boston's future. He's a control pitcher without a fastball, which hurt him in his tryout in the bigs last year.

But if he gets a tour around the AL to learn the hitters, he could be effective. He's 24, so he still has time. Plus, Darwin and Viola are getting up there in age so there will be room.

He won't remind anybody of Aaron Sele, but he may be starting regularly within a year or two, if he stays healthy.

Here's the (ticker) kicker. According to *Baseball America*, he has a heart ailment that could stand in his way. The diagnosis is 'atrial nodal tachycardia' which is a minor abnormality in the heart's electrical system. It's brought on by stress, but isn't considered life-threatening. It definitely sounds career-threatening, though.

ANGEL MIRANDA — BREWERS

W	L	SV	ERA	IP	H	BB	K	Ratio
4	5	0	3.30	120	100	52	88	1.267

Miranda was one of the best prospects the Brewers have had in ages. He threw in the 90s with an awesome screwball.

Of course, he wouldn't be a Brewer unless he was plagued by doom. His '93 performance was marred by a weak shoulder and he suffered a possible career-ending knee injury a month after the season ended. Even if he comes back, there's no telling what effect his health will have on his effectiveness.

It's a tough break for the Brews, but imagine how Miranda must feel.

LARRY MITCHELL — PHILLIES
A – Spartanburg

W	L	SV	ERA	IP	H	BB	K	Ratio
6	6	0	4.10	116	113	54	114	1.440

He has a good 92 MPH fastball, a hard curve and a solid changeup. Mitchell, 22, is rough around the edges, but is considered solid No. 2 starter material. If he progresses according to schedule, he'll be in Double-A by season's end.

DAVE MLICKI — INDIANS

W	L	SV	ERA	IP	H	BB	K	Ratio
0	0	0	3.38	13.1	11	6	7	1.298

He was all set to challenge for a spot in the Cleveland rotation when shoulder surgery effectively ended his season in late March. He came back for three meaningless no-decisions at the end of the season.

He's now throwing in the low 90s and he could have a chance for a spot in the rotation. He did have good strikeout totals before the surgery. But unless he conquered his control during his recovery, he could have difficulty adjusting to the majors and keeping the big boys from scoring on him.

MIKE MOORE — TIGERS

W	L	SV	ERA	IP	H	BB	K	Ratio
13	9	0	5.22	213.2	227	89	89	1.479

What can you say about a 34-year-old pitcher who leads the league with 35 home-runs allowed, posts a 5.22 ERA, a 1.48 ratio and still walks away with a winning record?

We guess you say he's a Tiger.

Sure, Tiger Stadium contributed to the HR total, but Mike didn't do much to help himself either. He led the team in hits-, runs-, earned-runs and walks-allowed. He averaged only 3.8 K/9IP; in fact, he threw as many walks as K's (89). He also led the AL in starts with 36, but managed only 14 quality outings. His 13 wins were largely due to the fact that he enjoyed the highest run support (6.32/9IP) in the AL.

Moore gave up 3 HR to Carlos Baerga in a game on June 1, but Detroit out-homered Baerga 5-3 and won the game 9-5. Dan Gladden said, "I think Baerga ought to send Moore part of his All-Star Bonus." If that's the case, Moore would be richer than Malcolm Forbes with all the checks he'd be receiving from guys he turned into AL Players of the Week.

To be fair, he did heat up in August, going 4-1 with a 2.45 ERA, and helped prolong the Tigers' pennant hopes. But where else could his stats translate to a winning season? He'll be back this year; avoid him like the plague.

MIKE MORGAN — CUBS

W	L	SV	ERA	IP	H	BB	K	Ratio
10	15	0	4.03	207.2	206	74	111	1.348

Morgan has a .500 record over the past five years and a respectable 3.14 ERA over that span. But his mediocre 1993 season might be the beginning of the end for this Cub.

He's 34 years old and has over 1800 innings on the old slingshot, which means he might start breaking down. If he does stay healthy, expect his performance to balance out somewhere between his '92 and '93 stats.

ALVIN MORMAN — ASTROS
AA – Jackson

W	L	SV	ERA	IP	H	BB	K	Ratio
8	2	0	2.96	97.1	77	28	101	1.079

Alvin, the No. 8 prospect in the Texas League, is a 25-year-old monster. He has a very good curveball and throws two heaters, a four-seamer (which can hit 94 MPH) and a two-seamer. The Astros aren't sure what he'll do in the majors (start or relieve). They say he'll be ticketed for the bullpen this year.

A strained rotator cuff kept his innings down last year, but he's a beauty.

JACK MORRIS — BLUE JAYS

W	L	SV	ERA	IP	H	BB	K	Ratio
7	12	0	6.19	152.2	189	65	103	1.664

The Blue Jays paid 5.425 million dollars for this??!! It was the most expensive fertilizer job ever spread on artificial turf.

Morris went down May 8 with a rupture of the anterior cruciate ligament in his ERA (but the Jays misdiagnosed this as a sore shoulder). He also missed the last three weeks of the season with a torn ligament in his pitching elbow. Between injuries, he was pretty rotten.

Jack's career has wound down about as far as it will go. He might surface with a pitching-poor club in '94, but what he has to offer, no team needs.

JAMIE MOYER — ORIOLES

W	L	SV	ERA	IP	H	BB	K	Ratio
12	9	0	3.43	152	154	38	90	1.263

Moyer made it back to the bigs in May and didn't disappoint. After an 0-3 start, he went on a 10-3 tear from June through August.

Jamie threw a lot of quality starts (16 out of 25 possible), but like his buddy Ben McDonald, he didn't get much support.

His 3.43 ERA was his best ever and he showed good control, throwing only 38 walks compared to 90 K's. His K-rate of 5.3/9IP is OK, but he's never been a strikeout pitcher.

The big question mark from last year was the number of hits he allowed (154 in 152 innings). Fortunately, most were singles and he kept his slug-allowed down to .376.

Also, home runs and walks hurt him in Camden Yards, pushing his ERA at home over two runs higher than on the road.

Moyer will be 31 next year and he's been inconsistent throughout his career. He may be able to keep his ERA at manageable levels and remain valuable, but he'll never be more than a No. 3 or 4 starter.

TERRY MULHOLLAND — PHILLIES

W	L	SV	ERA	IP	H	BB	K	Ratio
12	9	0	3.25	191	177	40	116	1.136

Terry was sidelined in early September after he hurt his hip flexor when his spikes caught on the bullpen mound during his warm-ups. Despite missing six or seven starts, Mulholland continued to pitch at his very solid level.

He only won 12 games for the National League pennant winner, but he lost a lot of tough decisions and went 1-2 in his last eight quality starts. He's still the same pitcher he was last year, which makes him one of the better starters in the league.

OSCAR MUNOZ — TWINS

AA – Nashville

W	L	SV	ERA	IP	H	BB	K	Ratio
11	4	0	3.08	131.2	123	51	139	1.322

AAA – Portland

W	L	SV	ERA	IP	H	BB	K	Ratio
2	2	0	4.31	31.1	29	17	29	1.468

Munoz, 24, was a terror for two seasons in Single-A, sporting 1.50-2.50 ERAs and 3.1K/W ratios. He's been slower adjusting to Double- and Triple-A, but he has improved with experience.

He averaged 9.5 K/9IP in Double-A last year and was getting his share in his brief appearance in Triple-A. Look for him to cut down on his baserunners and excel in Portland this year.

MATT MURRAY — BRAVES

A – Macon

W	L	SV	ERA	IP	H	BB	K	Ratio
7	3	0	1.83	83.2	70	27	77	1.159

Arm woes derailed this 23-year-old, but he stayed healthy and rebounded in 1993, impressing everyone who saw him pitch. Like his teammate at Macon, Darrell May, he needs to pitch for another year and we can place him properly.

MIKE MUSSINA — ORIOLES

W	L	SV	ERA	IP	H	BB	K	Ratio
14	6	0	4.46	167.2	163	44	117	1.235

The Orioles maintained that Mussina was not hurt in the June 6 Wrestlemania with Seattle, but the numbers tell a different story.

Up to and including that start, Mike was 8-2 with a 2.86 ERA.

In his next seven starts, he got through the seventh inning once and compiled a dismal 8.50 ERA. He finally went on the DL on July 22 with an inflamed muscle under his right shoulder blade.

Mike was reactivated in late August, but the injury nagged him the rest of the season, limiting him to only six more starts (although he went 3-2).

We suspect that Mike's season may have been hexed as early as May 16. After he threw 14 strikeouts in a 3-2 win against the Tigers, Sparky gave him the kiss-of-death by calling him the best pitcher in the league.

"He's the boss," the Sparkster proclaimed.

The fact that the then-24-year-old Mussina threw 141 pitches in the game probably didn't help either. One hopes that Johnny Oates will not work his young starter so hard.

Mussina's final record of 14-6 is nothing to sneeze at, but he is certainly capable of much more. With a sound shoulder, he has 20-win potential and could record 180-200 K's.

If he refrains from throwing at Mariners, he should reclaim his status as one of the premier pitchers in the AL and Cito 'Nepotism' Gaston will have to pitch him in the All-Star game.

JEFF MUTIS								MARLINS
W	L	SV	ERA	IP	H	BB	K	Ratio
3	6	0	5.78	81	93	33	29	1.556

The pitching-rich Indians tried to sneak him through waivers, and the Marlins snatched him up. Mutis, 27, started the '93 season in the Cleveland rotation, but was optioned to the minors on April 30 due to ineffectiveness. He went 6-0 with a 2.62 ERA for Charlotte before being called back up in July.

Despite solid numbers in the minors, Mutis has never been able to put it together in the show. He has decent control and he changes speeds well. The one thing he lacks, though, is that one quality strikeout pitch. He may help the Marlins this season, but he doesn't have much star potential.

DAVE MYSEL								TIGERS
A – Fayetteville								
W	L	SV	ERA	IP	H	BB	K	Ratio
5	2	0	2.61	72.1	69	16	46	1.175
A – Lakeland								
W	L	SV	ERA	IP	H	BB	K	Ratio
4	5	0	3.60	70	59	28	46	1.243

He's considered the hardest thrower in the Tiger system. This keeps his hits down, but it doesn't translate to as many K's as you'd like.

Still, he has good control and always comes in with a low ERA. Dave's 23 and he's still a couple years away, but he should be moving up next year.

CHRIS NABHOLZ								EXPOS
W	L	SV	ERA	IP	H	BB	K	Ratio
9	8	0	4.09	116.2	100	63	74	1.397

Chris got royally screwed up last year and it took half the season before he got straightened out. Part of his problem was definitely mechanical. He couldn't settle on a consistent delivery and his constant tinkering really gave him control problems. His strikeout rate didn't drop significantly, but his walks increased by over 40 percent.

He's 27 now, so he's at his peak. Nabholz can still be a consistent 15-game winner, but he's gotta stop futzing around and get in gear.

CHARLES NAGY								INDIANS
W	L	SV	ERA	IP	H	BB	K	Ratio
2	6	0	6.29	48.2	66	13	30	1.623

Surgery to "clean out" his shoulder ended his season in June, and there haven't been many reports over the winter about his recovery. But if he's healthy, we think he'll regain his status as one of the top pitchers in the AL.

Watch him close in spring. If the sinking fastball still has velocity and bite, he could lead the hapless Indians to their first division title since 1954.

JAIME NAVARRO								BREWERS
W	L	SV	ERA	IP	H	BB	K	Ratio
11	12	0	5.33	214.1	254	73	114	1.526

After bestowing praise on Jaime last year, he proceeded to let us down in big fashion.

He pitched 31.2 less innings and gave up 30 more hits. That's a big swing in the wrong direction.

As a result, Navarro led the league in earned runs with 127. A minor note, he also led the league in sacrifice-hits allowed for the second straight year.

The Brewers were really looking to Jaime to fill the gap left by Bosio's departure and the ace role didn't suit him. If Eldred steps in, as he should, perhaps the comfort of the two-spot will bring Navarro up to snuff.

ROBB NEN								MARLINS
W	L	SV	ERA	IP	H	BB	K	Ratio
2	1	0	6.75	56	63	46	39	1.946

Nen is your typical 24-year-old 97 MPH Steve Dalkowski/Nolan Ryan-type flameballer. ... With more emphasis on Dalkowski (who never made it out of the minors because he was wilder than an unfed tigress in a petting zoo).

Nen has as much control over his heater as a water buffalo does over the world's oil sup-

Starting Pitchers – 167

ply. When you look up "pitching project" in the dictionary, you'll see Robb's smilin' face sayin', "Right back atcha, babe!"

DAVID NIED							ROCKIES
W	L	SV	ERA	IP	H	BB	K	Ratio
5	9	0	5.17	87	99	42	46	1.621

In all probability, he was pitching hurt for most of last year. He spent the majority of the season sidelined with arm trouble and spent his active time getting rocked on the road. His road ERA was 6.86, home it was 3.60. Also, there was the baggage of being the No. 1 pick in the expansion draft and the carry-on pressure requisite with the position. He's a fine pitcher and could shine this year, but hey, he's in Colorado and we all know what that means.

RAFAEL NOVOA							CUBS
AAA – New Orleans							
W	L	SV	ERA	IP	H	BB	K	Ratio
10	5	0	3.42	113	105	38	74	1.266
W	L	SV	ERA	IP	H	BB	K	Ratio
0	3	0	4.50	56	58	22	17	1.429

Novoa is a talented package who came over to Milwaukee from the Giants' fold in 1992.

He doesn't possess blinding talent, but he's solid in terms of keeping men off the bases and he's young enough (26) to improve.

The Brewers could do much worse, so they promptly traded him for Bob Scanlan. While Scanlan may provide badly needed bad relief, he won't be worth a hill of beans if no one pitches well enough to need a save.

CHAD OGEA							INDIANS
AAA – Charlotte							
W	L	SV	ERA	IP	H	BB	K	Ratio
13	8	0	3.81	181.2	169	54	135	1.228

He got off to a slow start, but Ogea, 23, came on strong in the second half of the season to solidify his status as one of the top pitching prospects in the system. Coaches like his stuff, but they invariably point to his composure on the mound and knack for finding weaknesses in hitters as his keys to success.

After witnessing Embree and Mlicki go down with season-ending injuries, the Indians had to be pleased with Ogea's progress. Cleveland will give him a long look in the spring, and there's a good chance that he will break camp as their fourth or fifth starter.

BOBBY OJEDA							INDIANS
W	L	SV	ERA	IP	H	BB	K	Ratio
2	1	0	4.40	43	48	21	27	1.605

No matter what you think of his abilities, you've got to respect the guy for coming back from such a life-altering tragedy. The reports of his long and emotional recovery, his flight on an overseas jet, his thoughts of suicide, had baseball fans everywhere offering up prayers.

His first appearance of the season, shaky as it was, was testament to his character and his will to overcome grief. Whatever he does on the mound from now on won't matter one iota. He's a baseball hero and pretty darned deserving of the honor, too.

DONOVAN OSBORNE							CARDINALS
W	L	SV	ERA	IP	H	BB	K	Ratio
10	7	0	3.76	155.2	153	47	83	1.285

Osborne followed up on his exceptional rookie season with a 10-7, 3.76 performance in '93. It was quite comparable with what he did the previous year, and helped solidify his position as one of the better young pitchers in the league.

The strides that Osborne took in '93 might appear insignificant until one considers the environment he was pitching in. In an expansion season that saw ERAs skyrocket, he kept his at a stable 3.76. He also went from giving up 9.7 hits per nine innings in '92 to 8.85 per nine last year, exactly the kind of improvement one looks for in a developing pitcher.

Due to inflammation in his left shoulder, the Cardinals shut Osborne down for the last month of the season. Now, he's shut down for the year with a complete tear of his rotator-cuff. His career is in serious jeopardy.

GAVIN OSTEEN							ATHLETICS
AA – Huntsville							
W	L	SV	ERA	IP	H	BB	K	Ratio
7	3	0	2.30	70.1	56	25	46	1.152
AAA – Tacoma							
W	L	SV	ERA	IP	H	BB	K	Ratio
7	7	0	5.08	83.1	89	31	46	1.440

Gavin's the son of Claude Osteen. He throws a cut fastball, two-four seamer and can hit 87 MPH on the gun. His breaking stuff is good, so the A's have themselves another viable prospect. Hallelujah!

JOSE PARRA							DODGERS

AA – San Antonio

W	L	SV	ERA	IP	H	BB	K	Ratio
1	8	0	3.15	111.1	103	12	87	1.033

Parra was the hard luck kid in '93, and if people in your fantasy league weed out pitching prospects by wading through records, this guy will slip through the cracks.

Pitching in Double-A San Antonio at the ripe old age of 20, Parra's record and ERA weren't in line with his other numbers, which take the breath away.

His strikeouts were good, but it was his control (1.033 ratio!) that was most impressive. Parra should be able to increase his K's as his arm grows stronger, which is a pretty scary thought.

He would usually be a long-term prospect, but he could be up full-time by '95 if he continues to progress at this rate.

ROGER PAVLIK							RANGERS

W	L	SV	ERA	IP	H	BB	K	Ratio
12	6	0	3.41	166.1	151	80	131	1.389

Pavlik was rescued from Oklahoma City in May when Craig Lefferts went on the DL. He started out all right, but didn't really heat up until August. In his last 12 starts, he was 6-1 with a 2.18 ERA.

All in all, he posted the best numbers of his career last year; 12 wins, 166.1 innings, 18 QS/26 starts (69 percent), 131 K's. He averaged 7.1 K/9IP, which you definitely like to see in a youngster.

However, he gave up 80 walks, which you definitely don't. He doesn't allow a lot of hits, but the walks really hurt him. He also gives up a few long balls, 18 HR in '93, .97 HR/9IP.

Nonetheless, Pavlik has shown improvement over the last two years. He's earned a spot on the Texas rotation and will have the chance to work on his control.

MELIDO PEREZ							YANKEES

W	L	SV	ERA	IP	H	BB	K	Ratio
6	14	0	5.19	163	173	64	148	1.454

Melido's another one of those pitchers who's perennially expected to have an explosive year but never does.

In '92 his problem was run support from the Yanks, this year it was nagging injuries which limited his innings.

Perez retained his strikeout prowess, but he'll always have that going for him. We think it would be nice if he'd complement that with a winning record.

Perez is worth taking a chance on every season just because he's a power pitcher. Another year like this, though, and the Yanks will have him shopping for a new home.

HIPOLITO PICHARDO							ROYALS

W	L	SV	ERA	IP	H	BB	K	Ratio
7	8	0	4.04	165	183	53	70	1.430

Last year, we said that the jury was still out on Pichardo. Well, based on his '93 performance (which included a two-week stint on the DL), the jury came back and convicted him on all counts.

The league hit .282 off Hipolito, while averaging almost 10 hits per nine innings in his starts. Pichardo gave up nearly twice as many ground balls as fly balls, which may partially absolve him for the way the league hit him last season.

However, until he quits serving up sweet-spot souffles and the Royals switch to natural turf in '95, his rotation spot is in jeopardy.

JIM PITTSLEY							ROYALS

A – Rockford

W	L	SV	ERA	IP	H	BB	K	Ratio
5	5	0	4.26	80.1	76	32	87	1.345

Pittsley, 20, looked pretty good in his first season of professional baseball. His 9.8 strikeouts per nine innings confirmed what the Royals scouts have been saying about him; that he has a major-league average fastball, a decent curve and changeup, and excellent mechanics.

He pulled a back muscle mid-way through the season, so he didn't have a chance to advance past single-A Rockford. But he is healthy now and will report to spring training with a chance to pitch himself into Double-A Omaha's rotation. Keep an eagle eye on him. Pittsley could burst onto the scene rapidly.

MARK PORTUGAL							GIANTS

W	L	SV	ERA	IP	H	BB	K	Ratio
18	4	0	2.77	208	194	77	131	1.303

Dave: I guess I should take back what I said last year: "Even if he's healthy, he's nothing special."

If you go 12-0 to close out the season and bang out 26 quality starts in 33 games, you're pretty special. In addition, Portugal didn't allow more than five runs or four earned runs in any of his starts.

I don't like him as much as some other NL starters because his stuff isn't that great and I'm a big advocate of guys with good fastballs.

Portugal doesn't have a good health record and he doesn't work many innings.

Barring that, he's the best guy on the staff in terms of keeping the ball in the park (10 HR-allowed in '93) and there's little reason he can't continue to be successful this year.

JAY POWELL — ORIOLES

A – Albany

W	L	SV	ERA	IP	H	BB	K	Ratio
0	2	0	4.55	27.2	29	13	29	1.518

Baltimore took Powell with the 20th pick from Mississippi State last year. He's 22 and throws a 95 MPH blower.

With Olson and Pennington in the way, Jay will probably be groomed as a starter. That may change if Olson and the O's part ways this year, however.

ROSS POWELL — REDS

AAA – Indianapolis

W	L	SV	ERA	IP	H	BB	K	Ratio
10	10	0	4.11	179.2	159	71	133	1.280

Ross is fairly unremarkable and has been for most of his minor league career. He's a 26-year-old lefty, though, and that alone may earn him a spot if the Reds get in a jam.

He doesn't give up many hits, but the walks have always hurt him.

TIM PUGH — REDS

W	L	SV	ERA	IP	H	BB	K	Ratio
10	15	0	5.26	164.1	200	59	94	1.576

Pugh did not have a spectacular rookie season in the majors, but he doesn't belong on the scrap heap, either.

He gave up too many hits last year and posted a 1.576 ratio, which lead to several early departures and a lousy 5.26 ERA.

But he also put together a few impressive outings, including his final start on September 29 against the Padres.

Date	IP	H	R	ER	BB	K	Game Score
9/29	9	1	0	0	4	4	85

His K-rate of 5.2/9IP was decent for a rookie and you can usually expect a young pitcher's K's to increase. He has a lot of pitches to draw from; sinker, slider, change and a slip pitch which is basically a palm ball.

Pugh needs to work on his control and cut down on his baserunners. He has a tendency to overthrow his sinkers, producing non-sinking meatballs. He also tires easily and gives up a lot of hits after throwing 75 pitches.

If he can gain stamina, he might make a decent No. 3 or 4 starter. With better control, he could be used in long relief. Tim doesn't look like he'll ever be a world-beater, but with time, he could provide some quality innings.

BILL PULSIPHER — METS

A – St. Lucie

W	L	SV	ERA	IP	H	BB	K	Ratio
7	3	0	2.24	96	63	39	102	1.063

A fiery 20-year-old lefty with an excellent fastball, an excellent curve and an improving change. Bill made great strides with control in '93, but must temper his temper. He punched a picture frame last year and cut a tendon in his index finger. He came back and pitched to Florida State League hitters like they were picture frames, punching them out (this time without sustaining injury). Considered the best arm in FSL last year, he was the No. 3 prospect. He's flown through the system and could be in a Mets uniform between late 1994 and early 1996.

PAT RAPP — MARLINS

AAA – Edmonton

W	L	SV	ERA	IP	H	BB	K	Ratio
8	3	0	3.43	107.2	89	34	93	1.142

No, he didn't sing backup for Sir Mixx-a-Lot on "Baby's Got Back" and he doesn't tour with "2-Live Crew." He just blows his 95 MPH fastball past hitters in the PCL, a league where a 3.43 ERA means you're the new sheriff in town.

Rapp is 26 and they say his breaking stuff isn't that good. Who cares? His change is more than adequate and his performance in the PCL meatgrinder probably means he's ready to excel with what "little" he's got.

This man could really explode on the NL next year, so watch him with extreme care.

SHANE REYNOLDS — ASTROS
AAA – Tucson

W	L	SV	ERA	IP	H	BB	K	Ratio
10	6	0	3.62	139.1	147	21	106	1.206

He needs a major-league job now. He's 26 and it's awfully hard to pitch any better than this at the PCL level. He's got the stuff, he's got the command. According to talk in the off-season, look for Reynolds to become a long-reliever this year.

ARTHUR RHODES — ORIOLES

W	L	SV	ERA	IP	H	BB	K	Ratio
5	6	0	6.51	85.2	91	49	49	1.634

Everybody was expecting big things out of Rhodes last year, but arthroscopic knee surgery in May knocked him out until August. He never got it going after his return, either.

His K/9IP fell from 7.35 to 5.15 between '92 and '93, and that should be a concern. However, much of that has to be due to the injury and, at 24, he should bounce back.

Art still has a sweet fastball and curve. He could be ready for a breakthrough season.

DANA RIDENOUR — ROCKIES
AAA – Colorado Springs

W	L	SV	ERA	IP	H	BB	K	Ratio
8	8	0	5.21	121	156	58	105	1.769

You might see him on the ML roster this year, but he wouldn't have any business being there. He's 28 and has seen eight long years come and go in the minors without a taste of the big leagues. Two words, "No Prospect!"

JOSE RIJO — REDS

W	L	SV	ERA	IP	H	BB	K	Ratio
14	9	0	2.48	257.1	218	62	227	1.088

Everything you need to know about Rijo was explained in last year's issue. ... Oh, yeah, he's the guy we heinously omitted.

Well, this time we can tell you Jose was probably the unluckiest pitcher in baseball. Despite leading the NL in K's with 227 and lowering his ERA to 2.48, he ended up with a merely above-average record of 14-9. He threw a remarkable 28 quality starts (for reference, Maddux threw 29) and had a 13-6 record in those games, with nine no-decisions. With average support, Jose would've gone 18-9.

He started out pitching well enough, but the real story of his season came in the second half. In his first 11 starts after the All-Star break, he went 7-2 with 1.25 ERA, and averaged over a strikeout per inning.

He only had one poor outing in the second half, giving up 5 earned runs to the Dodgers on 9/20. Apparently, this upset him. In his next start, he threw a complete game, 1-hit shutout *in Colorado* on September 25.

Date	IP	H	R	ER	BB	K	Game Score
9/25	9	1	0	0	0	8	93

Still, without run support, he only went 8-3 in his 15 quality starts in the second half.

Jose's a tough fireballer who gets even tougher in the clutch. He allowed only a .188 batting average with runners in scoring position, getting 58 K's against 202 batters.

Plus, he rubs snake oil on his arm before and after he pitches, so he's got that going for him. He says it's a great anti-inflammatory. Maybe Jose Canseco should've used some.

If the Reds can stay healthy next year, Rijo's won-lost log could explode. A 25-win season is possible, but the only question is can Jose pile up 250+ innings again. Until 1993, he'd never pitched more than 211 innings.

BEN RIVERA — PHILLIES

W	L	SV	ERA	IP	H	BB	K	Ratio
13	9	0	5.02	163	175	85	123	1.595

Ben has good stuff and pitched well at times, but he was a lucky sonuvabuck in '93. He only had 11 QS in 28 appearances, but was an amazing 5-7 in his non-quality starts.

Basically, he pitched like crap in the majority of his starts, but was bailed out by his excellent offense. Last year he was pretty darn wild and the hitters could sit and wait for their pitch. The results were a .361 OBP and 16 homers allowed (not to forget 19 doubles and 10 triples) in his 163 innings.

If he can improve his control to four walks per game, he's got an excellent chance of winning big in next season. He's big, young (25) and strong as an ox; he's also got very few innings on his arm.

CHRIS ROBERTS						METS
A – St. Lucie						
W	L	SV	ERA	IP	H	BB	K	Ratio
13	5	0	2.75	173.1	162	36	111	1.142

Roberts was a first-round draft pick in '92, but because he pitched for the Olympic team that summer, he didn't pitch his first inning of professional ball until last year.

In St. Lucie of the FSL, Roberts, 22, displayed excellent control and a great sense for the game. From the looks of his record, he's had no problems adjusting. His fastball is mediocre right now, but he throws a devastating changeup for strikes.

He's a little raw, and could use a year in Double-A to refine his game and work on picking up some velocity on the heater.

FELIX RODRIGUEZ						DODGERS
A – Vero Beach						
W	L	SV	ERA	IP	H	BB	K	Ratio
8	8	0	3.75	132	109	71	80	1.364

Rodriguez was a catcher until the spring, but Lasorda wanted to see him pitch and converted him, Frankie Rodriguez style.

Felix was voted the No. 10 pitcher in the Florida State League, but his 95 MPH heater was voted the best.

Even though he has all this, and threw a no-hitter in his final start, his minor league manager thinks he's got a long way to go.

FRANKIE RODRIGUEZ						RED SOX
AA – New Britain						
W	L	SV	ERA	IP	H	BB	K	Ratio
7	11	0	3.74	170.2	147	78	151	1.318

Frankie averaged 7.96 K/9IP and allowed only a .228 batting average in the Eastern League last year.

He gives up too many walks, but he's only 21 and has showed signs of improvement in his short, two-year career. He's a good prospect – you know, the kind with the 96 MPH fastball – so keep an eye out for him.

KENNY ROGERS						RANGERS
W	L	SV	ERA	IP	H	BB	K	Ratio
16	10	0	4.10	208.1	210	71	140	1.349

Kenny became a full-time starter for the first time in '93 and was good for 16 wins in 33 starts, 22 of which were of quality.

Rotisse-owners concerned with the running game should know that he shut it down completely; only 26.7 percent of Kenny's base-stealers were successful (4 SB, 11 CS).

What you see is what you get with Rogers because he's consistent. His ratio has always been around 1.35 and his K-rate has always been around 6+K/9IP. These numbers are good, but are they worth 16 wins every year? Probably not.

Kenny got a ton of support last season (6.09 runs), and that doesn't happen every year. His ERA was below league average, but not stellar. He's a solid No. 2, but he's probably already peaked at 16 wins.

JOHN ROPER						REDS
W	L	SV	ERA	IP	H	BB	K	Ratio
2	5	0	5.63	80	92	36	54	1.600

Roper's knuckle curve was voted the best breaking ball in the American Association last year by *Baseball America*. He has a full repertoire to support it, including two- and four-seam fastballs, slider and change.

Major league hitters weren't exactly fooled by his stuff last year, but it was his first exposure to the bigs. He's 22 this year and will certainly be battling for a spot on the Reds' staff.

KIRK RUETER						EXPOS
AA – Harrisburg						
W	L	SV	ERA	IP	H	BB	K	Ratio
5	0	0	1.36	59.2	47	7	36	0.905
W	L	SV	ERA	IP	H	BB	K	Ratio
8	0	0	2.73	85.2	85	18	31	1.202

What a quick worker he is. He pitches like the ball is setting his glove on fire.

We're a little scared by him. With his stuff, it seems like he's living on the edge. Also, guys who average 3.3 K/9IP don't usually survive.

No pitcher ever has a 1.000 winning percentage, so for that reason alone, we don't recommend you draft him. His K-rate should improve and he was inordinately successful, but we think Brian Looney is a safer pick and that Rueter should be put lower on your draft list until he pitches another 200 innings.

SCOTT RUFFCORN						WHITE SOX
AA – Birmingham						
W	L	SV	ERA	IP	H	BB	K	Ratio
9	4	0	2.73	135	108	52	141	1.185

Ruffcorn is another among the cast of thousands White Sox prospect list.

He's one of the best.

He brings an excellent fastball and complements it with a good hard curve. It'd be nice to see him polish the changeup he's reportedly developing, but his pitches are quality enough to get him by for the time being.

Ruffcorn was ranked No. 5 in the Southern League by B.A. and he looks like he's got the best chance to succeed Jason Bere as the next prospect to make this talented staff.

Where are they going to fit Rod Bolton, James Baldwin and Robert Ellis?!?

NOLAN RYAN							HALL OF FAME
W	L	SV	ERA	IP	H	BB	K	Ratio
5	5	0	4.88	66.1	54	40	46	1.417

Todd: Yeah, we know no one's going to draft Nolan this year, but we couldn't just leave him out. Then again, who wants to hear about his '93 season?

Long live the king!

Dave: Doug and I were dragged down to Cleveland for our first and last game at Memorial Stadium by our rotisserie buddy Ken Godard. Not only did we have the distinction of seeing the "mistake by the lake" in its final season (and actually, I think it's kept up much more nicely than Tiger Stadium), but we had the honor of seeing his Lordship throw his final win. It wasn't a typical Nolan performance – he only got two strikeouts – but his dominance was unmistakable (he threw a two-hitter over seven innings). Doug and I only saw Nolan twice in his career, but it's a pleasure knowing his career ERA while we were at the park was a nice even 0.00.

ROGER SALKELD							MARINERS
AA – Jacksonville							
W	L	SV	ERA	IP	H	BB	K	Ratio
4	3	0	3.27	77	71	29	56	1.299

Salkeld, 23, has lost between 4-7 MPH off his fastball with his arm woes so that puts him in the 88-91 MPH range now. He seems to think that some velocity will return by the spring, but that remains to be seen.

He was impressive in his 14.1 innings with Seattle, but we all know that means little. Still, he was once the best pitching prospect in the minors (or damn close to it) and he still

could be a quality pitcher. If he can juice up the heat to 93-94 MPH, he could be a 20-game winner by the time he's 25.

SCOTT SANDERS							PADRES
AAA – Las Vegas							
W	L	SV	ERA	IP	H	BB	K	Ratio
5	10	0	4.96	152.1	170	62	161	1.523
W	L	SV	ERA	IP	H	BB	K	Ratio
3	3	0	4.13	52.1	54	23	37	1.471

Sanders is considered to have better stuff than his counterpart Tim Worrell. He has a sound fastball with a slider as his out pitch.

Sanders needs to use his change more. He'll need the junk seeing as how his cheese has some holes in it.

If he develops even remotely well then he'll be a Padre by the end of '94.

SCOTT SANDERSON							GIANTS
W	L	SV	ERA	IP	H	BB	K	Ratio
11	13	0	4.21	184	201	34	102	1.277

He showed his customary control, but also showed his inability to win big. If California doesn't want you, you can't be that good.

JASON SATRE							ORIOLES
AA – Bowie							
W	L	SV	ERA	IP	H	BB	K	Ratio
7	3	0	3.11	84	68	20	65	1.047
AAA – Rochester							
W	L	SV	ERA	IP	H	BB	K	Ratio
4	5	0	5.85	80	87	45	42	1.650

Jason's been a great disappointment to the scouting establishment (whatever that is) for quite some time. He's been in pro ball for 6 years now and has improved, but he's clearly not the sensation he was projected to be.

It's taken him a couple years to adjust to each level as he's moved up; notice the slight difference between his Double- and Triple-A numbers. By that reckoning, he's at least a year or two from the bigs. He's still only 23, so he has the time.

CURT SCHILLING							PHILLIES
W	L	SV	ERA	IP	H	BB	K	Ratio
16	7	0	4.02	235.1	234	57	186	1.237

Curt pitched a helluva lot better than his ERA would indicate. He had seven starts where he allowed 5+ earnies, and if you remove those starts, he had a line like this:

IP	H	R	ER	BB	K	ERA	Ratio
205.2	174	70	65	43	163	2.84	1.055

There was a run in July where Schilling gave up 27 earned runs in 20.1 innings (11.95 ERA), that alone pushed up his ERA from 3.22 to its mediocre burial plot of 4.02.

What I'm trying to say in a roundabout way is this: Schilling is excellent! If some dumb cluck in your league releases him, then go out and get him. He finished the season with quality starts in six of his last seven appearances and you saw what he did in the post-season.

Even with his subpar performance (for him, that is) he was one of the best pitchers in the game last year. There's an excellent chance he'll be way better in '94.

ERIK SCHULLSTROM — ORIOLES

AA – Bowie

W	L	SV	ERA	IP	H	BB	K	Ratio
5	10	1	4.27	109.2	119	45	97	1.496

Schullstrom was better than his dismal 5-10 record last year; Bowie's offense just wasn't giving him much support.

But, at 25, he's still no great shakes. He gets his share of K's but he also gives up a ton of hits and walks, which is basically the story of his career.

Bowie began using Erik in relief and that doesn't necessarily bode well for him, considering the Orioles' wealth of relievers. He's not bad, but he's got a lot of guys ahead of him, which means he needs to get real impressive real quick if he wants to go anywhere.

AARON SELE — RED SOX

W	L	SV	ERA	IP	H	BB	K	Ratio
7	2	0	2.74	111.2	100	48	93	1.331

This youngster, brought up in June when Clemens went on the DL, has since been touted in Boston as the new Roger Clemens.

Roger's rookie year stats:
IP	H	R	ER	BB	K	ERA	Ratio
133.1	146	67	64	29	126	4.32	1.313

Aaron's rookie year stats:
IP	H	R	ER	BB	K	ERA	Ratio
111.2	100	42	34	48	93	2.74	1.331

There are similarities, but they are definitely different pitchers. Besides, are Sox fans really that anxious to bury the old Clemens? Sele isn't the fireballer that Clemens is, although he does throw 85-88 MPH two- and four-seam fastballs. He's got good command of his slider and change, and improved his curve considerably last year.

His 7.1 K/9IP is certainly respectable, but not as respectable as Clemens' 8.5 K/IP. On the other hand, Roger would have loved a 2.74 ERA. Also, Sele didn't allow more than three runs in any of his 18 starts.

He had a rookie season comparable to the top active AL starters. His ratio is a little high, but he has plenty of time to improve his control. He also had a tendency of tiring late in the season last year, especially during a slump in September. This, too, shall pass.

Sele is a mega-prospect; look for a big year from him in '94.

FRANK SEMINARA — PADRES

AAA – Las Vegas

W	L	SV	ERA	IP	H	BB	K	Ratio
8	5	1	5.43	114.1	136	52	99	1.644
3	3	0	4.47	46.1	53	21	22	1.597

Seminara is a solid starter who's a little too old to develop into anything more.

His biggest enemy this season was poor mechanics. How he went 160 innings between Triple-A Las Vegas and San Diego without someone noticing sooner is a mystery.

Seminara has a solid fastball which relies on movement more than heat. It's good enough to make him a valuable contributor once he straightens out his control situation.

JOSE SILVA — BLUE JAYS

A – Hagerstown

W	L	SV	ERA	IP	H	BB	K	Ratio
12	5	0	2.52	142.2	103	62	161	1.157

A 20-year-old native of Mexico, Silva throws in the mid-90s with regularity.

In fact, he was clocked at 97 MPH the day he struck out 14 batters in a game last year. He showed enough command in '93 to be named the No. 3 prospect in the SAL by *B.A.* His star is just starting to rise. He's at least two years away, but he has the frame, the mechanics and the attitude to be a great power pitcher.

DAN SMITH — RANGERS

AAA – Oklahoma City

W	L	SV	ERA	IP	H	BB	K	Ratio
1	2	0	4.70	15.1	16	5	12	1.369

Dan's a good, 25-year-old prospect who had his season derailed last year by bone spurs in his left (throwing) elbow.

He was on Tulsa's DL in '92 as well, so there are definitely questions about his ability to stave off injury. Actually, everybody wants to know if he'll ever pitch a whole season. His 6-foot-5, 195-pound frame doesn't suggest health and longevity.

He has good control when he's healthy, but who knows when that will be.

PETE SMITH — METS

W	L	SV	ERA	IP	H	BB	K	Ratio
4	8	0	4.37	90.2	92	36	53	1.412

Smith got hurt again last year. He missed a lot of time due to shoulder tendinitis and was often ineffective. The Braves decided not to offer him a job and instead will give Mercker or one of the prospects a shot in the rotation.

Smith pitched well at times, but he's not really a safe pick. Now put him with the Mets and let the fun begin.

ZANE SMITH — PIRATES

W	L	SV	ERA	IP	H	BB	K	Ratio
3	7	0	4.55	83	97	22	32	1.434

Zane had problems all year with a rotator-cuff injury in his left shoulder (you get the feeling somebody put a hex on hurlers named Smith?). He missed the start and the end of the season and couldn't do much in between.

He gave up too many walks and his K/W, one of his strengths in recent years, was very low. His lack of control was clearly due to the injury, but this is the second year in a row that he's had problems with that shoulder. At 33, he's not exactly ancient, but it doesn't look like he's healing properly.

If Zane, Barry and the Bucs had ever done anything in the post-season, he'd be doing analgesic commercials with Brett and Ryan. They didn't, he's not, and you don't want him.

JOHN SMOLTZ — BRAVES

W	L	SV	ERA	IP	H	BB	K	Ratio
15	11	0	3.62	243.2	208	100	208	1.264

Smoltzie was nearly as "lucky" as his golf-partner Greg Maddux. After his third start, John had a 1-2 record with a 0.75 ERA!

How did he manage that? Well, he lost 1-0 on opening day when Jose Guzman fired a one-hitter; then he lost 1-0 to Billy Swift and the Giants on April 16.

Here's his "Maddux Line" (over 15 starts):

IP	H	BB	K	ERA
107.1	90	44	96	3.19

Like Maddux, he was 0-7 in these starts.

Think about it, his overall ERA was 3.62, he had an ERA almost a half-run lower during a 15-start run and couldn't buy a win. With reasonable luck, he should have gone 17-9.

His control was a bit off this year, but that was it. Anyone who thinks this unlucky Brave had an off year needs rotisse-counseling.

JOHN SMILEY — REDS

W	L	SV	ERA	IP	H	BB	K	Ratio
3	9	0	5.62	105.2	117	31	60	1.401

Smiley had a bone spur in his left elbow which forced the Reds to shut him down for the year on July 3. He ended up having arthroscopy to remove the spur in August.

Considering his 3-9 start and his 5.62 ERA, the premature end to Smiley's season may have been merciful.

John never quite found his old form last year and the injury was probably a major factor. We should also mention that he started slowly in 1992, but finished at 16-9 with a 3.21 ERA. He didn't get the chance to recover this time.

And although he wasn't exactly spewing out quality starts in '93, he didn't get much support in the ones he did throw.

If he is healthy in the spring, Smiley looks like a prime candidate for a comeback.

STEVE SODERSTROM — GIANTS

No Professional Experience

The Fresno State righty has a good 92 MPH fastball with a decent curve. He needs to improve his curve and develop a changeup to meet Giant expectations.

Some scouts were concerned he was overused at Fresno. In a college program? *Never!*

PAUL SPOLJARIC — BLUE JAYS

AAA – Syracuse

W	L	SV	ERA	IP	H	BB	K	Ratio
8	7	0	5.29	95.1	97	52	88	1.563

Spoljaric, 23, is a solid left-handed prospect. He throws in the low 90s with a good changeup. He needs work on the curve and hard slider, but he's shown he can strike out hitters with the stuff he's got. He also needs to work on hitting the catcher's mitt (i.e. throwing strikes), or else major league hitters will tee off on him when he gets called up.

Toronto will probably give him another season at Triple-A and if he shows promise there, he'll be in the rotation by mid-'95.

RUSS SPRINGER — ANGELS

AAA – Vancouver

W	L	SV	ERA	IP	H	BB	K	Ratio
5	4	0	4.27	59	58	33	40	1.542

Russ planted his feet firmly in the toilet with his lackluster 1993 season. He has a good sinking 93 MPH heater and a hard slider with good action. In fact, some scouts were saying he was better than his LSU teammate Ben McDonald at the beginning of the year. With the degenerative problem he has in three of the discs in his back, there's just no way he'll compete with Big Ben this year. He spent a lot of his spare time rehabbing, but the injury is not considered career-threatening.

DAVE STEWART — BLUE JAYS

W	L	SV	ERA	IP	H	BB	K	Ratio
12	8	0	4.44	162	146	72	96	1.346

Dave's letting his age show quite a bit now. He came out of the spring hurt, then limped through the end of August like a gut-shot deer. Eventually, he worked the rust out of his limbs because in September he went 4-0 with a 2.51 ERA and was named the ALCS MVP.

At 37, Stewart is losing it. He's not as far off form as Morris, but he's getting there nonetheless. He might be able to help come playoff time, but most teams can't afford to let him work out the kinks during the regular season. Besides, his health and stamina have to be questioned by any potential owner.

TODD STOTTLEMYRE — BLUE JAYS

W	L	SV	ERA	IP	H	BB	K	Ratio
11	12	0	4.84	176.2	204	69	98	1.545

There's got to be something better for him to do with his time than going out and getting shelled every fifth day. And he's been doing it for two years now. We don't know about Stottlemyre, but usually when you're 29-years-old, and the league hits .292 off you, it's time to get look at other career opportunities.

Real estate is always promising.

JEFF SUPPAN — RED SOX

R – Red Sox

W	L	SV	ERA	IP	H	BB	K	Ratio
4	3	0	2.18	57.2	52	16	64	1.179

Suppan's more than ready to bust out of the rookie league. He's been compared to Roger Clemens for his excellent mechanics, delivery and bulldog attitude.

He's only 20 and doesn't throw 90+ MPH yet, but his handlers expect him to as he fills out. Jeff's at least a couple years away, but he could be a rising star.

RICK SUTCLIFFE — ORIOLES

W	L	SV	ERA	IP	H	BB	K	Ratio
10	10	0	5.75	166	212	74	80	1.723

Last year, we said Rick's 4.47 ERA was unacceptable. His 5.75 ERA in '93 made him look like a reject from the Tigers staff.

His 1.85 ratio was ridiculous and he threw only 4.33 K/9IP. Basically, Sutcliffe turned the entire league into better hitters than Travis Fryman. Travis had a .379 OBP and a .486 slugging; Sutcliffe allowed a .385 OBP and a .496 slugging. The AL hit .314 off him.

You're dead meat if you gamble on him.

BILLY SWIFT — GIANTS

W	L	SV	ERA	IP	H	BB	K	Ratio
21	8	0	2.82	232.2	195	55	157	1.075

Swift is one of those guys who we kinda goofed on but we're still in the ballpark.

We were positive Swift was destined for short innings because his arm had given out last year. Well, he pitched 230+ innings and seemed to do pretty well.

On the other hand, we're still kind of right, because Billy stumbled badly in August, around the time the Giants really needed him and Burkett to stave off the charging Braves.

This face-off with the Braves was the scene for one of the most crass spectacles witnessed in baseball this year.

Many will remember the late-season series in which the Giants were swept by the Braves. In one game Swift was beaten severely. McGriff and Justice served up back-to-back homers and broke Bill's back in the bargain.

It was at this point that the San Francisco crowd began to boo Swift off the field in loud fashion, ridiculing and berating the guy who'd already won 17 games and was destined to win 21 on the year. Real classy, you ingrates!

The man pitches his butt off for 60 more innings than he's ever pitched in a season and you boo him because he gives up homers to two of the best sluggers in the NL. What the hell is in that Bay water, anyway?

Chances are slim to none Swift will repeat his performance in '94. At his age, the wear and tear of a year like this one will really take its toll. If he does fade early, look to Salomon Torres to step forward and assume the reins.

GREG SWINDELL							ASTROS
W	L	SV	ERA	IP	H	BB	K	Ratio
12	13	0	4.16	190.1	215	40	124	1.340

Swindell was bothered most of last season by inflammation in his pitching shoulder. He only went on the DL for three weeks, but he was ineffective for a good portion of the year. He finished the season with an eight-hit, 10-K shutout over Cinci, which was encouraging.

With rest in the off-season, Swindell has a good chance of coming back strong in '94. He retained the solid control and K-rate he had during his fine 1992 season with the Reds, so it looks like the arm is still intact. Remember that his '93 owners will be loathe to draft him, so keep an eye on how he does in the spring.

AMAURY TALEMACO							CUBS
A – Peoria
W	L	SV	ERA	IP	H	BB	K	Ratio
8	11	0	3.45	143.2	129	54	133	1.274

Talemaco was signed as a free agent out of the Dominican Republic in 1991, and the Cubs think they have themselves a steal. You can hardly blame them when you consider that he has excellent control with good strikeout numbers and a fluid delivery. Scouts think he will fill out and increase the velocity of his fastball. He needs a lot of polish, but the 20-year-old still has plenty of time. ETA – 1996.

FRANK TANANA							YANKEES
W	L	SV	ERA	IP	H	BB	K	Ratio
7	17	0	4.35	202.2	216	55	116	1.337

Old as dirt and apparently just as hard to get out of a uniform.

KEVIN TAPANI							TWINS
W	L	SV	ERA	IP	H	BB	K	Ratio
12	15	0	4.43	225.2	243	57	150	1.329

Tapani is definitely becoming hittable, and the ERA has been slipping the last few years, but he's still a winner.

He's beginning to throw a few walks, but 150 K's in '93 were his highest ever. A 2.63 K/W ratio doesn't exactly scream of control problems. His ratio was still decent in a hitter's year.

He was good for 35 starts, tied for third in the AL, 20 of which were quality starts. And according to STATS, Inc., Kevin only got 4.23 runs of support, over half a run below the league average. Despite this, he finished the season strong, going 5-2 with a 2.35 ERA in September and October.

If Kirby and the rest of the Twinkies return to the land of the living this year, Tapani will be good for 15 wins.

JULIAN TAVAREZ							INDIANS
A – Kinston
W	L	SV	ERA	IP	H	BB	K	Ratio
11	5	0	2.42	119	102	28	107	1.092

Tavarez, 21, won 15 games between Single-A Kinston, Double-A Canton-Akron and Cleveland last year. He was rated the top pitching prospect in the Carolina League, where he won 11 games with a 2.42 ERA.

He has a fastball that is clocked in the low 90s and he spots it well. But his best pitch is a hard sinker that churns out groundballs. With Baerga and Lewis working as a team, Tavarez should fare quite well in the majors.

Tavarez has been working out all winter in an effort to build some strength. Last season, he checked in at 6-2, 165 lbs. But he's just a kid. In a year or two, he could be 6-5, 225.

Although he got a look-see in September, Tavarez will probably spend the season in Triple-A Charlotte. But with his stuff and control, he's not far off from a permanent job in the Indians' rotation.

BRIEN TAYLOR							YANKEES

AA – Albany

W	L	SV	ERA	IP	H	BB	K	Ratio
13	7	0	3.48	163	127	102	150	1.405

He was still plugging away and working on his change last year. He was the No. 4 prospect in the Eastern League. Then he blew out his shoulder in a brawl during the off-season and *will miss this year*. He's supposed to come back as good as new (with his 95-97 MPH heater and beautiful yellow-hammer curve), but don't expect to see him in 1994.

BOB TEWKSBURY							CARDINALS

W	L	SV	ERA	IP	H	BB	K	Ratio
17	10	0	3.83	213.2	258	20	97	1.301

Tewks continued to display his pinpoint control in '93, allowing a scant 0.84 walks per nine innings. However, considering the league touched him for a .301 batting average and his ERA jumped from 2.16 to 3.83, the Cards might be wishing he missed the strike zone a little more often.

National League hitters came to the plate swinging, and more often than not, put the ball in play. Lefties especially enjoyed what Tewks had to offer, hitting .313 off him.

In 32 starts last year, Tewksbury allowed fewer that six hits only twice. He wasn't very effective holding runners on. The opposition was successful in stolen base attempts 78 percent of the time.

However, Tewksbury was inexplicably effective in keeping the baserunners he allowed from scoring. Sooner or later, it'll catch up with him.

J.J. THOBE							INDIANS

A – Columbus

W	L	SV	ERA	IP	H	BB	K	Ratio
11	2	0	1.91	132	105	25	106	0.985

A seventh-round draft pick in the '92 draft, Thobe, 23, came out of nowhere to win the Sally League ERA title last year. It was his first full season of pro ball, so time will tell if he's for real. But if he shows promise, it shouldn't be long before he's ready to replace Embree or Ogea in the upper-levels of Cleveland's minor league system. Stay tuned.

JUSTIN THOMPSON							TIGERS

A – Lakeland

W	L	SV	ERA	IP	H	BB	K	Ratio
4	4	0	3.56	55.2	65	16	46	1.455

AA – London

W	L	SV	ERA	IP	H	BB	K	Ratio
3	6	0	4.09	83.2	96	37	72	1.590

At 21, Justin's considered the Tigers' top pitching prospect. At times, he has a devastating fastball, but its usually just a good one.

He's improved his control and sports a solid K/W, but he's still a couple years away. He needs to cut down on his hits allowed and continues to have problems with his stamina. He averaged only 5.5 innings/start last year.

MARK THOMPSON							ROCKIES

A – Central Valley

W	L	SV	ERA	IP	H	BB	K	Ratio
3	2	0	2.20	69.2	46	18	72	0.919

So far, Thompson's two-year minor-league record is 14-6 with a 2.15 ERA and 196 strikeouts in 209 innings. Sounds like a good way to begin a career.

He started out the season in dominating fashion and recieved the promotion to Triple-A Colorado Springs in June. There he went 3-0 with a 2.79 ERA before going down mid-season with a torn labrum in his shoulder. He had an arthroscopic prodedure to correct it and missed the second half, but he is expected to be ready by spring.

Thompson, 23, throws two effective fastballs, a four-seamer and a sinking two-seamer. He also has excellent control. He's got the tools and the build, so he'll be a solid starter. Thompson will have to prove that his shoulder is sound in Colorado Springs this season, but if he remains healthy, he should get a callup in September.

RANDY TOMLIN							PIRATES

W	L	SV	ERA	IP	H	BB	K	Ratio
4	8	0	4.85	96.1	109	15	44	1.290

Tomlin was another Pirate starter plagued by injury last year and wound up with his first losing season. He'll be undergoing surgery to remove bone spurs from his left elbow.

Despite the injury, he kept his walks down and his K/W looks good. He got knocked around, though. The league slugged .485, including 11 HR's and 30 doubles.

He only pitched 96.1 innings, so its tough to make any generalizations from last season. But you know he's always given up a few hits. You'll want to take a long, hard look at him in the spring before you pick him up.

SALOMON TORRES							GIANTS
AAA – Phoenix							
W	L	SV	ERA	IP	H	BB	K	Ratio
7	4	0	3.50	105.1	105	27	99	1.253
W	L	SV	ERA	IP	H	BB	K	Ratio
3	5	0	4.03	44.2	37	27	23	1.433

From the beginning of the season, baseball fans were scratching their heads about the whereabouts of the highly touted Torres. Why wasn't he in a Giant uniform?

Apparently manager Dusty Baker didn't consider him ready. A few months later Torres was up and kicking major butt in the NL.

What was it that convinced you Mr. Baker? Was it the 166 K's in 188.2 minor league innings? Was it the fact that he walked only 39 batters in the same span? Perhaps it was the combined 14-8 record with a 3.15 ERA between Double-A Shreveport and Triple-A Phoenix.

Well, we're impressed even if Dusty wasn't. It's pretty clear that Salomon had the power to kick butt in Double-A and need never have wasted his time in Phoenix. Over-cautiousness may have cost the Giants some Torres wins and the NL pennant to boot.

Ironically, it was Torres' season which was marred by the season-ending loss to the Dodgers. To his credit he begged for the ball in the biggest game of the year. He's proven rich in talent, and he's obviously got some brass to go with it.

Torres threw in the mid-80s when he was 19, and now he's upped the ante to the mid-90s. Anything higher than that and he'll be overthrowing.

He's a composed player and definitely uses his head on the mound. He's one of the best to surface in recent years.

MARK TRANBERG							PHILLIES
A – Clearwater							
W	L	SV	ERA	IP	H	BB	K	Ratio
7	3	0	2.50	75.2	78	18	59	1.269

He's a finesse pitcher with exceptional control. He throws in the low 80s with three off-speed pitches (his out pitch is his split-finger).

He's 25, so he's not a mega-prospect, but he could be a comer this year.

STEVE TRACHSEL							CUBS
AAA – Iowa							
W	L	SV	ERA	IP	H	BB	K	Ratio
13	6	0	3.96	170.2	170	45	135	1.260

Steve, 23, was an eighth round draft pick in 1991 and he has been on the fast track to the majors ever since. He showcases a widow-maker curve to go with a decent fastball, slider and forkball. His repertoire is pretty polished, as is his command of the strike zone.

He'll battle for a job in the spring and if he doesn't make it, he'll be sent back to Iowa. But judging from the existing staff's health record, his wait in Triple-A shouldn't be too long. He's one of the Cubs' best prospects.

HECTOR TRINIDAD							CUBS
A – Peoria							
W	L	SV	ERA	IP	H	BB	K	Ratio
7	6	0	2.47	153	142	29	118	1.118

Trinidad is only 20 years old and it's likely that he will pitch a full season in high-A or Double-A ball. But so far, this youngster, only three years out of high school, looks pretty good. He is known primarily for his control and his ability to slip his 84 MPH fastball by hitters. He also throws a curve and change, both solid pitches.

Trinidad will need a few years to bulk up and build endurance, but he looks like a good long-range prospect.

UGUETH URBINA							EXPOS
A – Burlington							
W	L	SV	ERA	IP	H	BB	K	Ratio
10	1	0	1.99	108	78	36	107	1.056

This guy is scary. He's 20 and throws his riding heater up to 96 MPH on the fast gun. In addition, he's got a major-league changeup. His problem is that he needs a breaking ball.

He wasn't that impressive at Double-A and he'll start there again in 1994. He could be in the show by year's end, but he'll have to have his slider straightened out and it'd be nice if he could add 10-15 pounds to his 6-2, 170 pound frame.

FERNANDO VALENZUELA — ORIOLES

W	L	SV	ERA	IP	H	BB	K	Ratio
8	10	0	4.94	178.2	179	79	78	1.444

Valenzuela made a decent comeback to the majors last year, which included being named the AL pitcher of the month for July. He wasn't very impressive early on, however, and he absolutely disintegrated in the last third of the season. In his six starts in August he compiled a 13.96 ERA, while allowing 50 base runners (39 hits and 11 walks) in 20 innings.

Fernando's stuff is a fraction of what it was in his prime. If a team is desperate for a left-handed starter, they may pick him up. If not, he's done.

MARC VALDES — MARLINS

W	L	SV	ERA	IP	H	BB	K	Ratio
0	2	0	5.59	10	8	7	15	1.800

Valdes, 22, is a 6-foot, 170 pounder taken with the No. 27 pick in the first round of the 1993 draft.

He throws a hard sinker in the mid-80s and has a nice sharp slider. He hits a lot of batters because he pitches inside so much. Scouts question his ability because of his pitches and slight build. The Marlins are praying he can become someone like Billy Swift.

TODD VAN POPPEL — ATHLETICS

W	L	SV	ERA	IP	H	BB	K	Ratio
6	6	0	5.04	84	76	62	47	1.643

Van Poppel has spent the last couple years dealing with the hype of his lucrative contract.

In that time, he's grown stronger (his arm is compared to Clemens', sans Roger's unearthly control) and he's developed his curve and fastball into Nagasaki/Hiroshima territory.

The standout flaw is his lack of control. It's getting there, but he's so incomplete without it. The A's want him worse than an anxious prom date, but they'd be wise to protect their rather sizeable investment and continue waiting until he's fully ripe.

BEN VanRYN — DODGERS

AA – San Antonio

W	L	SV	ERA	IP	H	BB	K	Ratio
14	4	0	2.21	134.1	118	38	144	1.161

He faltered badly upon arriving in Triple-A Albuquerque, but his Double-A season had been spectacular, marked by his typical strikeouts and newly developed control.

His fastball is very good (a given) and he's improving a curve which Lasorda taught him. VanRyn says the key to his success, though, has been his slider.

Baseball America sent a mixed message by publishing him the No. 1 prospect in the Texas League, then leaving him off the list of Top Ten Dodger prospects. We'll stand by the higher ranking.

RON VILLONE — MARINERS

AA – Jacksonville

W	L	SV	ERA	IP	H	BB	K	Ratio
3	4	0	4.24	63.2	49	41	66	1.414

We're not sure what his future holds. In fact, neither are the Mariners. He probably has the second-best arm in the system behind Japanese relief sensation Makato Suzuki. He's huge, 6-3 and a muscular 230, and he throws in the mid-90s, peaking around 95 MPH. He adds a slider, a curve and a change.

Right now, he's a starter, but the Mariners are also thinking about making him a closer, which puts him in line with about 10 other guys (including superb arms like Ayala and Suzuki). This guy's wild, but his control is the only thing that's bush-league about him.

FRANK VIOLA — RED SOX

W	L	SV	ERA	IP	H	BB	K	Ratio
11	8	0	3.14	183.2	180	72	91	1.732

The Sox got their money's worth out of Viola last year. His 3.17 ERA was impressive in a hitter's year, and he led the AL in home-ERA at 2.19 (STATS, Inc.). He again kept his home-runs allowed down and his slugging-allowed average was only .372, well below the league average.

In that sense, he looks great.

But you have to be a little concerned with his decreasing K's and increasing walks. His ratio was less than stellar at 1.37. And he was bothered by injury last year. He missed a start for the first time in his career with a sprained ankle in early May, breaking a streak of 382 consecutive starts. Then, his season was ended in September by a bone spur in his left elbow which will require surgery.

If the surgery takes, count on Viola for another 10-12 wins, but not much more.

TERRELL WADE							BRAVES
A – Macon							
W	L	SV	ERA	IP	H	BB	K	Ratio
8	2	0	1.73	83	57	36	121	1.121
A – Durham							
W	L	SV	ERA	IP	H	BB	K	Ratio
2	1	0	3.27	33	26	18	47	1.333

The No. 1 prospect in the Sally League. Wade, 21, has a wicked 94 MPH sinker and a good changeup. He's really a consistent breaking-ball away from greatness.

He'll probably start at Double-A. He made it there in 1993, but his control was iffy. He needs more innings at that level before he jumps to Richmond. The Braves are figuring he'll be ready by 1995.

According to *B.A.*, scouts place Wade at the top of the class among minor-league pitchers. There are others, like Jose Silva of the Jays who are also in contention for this status, but at worst, Terrell is even with 'em. You have to be worried about his future, given the Braves' rotation, but Pete Smith is gone and, who knows, Mercker could bomb out or be traded.

BILLY WAGNER							ASTROS
A – Auburn							
W	L	SV	ERA	IP	H	BB	K	Ratio
1	3	0	4.08	29	25	25	31	1.724

Your basic 5-foot-10-inch lefty with a 98 MPH fastball who's taken in the first round.

In 1992, he had 19.1K/9IP and allowed 1.58 H/9IP at Ferrum College, both NCAA records. He slumped in 1993, allowing 2.64 H/9IP and fanning only 16 batters a game.

He already has a good curveball, so the Astros want him to work on a change and get his control in check. As soon as he can do the latter, he'll tie major-league hitters in knots.

PAUL WAGNER							PIRATES
W	L	SV	ERA	IP	H	BB	K	Ratio
8	8	2	4.27	141.1	143	42	114	1.309

Wagner got the nod as a starter in June and appears to have settled in to his new role comfortably. He's only started 18 games in his short career, but his numbers are decent and it looks like he'll stay with it.

His ERA was a little high, but if you take out his relief appearances, he was 6-5 with a 3.96 ERA. Not All-Star numbers, but good for a youngster adjusting to the long innings.

He has good control, as evidenced by his 2.71 K/W and 7.3 K/9IP averages. He needs to learn to pitch to lefties, however; they hit .301 and slugged .444 off him (STATS, Inc.).

Paul spent some time on the DL in August with a strained hamstring, but he came back strong, throwing 6 quality starts out of his last 7 attempts. Considering his competition on the Pirates' staff, we see no reason why he can't step in to be a consistent No. 2 or 3 starter for them in '93.

TIM WAKEFIELD							PIRATES
W	L	SV	ERA	IP	H	BB	K	Ratio
6	11	0	5.61	128.1	145	75	59	1.714

What a year! After starting 3-2 in April, Wakefield went 0-for-3-months (10 starts, 8 losses). The Bucs sent him down to Double-A Carolina for nine starts; he went 3-5 with a 6.99 ERA. But those numbers were good enough for a ticket back to Pittsburgh and they brought him back in September after losing Randy Tomlin. He did finish the season with two complete game shutouts, but it was too little, too late. One was in the second game of doubleheader, and the Cubbies were apparently too tired to see the knuckleball.

Tim looked promising in '92, but we warned you about one-pitch, junkball phenoms. Last season was nothing but junk. His knuckler was flat and high in the strike zone, his ratio and ERA were sky-high and his K/W was nonexistent.

He needs two more pitches and some control before he can be a decent starter.

BOB WALK							PIRATES
W	L	SV	ERA	IP	H	BB	K	Ratio
13	14	0	5.68	187	214	70	80	1.519

Walk appears to be at the end of the line. He led the NL in ER-allowed with 118, despite enjoying a league-high 1.2 ground double plays/9IP (STATS, Inc.). The Pirates' offense gave him 5.05 runs of support, but his 5.69 ERA was more than enough to offset this. He doesn't know what a quality start is anymore; he threw 10 QS in 32 starts (31 percent). Ugh!

His K/W has never been very good and in the last few years it's been plummeting faster than Wile E. Coyote down the Grand Canyon. It's time he hit the showers before the Road Runner drops a boulder on him.

B.J. WALLACE — EXPOS

A – West Palm Beach

W	L	SV	ERA	IP	H	BB	K	Ratio
11	8	0	3.28	137	112	65	126	1.292

Wallace, 23, is a lefty with a very good slider, a pretty good fastball and a nice change.

His main problem has been mechanical. He doesn't consistently maintain his delivery and the resulting shoulder tendinitis has hampered his ability to pitch 150 innings.

He'll get a shot at Double-A this year, but it seems unlikely that he'll have much of a role until at least 1995. He'll have to turn his game up a notch to place himself immediately in the Expos plans, but they do see him as someone who'll have a job in their rotation by 1996.

JASON WASDIN — ATHLETICS

A – Madison

W	L	SV	ERA	IP	H	BB	K	Ratio
2	3	0	1.86	48.1	32	9	40	.848

Wasdin's a Florida State hurler who came into the organization with the 25th pick. He arrived with a fastball and change and proceeded to develop a wicked slider in the Cape Cod amateur league.

His performance in Single-A Madison was impressive and he adjusted pretty well after being moved to A-ball Modesto.

Because he's 21, the A's will almost surely jump him to Double-A as soon as he shows signs of low minor mastery.

ALLEN WATSON — CARDINALS

AAA – Louisville

W	L	SV	ERA	IP	H	BB	K	Ratio
5	4	0	2.91	120.2	101	31	86	1.094

W	L	SV	ERA	IP	H	BB	K	Ratio
6	7	0	4.60	86	90	28	49	1.372

After going 5-4 with a 2.94 ERA for Louisville to begin the season, the Cardinal brass had seen enough. Watson was called up on July 6 when Mike Perez went on the DL.

Watson ripped off six wins in his first seven starts and, for about a week, it looked like he might garner the Rookie of the Year award. Then Watson lost his next seven decisions. His first two losses were blowouts, though. If you erase those debacles, Watson would have wound up 6-5 with a 3.45 ERA in 13 starts.

Watson was the Cardinal's first round (21st overall) draft pick in 1991. He spent just a little over two seasons in the minors where he displayed good control and struck out nearly a batter per inning.

Watson's repertoire consists of a hard fastball, a sharp slider and a decent, but improving, changeup. But what impressed manager Joe Torre most was his composure on the mound. Watson is a great competitor, and he displayed no signs of rookie jitters in his first big-league campaign.

We marked him as an A-1 prospect in last year's tome, and Watson more than lived up to our expectations. He's only 23, so look for him to improve markedly and take over the ace status from Tewksbury within the next two years.

DAVID WEATHERS — MARLINS

AAA – Edmonton

W	L	SV	ERA	IP	H	BB	K	Ratio
11	4	0	3.83	141	150	47	117	1.397

Mr. Weathers looks a mite purty. He throws 93 MPH and posted uber-nice numbers in the PCL, despite starting the season with a tired arm and the flu. He has had some problems in the past with tipping pitches with his motion, but he's worked hard on hiding the ball during delivery.

He's a good candidate for a rotation slot out of the spring and, like Pat Rapp, he could kick the league squarely in the butt in 1994.

BILL WEGMAN — BREWERS

W	L	SV	ERA	IP	H	BB	K	Ratio
4	14	0	4.48	120.2	135	34	50	1.401

Apparently Wegman was so disappointed by the lack of help from his team both defensively and offensively in '92 that he decided to simply slip into mediocrity and do the job for them.

He's not too old, but don't expect any radical comebacks.

BOB WELCH — ATHLETICS

W	L	SV	ERA	IP	H	BB	K	Ratio
9	11	0	5.29	166.2	208	56	63	1.584

Welch has been so bad since winning the Cy Young in '90 that we can only figure that a sense of remorse has caused him to prove how undeserving of the award he was.

Welch is dead in the water. Squeeze this grape and look for the whine.

DAVID WELLS								TIGERS
W	L	SV	ERA	IP	H	BB	K	Ratio
11	9	0	4.19	187	183	42	139	1.203

Wells contributed to the Tigers' fast start, going 9-1 with a 2.68 ERA in his first 15 starts. He was getting more innings than he was accustomed to, however, and the pace may have gotten to him. He started losing in July and an inflamed left elbow put him on the DL in August.

Wells wound up with only 11 wins, but he posted decent stats and should be considered the best of the Detroit starters. The Tigers apparently agree because they hesitated before deciding to re-sign him this season.

His control was excellent last year and his 3.31 K/W ratio was second highest in the AL. His 1.2 ratio was respectable and he was the only regular starter in the rotation to post an ERA (4.19) below the league average.

Wells can continue to be a valuable contributer, though he may have to cut down on his innings in order to stay healthy.

TURK WENDELL								CUBS
AAA – Iowa								
W	L	SV	ERA	IP	H	BB	K	Ratio
10	8	0	4.60	148.2	148	47	110	1.312

He's 27 now, so Wendell is starting to lose his luster. Actually, he wasn't that shiny to begin with. He has an average fastball and relies on his offspeed pitches and control to succeed. But if either one is off, he's in for a long day. Our guess is that more often than not, he'll have long days.

MATT WHISENANT								MARLINS
W	L	SV	ERA	IP	H	BB	K	Ratio
2	6	0	4.69	71	68	56	74	1.747

You don't need to major in particle physics to explain this guy's problem. When the last three digits of a pitcher's ratio are a Boeing jetliner, you know he's either getting tips from Bill Gullickson, or he's walking every dog on the block.

Well, Whisenant, 23, needs to stop walking 7.1/ 9IP. He has a good heater which (obviously) is anything but straight.

If he can get his breaking ball in order and fix his mechanics, he could be a fast mover. He looks like a project right now, though.

GABE WHITE								EXPOS
AA – Harrisburg								
W	L	SV	ERA	IP	H	BB	K	Ratio
7	2	0	2.16	100	80	28	80	1.080

The No. 7 prospect in the Eastern League. Gabe, 22, pitched quite well in Triple-A as well, going 2-1 with a 3.12 ERA and an exquisite 28/6 K/W ratio in 40.1 innings.

According to *B.A.*, Expo scouts liken White to Tom Glavine. He doesn't have an exceptional pitch, except for his change. He does hide the ball well and work up-and-down, in-and-out, deceiving and out-thinking hitters.

White got lit up in the AFL, his first bout with failure at the professional level. Despite this, he will be considered for a spot in the rotation in the spring.

WALLY WHITEHURST								PADRES
W	L	SV	ERA	IP	H	BB	K	Ratio
4	7	0	3.83	105.2	109	30	57	1.315

Wally spent the year in San Diego proving that he can't pitch any better as a starter than he did in relief.

CASEY WHITTEN								INDIANS
A – Watertown								
W	L	SV	ERA	IP	H	BB	K	Ratio
6	3	0	2.42	81.2	75	18	81	1.139

His name isn't as well known as Kirkreit, but Whitten has just as much potential to crack the Indian rotation in '95. Whitten, 21, was drafted in the second round out of Indiana State and assigned to Watertown in the NY-P League. There, the lefthander displayed a 91 MPH fastball and excellent control, and was named the No. 7 prospect in the league by *Baseball America*.

The Indians want to move Whitten and Kirkreit along at the same speed. They both have a chance to make Double-A this spring, and it's quite possible we will see them both in the majors within the next couple of years.

BOB WICKMAN								YANKEES
W	L	SV	ERA	IP	H	BB	K	Ratio
14	4	4	4.63	140	156	69	70	1.607

Wickman has got to be the luckiest sonuvagun in baseball ... and that's really annoying.

He had a 14-4 record, but a 4.63 ERA ... and that's really annoying.

He struck out 70 men and walked 69 ... really annoying.

The Yanks will probably keep him instead of giving one of their good pitchers a chance ... and that's the most annoying thing of all.

Mike Williams — Phillies

AAA – Scranton/Wilkes-Barre

W	L	SV	ERA	IP	H	BB	K	Ratio
9	2	0	2.87	97.1	93	16	53	1.120

A long-shot to get PT in the rotation, his best bet may be some long-relief innings. The thing is, he's spent almost all of his minor-league career as a starter.

Williams is 25, so he's not really going to take his minor-league game to a new level. This makes him marginal and his ability to strike out batters isn't good. Our best guess is that he is – at best – second-echelon material.

Trevor Wilson — Giants

W	L	SV	ERA	IP	H	BB	K	Ratio
7	5	0	3.60	110	110	40	57	1.364

Evan: At the insistence of one of my fellow authors (who shall remain nameless) I went against my better judgment and said that Trevor should be a fine pitcher for the Giants.

We went around and around about it, and he ultimately won me over with the timeless argument concerning the commodity on lefties who can throw hard.

Well, this year I'm gonna say what I thought last year.

I don't think Trevor Wilson is a very good pitcher. No sir, and there's nuthin' gonna make me change my mind.

Now go get 'em Trev.

Gerald Witasick — Cardinals

R – Savannah

W	L	SV	ERA	IP	H	BB	K	Ratio
4	3	0	4.12	67.2	65	19	74	1.241

Witasick, 21, was chosen in the second round of last year's amateur draft, and he earned a promotion to Savannah of the GCL before the season ended.

His fastball, clocked at 92 with the fast gun, is already major-league calibre, but he will need another season or two to develop the off-speed stuff. Judging by his control and durability, however, he could help the depleted St. Louis bullpen before long.

Bobby Witt — Athletics

W	L	SV	ERA	IP	H	BB	K	Ratio
14	13	0	4.21	220	226	91	131	1.441

Witt didn't exactly remedy the A's pitching woes. If anything he was a wash, losing almost as many games as he won.

Witt has always been the out-of-control type, too busy leading the league in walks to bother giving up hits.

Despite moments of brilliance last year, he's reaching the age where his value will drop like a Padre paycheck.

Mike Witt — Yankees

W	L	SV	ERA	IP	H	BB	K	Ratio
3	2	0	5.27	41	39	22	30	1.488

Witt came back after a year off to rejoin the Yankees. He didn't contribute much but neither did he hurt the team.

The sore point is that he got nine starts with a phenom's name written all over them. Shame on the Yankees.

Tim Worrell — Padres

W	L	SV	ERA	IP	H	BB	K	Ratio
2	7	0	4.92	100.2	104	43	52	1.460

Worrell's got three pitches: a sinking fastball, a circle change and a hard slider. Compared to teammate Scott Sanders, he's got better control.

Kelly Wunsch — Brewers

A – Beloit

W	L	SV	ERA	IP	H	BB	K	Ratio
1	5	0	4.83	63.1	58	39	61	1.532

Taken from Texas A&M, Wunsch had an excessively high ERA but struck out almost a man an inning.

He was considered one of the top players in the Cape Cod League last year.

Kip Yaughn — Marlins

W	L	SV	ERA	IP	H	BB	K	Ratio
0	0	0	6.86	21	25	13	13	1.810

Elbow problems kept him from doing anything last year, but he has a good live arm and throws both a power and slow curve. He's looking to make the club in the spring, but his elbow is still questionable.

Relief Pitchers – *Essays*

Mark Acre — Athletics

A – Madison

W	L	SV	ERA	IP	H	BB	K	Ratio
0	0	20	0.29	31.1	9	13	41	0.702

Acre had great control in A-ball Madison and wasn't too shabby in Double-A either. At his age (25), though, he wouldn't be a prospect if he wasn't mowing down this caliber of hitter.

The A's don't need Acre right this minute, but if the Eck falters badly, Mark will get a shot sooner than he expected.

Rick Aguilera — Twins

W	L	SV	ERA	IP	H	BB	K	Ratio
4	3	34	3.11	72.1	60	14	59	1.023

Rick's save total fell from 41 to 34 between '92 and '93, but that was more a function of the Twins' lack of offense than Aguilera's pitching. At 31, he saved 85 percent of his opportunities and improved his stats in almost every other category. He also earned Pitcher of the Month honors in June with 10 saves, a 10 K/W average and a 0.00 ERA.

With excellent control and an 8 K/9IP average over the last five years, he's one of the best closers in the game.

Larry Andersen — Phillies

W	L	SV	ERA	IP	H	BB	K	Ratio
3	2	0	2.92	61.2	54	21	67	1.216

When is this 41-year-old Henny Youngman gonna lose his stuff? He's still punching out a guy an inning! We'll tell you one thing. ... We wish he'd end his stand-up shtick right now. "Why do we drive on a parkway and park on a driveway?" That's just not funny. If he had any class, he'd come up with some nice dirty jokes we haven't heard. All he is, is a two-bit Andy Rooney with a slider.

Paul Assenmacher — Yankees

W	L	SV	ERA	IP	H	BB	K	Ratio
4	3	0	3.38	56	54	22	45	1.357

Paul isn't done yet, but it may be prudent to lower your expectations a bit. He still throws a great curve and uses it to strike out nearly a batter an inning, but his advanced age will eventually start hindering his effectiveness. The Yanks will use him in a set-up role in '94.

Bobby Ayala — Mariners

W	L	SV	ERA	IP	H	BB	K	Ratio
7	10	3	5.60	98	106	45	65	1.541

Todd: We are intrigued by the off-season trade that sent Ayala to the Mariners and Hanson to the Reds.

We expected big things out of Ayala last year, but were disappointed by the disappearance of his control and his tendency to set gopherballs on a tee for the opposition (16 HR in 98 innings... Ouch!).

Still, Bobby showed good control in the minors and we expect it to return. He has a full repertoire: fastball, slider, splitter, and change. Given his past record and youth (24), he should reward the Mariners for their faith in him.

Dave: The Mariners are looking at young Mr. Ayala as a setup man who'll be groomed for the closer's role. He definitely has the tools to succeed and if he gets a closer's job, his rotisserie value will sky-rocket.

Cory Bailey — Red Sox

AAA – Pawtucket

W	L	SV	ERA	IP	H	BB	K	Ratio
4	5	20	2.88	65.2	48	31	59	1.220

Bailey's a 23-year-old fireballer who's screamed through the Boston farm system. He started in the rookie league two years ago and made it to the show for 15 innings last year when Jeff Russell went on the DL.

He averaged over 12 K/9IP at Single-A, although his K's dropped slightly at Triple-A. Once he has a chance to adjust to the big leagues, he'll be mowing them down. He could cut down on his walks, but he doesn't give up many hits and keeps his ratio low.

The Sox may groom him to replace the aging Russell, although Ken Ryan may have something to say about that. Cory could get some serious time this year, but if not, you'll be hearing about him in a couple years.

Scott Bankhead — Red Sox

W	L	SV	ERA	IP	H	BB	K	Ratio
2	1	0	3.50	64.1	59	29	47	1.367

Bankhead's a 30-year-old ex-starter who's trying to hold on any way he can. After a successful year in Cinci, his return to the AL was last year was rather inauspicious.

He doesn't strike any body out, his ratio is too high and his ERA is less than stellar. He's an interloper and nothing more.

Rich Batchelor							Cardinals
AA – Albany							
W	L	SV	ERA	IP	H	BB	K	Ratio
1	3	19	0.89	40.1	27	12	40	0.967

Batchelor was the price tag when the Cardinals traded Lee Smith to the Yankees late last year. While he has yet to spend a full season at the Triple-A level and needs some work on his fastball, St. Louis is looking for him to win a bullpen job in the spring. They also indicated that he might eventually get a chance to win the closer job.

He throws a good forkball and has decent control, but he isn't a sure thing.

Jose Bautista							Cubs
W	L	SV	ERA	IP	H	BB	K	Ratio
10	3	2	2.82	111.2	105	27	63	1.182

He spent 1992 in the Royals' minor league system, where he went 3-10 between Omaha and Memphis. The Cubs picked him up before the beginning of the '93 season, and he ended up going 10-3 for them in 58 appearances, including seven starts. He was the surprise of the pitching staff in the unfriendly confines of Wrigley.

His stuff isn't overpowering, but he has excellent control and a knack for inducing ground balls. The Cubs might be tempted to put him in the rotation this year, but it would be a mistake. At 29, he's no spring chicken and probably wouldn't be able to handle more than 150 innings. The most he's ever worked in a season is 172 innings while with the Orioles back in 1988. If used in the bullpen, Bautista might be able to reproduce a semblance of his '93 season. If the Cubs make a starter out of him, there's a good chance he will break down.

Rod Beck							Giants
W	L	SV	ERA	IP	H	BB	K	Ratio
3	1	48	2.16	79.1	57	13	86	0.882

We knew Beck would be this good and he was more than ready to shoulder the responsibility of closer to a pennant contender.

Beck was as sharp as 1992, retaining his phenomenal control and saving 48 in 52 opportunities.

Beck will continue to be the cornerstone of the Giants pitching staff the way NL colleagues John Wetteland and Brian Harvey are theirs.

Steve Bedrosian							Braves
W	L	SV	ERA	IP	H	BB	K	Ratio
5	2	0	1.63	49.2	34	14	33	0.966

The story of Bedrosian's struggle to keep his son alive while making the bigs is heartwarming. The Braves now look like geniuses. ... For a song they picked up an excellent setup man (and it was great P.R., too).

It doesn't matter what Bedrock does on the field, his mission is accomplished. In addition, the Braves probably won't ever consider him for a few saves (he is 36 after all), so his value is strictly in middle relief.

Stan Belinda							Royals
W	L	SV	ERA	IP	H	BB	K	Ratio
4	2	19	3.88	69.2	65	17	55	1.177

Kansas City got themselves a good set-up man capable of stepping into the closer's role in their trade with Pittsburgh last August. Belinda, though inconsistent at times, bounced right back from his NLCS nightmare in '92 (the way Mitch Williams would have, had he been given the chance), and converted 19 of 23 save opportunities for the Pirates before the trade.

Belinda was used primarily as the right-handed setup man and the Royals plan to use him in the same capacity this season. His closer status is gone, unless Montgomery gets injured, but he is still a tenacious pitcher and can do the job as well as anybody else in the Royals' pen.

But Kansas City gave up two excellent prospects to obtain Belinda. Though he isn't dominating, John Lieber has a chance to be an effective major-league starter in a couple of years. And Miceli is no slouch either. Sure, the Royals' bullpen was a major concern, and they addressed the problem by acquiring a solid, if erratic, arm to fill the void. But the youngsters they gave up just might pay off big for the Pirates.

BILL BENE							DODGERS

AA – San Antonio

W	L	SV	ERA	IP	H	BB	K	Ratio
5	6	1	4.84	70.2	50	53	82	1.458

Renowned legend who, like the Wild Thing in the film "Major League," was made to throw to cardboard cutouts because of his wild throws.

Bene is also known for having walked 312 batters and striking out 226 in 251 career minor league innings.

The Dodgers took him with their first-round pick in '88 and have been waiting for him to develop ever since.

JOE BOEVER							TIGERS

W	L	SV	ERA	IP	H	BB	K	Ratio
6	3	3	3.61	102.1	101	44	63	1.417

Oakland released Boever in August and the Tigers, in yet another testament to the state of their staff, signed him a week later. He's 33 years old and declining, which means he's now worse-than-average.

PEDRO BORBON							BRAVES

AAA – Richmond

W	L	SV	ERA	IP	H	BB	K	Ratio
5	5	1	4.23	76.2	71	42	95	1.474

Pedro gets his K's and is a pretty good power-pitching lefty. He gives up a few too many dingers and too many walks, but if he can work the control a bit, he could be a valuable part of the Atlanta 'pen.

TOBY BORLAND							PHILLIES

AA – Reading

W	L	SV	ERA	IP	H	BB	K	Ratio
2	2	13	2.52	53.2	38	20	74	1.081

Definitely an option for the Phillies if Bottalico, Gomes and Doug Jones fall flat. Borland's build is just a wee bit scary: 6-7, 175! He's a damn rail! Other than that, the numbers speak for themselves. He'll get a job in the spring, or be in Scranton, waiting for the call.

SHAWN BOSKIE							CUBS

W	L	SV	ERA	IP	H	BB	K	Ratio
5	3	0	3.43	65.2	63	21	39	1.279

Just when the Cubs were ready to give up on him, Boskie started coming through. He made the switch to the bullpen and recorded a 3.11 ERA over the second half of the season. By doing so, he saved his job for another year.

But 1994 is a make or break year for him. He'll have to prove that last year was no fluke and that he can be effective coming out of the bullpen. His fastball is a shadow of its former self and his off-speed pitches don't fool anyone, so there is a strong possibility that he will go back into the toilet. Larry Himes is crossing his fingers and toes.

RICKY BOTTALICO							PHILLIES

AA – Reading

W	L	SV	ERA	IP	H	BB	K	Ratio
3	3	20	2.25	72	63	26	65	1.236

Considered to have a Dibble/Wetteland-like psycho mentality, Bottalico, 24, throws in the mid-90s with a hard slider.

With the trade of Mitch Williams, the only thing that stands in his way is 37-year-old Doug Jones. Down the road, he'll be challenged by Wayne Gomes, but Gomes needs to lose weight and throw strikes.

The bottom line: Bottalico could be closing games out for Philly by April. If he's sent to Triple-A, he'll get a shot as soon as he shows he's ready. He's one of the top reliever picks you can make for your fantasy team.

JEFF BRANTLEY							GIANTS

W	L	SV	ERA	IP	H	BB	K	Ratio
5	6	0	4.28	113.2	112	46	76	1.073

He really hit the wall in '93, allowing almost a hit an inning and pumping helium into his ERA until you wanted to paint "Goodyear" on his side.

Brantley should recover and he's been such a quality pitcher for so long that he can't be taken for granted.

He's lost a lot, but he's part of what makes the Giants long relief staff one of the best in the majors.

BILLY BREWER							ROYALS

W	L	SV	ERA	IP	H	BB	K	Ratio
2	2	0	3.46	39	31	20	28	1.308

One of the bright spots in the Kansas City bullpen in '93, Brewer, 26, had ERA's of 1.98 and 1.73 for the Expos in two single-A seasons. The Royals grabbed him in the 1992 Rule V draft and he won a job in their bullpen in the spring.

Relief Pitchers – 187

Brewer pitched effectively all season long, allowing just four of 39 inherited runners to score. He became lax in bases-empty situations, but when runners were in scoring position, he really hunkered down, allowing a measly .143 batting average. He's a flyball pitcher, and is helped immeasurably by spacious Kauffman stadium.

With another season like '93, Brewer's role in the KC bullpen could be expanded to include a lot more late-inning work.

BRAD BRINK — PHILLIES
AAA – Scranton/Wilkes-Barre

W	L	SV	ERA	IP	H	BB	K	Ratio
7	7	0	4.22	106.2	104	27	89	1.228

Brink's a 29-year-old with excellent control and a solid 7.5 K/9IP rate. He suffers from the same problems as every other Phillie: He has to wait for an injury before he'll get a few starts. Barring that (or the self-destruction of Ben Rivera via a 1/2 K/W ratio), he'll get a stab at a relief role in the spring. Brink is getting to the point where he has to get a major-league job now. He's been at Triple-A at four different stretches in his career and only has 47.2 major-league innings to show for it.

JEFF BRONKEY — RANGERS
AAA – Oklahoma City

W	L	SV	ERA	IP	H	BB	K	Ratio
2	2	14	2.65	37.1	29	7	19	.964

W	L	SV	ERA	IP	H	BB	K	Ratio
1	1	1	4.00	36	39	11	18	1.389

Jeff's control has come and gone throughout his extensive minor league career. He looked good in Oklahoma City last year, and that may earn him some time in Texas if anything happens to Henke.

But he's 28 and has moved down the depth chart as often as he's moved up. Don't bother.

JIM BULLINGER — CUBS
AAA – Iowa

W	L	SV	ERA	IP	H	BB	K	Ratio
4	6	20	3.42	73.2	64	43	74	1.452

In his two brief appearances last year, in June and September, Bullinger showed the Cubs that he wasn't quite ready to compete with the big boys. Playing with the kids in Triple-A was a different story, though, as he racked up 20 saves for Iowa.

While his pitches are considered to be average by major league standards, one fact looms large over his future. He is a 28-year-old man, and needs to make a definitive step out of the minors soon. If he doesn't turn the corner in '94, the chances are slim that he ever will.

DAVE BURBA — GIANTS

W	L	SV	ERA	IP	H	BB	K	Ratio
10	3	0	4.25	95.1	95	37	88	1.385

Burba showed outstanding K stats, but he still can't get the tough outs.

He looks vastly improved over last year's model, but he'll have to stop giving up runs if the Giants are going to pitch him 90+ innings.

ENRIQUE BURGOS — ROYALS
AAA – Omaha

W	L	SV	ERA	IP	H	BB	K	Ratio
2	4	9	3.16	62.2	36	37	91	1.165

Burgos came out of nowhere to put up some pretty daunting numbers for Omaha and earn a July promotion to the bigs in '93. Well, it wasn't actually nowhere. He spent the previous three seasons pitching in Taiwan.

Regardless of where he came from, Burgos, 28, is already as developed as he will be. He couples good control with a well above-average fastball and a forkball. He has what it takes mow down American Association hitters, he's proven that. Spring training will be his true test of his mettle.

CHRIS BUSHING — REDS
AA – Chattanooga

W	L	SV	ERA	IP	H	BB	K	Ratio
6	1	29	2.31	70	50	23	84	1.043

At 26, Bushing has bounced around for eight years in five different organizations. He's been used in every pitching role, but he seems to have been comfortable as a closer for Chattanooga last year.

Chris throws 90+ MPH and has a decent curve and change. His control has improved a great deal and his 10.8 K/9IP last year was outstanding. He'll get a chance to earn a few saves Triple-A this year and may get the call to Cinci if he's needed.

MIKE BUTCHER — ANGELS

W	L	SV	ERA	IP	H	BB	K	Ratio
2	3	3	2.86	28.1	21	15	24	1.271

There's nothing really special to write about Butcher, his control is a little lacking, but other than that, he's OK.

GREG CADARET								ROYALS
W	L	SV	ERA	IP	H	BB	K	Ratio
3	2	1	4.31	48	54	30	25	1.750

He might convince someone to give him a look in the spring, but it's obvious from his last two seasons that he is about done.

CRIS CARPENTER								RANGERS
W	L	SV	ERA	IP	H	BB	K	Ratio
4	2	1	3.50	69.1	64	25	53	1.284

Cris's season started well in Florida (2.89 ERA, 1.125 ratio), but they traded him off to Texas in July. His AL debut was a little tougher; they smacked him for 35 hits and a 4.22 ERA in 32 innings.

But those numbers certainly aren't terrible and neither is Carpenter. He's essentially a decent pitcher who'll do well for the Rangers as a set-up man for Henke.

JOE CARUSO								RED SOX
AAA – Pawtucket								
W	L	SV	ERA	IP	H	BB	K	Ratio
5	10	0	5.30	122.1	138	68	65	1.684

Caruso crashed back to earth last year after a stunning '92 season in Single-A.

To be fair, going from Single- to Triple-A is a big jump and Pawtucket used him as a starter for the first time... but he just stunk.

Joe's 23 and has shown much more promise in the past. He throws a 90+ MPH fastball and has a good slider, so he could definitely bounce back. We'll give him at least another year or two before we write him off, but he won't be on any of our teams in the meantime.

LARRY CASIAN								TWINS
W	L	SV	ERA	IP	H	BB	K	Ratio
5	3	1	3.02	56.2	59	14	31	1.288

Casian has good control, doesn't walk anybody and doesn't give up extra-base hits.

He does get nickel-and-dimed a bit, though. The league hit .268 of him, .345 with runners in scoring position. Still, his ERA and ratio are solid and he's a 28-year-old lefty. It doesn't look like he'll ever be a closer, but he's a solid middle-reliever. who'll be around for a while.

TONY CASTILLO								BLUE JAYS
W	L	SV	ERA	IP	H	BB	K	Ratio
3	2	0	3.38	50.2	44	22	28	1.303

The one significant thing about Tony's season that needs to be mentioned is that his ERA at the All-Star break was 2.22, but due to a rocky second half, it was 3.38 by year's end.

Last season was really his first effective campaign, as he allowed fewer hits than innings pitched for the first time in his career. But just by virtue of being a lefty, he will probably get his 50 innings of work in and draw his $185,000 paycheck.

NORM CHARLTON								MARINERS
W	L	SV	ERA	IP	H	BB	K	Ratio
1	3	18	2.34	34.2	22	17	48	1.125

Blew out his elbow in early August and after surgery, he isn't expected back until mid-season 1994. That cuts his value by more than half for rotisserie owners. We all know Charlton is excellent when healthy, so it might be worthwhile to use a couple of dollars on him as a gamble (especially if you have a minor-league draft and can get a quality long reliever with one of your picks).

TONY CHAVEZ								ANGELS
A – Cedar Rapids								
W	L	SV	ERA	IP	H	BB	K	Ratio
4	5	16	1.52	59.1	44	24	87	1.146

Chavez is 23. His control is the only question about him as he rises through the ranks. He'll start at Double-A Midland and should be in Triple-A, or the majors by year's end if he keeps plugging away.

STEVE CHITREN								ATHLETICS
AA – Huntsville								
W	L	SV	ERA	IP	H	BB	K	Ratio
2	1	1	5.17	55.2	53	35	39	1.581

Steve took a sabbatical to the minors last year to sort out some health and mechanical problems and he may have solved them.

His time in Double-A was typical of his control difficulties, but by the time he got to Tacoma he'd really lowered his walks and was throwing strikes.

He won't be more than average on the mound, but that makes him exceptional in Oakland.

MIKE CHRISTOPHER — INDIANS

AAA – Charlotte

W	L	SV	ERA	IP	H	BB	K	Ratio
3	6	22	3.22	50.1	51	6	36	1.133

Despite saving 22 games for Charlotte last year, and 26 games the year before that, he isn't the answer to the bullpen problems in Cleveland. What he lacks is a fastball, and the quality of his breaking pitches aren't helping him compensate. He's a man without a role right now, and at the age of 30, that is not a good sign.

JOE CICCARELLA — RED SOX

AA – New Britain

W	L	SV	ERA	IP	H	BB	K	Ratio
0	4	15	4.22	32	31	23	34	1.688

AAA – Pawtucket

W	L	SV	ERA	IP	H	BB	K	Ratio
0	1	0	5.60	17.2	27	12	8	2.20

We want Ciccarella to end up in the Cubs' organization just to hear Harry Caray butcher his name.

Joe had a good '92 season in Single-A, but he didn't impress anybody last year. He's only 24 and will have a chance to turn it around in New Britain this year. If he can't, he can always go back to hockey.

PAUL COLEMAN — CARDINALS

No pitching experience

The Cardinals passed on Frank Thomas in the '89 draft to pick Coleman as a power-hitting outfielder in the first round. But injuries have all but destroyed his chances of making it as a hitter. So what is he doing among the relievers, you might ask.

Well, he was discovered to have an impressive arm while at Double-A Arkansas and the Cardinals will try to make him a pitcher. He's a real longshot, but scouts had his fastball clocked at 94 MPH on the slow gun in the instructional league, and Cardinals GM Dal Maxville was quite impressed with his breaking ball. It's a crazy experiment, but if he can learn the knack of working hitters, Coleman could burst on the scene in a heartbeat.

DENNIS COOK — INDIANS

W	L	SV	ERA	IP	H	BB	K	Ratio
5	5	0	5.67	54	62	16	34	1.444

He has had good control throughout his career, and that fact is promising. However, all the other indicators are pointing down. If Cook pushed his game up a notch, he would still be mediocre.

DANNY COX — BLUE JAYS

W	L	SV	ERA	IP	H	BB	K	Ratio
7	6	2	3.12	83.2	73	29	84	1.219

He was very effective during the first half of the season, compiling a 2.47 ERA and striking out nearly a batter per inning. His second-half performance wasn't nearly as impressive though. After the All-Star break, he began suffering from back pain and Gaston had to reduce his workload considerably.

A cursory glance at his '93 season would indicate that he has finally returned to his old form. But even if he has, he'll have difficulty staying healthy over a full season and his work will be limited. Don't count on him to duplicate last year's success.

JOSE CORREA — TWINS

A – Fort Wayne

W	L	SV	ERA	IP	H	BB	K	Ratio
4	5	9	2.63	96	81	36	107	1.219

Correa is 22 and the Twins like his potential. Fort Wayne used him to close 18 games last year and that may be a sign of things to come. He numbers aren't stunning at this point, but they don't fall far from it.

He has an excellent K-rate and good control. If he can repeat this performance at Double-A this year, he'll be on the fast track through the Twins' organization.

OMAR DAAL — DODGERS

W	L	SV	ERA	IP	H	BB	K	Ratio
2	3	0	5.09	35.1	36	21	19	1.613

This lefty is rich in talent but a lightweight otherwise at 6-3, 160.

He's got a good curve and shows a lot of poise. The Dodgers like him and they need a closer, pending the possible arrival of Darren Dreifort.

VIC DARENSBOURG — MARLINS

A – Kane County

W	L	SV	ERA	IP	H	BB	K	Ratio
9	1	16	2.14	71	58	28	89	1.211

He's a small lefty, 5-10, 165, but Darensbourg throws a hard-moving 92-94 MPH fastball. He doesn't have much of a breaking ball yet. Despite this, there's a small chance that Vic can get a job in the spring with Florida. He's got a great arm and he's a lefty. At the very least, he should get a job in '95. All he has to do is keep succeeding at higher levels.

JEFF DARWIN							MARINERS
AA – Jacksonville							
W	L	SV	ERA	IP	H	BB	K	Ratio
3	5	7	2.97	36.1	29	17	39	1.266

Jeff is 24 and is the kid brother of 15-game winner Danny Darwin of the Red Sox.

You may remember Jeff as the guy who the Marlins traded Dave Magadan for. You may also remember him as the guy who the Mariners traded Dave Magadan for. Well, the Marlins got the best of the deal – They got Henry "Cotto Cheese" as interest on the deal! We're kidding, we're kidding!! We don't like Henry Cotto (actually, Henry, you're a nice guy, you just can't play baseball).

We do like Darwin, though. The fastball hits 94, the slider comes in at a pretty amazing 89 MPH. He doesn't have an off-speed pitch, so he's a reliever right now.

JIM DAUGHERTY							ASTROS
AA – Jackson							
W	L	SV	ERA	IP	H	BB	K	Ratio
2	2	36	1.87	53	39	21	55	1.132

He's your typical submarine/sinkerball-type. He changes speeds, mixing the fastball with an exceptional changeup and is currently trying to develop a slider to give hitters something else to think about. Daugherty is 26, so he's not a super prospect. In addition, with some of the arms the Astros have, he's probably not among the top three closer prospects they have. But hey, Doug Jones has had one helluva ride with similar stuff and there's no reason why Daugherty couldn't do the same.

CLINT DAVIS							CARDINALS
AA – Arkansas							
W	L	SV	ERA	IP	H	BB	K	Ratio
2	0	1	1.95	37	22	10	37	0.865

Davis, 24, has pitched beautifully in his first three professional seasons and is highly regarded in the organization. He throws a side-arm fastball with decent velocity but the Cardinals feel he needs another year of work on his breaking pitches. It's a good bet that Davis will pitch the entire season at Triple-A Louisville. But if he does well there, a promotion to the majors could come as early as April of '95.

MARK DAVIS							PADRES
W	L	SV	ERA	IP	H	BB	K	Ratio
1	5	4	4.26	69.2	79	44	70	1.765

As bad as he looked in Philadelphia, Davis looked exceptionally sharp in his homecoming, striking out batters left and right and lowering his ERA by a run and a half.

He may not be the reliever he was for that single shining moment in '89, but he has proven that he can throw long innings and throw strikes.

Used wisely, he'll be a valuable long reliever for the Padres.

TIM DAVIS							MARINERS
A – Riverside							
W	L	SV	ERA	IP	H	BB	K	Ratio
3	0	7	1.76	30.2	14	9	56	0.750

He basically did the same thing at Appleton for 78 innings, also.

Davis is 23 and no, he's not some 100-MPH fireballer. He is a junkballer with incredible command. He has a hard slider and an unbelievably deceptive changeup (at least to A-Ball hitters).

He's probably 12-to-18 months away, but if he can retain even 80 percent of his effectiveness, we'd like to be his agents.

STORM DAVIS							TIGERS
W	L	SV	ERA	IP	H	BB	K	Ratio
2	8	4	5.05	98	93	48	73	1.439

Davis was like two different pitchers last year. He was his normal lackluster self in Oakland, but the move to Detroit seemed to give him new life. In 35.1 innings for the Tigers, he recorded 36 K's, 4 saves and a 3.06 ERA. He could provide the solid middle-relief the Tigers are desperate for next year.

But don't forget Storm's normal lackluster self. He's still a risk.

Jim Dedrick — Orioles

AA – Bowie

W	L	SV	ERA	IP	H	BB	K	Ratio
8	3	3	2.54	106.1	84	32	78	1.091

Dedrick was impressive last year in his Double-A debut. He keeps guys off base and throws a few K's. But the Orioles don't know what they want to do with him; he started six games and finished 14 of his 38 appearances.

He probably deserves a shot in Triple-A next year, but he's 26 and may have missed his window of opportunity.

Jose DeLeon — White Sox

W	L	SV	ERA	IP	H	BB	K	Ratio
3	0	0	2.98	57.1	44	30	40	1.291

DeLeon doesn't look any more effective as a long reliever than he has as a starter in recent seasons.

He didn't have enough time to prove this as a White Sox, but he will given time. Chicago has too many quality pitchers to waste their time on old-timers like Jose.

John DeSilva — Dodgers

AAA – Toledo

W	L	SV	ERA	IP	H	BB	K	Ratio
7	10	0	3.69	161	145	60	136	1.273

DeSilva is reknowned for his fine K/W ratios and his inability to get a trial with the Tigers when he was n their organization. Now he's with the pitching-rich Dodgers and there's even less of a chance that he'll get a job. He could be an effective long-reliever, but he'll probably be someone with a 4.50+ ERA at Albuquerque.

Rob Dibble — Reds

W	L	SV	ERA	IP	H	BB	K	Ratio
1	4	19	6.48	41.2	34	42	49	1.632

Rob let loose a wild pitch on April 21 with the potential winning run on third, and broke his arm applying the tag at home plate. The arm required surgery and sidelined him for a month. He also suffered from a perforated eardrum early in the season which caused equilibrium problems and ruined his control.

We said last year that his weird mechanics may begin to cause injuries, and these freak events don't fall under that category, but we weren't too far from the mark.

Rob's attitude and his injuries should concern you. He may be able to turn in a couple more decent years, but he's embarked on a downward trend.

Frank DiPino — Royals

W	L	SV	ERA	IP	H	BB	K	Ratio
1	1	0	6.89	15.2	21	6	5	1.723

He is 37 years old. Somebody should clue the Royals on to the fact that DiPino isn't exactly the Nolan Ryan of relief. Incredibly, he's still on their 40-man roster.

Jerry DiPoto — Indians

W	L	SV	ERA	IP	H	BB	K	Ratio
4	4	11	2.40	56.1	57	30	41	1.544

DiPoto, 26, began his pro career as a starter. But he suffered through four lackluster seasons in the rotation, largely because he had difficulty doing two things; changing speeds and waiting the required five days to pitch again. The Indians moved him into the bullpen for the '92 season, feeling that his intensity would suit him well in that role. It paid off last year, as DiPoto posted 11 saves for the Tribe over the second half of the season.

DiPoto has yet to show the command of his pitches required of a closer. He likes to get ahead of the hitters, and when he does, he is very effective. But he gets in a lot of trouble when the count slips to 2-0 because he can't throw the breaking ball for strikes, forcing him to offer up the meaty fastball.

The Indians would like to see him step up in '94 and claim the closer job. But as a prospect, DiPoto is a longshot. His breakthrough season in Charlotte last year was a good sign, but unless his control improves, he will have little chance of repeating his success. He would be much better off serving as understudy to an established closer for a season or two before taking the reigns.

Steve Dixon — Cardinals

AAA – Louisville

W	L	SV	ERA	IP	H	BB	K	Ratio
5	7	20	4.92	67.2	57	33	61	1.330

Steve collected 20 saves for Louisville last year, but he also had an ERA that just missed the 5.00 mark. Don't invest a lot in his future until he gets a handle on Triple-A hitters.

Dixon has a tendency to stalk around the mound and mutter to himself and the baseball, ala Mark Fidrych. While the theatrics might indicate his intensity on the mound, they won't help him get big league hitters out.

Kelly Downs							Athletics
W	L	SV	ERA	IP	H	BB	K	Ratio
5	10	0	5.64	119.2	135	60	66	1.630

Downs' effectiveness as a starter was so poor (0-6 in his 12 starts) that he was relegated to the bullpen for good.

He still didn't pitch well. Despite lowering his ERA and winning some games, he walked a man for every one he struck out. He's too old and he's a terrible risk.

Brian Drahman							Marlins
AAA – Nashville							
W	L	SV	ERA	IP	H	BB	K	Ratio
9	4	20	2.91	55.2	59	19	49	1.401

His productive innigs were spent in AAA, but he was able enough to convince the Marlins to take a chance on him.

He's got good potential as a closer, but his lack of major league experience may work against him. He's a good low-dollar risk for fantasy leaguers.

Mike Draper							Mets
W	L	SV	ERA	IP	H	BB	K	Ratio
1	1	0	4.25	42.1	53	14	16	1.583

Draper, 27, allowed a .327 batting average and struck out only 16 batters in 42.1 innings, so it's safe to say he didn't intimidate anybody in the majors. To compound his miserable rookie season, he suffered a torn ligament in his elbow in mid-August and spent the remainder of the season on the DL. Draft him only if you're serious about finishing in the second division.

Darren Dreifort	Dodgers
Played in instructional league – no stats available	

Dreifort was an incredibly hard sign, as draft picks with his talent are prone to be.

He was the No. 2 pick and looks like he was worth it. Although he was an excellent hitter at Wichita State he was drafted for his 96+ MPH fastball and wicked slider.

Among drafted players, Dreifort's considered the most ready for the bigs and the Dodgers are running him with blinders on into the bullpen, where they intend to make him the regular closer.

A '92 operation on both knees hampered him in the instructional league but he should shake it off and jet through L.A.'s system.

Dennis Eckersley							Athletics
W	L	SV	ERA	IP	H	BB	K	Ratio
2	4	36	4.16	67	67	13	80	1.194

Eckersley didn't have a bad year, if he was anybody but the Eck.

Who would complain about an 80/13 K/W ratio but the Eck?

A lousy 36 saves? Not the Eck!

The secret to his downfall, lefties. They destroyed. They've always been a weakness held in check, until now. Lefties hit .323 against him, while righties only hit .197. Five homers and 34 RBI allowed in 130 lefty at-bats while allowing two homers and nine RBI in 127 innings against the right.

Eckersley is 39, lest we forget, so his newly exposed humanity should serve as little shock.

Despite this, he's still a lock to be one of the best relievers in the game. Fantasy owners, it's conceivable that he may go for less than $40 for the first time in years.

Tom Edens							Astros
W	L	SV	ERA	IP	H	BB	K	Ratio
1	1	0	3.12	49	47	19	21	1.347

Known in the common parlance as a "relief cheese-bomb." With his K/W ratio and age (33) you want to treat him like he's coming to twon with a bomb in his trunk.

Mark Eichhorn							Blue Jays
W	L	SV	ERA	IP	H	BB	K	Ratio
3	1	0	2.72	72.2	76	22	47	1.349

Earned Run Average is an invaluable tool to measure a pitchers' worth, but especially in the case of relievers, it doesn't tell the whole story. Mark Eichhorn, with his 3-1 record and 2.72 ERA, is a prime example.

Eichhorn has a lot of trouble keeping runners from scoring, and in the bullpen, that is a fatal flaw. In '93, he allowed 20 of the 48 runners he inherited to cross the plate. The fact that opposing hitters posted a .272 average against him probably had something to do with his ineffectiveness, don't you think?

Despite his 3.01 ERA over the past five years, Eichhorn has allowed 35 percent of his inherited baserunners to score over the same period. He is yet another example of a pitcher who is more valuable to a fantasy league team than he is to his own major league team.

STEVE FARR							YANKEES
W	L	SV	ERA	IP	H	BB	K	Ratio
2	2	25	4.21	47	44	28	39	1.532

Although Farr managed 25 saves, he's really deteriorating fast. His walks and hits allowed went up while his ERA skyrocketed from last year.

More importantly, with import Xavier Hernandez in town, "Farr Away" is going to be the operative phrase on everyone's lips.

MIKE FETTERS							BREWERS
W	L	SV	ERA	IP	H	BB	K	Ratio
3	3	0	3.34	59.1	59	22	23	1.365

Fetters returned to his sordid past of lousy control and average ERAs, looking more like the Mike Fetid we grew accustomed to. We predicted good things for him, and we weren't on target.

We feel confident that Fetters will be mediocre in '94. After all, he's done that before.

HUCK FLENER							BLUE JAYS
AA – Knoxville							
W	L	SV	ERA	IP	H	BB	K	Ratio
13	6	4	3.30	136.1	130	39	114	1.240

Flener, 25, has made steady progress through the Blue Jay system since being drafted in the ninth round of the 1990 draft, culminating in a six-game stint in the big leagues last year. In 1991, he struck out 107 hitters and posted a 1.82 ERA in a little over 79 innings for Myrtle Beach, so there seems to be little doubt about his ability to handle minor-league batters.

Considering that Toronto's bullpen is in need of young blood, he could win a job in the spring, though he will probably be limited to long-relief. He might struggle with his control at first, as many young pitchers do, but he has a good chance to become an effective set-up man within a couple of years.

JOHN FRANCO							METS
W	L	SV	ERA	IP	H	BB	K	Ratio
4	3	10	5.20	36.1	46	19	29	1.789

After two consecutive injury-plagued seasons, Franco seems to be nearing the end of his productive career. He might be able to hang on for a few more seasons, but the Mets cannot depend on him as their closer anymore. It's time they passed the mantle to someone else.

SCOTT FREDRICKSON							ROCKIES
W	L	SV	ERA	IP	H	BB	K	Ratio
0	1	0	6.21	29	33	17	20	1.724

Taken in the third round of the expansion draft, Fredrickson, 26, became the first player ever promoted to the Rockies in April. He spent the season being shuffled back and forth between the majors and the PCL, so it's no surprise that he never settled in anywhere.

Scott's a burly guy, standing 6-3 and weighing in at 215 lbs. He throws a hard slider and an above-average fastball that has good movement. The Rockies can use his arm in long relief, but he really needs a full season in Colorado Springs to hone his skills and build confidence.

MARVIN FREEMAN							BRAVES
W	L	SV	ERA	IP	H	BB	K	Ratio
2	0	0	6.08	23.2	24	10	25	1.436

Like Pedro Borbon, Marvin's control really led to his problems. He only allowed one dinger in his 23.2 innings and he struck out 9.5 per 9 IP, so there are positives here. Then again, he also let lefties tattoo him at a .286 clip. He's OK, but he atrophied on the pine. If he can get the innings, he'll be an effective middle-man. He's not much else, though.

KEVIN FOSTER							PHILLIES
W	L	SV	ERA	IP	H	BB	K	Ratio
1	1	0	3.93	71	63	29	59	1.296

A 25-year-old swingman, Foster looks okay, but he's just another guy on the depth chart until he moves his game up.

STEVE FOSTER							REDS
W	L	SV	ERA	IP	H	BB	K	Ratio
2	2	0	1.75	25.2	23	5	16	1.091

Foster suffered from numerous ailments last year, including inflammation in his right shoulder, bicep tendinitis and torn cartilage in his right shoulder. He was also on Nashville's DL in '92.

Steve recorded buku saves in his minor league career and has always done a good job keeping guys off base. But you have to wonder how much his 27-year-old arm can take.

He's an effective pitcher if he's healthy and he's young so he may recuperate well. But take a close look at him in the spring before you draft him.

STEVE FREY								ANGELS
W	L	SV	ERA	IP	H	BB	K	Ratio
2	3	13	2.98	48.1	41	26	22	1.386

It's like the Angels collect guys with terrible K/W ratios and give them save opportunities. Frey will do as a makeshift closer (he actually converted 81 percent of his save opps. last year), but he's going to get displaced as soon as Watson, Percival, or someone else is viable. Watch the battles in the spring, someone could show up and wrest this lefties saves.

TODD FROHWIRTH								ORIOLES
W	L	SV	ERA	IP	H	BB	K	Ratio
6	7	3	3.83	96.1	91	44	50	1.401

Frohwirth did an adequate filling in for injured closer Gregg Olson, last year, but he's definitely in a state of decline.

His ratio has increased and his strikeouts decreased for the second year. Now he's got younger and better guys behind him who are ready to come up and perform at the major league level.

He's not bad, but he's 31 and about to be pushed out in Baltimore.

PAUL GIBSON								YANKEES
W	L	SV	ERA	IP	H	BB	K	Ratio
3	1	0	3.48	44	45	11	37	1.273

Gibson improved exponentially after moving across town from Shea to Yankee Stadium. The biggest factor was defense. He had one as a Yankee.

Gibson should continue to be at least mediocre. He's not young, but a good infield will shave runs off his ERA like a Black and Decker hedge trimmer.

WAYNE GOMES								PHILLIES
A – Clearwater								
W	L	SV	ERA	IP	H	BB	K	Ratio
0	0	4	1.17	8	4	9	13	1.625

Taken out of Old Dominion with the Phillies No. 1 pick (No. 4 overall), Gomes is a classic lefty power reliever. He has a 95-MPH heater and a very hard-breaking curve. He has two weaknesses: 1) Cholesterol; 2) an inability to throw strikes.

In addition, he hasn't thrown much, so he has little experience (i.e. bad mechanics). According to the Phillies' time-table, Gomes is at least a year away, possibly even two.

GOOSE GOSSAGE								ATHLETICS
W	L	SV	ERA	IP	H	BB	K	Ratio
4	5	1	4.53	47.2	49	26	40	1.573

Gossage hung tough, striking out a lot of guys and walking few. The last time his K/W ratio looked this good was when he was a Padre in '87.

Considering how miserable the rest of the staff is, Gossage is a keeper. It's unlikely that he can keep this up for much longer at his age, but he looks a helluva lot stronger than his toddler colleagues.

JIM GOTT								DODGERS
W	L	SV	ERA	IP	H	BB	K	Ratio
4	8	25	2.32	77.2	71	17	67	1.133

Few remember (we didn't until we looked it up), but back in 1988 Gott saved 34 games for the Pirates.

After injuries ended his career in Pittsburgh he was shipped to L.A., where he had a distinguished but unremarkable career in long relief.

This year he exploded. His control and ERA were excellent and he was handed the closer role over McDowell and Worrell. He may save more games in '94, but L.A. still needs to find a relief ace. If Dreifort isn't ready, Gott is an adequate draft for fantasy teams.

JOE GRAHE								ANGELS
W	L	SV	ERA	IP	H	BB	K	Ratio
4	1	11	2.86	56.2	54	25	31	1.394

He's a right-handed Steve Frey, all junk and location and no K's. He hasn't developed the way the Angels hoped, so he's their stop-gap righty closer until someone displaces him.

RICK GREENE — TIGERS

A – Lakeland

W	L	SV	ERA	IP	H	BB	K	Ratio
2	3	2	6.20	40.2	57	16	32	1.795

AA – London

W	L	SV	ERA	IP	H	BB	K	Ratio
2	2	0	6.52	29	31	20	19	1.759

Greene, 23, was the Tigers' top pick in the '92 draft and his performance last year was somewhat less than they expected.

He's a youngster and has very good velocity of his fastball, but at this point, he's just a tad inconsistent.

JOHN GRIMM — TIGERS

A – Fayetteville

W	L	SV	ERA	IP	H	BB	K	Ratio
0	2	10	1.45	37.1	18	14	58	.857

A – Lakeland

W	L	SV	ERA	IP	H	BB	K	Ratio
2	1	3	2.45	18.1	12	11	17	1.255

Grimm turned in some outstanding numbers in Fayetteville before moving to Lakeland. He averaged 13.9 K/9IP, posted a 4.1 K/W and didn't let anybody on base.

He cooled off a bit in Lakeland but he only pitched 18.1 innings there. John's 23 and has to be considered an excellent prospect.

MARK GUBICZA — ROYALS

W	L	SV	ERA	IP	H	BB	K	Ratio
5	8	2	4.66	104.1	128	43	80	1.639

In the inaugural edition of the Advocate, we said that Gubicza's career was in serious jeopardy. Well, it still is. Like a good trooper, Gubicza took another pay cut and is volunteering to serve out of the bullpen if needed. Like he has a choice.

LEE GUETTERMAN — CARDINALS

W	L	SV	ERA	IP	H	BB	K	Ratio
3	3	1	2.93	46	41	16	19	1.239

Guetterman, who stands 6-8, has value to the Cardinals during the occasional bench-clearing brawls as a head-knocker. As a pitcher, though, he's weak.

MARK GUTHRIE — TWINS

W	L	SV	ERA	IP	H	BB	K	Ratio
2	1	0	4.71	21	20	16	15	1.714

Disregard this line. Guthrie missed the majority of the season with a blood clot in his left (throwing) shoulder and obviously wasn't himself when he was playing.

Mark can pitch and will be effective if he can recover from the injury. He's averaged 6.9 K/9IP for the last five years, including last year's disappointment.

He should return to his role of setup man for Rick Aguilera.

JOHN HABYAN — ROYALS

W	L	SV	ERA	IP	H	BB	K	Ratio
2	1	1	4.15	56.1	59	20	39	1.402

Habyan came over from the Yankees on July 30 in a crazy three-way swap that also involved the Cubs. In a nutshell, the Royals sent Karl Rhodes to Chicago and got Habyan from New York. By the way, the Royals also got hosed down in the deal.

Habyan hasn't pitched well since 1991, and he sure didn't win over his new team with his 4.15 ERA over the second half. He's losing steam quickly and should be considered a bad investment.

GENE HARRIS — PADRES

W	L	SV	ERA	IP	H	BB	K	Ratio
6	6	23	3.03	59.1	57	37	39	1.583

Same shoddy control, but he saved quite a few games. There's no way he should have been as successful as he was, and nobody wants to bet he'll do it again.

He could lose his job to someone like Hoffman or even Steve Hoeme, but he throws 95+.

MIKE HARTLEY — TWINS

W	L	SV	ERA	IP	H	BB	K	Ratio
1	2	1	4.00	81	86	36	57	1.506

Hartley's starting to get knocked around at age 32. The K's are decreasing and the walks and hits-allowed are increasing (as is his age).

Mike was, at one time, a fairly consistent middle-reliever, but now he's slipping.

BRYAN HARVEY — MARLINS

W	L	SV	ERA	IP	H	BB	K	Ratio
1	5	45	1.70	69	45	13	73	0.841

Harvey's arm was tender late in the year, so the Marlins treated him with great care. But apart from that, Harvey was a horse, perpetually sending National League hitters back to their kennels with their bats between their legs. We're not exactly sure how he fits in with the Marlins' long-range plans, but he's one of the best in the game.

If he can nail down 45 saves with an expansion team, you gotta figure he could save a bunch more if he was sent to a contender.

HEATH HAYNES								EXPOS
AA – Harrisburg								
W	L	SV	ERA	IP	H	BB	K	Ratio
8	0	5	2.59	66	46	19	78	0.985

Haynes, 25, is moving rather slowly up the ranks for someone with his performance level. We wrote about him last year and told you to keep an eye on him. It's obvious from the way he's been handled that he's not viewed as a top-level major-leaguer by Montreal. But when you have a ratio under 1.000 and a strikeout rate of 10.6 per nine, then you have to be doing everything right.

Dave: My guess is that he's a junkballer with excellent command. With his power-pitcher-like numbers, I'm betting he'd be a success in the majors.

KURT HEBLE								BLUE JAYS
A – Dunedin								
W	L	SV	ERA	IP	H	BB	K	Ratio
6	1	4	2.49	50.2	35	34	66	1.362

He's a long-range prospect and got hit pretty hard in his first taste of Double-A ball late last year. But he looked brilliant in the Florida State League and the Blue Jays will take a long, hard look at him in the spring. Look for him to be assigned to Double-A Knoxville at the beginning of the season.

JEREMY HERNANDEZ								INDIANS
W	L	SV	ERA	IP	H	BB	K	Ratio
6	7	8	3.63	111.2	116	34	70	1.343

Jeremy's claim to fame is that he is one of three players named Hernandez who were involved in two separate Cleveland trades on June 1 last year. Unfortunately, though, nothing he's done in his career to date distinguishes him from the run-of-the-mill reliever. He can eat up innings in the Indian bullpen, but that's about it.

XAVIER HERNANDEZ								YANKEES
W	L	SV	ERA	IP	H	BB	K	Ratio
4	5	9	2.61	96.2	75	28	101	1.065

He's probably been the best long reliever in the National League over the last two years. He was excellent in '92, and last year, the league's offense went berzerk, but X-man kept his ERA at an excellent level, while vastly improving his control!

Xavier has good stuff (excellent forkball) and his value may go through the roof. The Yankees intend to at least give him a shot at the right-handed portion of the closing job. Heck, they may give him the whole shebang. It's not like they have 15 options, everyone on that relief staff is a giant question mark.

TOM HENKE								RANGERS
W	L	SV	ERA	IP	H	BB	K	Ratio
5	5	40	2.91	74.1	55	27	79	1.103

The warm Texas air proved to be therapeutic for Henke. His total of 40 saves was his highest ever and was the third highest in the AL. Not bad for a 36-year-old, especially considering the fair amount of innings he pitched.

There has been some concern in recent years about Henke's injury-prone status, but he stayed healthy all year and averaged over 9.5 K/W to reward the Rangers for their faith in him. Apparently, he's not done yet.

But the fact remains that he's had problems with injury in the past and he is aging. He still has the stuff, but it's always a gamble when you draft a power pitcher who's over 35.

MIKE HENNNEMAN								TIGERS
W	L	SV	ERA	IP	H	BB	K	Ratio
5	3	24	2.64	71.2	69	32	58	1.409

Henneman tied his career high of 24 saves and recorded his lowest ERA since '88.

Last year, we graded Henneman a solid C+; his effort in '93 moves him up to at least a B-. He finished ninth in the AL with a .828 save percentage, which certainly suggests that he's a consistent performer.

But he still lets too many guys on base to be called dominant. He gets the job done, but he's not among the elite.

DOUG HENRY — BREWERS

W	L	SV	ERA	IP	H	BB	K	Ratio
4	4	17	5.56	55	67	25	38	1.673

He got 17 saves, blowing another seven opportunities, and watched his K/W ratio take a drastic turn.

He allows a shipload of baserunners and he can't save games when he gives up as many runs as he does.

He's not good, but he's probably all that Milwaukee has next year.

JULIAN HEREDIA — ANGELS

AA – Midland

W	L	SV	ERA	IP	H	BB	K	Ratio
5	3	0	3.12	89.1	77	19	89	1.075

There's really little about 24-year-old Julian that you can't like. He has excellent control, keeps the hits down and pitches like a long-reliever Clemens in a park that has more in common with Mile High, than the Astrodome (i.e. it's a great hitter's park). With numbers like these, you have to think he could pitch – and pitch damn well, thank you – if he got a major-league relief role.

ROBERTO HERNANDEZ — WHITE SOX

W	L	SV	ERA	IP	H	BB	K	Ratio
3	4	38	2.29	78.2	66	20	71	1.119

Roberto was just like Rod Beck in the sense that he made it so easy to see his potential as a closer last year.

He's already 29, so he's definitely less valuable than a veritable pup like Beck, but he's also got years of greatness before him by virtue of strength in a limited role.

BRYAN HICKERSON — GIANTS

W	L	SV	ERA	IP	H	BB	K	Ratio
7	5	0	4.26	120.1	137	39	69	1.463

Nowhere near as sharp as he was last year, Bryan misplaced his control over the winter.

Part of the problem was that he was starting 15 games along the way. Hickerson is prone to get racked up by righthanded batters. This tendency is only exacerbated by pitching long innings to guys who kill you in middle relief.

Hickerson gives up nothing to lefties, and may be one of the most effective pitchers against southpaws in the league.

He's better in relief, and the Giants have undoubtedly realized this point. He's not young, so the Giants should use him while he's still vital.

MILT HILL — BRAVES

AAA – Indianapolis

W	L	SV	ERA	IP	H	BB	K	Ratio
3	5	2	4.08	53	53	17	45	1.321

W	L	SV	ERA	IP	H	BB	K	Ratio
3	0	0	5.65	28.2	34	9	23	1.500

Milt, 28, is in serious jeopardy of missing his window of opportunity. A couple years ago, he looked a shoe-in for a middle-relief job, but he was used by the Reds last year only to fill holes when Dibble and Landrum went on the DL.

He's starting to get tagged by the hitters at both Triple-A and the majors. He needs to reverse this trend in Richmond this year because the Braves have younger guys who are more than willing to take his slot.

SHAWN HILL — INDIANS

A – Geneva

W	L	SV	ERA	IP	H	BB	K	Ratio
5	4	12	2.25	40	26	17	55	1.075

This 24-year-old displayed excellent control and over 12 strikeouts per nine innings last year in the NY-P League, so it's safe to say he's caught the organization's eye. But the Indians will surely want to see what he does against stiffer competition before they give him the call. He'll get a ticket to Double-A if he performs well in the spring and he could be in Charlotte before the year is out.

STEVE HOEME — PADRES

AA – Wichita

W	L	SV	ERA	IP	H	BB	K	Ratio
2	3	19	2.42	48.1	41	16	47	1.179

Hoeme had sweet ERA and save numbers with a fine K-rate and some control thrown in.

He's another guy just treading water at his present level. Sending him to the PCL will be the real test. He should make it to Triple-A in early '94 and could earn himself a tryout if he throws well.

JESSE HOLLINS — CUBS
No stats due to injury

He seemed to have made great strides with his control in '92, but arthroscopic surgery on his rotator cuff and a frayed tendon forced him to sit out all of last year.

Hollins, 24, slipped out of the organizations' top-ten prospect list, but the Cubs will give him a long look in the spring. If he can demonstrate he's healthy and has regained the 95+ MPH velocity he was famous for, he has a shot at breaking camp with the big leaguers.

BRAD HOLMAN — MARINERS

W	L	SV	ERA	IP	H	BB	K	Ratio
1	3	3	3.72	36.1	27	16	17	1.184

You may remember Holman because he took that vicious line-drive off his face late in the season. What a terrifying moment that was. ... Well anyway, he was extremely tough to hit while in Seattle, but didn't appear to be anything real special at Calgary (4.74 ERA, 1.530 ratio). What we're probably looking at is a marginal 26-year-old middle-reliever. His ERA will probably check in the high threes, low fours.

DARREN HOLMES — ROCKIES

W	L	SV	ERA	IP	H	BB	K	Ratio
3	3	25	4.05	66.2	56	20	60	1.140

He got off to a "Rockie" start and was demoted for a short time in April, but there really isn't anything wrong with Homes that a little more atmosphere wouldn't fix. While he got bombed for a 6.16 ERA before the All-Star break, he got his act together over the second half of the season, compiling 17 saves and a neat little 2.25 ERA. There shouldn't be too many concerns about him. He's not a blue-chip closer, but he was good enough to convert 25 saves out of 29 opportunities in mile-high country. He can get the job done until the Rockies can develop someone better.

TREVOR HOFFMAN — PADRES

W	L	SV	ERA	IP	H	BB	K	Ratio
4	6	5	3.90	90	80	39	70	1.322

While his control of the plate improved drastically upon his arrival in San Diego, his ERA climbed a full run and he gave up a lot more hits than he did as a Marlin.

Trevor's a talent to be reckoned with and he's reaching the age where his ability should ripen. Look for him to bloom and become a solid long reliever.

RICK HONEYCUTT — RANGERS

W	L	SV	ERA	IP	H	BB	K	Ratio
1	4	1	2.81	41.2	30	20	21	1.200

He had huge control problems, but didn't give up hits, thus keeping his ERA down.

When it comes down to it, he and former teammate Gossage (the two will combine for 82 years of age in '94), were far better than their younger brethren.

Honeycutt may not be as effective as he was in his prime, but he can still set the table better than the legion of 28-year-old nobodies which plagues the league.

STEVE HOWE — YANKEES

W	L	SV	ERA	IP	H	BB	K	Ratio
3	5	4	4.97	50.2	58	10	19	1.342

Evan: I have a confession to make. After penning a scathing essay on Howe and his drug problem I had the nerve to draft him in our Rotisserie league.

However, if the court will examine Mr. Howe's stats from '93, I'm sure they will agree that I have more than atoned for my hubris by suffering through his lousy season.

Even if the Yanks give him a reprieve you can rest assured that he won't be on my team. I've learned my lesson.

MIKE IGNASIAK — BREWERS
AAA – New Orleans

W	L	SV	ERA	IP	H	BB	K	Ratio
6	0	9	1.09	57.2	26	20	61	0.798

He needs to translate the control and moxie that he demonstrated in Triple-A New Orleans to the bigs. He can strike guys out but he allows too many base runners to be considered an effective reliever.

He's still young enough (28) to be of value to the Brewers.

JEFF INNIS — METS

W	L	SV	ERA	IP	H	BB	K	Ratio
2	3	3	4.11	76.2	81	38	36	1.552

Although his 4.11 ERA was more than a run higher than his career average, 1993 was a typical Innis performance. He continues to induce a ton of groundball outs with his submarine delivery, and as a result, only nine of 34 inherited baserunners scored while he was on the mound.

His control was off last year and the league compiled a .372 on-base average off him. But while it might be cause for a little concern, Innis hasn't given any indications why he can't come back strong in '94. He should again be a capable set-up guy for whoever the closer turns out to be in New York.

MIKE JACKSON								GIANTS
W	L	SV	ERA	IP	H	BB	K	Ratio
6	6	1	3.03	77.1	58	24	70	1.060

He continued the control streak he's been on the last two seasons and lowered his hits allowed to boot.

He's a career long reliever, so his experience is much greater than most reliever's his age. he's been doing it longer and he's one of the best. He should continue to be a valuable complement to Rod Beck.

JOHN JOHNSTONE								MARLINS
AAA – Edmonton								
W	L	SV	ERA	IP	H	BB	K	Ratio
4	15	4	5.18	144.1	167	59	126	1.566

Johnstone, 25, started off like crap in the Edmonton rotation. He started short-arming the ball and junked his excellent curveball, thus exacerbating his problems.

The Marlins got desperate, put him in the bullpen, and he turned it around. He's very intense and the increased activity he saw in the bullpen must have helped him. He's currently working on a split-finger and may win a job with the Marlins' bullpen this year.

CALVIN JONES								INDIANS
AA – Canton-Akron								
W	L	SV	ERA	IP	H	BB	K	Ratio
5	5	22	3.30	62.2	40	26	73	1.053

Lest you be deceived by the 22 saves he racked up for Double-A Canton-Akron last year, consider one thing. There's got to be a reason why this 30-year-old man is still playing in the bush leagues.

DOUG JONES								PHILLIES
W	L	SV	ERA	IP	H	BB	K	Ratio
4	10	26	4.54	85.1	102	21	66	1.442

1993 Advocate: "The Astros worked (Jones) alarmingly hard last year. (He) may be less effective because of the overwork."

The 111.2 innings they had him pitch in 1992 were 20 more than he'd ever worked in his career. At age 35, the Astros asked him to work 22 percent harder than he ever had (and he had that 91.2 inning season five years previously, in 1987!).

Imagine if the Red Sox asked Roger Clemens to pitch that many more innings at age 35 (it would be 343.2 innings, in case you were wondering)?!

In *Baseball America*, Peter Gammons said that Jones has lost something off his change. Well, that's not surprising. When you work a pitcher at an unprecedented level when he's 36, expect something to flunk flank.

We hope that the Phillies show more sense and use him wisely, but it may be too late.

TODD JONES								ASTROS
W	L	SV	ERA	IP	H	BB	K	Ratio
4	2	12	3.13	37.1	28	15	25	1.072

Jones worked on junking his slow curve for a cut fastball during the winter season in 1992. He seemed kind of mediocre at Triple-A. But of course, this is the PCL we're talking about and his ERA dropped by a run and change with the jump to the majors. He looks like a solid pitcher to us (as long as his control stays at its current level) and right now he's the No. 1 replacement if anything should happen to the Wild Thing.

PAUL KILGUS								CARDINALS
W	L	SV	ERA	IP	H	BB	K	Ratio
1	0	1	0.63	28.2	18	8	21	0.907

Kilgus pitched brilliantly for the Cardinals last year, allowing only one of the 14 baserunners he inherited to score. But one must be prepared for a recurrence of the control problems that have plagued him in the past. If he can control his wildness, there's no reason why he can't contribute solid numbers to the Cardinal bullpen.

Kevin King — Mariners

A – Riverside

W	L	SV	ERA	IP	H	BB	K	Ratio
3	2	5	1.57	46	37	20	28	1.239

AA – Jacksonville

W	L	SV	ERA	IP	H	BB	K	Ratio
2	0	1	3.14	28.2	25	7	13	1.116

King, 25, doesn't have the most impressive stats, but he pitched in the majors last year (quite ineffectively) and Piniella is seriously considering him for the pen in '94.

His K-rates are rather bad, while his control at Double-A looked very good. We don't know much about him, but it looks like he's a finesse pitcher.

Kurt Knudsen — Tigers

AAA – Toledo

W	L	SV	ERA	IP	H	BB	K	Ratio
2	2	6	3.78	33.1	24	11	39	1.05

W	L	SV	ERA	IP	H	BB	K	Ratio
3	2	2	4.78	37.2	41	16	29	1.514

Basically, Kurt can get the job done but not much more. He has a good fastball and hard slider and he gets a few K's with them.

But at 27, he's hardly a hot prospect. He's been playing more of a role in Detroit the last couple years and that will probably continue in '93, but he's average. Period.

Chris Kotes — Blue Jays

A – Dunedin

W	L	SV	ERA	IP	H	BB	K	Ratio
2	2	0	2.57	42	37	12	41	1.167

We haven't heard too much about him yet, but that will soon change, especially if he turns in another season like last year. Kotes is 25 and at least another two years away, but he's highly regarded by the organization and could find himself in Triple-A Syracuse before the year is out.

Bill Krueger — Tigers

W	L	SV	ERA	IP	H	BB	K	Ratio
6	4	0	3.40	82	90	30	60	1.463

Krueger's 36 and gives up more hits and walks every year. Plus, he missed almost two months last year with tendinitis in his left elbow. There's still room for him in Detroit, but not on your staff.

Les Lancaster — Cardinals

W	L	SV	ERA	IP	H	BB	K	Ratio
4	1	0	2.93	61.1	56	21	36	1.256

Lancaster has a four-pitch repertoire and can work hitters. But he's always been a little generous with the longball and shouldn't be trusted in later innings. He's a middle-of-the-road pitcher who could go either way in '94.

Richie Lewis — Marlins

W	L	SV	ERA	IP	H	BB	K	Ratio
6	3	0	3.26	77.1	68	43	65	1.435

Richie displayed adequate control in the minors, so we should probably look for a drop from 5.0 walks per game down to 3.5-4.0 or so. Other than that, he's a pretty solid middle reliever. He's 28 and doesn't look like he's good enough to move up the food chain.

Scott Lewis — Angels

AAA – Vancouver

W	L	SV	ERA	IP	H	BB	K	Ratio
3	1	9	1.37	39.1	31	9	38	1.017

W	L	SV	ERA	IP	H	BB	K	Ratio
1	2	0	4.22	32	37	12	10	1.531

Lewis, 28, has been futzing around like this for years. He has what it takes to pitch well in the majors, but he keeps screwing up when he gets a job. If things break well, he could get 15+ save chances. If they don't, he'll do more of the same.

Derek Lilliquist — Indians

W	L	SV	ERA	IP	H	BB	K	Ratio
4	4	10	2.25	64	64	19	40	1.297

Largely because of his bulky frame, Derek was never given credit for his ability to pitch. Given up for dead by the Padres in '91, Lilliquist signed with the Indians before the '92 season and has pitched excellent ball the past two years.

Lilliquist, 28, doesn't have awesome stuff, relying instead on his ability to get ahead of the hitters. He fell behind in the count to only 39 of the 271 batters he faced last season. Although he gives up a lot of hits, he is stingy with the extra bases and the free pass.

Lilliquist did his part to help compensate for the tragic loss of Steve Olin, converting 10 of 13 save opportunities. However, he lacks the tenacity and the overpowering stuff that true closers are made of. No matter what his role is, however, Lilliquist should contribute solid innings for the Tribe.

Chris Limbach							Royals
AA – Memphis							
W	L	SV	ERA	IP	H	BB	K	Ratio
3	4	6	2.73	92.1	85	22	82	1.159

Although he isn't a grade-A prospect, he has seen his share of success in his eight minor-league seasons, mostly because he throws strikes and is not afraid to challenge hitters. Also, he is only 26 years old, and has been pitching in relief his whole career – so you know his arm hasn't been abused. Limbach has a chance to break into the Royals' bullpen in '94.

Marty Lister							Reds
A – Charleston-WV							
W	L	SV	ERA	IP	H	BB	K	Ratio
1	2	32	2.08	52	38	31	57	1.327

Baseball Weekly picked Lister as the Reds' second best pitching prospect last year. He's a 21-year-old lefty who throws 90+ MPH with a decent hard slider. He's also pretty wild (31 BB, 6 WP), so South Atlantic League hitters were terrified of him. Marty idolizes Randy Myers and he's getting a reputation as kind of a looney.

Lister needs to improve his control; he'll get to work on it in Double-A this year.

Graeme Lloyd							Brewers
W	L	SV	ERA	IP	H	BB	K	Ratio
3	4	14	1.96	92	79	25	65	1.130

He put in some valuable innings for Milwaukee, showing decent control and an ability to keep men from crossing the plate.

He was developing as a closer for Toronto in their farm system until this year when he became a Brewer and was instantly promoted.

He's had some good minor league years, and has saved games on the Double-A level. You've gotta think Milwaukee considers him at least an outside candidate the replace the ineffective Henry as closer. How well Lloyd would respond to the role is anyone's guess.

Mike Maddux							Mets
W	L	SV	ERA	IP	H	BB	K	Ratio
3	8	5	3.60	75	67	27	57	1.253

Mike isn't pretty or dominant, but he gets the job done and is a useful pitcher to have on the roster. He should be good for another 70 or 80 innings of steady relief in '94.

Pedro Martinez							Expos
W	L	SV	ERA	IP	H	BB	K	Ratio
10	5	2	2.61	107	76	57	119	1.243

What a monster!

Take one look at his Ks and hits allowed and you start to drool. This guy is young and good.

The Expos look like they'll start him rather than use him in relief, as they already have one of the NL's most talented closers (the Expos seem to be making a habit of filching talented Dodger pitchers).

If his arm continues to develop, and the Expos know when to pull the plug on him, Pedro could turn into a solid starter with great strikeout numbers.

He does not have the physique to throw heat for long innings, so Alou must be very wary of Pedro's following in big brother Ramon's footsteps.

Pedro A. Martinez							Padres
W	L	SV	ERA	IP	H	BB	K	Ratio
3	1	0	2.43	37	23	13	32	0.973

P.A. had a good short season workout with the Padres. Compelling strikeout numbers and a tasty ERA present a nice package.

He's not as good as the A-less Pedro, but he's good.

Tim Mauser							Padres
W	L	SV	ERA	IP	H	BB	K	Ratio
0	1	0	4.00	54	51	24	46	1.389

Mauser had a 4.96 ERA for Philly, and had a 3.58 ERA for San Diego. His minor-league numbers were impressive (0.726 ratio, 10.9 K/9IP, 0.87 ERA in 20.2 innings at Scranton).

He's 27 and looks like he'll be a solid middle-relief cog.

Chuck McElroy							Reds
W	L	SV	ERA	IP	H	BB	K	Ratio
2	2	0	4.56	47.1	51	25	31	1.606

The Cubs tired of waiting for his control to arrive and traded him to Cinci for minor league pitchers Larry Luebbers and Mike Anderson and minor league catcher Darron Cox.

McElroy has always owned a good fastball, but he plays right into the hitter's hands by slipping behind in the count. The heater becomes a made-to-order sirloin that hitters gobble up like starving hyenas. If the Reds can get him to locate the strike zone with consistency, then they can make him into a reliable set-up man. If they can't, they'll have traded for a left-handed short-order cook.

It's sort of like Let's Make a Deal, and the Reds went for curtain number three.

KEVIN MCGEHEE								ORIOLES
AAA – Rochester								
W	L	SV	ERA	IP	H	BB	K	Ratio
7	6	0	2.96	133.2	124	37	92	1.205

McGehee came to the Orioles in the Luis Mercedes trade and if he thought that would move him up the depth chart, he was mistaken. He's a starter by trade, but the O's used him primarily in relief during his brief stint in the bigs last year. They basically have three hot minor-league starters they can use in relief and Kevin will be competing for that role in '94.

He throws 85-86 MPH, which is harder than O'Donoghue or Oquist, and he has a better breaking ball than either. The other two generally get more K's, but Kevin still has good control and keeps his ratio low.

The O's need a set-up guy; McGehee could be it, but he definitely has some competition.

GREG MCMICHAEL								BRAVES
W	L	SV	ERA	IP	H	BB	K	Ratio
2	3	19	2.06	91.2	68	29	89	1.058

Despite his so-called problems late in the season, it's hard to find a flaw in his numbers. Sure he's another Doug Jones-changeup type, but the bottom line is keeping the ERA down and not letting the other team back in the game. McMichael did those things very well.

Because he's a groundballer, he has problems on turf. But that's probably his sole weakness, except for the fact that the Braves have some concerns about him.

Hell, he had a 1.24 ERA after the All-Star break. Even though he was criticized for blowing a few saves at season's end, his September ERA and ratio were 1.89 and 1.158 (with only one HR-allowed), respectively. Even if he's only a long reliever, he's worth acquiring.

RUSTY MEACHAM								ROYALS
W	L	SV	ERA	IP	H	BB	K	Ratio
2	2	0	5.57	21	31	5	13	1.714

His prospects for a major league career keep getting slimmer. Last season, he spent most of his time on the DL after tearing a ligament in his elbow. If he makes it back to the show for another shot at it, it's a safe bet Rusty will live up to his moniker.

JOSE MELENDEZ								RED SOX
AAA – Pawtucket								
W	L	SV	ERA	IP	H	BB	K	Ratio
2	3	2	5.40	35	37	7	31	1.257
W	L	SV	ERA	IP	H	BB	K	Ratio
2	1	0	2.25	16	10	5	14	.937

Todd: Melendez was under a lot of pressure to perform last year after he came to the Sox in the Plantier trade. He ended up missing most of the season with a jammed thumb and, get this, a nerve-root irritation that caused knots in his neck. What?!

This was a terrible trade from the start (even given the Sox' less-than-stellar recent trading record under Lou Gorman). Get real; Plantier was projected as, and has become, a great young slugger. Boston, in typical fashion, traded him away after a subpar season for a 27-year-old middle reliever who's never been more than a remote possibility (and turned out to be a Nervous Nellie). Of course, these are the guys who kept banishing Mo Vaughn to Triple-A every time he struck out.

Melendez has the potential to bounce back next year and provide some solid innings in long relief, but he definitely isn't the ice-cube you want in there to close the game. Hate to say it, but score about fifteen for the Padres.

KENT MERCKER								BRAVES
W	L	SV	ERA	IP	H	BB	K	Ratio
3	1	0	2.86	66	52	36	59	1.333

Having Mercker pitch spot-starts and horse-hockey relief is like commissioning Michelangelo to whitewash the fence you had Christopher Wren design.

That might be overstating it a bit. It's more like using Dave Hollins as a utility infielder.

We stand by what we said last year. If this guy gets a real job, he could be incredible. As it is, he's pretty well smokin'.

Danny Miceli — Pirates

AA – Memphis

W	L	SV	ERA	IP	H	BB	K	Ratio
6	4	7	4.60	58.2	54	39	68	1.585

Pittsburgh acquired Miceli from the Royals in the Belinda trade in July. He's a 23-year-old fireballer with a 95 MPH fastball and a good hard slider. He's considered an intimidator and isn't afraid to pitch inside.

His 1.74 K/W last year in Double-A was respectable, but it's generally much higher.

The Pirates like him and gave him a tryout in September, so he's on the fast track and may see some significant time this year.

Mike Milchin — Cardinals

AAA – Louisville

W	L	SV	ERA	IP	H	BB	K	Ratio
3	7	0	3.95	111.2	108	43	72	1.352

After three consecutive subpar seasons, Milchin's status is beginning to erode. He was switched to the bullpen last year at Louisville in an effort to take some of the pressure off him. The Cardinals still like his live arm, and the fact that he is a left-hander might allow him some more time to prove his worth. But Milchin will have to put it together soon or risk losing his prospect label.

Alan Mills — Orioles

W	L	SV	ERA	IP	H	BB	K	Ratio
5	4	4	3.23	100.1	80	51	68	1.306

Mills improved his K/W a little last year, but he's another year older (27) and still doesn't throw excessive strikes. His ERA and ratio are slightly better-than-average, though, and they have been most of his career.

He isn't spectacular, but, at this writing, the Orioles and Gregg Olson are at an impasse and that may leave Alan first in line for the closer role.

Mark Mimbs — Dodgers

AA – San Antonio

W	L	SV	ERA	IP	H	BB	K	Ratio
3	3	10	1.60	67.2	49	18	77	0.990

Mimbs, 25, is a candidate for the Dodger closer position and, if he worked out, L.A. could afford to season Dreifort as they wished.

Mark's getting old to be a prospect, but he's not that old for a closer and he had killer stats. Look for him and Daal to battle it out for immediate control of the bullpen with the winner laying for Dreifort down the line.

Blas Minor — Pirates

W	L	SV	ERA	IP	H	BB	K	Ratio
8	6	2	4.10	94.1	94	26	84	1.272

Minor turned in a decent season in his first full year in the bigs last year. His 3.62 K/W was exceptional and he averaged over a strikeout an inning.

He only allowed a .265 batting average, but he had trouble with runners in scoring position, when he allowed a .316 average and .411 SL% (STATS, Inc.). He has good control and does a decent job keeping runners off base, but he needs to bear down when it counts.

Blas got a lot of attention in '92 when he recorded 18 saves for Triple-A Buffalo. Since the Belinda trade, Pittsburgh needs a legitimate closer and Minor is a candidate for the job. He finished 18 games for them last year, but he's 28 already and needs to get more innings in that role. He's no Belinda, but unless the Pirates get somebody in the off-season, they'll take whatever they can get.

Rich Monteleone — Yankees

W	L	SV	ERA	IP	H	BB	K	Ratio
7	4	0	4.94	82.2	85	35	50	1.452

It's hard to explain Monteleone's lack of success. He pitches long innings and has pretty decent control. Despite a tendency to give up the home run to lefties (on a very regular basis), he's not that much worse against them than he is versus righthanders.

Monteleone is getting older, having passed the safety net of 29 which saves so many mediocre relievers. He'll most likely lose his spot in the bullpen and be traded or dumped pending vast improvement.

Jeff Montgomery — Royals

W	L	SV	ERA	IP	H	BB	K	Ratio
7	5	45	2.27	87.1	65	23	66	1.008

After leading the league with 45 saves and posting a sub-3.00 ERA for the fifth consecutive season, Montgomery is considered by many to be the best closer in the AL. That argument certainly has merit now that Eckersley has become human again and Olson is recovering from season-ending surgery.

His consistency the last five seasons can be partly attributed to the way he's been used. The Royals have taken good care of him, as a cursory glance at his career workload will tell you. With his excellent health record, he should be good for another 35-40 save season.

STEVE MONTGOMERY — CARDINALS
A – St. Petersburg

W	L	SV	ERA	IP	H	BB	K	Ratio
2	1	3	2.66	40.2	33	9	34	1.033

St. Louis took him in the third round of the '92 draft, and while Montgomery signed with the club, he elected to delay his pro career until he finished his degree. Judging by his performance in St. Pete and his subsequent promotion to Double-A Arkansas, the Cardinals have to be glad they waited for him. They'll use him as a starter until they feel he has made up for lost time, but his future is in the bullpen. It's too soon to tell whether or not he'll be a star, but considering the St. Louis bullpen is pretty thin at the major-league level, he could be in the majors by 1995.

RICHIE MOODY — RANGERS
AA – Tulsa

W	L	SV	ERA	IP	H	BB	K	Ratio
3	2	16	2.18	66	58	34	60	1.394

Moody, 23, has an excellent hard curve and a tailing fastball, but his control is a bit iffy at this point in his career.

He's at least a couple of years away.

MARCUS MOORE — ROCKIES

W	L	SV	ERA	IP	H	BB	K	Ratio
3	1	0	6.84	26.1	30	20	13	1.899

Moore, 23, has some control problems he must address in Triple-A Colorado Springs before he can be considered a solid candidate for the closer job. He also needs to work on a breaking ball. But Moore, who stands 6-5, already has an excellent fastball that is clocked in the mid-90s and that's a start.

BOBBY MUNOZ — YANKEES

W	L	SV	ERA	IP	H	BB	K	Ratio
3	3	0	5.32	45.2	48	26	33	1.620

He spent the early part of the year in Triple-A relearning how to strike out more men than he walked. The days when he had a fastball seem to have been lost about four years ago when he was 22.

Munoz does throw hard and still has value. He doesn't allow many hits, he can save games and he's relatively young. He should make a competent reliever and could end up setting the table for Xavier Hernandez somewhere along the line.

MIKE MUNOZ — ROCKIES

W	L	SV	ERA	IP	H	BB	K	Ratio
2	2	0	4.71	21	25	15	17	1.905

Munoz looked fantastic against PCL hitters last year, but don't get excited.

Opposing major league hitters tagged him for a .309 batting average, a .408 on-base and a .506 slugging. Heck, the Tigers didn't even want him. That should tell you all you need to know about this pitcher.

ROB MURPHY — CARDINALS

W	L	SV	ERA	IP	H	BB	K	Ratio
5	7	1	4.87	64.2	73	20	41	1.438

He's 34 years old now and really can't be counted on anymore. He might have a job in 1994 simply because he throws left-handed.

JOSE MUSSET — YANKEES
AA – Midland

W	L	SV	ERA	IP	H	BB	K	Ratio
2	6	21	5.49	62.1	59	32	59	1.460

Not only was his ratio kinda nastee (an Anglo-American-French word used in Michigan by authors of the Advocate, pronounced "nah-staaay."), but he also served up nine taters in his 62.1 innings.

Musset, 25, was touted last year by Bill James as a smooth, power-submarine baller. His numbers aren't as bad as they look. He'll be proving himself again at this level and it wouldn't be surprising if he were to make it to the show. He looks like exactly the kind of fellow who could make an adjustment or two and become a valuable reliever.

RANDY MYERS — CUBS

W	L	SV	ERA	IP	H	BB	K	Ratio
2	4	53	3.11	75.1	65	26	86	1.208

As proof of his steadiness, just look at his '93 stats compared to what he has done over the past five seasons.

	1993	Last five years
ERA	3.11	3.10
Opp. BA	.230	.231

Granted, he tired over the second half of the season, as his 3.86 second-half ERA will attest, but even that follows his career trend. Over the past five years, Myers has posted a 3.43 ERA after the all-star break. That is more than a half a run higher than his first-half, ERA over the same time frame. Now, we're not saying he's capable of setting another NL saves record. He's not. In fact, there's a chance that he'll revert back to his disappointing '92 form. But if he isn't extremely overvalued in your rotisse league because of the gaudy saves total from '93, he could be a sound investment.

Doug: On the day he set the saves record, Myers took the opportunity to criticize certain unnamed Cubs players for not showing a desire to win. He guessed that about ten percent of the team could care less whether they won or lost. On another occasion, Myers suggested that there was a possible conspiracy around the NL to keep Cubs players off the All-Star team. That remark prompted a call from NL President Bill White and a quick retraction followed soon after.

Myers seems to enjoy the media attention just a little too much. He should learn to keep his mouth shut and concentrate on his job. If he did, there's no telling how good he'd be.

DENNY NEAGLE — PIRATES

W	L	SV	ERA	IP	H	BB	K	Ratio
3	5	1	5.31	81.1	82	37	73	1.463

The Pirates still haven't really decided what they want to do with Neagle; they had him start seven games, finish 13, and used him in long relief the rest of the time. He seems to be more comfortable as a reliever. In his 13 starts in the last two years, he's turned in ERA's of 5.40 and 6.61, respectively.

Neagle used to try to get as much giddyup on his cheese as possible after negative comments made by Tom Kelly when Denny was with Minnesota. He's determined to make a switch back to his old junkballing style.

But he already has good control, has been cutting down on his walks, and had an impressive 8.1 K/9IP last year. If he can stop trying to be Dibble, you can expect his K's to increase even more.

GENE NELSON — RANGERS

W	L	SV	ERA	IP	H	BB	K	Ratio
0	5	5	3.12	60.2	60	24	35	1.385

The Rangers signed Nelson in early September after the Angels sent him packing.

You can hit him. You can walk off him. The secret to his limited success last year seems to be that he didn't allow many extra-base hits. He only allowed a .358 slugging percentage and so kept his ERA down.

But he recorded ERA's of 6.45 and 6.84 the previous two years and the Angels weren't fooled by his sudden turn-around. We aren't either. He's 33 and will probably return to his hapless ways this year.

JEFF NELSON — MARINERS

W	L	SV	ERA	IP	H	BB	K	Ratio
5	3	1	4.35	60	57	34	61	1.517

He's one of those relievers you just have to have if you need to deliver ball four to a hitter. His control could improve, but all that would effectively do is increase his salary 20 percent. Don't draft him.

JERRY NIELSEN — ANGELS

AAA – Vancouver

W	L	SV	ERA	IP	H	BB	K	Ratio
2	5	0	4.20	55.2	70	20	45	1.617

Nielson came over with J.T. Snow and was expected by many to be an immediate left-handed complement to the short-relief corps of the Angels. Jerry's a hard thrower and displayed excellent control and the ability to keep the bat away from the ball prior to '93, so it seemed reasonable for those in the media (us included) and in the Angels' organization to think he was ready.

The ugly truth is that Vancouver wasn't the kindest place in the world to Nielson. His ERA was quite respectable, but his hits-allowed ratio was sinful. He's 27, so he's not going to have a 10-year career, but despite the negatives, he's probably ready to step into a job right now. With a little bit of luck, he might be able to get a few saves as the left-handed part of a bullpen-by-committee.

EDWIN NUNEZ — ATHLETICS

W	L	SV	ERA	IP	H	BB	K	Ratio
3	6	1	3.81	75.2	89	29	58	1.559

He throws strikes and keeps the walks down. Nunez' problem continues to be the fact that he gives up too many hits.

With Honeycutt gone, he and Gossage are the best of the A's long relief crowd.

John O'Donoghue							Orioles
AAA – Rochester							
W	L	SV	ERA	IP	H	BB	K	Ratio
7	4	0	3.88	127.2	122	41	111	1.277
W	L	SV	ERA	IP	H	BB	K	Ratio
0	1	0	4.58	19.2	22	10	16	1.628

O'Donoghue is another minor-league starter that the O's used as a reliever last year. He's a huge guy (6-6) with an 84 MPH blower and decent curve and change. His control is impressive, as was his 2.71 K/W in Triple-A.

He only got 19.2 innings at the major league level last year, which doesn't give you much of an indication, but he held his own and recorded 16 K's. He should get more time and be more comfortable this year, but he's still got to compete with McGehee and Oquist for the set-up job. He's the only lefty of the three and that may earn him a spot.

Omar Olivares							Cardinals
W	L	SV	ERA	IP	H	BB	K	Ratio
5	3	1	4.17	118.2	134	54	63	1.584

Olivares looked at being assigned to the bullpen last year as a step down and was miserable pitching in relief. His dissatisfaction showed, as he suffered through his worst season yet in the show.

If he can accept his role, whatever it may be, he'll certainly have better years ahead of him. He has a good fastball and decent complementary pitches. All he needs now is the right attitude and a little polish on his control.

Darren Oliver							Rangers
AA – Tulsa							
W	L	SV	ERA	IP	H	BB	K	Ratio
7	5	6	1.96	73.1	51	41	77	1.255

Oliver, 23, has been slowly moving up through the ranks for the last five years. He was rewarded with a brief tryout in the bigs last year, but it seems more likely that he'll spend most of '93 in Triple-A.

He throws a lot of K's and averaged 9.5 K/9IP last year, but his control has always been questionable.

Gregg Olson							? ? ?
W	L	SV	ERA	IP	H	BB	K	Ratio
0	2	29	1.60	45	37	18	44	1.222

Olson went on the DL with a sore shoulder and missed five weeks in August and September, forcing him to go below 30 saves for the first time since '89. Still, he got 29 saves in 35 chances and turned in his lowest ERA ever.

He's devastating when he's healthy; he's averaged almost a strikeout per inning and given up a .279 slugging percentage in the last five years (STATS, Inc.). Basically, Gregg's as effective as any closer in the game.

The O's aren't sure his injuries have healed, however, and they've been reluctant to sign him in the off-season. There's a long list of clubs talking to him and you can be sure he'll find another job if the Orioles drop the ball.

The doctors say he's healthy; he'll be a fine acquisition for somebody.

Mike Oquist							Orioles
AAA – Rochester							
W	L	SV	ERA	IP	H	BB	K	Ratio
9	8	0	3.50	149.1	144	41	128	1.239

Oquist is the third minor-league starter, with McGehee and O'Donoghue, that the O's are looking at in long relief.

Mike is the undisputed strikeout king of the bunch with his 8.68 K/9IP last year, but at 26, he's also a year older than the other two.

He has good control, keeps his walks down and his 3.1 K/W is outstanding. It should be an interesting year for the Orioles' management figuring out which pitching prospects to keep around, especially with an even younger crop preparing to make the jump. Too bad more clubs don't have problems like these.

Jesse Orosco							Brewers
W	L	SV	ERA	IP	H	BB	K	Ratio
3	5	8	3.18	56.2	47	17	67	1.129

What Jesse did last year was remarkable for a man of 36, but at 37 he topped it by a mile.

His strikeouts were phenomenal, and were matched only by his control.

'93 has to be some sort of aberration. How else do you explain a pitcher striking out 1.12 men/9 innings when he'd never struck out more than 1.05 in any previous season.

He could pile up saves as the Brewers see him as a closer in 1994.

AL OSUNA							ASTROS
W	L	SV	ERA	IP	H	BB	K	Ratio
1	1	2	3.20	25.1	17	13	21	1.184

Al spent half of 1993 proving to the Astros that he could pitch at the major-league level. Control has never been one of his strong suits and that and a combination of other factors led to his demotion to Tucson. He's not an exceptional pitcher, but he's an adequate lefty inning-burner.

JEFF PARRETT							ROCKIES
W	L	SV	ERA	IP	H	BB	K	Ratio
3	3	1	5.38	73.2	78	45	66	1.670

Although he took a big step backward last year, he still has some value to the Rockies. His 66 strikeouts indicate that he hasn't completely lost it yet, but the 45 free passes he allowed and the 11 wild pitches he uncorked gives reason for concern. He doesn't stink, but then again, he doesn't smell like roses either.

JEFF PATTERSON							PHILLIES
AAA – Scranton/Wilkes-Barre							
W	L	SV	ERA	IP	H	BB	K	Ratio
7	5	8	2.69	93.2	79	42	68	1.292

Patterson's control looks a bit iffy, but other than that, he looks like a competent long guy. He had a few saves at Triple-A, but he doesn't look like the sort to get more than 5-6 saves in the majors (he's 25) unless there are major injuries in the 'pen, or he moves his game up a huge step. Don't count on either.

BRAD PENNINGTON							ORIOLES
W	L	SV	ERA	IP	H	BB	K	Ratio
3	2	4	6.55	33	34	25	39	1.788

Pennington throws his cheese in the mid 90s and has a good slider. These pitches have helped him average well over 10 K/9IP for the last five years. He also has a decent change, but compared to his fastball, its generally considered a favor when he throws it.

His biggest problem has always been his control; he gives up a few too many walks and extra-base hits. Major-league hitters gave him a rude welcome last year knocking seven out of 34 hits into the seats (.477 SLG).

He may be wilder than a march hare, but any lefty who throws 95 MPH grabs plenty of attention. Thus, he's been named in several off-season trade rumors and there's some question as to where he'll be next year.

He's 25 and has time to improve his control (Did somebody say Mitch Williams?). He may develop into a fine closer, wherever he is.

TROY PERCIVAL							ANGELS
AAA – Vancouver							
W	L	SV	ERA	IP	H	BB	K	Ratio
0	1	4	6.27	18.2	24	13	19	1.982

He had surgery to remove bone chips and trim a ligament tear on his pitching elbow. Percival's heater hits the mid-90s consistently. Last year, we were touting him as about the best relief prospect in the game. He was pitching with that tender elbow and at first was making it work. ... Then his ERA sky-rocketed and next thing you know, his heater was checking in at 85 MPH tops. In the PCL, that's like chucking it in at 65.

Percival is still only 24. If his elbow is OK, all he has to do is throw strikes and start hitting 90+ again on the radar guns. Hell, with the disarray in the Angels bullpen, one out of two will probably be enough.

CESAR PEREZ							INDIANS
A – Columbus							
W	L	SV	ERA	IP	H	BB	K	Ratio
0	0	35	0.59	46	21	19	50	0.870

Perez, 23, was selected from the Yankees in the Rule V draft last year, and the 35 saves he racked up for the Columbus RedStixx makes it look like grand theft closer. He was a little old for the competition, but he struck out 9.8 hitters per nine innings and allowed a measly .133 batting average. Doing things like that will accelerate his program greatly. The Indians think he has one of the best arms in the organization, but they will probably start him out at Double-A Canton. Perez looks like a good candidate for a set-up job in '95.

MIKE PEREZ							CARDINALS
W	L	SV	ERA	IP	H	BB	K	Ratio
7	2	7	2.48	72.2	65	20	58	1.170

His ERAs the past few years in the minors have been downright scary, but he has been able to do the job at the ML level. The Cards would like to see him take the closer's job in '94, but he has little to offer besides great control. His fastball is barely adequate.

Tony Phillips — Mariners

AA – Jacksonville

W	L	SV	ERA	IP	H	BB	K	Ratio
1	3	5	1.78	30.1	34	5	23	1.286

A side-armer with an 85+ MPH fastball he can sink or run in on hitters. He keeps the ball down and allowed only two homers in 60.1 innings last year.

He's 25 and not exactly a front-line talent, but if you can jump two levels and keep the ball in the park, somebody will eventually find a job for you.

Jeff Pierce — Reds

AA – Birmingham

W	L	SV	ERA	IP	H	BB	K	Ratio
3	4	18	2.59	48.2	34	7	45	.843

Pierce has been virtually unhittable for the last two years in Single- and Double-A. His control is excellent and he records a ton of K's. He's been moving up a league each year and mastering each level so there's no reason to expect this year will be any different.

Jeff's 25 and on his way.

Erik Plantenberg — Mariners

AA – Jacksonville

W	L	SV	ERA	IP	H	BB	K	Ratio
2	1	1	2.01	44.2	38	14	49	1.164

According to *B.A.*, the Mariners only see this 25-year-old guy as a piece of middle-relief fluff. They picked him up in the Rule V draft because he's a local kid and he's a lefty. Still, his numbers look pretty nice and he didn't allow *any* homers in his 54.1 total innings last year. How many guys can do that?

Dan Plesac — Cubs

W	L	SV	ERA	IP	H	BB	K	Ratio
2	1	0	4.74	62.2	74	21	47	1.516

Plesac won't be counted on to work vital innings anymore and his role will be limited to that of long relief. He induces a lot of fly-balls and in a particular park on the south side of Chicago, that can be murder.

He'll be a terrible investment as long as he pitches in Wrigley.

Eric Plunk — Indians

W	L	SV	ERA	IP	H	BB	K	Ratio
4	5	15	2.79	71	61	30	77	1.324

He pitched 71 solid innings last year and converted 15 of his 18 save opportunities, but he lacks the fine control of a front-line reliever. If the Indians use him in the middle innings, he should be alright. If they depend on him to anchor the bullpen, they're in trouble.

Jim Poole — Orioles

W	L	SV	ERA	IP	H	BB	K	Ratio
2	1	2	2.15	50.1	30	21	29	1.013

Poole bounced back from an injury-filled '92 season and basically did everything you ask a spot reliever to do. He got a few K's and kept people off base; the league only batted .175 and slugged .240 off him. Wow!

His K/W could be improved, but he doesn't live or die by the strikeout, anyway. He's more of a control pitcher who just gets the job done however he can. If nobody's getting on base, it doesn't matter.

He's in his prime and getting better every year. If your league is competitive enough to make a middle reliever's stats significant, consider picking him up.

Dennis Powell — Mariners

W	L	SV	ERA	IP	H	BB	K	Ratio
0	0	0	4.15	47.2	42	24	32	1.385

A typical industrial-strength lefty pitcher. As long as he gets good defense in the infield, he'll be adequate.

John Pricher — Angels

A – Palm Springs

W	L	SV	ERA	IP	H	BB	K	Ratio
3	5	26	3.17	54	41	25	61	1.222

Pricher is one of these typical kids you see in the minors. His stats are decent and he's young (23), now it's just a question of how he rises through the ranks. Wait a a year or two on him, but remember he had a 10.2 K/9IP rate last year ... you gotta respect that.

Paul Quantrill — Red Sox

W	L	SV	ERA	IP	H	BB	K	Ratio
6	12	1	3.91	138	151	44	66	1.413

Quantrill's another starter by trade who gets used primarily in long relief, although he did get 14 starts with the Sox last year.

He has decent control but he just gives up too many hits. He led the league in intentional walks last year in only 138 innings; that should tell you something about the confidence Hobson has in his stopping abilities. Of course, Hobson also called for the most intentional walks in the majors, so maybe that tells you more about him.

Consider this; despite his 1.413 ratio, Paul only allowed 13.9 percent of his inherited runners score, which was the second lowest rate in the AL. Apparently, he was letting guys on, but not when it counted. So it depends on your point of view. If your league stresses ratio and won-loss percentage heavily (like us), you don't want him. If you're a Sox fan, however, you will appreciate his respectable ERA.

Scott Radinsky							White Sox
W	L	SV	ERA	IP	H	BB	K	Ratio
8	2	4	4.28	54.2	61	19	44	1.463

Scott made excellent strides in establishing his control of the strike zone but took a step backward in keeping runners from crossing the plate.

He should pull it all together by next year, showing that he's one of the best long relievers around.

Jeff Reardon							Reds
W	L	SV	ERA	IP	H	BB	K	Ratio
4	6	8	4.09	61.2	66	10	35	1.233

Jeff's presence in Cincinnati made the club look bad, simply because they wouldn't let him wear the beard and we're the ones who have to suffer looking at him.

It was an unusual season for Reardon. His normally low ERA shot up to 4.09, but he also corrected a recent problem by keeping 27 out of 28 inherited runners from scoring.

He did a good job finishing for the Reds when they needed it, but he's 38 this year and the ERA has been slipping. The Reds are ready to look at some younger guys, so Reardon's time this year will be limited.

Steve Reed							Rockies
W	L	SV	ERA	IP	H	BB	K	Ratio
9	5	3	4.48	84.1	80	30	51	1.304

Reed was going nowhere in the Giants' system, and Colorado wisely chose him in the third round of the expansion draft. He looks like he has an excellent career ahead of him if he can tackle some minor control problems. Reed should be the first one in line for the closer's job if Holmes should go down.

Carlos Reyes							Athletics
AA – Greenville							
W	L	SV	ERA	IP	H	BB	K	Ratio
8	1	2	2.06	70	64	24	57	1.257
AAA – Richmond							
W	L	SV	ERA	IP	H	BB	K	Ratio
1	0	1	3.77	28.2	30	11	30	1.430

Reyes has an excellent changeup and a decent curve and slider. He was taken in the Rule V draft from Atlanta by the A's. He's 25 and obviously not a top-line relief prospect. Still, he's a pretty good depth-chart pitcher and if you're in a rotisserie league where you can get guys in mid-season to replace injured guys, then you at least know who Carlos is and what his future probably will be.

Chuck Ricci							Orioles
AA – Bowie							
W	L	SV	ERA	IP	H	BB	K	Ratio
7	4	5	3.20	81.2	72	20	83	1.127

Ricci was turned into a reliever last year and turned in his best season ever. He cut down on his walks and increased his K's for an outstanding 4.15 K/W.

His control hasn't always been this good and it remains to be seen whether he can keep it up. He should get a chance to prove himself in Triple-A next year.

At 25, he needs to make some noise soon, especially with the myriad of guys ahead of him on Baltimore's depth chart.

Jeff Richey							Giants
A – Clinton							
W	L	SV	ERA	IP	H	BB	K	Ratio
2	1	28	1.03	52.1	19	17	75	.688

He looked just OK in A-ball San Jose and then exploded in A-ball Clinton.

He's not young (24), so he should rushed to the next level to see whether '93 was a fluke.

If he's for real, then he'll be a solid reliever on the major league level.

Dave Righetti							Oakland
W	L	SV	ERA	IP	H	BB	K	Ratio
1	1	1	5.70	47.1	58	17	31	1.585

Righetti was absolutely worthless to the Giants, so I can see why the A's want him.

Apparently their relief corps wasn't rotten enough last year and they're counting on Rigotoni to put them over the top.

He was once a fine pitcher, but he should have called it a day after this season.

BILL RISLEY							EXPOS

AAA – Ottawa

W	L	SV	ERA	IP	H	BB	K	Ratio
2	4	1	2.54	63.2	51	34	74	1.335

Risley is 27, a righty, and a candidate for middle relief. His control is questionable, but he looks like he could make it work at the major-league level if he got a job.

RICH RODRIGUEZ							MARLINS

W	L	SV	ERA	IP	H	BB	K	Ratio
2	4	3	3.79	76	73	33	43	1.395

His K/W deteriorated, his hits-allowed went through the roof and his ERA went up 60 percent. Sure the league ERA went up last year, but that was 15.4 percent. Until we find out what happened, we don't suggest you draft him. He's not going to get saves as long as Harvey's there and Darensbourg may steal whatever's left.

KEVIN ROGERS							GIANTS

W	L	SV	ERA	IP	H	BB	K	Ratio
2	2	0	2.68	80.2	71	28	62	1.227

Rogers looked very good, justifying predictions that he will one day soon be a quality Giant starter. His control of the plate was in line and he kept his hits allowed under the acceptable limit.

Rogers would undoubtedly make a fine reliever, but we look forward to seeing him racking up wins as one of the best starters in the National League.

MEL ROJAS							EXPOS

W	L	SV	ERA	IP	H	BB	K	Ratio
5	8	10	2.95	88.1	80	30	48	1.245

His season was less impressive than it looks. He blew nine save opps and his K/W stinks. He cost the Expos a couple of wins by converting only 53 percent of his save chances (but we're not going to be stupid and say he was the reason the 'Spos didn't win the division). Look for better performance this year.

BRUCE RUFFIN							ROCKIES

W	L	SV	ERA	IP	H	BB	K	Ratio
6	5	2	3.87	139.2	145	69	126	1.532

Don't put too much stock in his stats from last year. Over the last five years he is the owner of a 23-41 record and a 4.63 ERA. He has also allowed a .286 batting average over the same period. If you make the proper park adjustments to these averages, it becomes painfully obvious that he has no chance to repeat his performance in 1994.

JOHNNY RUFFIN							REDS

AAA – Nashville

W	L	SV	ERA	IP	H	BB	K	Ratio
3	4	1	3.30	60	48	16	69	1.067
W	L	SV	ERA	IP	H	BB	K	Ratio
2	1	2	3.58	37.2	36	11	30	1.248

Ruffin's a 22-year-old fireballer who throws 94+ MPH and has an excellent curve to complement his heat. He's considered the Reds' top pitching prospect.

Originally a starter, he's been in the pros for six years, five of which were in the White Sox' system. He struggled a bit in that role, however, and Chicago traded him off in the Tim Belcher deal.

The move to long relief seems to have settled him, but the Reds would still like to see him settle into the starting rotation after he gets some experience in the bigs.

His numbers weren't exceptional at the major-league level last year, but his youth and his heat make him a fine prospect.

JEFF RUSSELL							RED SOX

W	L	SV	ERA	IP	H	BB	K	Ratio
1	4	33	2.70	46.2	39	14	45	1.136

Russell came away last year with his third straight season of 30+ saves. The biggest difference in his game was that he averaged almost a strikeout an inning, which he hasn't done since he led the league in saves for Texas in '89. He also cut down on his walks, which was reflected in his low ratio.

Up until last year, though, he was pretty much in decline and you have to question his ability to repeat those numbers. He is 32 and about to leave his prime. Still, you have to consider him a top-notch closer until he proves otherwise.

Ken Ryan — Red Sox

AAA – Pawtucket

W	L	SV	ERA	IP	H	BB	K	Ratio
0	2	8	2.49	25.1	18	17	22	1.381

W	L	SV	ERA	IP	H	BB	K	Ratio
7	2	1	3.60	50	43	29	49	1.440

Ken spent most of the season in Boston last year and finished 26 games for them. He's 25 and throws in the 93-95 MPH range with an excellent hard slider. His curve and change aren't bad either. He clearly needs to work on his control, though.

Last year, with Jeff Russell coming off a lackluster season, it looked like Ryan was a lock for the closer role. Now, Russell's improved his game and upstart Cory Bailey looks like he's about ready, so Ken may have more competition than he counted on.

Bill Sampen — Royals

AAA – Omaha

W	L	SV	ERA	IP	H	BB	K	Ratio
1	2	8	3.41	37	37	13	34	1.351

The red flag went up in 1992 when his strikeouts fell dramatically. He never had the control to work the hitters effectively, so he got into trouble an awful lot with his fading fastball. He is 31 now, coming off a season that saw him spend most of his time hanging out with the kids in Omaha ... His value falls more with each passing year.

Julio Santana — Rangers

R – Rangers

W	L	SV	ERA	IP	H	BB	K	Ratio
4	1	7	1.38	39	31	7	50	.974

Julio only played in the GCL, but at 20, he was light-years ahead of the hitters. You don't see many 7.1 K/W averages at any level.

He throws 95 MPH with excellent control and was easily the No. 1 prospect in the league. He'll be 21 this year and will be moving up the ranks. It shouldn't be too hard to remember his name.

Tony Saunders — Marlins

A – Kane County

W	L	SV	ERA	IP	H	BB	K	Ratio
6	1	1	2.27	83.1	72	32	87	1.248

Saunders is just a little cub of 20 (since he's a Marlin, would that make a "spawn"?). His numbers obviously are impressive. There's little else to say about him. Watch him grow into a full-size fish.

Bob Scanlan — Brewers

W	L	SV	ERA	IP	H	BB	K	Ratio
4	5	0	4.54	75.1	79	28	44	1.420

The 6-foot-8 Scanlan throws pretty hard and has good movement on his off-speed stuff. But despite his size and the velocity of his fastball, he has never even come close to striking out a batter per inning in his pro career. It may be that he lacks the gene for finishing off hitters or something trivial like that.

The Brewers are grooming him for a set-up job in '94, but he will have to earn it by lowering his ERA. Being a peer of Andres the Giant is no guarantee of a promotion.

Carl Schutz — Braves

R – Danville

W	L	SV	ERA	IP	H	BB	K	Ratio
1	0	4	0.61	14.2	6	6	25	0.818

A 22-year-old lefty reliever who the Braves liken to Mike Stanton. His fastball checks in at 95 MPH and he adds an 83 MPH slider. He got rocked at Greenville, but hell, why was he moved from Rookie Ball to Double-A? Our guess is that he'll start in Durham or Macon. Right now, getting his control down has to be his priority (he had 22 walks-allowed in 21.1 innings at Richmond).

Jeff Schwarz — White Sox

W	L	SV	ERA	IP	H	BB	K	Ratio
2	2	0	3.71	51	35	38	41	1.431

Terrible control and he's getting too old. It's doubtful that he'll make much of himself as he's already spent 1/3 of his life pitching minor-league ball.

Tim Scott — Expos

W	L	SV	ERA	IP	H	BB	K	Ratio
7	2	1	3.01	71.2	69	34	65	1.437

He's a decent, unexceptional looking reliever. But he's just another cog in the long-relief machine.

Rudy Seanez — Padres

AAA – Las Vegas

W	L	SV	ERA	IP	H	BB	K	Ratio
0	1	0	6.41	19.2	24	11	14	1.779

The only reason he's a prospect is because he can throw 97 MPH. He's got rotten control and a history of arm trouble.

The Padres are attempting to change his delivery to reduce the injury factor. If it helps his control he could be transformed into a viable pitcher.

Scott Service — Reds

W	L	SV	ERA	IP	H	BB	K	Ratio
2	2	2	4.30	46	44	16	43	1.304

Service is 26 years old and has already played for 12 clubs in four separate organizations. Pretty popular guy!

The Rockies snatched him the from Reds, but Cinci claimed him back in early July. He did a decent job filling in when Wickander, et al, were on the DL, but the league got some big hits off him. He was tagged for a .445 slugging percentage, including 6 HRs in 46 innings. His control just needs some work.

The team likes his 8.4 K/9IP rate and he should get a shot at the set up job this year.

Jeff Shaw — Expos

W	L	SV	ERA	IP	H	BB	K	Ratio
2	7	0	4.14	95.2	91	32	50	1.286

Sort of a slightly inferior Tim Scott.

Keith Shepherd — Rockies

AAA – Colorado Springs

W	L	SV	ERA	IP	H	BB	K	Ratio
3	6	8	6.78	67.2	90	44	57	1.980

Shepherd's control is a major concern right now. But if he can get a better handle on his pitches, he could surprise a lot of people.

Steve Shifflett — Royals

W	L	SV	ERA	IP	H	BB	K	Ratio
1	4	0	2.60	52	55	17	25	1.385

At 28, Shifflett is a little old to be beating around in the bushes. If he doesn't stick in the majors by the end of the year, he'll be in danger of become a Rule V refugee.

His control is encouraging, though, as is his 2.99 career ERA in the minors. He was roughed up last year in Omaha, but it was his first sub-par season since becoming a pro in '89. He has the potential to become a solid contributor in the bullpen, much the same way Billy Brewer did last season.

Paul Shuey — Indians

AA – Canton-Akron

W	L	SV	ERA	IP	H	BB	K	Ratio
4	8	0	7.30	61.2	76	36	41	1.816

Taken with the second overall pick in the 1992 draft, Shuey, a reliever in college, started the season in the Canton rotation in order to straighten out his mechanics. The experiment failed, as he was creamed in his first seven starts. His manager likened it to putting a square peg into a round hole. The Indians then switched him back to the pen. It was too late, though. Shuey finished the season back in A Kinston, having been rocked all season long, both as a starter and as a reliever.

Shuey, 23, is still considered to be the best arm in the organization. He throws an above-average major league fastball and a devastating curve. If he can put it all back together, he could become a solid candidate for the closer role. The Indians need to quit tinkering with him and just let him pitch.

Heathcliff Slocumb — Indians

W	L	SV	ERA	IP	H	BB	K	Ratio
4	1	0	4.03	38	35	20	22	1.448

He has shown just enough promise in the minors the past few seasons to warrant being in someone's plans. He throws hard and challenges hitters, but he'll never be a quality pitcher in the show until he can draw a bead on the strikezone. He's in danger of being labeled a "should've been."

Lee Smith — ???

W	L	SV	ERA	IP	H	BB	K	Ratio
2	4	46	3.88	58	53	14	60	1.155

He showed excellent control and saved 46 games between St. Louis and New York.

Despite this, Smith is a marginal risk. He could continue to do what he's done for several more years or he could self-destruct. The save being the degraded stat it has become, his rising ERA is more noteworthy than the number of leads he preserved.

The Yanks are obviously thinking the same thing or they wouldn't have traded one of their best young pitchers for closer Xavier Hernandez. Smith and Steve Farr should stick around as veteran insurance, but they won't get save opportunities unless the X-man stumbles badly.

JERRY SPRADLIN — REDS
AAA – Indianapolis

W	L	SV	ERA	IP	H	BB	K	Ratio
3	2	1	3.49	56.2	58	12	46	1.235

W	L	SV	ERA	IP	H	BB	K	Ratio
2	1	2	3.49	49	44	9	24	1.082

Jerry's numbers in the bigs weren't too bad last year; he had an excellent ratio and a 2.7 K/W average. But, somehow, he let 10 out of 22 inherited runners score, much to the Reds' chagrin. It kinda looks like he got a raw deal.

He's always given up a few hits but his control has been good. Spradlin's 27 and his history suggests he'll be a solid middle-reliever. He'll get another shot this year and should have a little better luck.

MIKE STANTON — BRAVES

W	L	SV	ERA	IP	H	BB	K	Ratio
4	6	27	4.67	52	51	29	43	1.539

He was no great shakes before the All-Star break, but disintegrated after, posting a 8.27 ERA in July-August (STATS, Inc.).

His previously solid control evaporated and though hitters still couldn't drive the ball, they got on base off him at a once unheard of clip. He's obviously not viewed as front-line material right now, so it's probably wise if you let someone else have him in your draft. He has the talent, but he's going to have to prove himself to Atlanta and to us.

MAKATO SUZUKI — MARINERS
A – San Bernadino

W	L	SV	ERA	IP	H	BB	K	Ratio
4	4	12	3.68	80.2	59	56	87	1.426

Suzuki was the No. 6 prospect in the Callie League. There's a lot of speculation that this kid signed with Seattle because Nintendo owns the Mariners and Suzuki isn't exactly from San Pedro de Marcoris.

Anyway, he's a 19-year-old with a blower that hits 97 MPH, a hard curveball and a pretty good changeup. He's probably a year away, but Lou Piniella loves this kid's arm (wouldn't you if you had him in your organization?). He could be battling Ayala for the closer's role in 1995.

BILLY TAYLOR — ATHLETICS
AAA – Richmond

W	L	SV	ERA	IP	H	BB	K	Ratio
2	4	26	1.98	68.1	56	26	81	1.200

He almost made the Toronto roster after they took him in the Rule V draft last spring.

He uses his sidearm sinker and his slider on righties and his overhand two- and four-seam heaters, plus his curve and change, on lefties.

I guess he's your typical 32-year-old career minor-leaguer with six pitches. He really deserves a shot as he's been an excellent pitcher for the last four years. There's no reason to think he couldn't get out major-leaguers if he got a shot.

SCOTT TAYLOR — RED SOX
AAA – Pawtucket

W	L	SV	ERA	IP	H	BB	K	Ratio
7	7	1	4.04	122.2	132	48	88	1.468

Taylor's a sometime-starter, sometime-closer, usually in between, 26-year-old minor-league pitcher.

He's gotten a few innings in the show the last couple years but never really done anything with them. Actually, he's pretty mediocre in the minors, too. He might make it up on a regular basis, but who cares?

BOBBY THIGPEN — PHILLIES

W	L	SV	ERA	IP	H	BB	K	Ratio
3	1	1	5.83	54	74	21	29	1.759

If Mike Stanton drops off for another year or two, then he'll be in Thigpen's shoes. There's nothing really wrong with Bobby that a shrink and a really good pitching coach couldn't fix. Thing is, he's probably a lost cause already.

MIKE TIMLIN — BLUE JAYS

W	L	SV	ERA	IP	H	BB	K	Ratio
4	2	1	4.69	55.2	63	27	49	1.617

After two consecutive subpar seasons, Timlin has to be considered a shaky proposition. He has a good build and a decent fastball, but until he learns to fool major league hitters, his future is very much in doubt.

Rick Trlicek — Dodgers

W	L	SV	ERA	IP	H	BB	K	Ratio
1	2	1	4.08	64	59	21	41	1.250

Unusually young for a long reliever. Typically they're washed up starters whom someone believes can throw two or three good innings a game.

He was groomed as a starter by the Toronto organization and he didn't look too bad, so the Dodgers may work in some starts this year to see how he handles them.

If he remains a reliever he'll be a good one.

Mike Trombley — Twins

W	L	SV	ERA	IP	H	BB	K	Ratio
6	6	2	4.88	114.1	131	41	85	1.504

Trombley was disappointing last year in his first full season in the majors. The Twins tried him as a starter in 10 games, but he got shelled for a 3-5 record and 5.86 ERA... hence, his new role as a middle reliever.

Trombley looked very good in his minor-league career and it's probably that he just needs time to adjust.

He got his share of K's last year and had decent control. But the league's hitters had his number; they hit .290 and slugged .490 off him He could be able to improve now that he's been around the league a few times and seen the hitters.

He's only 27 and a starter by trade. If he looks sharp early on next year, he may slide into the starting rotation.

Matt Turner — Marlins

W	L	SV	ERA	IP	H	BB	K	Ratio
4	5	0	2.91	68	55	26	59	1.191

The Marlins rescued him from the Angels scrap heap and he rewarded them with a very fine season of no-glory relief. He's probably pitching as well as he can, but there's no reason he can't continue to pitch this well.

Sergio Valdez — Expos

AAA – Ottawa

W	L	SV	ERA	IP	H	BB	K	Ratio
5	3	1	3.12	83.2	7	22	53	1.183

Valdez, 28, doesn't seem to be high on the depth chart. He's not bad, but it might take another organization for him to get work.

Ed Vosberg — Indians

AAA – Iowa

W	L	SV	ERA	IP	H	BB	K	Ratio
5	1	3	3.57	63	67	22	64	1.413

He had a nice season for Triple-A Charlotte last year and his name has come up a few times in discussions about the Cleveland bullpen. But Vosberg is 32 years old folks. He's been pitching professional ball since Reagan was in office and he hasn't earned a big-league job yet. It's a good bet he never will.

Pete Walker — Mets

AA – Binghamton

W	L	SV	ERA	IP	H	BB	K	Ratio
4	9	19	3.44	99.1	89	46	89	1.359

The Mets selected Walker in the seventh round of the 1990 amateur draft, and he spent his first three professional seasons as an ineffective starter. But a switch to the bullpen in Double-A Binghamton last year resurrected his prospect status as he posted 19 saves in 35 relief appearances. He then went to the Arizona Fall League where he led the circuit with 10 saves an had a 1.47 ERA for Tucson.

The Mets are hoping that Pete can continue his new-found success in Triple-A Norfolk this year. He'll need to show them another solid season before they'll promote him, but the Mets like him a lot and he could be in Shea by the time September rolls around.

Bruce Walton — Expos

AAA – Ottawa

W	L	SV	ERA	IP	H	BB	K	Ratio
4	4	16	1.05	42.2	32	8	40	0.937

Walton was been floating about the A's organization for years before coming over to Montreal. He was treated with no respect by Oakland and it appears he's due for similar treatment at the hands of the Expos. He could do the job, but you have to be employed in order to be a good worker.

Ron Watson — Angels

AA – Midland

W	L	SV	ERA	IP	H	BB	K	Ratio
2	1	3	3.88	46.1	39	43	41	1.770

Think of him as Plan B if Troy Percival fails to wrest the big-league closer job.

Watson throws in the mid-90s and has a mid-80s slider. His control (if you can call a walk rate of 8.35 per nine ("control") is horrid. He needs to harness that if he's going to do much of anything.

DUANE WARD							BLUE JAYS
W	L	SV	ERA	IP	H	BB	K	Ratio
2	3	45	2.13	71.2	49	25	97	1.033

In last year's essay, we said that Ward would be better than ever in the closer's role largely because his workload would be reduced. Ward made us look like geniuses. While it doesn't exactly rate up there with "Dionne Warwick and her Psychic Friends Network," at least you're not paying $2.50 a minute to get such sage advice.

Barring injury, Ward should be just fine. He still throws in excess of 95 MPH and his slider bites as well as it ever has. He led the league with 45 saves last year and if the Jays can assemble a better supporting cast in the bullpen, he could even improve on that total.

TOM WEGMANN							METS
AAA – Norfolk							
W	L	SV	ERA	IP	H	BB	K	Ratio
5	3	2	3.23	86.1	68	34	99	1.182

Wegmann, 25, doesn't have a 90 MPH heater, but he racks up a ton of strikeouts with an outstanding changeup. Over four minor-league seasons, he has gone 30-15 with a 2.62 ERA and a nifty 3.6 K/W ratio.

The Mets sent him to the Arizona Fall League and he kicked some serious butt for the Tucson Javelinas, leading the league in strikeouts with 50. He'll have an opportunity to break camp with the team in spring training, but he'll probably start the season in Triple-A Norfolk. The Mets have some reservations about him because he has had difficulty developing a breaking ball. However, he has answered the call at every level so far and his minor league totals are just too darned good. He deserves a shot.

BILL WERTZ							INDIANS
W	L	SV	ERA	IP	H	BB	K	Ratio
2	3	0	3.62	59.2	54	32	53	1.441

Though he doesn't have outstanding stuff and isn't mentioned along with the top prospects in the organization, he has been doing the job in the minors since 1991. Last year was no exception, as he posted a 7-2, 1.95 record for Charlotte. Bill earned a promotion in May, but was overwhelmed by the level of play and was demoted two weeks later.

Wertz will have an opportunity to make the staff in the spring, and, judging by his record the last three years, you have to like his chances. It looks as if he can pitch middle relief as well as (if not better than) Wickander, Slocumb and their ilk.

DAVID WEST							PHILLIES
W	L	SV	ERA	IP	H	BB	K	Ratio
6	4	3	2.92	86.1	60	51	87	1.286

He's a damn mess. According to Peter Gammons in *Baseball America*, West's teammates swore he gained 30-50 pounds during the regular season because he's got an incredible eating problem. This is terrible, because he's a helluva talent.

Even if he can't get the walks down, he still murders righties and lefties (though lefties had a .385 OBP against this guy, they couldn't drive the ball off him). He's 29 and he could be a long-relief star in the NL for six or seven years, but with his weight problem, he could eat his way out of a job by the end of this year. Handle with care.

JOHN WETTELAND							EXPOS
W	L	SV	ERA	IP	H	BB	K	Ratio
9	3	43	1.37	85.1	58	28	113	1.008

The highest ERA he had in any month was 2.76. ... That's called dominating the opposition. In addition to holding the enemy to a paltry .260 OBP, they only slugged .276 off him. It's such a pleasure to watch him pitch. He comes in with that blazing heater and then turns over a couple wicked breaking balls. The opposition has a choice: Take strike three or hit a weak fly to the opposite field.

He didn't win the Rolaids Award (as we sorta predicted last year), but he probably had the best relief season in the National League.

Sure he doesn't have Beck's exquisite control, but he allowed only three homers to Beck's 11. This puts the classically trained guitarist with the psychotic disposition at the head of the class.

MATT WHITESIDE							RANGERS
W	L	SV	ERA	IP	H	BB	K	Ratio
2	1	1	4.32	73	78	23	39	1.384

Matt has pretty mediocre stuff at the major league level and his K's seem to come only by chance. But last year was his first chance to spend significant time in the majors, courtesy of Liebrandt's tendinitis, and he did get his share of outs.

Whiteside was a successful closer in the minors; he had a combined 61 saves and a 2.8 K/W in four years. Plus, he's only 26, so there's little reason why he can't adjust to major-league hitters. But he needs time to learn the hitters and develop his pitches.

KEVIN WICKANDER								REDS
W	L	SV	ERA	IP	H	BB	K	Ratio
1	0	0	6.09	34	47	22	23	2.029

Kevin came to the Reds in what amounted to a mercy trade with Cleveland for Todd Ruyak in May. Indians' pitcher Steve Olin was Kevin's best friend and his pre-season death in a boating accident was so devastating that Kevin felt he needed a change in scenery to recover. Olin was the best man at Wickander's wedding.

Then, Kevin spent a good part of the season on the DL with knee and shoulder injuries.

This is a truly sad story and you can't help but hope he bounces back and tears up the league. But the truth is that his control has never been good and he's been touted as a prospect for four years.

He'll be 28 this year. If he doesn't turn it up soon, his chances of having a major league career are slim.

MIKE WILLIAMS								PHILLIES
AAA – Scranton/Wilkes-Barre								
W	L	SV	ERA	IP	H	BB	K	Ratio
9	2	0	2.87	97.1	93	16	53	1.120

It looks pretty obvious that this guy has to throw strikes to even have a prayer. He's 25, so he's pretty much a finished product. At the big-league level, he has been used as a reliever and with the strength of the front-line staff, it looks like Williams will have to make it as a swing man. He hasn't been able to get his control going yet, but he has a good chance of making some good money. Of course, he's only of marginal help to a fantasy owner in the roles he's currently slated for.

MITCH WILLIAMS								ASTROS
W	L	SV	ERA	IP	H	BB	K	Ratio
3	7	43	3.34	62	56	44	60	1.613

Dave: Wild Thing, I know I don't love you. This is an Advocate first ... I'm sure we've never prefaced a comment with a paraphrase of Troggs' lyrics before (if we have, please send proof in writing and we'll give you an autographed copy of the '95 edition).

Oh, we're supposed to be writing about Mitch, aren't we. Here's my advice: unless you're desperate for saves, don't draft him. Word is that his stuff is a shadow of its former self. In B.A., Peter Gammons said he was routinely clocked only in the mid-80s. In addition he had only one 1-2-3 inning after the All-Star break. Those aren't the things one looks for in a relief ace.

MARK WILLIAMSON								ORIOLES
W	L	SV	ERA	IP	H	BB	K	Ratio
7	5	0	4.91	88	106	25	45	1.284

Williamson's 34 and starting to get clubbed all over the place. His control is still fair and he doesn't give up many walks, but the league hit .304 off him, so who needs them.

Now he's got to compete with a host of young and ready pitchers fresh from Triple-A. His innings are numbered from here on out.

CARL WILLIS								TWINS
W	L	SV	ERA	IP	H	BB	K	Ratio
3	0	5	3.10	58	56	17	44	1.259

Willis missed the first five weeks of the season with a strained right shoulder and got knocked around when he returned.

After the All-Star break, however, he posted a 0.72 ERA and a 2.9 K/W. If he can stay healthy, he can continue to provide solid innings in middle relief. He's 33, though, and the injuries may begin to play a role.

STEVE WILSON								DODGERS
W	L	SV	ERA	IP	H	BB	K	Ratio
1	0	1	4.56	25.2	30	14	23	1.714

Moderately talented long reliever who struck out some batters. He's always shown ability, but he never lives up to his potential. He's average.

Mark Wohlers — Braves

AAA – Richmond

W	L	SV	ERA	IP	H	BB	K	Ratio
1	3	4	1.84	29.1	21	11	39	1.091

W	L	SV	ERA	IP	H	BB	K	Ratio
6	2	0	4.50	48	37	22	45	1.229

Dave: I don't know what the hell this kid has got to do to impress the Braves, but if they don't want him, I'll start an expansion team just to have him pitch for me in relief.

At the beginning of the year, he was sent down to work on his control and learn a split-finger. In addition, there were concerns about the straightness of his heater voiced by the Braves coaching staff. Some of these coaches want the Braves to trade him. He's 24 this year, if they end up dumping him, he could only haunt them for, oh about 10-12 years, so I'd do it if I were them. Of course, I just picked up the habit of eating broth with a fork – take this advice with a carton of salt.

Todd Worrell — Dodgers

W	L	SV	ERA	IP	H	BB	K	Ratio
1	1	5	6.05	38.2	46	11	31	1.474

His control of the strike zone was pretty good, but he allowed way too many hits. He's never fully recovered from his arm surgery and has lost the velocity which made him a feared closer.

The Dodgers picked him up hoping to give him the closing role but the experiment was a failure. Worrell may still be valuable in short, middle relief.

Anthony Young — Mets

W	L	SV	ERA	IP	H	BB	K	Ratio
1	16	3	3.77	100.1	103	42	62	1.445

Anthony Young will go down in history as the pitcher who compiled the longest losing streak in major league history, but he is not as bad as his 1-16 record indicates. How does a pitcher lose 16 ballgames when he posts an ERA that is nearly a quarter of a run lower than the league average? The streak should be attributed equally to Young's ineffectiveness and the ineptitude of a Mets' lineup that gave him as little support as they could muster.

Regardless of who's to blame though, you've got to respect Young for the way he handled the pressure placed on his shoulders by the media. He never blamed his defense, which was shoddy, or his run support, which was non-existent. He accepted the consequences of losing without complaint, and he held his head up while those around him were hiding their heads in the sand. If a true winner is judged by the way he loses, then Young should have received consideration for the Cy Young award.

Pete Young — Expos

AAA – Ottawa

W	L	SV	ERA	IP	H	BB	K	Ratio
4	5	1	3.73	72.1	63	33	46	1.327

Young is 26. That's probably the most positive comment you'll hear positive from us.

There's really little else to say that's nice about him. He could be OK, but chances are his ERA would be in the 4.00 range and his K/W is indicative of someone who probably won't do much in the majors.

Team Essays – AL East

Baltimore Orioles

1993 Outlook: Expectations were high in Baltimore in the pre-season, with most of the attention centered on their young pitching staff. Mike Mussina was touted as a Cy Young candidate and Ben McDonald and Arthur Rhodes were thought to be rising stars. The offense was riddled with question marks. Could Cal Ripken and Glenn Davis bounce back from poor seasons and could Mike Devereaux and Brady Anderson repeat their great 1992 seasons?

Despite the unanswered questions, Baltimore was expected to compete with Toronto and New York for the division title.

April 8-13 (8-13, 6.5 games back)

The Orioles started off the season in lackluster fashion, going 4-10 in the season's first three weeks. Several of the losses were quality starts. But the offense couldn't get on track while Rhodes (10.47 ERA), Sutcliffe (5.13 ERA) and Valenzuela (11.05 ERA and a two-week demotion to Rochester) were getting clobbered.

Brady Anderson batted .351 during this stretch, but his performance was negated by the poor hitting of Devereaux, Reynolds and Davis (all hitting under .190). Gregg Olson also blew two saves during the same period that led directly to Baltimore losses.

The O's turned it around a bit, going 4-3 in the last week, but there seemed to be little consistency apart from Anderson and Mike Mussina (3-1, 3.12 ERA).

May 13-16 (21-29, 10 games back)

May was the official Baltimore Oriole Injury Month: Harold Baines, Arthur Rhodes, Sherman Obando and Mike Devereaux all were hurt during the month, so their 13-16 record was not too bad considering their circumstances.

The pitching didn't look too bad. Jamie Moyer replaced Arthur Rhodes and pitched fine in two starts. But poor support and a thrashing in his third start left him at 0-3 with Sutcliffe-like stats.

Mike Mussina continued to pitch excellently, finishing the month at 7-2, 2.89. Ben McDonald was still inconsistent (4.58 ERA).

But the veterans took some of the slack. Sutcliffe threw four quality starts among his six assignments. Most heartening was Fernando Valenzuela's four quality starts during the month. A pasting on May 28 raised his May ERA from 2.70 to 3.54. Poor run-support left him with a 1-2 record for the month.

The Oriole offense continued to sputter. Brady Anderson and Ripken were hitting under .230 and the Orioles scored over five runs in only seven May games (winning five of seven).

Glenn Davis, paramount in the Orioles' pre-season plans, continued to flounder. Davis finally accepted a demotion to Rochester on May 27. The Orioles were 10 games back and it looked like they were finished before the season was a third over.

June 20-7 (41-36, 6 games back)

Minor-leaguer Glenn Davis' nightmare season reached its apex on June 7 when his jaw was broken in a bar-room brawl while he was playing for Triple-A Rochester. Meanwhile, in the major-leagues, the Orioles finally woke up and started playing like solid contenders.

On June 2, the Orioles began a 10-game winning streak, culminating with a 5-0 run against Detroit and the Yankees. The Orioles' wins against Detroit basically killed the Tigers' '93 pennant hopes.

The Orioles were riding high, but on June 6, in their brawl with Seattle, the Orioles pennant hopes were probably dashed when Mike Mussina plunked Bill Haselman. Mussina officially wasn't hurt in the melee, but he was 8-2 with a 2.86 ERA through June 6. He was 6-4, but with a 6.37 ERA the rest of the year.

Ben "Bad-Luck" McDonald had a 1.69 ERA in 37.1 innings, but was only 2-2. In contrast, Rick Sutcliffe pitched in a consistently mediocre fashion (4.77 ERA), but went 3-1. Moyer went 3-0, 3.58.

Super-phenom Jeffrey Hammonds, recalled on June 25 after his 80-day probationary period in the minor-leagues, immediately justified his recall by going 6-for-11 with a two-run homer in his first three big-league games.

July 14-12 (55-48, 4 games back)

Baltimore was playing mediocre ball, but

with all the contenders treading water, the Orioles scrambled closer to the leaders.

Jamie Moyer, Valenzuela and Mussina went a combined 9-3, but Mussina's wins were misleading. He had only one quality start during the stretch and by July 22 he was on the DL with muscle problems in his shoulder blade. McDonald had four quality starts and one poor start and was 3-2. Sutcliffe was 0-2 with a lone QS in five appearances.

To give you an idea of the pennant race, on July 23, the Orioles were half a game out of first and were in fourth place. Toronto helped cure Baltimore's pennant fever by taking a tight two-game set at SkyDome by scores of 6-5 and 5-4. The 5-4 game was memorable because Cal Ripken booted a sharply hit Tony Fernandez grounder to end the game in the bottom of the 10th. The O's lost four of five, to drop back among the pack at month's end.

August 15-14 (70-62, 6 games back)

The Orioles started off August on an 8-0 tear by fattening up on weak-sisters Milwaukee and Cleveland. In doing so, they went from fourth-place, five games out, to second-place, a half-game out.

But their injury problem manifested itself again and this time, only the most crucial players were sidelined. Hammonds, Chris Hoiles and closer Gregg Olson all went down between August 3 and August 9. Olson's tender elbow led to a blown save on August 8. The next day he was done for. With Mussina still out, Rick Sutcliffe went down on August 23 and didn't return until mid September.

Detroit avenged their June smashing at Camden Yards with a 47-17 three-game pummeling at Tiger Stadium. The Orioles continued a disastrous road-trip by losing three to the Yanks and two to Seattle. When "The Trip" was over, the O's were 6.5 games out.

Mussina came off the DL and, along with Moyer, pitched excellent baseball, but Valenzuela, Rhodes and Sutcliffe were terrible. Without Olson, the bullpen was pretty effective. Todd Frohwirth had two relief wins and a save. The 'pen did blow two saves, but the starters were much more culpable.

Sept./Oct. 15-15 (85-77, 10 games back)

The pitching staff reeled off nine quality starts in ten games through Sept. 9, going 9-1 in that stretch and pulling within a half-game of Toronto. Hoiles led the charge and ended up hitting .374 and slugging .758 with 8 homers for the month.

Baltimore's luck ran out and they finished the month going 8-14. At the same time, Toronto was on a 17-4 tear, so the O's were doomed unless they played .864 ball. To put that in perspective, that's 140 wins over a whole season.

Park Effect. In its second year of existence, Oriole Park at Camden Yards provided a big boost to the offense in '93. Runs were up 11 percent last year, although the effect hasn't been that strong over the last two years (four percent). Note that some of this data may be skewed because baseball has only been played there for two years; take it for what it is worth.

The park doesn't affect spray hitters very much but it definitely squelches doubles and triples, down seven and six percent respectively over the last two years.

But power hitters need not despair; the short right and left field walls down the foul lines give them a shallow target and have pumped up HR production. Right-handed sluggers enjoy a 16 percent increase while lefties get a nine percent boost.

The park also contributed to an increase in errors last year, especially in the infield. The opposite was true in '92 and overall errors have been reduced 10 percent over both years.

Offense. Baltimore's offense was slightly above average last year, but only slightly. Actually, the only thing that pushed them over the hump was their plate discipline; their 788 walks was second only to Detroit and that pushed their OBP to a respectable .346. They also limited their K's, but their hitting and slugging were right around league averages.

The Orioles' running game, however, was atrocious. They only attempted 127 steals and were successful a paultry 73 times (57 percent); only the Yankees' oxen were worse. Also, they were tied for the second lowest total of triples with 24, so they're obviously slow of foot.

The addition of Rafael Palmeiro should help in the power and speed departments. The Orioles had to deal with a few injuries last year as well. If the regulars can stay healthy, the offense will get back on track.

Total Offense: 54.8

Pitching. Baltimore's starting rotation was also rather mediocre, due largely to the injury sustained by Mussina and the inconsistent performances of their aging veterans. The team had 82 quality starts, a nice number, but the rotation couldn't keep its head above water in the second half.

The veterans needed to be cleared out, but the prospects weren't ready for the most part. The rotation was not so much awful, as it was a smidge below-average. The team plays in a hitter's park and the rotation wasn't healthy and didn't fire on all cylinders.

The bullpen was much more solid. The problems mounted, however, when Gregg Olson was sidelined toward the end of the season. Long and middle relief was very good and the closing (as long as Olson did the work) was exemplary. There are still major questions, but if the O's can remove one 5.00+ ERA starter, they'll show tremendous improvement.

Total Pitching: 25.7

Defense:
Infield: At first base, David Segui didn't live up to his potential. Luckily, the rest of the infield was up to snuff. Second baseman Harold Reynolds provided smooth pivot-play.

At third, Leo Gomez and replacement Tim Hulett provided some of the best defense in the league. Hulett's glove work more than overcame his mediocre defense. At short, Ripken showed he was losing some ability, but he still flashed his intelligent positioning and excellent arm.
Pts: 31.4

Outfield: LF Brady Anderson has a great reputation defensively, but he wasn't that much above-average at all. Mike Devereaux provided slightly above-average work in center and Mark McLemore's play in right left something to be desired. Their's reputations were quite high, but the bulk of the defense was done within 50 feet of the mound.
Pts: 2.3

Catcher: Chris Hoiles moved from bottom of the class to its head in 1993. He calls a good game, doesn't make many errors and now has one of the better arms in the game. There's no weakness here, that's certain.
Pts: 18.6
Total Defense: 52.3

1994 Personnel:
Catcher: Chris Hoiles rules. Any game he doesn't play is bad. ... bery, bery bad.
Bench: Possible bench banditos include Jeff Tackett, Greg Zaun and Mark Parent all are competent, but unexceptional.
Starters: 44.6
Bench: C+

Infield:
1B: Rafael Palmiero is the man at first
2B: Mark McLemore was given the job on the strength of his team MVP season of 1993.
3B: At third, the battle will be waged with Chris Sabo holding the edge over Leo Gomez.
SS: Some generic dude is supposed to have this job, we can't think of his name, though.
DH: Harold Baines should lock up a lot of DH time.
IF Bench: At first and DH David Segui and Paul Carey should backup Palmiero. T.R. Lewis and Brent Miller are also possibilities. At second base, look for Brad Tyler and Manny Alexander – Manny can also spell wutsizname at short. At third, Tim Hulett should sop up any spare time.
Starters: 91.8
Bench: B-

Outfield
LF: Brady Anderson's sideburns have a lock on left.
CF: In center, Mike Devereaux is sinking slowly, but he still will get most of the PT.
RF: Young Gun Jeffrey Hammonds will shake the AL's collective booty in right.
Bench: Mark Leonard, Jack Voigt, Damon Buford, Sherman Obando, Mark Smith and Jim Wawruck are short-term solutions for outfield backup. Curtis Goodwin and Alex Ochoa are long-term solutions.
Starters: 28.0
Bench: B

Starting Pitching: The Orioles have four solid starters when Mussina is healthy and a prospect list a mile long, which will help them eliminate some dead weight this season. The staff may experience some growing pains in the next few years while the youngsters adjust but they should show some improvement immediately. In fact, their staff may be discussed with the same reverent terms as Atlanta's and Chicago's (AL) in a short time. McDonald and (a healthy) El Sid complete the quartet with Mussina. If Arthur Rhodes can come through, the AL better watch out. if not, then Rick Krivda, John O'Donoghue, Kevin McGehee, Jason Satre could step forward and be almost immediate help. In the long run, Scott Klingenbeck, Vaughn Eshelman, Jimmy Haynes, Brian Sackinsky and Jay Powell could step up. There's almost too many names here.

Front-Line: 104.6
Second-Echelon: A

Relief Pitching: The bullpen isn't a liability, either – The question is can Lee Smith replace Gregg Olson? They have a number of reliable guys to handle middle-relief. The 'pen allowed only a 3.81 ERA (fifth lowest in AL). After Lee Smith, there's Jim Poole, Ricci, Todd Frohwirth, Oquist, Mark Williamson, Alan Mills, Brad Pennington. In the long-run look for Armando Benitez and his awesome heater.

Front-Line: 35.1
Second-Echelon: B

Player Value: 259.5

Farm System: Baltimore is very rich in low-level pitching prospects. They have some fine outfielders, but are pretty poor in the infield. Jeff Hammonds, Alex Ochoa, Curtis Goodwin and Mark Smith head the outfield class. Paul Carey and T.R. Lewis, a pair of 1B/DH types are the best of the infielders. At pitcher, Jimmy Haynes, Armando Benitez and Rick Forney are A-Ball sensations. At higher levels, look for Jay Powell, Jason Satre, Chuck Ricci and Rick Krivda.

Infield: D
Outfield: A
Starters: B
Relievers: C
Farm Ranking: C+

Management and Ownership: Peter Angelos, William DeWitt, Tom Clancy and the rest of the new Oriole pack are kinda hard to figure. The Orioles need to get Clancy's football-fan ass out of the picture. According to *Baseball Weekly,* Clancy's arrogance nearly single-handedly eliminated the possibility of Will Clark's signing. In this case, the O's got a better player in Palmiero, but supposing Clancy pulls the same kind of stunts when free-agents like Robin Ventura or Juan Gonzalez come to town in 1997?

There is no doubt that these guys will spend the $$$, but the gang at *BW* ranks them below George, Marge and the San Diego Scourge, Tom Werner. To paraphrase our hero, Al Bundy, that's like having the bottom bunk under Oprah. Let's give them a year before we can pass a more fully realized judgment on them.

The front office is in a state of flux. Currently, new ownership is trying to figure out what to do with Doug Melvin, Rollie Hemond and Frank Robinson. It doesn't look like a top priority and as of early February, the situation hadn't shaken out.

The field-level situation is much nicer. Johnny Oates has provided solid leadership during his tenure with the O's. The team can't steal for beans, but is solid on the hit-and-run and the bunt. Oates didn't get much production from his bench last year, so he was conservative about using many lineups and among the 28 managers, only Cito Gaston used fewer pinch-hitters than Oates' 70.

Oates handled his staff in an average manner. He didn't pull starters too quickly, or too slowly; he didn't make them go inordinately high in their pitch counts and he didn't abuse his excellent bullpen. He didn't have a great staff and managed to use them pretty well. He did abuse Mike Mussina a bit, but let's hope he's over that.

Ownership: C-
Front Office: ? ? ?
Field Management: A
Overall: Incomplete

1994 Outlook: The Orioles have done quite a bit to address their problems. They've made sure third is shored up. They've added a quality (albeit, risky) starter in El Sid. And most importantly, they've added an excellent hitting first baseman in Rafael Palmiero. If they can get their closing situation settled, the Orioles could win the AL East. It'll never be easy with the Toronto juggernaut, but the Jays need to get their starting pitching settled and they haven't done that.

BOSTON RED SOX

1993 Outlook: The 1993 edition of the BoSox was expected to do one thing: stink. The team in 1992 had been absolutely awful and the Sox had really not gone out and addressed their problems. Sure they had the best pitcher in the game, but they had traded away a superb young hitter in Phil Plantier and were expecting weak-kneed Andre Dawson to replace him. The rotation apart from Clemens was in flux, as was the bullpen.

April 13-9 (13-9, 2 games back)

Boston won 11 out of their first 14 games to stake an early 1.5 game lead in the division. Clemens won three of four during this stretch, but Viola was the real story. Frank won three straight with a 0.75 ERA and a complete-game shutout against the White Sox. Both finished the month at 3-1. Danny Darwin, however, was a real concern going 0-4 with an 8.20 ERA and only three K's.

On the 21st, Randy Johnson blanked the Sox in the first of back-to-back shutouts in Seattle, which started a six-game West Coast skid that left them in fourth place, 2.5 games behind Detroit.

Meanwhile, Mo Vaughn was cementing himself in the starting role at first base by hitting .412 and slugging .735 with 10 doubles and four home runs. Scott Cooper, doing his part in erasing the memory of that Boggs fella, hitting .350. Tony Pena, on the other hand, hit .180 in a preview of things to come.

May 14-14 (27-23, 4 games back)

Clemens started the month with an 11 K, five-hitter over eight innings against the Angels to lower his ERA to 1.55. Darwin outdueled Chuck Finley 4-3 the next day and picked up his first win. Danny recorded five wins in May with a 1.33 ERA and a 26/6 K/W ratio. Viola couldn't get anybody out, though, and gave up a 4.55 ERA and three losses.

Billy Hatcher was the unlikely stallion for the month, hitting .375 with 13 RBI. Greenwell and Fletcher were also hot, hitting .316 and .304, respectively.

The Sox contributed to the Rangers' woes on the 29th, scoring 15 runs without a homer in Jose Canseco's infamous first and last pitching appearance.

June 11-16 (30-39, 9 games back)

Boston dropped 15 of the first 18 games in June and found themselves 10 games behind the Tigers. The entire offense was slumping while Clemens was struggling with a pulled groin and tendinitis. He went 1-2 on his way to the DL and the rest of the staff was just as bad. Viola and Darwin combined for six losses during the slide.

The Sox righted themselves with an 8-2 run to end the month behind the pitching of John Dopson. He won his last three starts with a 2.45 ERA. Aaron Sele also made his first start on the 22nd, throwing a five-hitter and recording eight K's over seven innings for the win.

July 20-7 (50-46, 1.5 games back)

Seattle helped the Sox on the road to recovery, surrendering six out of seven games by July 18. After winning eight in a row, Boston moved into a tie with New York and Toronto (Baltimore was a half-game out) to set up a first-class pennant race.

The race remained tight as Boston won its tenth straight and the other two held their ground. But the Sox split their last six games to finish 1.5 games out. Ominously, the final game had Clemens losing 4-0 to Ben McDonald.

Boston's offense was the spark to their success in July. Vaughn slugged .754 with eight homers and Hatcher hit .361 with eight doubles and 20 RBI. Andre Dawson finally got in the act and knocked in 20 runs of his own.

Sele also made his presence felt, going 4-0 with a 2.97 ERA.

August 11-16 (69-62, 6.5 games back)

The Sox were only a game behind Toronto on August 6, when Bill Gullickson outpitched Clemens and held them to three hits in a 5-1 Tiger victory. That was enough to ruin anybody's confidence. It actually did begin a 5-12 slump that left them 6.5 games out on the 26th and severely limited their playoff hopes.

The offense took the month off. Aaron Sele threw five quality starts and only got enough support for one win. Darwin and Viola both managed to go 4-1, but only because they posted low ERA's, 2.23 and 1.64, respectively.

Sept./Oct. 11-20 (80-82, 15 games back)

Despite the arrival of slugger Rob Deer, who contributed six homers and drove in 13 runs, and hot streaks for Valentin and Cooper, the Sox basically went out with a whimper.

The hitting was decent during the home stretch, but the pitching staff ran out of steam and posted a 4.96 ERA to seal their fate.

Park Effect. Fenway Park is excellent for run production; it has boosted runs scored 14 percent over the last three years. Its irregular outfield walls and wide gaps have increased doubles by a startling 30 percent. Hits and batting average are increased 13 and nine percent, respectively.

The Green Monster suppresses homers, however, but not as much as the deep right field wall. Left handed sluggers have knocked out 14 percent fewer homers since '91 while righties have hit 5 percent less.

For some reason, Fenway is also tough on the defense, especially the infield. Overall errors have been increased 26 percent and infield errors 32 percent. Maybe they need a new grounds crew.

Offense. Plain and simple, Boston's run production last year was pathetic. Their 686 runs were the third lowest in the AL and only 11 more than the Royals' league-worst 675. Despite the heroics of their young first baseman, they slugged only .380 and came in tied for last with 114 homers. Fenway's tough, but not that tough.

Their team speed is above average, but they don't use it much; they had a 66 percent stealing success rate (third in AL), but had only 111 attempts. They also led the league with 319 doubles.

The Sox are going to use a real man behind the plate this year and that should help their hitting somewhat. They haven't made any major moves in the offseason that would suggest a drastic turnaround, however.

Total Offense: -14.3

Pitching. Boston got some pleasant surprises from the starters just when they needed it. Of course, this doesn't include Roger Clemens, but their veterans and their rookie phenom did a commendable job in his absence. The starters' 3.81 ERA was the second lowest in the AL behind Chicago; the entire staff's 3.77 ERA was also second behind the other Sox. Their 96 quality starts easily led the league.

You can question whether the veterans will perform at this pace next year, but Clemens will be back and can pick up the slack.

The bullpen was equally effective saving 75 percent of their opportunities and posting a 3.71 ERA. Jeff Russell anchored the bullpen and their fortunes basically rely on him. Their middle-relief is adequate, but not exceptional. If there is a problem this year, it will be here.

Total Pitching: 82.7

Defense.

Infield: Vaughn is still not incredibly smooth, but he is becoming a pretty solid defender at first. At second, Scooter Fletcher is excellent on the DP and provides good range and grit.

At short, John Valentin is a very good defender, especially considering his lack of speed. He positions himself well, is solid on the double play and has a good arm. At third, Scott Cooper has a decent reputation, but his defense isn't on par with others' opinions.

Pts: 15.9

Outfield: The outfield defense last year was pretty abysmal. The only real bright spot was Rob Deer and he's taken his show to Japan. Zupcic isn't too bad.

Pts: 4.1

Catcher: Tony Pena had a good time calling a game and working the pitching staff, but he didn't do anything else right.

Pts: 4.0

Total Defense: 24.0

1994 Personnel:

Catcher:

Starters: Dave Valle should be OK this year if only because he'll be playing "wall ball" at the Fens.

Bench: The bench will consist of Flaherty and possibly Scott Hatteberg and Bob Melvin.

Starters: 19.2

Bench: D (B if Hatteberg gets a shot).

Infield:

1B: Mo Vaughn is the real thing at first.

2B: At second, it looks like Scott Fletcher's glove and ability to stay healthy will overcome the mighty club of Tim Naehring.

3B: At third Scott Cooper will get the nod.

SS: John Valentin is the best shortstop the Sox have had in many years.

IF Bench: At first, Carlos Quintana should

backup Vaughn. Jim Crowley, Ernie Riles and Billy Hall, Jeff Richardson and Luis Rivera could see some time in the middle of the infield. At third, Luis Ortiz could come up from Triple-A. Long-range prospects include Ryan McGuire and Bob Juday.

Starters: 51.5
Bench: C+

Outfield:
LF: Mike Greenwell will play left.
CF: Otis Nixon will start in center.
RF: Andre Dawson will get a chance if his knees can hold.
Bench: Jeff McNeely, Greg Blosser, Bob Zupcic and Billy Hatcher could get backup jobs. Look for Jose Malave and especially super-phenom Trot Nixon. Rumor has it that Nixon will come up in September and never leave. ... He's that good.

Starters: 18.7
Bench: C-B

Starting Pitching: Roger Clemens, Frank Viola, Danny Darwin and Aaron Sele will have slots 1-4. Other candidates include John "I honk" Dopson, VanEgmond, Frankie Rodriguez, Rob Henkel, Gar Finnvold, Joel Bennett and Gettys Glaze. Look for Jeff Suppan, or, "Clemens II," as he's called.

Front-Line:111.7
Second-Echelon: B

Relief Pitching: Ken Ryan, Cory Bailey and Jeff Russell will get first dibs on all saves. Long-relievers include Scott Bankhead, Nate Minchey, Taylor, Quantrill, Hesketh, Fossas and Jose Melendez.

Front-Line: 28.5
Second-Echelon: C+

Player Value: 229.6

Farm System: The farm system is in adequate, but unexceptional shape. There's a pretty good balance here. They have a decent catcher in Hatteberg, fine infielders with Ryan McGuire, Jim Crowley, Bob Juday and Luis Ortiz. Jose Malave, Greg Blosser and uber-kind Trot Nixon in the outfield. At pitcher, they have Frankie "96-MPH" Rodriguez, Gar Finnvold, Tim VanEgmond, Rob Henkel and Jeff Suppan. At relief, they're thin, but Cory Bailey is a comer.

Infield: B
Outfield: C+
Starters: C+
Relievers: D
Farm Ranking: C+

Management and Ownership: John Harrington is a pretty nice guy who works hard on ownership issues. He came out of the struggle with Haywood Sullivan in the driver's seat, but the front-office is the most disarrayed in the game. The team is willing to spend to get talent and is reasonably dedicated to developing it's own players.

Currently, the Sox are operating in quite a strange manner. They have no GM after Lou Gorman was demoted/promoted. This can only be seen as a positive as Gorman is a nitwit. This is the man that traded Phil Plantier and Jeff Bagwell, after all. At this stage in the game, it's bloody obvious that Gorman wouldn't know a Grade-A prospect if one came up from Double-A and bit him on the butt. Lord knows, he traded two of them away, and who knows how close the Sox came to getting rid of Maurice Vaughn. Gorman has his defenders, but how many GMs (still in the game) have traded away a 30-homer hitter and an All-Star first baseman for negligible gain *on a team starving for offensive help*? The answer rhymes with "hero," unless you factor in former GMs high up in the Boston front office. Right now, the Sox are searching and have their heart set on Dan Duquette of Montreal. ... Let's see what happens.

What's going on the field is something worthy of New York. The public perception of Butch Hobson when he was the manager at Pawtucket was that he was a player's manager who was exactly the kind of guy who could nurture young stars like Blosser, Sele, Vaughn and Plantier. Well, it seems Mr. Hobson blew his tact gasket when he hit the show. In 1992 alone, he feuded with Plantier until he was traded for a sack of beans. For an encore, he got into a celebrated fistfight with his young-star first baseman. Mo Vaughn has heart, however and smacked the hell outta the ball in 1993. Then to show his class, Hobson told his coaching staff they would all return for 1994 – the thing is, they were fired just a few days later. Whoops.

As an in-game skipper, Hobson's team

plays like it's the 1985 Cardinals. There's only one problem, the Sox don't get on base like the '85 Cardinals; they don't advance themselves on the bases like the '85 Cardinals; and they sure as heck don't play 'd' like 'em either.

Hobson doesn't let his starters get bashed and doesn't let 'em go too deep into their pitch counts, either. With his excellent bullpen, Hobson isn't afraid to remove starters, but he is the kind of guy who balances his pitchers' work.

Ownership: C-
Front Office: Incomplete
Field Management: C-
Overall: Incomplete

1994 Outlook: Last year we told you to look for the Red Sox to surprise. If Clemens had his normal season, the Sox would have gone 86-76. This year, expect the Sox to peddle around .500. They have the pitching, and the offense has to improve, but something is going to keep the Sox within a few games of where they are. Somebody in the rotation, or a couple once-reliable relief cogs will falter. The most you could expect would be 90 wins (unless Sele goes 20-7), but a realistic expectation would be around 79-88 wins. There are questions about the pitching consistency and not enough solutions on offense.

DETROIT TIGERS

1993 Outlook:
The Tigers were definitely considered a second-division team going into the '93 season. Their offense was continually underrated by many prognosticators and their shoddy pitching had obviously not been fixed (And no, we're not ignoring the acquisition of Mike Moore, et al.). Detroit was picked by many publications to finish last. Baseball Weekly was generous, giving them fifth place.

April 15-7 (15-7, 2 games ahead)
The season started inauspiciously. Detroit played listlessly in their first six games (2-4) and the negative predictions looked safe.

On April 13, Travis Fryman went 3-for-5 with four runs and five RBI, keying a 20-4 dissection of Oakland. With the rout as impetus, the Tigers went on an 11-1 tear that would leave the rest of baseball gasping.

During this stretch, the Tigers had wins by scores of 20-3, 10-6, 8-7, 12-4, 17-1 and 16-5.

That's not to say every win was a mediocrely pitched rout. The Tigers won some duels 3-2, 5-0, 3-1 and 5-3.

John Doherty was 3-1 with a 2.08 ERA, but David Wells was the sensation, going 4-0 with a 1.47 ERA. Michiganders started talking earnestly of the Cy Young for the first time since '84. The money guy, Mike Moore started off in a fashion typical of his '92 performance: 2-1 with a sexy 6.25 ERA.

Chad Kreuter, Fryman, Whitaker, Phillips and Gibson were providing the offense. Kreuter's strong play behind the plate and incredible offensive improvement led to Mickey Tettleton's move to first base. Our good friend Cecil was a wash, driving in 17 runs, but hitting only two homers. The big guy was already six HRs off the league-leading pace.

May 15-11 (30-18, 2.5 games ahead)
Gibson and Kreuter continued their early excellence (sustaining averages of .331 and .369 respectively), while Cecil cranked out seven homers.

Despite the terrible pitching of Moore and Gullickson (a combined 5.60 ERA in 80.1 IP), the pitching staff a 3.99 ERA, miraculous by Detroit's standards.

Dave: I must add that it was a royal pain to do call-in shows in the Michigan area during this time. It seemed like everyone was hooting about the poor reviews we'd given the Tiger pitching staff in last year's book. We just told everyone to get back to us by the end of July. In retrospect, the prescience of this statement was eerie.

June 13-16 (43-34, 4 games back)
Detroit started June playing .500 ball.
Feeling the heat after Toronto went on a hot streak, the Tigers took three of four games at Tiger Stadium (June 10-13), outscoring Toronto 23-5 in their three wins. Ominously, they lost the final game 13-4 when newly acquired Tony Fernandez drove in five runs against Mark Leiter. It didn't matter at the time because the Tigers had withstood the charge and held onto a four-game lead.

On June 20, they stood at 43-25. If you

look at the record the Tigers had in June, you can guess what happened next.

June 22 is now considered the day that the Tigers' hearts, spirit and backs were broken.

Mike Mussina walked into his start against the Tigers reeling after an unmerciful bashing at the hands of the Brewers on June 16. The Tigers had commented that Mussina was lacking in confidence and pounced on him for five runs, knocking him out before he could finish the second inning. The Tigers held onto a 8-3 lead going into the bottom of the sixth. Then all hell broke loose. Gullickson faltered, the bullpen failed and Chris Hoiles' grand slam capped an eight-run inning. Detroit lost 12-9.

Baltimore finished the series by taking two games by scores of 6-2 on June 23 & 24. Boston also helped continue the slump by drubbing Detroit three times, outscoring them 29-8 during their series.

When all was said and done, the Tigers had lost 10 straight and 13 of 14.

July 10-18 (53-52, 7 games back)

Amazingly, it seemed that no one wanted the division. As Detroit was swandiving into mediocrity, Toronto and New York were dogpedaling along at .500. On July 10, The Tigers were 48-39, only half a game out of first!

The Tigers then went 5-13 to put themselves out of the race.

The chief culprits were, of course, Gullickson and Moore, but the entire staff stank to high heaven (Wells had a 8.28 ERA in 29.1 IP). Gibson and Kreuter (explicably) fell to earth, but the offense was still on a pace to score 890 runs. It's safe to say that when the team ERA jumps from 3.67 to 4.89 over a two-month span, that the entire staff is pitching like they need arthroscopy.

August 18-11 (71-63, 6 games back)

Gullickson and Moore rebounded in August, going 6-0 and 4-1, respectively. Tom Bolton filled in admirably for the injured Wells with a 4-1 record and 2.87 ERA.

The offense remained awesome, except for a few notable occasions. Trammell (.405) and Fryman (.313) led the charge.

After being held to two runs in a doubleheader sweep by Milwaukee on the 13th, Detroit went on an 11-4 run to finish the month. It wasn't enough to catch Toronto. In fact, it only allowed them to overtake a plummeting Boston team, whose excellent pitching was being negated by lousy hitting.

Sept./Oct. 14-14 (85-77, 10 games back)

The staff fell back to earth and managed only 9 quality starts in 28 appearances, which helps explain their 5.23 ERA for the month. That was all she wrote.

The hitting slumped a bit, but it's impossible to fault a team for hitting .276 with a .361 OBP and a .412 slugging percentage. In essence, the hitters had to carry the team all season. Whenever the offense showed signs of mortality – i.e., whenever they played at the level of their AL competition – the Tigers' abysmal pitching staff ensured yet another loss. Hell, it's been that way for years. ...

Park Effect. Despite the deepest center field wall in baseball, it shouldn't come as any surprise that Tiger Stadium yields a ton of home runs. Of course, the Tiger sluggers are prolific but the park itself gives a 23 percent increase in homers. Lefties particularly enjoy the short right field fence as their homers are boosted 35 percent; righties only get a 17 percent increase.

Correspondingly, run production is 3 percent higher in Tiger Stadium.

Other than that, however, the park is kind to the defense. Its narrow gaps reduce doubles by nine percent and triples by 22. Strikeouts are increased two percent and errors are lowered by six percent.

Offense. The Tigers' offense is one mean machine. They easily scored the most runs in baseball with 899 and posted the highest OBP at .362. They were outhit and outslugged by both the Yanks and Jays in the AL but their ability to take walks *and* hit for power made them the most prolific scorers.

There are some questions whether this pace can continue this year; several key hitters are aging, Cecil is fading and Tettleton may be gone. A strong core of hitters will remain and the Tigers will be among the leaders in runs scored, but they may not have the same juggernaut they did last year.

On the other hand, their achilles heal, team speed, may be greatly improved with the arrival of Eric Davis and Danny Bautista. The Tigers stole only 104 bases last year with a mediocre 62 percent success rate.

Total Offense: 120.9

Pitching. The problems of the Detroit pitching staff are well documented. Everybody seems to know about it except Tiger management, however, and at this writing, they've done nothing to correct it. The same starting rotation that gave up a league-high 128 homers and posted a 4.78 ERA will be intact this year. Their fortunes may be improved somewhat if they can stay healthy, but it's doubtful.

The bullpen is rather mediocre as well... not as bad as the starters, but certainly no better than average. They allowed a 4.57 ERA, second highest behind New York, but still saved 67 percent of their opportunities. Henneman is coming off his best year, which suggests that the problems lie in long relief. Recent acquisitions Boever and Davis may help.

None of these guys are going to change Detroit's fortunes overnight, though, and the Tigers will need to score a ton of runs again this year to compete.
Total Pitching: -24.4

Defense.
Infield: Cecil Fielder is a joke at first. At second, Lou and the fill-ins are very solid. At third, Fryman could be Gold-Glove caliber. At short he was a bit lacking, last year, but in general he has been fine. Trammell was very solid at short.
Pts: 13.9

Outfield: In general, the outfield defense of the Tigers was adequate, but unexceptional. Gladden was OK in left. Cuyler was excellent in center; and Deer was very solid in right.
Pts: 14.3

Catcher: Kreuter was very good behind the plate, backup Tettleton wasn't so hot, but part of that could be ascribed to his utility status with the team.
Pts: 14.6
Total Defense: 42.8

1994 Personnel:
Catchers:
Starters: Chad Kreuter will start.
Bench: This is the best catching bench in the game. Tettleton and Rowland are both All-Star material.
Starters: 43.0
Bench: A

Infield:
1B: Cecil Fielder is a fine RBI man, an excellent power hitter.
2B: Lou Whitaker may be starting to show some signs of aging. He still looks good, but his power was not as prevalent last year.
3B: Travis Fryman will try to make the AL All-Star team at a new position this year.
SS: Trammell and Chris Gomez will split duties.
DH: There hasn't been a regular DH with the Tigers since Darrell Evans in the mid-1980s.
Infield bench: Skeeter Barnes, Scott Livingstone, Tony Phillips (when not playing the outfield) and Tettleton (when not batting No. 5) are all considered backups.
Starters: 62.9
Bench: B+

Outfield
LF: Tony Phillips plays here.
CF: Eric Davis is here.
RF: There will be a battle here, but look for Danny Bautista to take the job.
Bench: Milt Cuyler, Gary Thurman, possibly Kirk Gibson (if the Tiges re-sign him). Junior Felix (Ha!), Shawn Hare and Rudy Pemberton all are possibilities. Higginson and Burguillos are long-rangers.
Starters: 7.7
Bench: C-

Starting Pitching: A discussion of anyone here is ridiculous. David Wells is pretty good. Everyone else is a stinkbomb. Dave Mysel, Justin Thompson and the "Li-ars": Lira and Lima are prospects. Any ozzah starter in a Detroit uni vill be schott!
Front-Line: 4.6
Second-Echelon: D+

Relief Pitching: The relief scenario isn't much better. Henneman, Krueger, Boever, Gardiner, Bolton, Knudsen, Storm Davis, Bob MacDonald, Sean Bergman, Greg Gohr and a cast of thousands will attempt to pitch well (blindfolds and drumrolls, please).
Front-Line: 5.2
Second-Echelon: D

Player Value: 123.4

Farm System: Thin, thin, thin. Wafer thin. Paper thin. Rusty Meacham thin. This organization is (repeat after us) T-H-I-N!!! Rich Rowland is the position player closest to being ready, and he's a catcher! Top-flight prospects include Brian DuBose (a poor man's Bagwell?) and Danny Bautista. Bautista could be a star, but he'll have to draw a few walks, first. On the pitching end, the Tigers have Rick Greene as a possible closer solution, but he'll have to learn about "strike one." Dave Mysel and Justin (No, I'm not Jason!) Thompson are the two hard throwers in the organization. Lima and Lira are two other young guns, but aren't quite the "stuff" pitchers that Mysel and Thompson are.

Infield: D
Outfield: D
Starters: C
Relievers: D
Farm Ranking: D

Management and Ownership: Let's get our act together, eh? Mike Ilitch, the new owner, spent a lot of money renovating the Stadium and supposedly will spend to make a winner, but who's he gotten? We don't see no John Smiley's or Drabek's on this team, we see the Gullicksons and the Moores. BLECH!

When GM Jerry Walker was fired and replaced by Joe Klein, it was like Moe being replaced by Larry. When you substitute one guy who's done nothing, for another, what does it matter? Klein was the Tigers' scouting director, as was Walker. The Tigers have produced one good player since 1989, "utility infielder" Travis Fryman, but where's the rest of the farm system? The Tigers haven't made many trades and except for Eric Davis have nothing to show for 'em. This team needs to show they can make moves.

On the field, Sparky is Sparky. He doesn't handle his pitchers well, but they. He handles his veterans hitters well and seems to be competent at times during in-game managing. His lineup selections leave a lot to be desired at times, but really he's just a guy from the old school. He's no Casey Stengel, but he's the closest thing we have now.

Ownership: B-
Front Office: E
Field Management: C
Overall: C-

1994 Outlook: They'll do what they did in 1993: Kick butt and get their butts kicked. Their won-lost record will depend on how much their offense declines (which it probably will). Somewhere between 75-85 wins would probably be accurate. If everything were to break right, one of the kids could come up and pitch well, pushing Detroit to 88 wins, possibly even 90.

NEW YORK YANKEES

1993 Outlook

The Yanks looked spend-happy for the first time in a few years. The big story was their acquisition of SP Jim Abbott, and the lesser note at the time was the signing of veteran SP Jimmy Key. Time would tell which was the important pick-up. Thanks to the media, both pitchers were over-shadowed by the "one that got away", Greg Maddux.

Offensively they looked solid. Tartabull and Mattingly were poised to repeat their '92 performances and youngsters Bernie Williams and Pat Kelly had found homes at CF and 2B respectively. There was a host of aging bats in the infield thanks to the All-Geritol squad of Spike Owen, Wade Boggs, and Mike Gallego, but their collective defense helped save the bacon of the Yanks' lesser pitching lights throughout the season.

Rookie-wise, New York was swimming in prospects. Russ Davis and Kevin Jordan were waiting in the wings for greatness, and pitchers Domingo Jean, Mark Hutton and Sterling Hitchcock would vie for the spot left open by injured diaper dandy Sam Militello. Toronto looked tougher, but the Yanks had the clout to keep up.

April 12-9 (12-9, 2.5 games back)

All eyes were on Jim Abbott. Jimmy Key won his first two starts with an ERA of 0.60, but everybody was waiting to see Abbott's Yankee Stadium debut. Fortunately he pitched beautifully, after having lost his first start on April 7 in Cleveland. Steinbrenner was ecstatic with fan reaction and told *Baseball Weekly*, "He's turned on by New York as much as they are by him."

Key no-decisioned his third start, lowering his ERA to 0.38 in the process. Still, nobody was paying attention. Bob Wickman accounted for two of the Yanks first five wins despite the lack of quality in his performance. He would win many starts in this manner, causing sudden bouts of nausea in AL teams and their fans.

DH Jim Leyritz began his season well, hitting for average and slugging. C Mike Stanley had also started the ball rolling on what would be a fantastic season for him. Mattingly was on fire the first two weeks but ended the month hitting .233 while Boggs was living up to expectations, hitting .300.

May 17-13 (29-22, 2.5 games back)

Key began May with another gorgeous no decision which the Yanks ended up winning over seattle 3-2. Abbott was not faring as well. By May 3 he was 1-5 with a 3.53 ERA. Although Yankee bats were booming, they weren't showing up for his starts.

Wickman, on the other hand, was 3-0 with a 3.67 ERA. He was pitching well when he won, but his pitching in no decisions redefined awful. Somehow, he was sucking all of Abbott's run support away.

Closer Steve Farr and Wickman had a curious relationship going which stemmed back to the '92 season: Farr had seven saves in Wickman's nine career wins (credit *Baseball Weekly*).

June 17-11 (46-33, 2 games back)

The Yanks were hanging in among there AL East elite, constantly in contention for the top seat as detroit and Toronto spent the early months jousting.

The pitching was a mixed blessing. Good pitchers like Abbott and Melido Perez couldn't get on track, and guys like Wickman were rising to the occasion unexpectedly. The bullpen was a joke, with Monteleone, Howe and Habyan routinely blowing the leads Key handed them.

Batters like Leyritz and Velarde were still hitting solidly well into June, which helped balance the productive if misspent at-bats by Nokes and Tartabull. Mattingly was climbing back on the average train and journeymen Spike Owen and Mike Gallego were hitting smoothly.

The best hitter on the team for June was probably RF Paul O'Neill, acquired in the much discussed trade for Roberto "Bobby" Kelly. Paul hit .343 with 7 HRs and 18 RBI.

July 14-12 (60-45, tied with Toronto for AL East lead)

By July 2, Wickman was 8-2 with a 4.38 ERA, having picked up a couple of extra wins in long relief. Perez was 5-7 with the exact same ERA and Abbott was 5-8 with a 4.42.

Every starter had at least a respectable average, and O'Neill was still rolling along.

New York's best game in July was a 13-6 smiting of Oakland, accounted for primarily by a 10-run seventh inning. The heroes were Mattingly who had two of his four hits there and Mike Stanley who powered a grand slam, prompting Yankee fans to toss hundreds of pairs of souvenir socks on the field

The team won nine of their last ten games for july to finish the month in a tie with Toronto atop the East.

August 15-13 (75-58, 1.5 games back)

In August, it began to look as if the Yanks had made the same miscalculation teams such as Atlanta and San Francisco had made. All three teams had excellent prospects moldering in the minors while the mother club struggled to win. In the Yankees case they were unwilling to use their talented young pitchers until it was too late.

Rather than replace losing pitchers like Perez and Kamieniecki with Jean and Hutton early enough to avoid damage, they waited until they were pretty much done for to bring up the rookies. Even then, trials were short and there was no commitment to keeping either of the phenoms in the rotation. New York needed pitching and they weren't doing anything to stop the bleeding.

Sept./Oct. 13-16 (88-74, 7 games back)

This month of the season was filled with bitter disappointment. After having overcome mediocre pitching for much of the season the Yanks finally died for want of a closer. The lone saving grace was Abbott's no-hitter on Sept. 4, the first by a Yankee in 10 years.

What had developed into a possible pennant run, the first in years, had deteriorated into going through the motions. The Yanks had much to look forward to in the next year, but there was no reason why they had to manage '93 as they did.

Park Effects: Yankee Stadium's unique configuration creates extremes in power and favors left-handed hitting.

While runs and batting average are only slightly below average, home run potential (14 percent greater) contrasts radically with double and triple potential (12 and 39 percent lower respectively). The tradition of Yankee sluggers is not a coincidence.

The percentage for errors is lowered, and infield errors are especially low at 8 percent under league average. This a moot point at present, as the Yanks are staffed with fine fielders (e.g. Gallego, Kelly and Mattingly).

While right-handed batters view the stadium as a wash, left-handed power hitters are in heaven. The HR rating is 36 percent higher than the rest of the league. This may account for Mattingly's being able to muster power despite his decline in other areas of hitting.

Offense: The Yanks couldn't complain about power this year. Acquiring players like Paul O'Neill helped them to 178 homers (matched by Detroit and bested by Texas, who only have the best slugger in the AL). The age factor came into play as New York was high in doubles (tied for third at 294) but extremely low in triples at 24. The Yanks only stole 39 bases in '93!!! The next closest were Boston and Baltimore who both had 73. To compound matters, the Yanks were caught 35 times, negating even the slightest amount of good which their paltry stolen bases could provide. No other team wounded themselves even close to this terminally on the basepaths. Apparently, any advance to second on anything but a hit-and-run should be considered a suicide mission.

Despite the abysmal lack of even snail-caliber wheels, the team did manage to score 821 runs and keep themselves in the race for the AL East crown well into the last month. The Yanks will be experiencing a youth surge in the next couple of seasons, so the speed should pick up. It was really their only outstanding offensive flaw.

Total Offense: 121.4

Pitching: If you asked a Yankee fan what the outstanding pitching flaw was, they'd almost invariably reply, "Closing!!!" The tandem of Steve's Farr and Howe was much less effective than in past seasons, while the late-season acquisitions of Lee Smith and Paul Assenmacher came to late to stem the flow of blood from the bullpen.

In other respects than saving games, the 'pen wasn't that terrible. It was never really set, with the likes of cats like Scott Kamieniecki and Bob Wickman doubling as starters and long relievers.

On the other hand, those two guys alone won quite a few games between themselves.

Starting pitching was marred by the initially poor performance of mega free agent signee (say that ten times fast) Jim Abbott and the constantly poor performance of perennial disappointment Melido Perez. It was Jimmy Key's spectacular hurling coupled with long relief success which saved the day.

Considering the list of recruits waiting in the wings (it's as long as a Moscow bread line) this should not be a problem by the middle of '94. If Xavier Hernandez pitches up to snuff, the save situation will be much less critical as well.

Total Pitching: 11.7

Defense:
Catcher: While Mike Stanley's bat did most of the talking, his defense was pretty good too, comparable to that of Oakland's Terry Steinbach. Nokes' defense is self-explanatory by its absence.
Pts: 4.1

Infield: Mattingly had the third best AL glove-ranking after Wally Joyner and John Olerud, and 2B Pat Kelly had the best ranking in the AL.

Boggs was by far the best Amercian League third baseman, and short was anchored by able journeymen Mike Gallego and Spike Owen.
Pts: 36.6

Outfield: LF Dion James was a wash defensively, but CF Bernie Williams and RF Paul O'Neill were both above average with the mitt. Williams has proved his worth with the glove if not with the bat.
Pts: 15.2
Total Defense: 55.9

1994 Personnel:
Catcher: Mike Stanley will be getting the loin's share of playing time after last year's revelatory performance.

Bench: Matt Nokes will undoubtedly be back, much to the pleasure of pitchers across

the American League. Jim Leyritz should be able to pick up the slack behind the dish.
Starter: 20.7
Bench: A

Infield:
1B: Don Mattingly is the starter and looks to be for the near few years. J.T Snow was the closest thing to a mature prospect and he died and went to California.

2B: Pat Kelly should start most of the games this year. His defense is excellent and his bat has improved enough that a platoon isn't really necessary.

3B: Wade Boggs will begin the year as the starter, but the question is, will he end it on the bench? His lucrative contract, foolishly tendered by the Yanks, may ensure that he spends at least the rest of this year anchoring the hot corner.

SS: Now that Spike Owen is gone, it's a toss-up as to whether Randy Velarde or Dave Silvestri will get more time. They can both hit competently, but neither of them is a world-beater with the glove.

DH: If the Yankees can find a full-time left-fielder as they'd like, then Danny Tartabull will ease his aches and pains in the DH spot. This would serve to lengthen his career and might even result in improvement at the plate.

IF Bench: Kevin Maas is still around, but we all know the book on him by now. Prospect Tate Seefried may see some spare time at first, but he's not really good enough to stick at this time. He's only 21, he's got decent power and he strikes out like the pup Single-A ballplayer that he is. He's a decent prospect, but he needs seasoning like creole gumbo.

Second base is Kevin Jordan territory. It's only a matter of time until Pat Kelly is knocked out of the hole by this young buck. Baseball America failed to list him among their top ten prospects for the Yanks, but he looks as good as any of the other position prospects New York has in the top levels.

Third has Russ Davis champing at the bit to begin his major league career. He may not be the prospect everyone thinks he is, but every team that talks trade with the Yanks raises his name sooner or later. He would have been gone by now if the team didn't plan to use him. It's just a matter of when they decide to dis Boggs for the kid.

Whoever loses the Silvestri/Velarde battle will be the primary backup at short. Spike Owen is veteran insurance, yet again. 26-year-old Robert Eenhoorn (.280-6-46) is also a possibility, although he doesn't bring exceptional tools. Once again, the Yanks have a fine position prospect whom these veterans will yield to upon his delivery. In this case it's Derek Jeter, only the organization's No.1 prospect. They'll have to anchor short for '94 though. Bringing up Jeter this early would be devastating. Heck, bringing him up to Double-A too early could be devastating. He may be only a year and a half away.
Starters: 80.5
IF Bench: B+

Outfield:
LF: Since the Yanks propose to move Danny Tartabull to DH permanently, the slot probably belongs to Luis Polonia, light-hitting, former speed-merchant.

CF: It'll be Weekend at Bernie's ad nauseum as young Bernie Williams plies his trade. Let's hope his bat has more life than his silver screen counterpart.

RF: Paul O'Neill will be in right. He's generally good for 140-150 games a season, so some skirt-wearing second banana can pick up his slack.

Bench: Perennial backup Dion James is gone and that's a shame. Gerald Williams and Mike Humphreys are around, but neither of them is the hitter Dion is. These are the guys who'll spell O'Neill and Polonia for a few innings here and there.

Billy Masse is the guy who can really hit. He's insurance for Polonia and that should be reversed. Masse is one of those guys who is in imminent danger of being 35 and having accumulated 500 excellent major-league AB. If Polonia falters in spring the Yankees better darn well see to it that Masse gets his shot.

Randy Velarde isn't a longshot to play in left, he did it quite a bit last year. But with all these outfielders he'd be poaching on others' PT. Jalal Leach (.282-14-79 at Double-A) looks pretty good also.
Starters: 28.8
Bench: B

Starting Pitching: Key and Abbott are locks for the rotation. The remainder of the rotation, including guys like Perez, Wickman and Kamieniecki, are more likely to feel the knife when the new kids reach the block. Mark Hutton, Sterling Hitchcock and a presumably healthy Sam Militello are poised for full-time start duties.

Brien Taylor is the top organization prospect who won't see time in the majors in 1994. His injuries will ensure that he sits for much of the year and he'll be back in double-A if he returns early. Keith Heberling and Matt Drews are outside chances who most likely show up too late to make an impact this season.

Front-Line: 85.7
Second-Echelon: B+

Relief Pitching: The bullpen was significantly improved by the addition of closer Xavier Hernandez. He was striking out over a man an inning in Houston last year and his ratio was a sign that he's poised to become one of the bets closers in the business. He's 28, and many noted relievers have come into their own at his age. Paul Assenmacher will get stray saves and set the table with typical aplomb. Steve Howe should play set-up also.

Paul Gibson provides lackluster middle relief. If the starting pitching shakes out as it should, Kamieniecki and Wickman will make competent long relievers.

Front-Line: 13.5
Second-Echelon: D

Player Value: 229.2

Farm System: Key position prospects are the top-notch Jeter, potential stars Jordan and Davis as well as oft-overlooked catching prospect Jorge Posada. It's a sign of minor league excellence that so many of the Yanks' prospects are infield candidates. Outfielders are generally a year or two away, but boys like Ruben Rivera and Shane Spencer are super-prospects.

Pitching is somewhat depleted from years past, but this is only because four of the top prospects of the recent past (Hutton, Hitchcock, Militello and Jean) are either ready to start as Yankees or for other teams. Brien Taylor, considered to be the best of that lot, is the most notable pitcher left behind in the shift. The new guard is comprised of such notables as Keith Heberling, Matt Drews and Andy Pettitte (11-9 3.04 in Single-A). If Taylor isn't careful, his late arrival to the show may cause him to be passed up by these guys as well.

Bobby Munoz is the only closer who's been developed enough to be considered a real prospect and he didn't make the transition to the mother club as well as New York would have liked. This was obviously a factor at the end of the season, when the Yanks felt the lack of a finisher and fell out of the AL East race. They also traded Rich Batchelor, the other developed closer, in order to acquire Lee Smith in September.

Infield: A
Outfield: B
Starters: A
Relievers: D
Farm Ranking: A-

Management and Ownership: The Yankees have flourished since King George was overthrown and exiled for his Winfield transgression. The Yanks have cooled on making their usual tons-'o-prospects-for-some-bit-part trades and are possibly too conservative in keeping too many of their kids. That's a nice problem to have.

GM Gene Michael isn't a genius, but he's surrounded by excellent support staff who acquire great talent and keep the big club stocked with good young players. He doesn't need to make big trades, but can deal from strength and has the ability to sign players when needed. It's just that New York is a hard sell to free agents after Steinbrenner made Stade Yankee over into the "Bronx Zoo" in the late 1970s.

Manager Bucky Showalter has a great reputation among his peers and in other baseball circles. His managing tendencies appear to be across-the-board average, but he seems to get good production from his players. Since he's so good, should we expect his firing soon?

Ownership: D+?
Front Office: B+
Field Management: B
Overall: C+

1994 Outlook: There's no reason why the Yankees can't win the AL East in '94. They made do with inconsistent pitching last season, and that should be no problem at all this year. They've developed a nice squad, which balances hitting, pitching and excellent defense all the way around.

The Yankees didn't make very many significant moves over the winter, but with their talent they didn't have to. The time has come when they have to stop signing veterans like Boggs and Owen and give the prospects a chance to make this team what it should be. As well as the Yanks did last year, they are a much better team this time around. The AL East should be competitive. Boston and Detroit still haven't addressed perennial shortcomings (power and pitching respectively), but Baltimore looks like a new clubhouse and Toronto is ...well, Toronto. All things considered, the Yanks look as promising as any team in baseball. If things break right they'll be the Braves of the American League.

TORONTO BLUE JAYS

1993 Outlook: When opening day rolled around, most pre-season sources were predicting that the World Champion Toronto Blue Jays would make a repeat appearance in the post-season. There were never any questions about their ability to score runs, which was augmented even more by the signing of veteran Paul Molitor to replace popular DH Dave Winfield. But the starting rotation was a concern, considering that Dave Stewart and Jack Morris were way past their prime, and that Stottlemyre, Hentgen and Leiter were unproven commodities. Juan Guzman was the only pitcher considered to be strong enough to stand on his own. Could the veteran leadership last long enough to lead the rest of the staff to a pennant?

April 13-10 (13-10, 2.5 games back)
Three games over five hundred might be considered a satisfactory start for some other teams, but for the World Champs, their 13-10 record just wasn't up to standards. As expected, it was the starting corps that let the Blue Jays down in the first month. Stewart tore a flexor muscle in his right forearm during spring training and started the season on the DL. Morris pitched like he belonged on the DL, losing his first three starts and allowing 29 earned runs in 22.2 innings. Guzman was beaten up in his first two starts, but settled down to post solid performances in the latter half of the month, including a five-hit shutout April 29th.

It was a rosier picture on the offensive side of things. John Olerud began in spectacular fashion, hitting .450, slugging .650 and posting a .527 on-base average. Joe Carter pounded six homers and put up a .509 slugging average. Robby Alomar hit .302 and complemented it with a .400 on-base. The lineup maintained a respectable .277 average for the month. With the 4.80 ERA the pitching staff contributed though, it added up to a less-than impressive third place tie with the Yankees.

May 16-12 (29-22, 2.5 games back)
The month of May saw Detroit pummel opposing pitchers and rise to prominence in the AL East. But north of the border, the Blue Jays were playing good enough to keep up with the torrid pace the Tigers were setting. Once again, though, it was primarily their hitting that kept them in the hunt, although Pat Hentgen stepped into the spotlight by registering five quality starts in his six opportunities and lowering his ERA to 2.78. In the geriatric ward, Stewart came off the DL May 13, but by that time Morris had faltered with a sore elbow and back. Olerud (.348 average, .652 slugging) and Carter (7 HR, .617 slugging) continued to play their hot hands, while Paul Molitor suddenly came alive and made everyone forget about the loss of Dave Winfield. Molitor hit .374 in the month and slugged .539, striking out just eight times in 115 at-bats. Toronto was still not hitting on all cylinders, but their offense, which recorded a .284 average and slugged a league-leading 42 home runs, enabled them to stay within striking distance of the lead.

June 19-9 (48-31, 2 games ahead)
The Jays entered the month of June tied for second place with New York, 2.5 games off the pace. However, the pitching staff finally began looking like a big league rotation and Toronto stormed to the top of the pile with a 19-9 record. The Blue Jays rode a seven-game winning streak in the middle of the month, highlighted by back-to-back complete game shutouts recorded by Jack Morris and Al Leiter. Hentgen (5-0 in June) and Guzman continued to pitch well, and the bullpen, led

by Duane Ward's seven saves and 1.46 ERA, protected the leads they were entrusted with.

It was the right side of the infield that led the offensive attack this time. Olerud launched a 26-game hitting streak, hit .427 and slugged .760, while Alomar hit .369 with five homers and got on base at a .431 clip. Because of injuries to Luis Sojo and Dick Schofield, Toronto acquired Tony Fernandez from the Mets in the second week of June and he put in a .326 average for his new club. Everything seemed to be coming together for the SkyDome residents as they ended the month leading the division by two games.

July 12-14 (60-45, tied for first)

The potent Blue Jay lineup finally came down to earth and allowed the Yankees and the Tigers to creep into the picture. Toronto's starting corps cooled off considerably, going 4-12 with 10 no-decisions in July. It didn't help any that their formidable offense took a holiday in the first eight games, averaging only 2.25 runs over that stretch. Not coincidentally, they lost eight of their first nine games and played first-place tag with New York for most of the month. The main culprits in the offensive collapse were Joe Carter and Devon White. Carter struggled to hit .219 with little power, while leadoff-hitter White couldn't even stay above the Mendoza line. Olerud's .389 batting average, .491 on-base and .700 slugging percentage couldn't quite overcome the Jays' offensive malaise. Toronto spent eight days in July tied with the Yankees, and a heated pennant race was on.

August 17-12 (77-57, first place)

The Blue Jays spent nine days tied for first place in August, and for three weeks, all eyes were trained in the direction of the AL East. Every time the Yankees would get close to claiming the league lead for themselves, the Blue Jays would rip off two or three wins to wrestle control out of New York's hands. In mid-August, with the pressure mounting daily, the Blue Jays put together a string that may well have been the turning point of their season. Beginning August 14, Toronto won five consecutive games against the Red Sox and Indians to give themselves some desperately-needed breathing room. The Yankees lost three of four games in that span. And while they would eventually give up the two-game cushion they had built, the Blue Jays showed the rest of the league that they knew how to come through at crunch time.

Feeling hot Yankee breath on their necks, the Blue Jays acquired Rickey Henderson just before the July 31 deadline in a trade that involved sending their best pitching prospect, Steve Karsay, to the A's in payment. But Rickey, suffering from injured hands, was a non-factor, hitting only .208 for his new team. As was the case all season long, the Jays were paced by Alomar (.360 average, .423 on-base), Molitor (.355 average, .410 on-base) and Carter (nine home runs, .505 slugging).

Sept./Oct. 18-10 (95-67, 7 games ahead)

The Blue Jays lost six of their first seven games in September, but the Yankees didn't seem to want the pennant either, and Toronto maintained their share of the lead. But, beginning with a 10-4 drubbing of the Angels on September 10, the Blue Jays ripped off a string of nine consecutive wins to put the pennant in the bag. Dave Stewart, who has made a habit of gearing it up in the fourth quarter, led the pitching staff, going 4-0 with a 2.51 ERA. Guzman contributed a 4-0 record, while Hentgen and Stottlemyre each won three games. Toronto clinched the division with a 6-4 win against the Milwaukee Brewers on September 28.

Park Effect. The symmetrical confines of SkyDome have been a great boon to hitters so far in its three-year life-span. Since its inaugural 1991 season, SkyDome has boosted runs by seven percent and home runs by 21 percent. Joe Carter is especially enamored of his home stadium, as it increases right-handed homers by a healthy 52 percent margin. Last year alone, righties hit 82 percent more homers in SkyDome than anywhere else.

The fast Toronto lineup, and the faster Toronto carpet, contributed to a 101 percent increase in triples last year, and a three-year boost of 47 percent. Skydome also pushes up batting averages, but to a lesser degree. A scant three percent advantage is given to hitters in Toronto. Infield errors were reduced by 24 percent last year.

Offense: The Blue Jays had one of the most potent offense in the major leagues last year. They boasted the top three finishers in the race for the batting title and the team combined to hit .279, tied with the Yankees for best in the majors. The Blue Jays also led the majors in slugging percentage and only two teams, the Tigers and the Phillies, outscored them. To top things off, Toronto's balanced lineup also paced the AL in stolen bases and in stolen-base percentage. Perhaps the most telling statistic concerning the Toronto offense, however, is the .287 batting average they maintained with runners in scoring position. They simply knew how to push runners across the plate, and they did so with regularity all season long.

Total Offense: 102.9

Pitching:

Pat Hentgen was simply the best pitcher on the Blue Jays staff last year, coming out of nowhere to lead the club with 19 wins. Juan Guzman had a 14-3 record and 194 strikeouts. The two teamed up for a 33-12 mark and a .733 winning percentage. The rest of the rotation combined for a 37-38 record and a .493 winning percentage. It didn't help that Morris, Stewart, Stottlemyre and Al Leiter all spent time on the DL. Stewart did come through with a nice post-season, but in the summer heat of the real season, he and his mates stunk.

Duane Ward anchored a solid bullpen that went 25-17 and recorded a stellar 3.30 ERA. Eichhorn (3-1, 2.72 ERA), Danny Cox (3.12 ERA in 83.2 innings) and Tony Castillo (3.38 ERA in 50.2 innings) all deserved credit as an effective supporting cast. But Ward, who converted 45 of 51 save opportunities, was the real star of the bullpen.

Total Pitching: 38.1

Defense:

Infield: At first base, Olerud was one of the steadiest gloves in the league. Oddly, Alomars' range factor at second base was below average last year, but anyone who watches baseball knows of his fine fielding mobility and knack for turning the double play.

Sprague is in no danger of winning the gold glove, but his work last year was adequate. At short, Tony Fernandez did the job he was acquired to do, provide solid defense and augment that with a little offensive punch.

Pts: 10.7

Outfield: Devon White continued to prove why he is considered one of the best center fielders in baseball committing only three errors in over 1200 defensive innings. Joe Carter, while still a steady fielder, slowed a bit last year, and his range dropped nearly a third of a point. Left field was basically a revolving door all season, with nobody but mercenary Rickey Henerson playing the position the way it should be played.

Pts: 16.3

Catcher: Pat Borders provided good hands behind the plate and performed decent work with the pitchers, but that was about it. He managed to nail 33 percent of the runners trying to steal against him, but that is a rather lukewarm total. Randy Knorr didn't impress anyone with his skills last year, but he does have the reputation of having a strong arm.

Pts: 1.2

Total Defense: 28.2
1994 Personnel

Catcher: If he isn't traded by opening day, Pat Borders will probably get the starting job again simply because Toronto will need to justify his salary. But the Blue Jays would really like to have Carlos Delgado as their catcher and may trade Borders to clear the way for his arrival. If he wins the job, Delgado could be an impact player this year.

Bench: Randy Knorr will again be available to fill in as a back-up, but as in the past, his playing time would be limited to unimportant games and the late-innings of blowouts.

Starters: -3.0
Bench: B-A

Infield:

1B: While he probably won't challenge the .400 mark again, John Olerud is still capable of hitting well above .300 with 100+ walks. And as long as he has White, Alomar and Molitor hitting in front of him, he should drive in a healthy amount of runs again.

2B: Roberto Alomar broke his leg playing winter ball for his father's team in the Puerto Rico League. But doctors have assured the Toronto front office that he should be completely healed by opening day. If he's healthy, Robby will continue building his reputation as one of the best all-around players in the game.

3B: The word was that Sprague began pressing to hit the long ball after the All-Star break last year, and his work at the plate suffered as a result. Now that he has a full season at third base behind him, look for him to relax and be a little more consistent with his production.

SS: Tony Fernandez is again an ex-Blue Jay, which means that super-prospect Alex Gonzalez will get every opportunity to win the starting job in the spring. He already has the fielding skills of a major-leaguer, but if he struggles at the plate, Toronto may opt to demote him so he doesn't lose confidence.

DH: Veteran Paul Molitor will be back, and the Skydome faithful will worship the ground he walks on. He still has a potent bat and an excellent eye.

IF Bench: If things pan out the way the Blue Jays hope, Dick Schofield will back up Gonzalez at short. Eddie Zosky, who had bone chips removed from his throwing shoulder last year, will have to prove both his health and his bat in the spring to win a job. Domingo Cedeno, who bravely tried to claim the shortstop job in '93, could be a middle infield backup, but he doesn't have much star potential. Third baseman Howard Battle has shown excellent power in the minors and could surprise a few people if given a chance. It is likely, that he will spend another season in the minors polishing his strike zone. At first base, Domingo Martinez has excellent power potential and the terrible strike zone that accompanies it. But since Olerud is close to being a deity in Toronto, Martinez may be trade bait. Darnell Coles could also serve as a spare tire.

Starters: 117.0
Bench: B

Outfield:

LF: There will be some juggling done in the Toronto outfield, but Rob Butler has a good chance of nailing down the third outfield slot in the spring. He makes contact and has decent speed and a good defensive reputation. He's also a left-handed hitter, which doesn't hurt his chances any.

CF: Because of his defensive value, Devon White would benefit the Blue Jays even if he couldn't hit. But Toronto got the bonus plan last year as White put up great numbers in the leadoff spot. If he's healthy, White is a safe bet to steal 30 bases and score 100 runs in '94.

RF: The time is coming when Joe Carter must turn in his mitt and accept the DH job.

But for as long as Molitor is in a Blue Jay uniform, Carter will stay in the outfield. There are absolutely no questions about the potency of his bat.

OF Bench: The Blue Jays are strong in their outfield reserves, with young hitters aplenty to fill in gaps. Willie Canate finally has recovered from his severe case of "Rule-V-itis" and has a good chance to make the club Gaston likes him because he has plus speed and could turn in a decent batting average. Robert Perez, who hit .294 and 12 home runs for Syracuse, could emerge in the spring and win a job as well-- at last glance, he was hitting .329 in the Venezuelan League. Another name to keep in mind is Juan de la Rosa. Although his '93 debut in AAA was ruined by injury, should play full time in Syracuse and could be summoned in the event of an injury. Shawn Green and Rick Holifield are a bit far off to get excited about, but they both could progress rapidly this year.

Starters: 34.5
Bench: C

Starting Pitching:

This is where the formidable Blue Jay roster starts to look a little thin. Last year, the rotation seemed more like a M*A*S*H* unit than a pitching staff, and the front office hasn't done a thing to change matters over the winter. Guzman and Hentgen should be OK. But the broken-down trio of Stewart, Stottlemyre and Leiter will again be asked to at least impersonate real pitchers, and even that might be too much for them. Paul Spoljaric and Huck Flener will be waiting in the wings for the eventual breakdown that will occur.

Front Line: 77.6
Second Echelon: C

Relief Pitching: The Blue Jay's bullpen is not nearly as bad as its press. Duane Ward is one of the better closers in the game right now, and playing for the Blue Jays will guarantee at least 50 save opportunities again this season. Other than free-agent Mark Eichhorn, the pitchers primarily responsible for the bullpen's 3.30 ERA last year will return. Timlin and Cox will set the table from the right side and Tony Castillo will do the same form the left side. Woody Williams could stand in for a season until minor-leaguers Kurt Heble or Aaron Small is ready .

Front Line: 35.9
Second Echelon: B
Player Value: 265.0

Farm System: The system is absolutely busting at the seams with position players, and the front-line talent looks pretty sharp. Carlos Delgado leads the pack at catcher and is on the short list of Rookie-of-the-Year candidates. Alex Gonzalez will get a long look in the spring, and if his hitting is anywhere near the quality of his fielding, he could be the opening-day starter at short. No one will displace John Olerud at first base, or Paul Molitor as DH, but Domingo Martinez is still a highly regarded prospect. D.J. Boston is an excellent long-range prospect at first base, and his development as a hitter could determine Domingo's fate. Ray Gianelli and Domingo Cedeno are the closest middle-infield prospects in the system, but their abilities are still in doubt. Outfield prospects Robert Perez, Shawn Green and Lee Stevens are all expected to do battle for an outfield job, with an edge going to either Perez or Stevens because of their experience. Rotation candidates Spoljaric and Small are closest to the show, and kids like Alanso Beltran, Tim Crabtree and Joe Silva will be taking their places in the AAA Syracuse rotation. A stockpile of arms for the bullpen includes the likes of Huck Flener, Chris Kotes, Kurt Heble and Mark Ohlms.

Infield: A
Outfield: C+
Starters: A
Relievers: C+
Farm Ranking: B+

Management and Ownership: Although John Labatt Ltd., bottlers of Labatt's beer, is the parent company that holds the title and makes the payments, president and CEO Paul Beeston is the man that the front office answers to. He is a longtime baseball fan with an understanding of what it takes to build a winning organization. Beeston has always provided the capital required to support a large scouting and player-development system. And while he didn't spearhead the movement to scout and sign Latin American players, he certainly helped the organization maintain its reputation in that department. As proof, he allocated the $700,000 needed to sign the 16-year-old Brazilian pitching phenom, Jose Pett.

GM Pat Gillick is the one chiefly responsible for building the Toronto player development program, which has recently produced prospects Carlos Delgado and Alex Gonzalez. Once known as "Stand Pat", he has, over the past few years, shown the willingness and ability to acquire front-line talent late in the season to guarantee a pennant. Last year's swap for Henderson has been widely criticized, especially after Gillick let him go back to the A's as a free agent. However, it's hard to argue a case against Gillick when confronted with Toronto's back-to-back Championship seasons and three consecutive division titles. He is one of the best and most influential GMs in the game, and 1993 will be his last season in charge of the Blue Jays.

Cito Gaston's job last year was to provide a steady atmosphere both in the clubhouse and on the field. Once stability was achieved, his managerial style followed the watchmaker's theory, wind it up and let it tick. Gaston used the fewest starting lineups in the majors last year. But he was fortunate enough to have an extremely talented and healthy group of everyday players who made him look very good. He is generally slow in pulling his starters, but again, his powerful lineup affords him the luxury of resting his relievers when they need it. One thing is certain about Gaston, he has gotten his share of post-season experience the last three seasons – and that looks awfully good on a resume.

Ownership: A
Front Office: A
Field Management: A
Overall: A

1994 Outlook: The Blue Jays again appear ready to unleash their powerful offense on the AL East. There is no team in the division that can match up with them position by position, especially if they can be persuaded to utilize the talent they have in the minors. They have been quiet over the winter, concentrating on trimming the fat from the roster and locking up the remaining players with contracts. They said good-bye to Jack Morris, Rickey Henderson, Tony Fernandez, Mark Eichhorn and Alfredo Griffin and chose not to pursue any free-agents. Pitching will be a problem for them, as the walking-wounded will again try to motivate their bodies through another grueling season. But affordable, young talent is a precious commodity in these times and the Blue Jays will probably have to part with some of theirs for a reliable pitcher.

Team Essays – AL Central

Chicago White Sox

1993 Outlook: The Sox looked tough heading into the season, and they would turn out to be too tough for their AL West brethren by season's end.

The big news with the bat was the perennially powerful corner-duo of Thomas and Ventura as well as the acquisition of OF Ellis Burks from the Red Sox, who were still doing their best to ship anyone who could hit a home run out of Fenway.

Pitching was pretty much the same as in years past. Black Jack anchored the rotation, followed by the "always-poised-for-greatness" Alex Fernandez and comer Wilson Alvarez. The other starters were has-beens like Kirk McCaskill, but they would be easily replaced by the likes of Rod Bolton and Jason bere as need arose.

Defensively the Sox were sharp. Ozzie Guillen was back at short and would complete the double play with the able 2B platoon of Joey Cora and Craig Grebeck. LF Tim Raines was still running warning-track flies with aplomb and the fleet Lance Johnson was roaming CF.

The big story to kick off the year was the return of Bo Jackson. While he was a huge question mark, management made it clear that it was counting on its known quantities to pull the team. Bo may know rehab, but Gene Lamont made it clear that he preferred to know The Big Hurt.

The order was a canny combination of power and speed and the pitching was very good with more waiting on deck. The Sox were one stacked club.

April 13-9 (13-9, 1.5 games back)
McDowell's opening day line, 6IP 7H 4ER 5BB 4K, yielded him a win, and was typical of how many of his wins looked (i.e. cheap and sleazy).

He ended up 5-0 with a 4.33 ERA at month's end, striking out 17 batters and walking 14. How many pitchers can claim that kind of luck. As well, McDowell would end up pitching into August before he finally had a no decision.

April was an important month for Alex Fernandez, as it heralded his arrival as the pitcher he'd been hyped as for three years running. No more disappointing Aprils for Fernandez as he posted a 2.17 ERA and struck out 28 men in 37.1 innings. His control was excellent all year, and he showed that at 23 years of age he had become the youngest veteran pitcher in the game.

May 11-14 (24-23, 2.5 games back)
May was not a pleasant sequel to a successful April as the Sox took a slight tumble, barely keeping themselves above .500. While Alvarez and Fernandez saved bacon by going a combined 6-2, McDowell was busy working on a 2-4 record, proving that giving up four runs a game doesn't guarantee a 5-0 record as it had the month before.

June 15-13 (39-36, 0 games back)
The biggest moment in the otherwise bland July was Joey Cora's first major league home run which he belted into the upper deck of Tiger Stadium off Mike Moore on June 2.

Thomas's season really began in June. Although he'd been his usual solid self, from June through August he lived up to his billing as arguably the best hitter in baseball.

He hit around .340 with 29 homers and 74 RBI and had an OBP+SLG of over 1.000 for each of those months.

Inexplicably, Robin Ventura had one of his slumps in June. As hot as he'd been the month before, he suddenly caught cold and barely managed to keep his batting average above .200. His plate discipline was terrible (for him) at 13 BB and 23 K, as he usually walked much more than he struck out. Someone slipped him a mickey and he took a tumble.

On June 21, the Sox tied California and K.C. for the West lead, and by June 23 they held sole possession. they never looked back, despite several month-ending losses.

July 18-9 (57-45, 0 games back)
Alvarez headed in the opposite direction of Thomas during the month of July. It wasn't so much his 1-2 record which was alarming, but rather the fact that he walked 30 batters while striking out only 16. His control shot, he was demoted to AAA to work with his old pitching coach and get his game together. It was a pivotal moment for a pitcher who badly wanted to prove he was ready for the show.

Despite the loss of a key pitcher, Chicago rolled on. Fernandez and McDowell combined to go 8-3, while rookies Bolton and Bere combine for another five wins.

Most impressive was the performance of lefty reliever Scott Radinsky, who won four games in relief, improving his over-all record to 6-0 by the end of the month. The Sox rotation was proving to be a multi-faceted machine.

The use of Bolton and Bere was a marked difference from usual MLB strategy. Considering the Braves' and Yankees' refusal to throw rookies into the fray, which cost New York a division championship and almost cost Atlanta as well, the Sox can proudly attribute their success to sensible use of young talent.

August 17-12 (74-57, 0 games back)

August was the month of the McDowell. He went 4-1 with a 1.74 ERA, striking out 38 men and walking only 10. Traditionally, June and August have been the best months for Black Jack as a pitcher, and '93 was no exception as he posted his best ERAs and K/BB ratios in those months.

When Mcdowell won his 17th game on August 1, it marked the third time in the season that he had a five game winning streak.

Jack's co-conspirator in August was the talented Roberto Hernandez, whose closing skills were fast making him a household name in the AL. He may well have been the nastiest reliever in the majors for the month, saving 8 games while striking out nine and walking none. His ERA was a delectable 0.68.

Entrepreneur that Ventura is, he decided to combine the thrill of a hockey brawl with the more staid atmosphere of a baseball game. To do so, he charged Nolan Ryan in an Aug. 4 match-up between the Sox and the Rangers. The only problem was that Ventura hit like Little Lulu and Ryan began to resemble Jack Sullivan as the bout wore on. Six punches later the fight was broken up, but not before Ventura had undoubtedly reconsidered selecting his opponents on the basis of age.

Sept./Oct. 20-11 (94-68, AL West champs)

Sept. belonged to Messrs. Alvarez and Bere. While McDowell and Fernandez were feeling the fatigue of the season, the two youngsters were busy going 14-0 in their last 14 decisions.

Hernandez was still feeling his oats. He began to relish the closer role and became more comfortable as the season ended. His ERA was a far cry from August's at 3.12, but he saved another eight games and won two for good measure. He gave up more hits than usual (22 in 17.1 innings) but he seemed to be taking more risks with the strike zone. The gamble paid off as he struck out 19 men and walked only five, cementing himself as Chicago's relief ace.

Thomas celebrated September's arrival by breaking the Sox single-season home run record of 37 previously shared by Carlton Fisk and Dick Allen. He would go on to set it at 41. He also tied Luke Appling for second on the Sox single-season RBI list with 128.

Unfortunately, late-season performance would haunt the team, as McDowell dropped two games to Toronto in the ALCS and the batting order was weakened as Thomas recovered from a wrist ailment. The Sox were a talented club, but they were not yet complete enough to compete.

Park Effects: Comiskey II is yet another in the recent trend of generic stadiums, where the distance to all fields is equal.

This does tend to keep things equal in terms of left-handers and righties, but it can make things a little boring at times. Imagine the horror if every park had the same shape and dimensions.

Batting average is at league standard, and run scoring id lowered only a bit. Comiskey favors homers (8 percent higher than league) over doubles and triples (13 and 9 percent lower respectively). In case you're curious, Lance Johnson hits about the same number of triples at home as he does on the road, which is an impressive testament to his fleetness.

The percentage of errors is 6 percent lower thanks to the park, and obviously much lower when Guillen and Grebeck are holding down the infield.

As stated before, power is raised for both sides of the plate (7 percent for righthanders and 12 for lefties).

Offense: Interestingly, Chicago's offense (.265 BA, .338 OBP and .411 SLG) defined "average" in the AL last year. Apparently it was good enough to win the roller-coaster AL West. The Sox compensated for an extremely low number of doubles (228) by racking up an AL-leading 44 triples (thanks primarily to Lance Johnson).

Other than Johnson, the team speed wasn't anything remarkable. When guys like Thomas, Karkovice and Ventura are filling the batting order this is prone to happen. There won't be any major changes in the offense in the near future, but the pitching should continue to be fine enough to render this moot.

Total Offense: 64.3

Pitching: Excellence was the calling card of Sox pitching as they barnstormed the AL, racking up a .580 winning-percentage, best behind Toronto's .586. Cy Young winner Jack McDowell and Alex Fernandez led the charge while youngsters like Jason Bere and Wilson Alvarez as well as long relief lefty Scott Radinsky picked up the remaining wins. Because the offense was not over-whelming (we're not even positive it was whelming at all) the pitching was the factor that propelled Chi into the post-season. It is also the reason that they lost the ALCS, as the breakdown of starters (most notably Mr. Cy Young himself) was too much for the overmatched offense to compensate for.

In closer Roberto Hernandez, Chicago has found one of the best young closers in the game. He was especially key in their stretch run, posting incredible strikeout numbers and saving 38 games in 44 opportunities on the year, 16 of them in the last two months.

Alvarez and Bere really helped themselves at the end of the year, but either could be pushed by the likes of James Baldwin and Scott Ruffcorn.

Total Pitching: 87.8

Defense:
Catcher: Karkovice was easily the best defensive catcher in the AL, due in large part to his arm. He's not great with the bat, but his maturity behind the plate prompted the Sox to give Fisk the boot.
Pts: 23.5
Infield: Frank Thomas' defense was still pretty pathetic, but something tells us that Chicago just didn't care very much. Despite a reputation for quickness, Joey Cora was not a good second baseman.

Ozzie Guillen was his usual exceptional self (as well as his usual horse's butt self) and Robin Ventura's defense was good enough to make him the best third baseman in the business after Matt Williams.
Pts: 23.9

Outfield: Left field was fine after Rock Raines brought his solid glove back from his injury. CF Lance Johnson was the only guy close enough to smell glove-meisters Chad Curtis and Kenny Lofton and Ellis Burks was a nice change from the usual bozos patrolling right field.
Pts: 25.0

Total Defense: 72.4

1994 Personnel:
Catcher: Karkovice will start. His bat and glove should be a solid addition to a championship-calibre team.

Bench: Matt Morello has backed up Pudge and he'll be the reliever for the receiver yet again.
Starter: 23.3
Bench: C

Infield:
1B: Frank Thomas will be the starter ... of course!!! Let's hope he's improved his glove so he can send his final few detractors into the woodwork.

2B: Joey Cora will start at second despite Julio Franco's acquisition. The Sox want to use Franco as a DH and preserve his health.

3B: Ventura will prove himself the best young third baseman in the game (with the possible exception of Fryman, now). There's a pretty thin line-up on the bench if he goes down.

SS: Ozzie Guillen is a hole in the order, like Cora, but, unlike Cora, he provides invaluable defense in the middle.

DH: Franco is supposed to be the DH, but it would be a shame if a guy like 1B Drew Denson didn't get a shot.

IF Bench: Drew Denson is the backup at first, but like Cris Cron before him he'll be stymied by Big Frank. Denson might get some time at DH. Craig Grebeck should back up both short and second with his great glove. 27-year-old Norberto Martin is a possible 2B backup, and we wouldn't want to rule out Steve Sax.

Esteban Beltre and Glenn DiSarcina are marginal support at SS, but 24-year-old Brandon Wilson may get some development P.T. and show what he's got.

Starters: 107.9
IF Bench: C

Outfield:
LF: Left field didn't land on Rock Raines, Rock Raines landed on left field. And he's there to stay.

CF: With the puzzling acquisition of Darrin Jackson, Lance Johnson's future is in flux. He's an excellent center fielder and they can't help but trade him or use him. Neither is great with the bat (except Johnson's triples of course).

RF: Right field should be a platoon of aging talent Warren Newson and Mike Huff. It will probably factor in a heavy use of Dan Pasqua. This is not good.

Bench: Huff, Newson and Huff are the backups, so it makes sense that they would platoon. This is one area in which the Sox are less deep than they should be.

Starters: 52.4
Bench: C

Starting Pitchers: After Ace McDowell, Fernandez and Alvarez are locks for the rotation. As well as Bere did down the stretch, he could be displaced by Ruffcorn or Bolton. James Baldwin, Robert Ellis and Scott Christman are all candidates for starts sometime during the year.

Front-Line: 102.1
Second-Echelon: A

Relief Pitching: The long relief corps is pretty thin, but Radinsky won a lot of games in under 55 innings last year. Guys like Jeff Schwarz and Jose DeLeon are guaranteed to eat up innings, but effectiveness is a worry. . Roberto Hernandez will join the elite at closer.

Front-Line: 32.0
Second-Echelon: C

Player Value: 294.4

Farm System: The Sox are heavy with pitching prospects. Most of the backups in the pitching essay were grown at home. As well, young Luis Andujar look likes like a future winner, while Steve Schrenk looks like he's getting too old to compete with this bunch.

In the field, Chris Snopek is a quality backup at third while Brandon Wilson at short and Ray Durham at second could shore up the middle in coming years. Beware of old guys like Scott Cepicky when evaluating position talent.

Infield: C+
Outfield: D
Starters: A
Relievers: C
Farm Ranking: C+

Management and Ownership: Jerry Reinsdorf is a twit. He's more concerned with coining superlatives for the Pete Rose of basketball, than he is in putting together a championship baseball team. Reinsdorf is much more interested in putting together a circus (getting Bo Jackson? What made him a necessity?), than promoting an exceptionally good baseball product. He'll spend some money and his front office isn't half bad, but Steinbrenner was right when he called vice-chairman Einhorn and Reinsdorf "The Katzenjammer Kids." These two need to re-evaluate the way they handle baseball operations. Michael Jordan's retirement should not have been announced during game one of the ALCS. To us, that mess was enough of a conflict of interest to suggest that people shouldn't own teams in more than one major sport. But hey, we don't need to really go into great detail about these goofs, just read the paper every month and we're sure you'll read some other inanities from Reinsdorf's lips.

GM Ron Schueler is not bad at all. He got Tim Raines for Ivan Calderon, not a bad trade at all. This team has made decent moves (but, we'll not dog them too much for the acquisition of Darrin Jackson). They will do what they have to do.

Gene Lamont is a very good manager. He survived the race and the quirks of a pretty strange clubhouse mix. In addition, he was able to avoid the Bo Jackson zoo. Finally, he was able to circumnavigate the Pudge Fisk fiasco coming out unscathed. The Sox are not a flawless team and Lamont was able to make winners out of them.

Ownership: D+
Front Office: B

Field Management: B
Overall: C+

1994 Outlook: The 1994 outlook is not as cloudy as for 1993. The team is a lot more settled. The rotation has been filled out and the offense is in place. The only questions remaining are regarding the hole in right field and the holes in the bullpen. The Sox are co-favorites (with Cleveland) to win the division.

CLEVELAND INDIANS

1993 Outlook
How do you discuss the outlook of the Cleveland Indians in April of '93 without mentioning the word tragedy? The Indians' season essentially ended before it began, on the night Tim Crews and Steve Olin were killed in a boating accident that also left Bob Ojeda seriously hurt. More than the loss of talent, the tragedy left both the young Indians clubhouse and the Cleveland front office in a state of shock. If things weren't bad enough, highly regarded pitching prospects Alan Embree and Dave Mlicki both landed on the DL before the season even started. Sandy Alomar Jr. and starter Scott Scudder went on the DL in the spring as well. Outlook, you ask? Better not ask.

April 7-15 (7-15, 8 games back)
The Indian offense got off to a decent start as the team hit .284 in April. The bulk of the hitting came from Albert Belle who produced a .302 average with eight home runs and a .640 slugging. Paul Sorrento also contributed five homers and a .557 slugging. And on April 8, Carlos Baerga became the first major leaguer to ever homer form both sides of the plate in the same inning.

The starters, however, weren't having such an easy time of it. In their 22 starts, the rotation recorded just five quality starts. Charles Nagy had a 1-4 record and a 6.15 ERA by the end of the month. In fact, the only Indian starter that didn't have an ERA above 5.00 in April was Jose Mesa, who posted a 1-1 record in four starts.

May 12-17 (19-32, 12.5 games back)
The rotation continued to be the major short-coming of the Indians, and things would only go form bad to worse.. Charles Nagy left his start May 15 with what he described as a "dead and sore" arm and he went on the DL two days later. He eventually had surgery to clean out his shoulder, and he missed the rest of the season. On the bright side, however, Jose Mesa put together a 4-2, 2.85 record and Tommy Kramer won his second start of the season with a one-hit, one-run complete game. He struck out eight batters in the start. Unfortunately, the rest of the staff was getting hammered on a regular basis. Belle and Sorrento, both continuing their power display with 13 homers between them, couldn't drive in enough runs to bail out the starters. Kenny Lofton also got hot in May, hitting .373 with a .443 on-base.

June 17-10 (36-42, 11.5 games back)
June was by far the Tribe's best month. They continued to search for pitchers to come to the aid of a beleaguered and over-matched staff. But GM John Hart busied himself, releasing Bielecki and trading for Heathcliff Slocumb and Jeremy Hernandez. Tommy Kramer continued to impress manager Mike Hargrove with a 3.37 ERA in five June starts. The Indian's bullpen was much improved. Lilliquist and newcomer Jeremy Hernandez seemed unstoppable at times and Eric Plunk had taken over the closer's role and was rolling right along. The rotation floundered, but the entire staff registered a 3.63 ERA in June, so you know the bullpen was doing its job.

The heart of the batting order was still producing steadily. Baerga, who had been relatively quiet, had a .333 average, seven home runs and 24 RBI. He also rode a 17-game hitting streak. Not to be left out, Belle contributed five homers and 19 RBI.

July 12-14 (48-56, 11.5 games back)
The Cleveland pitching staff took a turn for the worse, so the Indians started their auditions for '94 early, calling up Albie Lopez to replace Tom Kramer when he went on the DL with a sore elbow. Lopez turned in a couple of nice starts before being shelled for nine runs in an inning and a third July 28. Cleveland also put an early call in for their superstar-in-waiting Manny Ramirez, just to give him a taste of life in the big leagues. Meanwhile, Albert Belle became an offensive force. He tagged AL pitchers for a .341 average, nine

home runs and 25 RBI in July. Baerga was also cruising right along, with a .337 average in 104 at-bats.

August 14-14 (62-70, 14 games back)

To the Indians, August seemed like just a rehash of July. The rotation continued to struggle while the combination of Belle and Baerga continued its lethal attack. This time, it was Baerga's turn to shine. He banked a .341 average for the month with a .390 on-base and 23 RBI. Belle only hit .282, but he hit five home runs and drove in 23 runs. Ed McMahon's Star Search continued in August. Jim Thome joined the team mid-month for his tryout and homered in his first game. He hit seven home runs for the Indians over the rest of the season.

Sept./Oct. 14-16 (76-86, 19 games back)

The final month of he season couldn't come fast enough for the city of Cleveland. October 3rd. came and went, and the Indians could finally walk away from a season that seemed more like a test of mental and emotional strength than a sport. There were a few bright spots in their season, though. Albert Belle edged Frank Thomas by one run to win the AL RBI title. Charles Nagy started and pitched three innings in the team's final game, giving the Indians hope that he will be fully recovered from surgery for the '94 opener. Bob Ojeda recovered from the boating accident and provided an emotional lift to the club and its fans. And Cleveland's hitting prospects, Ramirez, Thome and Mark Lewis, all impressed management in their major-league appearances. The team's outlook was a heck of a lot better than it had been at the start of the season.

Park Effect. Cleveland Municipal Stadium is now a football-only venue. The Indians are moving into a new ballpark called the Gateway for the 1994 season and no one can predict how it will affect scoring. However, in the interests of history, here are the park effects of the Indians' former home.

Over the past two seasons, the park has been pretty neutral, reducing runs by just one percent. In 1993 however, runs were down 15 percent. Home runs hit by left-handed batters were up five percent last year, while right-handers were at a 13 percent disadvantage. And for some reason, errors were reduced last year by 21 percent. It was probably just an anomaly, as the park has had a tendency to induce errors, albeit at a negligible rate, over a two-year stretch.

Offense: Although the Indians were the youngest team in the majors to begin with, they featured a balanced attack that scored a healthy amount of runs. The 4.92 runs per nine innings in support the lineup supplied to the pitchers was more than generous. The offense did a lot of things well last year. They hit .275 on the season and .281 with runners in scoring position. They were successful on the basepaths 74 percent of the time, swiping a total of 159 bases. They received a .317 average and a .398 on-base from the leadoff hitter and they hit .290 with a .551 slugging average in the cleanup spot. They also had the second-lowest strikeout total in the AL.

Total Offense: 60.9

Pitching: It's hard to know where to start in describing the pitching staff of a team that used 18 starting pitchers last year. Nagy missed almost the entire season with a shoulder ailment that would require surgery, and injuries to rotation prospects Alan Embree and Dave Mlicki took their toll on a pitching staff that was already thin to begin with. It's not surprising that rotation limped to a 42-54 record and compiled a 5.25 ERA. The bullpen that was so seriously depleted with the deaths of Olin and Crews pitched their butts off to record a respectable 3.51 ERA and convert 45 saves. However, if the Cleveland offense couldn't compensate for the shabby starting pitching they received, nothing could.

Total Pitching: -28.1

Defense:

Infield: Carlos Baerga was the primadonna of this infield, displaying fantastic range at second base and making the DP look as easy as tying his shoe. The rest of the infield was nothing to write home about. The trio of Sorrento, Milligan and Jefferson at first base were adequate. Treadway and Espinoza were below-average fielders at third base, and Felix Fermin was down-right pitiful at shortstop.

Pts: 0.2

Outfield: In left field, Albert Belle provided decent work with the leather. Kenny

Lofton is one of the better center fielders in the league and has the quickness to get to almost anything hit near him. Wayne Kirby's defense was a pleasant surprise in right field, but Glenallen Hill's played the field as if there were spiders all over the place.
Pts: 30.2

Catcher: Sandy Alomar didn't contribute much due to his back injury and he's injured so often that it's anybody's guess what his defense is like anymore. The catching duties were split between Junior Ortiz and Jesse Levis. Both had good hands, but Ortiz was more successful against the running game and he goaded a better ERA out of his staff.
Pts: 8.2
Total Defense: 38.6

1994 Personnel:
Catcher: At last glance, Sandy Alomar Jr. was playing ball for his father's team in Puerto Rico, so there is hope that his health has finally returned. He will get the starting job in the spring if he passes the physical, and could amaze everyone by fulfilling his star potential as a hitter. But no one in the Cleveland front office will be holding their breath for that to happen.

Bench: Junior Ortiz can't do much with the bat, but the rules state that every team must field a catcher, and Ortiz fits the bill as well an anyone else the Indians have. Jesse Levis will remain in the depth chart and could steal some playing time from Ortiz if Alomar stays healthy.
Starters: -3.6
Bench: D

Infield:
1B: Cleveland traded Randy Milligan to the Expos for Brian Barnes during the winter. Paul Sorrento, who submitted his claim on the job last year with 18 dingers, now owns it outright.

2B: There's been a harvest of young all-star second basemen in baseball the last several seasons, but Carlos Baerga is he cream of the crop. He provides stellar defense and a dangerous bat. Put simply, he is the driving force behind the Cleveland Indians.

3B: Jim Thome will finally receive his inheritance and become the starting third baseman. His potential at the plate have a lot of people excited in Cleveland.

SS: John Hart improved the team defensively by trading Reggie Jefferson and Felix Fermin to the Mariners for Gold-Glover Omar Vizquel. The move consolidates a crowded infield and makes the Indians very solid up the middle.

DH: Eddie Murray was signed over the winter to fill the Indians' need for a full-time DH. It's hard to predict how he'll hit in the AL after a five-year absence. It's equally difficult to name a more consistent performer.

IF Bench: Mark Lewis (if he's not traded) and Alvaro Espinoza will probably be the main infield backups. But the Indians signed former St. Louis shortstop Tim Jones and invited him to spring training, which makes a Lewis trade even more likely. The Indians also let big Sam Horn go on waivers, and the top level of their minor league system is tapped out of infield prospects. A serious injury to their starting infield would force the team to go with a below-average replacement-level player.
Starters: 83.9
Bench: B

Outfield:
LF: Albert Belle will bring his intense style of play and run-producing bat back to the Cleveland outfield this year. Even if he isn't able to maintain his defensive improvements from last year, he should continue to fuel the Indians' attack with solid power and plenty of RBI.

CF: Kenny Lofton has a headlock on this position and as the leadoff hitter in the lineup. Lofton's speed on the basepaths compliments the power of Belle and Baerga nicely.

RF: If GM John Hart is serious about contending in '94, he should install Manny Ramirez as the starting right fielder on opening day. Young Manny is a rookie-of-the-year candidate that can hit for average with decent power in the show right now.

OF Bench: With a strong everyday outfield already in the works, Cleveland may not need very substitutions. But just in case things don't fall into place, the Indians still have Candy Maldonado and Wayne Kirby to fill in any gaps. Omar Ramirez (no relation) and Ken Ramos don't have very much star potential, but will be stationed in AAA Canton in

the event of an emergency.
Starters: 79.8
Bench: A (Manny Ramirez)

Starting Pitching: John Hart has been active in the talent market this offseason and has acquired a couple of arms he feels can help the rotation. Dennis Martinez signed as a free agent and will step in right behind a healthy Charles Nagy as the No. 2 starter. Brian Barnes, acquired in trade for Randy Milligan, will get a chance to start again and could surprise a lot of people if he gets his curveball on-line. The Indians are going to audition a cast of thousands for the final rotation spots in spring training. Those pitchers will include Albie Lopez, Julian Tavarez, Alan Embree, Dave Mlicki, Jason Grimsley, Jose Mesa, Paul Byrd and Tommy Kramer. And in case they can't find enough talent among those guys, they could still package Mark Lewis off for someone who can contribute 150-200 worthwhile innings.
Front-line: 31.6
Second-Echelon: B+

Relief Pitching: At the time of this writing, the Indians had yet to sign or trade for a closer. Unless they acquire an ace, they will probably go with a closer-by-committee format featuring Jerry DiPoto, Derek Lilliquist and Eric Plunk. Paul Shuey, 23, has a fantastic arm and is being groomed as a closer in the minors, but it's likely that Cleveland will wait another year for him to mature and build confidence. Both Bill Wertz and Jeremy Hernandez can earn a bullpen job in the spring. Young guts with a chance include Apolinar Garcia, Calvin Jones and Cesar Perez.
Front-Line: -7.6
Second-Echelon: C

Player Value: 184.1

Farm System: The farm system is going to pay off in 1994. OF Manny Ramirez and 3B Jim Thome are poised to win starting jobs with the Indians this year and although SS Mark Lewis is blocked by Vizquel, he is a quality prospect that should bring good value in a trade. After Ramirez, Thome and Lewis, though, the talent starts to thin out in terms of position players. There are no catchers of special value in the system and infield prospects are a rarity. Outfielders John Cotton and Brian Giles could make some noise within a few years though, but with the outfield the Indians already have locked up in long-term contracts, they probably won't be needed.

The organization is well stocked with pitchers. Ogea, Embree and Mlicki are healthy enough to put their frustrating seasons behind them and make a push for the majors. One or two of them should make the show by season's end. John Carter, who went 17-7 2.79 at Class A Columbus last year and is considered one of Cleveland's best arms could pitch himself into the picture and wind up in AAA Canton. Relievers Paul Shuey, Apolinar Garcia and Calvin Jones have all shown promise and will climb into prominence soon.
Infield: B
Outfield: C
Starters: B
Relievers: B
Farm Ranking: B

Management and Ownership:
Real-estate mogul Richard Jacobs owns the club and is known as a fan-oriented civic leader. He spearheaded the movement to build Gateway stadium as part of the Gateway sports complex in Dayton Cleveland. He has also provided the capital to restock the franchise with pitching at least until some of their minor league prospects come through. More notably, however, he has provided the cash necessary to sign his young and talented players to long-term contracts. It was an action that would provide long-term security for his franchise and buy some time to restock its minor league system.

General Manager John Hart did the best he could to piece together a pitching staff last year. He wouldn't trade prospects Manny Ramirez and Jim Thome, the asking price for most of front-line starters they inquired about. Instead, he signed a couple of free agents and traded a few marginal players for a few marginal pitchers. Hart had basically written off the season, concentrating instead on '95. This winter, he signed free-agent Dennis Martinez and traded for Brian Barnes in an effort to bolster his rotation. He also signed Eddie Murray to DH for the Indians and traded for Omar Vizquel. Hart has pulled out all the stops for the upcoming season.

Manager Mike Hargrove deserves a lot of credit for guiding his young team through the tragedy that struck in the spring. He communicates well with his players and there have hardly been any signs disunity in his clubhouse. He isn't the greatest in-game strategist in the world, preferring a conservative game plan most of the time. But Hargrove doesn't overwork his pitchers and plays the platoon differential well. His players responded well to his leadership last year, and this year he has even more talent to work with.

Ownership: B
Front Office: A
Field Management: B
Overall: B+

1994 Outlook: Their long nightmare over, the Indians are about to go on a warpath in the AL Central. Offseason moves were made to improve the rotation, weed out some existing infield talent and shore up team defense. Time will be the determining factor in how successful the moves will be, but with the everyday lineup already in place and the emergence of Jim Thome and Manny Ramirez, the Indians should have an offense capable of outscoring the White Sox. In order to make the inaugural season of the Gateway one to remember though, the Indians need some of the 101 pitchers they have accumulated to produce.

KANSAS CITY ROYALS

1993 Outlook

The Royals were a busy team over the winter of '92, as they revamped their roster to include a big-gun pitcher (David Cone) and a couple of middle infielders (Jose Lind and Greg Gagne). They also traded third baseman Greg Jefferies to the Cardinals for right fielder Felix Jose. The swap accomplished two of Herk Robinson's goals. It allowed him to move Keith Miller to third base and it added a little more quickness to the traditional speed-burning/solid-defense formula that great Royals teams of the past have been built around. They also boasted the return of Jeff Montgomery, one of the best closers in the game. Kansas City's critics pointed out that the starting rotation was mighty thin behind the 1-2 combo of Appier and Cone, and that the offense lacked a true impact player. Most prognosticators had the Royals placing between second and fourth in the AL West.

April 9-14 (9-14, 6 games back)

While their five-game losing streak to begin the 1993 season wasn't nearly as catastrophic as their 1-18 start in 1992, it was enough to cause some concern in the clubhouse and speculation in the press about Hal McRae's future. Keith Miller strained a groin and went on the DL. Phil Hiatt, who performed well in the spring, was called up to replace him, but he couldn't find his stroke. The rest of the offense was no better, as Brian McRae, Joyner, Brett and Felix Jose all had a miserable month. Despite his three quality starts and a 3.79 ERA, Cone was 0-4 in April. Appier won only two games even though he posted five quality starts and a 3.70 ERA. Pichardo, Gubicza and Gardner were all ineffective early on, but the lack of run-support had taken its toll. Hal McRae couldn't even awaken the Royals' bats with a tirade against reporters April 26 that earned him a cautionary letter from AL president Dr. Bobby Brown. The Royals found themselves six games behind the Angels, looking up at every other team in the division except the lowly Twins.

May 16-9 (25-23, 2 games back)

After seven attempts, David Cone finally won his first game of the season May 14. Worse still, after nine starts Cone had a 2.70 ERA, but only a 1-5 record to show for the effort. His run support was dismal, and he was building the reputation around the league as the hard-luck pitcher of '93. Fortunately, Appier enjoyed slightly better fortunes in May. He put in a 3-1, 3.28 performance, and his five-hit complete game win May 22 lifted the Royals to the .500 mark for the first time.

By May 27, the Royals had won eight of their last ten games and had climbed into fourth place, just one game behind the White Sox and the Angels. The Royals offense was starting to come alive, with a veteran catcher leading the way. Mike Macfarlane sparked the offense with a .338 average, six home runs and 20 RBI. Brian McRae chipped in a .330 average and Wally Joyner helped out with a .322 average and a .423 on-base. The Royals' improved defense even decided a few ballgames. By the end of May, the Kansas City had a 15-8 record in games decided by one run. It was the best one-run winning percentage in the league. They had climbed into second place in the west, and the Angels had a loose grip on the lead.

June 13-15 (38-38, 1.5 games back)

The Royals won their first four games and had sole possession of the league lead by June 3. They held that distinction until June 21, which was quite a feat, considering they went 7-9 during that stretch. But when the dust cleared at the end of the day, California, Chicago and KC all had a share of the lead. The Royals went 3-6 over the final nine days of June, and the Angels went 2-6. Chicago payed .500 ball over the span and emerged from the month one and a half games ahead of the pack.

Appier put up Cy Young numbers in June, with a 4-0, 2.23 performance. Cone allowed 13 runs in his first two games, but tossed three nice starts in the latter half. But the reason why the Royals couldn't contend with the White Sox was the shaky performance of the rest of the staff. Haney (5.59 ERA) and Gardner (5.88 ERA) were especially disappointing, but the Royals had no one else to take their places.

July 16-12 (54-50, 4 games back)

The Royals made their push, and for a while there they were nip-and-tuck with the White Sox. But on July 27, Kevin Appier lost a 1-0 ballgame in which he went the distance, allowing just one walk and striking out 11. That game ended the Royal's season in a rather definitive way. He had pitched his butt off, but just couldn't get the run-support he deserved. He came away with a 2-1 record for the month despite having allowed just 17 hits and nine walks in 29.2 innings. It was the inability of the Royals to score runs at key moments that led to their downfall, and the large number of one-run games they had played up to that point started looking like an omen.

August 15-14 (69-64, 6 games back)

August was the same old story for the pitching staff. Appier (3-1, 2.89) and Cone (3-1, 3.50) led the way and the rest of the rotation stumbled to a 6-8 record. Jeff Montgomery spoiled Appier's last two starts (which were beauties), losing both games in extra innings. Meanwhile, the offense took a terminal dip, struggling to hit .244 for the month. Nobody, and we mean nobody, could hit for beans in August. It was like someone had turned off a switch.

Sept./Oct. 15-14 (84-78, 10 games back)

Again, it was a horrible lack of run-support that caused the demise of the Royals. Brett hit .280 and five home runs over the final month of his career. It was nice to see him go out with a bang. But it was a shame the rest of the lineup couldn't muster enough production to allow a Kansas City icon some excitement in his final summer of ball.

The Royals were eliminated from the AL West race on Sept. 24, even though they beat the Angels 7-2. that night. Prophetically, a wounded bird landed at second base, then attempted to fly away, crashing into the left field wall and falling lifelessly to the turf. The bird, and the Kansas City Royals, were pronounced dead that evening.

Park Effect. Ewing Kauffman Stadium's spacious outfield and fast turf are the primary reasons why it is such a hitter-friendly park. Those two factors were responsible for a 46 percent increase in the amount of doubles hit, and a 90 percent jump in triples last year. The stadium also hampered home run totals, limiting the four-baggers by 28 percent. Line-drive hitters with speed have always thrived on the carpet in KC.

The park effects for 1994 should hold steady, increasing run production at a nominal 5-10 percent. But in 1995, the Royals will have replaced their artificial turf and will play their first season on natural grass. Finally, the real stuff. Scoring will almost certainly drop, and it is likely that they will also move the fences in a tad to help keep games in Kansas City from becoming yawn-fests.

Offense: One word sums up the Kansas City offense last season. Dismal. The Royals scored the fewest runs in the AL and ranked dead last in total walks and on-base percentage. Their attack, far from balanced, featured an above-average number of doubles and triples, but home runs were very scarce, especially at home. Part of the problem was that the Royals built a lineup to suit their ballpark, collecting players with speed that could hit the ball on the ground. And while their .283 average at home was the best in the league, they suffered a .244 average in away games, the worst in the league. Herk Robinson would be wise to consider that Kansas City plays half of their games out of their home town and that the addition of a slugger or two couldn't hurt. The anemic offense produced only 4.20 runs per nine innings for the pitching staff, the worst run-support in the league.

Total Offense: -17.6

Pitching: On paper, the Kansas City pitching staff looked pretty competitive. According to the Pythagorean Won-Lost Formula created by Bill James, the Royals pitchers should have won 79 and lost 83. In actuality, the staff went 84-78, posting a 4.04 ERA that was good for third in the league. The Pythagorean formula is designed to predict a winning percentage based on the relationship between runs scored by the offense and runs allowed by the pitching staff. Considering the lack of run-support, though, the Royals were fortunate to win as many games as they did.

Behind Appier and Cone, the staff thinned considerably. Tom Gordon re-discovered his curveball and went 8-4 with a 3.36 ERA as a late-season starter, but his performance came too late in the season to help the rest of the rotation that struggled to a 20-23 record. Mark Gardner, Hipolito Pichardo and Chris Haney all tried to fill out the remainder of the rotation, but none of them could post an ERA below four or allow less than a hit per inning.

The bullpen, which already featured a solid closer in Jeff Montgomery, was improved by the mid-season acquisition of Stan Belinda. However, it suffered from the same trouble as the starting rotation--nobody but the top two or three guys could produce quality innings. Montgomery was his usual consistent self and Belinda did the job he was acquired to do. Even Billy Brewer and Mark Gubicza were viewed as pleasant surprises. But calling Habyan, Meacham or Sampen into a close game was akin to handing a flamethrower to a pyromaniac.

Total Pitching: 66.5

Defense:
Infield: Back trouble caused Wally Joyner to miss quite a few games the last month of the season, but up until that point, he had provided solid defense. Chico Lind made all the routine plays, and turned just about everything he touched into outs. But his range factor slipped a little as he had some difficulty adjusting to the new carpet. Mike Tucker will eventually win the second base job, but he has the tools to become a solid fielder, especially when the Royals switch to grass in '95.

Greg Gagne continued to prove his worth in the field. He recorded 265 put-outs in '93, good for second in the league behind Oakland's Mike Bordick. Third base was a problem spot for the Royals. Keith Miller spent more time on the DL than he did on the field. Phil Hiatt committed 16 errors in half a season's worth of play and struggled at the plate to boot. When Gary Gaetti was released by the Angels, Kansas City snatched him up for his reliable glove. Gaetti made just five miscues in 72 games, justifying his $109,000 salary.

Pts: 31.7

Outfield: In left field, Kevin McReynolds and Chris Gwynn both provided seamless defense, with a slight edge going to Gwynn because of his arm. In center, Brian McRae didn't set the world on fire, but we all know he has the athletic ability to improve greatly. Felix Jose, who battled his shoulder all year, was a non-entity in right field.

Pts: 19.2

Catcher: Macfarlane put in adequate work behind he plate last year. He handled the pitching staff well and shot down 43 percent of opposition baserunners. Brent Mayne proved his defensive work was up to snuff and won the starting job at the beginning of the season. But he couldn't hit well enough to keep his job, and wound up playing back up to Macfarlane for the rest of the season.

Pts: 18.0
Total Defense: 68.9

1994 Personnel
Catcher: The Royals are hoping Macfarlane can come close to duplicating his production of last year and will hand him the starting job in the spring, like they should have done in '93.

Bench: Mayne, ever the bridesmaid, will have to come through in a big way with the bat if he wants any significant playing time or attract any trade offers. Realistically, the Royals don't have anybody in the minors who could hold their own at the major league level, except maybe Nelson Santovenia if he's still around.

Starters: 24.3
Bench:

Infield:

1B: Because of their paltry offensive production, the Royals will ask Joyner to supply an inordinate share of the run production. He is rehabbing a lower back injury that caused him to miss the final 17 games of 1993. If he is healthy enough to contribute a typical Joyner season, he will be fine. But he isn't the impact player the Royals need him to be.

2B: Jose Lind will be the starter again, and although his spot in the batting order is a black hole, his defensive contributions will warrant his having a job. Michael Tucker, 23, should start his second pro season at AAA Omaha this year. If he hits the way he did last year though, the Royals might be seduced into calling him up around mid-season.

3B: The Royals have locked up Gary Gaetti with a minor-league contract and have discussed moving Keith Miller into the outfield to accommodate his aching body. Gaetti, who was reborn at the plate with KC last year, will field well enough to hold the position for a while. But if Phil Hiatt, who struggled in all aspects of the game last year, can polish his tools to McRae's satisfaction in Omaha, he would push Gaetti aside in a heartbeat.

SS: Greg Gagne's hitting will probably fall off quite a bit, but he plays close to flawless defense and will fill out one of the best fielding infields in the majors.

DH: Brett is now working in the front office which means the Royals will be having open auditions for the DH job in the spring. They haven't pursued any free-agent hitters over the winter so they'll probably go with either Bob Hamelin, 29 dingers in Omaha, or his teammate Russ McGinnis, who hit .291 with 16 homers.

IF Bench: If Joyner should go down with an injury, Bob Hamelin could step up and fill in. The Royals also have a promising hitter in Joe Vitiello, but they would rather see him spend another season in the minors. They would also like to see Mike Tucker simmer for a year at AAA, but he could be ready if Lind plays himself out of a job. Terry "Slumpert" earned his nickname last year, but will get a job backing up Lind and Gagne because of his previous experience. The Royals don't have a lot of options at short if Gagne gets hurt, but they are still high on prospect Shane Halter, who could find himself stationed in Omaha by summer's end. Russ McGinnis is a natural third baseman, and he could finally earn a major-league job as a third base backup.

Starters: 20.0
Bench: C+

Outfield:

LF: Kevin McReynolds had difficulty erasing his reputation as a reticent, reluctant team player and wore out his welcome in the Kansas City clubhouse. He was traded back to the Mets in exchange for Vince Coleman. Apparently, Herk Robinson figured there was nothing wrong with either player that a change of scenery wouldn't fix. But the explosive personality aside, Coleman has been mighty frail the past three seasons and shouldn't be trusted with either playing time or nitro glycerine.

CF: Brian McRae is still trying to draw a bead on the strikezone, but he hit over .300 as a leadoff hitter last year and should continue to improve defensively. His speed will also come on-line soon, which will give a little more luster to his stats.

RF: Felix Jose underwent arthroscopic surgery over the winter to fix his ailing shoulder and should again be able to switch-hit in the spring. He will have to bounce back to his 1992 form to save GM Herk Robinson from being run out of town on a rail.

Bench: Chris Gwynn and Darryl Boston are hold-overs from '93, and will probably win roster spots because of their major-league experience. Former L.A. prospect Tom Goodwin was signed off waivers over the winter and will have a chance to earn a job in the spring because of his great speed. Les Norman will probably start the season out in Omaha, but he could be summoned as a fill-in. The organization's best outfield prospect, however, is 20-year-old Johnny Damon, who could start the season at AAA Omaha and get a call-up in September.

Starters: 5.0
Bench: D-

Starting Pitching: Kevin Appier and David Cone are the only pitchers in the KC rotation that are dependable enough to be considered a lock for their jobs. Tom Gordon, who re-discovered his hard-breaking curve and ability to win late last year, will probably get the number-three spot in spring. The other two rotation spots will be filled in the spring. Candidates for those spots are Mark Gubicza, Billy Brewer, Chris Haney, Hipolito Pichardo, Mike Magnante and minor league prospect Jeff Granger. The Royals have also been active signing homeless fringe pitchers to minor league contracts. We might see someone like Bob Milacki, Scott Ruskin or Paul Abbott win a job with the staff in '94.
Front-Line: 117.7
Second Echelon: C-

Relief Pitching: The Royals have Jeff Montgomery to lead the bullpen, and he is just about as reliable as they come in the AL. Stan Belinda, in his second term with the Royals, will again set the table and will close once in a while to save Montgomery some work. Rusty Meacham is said to be recovered from the elbow injury that limited him so much last year and is pitching well in winter ball. The remainder of the bullpen will be comprised of whoever isn't in the rotation. Brewer and Gubicza both spent time pitching long-relief last year, they could find themselves there again if they don't make the grade in the spring. Minor-league veterans Steve Shifflett and Enrique Burgos can also contribute some innings, but aren't star material.
Front-Line: 42.0
Second-Echelon: C

Player Value: 209.0

Farm System: Pitching prospects Jeff Granger and Jim Pittsley are progressing quickly and could both become dominant major league pitchers within three or four seasons. Their second tier pitching talent includes hurlers like Melvin Bunch and Brian Bevil, guys who might take longer to develop, but could pitch themselves onto the roster in the next two years.

Second baseman Mike Tucker and outfielder Johnny Damon are the best hitting prospects in the organization. Tucker is closer to a major league career, but Damon is three years younger, and therefore, has a higher ceiling. Infielders Bob Hamelin, Joe Vitiello and Shane Halter and outfielders Adam Casillas and Kevin Koslofski all could reach the majors this year, but aren't of the same calibre as Tucker and Damon.
Infield:
Outfield:
Starters:
Relievers:
Farm Ranking:

Management and Ownership: The late Ewing Kauffman was a very generous man who took immense pride in his community. Once every few years, he would pop up at a local high school and offer to pay the college tuition of every graduating senior that stayed out of trouble and completed their courses. His philanthropic ways extended to the baseball team he owned since its inception in 1968. As a result of his financing, the Royals were always able to take part in free-agent signings and compete with bigger market teams for top-of-the-line talent. Kauffman was so devoted to his team and his community that he set up the mechanism for selling the team well in advance of his death last year. His one stipulation for the eventual buyer: keep the team in Kansas City. A five-man board of directors in now in place, and since they will have to sell the franchise in a few years, they may be far more conservative in the allocation of operating expenses.

The man in charge of putting a team on the field is still GM Herk Robinson. Despite Kansas City's contention for the AL West last year, Robinson's recent roster moves have been questionable. His Gregg Jefferies for Felix Jose trade in the winter of '92 was either a case of inspired lunacy or utter ignorance of player talent. He gave up too much talent (namely OF Karl Rhodes, and pitchers Jon Lieber and Dan Miceli) for relievers Stan Belinda and John Habyan in trades during the course of the '93 season, considering that Habyan would be cut loose just a few months later. And last, but certainly not least, the one trade he pulled off during the winter of '93 was Kevin McReynolds to the Mets for bad-news Vince Coleman. Robinson can't be accused of trying to win any popularity contests in the Kansas City area.

We'll ignore his famous tirade in April last year because it has little relevance here. Besides being a demi-god in the eyes of hardcore Royals fans, Hal McRae is adept at handling his players and providing on-field leadership. McRae sets high standards for his players and expects them to work hard to meet those marks. If he doesn't see the work, the player in question doesn't see the playing time. He's a former batting coach, so he has a tendency to work closely with the hitters in the cage. McRae is a good offensive strategist, a by-product of his playing days, but he needs to learn how to handle a pitching staff. He is generally slow to give the starter the hook, and once he does, he has a proclivity to ride his ace reliever too hard. Last year, he let his closer work more than inning 20 times.

Ownership: ????
Front Office: E
Field Management: C
Overall: D

1994 Outlook: Hal McRae has built a solid defense in Kansas City, now he needs some more offense to go with it. If the Royals can sift through the rubble and piece together a starting rotation behind Appier and Cone or add one or two solid hitters to their lineup, they can contend for the AL wild-card slot in the playoffs. In light of Herk Robinson's recent attempt to make the Royals the Boy's Town of baseball, though, (with the signings of every hard-luck young pitcher in baseball and the acquisition of bad-boy Vince Coleman) the chances of them acquiring such players from the outside are relatively low. They have a strong minor league system, but it won't start paying off until after the '94 season is in the books.

MILWAUKEE BREWERS

1993 Outlook: The Brewers can't have started the season on a very high note. They'd lost two veteran players in pitcher Chris Bosio (to Seattle) and Paul Molitor (to Toronto) and the loss of even a mediocre outfielder like Dante Bichette to expansion didn't help matters. They were relying on a combination of aging talent (Yount, Thon and Brunansky) and unproven youth (Nilsson and Jaha).

The up side was supposed to be the return of AL Rookie of the Year Pat Listach, who immediately dashed that hope by injuring himself for much of the first part of the season. Cal Eldred was hoping to pitch as well as he'd finished '92, but would it be enough?

The Brewers and their fans weren't deluding themselves, they knew the season would be an uphill battle ending in a downhill retreat.

April 9-11 (9-11, 5 games back)
Bill Wegman was the Opening Day starter. After the tough luck and lack of run support which plagued him in '92, he showed up with a quality start and the first loss of many he would suffer through this year.

In the same game, OF Greg Vaughn established himself with his first homer and the team's only run. All in all, this game is a fairly accurate microcosm of the trend the Brewers' season took.

The series against Cali was a split with a convincing win by Eldred. Cal began shakily however, alternating excellent starts with appearances where he was blown off the mound. His best start was a one-hitter on April 23, testament to his explosive abilities. After giving a one-out double to Rafael Palmiero, Eldred sat down the next 23 Rangers he faced, striking out nine in the first five innings and ten for the game.

The worst problem was middle relief. In a 12-2 loss to Cali, in which Jaime Navarro pitched one-run ball for seven innings, three middle relievers conspired to lose the game and inflate their ERAs (Orosco 27.00, Austin 14.73 and Manzanillo 15.43).

It seemed as if the Brewers were on a crusade to prove they could beat any team...one out of three times.

May 13-14 (22-25, 7.5 games back)

The Brewers were still hovering around .500 and steadily dropping out of contention. They began and ended May ahead of both Baltimore and Cleveland and it looked as if they had a prayer of finishing somewhere near the middle of the pack.

On May 3, the Rangers exercised revenge on Eldred for his hubris of April, ringing him up for six runs in 3.1 innings. This typified his roller coaster starts.

The Ricky Bones Experiment continued ... unsuccessfully for the most part. He looked sharp for the late part of June, but he had trouble getting batters out, and received no run support even when he pitched competently.

Long relief was still a shambles, with the best pitchers being those who'd gotten their ERA under double-digits.

Listach and Jaha could barely hit higher than their weight, Listach batting .210 for the month of May and Jaha pulling himself out of his April slump of .217.

Vaughn was the lone beacon of hope, chalking up 5 homers by May 1 and seven more by the end of the month. He drove in 25 runs during this stretch and hit .290 with 17 walks.

June 10-19 (32-44, 14.5 games back)

By June 2, Eldred was 6-6 and well on the road to a .500 season. Through the end of June, he did not record a single no decision. By the end of the month he was 9-8 in 17 starts and had a solid ERA in the vicinity of 3.50 to show for it.

Jaha continued his slump and was suffering various health ailments. He seemed to be losing confidence as a hitter. C Dave Nilsson was also having problems, and was forced to share backstop duties with Joe Kmak and Tom Lampkin as a result. Needless to say they were worse than he was.

The rotation was so weakened that Mike Boddicker was pressed into service. He wasn't very good, but neither was he so bad that Milwaukee could afford to remove him.

By the end of the month the team was irreparably removed from contention. 14.5 games may not seem so bad, unless you compare it to the AL West, where Oakland and Minnesota were sharing cellar space at 6.5 games back.

"The Trials of Wegman" melodrama continued. On June 4 he lost, bringing his record to 4-8 with a very good 3.17 ERA. He would lose his last six decisions and see his ERA rise to 4.48! Some folks just can't get no justice I reckon.

July 9-17 (41-61, 16.5 games back)

Pitching prospect Angel Miranda started serving up quality starts after the All-Star break. His 4-4 record for the second half of the season belied his stinginess at giving up hits and a shoulder ailment cut down on his strikeouts.

15 of the Brewers 26 games in July were decided by two or less runs, and they came away with a 6-9 record.

Their best game was a July 8 drubbing of Minnesota to the tune of 15-3. Of course, the Brewers were beating up on the hapless Kevin Tapani, owner of a 3-10 record at the time. Strangely, the Brewers were able to score all their runs without the aid of a single HR.

August 16-16 (57-77, 20 games back)

By August 1, the Brewers had begun to decorate the AL East cellar, realizing that they would be spending the last two months of the season there.

August's 16-16 record was an improvement for the Brews, but it wasn't even good enough to hold them in stasis, as Toronto, Baltimore and New York took off for parts north of .500 in the race for the AL East championship.

Sept./Oct. 12-16 (69-93, 26 games back

The Brewers ended the season as they'd played it all year, consistently and badly. They had almost exactly the same record as the A's, both teams ending up 26 games back in their respective divisions.

Worst of all, nothing that transpired in '93 could lead the Brewers to believe that their problems had been salved heading into '94. Jaha was coming along well, Vaughn had performed better than expected and Eldred had shown promise, but this did nothing to dispel disappointment in the entire pitching staff and most of the batting order.

Park Effects: County Stadium gives a slight edge to pitchers. Batting average and runs are both slightly lower than they would be on the road. It's very difficult to take the extra base here. Doubles aren't too far off the norm, but triples are lowered by 11 percent and homers lowered by 15 percent (which helps explain Greg Vaughn's tendency to hit for increased power in states other than Wisconsin).

County Stadium is bane to good pitching, much less the jokers that the Brewers assemble on the mound. With a percentage of errors 10 percent above league average, guys like Bill Wegman (who's got the collective bad luck of "The Voyage of the Damned") are living in a world of hurt. Put average fielders behind him and he'll be ready for a straitjacket by the All-Star break.

The symmetry of the park (it is equidistant to all fields) ensures that both left and right-handers are robbed of at least 10 percent of their power.

Offense: It sounds trite, but Milwaukee's biggest problem was an inability to score runs. They had the worst slugging of any AL team at .378 (the Marlins at .346 were the only major league team worse in this respect) and their OBP was lower than every AL team except the Royals.

Despite this, the Brewers did manage to score more runs than scrub squads like Oakland and California. Unfortunately they didn't score enough to prevent losing 26 games.

Their power and speed were weak points. While they did hit more doubles than the White Sox, the Sox kinda lapped them in homers by 37. The Brewers were also firmly mired in the echelon of AL teams with 25 or less triples. Only Cali and Cleveland stole more bases than Milwaukee's 138, but the Brewers' below-average SB% (60%) is explained by the 93 times their runners were caught pilfering.

The speed should recover along with the return of a healthy Listach (look how much of the Indians' SB stats are provided by speed-merchant Kenny Lofton). As for the bats, the Brews are a crap-shoot at the plate until they can come close to sewing up the batting order.

Total Offense: 1.0

Pitching: While the Brewers were better than powerhouse staffs like the A's and Tigers, they were easily one of the most plague-ridden rotations in the AL.

Everybody knows about Bill Wegman's bad luck on the mound, and apparently the bug bit Jaime Navarro (11-12 5.33) and youngster Angel Miranda (mid-season and post-season injuries). Sophomore Cal Eldred escaped relatively unscathed, and the Brewers could thank him for pitching enough innings to keep their ERA down to 4.45 (10th best in the AL).

While Listach's return to short should aid in sewing up the defense behind the starters, the Brewers' '93 ERAs indicate that their starters and long relievers have too many problems of their own for improved glovework to solve. It would really help if the aging Orosco pulled some saves out of his bag of tricks since Doug Henry seems played out.

Total Pitching: -7.3

Defense:
Catcher: The Brewers used three catchers, but the primary receiver was Dave Nilsson, whose defense just wasn't that great. However, he looked like Johnny Bench compared to mates Tom Lampkin and Joe Kmak.

Pts: -1.2

Infield: John Jaha looked pretty good at first. He wasn't in the same league as Mattingly or Joyner, but he was a lot better than the supposedly sure-handed Cecil Fielder.

Bill Spiers was terrible at second, and platoon-mate Bill Doran wasn't much better. Surhoff was in Ventura territory at third while short was safe in the hands of Pat Listach, whose glove made up for his lackluster season at the plate.

Pts: 11.7

Outfield: Greg Vaughn was the best all-around leftfielder in the AL after Rickey Henderson, Henderson being the only one who could touch him defensively.

Robin Yount was his typically reliable self and Darryl Hamilton was adequate.

Pts: 12.8

Total Defense: 23.3

1994 Personnel:
Catcher: Nilsson is the starter, plain and simple. He may not be the greatest glove in the world, but he could be one of the batting surprises of the 1994 season.

Bench: Now that Lampkin is gone, the closest thing to a veteran backup within 100 miles is Joe Kmak. If Nilsson gets hurt, be afraid ... be very afraid. It's also possible that Surhoff could return behind the plate. Mike Matheny (.254-2-28 in Double-A) and 24-

year-old Mike Stefanski (.322-10-57 in Single-A) are remote contingencies.

Starter: -1.5
Bench: D - A (depending on Surhoff)

Infield:
1B: Jaha will be starting, and the Brews seem ready to stick out his slumps as they did in '93. Even when he isn't hitting, he's the best qualified man to fill the position.
2B: With Spiers re-signed, second will likely be doomed again. It's not as if Spiers boots grounders like a Little Leaguer; he's adequate defensively. However, he can't hit
3B: Third will be an interesting stand-off between Surhoff and Seitzer. They might platoon, or one may knock the other off. All things considered, Surhoff performed excellently with the glove last year and Seitzer had an offensive renaissance, so using both might not be a bad idea.
SS: Listach should return in full health to nail down the middle. His presence will be helpful, but it's not as if Thon was such a slouch on defense last year. What Listach must bring to the party are his bat and running shoes.

DH: The primary DH for the last couple of years was Kevin Reimer. Well, he's gone for good, leaving a void in the order. Vaughn is too good a fielder to waste as DH, and there's a dearth of non-position hitters on the Brewer roster.

IF Bench: The question marks at first and DH may be answered by player signings (remote possibility at best) or spring performances. Don Barbara has a chance to fill in some at first, but he's a light hitter. 24-year-old Scott Talanoa (.287-25-66 in Single-A) could also find himself on an accelerated track to the majors due to his aging status. Matt Mieske, who can hit powerfully when healthy, is a possibility for the DH spot if he makes the club.

Jeff Cirillo is the best bet for rookie backup at third, while known quantities Juan Bell and Jose Valentin provide uninspiring relief at short.

Starters: 15.6
IF Bench: C-

Outfield:
LF: Greg Vaughn is the man...again.
CF: The re-signing of Robin Yount will clear up a lot of mysteries in the outfield. If he isn't back in '94, Darryl Hamilton could move over from right or the Brewers could use one of their lesser farmhands. God knows they can't sign free agents or trade for talent, two factors which further limit their ability to compete as veterans like Yount and Molitor depart.

RF: Hamilton is the rightfielder going into 1994. He's been solid for the last couple of seasons. His speed would allow him to play center if needed.

Bench: Right is an easier position to fill than left or center with the likes of Matt Mieske, Troy O'Leary and the impressive (.293-22-108 in Single-A) if aging (23-years-old) Derek Wachter. Any of these three who sees major league time will be seasoned by DH at-bats in the wake of Kevin Reimer's departure. Other candidates are Alex Diaz, who saw time last year, and the newly acquired Turner Ward, who doesn't bring many tools.

Starters: **44.1**
Bench: C

Starting Pitching: The top pitcher will again be young Cal Eldred. The rest is a crapshoot. Bill Wegman is Unlikely to recover from the devastating luck of his last two seasons, but he's one of the few experienced pitchers Milwaukee has. Jaime Navarro, also victim of bad luck in 1993, is young enough to shake it off and return in top form. Angel Miranda should have been the fourth starter, but his injuries have effectively removed him for the season, if not his career. Instead, Ricky Bones is the most likely candidate for the rotation. Ted Higuera continues to warm the bench, but he shouldn't get 20+ starts unless the Apocalypse is upon us.

While the Brewers have several talented pitchers on the farm, few of them are ready to be pressed into major league service. Ty Hill is their top prospect, but he's a couple of years away. Donnie Blair is a possibility, but he'd have to jump from Double-A after only half a season. Marshall Boze is the most likely rookie to arrive early. He should start the season in Double-A, but the starving Brewers could conceivably start him in Triple-A. Scott Karl is probably as ready as any other prospect, and he's really honed his control. The

Brews could use a groundball pitcher or two. On the other hand, a strikeout pitcher would be a nice change of pace. None of the older prospects have overpowering stuff, and this should worry Milwaukee. Kelly Wunsch could prove to be an exception, but his schedule is completely up to the Brewers.

Among others candidates are Francisco Gamez and Byron Browne (who made the 40-man despite a 117/110 BB/K).
Front-Line: 55.9
Second-Echelon: C-

Relief Pitching: The closer role should be a dogfight between Jesse Orosco and new arrival Bob Scanlan. Don't be surprised if the talented Orosco wins in the short term. Doug Henry has lost the job and doesn't appear to have much chance to win it back.

Talented 25-year-old Charlie Rogers (4-3 23 SV, 1.74 in Double-A) will almost surely be tested by mid-season.

Long relief should assemble the usual suspects in Mike Fetters, Mike Ignasiak and Mark Kiefer. Graeme Lloyd, solid if unexceptional, will probably be better than the lot of them. Any of the young starters listed above could end up in the bullpen until the Brews feel they're ready.
Front-Line: 0
Second-Echelon: C-

Player Value: 114.1

Farm System: The Brewer farm isn't the worst around, but it is weighted down by pitching and outfield prospects. They aren't developing middle infielders (with the recent exception of Listach) and the phenoms they laud as superstars are merely competent (like Dave Nilsson and the emerging Jaha).

Ty Hill will be a legitimate candidate for All-Star ... someday. None of their pitchers are ready. Guys like Boze, Blair and Karl really need to mature in Double-A this year. High-schooler Jeff D'Amico was a smooth pick, but it'll be several years before he sees the inside of County Stadium as anything but a spectator. Kelly Wunsch could be a big surprise to the uninformed. His performance among other amateurs in Cape Cod opened a lot of eyes.

Look for Mieske and O'Leary to arrive in 1994. The infield is woefully understaffed with top-notch prospects.
Infield: D
Outfield: C
Starters: C+
Relievers: D
Farm Ranking: D

Management and Ownership: The Brewers are in trouble financially. Their fan-base is small and only the Expos and Padres under-drew them last year. Bud Selig puts his hands in his pockets and pulls out lint, there's no doubt. The team doesn't acquire free-agents and since it's bereft of talent, it doesn't make many trades. The last major trade the Brewers made was the Sheffield trade with San Diego (and that isn't exactly one the Padres got smoked on). Because of this, it's really hard to grade Sal Bando.

As for management, what can you say about Phil Garner? He doesn't have any horses. Before you can say anything and rate these guys, you actually have to see them do something. We haven't seen them do squat, so they get incomplete's
Ownership: C
Front Office: Incomplete
Field Management: Incomplete
Overall: Incomplete

1994 Outlook: The Brewers will be bad again in '94. It can't be stated more baldly than that. They are a small-market franchise which generates poor revenues and their owner carries the weight of baseball's woes as no other owner.

Lack of money prevents them from signing the big names they need to fill seats, and poor attendance keeps them from making enough money to ink big contracts. The only route out of this Catch-22 is the minors, and they've lapsed in that arena as well.

In terms of competition, the White Sox and Indians should duel for Numero Uno. This leaves the Royals and Twins as Milwaukee's other roommates. The Twins are rebuilding and the Royals could go either way. It's conceivable that the Brewers could find themselves in the middle of the pack by season's end. Without pitching, which they must acquire by hook or by crook, they're more likely to find themselves in fourth or fifth.

MINNESOTA TWINS

1993 Outlook: The Twins weren't really looked at to be right at the top of the hunt. The White Sox, the Mariners and the Rangers all looked more potent. Oh, the Twins had their proponents, but they weren't as plentiful as those who championed the other teams. The Twins were expected to check in somewhere in the 82-87 win range: not enough to win it all, but enough to put them near the edge of the race.

April 8-14 (8-14, 6.5 games back)
The Twins played .500 ball for the first few weeks and were as high as third place on April 22 with an 8-6 record.

Willie Banks won his first two starts and Jim Deshaies went 4-1 in five quality starts for the month with a 2.36 ERA.

Hrbek also got off to a fast start, slugging .530 with 14 RBI for the month.

But on the 23rd, the Twins welcomed the Tigers for a weekend series in the 'Dome, a series in which they were swept and outscored 45-10. By the time they could recover, they had lost eight straight and were in sole possession of the West Division cellar.

Not coincidentally, Scott Erickson returned from the DL during this period and got an early jump on his pathetic season. He recorded three losses in his first three starts with a *9.60* ERA and a *1.8* ratio.

May 12-13 (20-27, 6.5 games back)
The month started with a little sweet revenge in Tiger Stadium. The Twinkies beat Bolton and Moore to take the series and move out of last place.

Minnesota played sub-.500 ball for most of May and dueled Oakland for sixth place. A dramatic 12-11, last-at-bat win over the A's on the 26th, and then a sweep over the Indians, finally propelled them out of last.

As it turned out, May was one of Minnesota's most productive months. While no one was playing exceptionally well, the team managed to put together some consistent .278 hitting and the pitchers kept their ERA under 4.90. Not stellar, but good enough to finish one game under .500 for the month, a feat they wouldn't repeat until September.

June 12-15 (32-42, 6.5 games back)
The Twins mounted a strong rally in early June, starting the month 9-3 and winning two series' against Texas and one each against Oakland and Cleveland. They were within three games of first-place K.C. on the 14th.

This proved to be their last hurrah, however. Eight straight losses, including two each to Toronto and Boston and a four-game sweep at the hands of the Yanks (in which they were outscored 27-9) left them 7.5 out again.

They finished the month tied for last, but they were only 6.5 out, the closest they would get for the remainder of the season.

Deshaies and Rick Aguilera were the stars of the staff and were largely responsible for their early run. Aguilera recorded 10 saves in June with a 10/1 K/W ratio and 0.00 ERA. Deshaies went 3-1 with a 3.34 ERA.

July 11-16 (43-58, 13.5 games back)
A 4-7 start in July sent the Twinkies into the All-Star break 8.5 games out and in firm possession of last place. On their return, three losses to the Orioles continued the trend and set the tone for the rest of the year.

By the end of the month they were 13.5 out and any playoff hopes, if they survived this far, were extinguished. On the brighter side, Oakland was losing just as frequently and a first-class cellar race was developing.

The hitters did their part and enjoyed their best month, hitting .279 and slugging .414. Dave Winfield was setting up his chase for the 2,000th hit by hitting .355 and slugging .710. Shane Mack hit .394 with 10 doubles and 14 RBI while Brian Harper hit .298 with 17 RBI, although, as it turned out, the Twins management wasn't paying any attention.

August 13-17 (56-75, 18 games back)
Oakland kept it close for the first week, but Minnesota finally broke out of the cellar for good with a win over the Yanks on August 7. A four-game winning streak, including a sweep of the Angels, put them five games ahead of the A's on the 15th. But they couldn't pull away and Oakland tightened it up.

Sure, this race didn't get the same billing that the Atlanta-San Fran race did, but it was the 'last great AL cellar race.'

You're right, who cares?

The Twinkies finished the month four games ahead of the A's.

Sept./Oct. 15-16 (71-91, 23 games back)

More of the same. The Angels tumbled into the picture and the three teams were neck-and-neck for much of the month.

Last-week surges by Cali (2-5) and Minnie (4-2), however, left them both 23 games out and three games ahead of Oakland, all alone in the stinkhouse.

End of story. So be it.

Park Effect. The Hubert H. Humphrey Metrodome aids offense in all categories except homers. It helps run production by six percent despite reducing home runs seven percent. Most of the difficulty is felt by righties (12 percent reduction) who have to shoot for the deep left field wall.

The difference is made up with a five percent increase in hits, including a 14 percent boost in doubles and an incredible 49 percent in triples.

Errors are scarce in the Metrodome; they're lowered a healthy 12 percent.

Offense. The Twinkies didn't have much punch last year, scoring only 693 runs. They sprayed enough singles around, but they refused to take walks and turned in a horrid .327 OBP (second worst in AL). Nor did they have any power; their .385 slugging percentage was the third worst.

And the Twins may be the slowest team in baseball. They hit into a league-high 150 double plays and managed only 83 stolen bases.

Their star hitters are slowing down with age and everybody else was on the DL last year. Simply by staying healthy, the Twins' offense could improve by 70 runs this year, which would put them around the league average. But they haven't made any moves that would suggest they could be anything more than average.

Total Offense: -18.4

Pitching. The starting rotation was even worse than the offense, largely due to the heroics of Scott Erickson, who single-handedly accounted for 19 losses. Nobody else posted an ERA under 4.00, though, so he can't take all the credit for their collective 4.92 ERA and 50-78 record.

Now that Banks (a former No. 1 pick) and Deshaies have been traded away, the Twins will rely heavily on unproven youngsters this year. This doesn't mean they can't perform up to the rigorous standards set last year, but their lack of experience doesn't bode well.

Their middle relievers last year were mediocre; the bullpen allowed a 1.423 ratio and a 4.35 ERA. Dave Stevens, a prospect who came over in the Banks trade, may be able to help, but he is also unproven. Rick Aguilera, however, is a talented veteran who handles closer duties as well as anyone.

Total Pitching: -36.0

Defense:

Infield: Kent Hrbek may need to lay off the pastries, but he still can field for a guy who needs to jog in a rubber suit. Chuckie K. needs to get back to where he was in 1992. There's no doubt he can be one of the best defensive players at his position.

At short, Meares was nothing special. His zone rating was well below-average and his hit-happy staff didn't get many DPs turned behind them. Pagliarulo was nothing special at third, either.

Pts: 5.3

Outfield: Overall outfield defense was atrocious. Kirby is losing it in center; Munoz has always been pretty mediocre, and McCarty showed he should play first. Mack was the only adequate defender, but one OF does not an outfield make.

Pts: 0.3

Catcher: Harper was pretty surprising with his arm, but overall he's not the greatest with the glove. His reputation is weak, but he's nowhere near as bad as people say he is.

Pts: 9.6

Total Defense: 15.2

1994 Personnel:

Catcher: Matt Walbeck has dibs, but his bat might force Derek Parks to take over.

Bench: Lenny Webster and Mike Durant are the two possible backups now.

Starter: 0.0

Bench: C-

Infield:

1B: Dave McCarty and Kent Hrbek should fight here.

2B: Chuck Knoblauch will have it all alone.

3B: Stahoviak, Chip Hale and Scott Leius will fight here.

SS: Pat Meares, Denny Hocking and Jeff Reboulet will fight here.

DH: Dave Winfield will DH most of the time. The loser of the fight at first, Gene Larkin or Mike Maksudian, could see time here.

IF Bench: The bench will consist of the guys above (call them losers), plus Gary Scott. Long-range prospects include Steve Dunn, Jeff Carter, Brian Raabe

Starters: 17.8
Bench: B-

Outfield

LF: Mack and Munoz will be fighting.

CF: Shane Mack could play CF, but Rich Becker could win the job outright.

RF: Kirby's been talking about a full-time move to right and this would be a good year.

Bench: Randy Bush, Derek Lee, Brito, J.T. Bruett look like big-league bench bait. Long-rangers are: Anthony Byrd, Marty Cordova, Lawton and Torii Hunter.

Starters: 11.9
Bench: D+

Starting Pitching: Scott Erickson stinks. Kevin Tapani could bounce back hard. Pat Mahomes, Mike Trombley, Oscar Munoz and Guardado, Tsamis and Greg Brummett are the possibilities. Long-term uber prospect LaTroy Hawkins could surprise late in the year.

Front-Line: 24.6
Second-Echelon: D

Relief Pitching: Rick Aguilera is supposedly trade-bait, but he could be very effective for the Twins. Others include Carl Willis, Larry Casian, Rich Garces, Mark Guthrie, Brett Merriman, Dave Stevens, Ontiveros, Correa.

Front-Line: 15.2
Second-Echelon: B-

Player Value: 69.5

Farm System: With the trade of Banks, the Twins are rich with young catching. Derek Parks and Matt Walbeck both look quite nice. Scott Stahoviak and Denny Hocking are the young hopefuls in the infield. In the outfield, Rich Becker, long-rangers Torii Hunter and Anthony Byrd look very nice. The Twins have several excellent pitching prospects. Perennial hopeful Pat Mahomes heads the list, but look for LaTroy Hawkins and Oscar Munoz.

Infield: C
Outfield: B
Starters: C
Relievers: D
Farm Ranking: C

Management and Ownership: The owner, Carl Pohlad is famed for his frugality. Hey, Minnesota is not Chicago, so it's not like the Twins have billions to spend. Still, the Twins don't make major moves. GM Andy MacPhail is considered one of the finer minds in the game, but he is hamstrung by his owner.

As for Tom Kelly, he may be gruff and hard to deal with (from the media's perspective), but he's pretty damn good. The man is pretty uncanny at reading stealing situations and last year he called for very few pitchouts, but was usually right on when he did. This had to have helped weak-armed Brian Harper. The offense is composed of bashers, so there isn't the strength in fundamentals that used to characterize Kelly's old teams, but he knows his team's strengths and isn't afraid to try something new to shake things up. With his staff, he was quick to pull them and go to the pen. He did work his short relievers a bit hard. All in all, he did a pretty canny job in a tough situation.

Ownership: C-
Front Office: B+
Field Management: B
Overall: B-

1994 Outlook: The Twins are still in rebuilding mode. They'll probably need a year or two before they can jump back in it. Their infield is in a state of flux, as is their catching, pitching and outfield. Well, that about covers their entire team, doesn't it? If there's a team that can stay with the rebuilding until they have to, it's the Twins. Slow and steady wins the race and the Twins have always had the patience.

Team Essays – AL West

California Angels

1993 Outlook: The Angels were expected to be a periphery team. Not a real contender, but a threat to be around .500 if things broke right. There were many question marks. Could Chad Curtis continue to play well in center? Could Tim Salmon play well in left? What about the holes in the infield? Could J.T. Snow, Russ Springer and Jerry Nielsen do enough to justify the trade of Jim Abbott? What about the offense? Is there depth in the rotation? Could the Angels find a closer? There were no answers – only more questions. ... And that made the Angels pretenders.

April 13-6 (13-6, 1.5 games ahead)
California started off the year 2-2 before going on a 10-2 run to put themselves 2.5 games ahead of Texas on April 26. Leading the charge was the Angels pitching staff. Mark Langston, Chuck Finley and Scott Sanderson finished the month with a combined 8-1 record and a 2.99 ERA.

J.T. Snow hit .343 with six homers. Tim Salmon only hit .254, but he had an impressive .392 OBP and hit five homers for a .559 slugging percentage with 14 RBI.

May 27-21 (14-15, 2 games ahead)
The Angels didn't show a consistent pattern during the month. They mixed mediocre winning streaks with small losing streaks and ended the month on a 5-5 "tear."

Chad Curtis went bonkers hitting .354 with a .463 OBP and Rene Gonzales added a .407 OBP to set the table. Salmon continued to consistently excel. But as the gang (and fill-in Torey Lovullo) were hitting stride, Snow was plummeting, hitting four dingers, but posting a .124 average. The pitching staff continued their solid work, posting a 3.62 ERA for the month.

June 37-38 (10-16, 2 games behind)
Quite simply, the pitching self-destructed. The entire staff posted a 5.73 ERA for the month. Langston went 4-1 with a 3.09 ERA and Chuck Finley was 4-1, 1.91, but with beauties like Sanderson (0-6, 6.06) showing the way, the team was only in 13 of the 26 games they played. In addition, Curtis, Gonzales and Polonia hit a combined .219, making sure there was no one on base for the boppers. Chili Davis, pretty much unheard of before June, hit six homers and drove in 27 RBI (he only had a .274 OBP, though.).

July 48-55 (11-17, 9.5 games back)
On July 1, the Angels were two games out. Between the 17th and the 26th, the Angels posted a spritely 0-10 record during a nine-game road trip (they also lost to Oakland, the first game back). They were outscored 60-29 during this disaster. It's safe to say that an offense which averages less than three runs a game will kill ya every time. DiSarcina, Lovullo and Snow were among the stinkiest of stink-bombs.

August 59-72 (11-17, 15 games back)
The race had ended by mid-July and the Angels went into "rebuilding" mode. The offense was lackluster and the pitching had settled in a mediocre groove. When the month started, the fates had already determined California's destiny, it was just a matter of going forward in time and letting the string play out.

Sept./Oct. 71-91 (12-19, 23 games back)
See August.

Park Effects: Anaheim Stadium, for all practical purposes, is a neutral park. Over the last three years, the Angels and their opponents have scored as many runs in Anaheim as they have on the road. The park slightly lowers batting average. More drastically, it cuts doubles by 14 percent; triples by 32 percent; and increases HR by about 7 percent.

It appears that the park induces a lot of errors (16 percent above AL average), which helps neutralize the run-suppressive features of the park.

Anaheim seems to favor right-handers, increasing their average slightly, while giving a decent boost in homers. Left-handers get a slight nudge in power, but lose eight percent off their B.A.

Offense: California's overall offense was very weak last year (they finished second-to-last in the AL with 684 runs). Callie's OBP was below average and the team's base-stealing was quite poor. The Angels finished second in the league in steals with 169, but also led the AL in caught stealing (with 100) –

effectively negating their speed. The Angels also hit very few triples (adjusting for the fact that the Angels are going to lose triples in this park) and grounded into an average number of double-plays, suggesting they merely have average, or slightly above-average team speed.

The real weakness, however, was the Angels' lack of power. They finished second-to-last in slugging percentage (the Brewers had a .378 SL% to the Angels' .380) and tied for last in homers with Boston (114). They have done nothing to address their deficiencies in the off-season and there are no good-hitting prospects on the horizon.

Total Offense: -9.3

Pitching: The rotation had two exceptional starters and after that was a giant head cheese – old guys pitching themselves out of jobs – plus inexperienced kids trying to wrest those jobs away. To look at it positively, the Angels had 89 quality starts, tied with Seattle and Kansas City for the second-best total in the league behind Chicago's 93, but their second-echelon starters drove their ERA sky-high.

The bullpen was rather scary. Their 4.47 ERA was abysmal and their inability to strike out hitters made the defense work extra hard behind them. Finally, the Angels didn't lose any extra games because of blown saves, but there's no doubt that the people slamming the door in '93 are not the guys you want to have.

There are decent prospects for both rotation spots and relief spots in 1994, so the pitching could be improved, especially the bullpen if one of the two fire-balling prospects (Watson and Percival) can develop quickly.

Total Pitching: 12.9

Defense:
Infield: At first, J.T. Snow showed excellent defensive tools, but was inadequate. At second, Torey Lovullo and Damion Easley were both very solid.

At third, Rene Gonzales was smooth, but the jury was out on Eduardo Perez – But Perez may end up in left field anyway. At short, Gary DiSarcina is a healthy season away from challenging for the Gold Glove.

Pts: 26.8

Outfield: In left, Luis Polonia continued his lackluster ways. In center, Chad Curtis is an absolute vacuum cleaner. In right, Tim Salmon is also exceptional.

Pts: 30.5

Catcher: Starter Greg Myers was your typical industrial-strength catcher. He had an average catcher's ERA and had an average arm. Ron Tingley, Chris Turner and John Orton were the backups. Orton could call a good game, but couldn't throw and Tingley could throw and couldn't call a game. Turner split the difference, calling a mediocre game and showing an inability to gun down Marge Schott with an M-16 on full-auto.

Pts: -0.3
Total Defense: 57.0

1994 Personnel
Catcher: California has been infamous as a clearinghouse for adequate defensive catchers who can't hit for beans. This year, expect more of the same. The Angels are looking to platoon Greg Myers and rookie Chris Turner. Neither of these two look like they'll be that good, but they're adequate.

Bench: The Angels have Jorge Fabregas, Mark Delasandro and possibly John Orton on the pine. These players are wildcards and shouldn't be much if they're forced to come in and play.

Starters: -2.6
Bench: D

Infield:
1B: J.T Snow was probably the worst all-around first baseman in the league last year. With a year under his belt, it's quite likely he could improve enough to put himself solidly in the middle of the pack.

2B: This position is kind of a mess. Frontline competition for the job will be among Kevin Flora, Spike Owen and Torey Lovullo. Each has various strengths and weaknesses, but Lovullo might be the best of the bunch right now. Owen will be the primary reserve if Flora or Lovullo wins out.

3B: Doctors suggested the Angels move Eduardo Perez to left to lessen strain on his throwing elbow. So Damion Easley shifts over and hopes to heal his shin splints at the less-taxing hot corner. The question is this: Can Easley's offense make him a viable third baseman – his defense will definitely be up to task.

SS: If Gary DiSarcina can play 150 games,

he could win the AL Gold Glove. The thing is his bat is awful. He's entering his prime, so it's possible he can hit better.

DH: Chili Davis is a decent bat, but with age and other factors, we're inclined to look for a decline in his performance.

IF Bench: Chris Pritchett and Ty Van Burkleo (.274-6-56 at Triple-A) are likely backups at first and DH. At second, look for 26-year-old P.J. Forbes (.319-15-64 at Double-A) and Jim Walewander (.305-1-43) as bench possibilities. Eduardo Perez and Mike Brumley (.353-0-46, 24 SB at Triple-A) might see some time at third. At short, Callie has plenty of possibilities, including: Rod Correia, Brian Grebeck and Brumley.

Starters: 23.0
Bench: C

Outfield:

LF: Eduardo Perez is a fine athlete, so it wouldn't be surprising if he were to shine defensively. The question is, can he hit? In all probability, right now he can't. He'll have some power and speed, but he won't walk and he probably won't hit for much average. Still, the Angels love him and he's 24, so he can definitely improve his skills.

CF: Chad Curtis is already one of the best leadoff men in the league. He's 25 now, so he could score 115 runs and steal 60 bases if things break right.

RF: Tim Salmon is possibly the best all-around right fielder in the game. If he can come close to duplicating 1993 this year, he'll supplant Walker and Gwynn. If Callie's pitching can keep them in the race, he could get serious MVP consideration.

Bench: Garret Anderson, Jim Edmonds, Orlando Palmiero and Mark Sweeney, John Jackson, 27, (.325-3-34 at Double-A) and Reggie Williams, 28, (.274-2-53, 50 SB at Triple-A) are the best bets as bench players. Marquis Riley, 23, (.264-1-42, 69 SB at A) and Tyrone Boykin, 26, (.325-3-40, 22SB at A) are long-shots to get some PT by the end of the season.

Starters: 50.0
Bench: C

Starting Pitching: Chuck Finley and Mark Langston (if he's not traded off) are the only two consistent starters the Angels have. Every one else we can discuss is at best a question mark. Phil Leftwich, Hilly Hathaway and Mark Holzemer are going to get good looks, as will John Farrell (3.99 ERA, 71/28 K/BB at Triple-A) and Brian Anderson. Other possibilities include John Fritz, Korey Keling, Joe Magrane, Russ Springer and Julio Valera. The best bets in terms of quality are Anderson, Springer and Leftwich. If these guys get jobs, they could be very good.

Front-Line: 66.8
Second-Echelon: C

Relief Pitching: At least the starters have one or two roles filled. The pen really has nothing in stone. Joe Grahe and Mike Butcher are the only pitchers with established value. Troy Percival will get a shot at closing if he's healed up and can throw strikes. Julian Heredia also has excellent potential. Other possibilities include Jerry Nielsen, Tony Chavez, Bob Gamez, 25, (5-2, 3.26 ERA and a 50/18 K/W ratio at AA), Scott Lewis and super long-shot Ron Watson.

Front-Line: 14.3
Second-Echelon: B

Player Value: 151.1

Farm System: The Angels' farm system is almost bone dry when it comes to hitting. They have some decent pitching prospects, like relievers Troy Percival, Ron Watson and Julian Heredia; and starters Russ Springer and Brian Anderson, but the closest thing to a young hitter with ability is Kevin Flora.

Infield: D
Outfield: E
Starters: C
Relievers: B
Farm Ranking: D

Management and Ownership: The Angels are a mess and in transition. Whitey Herzog, probably tired of the oft-inexplicable penny pinching ways of Jackie Autry, quit as V.P and G.M. on January 11, leaving the front office in a state of turmoil. Herzog is one worthy of immense respect; in the past, he would never back down from a fight. It's true he's getting up there in years, but the situation must be pretty grim indeed for him to just bail out on the Angels.

The reputation that the Autrys have has been massively reworked over the past few years. When "The Cowboy" was still making decisions, the club was a means of therapy for him. Free-agents like Reggie, Don Baylor and Nolan Ryan were pursued (and often acquired) doggedly to make them contenders. Now, his wife, Jackie, is in charge and the Angels are seen as a business. We are hearing about hard times in the land o' plenty. The Angels are suddenly raiding the cookie jar cash stash to pay for Mark Langston. Either that, or he's gone. Players making cash won't make it for Cali, it's time for the farm system to pay dividends. There's only one problem: The farm system is quite weak.

On the game-level management level, the Angels are doing quite well. Buck Rodgers has a good reputation as a baseball man and it's not too hard to see that he did an adequate job with the talent he had.

He's an aggressive manager, making his club steal and hit-and-run a great deal. His team doesn't bunt a great deal, but they are fundamentally sound. They make contact, hit behind the runner and get the sacrifice when they try for it. They are quite a bit better than average teams in this regard. If the Angels had better base-running judgment, you'd have to say they were one of the best "small ball" clubs in the game.

With his pitching staff, Rodgers seems pretty patient. He is slow to pull them, letting them work out of jams. With his shoddy bullpen, though, he's quite different. He makes his closers earn their saves, often pitching them more than one inning. He's aware how valuable it is to get outs and makes his best relievers throw a couple more outs than managers with better pitchers would.

As a manager with Montreal, we saw that Rodgers could do a good job of handling rookies and inexperienced players. He hasn't done much with California because he doesn't have much to work with.

Ownership: D
Front Office: ? ? ?
Field Management: B
Overall: D

1994 Outlook: To put it bluntly, the Angels are a weak team. They could surprise the division, but there are a lot of "buts" here. Their established talent level is very low. They have the makings of a decent infield and already have a pretty good outfield, but they need to score runs and put together a good bullpen. Meanwhile, the guys running the show seem to be running around like chickens with headectomies. If they can push themselves to .500, it'll be a very successful season.

OAKLAND A'S

1993 Outlook: Despite manager Tony Larussa's miraculously making something out of Oakland in '92, nobody who looked at their squad heading into '93 could have predicted greatness.

The pitching staff was a shambles. Washed-up starters like Ron Darling and Bob Welch were expected to carry the load in the wake of so-called "ace" Dave Stewart's move to Toronto and phenoms Todd Van Poppel and Kirk Dressendorfer hadn't justified the A's faith in them.

There were still potent bats. Mark McGwire was back after an injury-filled '92 and Rickey "The Mouth" Henderson was great, despite his contract whining. On the flipside, it was obvious that characters like Dave Henderson weren't aging well. Replacements were needed at several positions.

Enter the rookies of yesteryear. Brent Gates appeared to have found home at 2B, and multi-position understudies Mike Bordick and Lance Blankenship were still on active duty. This crew was soon followed by whiff-meister Craig Paquette, who claimed 3B for his own at the insistence of starry-eyed A's management.

While these youngsters were better than the A's could have hoped, it was unlikely that they were the spark needed to key the order. Even if they were, the pitching was so rotten (who expected the Eck to follow the trend?) that there was little hope of finishing above the middle of the pack.

April 7-11 (7-11, 5.5 games back)
Eckersley began his season in uncharacteristic fashion. He hadn't lost a game until Aug. 25 the year before, but it only took him until April 15 to do it this time.

He came into the ninth inning and gave up two singles and a double to the Tigers, retiring only one batter before being saddled with the loss. considering the way Eck has pitched in the past, three hits is about his quota for four or five appearances rather than a single outing. Oakland's loss was Detroit manager Sparky Anderson's gain, as he managed his 2,000th victory, becoming only the seventh skipper to accomplish the feat.

To compound matters, Oakland lost to Milwaukee two days later and dropped below .500 for the first time since Sept. of 1987.

May 12-16 (19-27, 7 games back)

May was kicked off in kooky (and pathetic) fashion when 3B Kevin Seitzer replaced the ejected Kelly Downs and retired Glenallen Hill on a called third strike. Seitzer hadn't pitched since high school, but with his initial success he was immediately more qualified than 3/4 of the Oakland bullpen.

Mark McGwire was murdering the fraternity of pitchers. He hit two homers against New York on May 3 to bring his total to 5 on the year.

On another up note, Oakland continued to be the only team with a winning record against Boston ace Roger Clemens, clobbering him for five runs on May 6 and leaving him 5-10 for his career against the A's. Of course, many of those losses came against Dave Stewart in his heyday, and it was his ability to shut down the Red Sox more than The Rocket's pitching which swayed the tide.

Oakland seemed to have some good bats. McGwire was still healthy, C Terry Steinbach was as smooth as ever, and Ruben Sierra hadn't had any major slumps. Of course, when Dale Sveum is your DH, you know something is terminally wrong.

By the middle of May, Bobby Witt (over from the Canseco trade of Aug. '92) was the best starter on the staff, with a 3-1 record. On May 11 he recorded his sixth career shutout (this was slightly overshadowed by Clemens nailing his 35th).

On May 15, Oakland beat Seattle for the 16th consecutive time in the Coliseum. This didn't change the fact that they were 6.5 games out and in last.

June 12-14 (31-41, 6.5 games back)

Oakland began the month 2-8 before a win at Minnesota on the 13th pulled them from their rut. They looked strong for the remainder of June, capitalizing on other teams' errors for a 10-6 record, possibly their best stretch of the season.

July 12-17 (43-58, 13.5 games back)

On July 5, Rickey Henderson did what only one player had previously done, namely lead off both games of a doubleheader with home runs. The always modest Henderson demurred praise, saying that scoring runs for the team was what mattered most to him.

One bright spot in yet another sub-.500 month was the arrival of slugger Troy Neel. He'd been up for some time, but his two homer, seven RBI performance in a July 8 loss to Boston really turned heads. He then encored by homering twice against Boston the next day. Neel looked like he was for real.

In that same start, struggling pitching phenom Van Poppel was absolutely torn to shreds by the Sox, serving up a juicy grand slam to Mo Vaughn.

By the third week of July, the A's were grasping at straws, attempting to stave off the inevitable. After Van Poppel lost to the Indians on the 18th, LaRussa tried a format where several long relievers were pitched to try and find a cohesive unit that could replace the void in the starting rotation.

August 9-21(52-79, 22 games back)

August saw the departure of Rickey to Toronto. The Jays were indulging in their usual season-ending shopping spree, and, considering what Henderson had done to their pitchers in the 1989 ALCS, it was little wonder that Rickey was atop their wish list.

The good side for the A's was that talented pitcher Steve Karsay arrived as the Jays part of the deal. In his first start on Aug. 17 (first time he'd pitched above AA) he pitched convincingly, unveiling his truly wicked curveball only after he'd baffled Brewer hitters with his cheese. His history of arm problems was nowhere to be seen.

Sept./Oct. 16-15 (68-94, 26 games back)

On Sept. 3, McGwire returned to the lineup after having missed 100 games due to foot surgery. He was cheered in his only at-bat.

Oakland waylaid the Blue Jays for the umpteenth time on Sept. 7. Though the Jays were apparently the team to beat in baseball, Oakland seemed to have their number the whole season, ambushing them 11-7 in extra innings in this particular meeting.

Bobby Witt was once again the best pitcher on the staff as he went 5-1 with a 2.72 ERA for the month. Of all the principals in the A's/Rangers trade, he seemed to be of the highest value when 1993 ended.

The season ended ignominiously. for the first time in what seemed to be centuries, the A's weren't the cream of the AL West crop. LaRussa, miracle worker that he may be, was not able to cobble together a team from the motley roster he was handed. It was the end of an era. But with the talent lurking on the A's farm, a new era may not be so far away.

Park Effects: The Coliseum isn't nicknamed the "Mausoleum" for naught, it is where hits go to die.

Batting average is lowered by 6 percent and runs are lowered by 12 percent (factor that into your next discussion concerning Rickey Henderson's many talents).

While homers aren't really affected (they're actually slightly encouraged), doubles are reduced by 15 percent and triples are relatively unknown at 27 percent below the league.

Errors are about league average, which means that Paquette's play is much more important than it would be in say...Riverfront or the Astrodome.

Neither side of the plate gets benefits in terms of average (they're both lowered by about 5 percent) but righthanders experience a 5 percent power surge while the same percentage is stolen from lefties.

Offense: The A's didn't finish last for no reason; their offense stunk. They only scored 715 runs and slugged .394 as a team (Boston outslugged them at .315!!).

On the up side: They hit a lot of homers and were solid on the basepaths (131 SB with a 69% success rate).

There should be an influx of young talent rounding out the batting order over the next couple os seasons. This accompanies the changes in the rotation, which will also be filled with farm talent. In terms of hitting, the A's should hope for more Troy Neels and fewer Craig Paquettes.

Total Offense: 46.2

Pitching: Oakland's pitching was easily the worst in the AL, posting a 68-94 record with a 4.90 ERA. It was the lack of starters more than their mediocre offense which doomed them to Basement City in the West.

The A's staff was hampered by has-beens like Ron Darling and Bob Welch, who were forced to pitch long, unproductive outings because Todd VanPoppel and Miguel Jimenez were still developing. The only veteran who performed adequately was Bobby Witt, and he was awful a lot of the time as well.

The Eck wasn't as bad as everyone says, but he was a monumental disappointment after his string of untouchable relief seasons. Whether he recovers or not, it's obvious that the A's need a rotation before they can worry about saving wins.

VanPoppel and Jimenez will definitely improve the rotation, and the newly acquired Steve Karsay should be an All-Star pitcher within 2-3 years. Look for the sequel to "Reversal of Fortune" as the Oakland rotation improves drastically in 1994.

Total Pitching: -37.8

Defense:

Catcher: Steinbach is one solid catcher. When the A's need to go to someone else (as they did for the last six weeks of the season) they're hating life.

Pts: 4.1

Infield: McGwire is a pretty crappy first baseman, even when he's healthy, but that's not what he gets paid for. As much of a revelation as Brent Gates was with the bat, he was just as bad as a second baseman. Chances are, he'll improve.

By the same token, Paquette turned out to be a good third baseman but a wild swinger at the plate. Mike Bordick was merely adequate at short.

Pts: -10.9

Outfield: The outfield was a shambles. LF Rickey Henderson was the only one who had a clue about catching and throwing the ball.

Lance Blankenship (who was probably out of position) and Dave Henderson were the definition of mediocrity in center while the much-vaunted Ruben Sierra performed as badly in right as he had at the plate.

Pts: 9.6

Total Defense: 2.8

1994 Personnel:
Catcher: Steinbach will be back and as reliable as ever.
Bench: Eric Helfand and Scott Hemond should back Steinbach.
Starter: 14.1
Bench: C

Infield:
1B: McGwire will also return in full health with a mighty bat.
2B: Brent Gates must improve his glove so that his bat stays at second.
3B: Craig Paquette has the weight on his shoulders. The A's ensured this when they let both Kevin Seitzer and Jerry Browne walk.
SS: Mike Bordick is a wrinkle which needs to be ironed out of the line-up. Nobody's ready to do it yet.
DH: Troy Neel should be the DH again this year. His bat is the start of whatever youth wave the A's can muster from their farm.
IF Bench: Mike Aldrete returns as experience at first, while Fausto Cruz brings youthful zeal in an attempt to learn short in the bigs.
There's really no one experienced to back second and third, so this should be addressed in the spring.
Starters: 33.1
IF Bench: D
Outfield:
LF: Who else, but the re-signed Rickey.
CF: Dave Henderson is probably toast, although he'll get P.T. out of an Oakland sense of obligation. Stan Javier should get the biggest share of at-bats with Blankenship getting the rest.
RF: Ruben Sierra will be in right collecting another eight million at-bats for his record books.
Bench: The A's have some warm bodies to back up the starters. We've seen what Scott Lydy and Scott Brosius can do and we're not impressed. Speedy Kerwin Moore may save the outfield bench if his hitting is as good as it looks.
Starters: 50.2
Bench: C+

Starting Pitching: If pitching developments optimally, then Steve Karsay, Todd Van Poppel and Miguel Jimenez will lead the rotation. After that trio, however, it's a crapshoot.

Bob Welch, Bobby Witt and Ron Darling are veteran candidates for the fourth and fifth spots and they could be higher if one or more of the rookies doesn't pan out. Last resort Kelly Downs will probably get some spot starts. Gary Haught is a prospect with a chance to break in for some innings.
Front-Line: 0.0
Second-Echelon: B

Relief Pitching: Relief is still stronger in terms of closing than the middle innings. Eckersley remains among the top closers despite the loss of his godhood. The A's even signed Dave Righetti in an inscrutable attempt to aid Eck. The names in long innings are the same old boys who turn LaRussa hair whiter every year: John Briscoe, Vince Horsman Roger Smithberg and the nominal best of the lot, Edwin Nunez. Steve Chitren is rumored to be returning with improved stuff. Since goose Gossage is gone (although he could show up sometime in the spring), closer prospect Mark Acre might be promoted to learn the ropes from Master Eckersley.
Front-Line: 12.1
Second-Echelon: B

Player Value: 109.5

Farm System: Among the best bets for success are 3B Jason Giambi, SP Haught and SS Cruz. Acre seems like he's got the stuff, but it's risky to draft relief prospects. When evaluating talent, once again compensate for age. Webster Garrison looks decent (.303-7-73), but he's 28. 29-year-old Jim Bowie and 26-year-old Scott Shockey are the same story. Mike Wolff and 30-year-old Eric Fox could vy for outfield time, but there's little room for outfielders with Rickey re-signed and Ruben Sierra sewing up right so tightly.
Infield: C-
Outfield: D
Starters: B-
Relievers: B-
Farm Ranking: C-

Management and Ownership: The Haas family provides a steady hand of leadership for the Athletics. The team is run with a financial framework not too dissimilar to that of the Brewers, Minnesota, or Montreal, but there's more flexibility involved here. Big names are traded back and forth, free agents like Rickey Henderson are signed and big money is paid to prospects. The A's were once the flagship organization in the majors and that status is long gone. Despite this, the team is trying to rebuild and is doing this rebuilding primarily from within.

GM Sandy Alderson has worked a decent overhaul of the team, dispensing with many of the aging vets, while garnering kids who can do the job in the future. With tactics like the Karsay trade (swindle) and the reasonably canny drafting the team has done of late, it's hard to find too much fault with them.

Tony LaRussa is considered the class of the AL. He's not "the dean of AL managers" like Sparky is, but he's had the most post-season success in the last 10 years of any AL manager, except possibly Tom Kelly (and some of that was a fluke).

Ownership: C+
Front Office: B
Field Management: B+
Overall: B

1994 Outlook: The A's haven't really done enough to improve their lot for 1994. They got Rickey, but their pitching hasn't shaken out yet. Because of this, it's really hard to see them challenging Texas and Seattle. Could it happen? Yes. But it would take an awful lot of things to go right for it to happen. Chances are these things won't go right, so let's be safe and call them a third-place or fourth-place team.

SEATTLE MARINERS

1993 Outlook: The Mariners were a legitimate contender. They had speed, power, pitching and good defense. Or so everyone thought. With a rotation of Randy Johnson, Erik Hanson, Dave Fleming and Chris Bosio; an offense built around stars like Ken Griffey and Edgar Martinez; and a bullpen with a quality closer like Norm Charlton, the team looked like it could easily win 90+ games.

April 11-11 (11-11, 3.5 games back)
The Mariners yawned out of the gate, winning a game, then losing a game until April 16-18 (the fact that catalyst Edgar Martinez was unavailable obviously hobbled Seattle). The Tigers outscored Seattle 39-20 on those dates, taking three of four games. Randy Johnson righted the ship on April 21 with a four-hitter over the Sox at the Fens, spurring the Mariners to a modest 6-3 spurt. Richie Amaral (.324 B.A.), Erik Hanson (3-0, 1.53) and Big Randy (3-1, 2.97) were among the stars. The pitching staff pitched at its level, the offense had an impressive OBP (.348), but their .385 SL% held down their record.

May 25-26 (14-15, 3.5 games back)
Erik Hanson and the rest of the pitching staff improved dramatically in May, posting a 3.77 ERA. Despite the better pitching and improved offense, the team's record fell under .500 for the month. The Mariners' problem was bad luck. They lost 11 one-run games, which basically sealed their fate for May. Hanson's ERA was a torrid 2.28, but he posted a 2-2 record. Johnson didn't fare much better, going 3-2, 2.45. On offense, Edgar Martinez's replacement, Mike Blowers was .313-3-17, numbers actually better than the average Martinez performance. Rich Amaral continued his solid work and Tino Martinez blossomed with a .306-6-15 month.

June 38-40 (13-14, 2.5 games back)
Ken Griffey, the best 23-year-old the league has seen in 35 years, rolled out of bed and started whacking the cover off the ball. His .353-10-22 June was the start of a three-month tear that brought him within striking distance of 50 homers. Tino Martinez, Jay Buhner (.300-4-15), Dave Fleming (3-1, 2.51) and Randy Johnson (4-1, 3.11) followed suit, but Erik Hanson (0-4, 6.19) and sundry others kept the treadmill going. The Mariners were within 2.5 games on June 3. By June 8, they were six games out and in sixth place. By the 25th, they had pulled within 2.5 games and stayed at that level.

July 51-53 (13-13, 7 games back)
During the dog days, the offense went berzerk and the pitching staff went on vacation, leaving a bunch of Pirates, Tigers and Rockies to handle the chores. The team hit .283 and slugged over .450, but had a 5.03 ERA, leading to yet another +/- .500 monthly record.

Randy Johnson self-destructed, going 0-3 with a 7.36 ERA; Tim Leary checked in with a 5.05 ERA; and Chris Bosio had a 6.21 ERA. If that wasn't enough, Dave Fleming added a 5.49 ERA. Griffey, Buhner, Blowers and Tino all hit like banshees, but it wasn't enough to overcome the shoddy hurling. ... only Erik Hanson (3.49 ERA) was consistent among the starters. Seattle lost games by scores of 6-5, 6-0, 6-3, 5-3, 7-6 and won games with scores of 9-8, 12-4, 6-5, 6-4, 7-6, 5-4. That's 11 games where the pitching allowed 5+ runs.

August 65-66 (14-13, 9 games back)

The pitching problems continued as the team posted a 4.97 ERA for the month. What is amazing is that the hitting went completely south (.224 B.A., .308 OBP, .377 SL%). They basically won a bunch of pitcher's duels and got clobbered in their losses. By this time, it was too late.

Sept./Oct. 82-80 (17-14, 12 games back)

With the race over, the offense continued to tank, but the pitching staff, led by big Randy (5-0, 1.73) and Chris Bosio (2-2, but a 1.91 ERA).

Park Effects: The Kingdome has gone through quite a few changes over the last few years and is now a park that gives a slight edge to offense, increasing runs-scored by 2 percent. Since 1992, the park hasn't affected batting average, but has boosted doubles by 24 percent, cut triples by 18 percent and lowered homers by 6 percent.

The Kingdome has had a severe dampening effect on errors, lowering them by 14 percent over the last two years.

The park dimensions were shifted about for its left-handed center fielder. It gives him a small nudge in power and average. Righties don't see much effect in average, but lose a decent amount of power. The park is built for left-handed hitters of all kinds and righties with line-drive bats.

Offense: Seattle was a little below-average offensively. They had a good on-base percentage and good homer power. The Mariners were subpar at hitting for average, but compensated somewhat by having good plate discipline.

The Mariners were a pretty poor running club, losing 68 men on the basepaths while garnering an equally fetid 91 steals.

In addition, the Mariners kicked the tar out of lefties. In fact, they were extremely top-heavy in this regard. Their biggest offensive need is another power bat that can chop up righties. If Eric Anthony can adjust to the league and Edgar Martinez can come back strongly, then the Mariners will be better in this regard. In addition, with Marc Newfield on the horizon, the Mariners' offensive prospects look very good indeed.

Total Offense: 29.3

Pitching: The team had 89 quality starts, tied for second in the AL. Despite the injury to Bosio, there was little to complain about on this front last year.

The bullpen was atrocious, though. Their 4.74 ERA was tied with Pittsburgh for second-worst in baseball. And we don't think that the Rockies should be held 100 percent accountable because their park is – how shall we say it – unique in the way it shapes offense?!

After Norm Charlton went down, the guys brought in to slam the door were handing out latchkeys to burglars. Charlton was very good, converting 18-of-21 save opportunities. The rest of the Mariners' pen converted 53.5 percent of their save opps (23-of-43). That probably meant a two- to four-game swing in the standings right there.

For 1994, the question is, how can Erik Hanson be replaced? Sure there were monetary constraints, and Bobby Ayala has a great arm, but the loss of Hanson and his 22 quality starts will be felt. A replacement-level pitcher should give the Mariners 12-15 quality starts in the same amount of playing time, and that could mean five to seven extra losses for the team. One has to expect that Bosio will get 200+ innings and that Fleming will be better, but one of the kids will have to take two steps forward. Ayala should be better this year, and one of the kids has to be better. Still, the off-season has added questions about the staff's quality, not answered them.

Total Pitching: 38.9

Defense:

Catcher: Former starter Dave Valle was an exceptional defensive catcher with a solid all-around game. Dan Wilson and the backups are a solid question mark.

Pts: 18.7

Infield: Tino Martinez is an average to above-average first baseman with upward potential. The second base situation has not been determined, but we're assuming that Amaral will get the nod here. He is below-average. At third, it'll be the solid Edgar Martinez if he's healthy. Mike Blowers is an adequate replacement.

Omar Vizquel was the crazy glue of this infield and one of the best defensive players in the game, comparing him to Felix Fermin is like comparing Michelangelo's Pieta to a misshapen lump of excrement.

Pts: 24.8

Outfield: Overall, the Mariner outfield had good defensive reputations, but their statistics didn't support them.

Pts: -10.0

Total: 33.5

1994 Personnel

Catcher: The obvious starter from the Mariners' pack of suspects is Dan Wilson. Wilson has great "leadership" skills and good "intangibles," but he's quite bereft of "tangibles." It remains to be seen if he'll be more than a shadow of Dave Valle's ability.

Bench: Bill Haselman is the primary catching bat off the bench. Brian Deak (if resigned), Chris Howard (.320-6-55 at Triple-A), Mackey Sasser and former-Giant rehab case Eric Christopherson make up the other possible scrubs. A sleeper is James Bonnici who could jump from Double-A to the majors if he can hit enough. The depth here looks quite good.

Starter: 0
Bench: B

Infield:
1B: There will be a fight between Tino Martinez and newly acquired Reggie Jefferson. Our money is on Tino because he provides a solid power bat and very nice defense. Jefferson is quite lacking in the latter regard.

2B: Look for Richie Amaral, Anthony Manahan, and Ruben Santana to battle in the spring. Manahan is a Seattle favorite, but Santana and Amaral can play the game better right now. Our money is on Amaral, but his defense is weak and Santana's power could surprise.

3B: If Edgar Martinez is healthy, he'll force Mike Blowers to the bench. End of story. If Edgar isn't 100 percent, you'll probably see Blowers come in against lefties.

SS: The Mariners are very weak at short. Felix Fermin isn't that good and the Mariners aren't deep at short.

DH: Expect Marc Newfield or Reggie Jefferson to see the majority of time here. Because of Newfield's youth, Jefferson will probably get the most ABs. But then again, Newfield is an amazing young hitter.

IF Bench: At first base, Greg Pirkl is probably the only real backup with the retirement of Pete O'Brien. At second, if you see Fernando Vina (.230-4-27 at Triple-A) playing, it means the Mariners are in trouble. Otherwise, look for super-prospect Arquimedez Pozo. If he plays up to his ability, he could be in the majors this year. At third base, the Mariners have only Dale Sveum (.300-6-26 at Triple-A) as insurance. At short, the Mariners have Bobby Holley, 26, (.247-13-66 at Double-A) and nothing else. Simply put, the Mariners need to put some kind of bench together in the spring.

Starters: -2.2
IF Bench: D
Outfield:

LF: Eric Anthony is a solid glove and a decent bat. If he can adjust to the pitching in the AL, he could blossom this year and be a 20-25 HR threat. His plate-discipline is getting much better and this could be his breakthrough year.

CF: We tend to disagree with what the Advocate Ratings say in center field, we believe Ken Griffey is the best outfielder in the American League and he could be the MVP this year.

RF: Jay Buhner's defense may be overrated, but he's a solid all-around performer and is a good reason why the Mariners have one of the best outfields in the game.

Bench: The bench isn't really long on numbers, but there's a decent amount of talent here. First off, don't look at Junior's brother, Craig Griffey. Craig has one talent – speed – and he's almost too old to develop other skills. Marc Newfield is the superstar among this pack. Others who could get some PT include Darren Bragg, Dann Howitt, Quinn Mack, 28, (.308-6-39 at Triple-A), Lee Tinsley and

Brian Turang. These guys all have pretty similar skills, so whomever has the hot spring will be the one to grab the bench spots.

Starters: 53.9
Bench: C

Starting Pitching: The Mariners have three bona-fide starters in Johnson, Bosio and Fleming. The Mariners will rue the day they shipped Erik Hanson out of town, however. The rest of the rotation will have to be filled out with the likes of Jim Converse, John Cummings, Roger Salkeld, and, if they are unlucky, Tim Leary. A real long-shot is Ronnie Villone, another is Craig Clayton.

Front-Line: 95.7
Second-Echelon: C

Relief Pitching: If the Mariners don't re-sign Norm Charlton, they'll blow 35-45 percent of their save opps. Right now, they're planning on putting Bobby Ayala in long relief, keeping an eye toward a future closing role for him (possibly as early as July). The rest of the pen is a bunch of decent unproven arms and a bunch of veterans that can't get outs. Amongst the pack of veterans are Rich DeLucia, Jeff Nelson, Dennis Powell, Ted Power and Dave Wainhouse.

The kids include Travis Buckley, Jeff Darwin, Tim Davis, Reggie Harris, Brad Holman, Kevin King, Tony Phillips, Erik Plantenberg, Makato Suzuki and Mike Walker.

Front-Line: 10.8
Second-Echelon: C

Player Value: 158.2

Farm System: The Mariners are a pretty good organization. They have a good catching prospect in Bonnici and have fine middle infield prospects like Pozo and Santana at second and Alex Rodriguez at short. In the outfield, they only have one prime-timer, Marc Newfield, but he's incredibly gifted. At starter, there aren't any Grade A eggs, but Roger Salkeld, Jim Converse, John Cummings and Ron Villone all have star potential. Reliever is a little more thin, but Jeff Darwin, Tim Davis, Tony Phillips and Makato Suzuki could all do the job. Suzuki could be the next Rob Dibble.

Infield: A
Outfield: C

Starters: B
Relievers: C
Farm Ranking: B

Management and Ownership: The Nintendo people (led by John Ellis) who bought the Mariners are movers and shakers considering their small market. They've made a commitment to Junior and Randy, their two biggest stars, so they at least have the appearance of caring. They also have an idea of what they're doing. They may not be taking the wisest course of action, but at least they have a self-concept and a sense of direction.

GM Woody Woodward oversees an active organization that drafts well; makes an abundance of off-season moves (not much happens during the season); and often holds onto its players (keeping in mind the team's profit-loss statements). Trades like the one for Eric Anthony are a sign of strength, but the virtual giveaway of Erik Hanson was distressing (Bret Boone right now is about as valuable as Bobby Ayala; Dan Wilson had better catch like Johnny Bench to be worth half a season of Hanson). The Reggie Jefferson-Felix Fermin trade may backfire, but still Woodward has to count his pennies carefully.

On the field, the Mariners are well-handled by Piniella. A solid motivator, it's probably not an accident that Ken Griffey slugged .617 last year. It's also probably not an accident that Big Randy got his poop together.

Piniella plays an NL game. He doesn't have much team speed, but he bunts a lot and likes to hit-and-run. With boppers like Buhner and Junior, the team doesn't bunt or run too well, but they put the bat on the ball. He isn't fanatical about platooning, but he isn't afraid to wheel out a pinch hitter in the late innings.

When it comes to pitching, only one thing really distinguishes Sweet Lou: A penchant for working his starters very hard. This may come back to haunt him.

Ownership: C
Front Office: B
Field Management: A
Overall: B

1994 Outlook: The Mariners have many questions regarding their fourth and fifth starters and their bullpen, but their offense and the anchors of their rotation are solid. In the AL

West, that makes them contenders. If they can get a full season out of Tino and Edgar Martinez, plus one of the kids in the rotation and Bobby Ayala comes through, the Mariners could win 95 games. If not, they'll hope to shoot for 85 wins.

TEXAS RANGERS

1993 Outlook: The Rangers were figured to contend in '93, mostly on the strength of their offense. Texas expected big contributions from Canseco and Gonzalez and hoped for a modest recovery from Palmeiro.

The starting pitching was questionable. They were going to have to rely on some youngsters and keep veterans like Nolan Ryan and Charlie Leibrandt healthy.

The bullpen looked strong with Henke closing and Rogers and Whiteside assisting.

Basically, little turned out as expected.

April 11-10 (11-10, 3 games back)

The Rangers jumped out to an early lead, going 6-1 against East Coast Lily-livers Baltimore and Boston. The starters were on fire; Kenny Rogers, who hadn't started in two years, and Kevin Brown threw quality wins, while veterans Ryan and Leibrandt combined for 13 innings without an earned run in their first starts. Things were looking good!

But a trip through Detroit, Milwaukee and Toronto cooled them down and Texas went into a 5-9 slump to finish the month three games behind the Angels.

Brown, Rogers and Leibrandt combined for 11 QS and went 7-3, which was most promising. Craig Lefferts, however, went 1-4 on his way to the scrap heap and Nolan suffered his first injury, torn cartilage in his knee.

The offense was also a mixed big. Dean Palmer slugged .686 with seven dingers and 15 RBI for the month. Gonzales hit .321, also with seven homers, and Ivan Rodriguez hit .349 with 19 RBI. On the other hand, Doug Strange (.198) and Palmeiro (.183) were pathetic and Canseco (.256) was mediocre.

May 14-14 (25-24, 2.5 games back)

Texas again started well, paying Milwaukee and Toronto back and going 6-2. On the 10th, they were within 1.5 games and looking like they were ready to take off. But a dismal 1-6 stretch on the road, including a sweep in 'Lily-livered' Boston, ended the month and brought them back to earth.

Leibrandt still looked strong, going 3-1, but Lefferts was shelled out of existence, Rogers went 1-3 and Nolan injured his hip in his first start back.

Palmeiro awoke from the dead and hit .286, but he hadn't quite hit his stride yet. Canseco had ended his season and pitching career on May 29, which was a nice follow-up to his May 26 head-butt (butt-head?) dinger. And Gonzalez continued his reign of terror slugging .773 with 17 RBI.

At the end of May, the Rangers looked like they could go either way.

June 10-16 (35-40, 4 games back)

Halfway through June, you still couldn't tell. But once again, a disastrous 2-8 road trip seemed to supply the answers. On the 16th, they arrived in Anaheim and laid down for the Angels, 5-2. The next night they ripped Sanderson and half the bullpen for 18 runs on 18 hits, but they should've saved some of those. They split the remaining two games and headed off to consecutive sweeps at the hands of the Mariners and White Sox.

They returned home at their lowest point, 6.5 games behind Chicago, and looking like they may never win another road game.

The only bright spot in this whole affair was the emergence of Palmeiro. He hit .348 with six homers and 14 RBI.

July 17-11 (52-51, 5.5 games back)

The Rangers answered the critics, going on a 12-2 tear before the All-Star break (including three wins at the end of June). At the break, they were one game behind Chicago. Most of the division was in the hunt, though, as five teams were within two games.

And Texas seemed to be sending a message in the first game back. They hammered Mike Moore for 6 ER in the first 2 innings and went on to post 12-7 and 9-6 victories over Detroit.

But the Tigers took the last two and sent the Rangers on another .500 stumble to finish the month. Meanwhile, the Sox couldn't lose and the Rangers ended up 5.5 games out.

Still, it was an impressive month. Texas scored 162 runs, thanks primarily to Palmeiro and Gonzalez, who combined for 21 HR and

63 RBI. Rafael alone slugged .852 with 13 doubles, 11 HR and 34 RBI. Unbelievable!

Rogers snapped out of a slump to lead the staff with a 3-0 record and 23/8 K/W. Roger Pavlik also made his presence felt, going 3-1.

August 17-12 (69-63, 5.5 games back)

The scene was set for the August 2 showdown with the Sox in Arlington. Texas was 6.5 out and needed to make up some ground.

The first two games were slugfests; Texas rallied in the bottom of the ninth to win the first 9-8 and Chicago repaid them the next night in an 11-6 drubbing. But Ryan, Brown and Henke held the Sox to three runs in the final two games, winning both and pulling Texas back into the race, 4.5 games out.

They went 14-10 for the rest of the month, primarily against Eastern Division opponents, and fought their way into second place, but Chicago was still a game better and increased their lead to 5.5 games.

Rogers and Pavlik again led the staff, combining for a 9-2 record, but the Rangers lost Leibrandt for two weeks to tendinitis and Ryan for good to a rib cage muscle injury.

The team was playing well, but the staff didn't look poised for a stretch run.

Sept./Oct. 17-13 (86-76, 8 games back)

But that didn't prove to be the case. The staff posted a 3.95 ERA, its lowest since April. Brown went 5-1 and Pavlik 3-0 to compensate for Ryan and Leibrandt, but the Rangers' offensive production fell at the same time. They hit 26 HRs, their lowest total since April, and slugged .418, their lowest all year.

They played well enough to claim second place, but Chicago proved too powerful down the stretch to be overtaken.

Park Effect. Venerable Arlington Stadium will be relegated to parking lot status this year, so any discussion of its park effects won't apply the Rangers' of the future. But for past reference, it generally lowered run production and hits. Homers were down three percent and righties suffered the worst disadvantage with a six percent reduction.

Little can be said of the new stadium, the Ball Park at Arlington, other than it has an extremely lame name. You can expect the park to be generous to right-handed power hitters like Dean Palmer and Juan Gonzalez.

Offense. The Rangers got plenty of production out of their sluggers last year, scoring 835 runs and smashing a league-high 181 dingers. They also tied the Yanks for the highest batting average with .279, but they were held back by a .329 OBP. The only thing they lacked, of course, were walks; they had only 483, the second lowest total in the league.

The effect that the Clark/Palmeiro fiasco will have on Texas' production may be this offseason's hottest debate. Clark is virtually guaranteed not to hit 37 homers this year, but then, Palmeiro may not either.

One thing is sure; Texas' running game was fairly bland last year and Clark will do nothing to improve it. Despite Palmeiro's 22 SB out of 25 attempts (88 percent), Texas stole 113 bases and were successful only 63 percent of the time. Clark *will not* steal 22 bases.

OK, two things are sure; Canseco *will not* pitch this year, so he may stay healthy and be able to pick up the slack for Clark.

Total Offense: 76.0

Pitching. The Rangers' rotation was hampered last year by injuries to their veterans and a slow starting youngster. They still managed to go 63-59 with a 4.39 ERA, which was slightly better than average.

They have a good core of three young, solid starters, but they'll have rely on some prospects and perhaps Charlie Leibrandt this year to fill the holes.

The Rangers' bullpen was already stocked with prospects last year and their inexperience showed. But they combined for 45 saves, 40 of which were veteran Tom Henke's, and kept 71 percent of their inherited runners from scoring. With more experience this year, the bullpen should be solid.

Total Pitching: 23.4

Defense:

Infield: Rafael Palmiero was decent at first and Doug Strange was league average. At short, Manuel Lee was exceptional, but Dean Palmer was lackluster at third.

Pts: 23.2

Outfield: In the outfield, Juan Gonzalez was OK in left, David Hulse was OK in center, but the mishmash of right fielders were inadequate.

Pts: 6.1

Catcher: Pudge Rodriguez is one of the best catchers in the game defensively.
Pts: 18.6
Total Defense: 47.9

1994 Personnel:
Catcher: Pudge Rodriguez will start at catcher, of course.
Bench: John Russell and Geno Petralli will be inadequate, but will backup.
Starter: 20.9
Bench: C-

Infield:
1B: Will Clark takes over at first. Will his bat and glove return?
2B: If Jeff Frye can get healthy, he'll try to get second back. Look for Doug Strange and an assortment of characters here.
3B: Dean Palmer is the Dean at third here.
SS: Benji Gil should have a good chance at getting this job.
DH: Dan Peltier, Steve Balboni will backup the handsome, muscular moron, Canseco.
IF Bench: Billy Ripken, Jeff Huson, Manuel Lee, Mario Diaz, Jon Shave and a pack of kids will take up the slack.
Starters: 43.3
Bench: C

Outfield
LF: Juan's the one.
CF: Look for Hulse, or maybe Rob Ducey.
RF: Dan Peltier, Gary Redus, Terrell Lowery or some other scrub could get the job.
Bench: Doug Dascenzo, Greer and Donald Harris could backup.
Starters: 48.1
Bench: D

Starting Pitching: Kevin Brown, Kenny Rogers and Roger Pavlik have the 1-3 slots locked up. Look for Rick Helling, Charlie Leibrandt, Dan Smith, Hector Fajardo, Daryl Henderson or Bruce Hurst to fight for the last two slots.
Front-Line: 68.3
Second-Echelon: B-

Relief Pitching: Henke will close and Whiteside will setup. Rick Honeycutt will get key lefties out. Jeff Bronkey, Cris Carpenter, Todd Burns, Patterson, Dreyer, Duff Brumley, Scott Eyre and possibly 95-MPH monster Julio Santana to get shots at 'pen jobs.
Front-Line: 14.3
Second-Echelon: C+

Player Value: 194.9

Farm System: The Rangers' farm system is rather thin. Terrell Lowery and Benji Gil are the only two position players who are both young and have good ability. Duff Brumley, Hector Fajardo, Dan Smith, Oliver, John Dettmer and Scott Eyre are good starting candidates. Keep an eye on this Santana kid in the low minors: He's got a marvelous fastball.
Infield: C-
Outfield: D
Starters: B
Relievers: C
Farm Ranking: C

Management and Ownership: George W. Bush and his partners will spend money. They want to put a winning product on the field and they, along with GM Tom Grieve, have a decent track record of signing and developing talent. The three big, young stars on this team: Gonzalez, Rodriguez and Palmer (soon to be including Gil), are all home grown; as are Kenny Rogers, Kevin Brown and Roger Pavlik. Right now, however, the team is thin on farm talent. They're pretty rich in the majors, though. Grieve is not a man inclined to making all the moves. When he does, they're not always the wisest. Giving up Kurt Miller for Cris Carpenter being an example. Still, he doesn't do too much and that's good.

Field manager Kevin Kennedy needs one more year on the battlefield before we can give him a proper grade. But as of right now, he looks like a decent one. His young players flourished behind him and that's a sign that his years of work in the Dodger farm system have instilled upon him the skills it takes to work with the little 'uns.
Ownership: B-
Front Office: C
Field Management: B-
Overall: C+

1994 Outlook: In the weak AL West, the Rangers and the Mariners are the teams to beat. Neither team is a power house, but whoever gets out of the gate the fastest will probably take the division. Now, flip your coin.

Team Essays – NL East

Atlanta Braves

1993 Outlook: The Atlanta Braves were expected to dominate. *End of story.* They had great pitching, a solid offense and a good defense. They were perceived as being flawless ... 100-105 wins were considered in the bank. In addition, it was expected that no team in the division had the firepower to match them. Anything short of a World Series victory would have been seen as failure by the world-at-large.

April 12-13 (12-13, 3.5 games back)
As the season opened, the pitching performed as advertised, but the strong lineup didn't. The Braves opened up with nine-straight quality starts. Their ERA for the month was 2.91, yet they were a game under .500. John Smoltz lost 1-0 twice in the span of 10 days (Smoltz was 2-2, 2.15 for April), Steve Avery was 1-2, 2.75, Maddux was 2-2, 3.09. Only Tom Glavine held up, going 3-0, 2.81, but he was getting unbelievable run-support. The team hit .229 and slugged .336. Pendleton hit .158 and Gant hit .206. Not to be outdone, Justice hit .157 with a .326 SL%. Only Blauser (.330) and Berryhill (.325, .575 SL%) were keeping the Braves from being shutout daily.

May 29-23 (17-10, 4.5 games back)
The pitching staff's output dropped a bit. Smoltz had a 5.54 ERA, but Avery, Glavine and Maddux went 11-3. On May 6-9, Atlanta showed the Rockies what a decent offense could do in Mile-High. The Braves scored 46 runs in a four-game sweep and held the Rocks to a mere 22 runs. The Braves pulled to 18-15 and were two games out. On May 15, they posted a 5-3 win over Curt Schilling and pulled within 1.5 games. It was as close as they'd get all month. During the month, Gant went berzerk, hitting .309 with seven homers and a .617 SL%. Justice also hit eight HR and slugged .573. The duo combined for 45 RBI.

June 44-34 (15-11, 7.5 games back)
The offense again fell to earth, posting a .306 OBP and a .384 S%. Glavine, Maddux and Smoltz were a combined 7-7, but posted a sparkling 2.50 ERA. Smoltz allowed 6 runs (5 earned) in his three losses. Avery was 4-0, 2.16. In all, the Braves fired 20 quality starts, going a pretty weak 13-7 in those games. Gant slugged .586 and drove in 17 runs and Pendleton rallied to hit .324-3-11, but the rest of the team's bats were AWOL.

July 63-43 (19-9, 7.5 games back)
For the first time all season, the fire seemed to be back. Sure, there was a fire in Fulton-County in late July the day McGriff came over, but that lasted only about four or five hours. The conflagration the team was to fuel would cast a pall over the entire NL until season's end.

The Braves started off 10-7 for the month, playing their (for this season) usual lackluster ball. Freddie M. came over and the Braves went on a 9-2 run to end the month. Mr. McGriff only hit seven HR and had 12 RBI in his 11 games. The bullpen saw some upheaval as Stanton posted a 5.59 ERA and Greg McMichael nailed down his first two saves, flashing a sterling 1.69 ERA and a 23/3 K/BB ratio. The offense came alive, Gant, Justice and Pendleton hit 19 homers and drove in 63 runs between them. Justice slugged .643!

August 82-50 (19-7, 3.5 games back)
On August 7, the Braves were 9.5 games back. On August 11, they were dead: 9 games back. But the Braves refused to die. From August 12-22, they ran off a 10-2 record, outscoring the opposition 71-36. On August 23, the Braves and the Giants squared off at Candlestick. The rotations were set as follows: Avery vs. Trevor Wilson on Monday; Glavine vs. Buddy Hickerson on Tuesday; and, in the Wednesday show-down, Maddux vs. Swift.

Jeff Blauser went 3-for-5 with two doubles and a homer in game one as Avery gutted out an eight-hit 5-3 win. Robby Thompson's fifth-inning homer keyed a three-run inning for San Fran., this raised tensions to nail-biting levels, but Bonds, Williams and Clark were held to three scratch singles by the baby-faced lefty. And this effectively shut down the Giants.

In game two, Pendleton, Justice and Gant homered and the Braves bullpen held, as Glavine beat Hickerson 6-4, for his 15th win. Atlanta held a 5-1 lead by the sixth and didn't really look in trouble throughout the evening.

Game three was a joke, McGriff and Justice hit back-to-back dingers in the first, then repeated the feat in the fifth! While this was going on, Maddux was taking a no-hitter into the sixth. Maddux went eight one-run innings and McMichael struck out the side in the ninth to complete the sweep. The Giants' 4.5 game lead held until the final day of the month when the two teams met at Fulton-County for their final three games of the season. Game one was a rematch between Maddux and 17-game winner Swift. Bonds managed just one single off Maddux in SF and he wasn't to be denied in Atlanta. He went 4-for-4 with a homer and two steals. But Atlanta took a 5-1 lead in the fourth and Maddux cruised along, picking up a complete-game 8-2 win. The lead was 3.5 games.

Sept./Oct. 104-58 (22-8, 1 game ahead)
September 1, seemed a day rife with harbingers of doom for Atlanta. John "tough-luck" Smoltz was the starter and Buddy Hickerson was going for the Giants. Hickerson was at his peak and Smoltz was wild in the strike zone, so it was an even matchup. Hickerson tired in the sixth and was yanked losing 2-1. In the seventh, Smoltz, struggling at the 110+ pitch mark, allowed the tying run and wasn't brought out for the eighth. Mark Wohlers came in. In the ninth, John Patterson, recently recalled from Triple-A swung and knocked Wohlers' fastball down the right-field line and into the night to give the Giants a 3-2 win and push the lead back to 5.5 games.

The next night seemed like a dream: Giant Killer Avery was gone after 3.2 innings having given up a homer to Bonds and a double to Williams. But the bullpen pitched over five scoreless innings and Jeff Brantley gave up three runs and recorded only one out, spoiling John Burkett's chance at winning his 19th game. The Giants were reeling.

On 9/9, Kent Mercker threw six no-hit innings over SD, winning 1-0. St. Louis beat San Fran. 9-4 and the lead was one game. On the 11th, Smoltz stomped Andy Benes 13-1 and Tewksbury outdueled Swift 3-1. The teams had swapped spots and Atlanta had a one-game lead. By the 17th, the Braves were up by four games. On the 22nd, Billy Swift overcame a 10-K performance by Pete Harnisch and beat the Astros 1-0, pulling the Giants within 2.5.

On the 28th, the spurned Harnisch threw a five-hitter over 8.2, posting a 5-2 victory over Atlanta. The Giants and the Braves were in a flat-footed tie with 100-57 records. On 9/29, Glavine nailed his 21st win, pasting Doug Drabek, 6-3. Meanwhile, phenom Salomon Torres tasted the steely blade of rejection via Darryl Boston's two HR as the Rockies clobbered him for four runs in under three innings.

The next day, Smoltz was lit up for six runs in four innings, losing his 11th, while Swift fired a two-hitter over seven, pulling the teams back into a tie. On October 1, Steve Avery picked up his 18th win, striking out seven and scattering five hits over eight innings, besting Colorado 7-4. The San Francisco bullpen barely out-lasted LA 8-7 behind Bonds' incredible 3-for-3, seven RBI night. On 10/2, Atlanta pounced on Colorado 10-1 behind Maddux's 20th win. The Giants thumped Orel Hershiser and the tie remained with one game left to play.

Most everyone following the race remembers October 3. It was a lazy Sunday and the Advocate crew was busy talking on the phone while watching the Giants dismantling on ESPN. The cursed LA curtain calls were finally welcomed by non-Giant fans around the NL. The Dodgers got their revenge for '91. Piazza's homers anointed him as the rookie sensation of 1993. It wasn't surprising that his dynamic play would highlight a game which his team dominated.

In retrospect, the Braves had done what no one had dreamed was possible in June. They had gone 50-18 down the stretch to overtake a team that had a nine-game lead on August 11. ... A team that won 103 games. Sure they got creamed in the playoffs, but they've got to work on something for 1994, don't they?

Park Effects: Fulton-County Stadium is obviously a hitter's park, boosting runs-scored by 10 percent from 1991-1993. Over the last three years, it has boosted batting average by 6 percent, doubles by 2 percent and homers by 14 percent. Fulton-County isn't very kind to Deion, it cuts triples by 30 percent.

Errors are way up here. Infield errors are up 22 percent and all errors are 22 percent above league-average.

The park pumps up righties a bit, but gives lefties 28 percent more homers and boosts their average by 8 percent.

Offense: Last year, the Braves had an average offense. Their 767 runs-scored was third-best in the league, but if you adjust for their park, the Braves probably were closer to 730 runs. They didn't hit for average that well and they didn't hit doubles, but they had good HR power, good speed and drew a decent amount of walks.

The Braves were much more adept at clubbing lefties. The addition of McGriff and the possibility of some of the other kids getting playing time will help balance their lineup.

The primary offensive needs of the Braves are getting rid of their deadwood at catcher and third. The release of Olson is a step in the right direction on the first count.
Total Offense: -13.9

Pitching: The pitching was across-the-board-exceptional. The Big Four were about as good as any four-man rotation in baseball history. The performance-level they set from 1991-1993 is as good as that of the Indians' staff of the early-to-mid 1950s and there doesn't seem to be any reason why they can't continue to dominate (they reeled off 107 quality starts last year – seven QS more than the runner-up Astros – and almost 25 percent more than the NL average in a park tilting clearly in favor of the hitter!).

In addition, with Kent Mercker and all the young starting prospects in the minors, there's no reason the Braves couldn't come up with a quality fifth starter.

The bullpen was also very good. The sole weakness seems to be the team's lack of faith in any of the closer candidates they have. The Braves also let a rather high 37.4 percent of inherited runners score (NL average was 32.3), leading to about eight extra runs-allowed. All in all, there is nothing wrong with the Braves pitching. They might want to unload a lot for a front-line closer, but they don't really need one.
Total Pitching: 190.8

Defense:
Catcher: The tandem of Berryhill and Olson effectively cancelled each other out. Olson had no arm, but called an adequate game and was relatively sure-handed. Berryhill called an excellent game and couldn't throw anyone out.
Pts: 0.1

Infield: At first, McGriff and Bream were solid above-average defensively. At second base, Lemke was one of the league's top five or six defenders.

Pendleton slipped somewhat at third, but still played very good defense.

At short, Jeff Blauser made two giant strides forward and moved from solid below-average to one of the league's best.
Pts: 32.3

Outfield: In left, Gant was very solid. In center, Otis led the charge with very solid defense, but Deion wasn't a slouch, either. Combined, they were one of the best CF units in the league. Justice was quite nice in right.
Pts: 24.2
Total Defense: 56.5

1994 Personnel

Catcher: We are talking about the Braves, here, so anything is possible. If the Braves do the smart thing (and they're 90 percent there by dumping Berryhill and Olson), Lopez will be the starter, or platoon with Charlie O'Brien. Note there is no value given for starting catchers, but Lopez could have a 15-25 point season if he gets 110+ starts.

Bench: Possible backups include Tyler Houston, 23, (.279-5-33 at Double-A) and old Mr. Standby himself, Jerry Willard (.319-8-44 at Triple-A). Whether Frankie Cabrera will have a seat on the bench will depend on the caprice of Ted Turner and John Schuerholz.
Starters: 0
Bench: C

Infield:
1B: It looks like the Braves are going to be perfectly willing to fork over the $$$ to keep Fred McGriff, leaving Ryan Klesko as a reserve 1B/OF. McGriff is one of the best in the biz, so it obviously isn't going to hurt the team to keep him. If McGriff were to get hurt, Ryan K. could detonate on the league.

2B: The Braves are kinda high on Ramon Caraballo, but he stinks. Mark Lemke is a solid glove and he hits way better than Caraballo would if Ramon got a full-time job. Unless Chipper gets a starting role, it has to be Lemke.

3B: Barring injury induced by having a keister the size of Botswana, Terry Pendleton will get every chance to show off his svelte, girlish figure at third base. Look for continued decline in ability.

SS: The only question here is "Wither Chipper?" What is the team going to do with their best prospect? Does he get any playing time at short? At third? At second? The Braves move like the Soviets did during the Cold War: slowly, suspiciously and mysteriously, like a bear. Expect Blauser to get all the PT, but something goofy could happen.

IF Bench: At first, look for Tim Gillis, 26, (.251-14-62 at Double-A) and Boi Rodriguez, 28, (.267-10-22) as possible scrubs. Jose Olmeda and Tony Graffagnino are sleepers at second. Graffagnino looks like a beauty, but he probably won't make it to the varsity this year; Olmeda, 26, (.279-9-51 at Double-A) is not "da thang" like Tony G., but he could see some ML PT. At third base, the best bets look to be Jose Oliva or Bill Pecota (.323-0-5). At short, Rafael Belliard or Mike Mordecai, 26, (.268-2-14 at Triple-A) could play. Of course, Chipper could play anywhere.

Starters: 85.4
Bench: A

Outfield:

LF: Ronnie Gant had a nice comeback last year and should place himself higher among league left fielders. He's not an exceptional player in any aspect (except maybe power), but he is above-average across-the-board.

CF: Deion Sanders' rating is a bit misleading. If he can play at his 1993 level for a full season, he'll be worth anther 5-10 points. This is the year to determine whether Deion is anything more than a platoon OF.

RF: David Justice has done it once, if he can hit 30+ HR again, he'll remain at his lofty perch among the best right fielders in the NL.

Bench: The Braves bench is a combination of adequate replacements and star-caliber rooks.

Jarvis Brown, Dave Gallagher (.274-6-28), Troy Hughes, Mike Kelly, Tony Tarasco all were on the 40-man roster and all could see time backing up the stars.

Starters: 48.0
Bench: B

Starting Pitching: Health permitting, Avery, Glavine, Maddux and Smoltz have their rotation slots etched in marble. With the trade of Pete Smith, look for Kent Mercker to get dibs on the fifth-starter's job. The other real candidate would probably be Terrell Wade, but he probably needs some time at AAA. All the other decent pitching prospects, except for Brian Bark (12-9, 3.67 110/72 K/BB at AAA) will start off as AA fodder.

Front-Line: 155.4
Second-Echelon: B

Relief Pitching: Greg McMichael, Mike Stanton, Mark Wohlers and Steve Bedrosian are obvious candidates for the first four slots of the bullpen.

Pedro Borbon, Mike Birkbeck (13-8, 3.11 136/41 K/W at AAA – he's really a starter, but he'd never be one for Atlanta), Marvin Freeman, Milt Hill, Mike Hostetler (8-5, 2.72 105/36 K/W at AAA), Judd Johnson (4-2, 2.65 55/22 K/W at AAA), Mike Loynd (8-5, 3.85 85/34 K/W at AAA), Dale Polley (8-1, 4.12 66/21 K/W at AA) and Don Strange (3.88 ERA 34/19 K/W at AAA) round out the rest of the pack.

Borbon, Hill and Freeman all have ML experience so they'll get dibs on PT.

Front-Line: 44.4
Second-Echelon: B

Player Value: 333.2

Farm System: It kinda goes without saying that the Braves are the envy of baseball. There's maybe one or two organizations that can rival them in pure talent, but it would be hard to find any one team that has more players who could be stars (maybe the Expos). The Braves' strengths are position players. There is at least one nice prospect at each infield position. Javy Lopez is a brilliant young catcher; first baseman Ryan Klesko and shortstops Chipper Jones and Glenn Williams are only beautiful. And Jose Oliva and Tony Graffagnino are both nice at third and second, respectively. In the outfield, Tarasco and Kelly are on the horizon, with a pair of diaper dandies, Damon Hollins and Andre King waiting in the low minors.

Pitching is a bit thinner, but with Grade A starter Terrell Wade, Grade A reliever Carl Schutz and a nice supporting cast of rotation and bullpen possibilities, the "B-Team" could really shine if pressed.

Infield: A
Outfield: A
Starters: B
Relievers: C
Farm Ranking: A

Management and Ownership: Ted Turner has made an about-face from his past as "Captain Outrageous," (could Jane Fonda really be a mellowing influence on him?! If so, that's amazing, eh?). He still meddles a lot in team affairs (Deion the Brave, we wish we hardly knew ye), but he isn't anywhere near as bad as he used to be. Turner isn't afraid to spend money (Greg Maddux, Fred McGriff); he surrounds himself with good management personnel; and he funds a minor-league system par excellence.

GM John Schuerholz oversees a pretty good team. They have a decent lineup and a pitching staff of a quality that hasn't been seen since possibly the "Hitless Wonder" White Sox teams of the turn of the century.

The weakness of the team is that it's so good, management stays on the treadmill during bad times rather than acting quickly and decisively to rectify problems.

Bobby Cox and Schuerholz were very slow to use the farm system to plug leaks in the infield and at catcher. It's obvious that Klesko and Lopez should have gotten lots of PT (in Ryan's case, at least until the McGriff trade).

Cox is a rather average manager regarding the running game. His team has decent speed, settling for an average number of steals at a good percentage. Cox's team bunts an average amount, but isn't too good at it. The team doesn't hit-and-run much, but they can execute the play very well when they have to.

Cox likes a set lineup. He doesn't fudge much with platooning, preferring to keep his regulars in as much as possible. He doesn't pinch hit super frequently, but he's gonzo about substituting runners late in the game.

When it comes to pitching, Cox is rather moderate, he doesn't pull starters at the start of trouble, but he doesn't wait until they've given up eight earnies, either. Despite his fine pitching staff, he doesn't work the starters inordinately hard and he doesn't work his 'pen that hard either.

Cox is a conservative guy, he doesn't like to make waves and he doesn't like anything to ruffle his calm. This might have worked against the Braves down the stretch last year, they need to work their kids in, or the Braves'll waste that beautiful talent they have in such bounteous quantity.

Ownership: B
Front Office: B+
Field Management: B-
Overall: B

1994 Outlook: If anything, the Braves are even stronger for 1994. They have all their pitching (probably substituting the most excellent Kent Mercker for the blechy Pete Smith in the No. 5 hole); they are installing Javy Lopez in at catcher; McGriff will play first all year; and there's tons of help waiting in the wings if injuries should hit. The Braves should win 95 games ... with an *insignificant* amount of luck, that number could be 110.

FLORIDA MARLINS

1993 Outlook: Anything the Marlins could do (except win the pennant, or 95 games) would have been considered under the realm of possibility. Everyone fully expected them to finish in last place, but a surprising showing wouldn't have been a shock: The Marlins showed quite a bit of moxie when they picked their players during the Expansion Draft. These guys showed they had a clue about talent and if they could teach that talent, then they could do some damage in the NL East.

April 10-13 (10-13, 7.5 games back)
Florida won on opening day in dramatic fashion against L.A., but promptly fell into the toilet. After dropping to 5-11, the Marlins went on a mini-tear of 5-1. The staff displayed amazing poise, reeling off quality performances and flashing a respectable 3.63 ERA. The offense hit 10 homers. The Orioles hit only 11 in April, but they averaged over 29 per month from May-October. The Marlins hit 10 homers in May *and* Sept./Oct. and averaged only 17 homers a month from May on. Their April .329 SL% demonstrated what their weakness would be in 1993.

May 21-28 (11-15, 13 games back)
The pitching deteriorated as their ERA rose

to 4.06, but again the offense was the problem as anti-stallions like Destrade – .202 B.A., .293 SL% – led the charge. Chuck Carr played like he was on a mission (for him at least) getting on base at a .388 clip and banging home 18 RBI (44 percent of his season's total!); in addition, Walt Weiss had a .423 OBP and a .333 B.A! Benny Santiago kept the flag flying for Tony-Pena wannabes, proudly flaunting his .189 B.A.

June 34-42 (13-14, 17.5 games back)

Santiago rallied, posting unbelievable an .281 B.A. and a .354 OBP with a .472 SL%! The pitching was nothing short of very purty. Chris Hammond justified his expansion draft choice, using his slider to compile a 6-0, 2.53 log. Charlie Hough flashed a nice 2.48 ERA, but was only 1-2. In all, the team ERA was 3.39. The offense slugged .403! This would be only the second time the team's SL% would be over .380. Orestes Destrade hit .316 and slugged .531; Bret Barberie hit .312 with a .407 OBP and Conine had a .369 OBP with a nice .469 SL%. All in all, things were looking really nice for the new kids. Could they top .500 (or get 75+ wins, at least?)?

July 43-60 (9-19, 22 games back)
August 55-76 (12-16, 26.5 games back)
Sept./Oct. 64-98 (9-18, 33 games back)

In July, the wheels came off the snake; the skin came off the wagon; the wings came off the boat and the plane got a big hole below the water-line. Well, you know what we mean: The Marlins played like an expansion club.

Their 30-49 crawl from July through season's end pushed them down. The Rockies finished 31-28 from August through October to give them three more wins than their Floridian brethren. The Marlins ERA in the second half rose to 4.46 (pre-break 3.87); their OBP dropped 17 points (from .322 down to .305) and their slugging dropped to .335 from .357. That's an offensive drop of between 12 to 14 percent: the difference between finishing first in runs and finishing eighth.

Park Effects: Joe Robbie Stadium has only been in the bigs for one year, so we don't have the most reliable data in the world.

In 1993, the Marlins' park increased runs by 5 percent. It increased B.A. by 2 percent, doubles by 1 percent and was neutral in allowing homers. It suppressed triples by 9 percent.

Joe Robbie increased errors by 12 overall percent last year and by 24 percent in the infield.

Apparently the park favors lefties, giving them 6 percent edges in homers and average. Righties lose a bit off their average and 5 percent off their HR.

Offense: In a word, their offense is terrible. The Marlins don't reach base. Their .314 OBP was the third worst in baseball (only the Mets and San Diego were worse). To top it off, they have absolutely no power. Their .346 slugging percentage was the worst in baseball by 32 points! Finally, despite having Chuck Carr, they have little in the way of a running game.

The Marlins scored 91 fewer runs -- 581 -- than the second-worst team in baseball (the Mets with 672 runs). But base-running is insignificant. The bottom line is this team can't steal first and it can't drive in the paltry few hitters that reach base.

The Marlins' front-line prospects look like they can hit some homers. That, and having Gary Sheffield for a year, can address a good-deal of the power shortcomings. The problem is that it doesn't like these kids are going to get on base.

Pitching: The Marlins had a mediocre rotation and a pretty decent bullpen, headed by one of the top closers in the game. It's hard to find the ace of this staff, or the chump. All the pitchers had bad records and ERAs in the low-to-mid-four range. The staff only completed four games and the entire pitching staff collapsed in the second half (3.87 ERA before break, 4.46 ERA after). Charlie Hough was in his late 40s and two of the remaining starters (Bowen and Hammond) had never pitched more than 150 innings in the majors before, so stamina was obviously a question. In addition, the team allowed a ton of walks (an NL-worst 598). They were an average power-pitching staff.

The pen, headed by Bryan Harvey, was quite impressive. They were pretty much responsible for the walks-allowed problem (if you remove Harvey, the bullpen allowed 4.55 BB/9IP), but they were tough to hit, converted their saves and stranded the runners the starters left on base.

The rotation could get immediate help in 1994 because there are several kids poised to make the club with the potential to dominate.

There are major questions about Harvey's whereabouts in 1994. Of course they don't have a replacement for him, but the Marlins do have a couple of relief candidates on the farm that could help this year.

Defense:

Catcher: Santiago's arm is slipping bigtime, but it's still OK. The rest of his game has never been that great, but it was adequate in 1993. The backups didn't get enough PT to really judge.
Pts: 4.8

Infield: Destrade can't hit, but he's an adequate defensive first baseman. At second, Barberie is excellent.

At third base, Magadan was surprisingly solid, but Gary Sheffield redefined disgraceful, negating Magadan's decent fielding.

At shortstop, Walt Weiss returned to post solid work.
Pts: 16.1

Outfield: Conine was atrocious in, posting the worst left-field defensive numbers in baseball. In center, Chuck Carr's excellent throwing arm allowed him to post adequate numbers. Darrell Whitmore's excellent throwing arm helped cancel out his relative inexperience in right.
Pts: -5.9
Total: 15.0

1994 Outlook:

Catcher: The Marlins don't like it, but they're stuck with Benito as their starter. Thing is, it looks like his skills are deteriorating to the level of "Il Duce."

Bench: Ron Tingley, Greg O'Halloran (.267-3-35) and Rob Natal are the catch-and-throw portion of the Marlins bench. Natal and Terry McGriff (.345-7-55 at Triple-A) and Mark Skeels (though it's unlikely Skeels will get an ML job this year) are the hitters. Anyone at this position is just a holding action for Charles Johnson, however. Johnson could be in the majors by season's end.
Starters: -1.0
Bench: B

Infield:
1B: Orestes Destrade was a pretty big disappointment last year, so it's quite possible that Greg Colbrunn and possibly Jeff Conine will get a shot at supplanting Orestes this year.

2B: If he's healthy, look for Bret Barberie to hog up most of the playing time. He still hasn't shown everything in his arsenal (even though he's shown enough for us).

3B: Florida fave Dave Magadan is back and he should provide workman-like play at third base.

SS: With the loss of Walt Weiss, look for Kurt Abbott to get the biggest shot at winning the position. After that there's a melange of possibilities ... none of them nice.

IF Bench:

At first, John Toale is an extreme long-shot as a backup. At second base, Alex Arias and Rich Renteria and (if he can develop) Ramon Martinez will get reserve time. It's quite possible that we'll see new OF Gary Sheffield at third in a pinch, otherwise we'll see the usual mix of infielders. At short, look for lifelong bench banditos Al Pedrique and Gus Polidor as reserves. This is a weak bench, ladies and gentlemen. The Marlins have little behind their front-line talent.
Starters: 8.5
Bench: D

Outfield:
LF: Jeff Conine must improve. His offense was OK, but his fielding was awful. He has the athleticism and ability to hit much better. He's like an NL version of J.T. Snow, he can be much better this year. ... He has to be if he's going to hand over the mantle of decided non-greatness to some other schmuck.

CF: Chuck Carr is seen as a holding action until some of the kids are ready, but from what we've seen, none of them will be by this spring. He sure as hell isn't much of a player (unless you think baserunning is the entire game of baseball), but he's not the worst player in this outfield.

RF: At first there was been talk of Gary Sheffield in left field, but with his good throwing arm, it might not be a bad idea to stick him in right. Sheffield, of course, isn't happy about being shifted from the infield, but the Marlins don't like to have their players caught driving under the influence, so the ill feelings wash out. In this case, the shift might be for the best as Sheffield's defense was terrible last year. Maybe he can concentrate on hitting and whack like mad.

Bench: The Marlins are extremely top-heavy with good, unexceptional prospects. Carl Everett, Nigel Wilson and Darryl Whitmore immediately come to mind as reserves, but one or two of them will probably start at Triple-A. Geronimo Berroa, Peewee Briley, Tim Clark, Matias Carrillo (.255-0-3?! why even bother with this guy? Oh, well ...), Henry Cotto-Cheese, Monty Fariss, Scott Pose and Jesus Tavarez are also possibilities. Junior Felix fans: rest assured, your beloved redefined "jake" during his Marlins career, so he is redefining "released" now.

Starters: 10.6
Bench: C

Starting Pitching: Luis Aquino may be back. Ryan Bowen and Chris Hammond will get two spots and look for Pat Rapp and David Weathers to fight for two others. Lest we forget, there's also the crafty veteran, Charlie Hough. Second-echelon possibilities include Robb Nen and Kurt Miller. The team is long on good possibilities, but short on established talent.

Front-Line: 15.8
Second-Echelon: B

Relief Pitching: The Marlins still haven't dished off Brian Harvey, so are we (un)safe in assuming he'll be the closer? Rich Rodriguez, Matt Turner and Richie Lewis will get first shots at the other slots. John Johnstone, Vic Darensbourg, Brian Drahman, Joe Klink, Kip Yaughn and Mike Myers also should get consideration. Keep your eye on Darensbourg, he could be a relief ace by 1995.

Front-Line: 37.1
Second-Echelon: C

Player Value: 71.0

Farm System: The Marlins system isn't in bad shape considering their short history. Charles Johnson is an excellent catcher, the infield is a bit dry with only the raw Edgar Renteria as a prospect. In the outfield, Everett, Tavarez and Whitmore look nice. Andy Larkin, Kurt Miller, Dave Weathers, Pat Rapp are decent starter prospects, but the bullpen is thinner, with only Vic Darensbourg, John Johnstone and Tony Saunders providing any long-term help as of now.

Infield: C
Outfield: C
Starters: C
Relievers: D
Farm Ranking: C

Management and Ownership: The Marlins are one of those teams with a management and ownership group that really knows what it's doing. The Marlins aren't afraid to add talent and aren't afraid to spend a bit to do it. The great irony of 1993 was watching the Padres, an "established" team, trade their finest player, Gary Sheffield, to the Marlins (has a team ever dumped their youngest star's salary on an expansion team before?). One needn't worry about H. Wayne Huizenga, the man has deep pockets and has excellent subordinates.

GM Dave Dombrowski, pirated from the Expos, was the architect of Montreal's incredible minor-league system and is busy doing the same in Miami. The Marlins already have an average farm system and they could have a world-class one by 1996. All they need to do is go through another draft or two with their ability to sniff out the talent. Dombrowski is a fine trader because he is among the best at evaluating ability and milking other GMs. without letting them know they got the hose.

Marcel and Rene Lachemann are an excellent management team. Of the two, we have the most respect for Marcel (who has an exceptional track record of developing young pitching), but the skipper ain't a slouch either.

Lachemann plays for the big inning, choosing to eschew the bunt and the hit-and-run. The team can't steal and it can't bunt, but they were exceptional at executing the hit-and-run.

They are pretty much a conservatively run team, but the talent isn't there right now. In other words, you can only be radical if you have players to be radical with. That isn't the case now. These guys are doing the best possible with what they have.

The only reason this team doesn't get higher marks for management and ownership, is that they need to spend another year putting

it all together before we can give them an A. They're 80 percent there, anyway.
Ownership: B
Front Office: A
Field Management: B
Overall: B+

1994 Outlook: The Marlins need another year or two for their plan to start coming together. Realistically, the Mets have more front-line talent in the majors and minors and if there is any semblance of order in the NL East this year, the Mets should stomp on the Marlins. If the Marlins don't finish last, then it will have been a fine year. If they do, then they did what was reasonable to expect.

MONTREAL EXPOS

1993 Outlook: The Expos, along with the Phillies, were expected to contend for the divisional title. Basically, Montreal was the favorite. They had a fine young talent corps on offense and a good pitching staff with an excellent closer. Pundits figured it would only take 88-93 wins to win the weak NL East and the Expos could do that, couldn't they?

April 13-10 (13-10, 4.5 games back)
The offense was the key in the first month, as the pitching stank. The team had a .346 OBP and slugged .441, overcoming their 4.25 ERA. Larry Walker led the charge, hitting .364 and slugging an incredible .745. DeShields got on base at a .412 clip and utility sensation Mike Lansing hit .342 and slugged nearly .550. The problem was emergency closer Mel Rojas – 5.00 ERA – and Denny Martinez who was 1-4 with a 4.70 ERA. Only Kenny Hill (4-0, 1.80) pitched with any consistency.

May 27-22 (14-12, 5 games back)
The pitching started falling into place (3.81 ERA), but the offense plummeted (.256, .325 OBP, .369 SL%). Moises Alou hit .322 and Grissom hit .326 with 17 RBI, but Walker fell off to .238 with a .357 slugging and Darrin Fletcher dropped from a .327 April to .196 with no extra-base hits and a .226 OBP. Martinez bounced back, going 2-1, 3.6 and Ken Hill moved to 6-0 with a 2-0, 3.20 month. The bullpen was really glad to see John Wetteland back. He went 2-0 with seven saves and a 2.08 ERA.

June 41-36 (14-14, 11 games back)
The race seemed over. Montreal's attack was absolutely scattershot at best, anemic normally and consisted of occasional drooling on the enemy at worst. The team hit .226 and had no power or walks. By grace of a 3.63 ERA, the team played .500 ball. Ken Hill posted the same 3.20 ERA he did in May, but went 0-2. Martinez went 5-0, 2.17 and Wetteland saved 57 percent (eight) of Montreal's June wins with an ERA of 0.51.

July 56-48 (15-12, 9.5 games back)
The offense was chugging along with a normal output, the pitching was improving as the team ERA dropped to 3.50. Moises Alou was a killer, going .323-7-24 with a .646 SL%; Darrin Fletcher hit .349 with a .506 SL% and a .439 OBP. DeShields didn't walk much, but hit .393 with a .479 SL%, his 10 RBI were 35 percent of his season's total. The thing is, Grissom tanked, hitting .224, Hill only pitched 18 innings as his groin was acting up, and sundry mediocre performances added up to little gain on Philly.

August 73-60 (17-12, 9.5 games back)
The pitching staff put together an unbelievable 2.83 ERA that was negated by a .319 OBP and a .373 SL% by the offense. Martinez was a chump, posting a 6.47 ERA and Hill was a semi-mediocre 3.31, but Mel Rojas 0.96 ERA; Wetteland 1.15 ERA, 9 saves; Jeff Fassero 3-2, 2.2; and Gil Heredia, Chris Nabholz and Duane Henry (who all pitched excellently in their starts) were crucial.

Sept./Oct. 94-68 (21-8, three games back)
The team played exceptional baseball during their last 36 games, going 27-9. From August 24-Sept. 5, the Expos went 9-0, reeling off seven quality starts, winning five games by 3+ runs and scoring 5+ runs six times. Montreal's dominance was evidenced by their average margin-of-victory during the streak: 5 runs (average score of these games was 7-2!). After losing their game on the 9/5, the Expos won seven-straight. On 9/14, they withstood a seven-run Cardinal rally in the 8th and 9th innings to post a 12-9 victory and pull within 4.5 games of Philly.

On 9/17, the enemy came to town for a three-game set. It was the series NL East fans had been waiting for. ... Les Expos were five back. A sweep would put them two back with 13 games left in the season. Attendance was 136,242 for the series (over 8 percent of Montreal's season attendance – at that rate – nearly 3.7 million fans would have attended Stade Olympic last season).

Game one on 9/17 featured the inconsistent Ben Rivera vs. the rejuvenated Denny Martinez; 9/18's game two was a matchup of Curt Schilling and the surprisingly effective Denis Boucher; Sunday, September 19th's game three had rookie sensation Kirk Rueter vs. Danny Jackson.

Friday's game started out with Rivera and the curveballer trading zeros for the first three-and-a-half frames. Montreal scored a run in the fourth and a pair in the fifth to take a 3-0 lead.

The sixth inning was a disaster for Montreal. Martinez faltered and allowed a three-run homer to Daulton. Felipe Alou, sensing the enormity of the situation brought in his setup man, Rojas to quell the fire. He did, but not before errors by Mike Lansing and Randy Ready put four unearned runs on the board, giving Philadelphia a 7-3 lead going into the seventh.

For once, Montreal took a page out of Philly's book and drew walks like demons. Rivera, David West and Mitch Williams were wilder than Madonna after four 40-ouncers of King Cobra. Montreal gleefully took the walks they doled out and converted them into runs. In the seventh, Curtis Pride's first ML hit, an RBI double, knotted the score at seven apiece.

For four-and-a-half innings, the Expos and Phillies traded zeros again. In the bottom of the 12th, Marquis Grissom led off with a double. He stole third and coasted home on Delino DeShields sac fly.

The lead was four games.

Game two started inauspiciously for Montreal. The Phillies scored twice in the third to take a 3-1 lead. Boucher was effective, allowing two earnies in five innings (Cordero's throwing error allowed the third run to score), but Gil Heredia and Duane Henry were poor in relief allowing the score to move to 5-1. The eighth provided some fireworks as Cordero redeemed himself+2 by cranking a three-run homer with no outs to pull within 5-4, but that was the final margin. West and Williams, atoning for their misdeeds in game one, shut down the Expos for the last six outs.

Jackson and Rueter were both ineffective in game three. By the sixth, it was 5-4 Philly, with both starters gone. The score held until the ninth. With two outs, Cordero singled off Mitch Williams, driving in DeShields and Rondell White to give the Expos a 6-5 win and knock the lead back to four games.

In the end, their 8-5 record to close the season out would have to have been 11-2 for them to have tied, 12-1 for 98 wins and the division. We should hail the Expos for their valiant charge, but they didn't have the horses.

Park Effects: Olympic Stadium slightly favors the pitcher, lowering runs-scored by 4 percent. The park increases doubles by 13 percent, but lowers B.A. 3 percent, triples by 1 percent, and homers by 14 percent.

The park is a fielding-percentage maven's dream, lowering errors by 14 percent. Of course this helps keeps runs-scored down.

Montreal seems kinder to lefties. It raises LH B.A. 3 percent and lowers their HR by 10 percent. Right-handers lose 6 percent off their B.A. and 16 percent off their homers.

Offense: Montreal had a slightly above-average offense last year. They overachieved because they scored more runs than the runs-created method suggested they should have. Montreal doesn't hit for average, but they draw some walks; put the ball in play; hit an average amount of doubles and triples – and if you adjust for park, they hit an average amount of homers, too.

Of course it goes without saying that they have the most amazing running game in baseball. Because of their exceptional team speed, the Expos ground into only 95 DPs last year, the fewest in baseball.

Montreal lost a real sparkplug in DeShields, but with the young corps of good hitters in their system, they should be able to improve at first and possibly at third. If one of the big-three outfielders got hurt, the Expos have a flock of kids that could come up and be stars. The Expos are about neck-and-neck with the Braves in bush-league talent.

Pitching: Last year they had an above-average staff. The team seems to be suited for the park, giving up a bunch of grounders -- which are gobbled up from their true bounces on this error-free turf by the team's solid infielders.

The Montreal rotation last year had a good ERA, but only made 80 quality starts (NL average is 86), several pitchers didn't have good years for Montreal, so a good deal of the problem can be attributed to that. The staff was in a shambles during the first half of the season, but the team made a furious charge at the end of the season and the pitching staff (3.19 ERA after the All-Star break) was the reason that the Expos stayed in the race almost until the end.

The pen wasn't quite as impressive as the rotation, but was still solid. The closing is close to non-pareil and the rest of the relief staff is adequate. The team is right at the league average in stranding runners and was good at slamming the door in save situations.

Les Expos will replace Denny Martinez with Pedro Martinez. Behind that they have two or three solid starters and a bunch of candidates to sort from. The problem they had last year was they spent too much time trying to figure out who to use and that ruined their first half and eventually ruined their bid for the NL East. They need to find their pitchers and stick with them. They have tons of prospects, so expect to see a lot of turnover in the rotation over the next three years.

Defense:
Catcher: Starter Darrin Fletcher didn't make too many errors and called a solid game, but his throwing was very weak. Backup Tim Laker showed nothing.
Pts: -1.0

Infield: The three-man gang of Colbrunn, VanderWal and Bolick provided solid defense at first. At second, the now departed DeShields provided excellent defense. Mike Lansing, the backup was subpar (he played excellent 'd' at short and third, though).

At third, Sean Berry was a smidge above-average. Shortstop Wil Cordero was below-average, but Lansing helped negate that with his backup play.
Pts: 17.9

Outfield: Moises Alou is an above-average fielder in left. Marquis Grissom is excellent in center and Larry Walker would be non-pareil in right if he could stay healthy.
Pts: 23.0
Total: 39.9

1994 Personnel

Catcher: Darrin Fletcher isn't as bad as all that. He calls a good game and he can do a little something with the bat. It's quite possible that the rating system for catchers is too harsh on guys who can't throw, but have good CERAs. He's nothing special, but he's adequate until they come up with their next Gary Carter.

Bench: Montreal's bench is quite bare of good players and guys not named Tim. Messrs. Spehr and Laker can't hit and haven't shown whether they can catch the ball.
Starters: -3.3
Bench: D

Infield:
1B: There are a hundred candidates for the job, but the front-runners are Cliff Floyd and Randy Milligan. Randy is, of course, Cliff's dad, so look for the kid to get the most shots at the job. Cliff's not much of a talent – if things break right, he'll only go 30-30 as a rookie.

2B: The Expos may fall on their swords when they realize what Delino meant to this team, but they've got two gritty gamers in Mike Lansing and Randy Ready. Neither is a star, but both are fine lead-off/No. 2 hitters.

3B: Sean Berry and Shane Andrews look like they'll fight it out. Berry's proven he can play well at the ML-level; Andrews has proven (via his birth certificate) that he's six years younger than Berry. It may not be this year, but Andrews will win out soon. If the Expos are as dumb as they look, then it's possible they'll start fudging with Cordero at third. This would only screw up their team for a year or two.

SS: If the Expos flash some moxie, expect Cordero to continue to play and improve at short.

IF Bench: At first base, Frank Bolick, Oreste Marrero, John VanderWal, Derrick White and Randy Wilstead, 28, (.333-3-35 at

A, .259-4-15 at Double-A) are other possibilities. Look for Bolick, Marerro and VanderWal to get dibs on any non-Milligan/Floyd time, though. At second base, Chris Haney, Mike Hardge and Charlie Montoyo are the front-line backups. Because Hardge is young, he looks like he'll get the most chances at a decent job. Matt Rundels, is a wildcard, but his bat looks like it could be excellent. Short is a position where Montreal is a bit thinner. Tim Barker may be decent, but Chris Martin looks pretty bloody impressive. If he can field a bit, he'd be a fine infield bat off the bench.

Starters: 14.2
Bench: B

Outfield:
LF: Moises Alou looks like he'll be back and healthy in left. Alou is 27 this year, so it wouldn't be surprising to see him hit .300 with 25+ homers.

CF: With Marquis Grissom it's the same story: He's 27 as well. He should squeeze out his peak seasons in the next two to three years.

RF: Will you let us say it?! Would you believe Larry Walker is 27 as well?! Folks, there are two, maybe three MVP candidates in this outfield. If we had to pick one it'd be Larry as his breadth of skills eclipses his teammates'.

Bench: The Expos are just stacking up beautiful OF prospects like coal for a tramp steamer. Pretties like Rondell White and Curtis Pride alone are worth the price of admission, but when you toss in cuties like Glenn Murray, Tyrone Woods and Tyrone Horne, you have five players that could start for many major-league teams. In terms of real bench players, Lou Frazier and Ted Wood are the best bets for the scrubeenie roles.

Starters: 78.2
Bench: A++

Starting Pitching: Kenny Hill, Chris Nabholz, Jeff Fassero, Pedro Martinez and Kirk Rueter look like they could fill up the rotation themselves. Tavo Alvarez, Denis Boucher, Gabe White, Rod Henderson, Chris Looney, Ugueth Urbina and B.J. Wallace are other candidates. Boucher and White probably would get first shot. Urbina and Wallace are probably the farthest away.

Front-Line: 63.5
Second-Echelon: A

Relief Pitching: John Wetteland will close and Mel Rojas will setup. Ace starter candidate Joey Eischen will get serious consideration for a long-relief job, as will Heath Haynes, Gil Heredia and Tim Scott. Second-echelon candidates include Joe Ausanio, Reid Cornelius (10-7, 4.17 119/82 K/W at AAA), Yorkis Perez (3.45 ERA, 58/20 K/W in 44IP at AA), Bill Risley, Jeff Shaw, Sergio Valdez, Bruce Walton and Pete Young.

Front-Line: 47.7
Second-Echelon: B

Player Value: 200.3

Farm System: The Expos are in absolutely beautiful shape. In the infield, Cliff Floyd, Mike Hardge, Jose Vidro, Shane Andrews and Brad Fullmer all are very nice prospects. The outfield is stacked with Rondell White, Curtis Pride, Chris Schwab, Benitez and Murray. The bullpen is rather bare, but the starting corps could be helped out by Joey Eischen, Rod Henderson, Chris Looney, Ugueth Urbina, B.J. Wallace and several others. An incredibly deep system.

Infield: A
Outfield: A
Starters: A
Relievers: C
Farm Ranking: A

Management and Ownership: The Expos have a ridiculous following in their home country and city. The team won 94 games and finished second-to-last in major-league attendance with 1.64 million customers. This is a @#%&*! joke. Quite simply, they are an exceptionally well handled team that doesn't have any fan base. It's hard to find fault when there's no way the team can scrape up the funds to compete with the big dogs. These guys could really use revenue sharing. Owner Claude Brochu doesn't have a great reputation (*Baseball Weekly*) ranked him 19th among the 28 owners), but it appears his hands are tied. He hasn't really shown any incompetence

Dan Duquette looks like a very competent, but unexceptional GM. He has orchestrated some good trades, but he lacks former GM

Dave Dombrowski's incisive ability to trim talent from another team's flanks while giving up relatively little. The Expos continue to draft intelligently and continue to keep their players interested in staying together. In Montreal, the Gallic land of baseball apathy, that alone is reason to cheer.

Felipe Alou is a champion of first-run strategies. His team runs like the wind; drops down more bun(d)ts than the Pillsbury cake-mix factory, and puts on the hit-and-run very often. It isn't for naught, as the Expos are only brilliant at this stuff.

Alou isn't afraid to play around with his lineups and he definitely isn't psychotic about platooning purely along righty-lefty lines.

In regard to pitching, Alou is one to spare the starter and spoil the closer. He yanks his rotation at the first sign of trouble, but his bullpen led baseball in a most dubious category: saves over 1+ inning pitched (with 30. ... No other NL team was over 14!). Wetteland is the kind of pitcher that goes deep in the count to hitters anyway, so you can't be too happy about a manager who makes his closer throw 35-40 pitches to earn a save. If he can keep from blowing Wetteland out, Alou is fine, however.

Ownership: B
Front Office: B
Field Management: B
Overall: B

NEW YORK METS

1993 Outlook: Injuries to key players and free-agent signings ruined the Mets' season in 1992. So in the spring of '93, they were worried more about the health of their roster than they were about the division title.

There were encouraging signs. Even though David Cone departed a season earlier, a healthy Saberhagen joined Gooden and Sid Fernandez to go three deep with quality starters in the rotation. Tony Fernandez was to give the Mets the best shortstop they had in several years. And Howard Johnson's experiment in centerfield was called off as he was installed back at third base in an effort to increase his comfort level. Rookies Ryan Thompson and Jeff Kent were the major question marks. If the Mets were to contend for the title, the two young platers acquired in the Cone trade would have to come through with big seasons.

April 8-13 (8-13, 8.5 games back)

Dwight Gooden dealt the Rockies a beautiful four-hit shutout on opening day, but unfortunately, it would be the closest the Mets would ever be to first place. The rotation pitched well throughout the first month. Gooden looked sharp, posting a 2.68 ERA for the month, and Saberhagen shook the rust off with three quality starts. Heck, even Frank Tanana had a nifty 1.71 ERA after his first three starts.

But the offense didn't give them much support with their measly .229 average. Ryan Thompson limped out of spring with hamstring troubles. Bonilla struggled to a .234 batting average and Tony Fernandez barely topped the mendoza line with a .203 effort. But Bonilla and Fernandez were only symptoms of a disease that infected the entire roster. By the end of April, the Mets were in the basement, a position they would grow accustomed to.

May 9-18 (17-31, 16.5 games back)

As May unfolded, the Phillies were busy winning games and the Mets were busy burying themselves in the standings. Gooden continued to be one of the hottest pitchers in the league, tossing a another four-hit shutout in the first week-- this time against he other expansion team. Saberhagen followed three days later with a three-hit shutout, but he had his next two solid starts wasted by a lack of support. On the darker side, Sid Fernandez went on the DL with a cartilage tear in his knee and Pete Schourek was systematically demolished all month long.

The hitting hadn't shown up yet, and the Mets could manage a mere .236 average. The front-office, unable to stand the losing any longer, fired Jeff Torborg May 19 and replaced him with Dallas Green. Torborg was let go primarily because he had trouble getting his players to toe the line. Green's authoritarian ways were supposed to bring a little discipline back to the team.

June 6-21 (23-52, 28 games back)

Things went from bad to worse in June, as the Mets failed to post a double-digit win total for the third consecutive month. The rotation continued to perform as advertised with Anthony Young and Doc Gooden each turning in four quality starts. But again, there was no run-support coming from the lackluster offense. The Mets lost eight of the 15 quality starts turned in by the rotation. Green tried shaking up the roster, as Tony Fernandez was traded to the Blue Jays for Darrin Jackson. But neither his moves nor his threats could wake up the Mets, and they slipped even further in back of the Phillies. Their season was essentially through by the end of June.

July 12-16 (35-68, 30 games back)
The Mets were beginning to come out of their offensive coma, but it was too little, too late. Although Eddie Murray caught fire and Bonilla continued hitting balls out of the park, the offense had slept too long and the team defense was porous. Injuries also took their toll in July. Howard Johnson was lost for the season when he had bone chips removed from his thumb and Sid Fernandez missed most of the month with his knee injury. And just when things seemed like they couldn't get any worse, Vince Coleman's firecracker tossing incident unfolded in late July and the Mets clubhouse became a war zone. Everything seemed to conspiring against a Mets resurgence, and the team just wasn't strong enough to withstand the misfortunes.

August 11-18 (46-86, 36 games back)
Same story, different month. The offense suffered a relapse and the pitching staff couldn't buy a run. The Mets staggered around the ring, reeling from so many body blows and powerless to prevent any further beatings. They waited for the final bell to sound.

Sept./Oct. 13-17 (59-103, 38 games back)
Mercifully, the Mets' pitiful season came to a close with a 9-2 victory over the Florida Marlins October 3. Like children on the final day of school, the players couldn't empty their lockers fast enough.

Park Effect: Shea stadium reduced scoring by four percent last year and home runs by only two percent. The same effects are apparent over the last three years. Shea stadium has always been a fairly neutral place to play so there's nothing new to hash over. In fact, the fans and the media in New York probably affect hitters more than the ballpark does.

Offense: Without question, the worst in the major leagues last year. New York hitters had the lowest batting average in the league, the lowest on-base and the second-lowest slugging average. Only the Florida Marlins rivaled the offensive ineptitude of the Mets. Granted, outside factors like nagging injuries to key personnel and a little girl being blown up played a role in the team's performance. Of course, it's awfully hard to build an offense with team chemistry that would be better served as biological weapon material for an Iraqi SCUD.
Total Offense: -80.8

Pitching: The Mets received adequate pitching throughout the season, but an inconsistent bullpen and injuries to Sid Fernandez, Bret Saberhagen and John Franco took their toll on what could have been an above-average pitching staff. One thing is clear, with 94 quality starts and only 45 wins to show for the hard work, the rotation didn't get the run-support they deserved.
Total Pitching: 75.1

Defense:
Infield: Not only did the Mets suffer a horrendous offensive season, but their defensive lapses contributed just as much to their losing ways. Both Eddie Murray and Jeff Kent showed their respective ages defensively-- just at opposite ends of the spectrum. The tag-team of Bonilla and Ho Jo were adequate at third. Tony Fernandez was beautiful at shortstop, and when the Mets traded him to Toronto, Tim Bogar got a chance to display his solid hands.
Pts. 10.3

Outfield: The platoon of Coleman and Orsulak in left field provided solid defense, with Coleman getting the edge with the mitt. In center, Ryan Thompson justified his playing time by turning in a nice season in the field and leading the majors in range factor. Bonilla was a butcher in right field, but Jeromy Burnitz came up and put in solid work.
Pts. 16.7

Catcher: Todd Hundley didn't win anybody over with his defensive work last year, catching just 25 percent of the runners trying

to advance on him. Charlie O'Brien looked much better on the field, but the last thing the Mets could afford to do was carry another offensive liability.
Pts. -4.6
Total Defense: 22.4

1994 Personnel:
Catcher: There's plenty of depth here with Hundley getting the starters' job to begin with. But if he should falter, Greg Olson, picked up in the free-agent bazaar, could take the job away from him. The Mets also acquired Joe Kmak on waivers from Milwaukee and Jeff Manto as a free agent. They also have Brook Fordyce fighting for a roster spot.
Starters: -14.3
Bench: C+

Infield:
1B: The Mets let Eddie Murray walk and could roll the dice on prospect Alan Zinter in '94, depending on how the rest of he infield shakes out. The other possibility would have Bonilla playing first if he isn't needed at third.
2B: After hitting 21 homers and driving in 80 runs, Jeff Kent has been given the second base job with a lot of fanfare. Expect some defensive improvements out of him as he learns the requirements of the position
3B: The Mets are leaning toward letting Butch Huskey develop for a year in AAA Norfolk. But if Bonilla is needed to play first and the Mets don't acquire a third baseman by opening day, Huskey just might find himself with the job.
SS: There's no telling what the Mets plan to do here. At this writing, they were shopping Saberhagen or Bonilla around the league, so there's a chance they will fill the position with an outsider by opening day. If their search comes up dry, then either Tim Bogar, Tito Navarro or Jeff McKnight should get the job in the spring while the quest continues.
Bench: Unless the Mets act to fill the holes in their infield, the bench should get plenty of work this summer. Those not already mentioned include shortstop Aaron Ledesma and second baseman Quilvio Veras. They're both mighty young, so they'll probably start the season in AAA.
Starters: 13.8
Bench: C

Outfield:
LF: Joe McIllvaine actually found a taker for Vince Coleman, trading him to the Royals for Kevin McReynolds. Next to Vinny's felonious behavior, McReynolds' sulking will seem like a vacation.
CF: The Mets are going to stick with Ryan Thompson in center because he plays excellent defense and has great speed. If he can shorten his swing and make better contact, he'll surprise a lot of people with his bat.
RF: Jeromy Burnitz has climbed into the saddle and will start showing his power at the major league level. He is an excellent athlete with plus speed and he can also play solid defense.
Bench: Orsulak and Jackson will be back, but they'll be fighting for playing time with new acquisitions Doug Dascenzo and Tracy Sanders.
Starters: 40.3
Bench: D

Starting Pitching: Gooden returns to lead the staff but Sid Fernandez will be absent, having signed with the Orioles. Saberhagen, if he's not traded, will step into the number-two job, and you can bet the Mets will be praying for his health. Eric Hillman, Bobby Jones and Pete Schourek will fill some spots in the rotation, but they'll also be competing against newcomers Pete Smith and Frank Seminara. Dave Telgheder will also have an opportunity to earn a job.
Front-Line: 40.7
Second-Echelon: C-

Relief Pitching: The New York bullpen will be a mix of veterans and rookies in '94 as the Mets plan to take advantage of some of the young arms they have stockpiled. If John Franco is healthy, he'll retain the closer's role. The supporting cast will likely feature set-up men Jeff Innis and Anthony Young. Mike Maddux might earn a job in the spring, but he'll have to beat out youngsters Tom Wegmann, Pete Walker, Kenny Greer and Joe Vitko to get it.
Front-Line: 0.0
Second-Echelon: C-

Player Value: 80.5

Farm System: Most of the top talent in the Mets system is located in the lower leagues, but they have a lot of really good prospects. They have tapped AAA Norfolk for most of its stars but Butch Huskey and Brook Fordyce might return there in the spring. It shouldn't be too long before they're joined by second baseman Quilvio Veras. Bill Pulsipher and Kirk Presley are the two best arms in the organization, but they're at least two years away from helping at the major league level. OF Preston Wilson has the best tools of any position player in the system and Edgardo Alfonzo has excellent instincts, but they too are at least two or three years from being ready.

- Infield: A
- Outfield: C
- Starters: A
- Relievers: D
- Farm Ranking: C+

Management and Ownership: Owner Fred Wilpon maintains a low profile. Can you blame him? Would you lay claim to such a mess? Seriously, he has taken more control over the operations of the team of late, emphasizing that fact by bluntly stating that Vince Coleman was through as a Met in August of last year. Wilpon has always doled out the necessary cash to sign free-agent talent, but he was burned by Saberhagen and promises not to make the same mistake again.

Joe McIllvaine has been a busy man over the winter trying to fill in the holes from last year, and he's not finished yet. First off, he trimmed the payroll by letting Sid Fernandez, Howard Johnson and Charlie O'Brien walk as free agents. Then he began rebuilding with trades and free agent signings that wouldn't cost him any draft picks. He picked up starter Pete Smith from Atlanta for outfield reserve Dave Gallagher. Then he traded minor leaguer Randy Curtis to the Padres for starter Frank Seminara and outfielder Tracy Sanders. He even picked up a couple of free-agent catchers-- Greg Olson from Atlanta, and Joe Kmak form the Brewers. All this done, and he is still trying to trade Bobby Bonilla and Bret Saberhagen by opening day.

Jeff Torborg was relieved of duty last year when the clubhouse began resembling Animal House and replaced with Dallas Green. Green has no tolerance for players that don't want to work, and will clean house if given the chance. He is a competent field general whose only short-coming is a tendency to stay with the starters a little longer than he should.

1994 Outlook: The Mets have turned over a lot of players in the hopes of exorcising their ghosts of 1993. If their young players (Burnitz, Thompson and Kent) improve with experience and the new-comers play up to expectations, the Mets' team offense looks to be much improved. There are still holes to fill, most notably a shortstop and another dependable starter. But the Mets are more willing to bring up youngsters from the minors now. And even if they continue losing, they will at least be losing with players they have drafted and developed themselves, instead of a team built on free-agents and mercenaries. One thing is for sure, if the prospects don't pan out, the Mets won't be going very far.

PHILADELPHIA PHILLIES

1993 Outlook: Despite a horrid 1992, scribes and seers looked to 1993 as a year of great potential for the Phils. The Phils possessed the best offensive talent in the league and the majority of their problems the previous year were due to injuries to the pitching staff. With Curt Schilling and Terry Mulholland, the Phillies had two excellent starters. With the additions of Danny Jackson, Ben Rivera and a healthy Tommy Greene, the league had to take notice: The Phillies had the arms to make them competitive. Many predicted a division title, others saw them as a second- or third-place team.

April 17-5 (17-5, 4.5 games ahead)
Out of the gate, the pitching screamed. With Tommy Greene 2-0, 2.45 and Curt Schilling 4-1, 2.54 leading the way, the Phils compiled a 3.25 team ERA and started the season 8-1. The offense was OK, but not in gear yet.

Daulton's .438 OBP and .516 SL% and Kruk's .343-5-15, .459 OBP, .657 SL% keyed the offense.

May 34-15 (17-10, 7 games ahead)
In May, the thunder came around. The team slugged .440. Darren Daulton hit 9 homers,

slugged .625 and drove in 30 RBI! Hollins posted .317-6-26 numbers and slugged .587; Inky slugged .662; and Kruk had an Olerud-esque .517 OBP. Three cogs in the rotation were on fire: Greene 5-0, 1.4; Mulholland 4-1, 2.83; Schilling 2-0, 3.00. The Phillies were threatening to run away with the division in April. By the end of May, they were in danger of making the race a joke.

June 52-25 (18-10, 6.5 games ahead)

The Phils continued to play excellent ball in June, but still lost half a game in the standings. The team hit .279, got on base at a .356 clip and slugged .443. Mariano Duncan hit .302 with 14 RBI. A semi-dormant Dykstra lit up the league, with .337-.466 OBP- .538 SL% numbers; and Jim Eisenreich hit .351.

Among the pitchers, Danny Jackson went 3-2, 2.91; Mulholland was 3-1, 2.06. Ben Rivera, the wild man from Borneo was 5-1, 3.69 (with an amazing [for him] 34/11 K/W!). Mr. 7-0, Tommy Greene fell to earth with the grace of a feather tied to an anvil, going 2-2, 6.98. In addition, the Phils lost their No. 1 headcase: Dave Hollins hit .189 before discovering he had broken his hamate bone.

July 66-39 (14-14, 6 games ahead)

The pitching staff started folding (4.50 ERA) as the second-half of the season beckoned. The offense wasn't awesome, but helped out enough. A .500 record for the rest of the season would yield 95 wins and most thought that would be enough to hold off the competition. With Duncan hitting .349. Dykstra's .485 OBP and .589 SL% and Kruk's .491 OBP, everything looked like business as usual in the city of brotherly spite.

August 82-50 (16-11, 9.5 games ahead)

The pitching continued to smell (4.37 ERA), but the offense was devastating. The team hit .287 with a .364 OBP and an excellent .484 SL%. Leading the charge was Inky with his .368-8-21 (.765 SL%). Danny Jackson 2-1, 1.35 was the only decent starter among the pack. But still, the Phils were able to push up their lead by 3.5 games.

Sept./Oct. 97-65 (15-15, 3 games ahead)

Quite simply, the Phillies avoided the 'el fold-o' syndrome. They could have fallen to two games back if they had been swept in their September three-game set against the Expos, but they won a game and went 7-5 to close out the season. They got the huge lead early, had a scare or two, and outlasted the competition. Let's give them their due.

Park Effects: Philadelphia is a neutral park that doesn't affect runs-scored or overall batting average. The park increases doubles by 4 percent and triples by 2 percent, but lowers homers by 3 percent.

The park helps neutralize offense by lowering errors by 7 percent.

The park heavily favors left-handed power hitters. It lowers their B.A. by a smidge, but gives them a 17 percent increase in home runs. Righties get a 1 percent bonus in B.A., but lose 17 percent of their homers here.

Offense: If you adjust for the lack of the DH in the NL, then you have to say the Phillies are the best offense in baseball. In this very even ballpark, the Phils hit for high average, hit tons of doubles, tons of triples and a good deal of homers. Also, they are the most patient team in the league. They didn't have a ton of steals, but had the third-best SB% in baseball last year (74 percent, tied with Cleveland) and grounded into very few DPs, indicating that their team speed is quite good.

These guys know what they're doing. They have the best bunch hitters on the planet and are smart enough not to run themselves out of an inning. They have every offensive tool in the box and they don't need to run, hell they only finished 22 runs-scored behind the Tigers and led the NL by 69 runs.

There are some decent replacement-level hitters in the minors, but no real star-caliber prospects. Most likely, the kids could replace an injury with an above-average player, but there are no Manny Ramirezes or Marc Newfields here.

Pitching: The pitching fell apart down the stretch (4.31 ERA from July through season's end), but the team has a darn nice rotation. The bullpen was doo-doo-ish, however. Ironically, this staff is much better on grass than turf (3.69 ERA on grass, 4.09 on turf).

The starters threw 92 quality starts, pitched tons of innings and had lots of complete games. Thanks to dominating performances by the big three, the team also had a solid 11 shutouts. They keep runners off base and do a great job of keeping the ball in the park.

Enough of the good things!

The bullpen was average in letting inherited runners score, but wasn't so good at converting save opportunities. The pen had horrendous control problems, allowing 4.73 BB/9IP. The bullpen's ratio (1.433) was one of the worst in the National League. The Phillies relievers did manage to keep their homers down to an average amount, though.

The Phillies' pen looks to improve just by the addition of phenom Ricky Bottalico. There are several decent prospects that could help improve the bullpen, but the main question is whether or not the Phils can afford to keep their rotation intact. If so, they won't have to rush Tyler Green if he isn't ready.

Defense:
Catcher: Darren Daulton is a solid fielder. His catch/throw skills are diminishing, but his leadership and intangibles are above reproach.
Pts: 5.1

Infield: Surprisingly, John Kruk is a pretty spritely defensive first baseman. He's not smooth, but he's adequate. At second, Duncan and Morandini are a different story. Neither is terrible, but neither's doing the job, either.

At third, Dave Hollins is blah. Again, he's not terrible, but he was adequate in 1992 and needs to get back to that. Backup Kim Batiste is even worse!

Kevin Stocker was average, but his backups, Batiste and Duncan, were both bad.
Pts: -12.2

Outfield: In left, Inky and Thompson provided decent defense. In center, Dykstra was a monster, tracking down flyballs and gunning down enemy base-runners.

Jim Eisenreich really surprised in right, compiling the second-best defensive numbers in the league.
Pts: 27.4
Total: 20.3

1994 Personnel
Catcher: Darren Daulton may be replaced by Wilkins or Piazza this year, but currently he's the best in the league. His bat is excellent and his defense is above-average. With the strength of the bench, the Phillies have the best catching in baseball.

Bench: Todd Pratt, Jason Moler and Mike Lieberthal are the ones who'll duke it out in the spring to backup the man. Pratt can hit, but the Phils hate his fielding. Moler can hit, but the Phils are afraid he'll hurt his arm with his funky throwing motion. Lieberthal can catch, but the Phils think he's too scrawny. Compared to the usual idiots you see on ML benches, these guys are like Johnny Bench, Thurman Munson and Chris Hoiles.
Starters: 32.5
Bench: A

Infield:
1B: If John Kruk doesn't get 130+ games in for the Phils, they'll be in trouble. The question is, when will he slow down a bit. Our guess is this year, but expect a .300 average and a .400 OBP, though.

2B: Mariano Duncan and Mickey Morandini look to get the PT initially. Neither is an exceptional player, so there's a hole waiting to be filled by minor-league Phils.

3B: David Hollins, Sir Psycho-Scary, needs to hone his fury and get his defense back in order. Other than that, he can continue being one of the top five or six third basemen in the game. It's doubtful that he'll get better with the bat, but he's still up there with just about anyone not named Ventura as an all-arounder.

SS: Kevin Stocker came up and sparked the Phils up the middle, playing above-average 'd' and hitting! WOW! Everyone is asking one thing, though: Can this kid keep it up? With the glove, the answer is yes. With the bat? We don't really know, but we suspect he'll be decent at the very least.

IF Bench: At first base, Ricky Jordan and Gene Schall look like they'll be solid backups. At second, look for Greg Legg (.280-0-25 at Triple-A) or possibly Kevin Sefcik (if he can make the jump from Double-A) to get some PT. Kim Batiste will be the primary third base backup, with Rob Grable and Vic Rodriguez, 32, (.305-12-64 at Triple-A) as other options. At short, if you see Joe Millette playing and you're a Phils fan, slit your wrists and save yourself some anguish. A much prettier option is Keith Kimberlin, 26. Kimberlin isn't Arky Vaughn, but his Triple-A line, .264-2-29, beats the hell outta Millette's .224-1-24.
Starters: 59.3
Bench: C

Outfield:
LF: It looks like Inky will get the lion's share of the work in left, with Milt Thompson getting lots of time as well. Both players have complementary skills so this is a solid platoon.

CF: Len Dykstra showed again that he can stay healthy for a full season. You can't like the fact that he's 31, but with his desire, he's the equivalent of 25. As long as everything's still in one piece (and has tobacco juice on it), he's one of the best.

RF: Jim Eisenreich and Wes Chamberlain are similar to the Phils left fielders. Eisenreich can reach base and play some defense, while Chamberlain can provide some thunder. Neither is a star, or will ever be one, but both are quite valuable.

Bench: Of the kids that could comprise the bench, Phil Geisler looks like the best for 1994. Jeff Jackson is attractive because he's only 22, but he needs to hit much better to be viable. Tony Longmire and Dave Tokheim look like decent line-drive hitters; Tom Marsh and Sam Taylor are veteran bats; and Chad McConnell is the wildcard. He's supposed to be a star-caliber bat, but he's not done a thing as of yet.

Starters: 60.1
Bench:

Starting Pitching: Tommy Greene, Curt Schilling, Danny Jackson and Terry Mulholland (if he's not traded) will get the first four slots. Ben Rivera will get the first crack at No. 5. Jeff Juden, Tyler Green and Mike Williams are the most like candidates to get shots if someone should falter.

Front-Line: 92.4
Second-Echelon:

Relief Pitching: Look for Doug Jones and Ricky Bottalico to battle for the closer spot. Jones is, at best, the present, Bottalico could be the present and is bloody well the future. Larry Andersen and Dave West will handle the setup roles from the right and portsides respectively. Look for Roger Mason, Don Pall and possibly Bobby Thigpen to pick up long work. Others include Toby Borland, Brad Brink, Kevin Foster, Drew Hall (2.76 ERA, 62/23 K/W in 65.1 IP at AAA), Jeff Patterson, Heathcliff Slocumb, Bob Wells (2.79 ERA, 99/34 K/W in 86.1 IP at AAA). The final possibility (but a real long-shot) is Wayne Gomes.

Front-Line: 34.2
Second-Echelon: A

Player Value: 278.5

Farm System: It isn't impolite to point out that the Phillies don't have the 1975 Reds at Scranton. The Phils have Moler and Lieberthal to shore up the catching, but 1B Gene Schall is the sole decent infield prospect. In the outfield, There's Phil Geisler. Ty Green, Jeff Juden are the prime starters and Borland, Bottalico and Gomes are the young reliever guns. There's great depth at catcher and closer, but a wasteland elsewhere.

Infield: D
Outfield: D
Starters: D
Relievers: A

Ownership and Management: Bill Giles is an old-school owner, smart and wise in many ways, but also archaic in his thought-patterns (he said some crazy, borderline racist stuff during the Marge Schott debacle of 1992). He also has the reputation of being a tightwad. If you look at the 1994 payroll, you'd probably disagree with that assessment. Compared to his peers, Giles is not a meddlesome owner.

Lee Thomas is a major-league level Manfred von Richtofen. Like Richtofen (a world-class shot, but not much of a flyer), Thomas has pulled the trigger on innumerable trades, sneaking up on unassuming GMs and swatting them from the sky before they know what hits 'em. Giles has not overseen a rich farm system, however, and that is really the way a team needs to be built. Kruk, Hollins, Dykstra, Greene, Rivera, Schilling and Mulholland – 85 percent of the team's guts – were acquired from other organizations.

Manager Jim Fregosi is a reasonably smart man. He knows he's got the big boppers and doesn't try to one-run-inning his way out of the game. The team bunts quite a bit, but they never hit-and-run (though they are reasonably adept at it), and they don't try to steal often (though they are quite adept at this, too).

Fregosi doesn't pitch out much, or issue intentionally walks. He'd rather his offense have the big inning and let his pitchers quell opponents' chances of having them. He likes a stable lineup and because of health and talent, he doesn't pinch-hit or pinch-run much.

Fregosi is pretty much the anti-Alou. He works his starters very hard, but doesn't give his closers more than an inning. Phillies starters threw 32 120+ pitch games (only Tommy "Aorta," the infamous "Orel and Ramon" killer was even close, forcing the Dodgers to throw 30 such games). The Braves only had 18 120+ pitch games and the league average was 13 per team. Fregosi needs to lighten up, or his starters will go up in flames in by July.

1994 Outlook: The Phillies look pretty tough. Ben Rivera can only get better and the Phils have much better bullpen depth. The question is this: Can Dykstra, Kruk and Co. continue to produce? We don't think Lenny can duplicate 1993 and we're not sure if one or two other players will fall to earth this year either. Couple this with addition of the Braves in the NL East, and there could be trouble in paradise. The Phils could still win 95+ games, but the cost of victory has risen. The Phils have not gained on the leaders, they've only treaded water this off-season.

Player Essays – NL Central

CHICAGO CUBS

1993 Outlook: The Cubs were never considered to be a serious threat in the division. They lost Greg Maddux to the Braves as a free agent, and the rotation would never be the same. The Cubs signed Jose Guzman during the winter, but they didn't seem to understand that you just don't replace a pitcher like Maddux. Mike Morgan seemed a capable pitcher to lead the staff, but the rest of the rotation was questionable. Harkey had yet to prove his health, and Boskie had yet to prove his worth. Because of a broken hand sustained in an exhibition game, Sandberg was expected to miss the first two weeks of the season and would have to report to the Cubs without the benefit of spring training. Shawon Dunston opened the season on the DL, which came as a shock to no one but him, and the quality of infield replacements Sanchez and Vizcaino were in doubt.

April 11-11 (11-11, 6 games back)
The Cubs tinkered around at a .500 pace throughout the month. They just couldn't seem to score runs with any consistency or find the quality innings when they needed them. Derrick May got off to a fast start, hitting .345 and slugging .517. Grace (.325 average) and Vizcaino (.347 average, .383 on-base) also started the season in stride. Harkey (3-0 in three starts) and Guzman (3-2, 2.82) were the only starters enjoying any success against opposing hitters. The rest of the rotation went 2-7 to help the team amass a six-game deficit for their efforts in April.

May 13-12 (24-23, 9 games back)
The Cubs shook off their offense malaise, hitting .285 for the month. Grace caught fire, leading the offensive attack with a .364 average and 22 RBI. Vizcaino continued his torrid hitting, carrying a .372 average in 94 at-bats through the month. To top things off, Ryne Sandberg returned to the lineup without the benefit of a spring tune-up and hit .274, further boosting the confidence level of the Wrigley faithful.
Frank Castillo (1-1, 2.42) and Greg Hibbard (4-2, 2.52) pitched well in May, and the rest of the rotation seemed to show some signs of life. But the bullpen crumbled, the main culprits being Paul Assenmacher and Bob Scanlan, and the Cubs were unable to make up any ground on the Phillies.

June 13-15 (37-38, 14 games back)
The Cubs' rotation suffered its first breakdowns in June, and by mid-month the team orthopedist was the busiest man in the organization. Within a three day stretch, Morgan, Harkey and Hibbard all went on the DL with knee injuries. Guzman tried valiantly to hold the staff together, but the rotation struggled to a 10-12 record in 26 games.
The offense dropped off a bit, but was still scoring enough runs to win. Grace cooled down with a modest .302 average, and the production of the outfield began dropping as well. But the bottom of the batting order came suddenly started putting the bat on the ball, leading the offense to respectability. Most notably, Rick Wilkins hit .414 and Rey Sanchez kicked in a .395 average.

July 15-12 (52-50, 12.5 games back)
In July, the Cubs started realizing they didn't have a prayer of catching the Phillies. Their offense scored runs at a feast or famine pace all month long, getting shut out one day and coming back to win by six runs the next. The rotation returned to health, but by that time, Morgan and Guzman were the only pitchers worth their salt. Hibbard couldn't find his rhythm after coming back and Mike Harkey never had his going in the first place.

August 12-18 (64-68, 18 games back)
They remained relatively healthy and had a couple of players go on hot streaks, but for the Cubs, who started the month 12.5 games behind the red-hot Phillies, August was just an exercise.
Grace (.336 BA, .410 OBA), Sosa (nine home runs) and Sandberg (.348 BA) all deserve credit for driving the offense, but the pitching staff's 4.31 ERA undermined their efforts and put the Cubs even further behind Philadelphia.

Sept./Oct. 20-10 (84-78, 13 games back)
The hitters wouldn't let the Cubs go out with a whimper, leading the pitching staff to 20 wins, including six straight early in the

month. Chicago played spoiler at the beginning of September, winning three of four from Philadelphia and sweeping the Giants in three games. While they had no hope to catch the leaders, those six wins enabled them to get a few games closer toward respectability. Wilkins had a .352 average for the last month of the season and Grace finished strongly with a .317 average and 21 RBI.

Park Effect: Because of its short dimensions in the power alleys, Wrigley field has always been a hitter's park, especially generous to sluggers. Almost every offensive statistic was above league average in Wrigley last year. Runs were increased by six percent, doubles by nine percent, triples by 24 percent and home runs by 16 percent. Right-handed hitters enjoyed a whopping 62 percent advantage in homers last year. The effect that Wrigley has on offensive stats is incontrovertible, and has been for generations. It's a no-brainer, hitters' stats in Chicago need to be adjusted down to determine true levels of ability.

Offense: The Cubs had a decent offense last year, scoring a little over four and a half runs a game for their pitchers. Their 161 home runs were the third-best total in the league, ranking just behind Atlanta and San Francisco, and the Cubs were fortunate enough to have established players like Grace, Wilkins and Sosa climb up to the next level of performance. But the Cubs failed to take full advantage of their offensive capabilities. They took a very low number of walks and stole only 100 bases on the season, and as a result, they weren't putting as many runners in scoring position as they could have.

Total Offense: -0.3

Pitching: Save for a few minor knee injuries in June, the Cubs' pitching staff enjoyed good health last year. Unfortunately, they didn't fare very well, allowing 4.18 earned runs per game and an opposition batting average of .273. With Morgan, Guzman and Hibbard, the Cubs had three decent number-two starters, but no one was capable of taking over the ace role. Harkey and Frank Castillo rounded out the rotation, but had disappointing seasons.

Randy Myers broke the NL single-season save record last year, but he was the leader of an average bullpen. Set-up men Scanlan and McElroy suffered through dismal seasons, and the rest of the pen seemed to follow their examples. Jose Bautista had an encouraging season as their most effective middle reliever, but his quality pitching was definitely in the minority last year.

Total Pitching: 59.0

Defense:
Infield: Grace played all but eight games last year and was nearly flawless in the field. Sandberg's range factor slipped a bit last year, but it's too soon to tell whether his actual range in the field is declining. He did come back from a broken hand with no ill effects on his glove-work or throwing. The word for Sandberg's defensive work is still "solid".

Steve Buechele battled a painful achilles tendon injury most of the season, and consequently, his mobility was affected. With good health, he is one of the best fielding third-basemen in the league. Rey Sanchez and Jose Vizcaino split time at short in '93. While Sanchez had slightly better numbers, both players are excellent fielders.

Pts. 52.1

Outfield: In left field, Derrick May didn't do anything to embarrass himself, but he really is a subpar fielder. Last season, Dwight Smith proved once again that he can't play the field. Willie Wilson was adequate in center. In fact, he played darn well for a 38-year-old man. In right field, Sammy Sosa made all the plays he was supposed to and recorded 12 assists with a strong, accurate arm.

Pts. 8.6

Catcher: In '93, baserunners trying to steal second off Rick Wilkins were pronounced dead 46 percent of the time. He is a very good defensive catcher who saves more than his share of runs with his arm. He prevented 56 runners from advancing into scoring position last year by stopping the running game. For that, he was one of the best defensive catchers in the NL last year.

Pts. 16.7
Total Defense: 77.4

1994 Personnel:
Catcher: Rick Wilkins will attempt to duplicate his offensive surge, but might very

well fall back to earth as he will undoubtedly be facing more left-handed pitchers.

Bench: The Cubs traded Matt Walbeck, so there is a large void that needs to be filled. There's nobody in the minors right now capable of backing up Wilkins, but the Cubs aren't through dealing. A backup could be attained as a throw-in for a larger package.

Starter: 31.5
Bench: Incomplete.

Infield:

1B: Mark Grace might have hit his peak last year, but he still offers a pretty complete package. He hits in the heart of a pretty capable lineup, so he should produce a healthy amount of runs again.

2B: Sandberg's loss of power last year is generally attributed to his broken hand. He will rebound in '94, there's no doubt about it.

3B: Steve Buechele will provide rock-solid defense at third base if he's healthy. But don't expect a lot of offense from him. Wrigley will help him maintain his 15 homer plateau, but he contributes much more in the field than he does at the plate.

SS: Shawon Dunston might make another comeback attempt, but the Cubs will have little patience with him. They will fall back on the Vizcaino, Sanchez platoon in a heartbeat if they hear so much as a whimper out of Dunston.

Bench: The Cubs have a pretty stable infield, and shouldn't need too many substitutes. Tommy Shields will sit on the bench and act like a ballplayer, but figures to get little playing time. Either Doug Jennings or Matt Franco could make the roster and could fill in if Grace should go down. If Dunston doesn't make it back, SS Jose Hernandez, 20, might get a shot at a bench job as well. Mike Grace, no relation, is a longshot, but he could displace Shields as the guy who sits next to the water cooler.

Starters: 101.6
Bench: C

Outfield:

LF: Derrick May is technically in possession of he job until spring training, but whether he can fight off Glenallen Hill for the position remains to be seen. May was bothered by a persistent shoulder injury last year, and figures to rebound in '94. But Hill made a good impression on his new employers in his late-season audition and could wrest control of the job away from May.

CF: Dwight Smith was cut loose over the winter and won't be playing for the Cubs in '94. Karl Rhodes, who hit 23 homers for AAA Omaha last season, is the front-runner for the job and the leadoff spot in the batting order.

RF: Sammy Sosa emerged as a legitimate home run threat last year and will be expected to continue the power surge. But he really needs work on his plate discipline.

Bench: Switch-hitting Kevin Roberson will be on the bench, but he could see a lot of pinch-hitting appearances if he can refine his strike zone a tad. Willie Wilson might be around next year, but shouldn't see much playing time. The Cubs have some good, young players who deserve the playing time much more. Eddie Zambrano has emerged as a power prospect the last two seasons in the minors and could back up first base as well as the outfield. Ozzie Timmons is a longshot to make the show this year, but he's the best power-hitting prospect in the system.

Starters: 14.3
Bench: B

Starting Pitching: The Cubs got tired of paying high salaries for pitchers who couldn't produce quality innings, so they dumped Mike Harkey and Greg Hibbard over the winter in a payroll-cutting decision. Mike Morgan, if his contract isn't dumped by opening day, will be that ace of the staff again this season, only because it's traditional that every team have one and he has the most seniority. Jose Guzman is a capable number-two pitcher, but then again, so is Morgan. Frank Castillo, Steve Trachsel and newcomer Willie Banks will fill out the rest of the rotation. And the door is open for prospects like Blaise Isley, Lance Dickson and Kenny Steenstra to earn jobs with the staff. Newly acquired minor leaguers Larry Luebbers and Raphael Novoa will also get long looks in the spring.

Front-Line: 57.8
Second-Echelon: C-

Relief Pitching: Randy Myers is about the only Cubs pitcher with his name carved in stone for the bullpen. Set-up men Chuck McElroy and Bob Scanlan were traded last year, which leaves Shawn Boskie, Jose Bautista, Dan Plesac and Jim Bullinger as the hold-overs. Jesse Hollins is still very much in the plans, but he will have to prove his health after rotator-cuff surgery ended his '93 season. Other minor leaguers with a chance to make the bullpen are Bill Brennan and Shawn Hill.

Front-Line: 12.3
Second Echelon: D

Player Value: 186

Farm System: The injuries to top pitching prospects Lance Dickson and Jessie Hollins left the organization a bit thin on arms. But Kennie Steenstra may be ready to continue his world-domination tour and fringe prospects like Derek Wallace and Steve Trachsel stepped forward to fill the gap.

The premier player in the Cubs organization is Brooks Kieschnick. An outfielder taken with the number-one pick in the '93 draft, Kieschnick displayed his refined swing in three rookie-level leagues last year and should start the season in AA. SS Kevin Orie and OF Ozzie Timmons are farther away from the majors, but both of them are young and have excellent tools. First baseman Matt Franco and outfielder Doug Glanville will both get opportunities to climb the organizations' ladder as well.

Infield: B
Outfield: B
Starters: D
Relievers: D
Farm Ranking: C

Management and Ownership: The Tribune Company, owners of superstation WGN-TV and the Chicago Tribune, has held the title of the Cubs and Wrigley field since 1981. Stanton M. Cook, chairman of the board of the Cubs, runs the show and signs the checks. And Mr. Cook has recently decreed that the checks he signs hereafter shall be smaller. He should have thought about that before he decided to pay Sandberg seven million dollars a year.

Larry Himes and Al Goldis built the White Sox into contenders, but last year they moved across town to work for the Cubs. Their '93 amateur draft, namely SS Kevin Orie and OF Brooks Kieschnick, addressed some of the club's immediate needs, but it was a draft made easier with three number-one picks. Himes has been busy over the winter, trying to shore up the major league roster and trim his payroll at the same time. He has released veterans like Harkey, Hibbard and Dwight Smith and he has acquired young, inexpensive talent to replace them. The test of his skills will come when Willie Banks, Karl Rhodes and Steve Trachsel are asked to perform next year.

Jim Lefebvre actually did a reasonable job squeezing runs out of the Cubs offense, but in the end it just wasn't enough. He didn't live up to the front office's expectations last year (the ten-games above .500 comment to the press didn't help him any) and was fired shortly after the season ended. Tom Trebelhorn, former skipper of the Brewers, endured two days of psychological testing to win the manager's job, but those doing the testing couldn't figure out why he was crazy enough in the first place to want it. Trebelhorn has a reputation for working well with young players, and the Cubs roster will have plenty of rookies on it. The hiring of Trebelhorn may turn out to be Larry Himes's best move.

Ownership: D
Front Office: C+
Field Management: ? ? ?
Overall: C-

1994 Outlook: The Cubs look like they have a pretty decent offense going into the season. The steady leadership of Grace and Sandberg compliments a bevy of young hitters challenging for jobs in the outfield. The Cubs are also pretty solid defensively, especially in the infield. The big question will be whether the starting pitching can hold up over the season. Behind Morgan and Guzman, the rotation is pretty thin and the Cubs will rely on rookies and unprovens to fill it out. Willie Banks is a groundball pitcher and should be alright in Wrigley, but Frank Castillo and Steve Trachsel are question marks. If the Cubs are going to contend in the National League Central, they will need two or three of their pitching prospects to come through with big seasons.

CINCINNATI REDS

1993 Outlook: The Reds were considered by several prognosticators as the one team that could surprise the Braves and steal the division. They had a powerhouse offense, a fine bullpen and a two excellent starters in Rijo and Smiley. They didn't have it all, but if the Braves faltered, the Reds could swarm through the cracks and take the division with 95 wins, or so.

April 8-14 (8-14, 6 games back)
The Reds started the season with a whimper, losing their first four series including a sweep in Philadelphia. Before they knew it, they were 3-9 and in firm possession of the cellar. They righted themselves to play .500 for the rest of the month and move out of last place by a half-game, but it was beginning to look like the season might be devoted to staying ahead of expansion-Colorado.

The pitching staff was doing an adequate job posting a 3.89 ERA, their lowest all year. But the offense was AWOL. Reds' hitters managed only a .252 batting average and 77 RBI. Bip Roberts and Reggie Sanders were especially conspicuous, hitting .169 and .240, respectively (*not* respectably).

May 17-12 (25-26, 8 games back)
Cinci continued their funk until May 10, when they settled in for a seven-game homestand against the hapless Padres and Rockies.

They outscored their opponents 52-20 and swept both series', proving to the world that they weren't quite as bad as these guys.

Upon re-entering the respectable baseball world, however, they were immediately swept by the Dodgers and dropped three out of four to the Giants. They clearly weren't as good as these guys, either.

Injuries, which eventually decimated their season, were already beginning to take a toll. Rob Dibble and Hal Morris were out for the entire month and Steve Foster and Chris Sabo also missed some time.

Somehow, the offense still managed 134 RBI behind good hitting by Barry Larkin (.342), Roberto Kelly (.328) and Sanders (.308, 15 RBI). Jose Rijo finally arrived as well, going 4-0 with a 3.32 ERA.

June 13-14 (38-40, 13.5 games back)
The Reds settled into a nice, boring .500 groove, which was to last for three months. Not even this month's week against the Padres and Rockies could lift them out of the doldrums, although the June 22 game did provide some fireworks. Cincinnati outscored Colorado 16-13 on 18 hits. The Rockies got their revenge the next day, pounding the Reds 15-5.

Oh, to be a Rockie with incentive clauses.

July 15-13 (53-53, 17.5)
The busiest guys in Cinci were the team trainers and physicians. All they had to deal with in July was Roberto Kelly's separated shoulder, Kevin Mitchell's strained hamstring, Bip Roberts' sprained thumb, John Smiley's bone spur, John Roper's strained muscle in his side and Kevin Wickander's sore shoulder.

Not a healthy ball club!

They still managed a 7-4 run going into the All-Star break and slid back to the .500 groove afterward. Actually, it's amazing they could win at all missing half their starters.

But San Fran was the hottest team in baseball and the Reds found themselves 17.5 behind at the end of the month. They must have felt cursed.

August 13-15 (66-68, 20.5 games back)
This month they lost Tom Browning, Willie Greene, Larkin and Roberts (again).

They also lost three games on the Giants, who were slumping at 15-11 in August.

Like it mattered.

Sept./Oct. 7-21 (67-95, 31 games back)
The Reds lost Kevin Mitchell again and, like the rest of us, they took the month off to enjoy the 'last great pennant race.'

Who could blame them?

Park Effect. Riverfront Stadium is more generous to home run hitters than any other park in the majors; it yields a 34 percent increase in dingers. As you might expect, it also boosts run production by six percent. Doubles are increased 8 percent but this is offset by a 21 percent reduction in triples.

The park is especially kind to lefties, boosting their HR a whopping 48 percent and their BA 4 percent. Righties have to suffer through a mere 28 percent bump in homers and their averages are actually reduced two percent.

Fielders love its smooth turf; 20 percent

fewer errors are committed in the infield, 15 percent overall.

Offense. The Reds couldn't keep anyone healthy last year and the offense really suffered. They still managed to post batting and slugging percentages right around the league averages, but you can expect their production to increase next year. Their DL last year was as long as Steve Howe's rap sheet and that won't happen two years in a row.

One bright spot was their running game. They recorded 124 steals with a 71 percent success rate and grounded into 104 double plays, the second lowest total in the league.

Total Offense: -35.7

Pitching. Jose Rijo is one the finest starters in the game but he didn't get much support last year. And nobody else on the staff deserved any. The staff posted a 1.399 ratio and 4.51 ERA to go 49-62; only Pittsburgh and Colorado were worse (but don't forget the trials of pitching in Colorado).

To be fair, Browning and Smiley suffered injuries, but they just aren't top-flight starters anymore. The addition of Erik Hanson should go a long way to improve the staff and the Reds have some promising youngsters who are ready for a full shot.

The bullpen was a bit chaotic last year with Dibble out and a host of converted starters filling in. They saved 67 percent of their opportunities and only allowed 27 percent of their inherited runners score. But they allowed plenty of their own guys on (1.424 ratio), and that pushed their ERA to 4.55. If Dibble stays healthy and the new guys are allowed to settle in, the bullpen could stabilize this year. But the question marks remain.

Total Pitching: 33.6

Defense:
Infield: Hal Morris is a decent defensive first baseman. The mess at second was exacerbated by Bip Roberts' injury, but neither he, nor Juan Samuel were that great.

At short, Barry Larkin played very well at times, but was hampered by his injuries. At third, Chris Sabo was slipping quite fast. His once facile play at the position was not readily apparent last year.

Pts: 13.6

Outfield: The Reds outfield looks very athletic (in right and center), but it wasn't really that great. Sanders was reasonably good and Kelly was a smidge above-average. Surprisingly, the less-than-slim Mitchell didn't do too badly.

Pts: 7.9

Catcher: Joe Oliver's defense has been up and down the last few years. He's got a decent arm and is reasonably sure-handed. It was hard to talk about his leadership skills and ability to call a game as his staff was AWOL except for Rijo.

Pts: 5.3

Total Defense: 26.8

1994 Personnel:
Catcher:
Starters: Joe Oliver will start at catcher.
Bench: Brian Dorsett, Darren Cox and a vacuum will vie for the job of doing nothing behind the plate for the Reds.
Starters: 2.7
Bench: Z-

Infield:
1B: At first, Tim Costo and Hal Morris will fight for time.
2B: Bret Boone and Calvin Reese will fight, but the job will likely go to Boone.
3B: Willie Greene and Costo will fight here. Possibly Boone, too.
SS: Larkin, Larkin, Larkin.
IF Bench: Brian Koelling, Keith Kessinger, Jamie Dismuke, Jeff Branson, Juan Samuel, Casey Candaele and possibly Bubba Smith could all see time as backups or replacements.
Starters: 58.2
Bench: B-

Outfield:
LF: Mitchell will be in left.
CF: Kelly will be in center.
RF: Reggie Sanders will be in right.
Bench: Possible bench banditos include: Cecil Espy, Tommy Gregg, Keith Gordon, Gary Varsho, Thomas Howard, Jacob Brumfield, Greg Tubbs and long-range prospects Chad Mottola, Steve Gibralter and Cleveland Ladell.
Starters: 44.9
Bench: C-

Starting Pitching: Jose Rijo, Erik Hanson and John Smiley will get three slots. Tom Browning, Tim Pugh, John Roper and Mike Anderson will vie for the remaining spots.
  Front-Line: 67.4
  Second-Echelon: C

Relief Pitching: Rob Dibble will get the first shot at closing. Look for Johnny Ruffin to get some shots at the job if Dibble stinks. Other relief possibilities include Jerry Spradlin, Steve Foster, Landrum, Jeff Reardon, Scott Service, Powell, Wickander, Chris Bushing. Long-rangers include Lister, Ferry, Jarvis, Jeff Pierce, Patterson.
  Front-Line: 3.2
  Second-Echelon: C

Player Value: 133.4

Farm System: The Reds are pretty darn thin. They have only two decent young 'uns in the infield, Calvin Reese and Jamie Dismuke. Costo and Greene are beautiful, but they're being counted on at the big-league level. In the outfield, there's Chad Mottola and Steve Gibralter. Both have great potential, but they're the only pair that really project well. Lister, Johnny Ruffin and Chris Bushing look to shore up the bullpen in the future, but the starting prospects are either gone or are going to be vying for jobs anyway.
  Infield: C
  Outfield: C
  Starters: D
  Relievers: C+
  Farm Ranking: C

Management and Ownership: Need we restate our opinion on the Reds ownership and front-office management? The declasse way they dumped Tony Perez (who seemed to be a sacrificial lamb to "racial sensitivity" anyway) made anyone in touch with the baseball world sick. GM Jim Bowden has made some good moves and pulled some boners, but overall, he seems adequate. The fact that he has less character than Stalin and has the demeanor of the now-deceased Ayatollah Khomeini must be factored in somehow. He'd be a 'C' if he wasn't a jerk. As for Marge, she's quite homely (but we can't hold that against her) and her handling of the Reds has been even homelier.

Davey Johnson has the reputation of being a managerial genius. He may be, but he sure as heck didn't get a chance to prove it with his injury-riddled 1993 personnel He'll get more of a chance in 1994, but there's trouble brewing as Large Marge don't like him. Don't expect him to last the year. Former *Baseball Tonight* analyst Ray Knight looks like he'll get dibs when the genius falls, let's hope he can teach better than he hit. He always picked apart everyone's swing, but he never hit .300 with 20+ homers. Not even once.
  Ownership: E
  Front Office: D
  Field Management: Incomplete (B?)
  Overall: D

1994 Outlook: Give us a break. This team is so screwy, trying to predict what the Reds will do is like trying to predict what Ross Perot'll say next. You can be sure something nuts'll happen, but what exactly? The Reds are a decent team. They have a good offense and they have the potential to contend. But they are also injury prone and have a good chance of being the "Midwestern Mets" if things don't go right. Hey, Kevin Mitchell's here. That's enough right there. We predict somewhere between 70-95 wins.

HOUSTON ASTROS

1993 Outlook: Sure the Braves were the odds-on favorites, with the Reds being a close second, but you couldn't count out those crafty Astros. Houston had improved its staff immensely with Drabek and Swindell and with the cadre of young talent, led by Mr. Bagwell, why couldn't the Astros surprise the league? Sure they wouldn't win 100 games, but supposing Atlanta and Cinci got caught in a war of attrition ... Couldn't Houston step into the breach and kick both their booties off the top of the mountain? This is baseball after all, anything is possible.

April 14-8 (14-8, 0 games back)
The Astros finished 14-5 for the month after losing their first three games of the season. Doug Drabek keyed an exceptional 3.06 ERA month for the staff with his 1.98 ERA. His 2-3 record left something to be desired,

though. Pete Harnisch was 2-0, 3.30; Doug Jones had a 1.72 ERA and four saves and Greg Swindell was 4-1, 3.08 – the free agents looked like a Godsend. The hitting also was pretty strong. Eric Anthony hit .338 and Luis Gonzalez hit .315-4-13, slugging .534.

May 27-22 (13-14, 5 games back)
The offense surged while the pitching dipped. The lead started evaporating. Harnisch fired a 10-K 6-3 win over the Reds on 5/9, pulling Houston within half a game of the Giants. As late as 5/16, the Astros were only one back, but by the 21st, they were knocked 5.5 games back when Derek Bell hit a two-run homer off Doug Jones in the ninth at San Diego. During the month, Bagwell exploded, hitting .412-7-25 and slugging .676! Biggio also keyed the offense going .324-6-10 (.581 SL%). Swindell and Jones were a combined 2-7 (Jones 4.58 ERA, Swindell 7.71), pushing the pitching down.

June 38-37 (11-15, 12 games back)
The offense went AWOL and the pitching joined for the ride. Drabek, Harnisch, Jones, Portugal, Hernandez and Swindell were a combined 5-13 with a 4.86 ERA, with such notable singular performances as Jones' 9.95 ERA and Harnisch's 5.02. Only Kile's 5-0, 1.16 month kept them afloat. The team went on an 8-2 run early in the month, but kept getting blown out. They lost games by margins of 7-5, 8-0, 14-11, 9-1, 5-0, 10-3, 8-5, 7-0, 8-2 and 6-5: A combination of Tiger losses and Angels losses.

July 54-50 (16-13, 15.5 games back)
Houston kept treading water while the Braves and Giants were playing on a higher level. That's not to say that the Astros weren't playing well, it's just that they couldn't keep up with the torrid play of the pack leaders. Harnisch started turning around his year with a 4-2, 3.24 month; Portugal also went 4-1 2.39. On the offensive side, while kid sensation Andujar Cedeno was going .232 with a .305 SL%, Luis Gonzalez was posting a .366-4-16 month with a nice .600 SL%. Even Steve Finley slugged .455!

August 69-63 (15-13, 16.5 games back)
The race was over. With the pressure off, Bagwell and Biggio went mad, Bagwell hit .352 and slugged .574, Biggio hit .318 with five homers and slugged .545. Harnisch, Portugal and Swindell were combined 10-3, but it didn't matter.

Sept./Oct. 85-77 (16-14, 19 games back)
Harnisch was amazing, posting a 1.16 ERA. What was more amazing was that he lost a game! Portugal was no slouch, posting a 1.62 mark, but he went 5-0. Pity, Petey, sometime's there ain't no justice. The pitching remained solid, but the offense dropped down a notch. It was a long, hot summer and the Astros just flat-out didn't have the horses.

Park Effects: The Astrodome is the third most-extreme pitchers' park in baseball, cutting runs-allowed by 10 percent. The 'Dome cuts B.A., doubles and triples by 4 percent, and homers by 19 percent.

The park builds on all these negative effects by suppressing errors by 20 percent.

This is a park for right-handed hitters (to put it another way, it's the bane of Luis Gonzalez' existence. It cuts homers by 10 percent and doesn't affect their averages. Lefties lose 29 percent of their homers(!) and 9 percent off their average.

Offense: The Astros had an above-average offense last year. Adjusting for their park, they had a good on-base percentage and very good power. They for a high average; they hit lots of doubles and triples and smack a decent amount of homers. They drew an average amount of walks. Their sole weakness is a poor running game, but that's something you can live with (they can cure 60 percent of that by getting Craig Biggio back on track).

The team needs to get rid of some older bats and make room for some of the kiddies. There are four or five potential-impact bats sitting in the minors waiting for jobs to be freed up. Weaknesses on the major-league roster can certainly be fixed from within.

Pitching: Adjusting for the park, the team had an excellent rotation and a good bullpen.

The rotation featured the second-best four-man rotation in baseball (and if you consider Swindell to be the fifth starter, even at his '93 level, he wasn't that bad!). These guys ha excellent stamina, good walk- and K-rates and they reeled off 100 quality starts (despite two of the starters having very poor seasons).

The rotation got stronger as the season progressed. Led by Harnisch and Portugal, the Astros ERA in the second-half improved from 3.73 to its final 3.49 mark (3.21 second-half ERA).

The bullpen was great at stranding runners and about average at converting saves. With the help of the park, they also kept the ball in the park and didn't allow many base-runners.

The loss of Xavier Hernandez will probably hurt the bullpen quite a bit, but the addition of Domingo Jean could easily offset that loss. The Astros also lost Mark Portugal, a fine starter last year, but it's improbable he'll match his 1993 performance. They are looking to dump another starter to save money (possibly Pete Harnisch). If they do, it's improbable that they'll contend.

The team has a lot of nice pitchers high up in the system and look to use them to fill out holes in the staff. Still, prospects have a learning curve and with pitching there are no guarantees. It remains to be seen whether the Astros will have enough guns for this season.

Defense:

Catcher: Taubensee and Servais were offensive complements, but they combined to be almost nothing. Neither can throw worth a damn, but they're adequate otherwise.

Pts: - 0.4

Infield: Three fourths of this defensive unit is amazing. Bagwell, Caminiti and Biggio are among the best fielders in the game. Cedeno negates about half their value with his ineptitude (he's by far the worst defensive shortstop in baseball).

Pts: 14.9

Outfield: Gonzalez was very good. Finley and Anthony were solidly above-average, but unexceptional.

Pts: 11.6
Total: 26.1

1994 Personnel

Catcher: Scott Servais and Eddie Taubensee are a nice platoon offensively. Defensively, they both keep the pitchers in line, but neither is really much of a thrower.

Bench: Tony Eusebio and Scooter Tucker are the tentative reserves. Eusebio, 27, (.324-1-43 at Triple-A) doesn't look like a whole lot. Tucker, 27, (.274-1-37) is more of the same. The Astros better hope their platoon stays healthy.

Starters: -4.1
Bench: C

Infield:

1B: Jeff Bagwell is the glue on this team. He's the Astros best hitter and even though he plays first, he's one of the best defenders on the team, too. If the Astros have an MVP candidate, he is it.

2B: Craig Biggio, like Bagwell, is an indispensable. He is a solid bat, but with his incredible defensive growth last year, he moves right up to the head of the class with the Baergas and the Alomars. He just needs to maintain consistency to stay in the stratosphere.

3B: Ken Caminiti is more replaceable than his right-side-of-the-infield mates, but he's still a valuable cog. Right now, the question is how much is his offense going to deteriorate. We're guessing that it will be enough to warrant his replacement within two years.

SS: It is imperative that Andujar Cedeno improve his defense. His bat places him amongst the best in the game, but his glove knocks him 10 steps back. He certainly has the tools to do it, but in non-rotisse terms he hurts the team with his sickly shortstop play.

IF Bench: Roberto Petagine could be NL Rookie of the Year if he got 450 at-bats. Other first base options, Jack Daugherty and Jim Lindeman are merely stopgaps. Both could hit, but who would want them to? At second base, Dave Hajek, 26, (.292-5-27 at Double-A) and James Mouton look like possibilities. In all honesty, Mouton is overmatched at second and he should get a look at left or right with the trade of Eric Anthony. Phil Nevin is the most viable candidate to backup third base, but if Mike Groppuso can push his game up five notches, he might see some PT, too. The logical winner at short would be Andy Stankiewicz. Major-League pisspot Orlando Miller and possibly Frank Kellner (.301-4-36 at Double-A) might also get some work.

Starters: 74.3
Bench: B

Outfield:

LF: Luis Gonzalez is what they call a solid little ballplayer. He's not exceptional, but he has nary a weakness and he's a fine fielder.

He's sneaking into his prime, so he could spank 20+ homers this year.

CF: Steve Finley is an adequate center fielder, possibly one that can play an important role on a division-winner, but he's not anything if he plays like he did in 1993. He has to draw more walks, stay healthy and hit closer to .290.

RF: Who will play right field in 1994? You probably need to read the bench section to get an idea of who'll vie for the job.

Bench: Jesse Barfield, formerly of Japan, Brian Hunter, Kevin Bass, Mike Felder, Willie Ansley and Rick Parker (.308-2-12 at Triple-A) will all be in the right field (and reserve mix). Because Hunter is considered a grade-A prospect by many, expect to see him get the best shot at the job. Prospects like Bob Abreu, Ray Montgomery, Gary Mota and Buck McNabb are longer shots to get playing time. Braulio Castillo, 26, (.363-2-37 at Triple-A) and slug(ger) Lance Madsen (.221-23-65 at Double-A) are also warm bodies.

Starters: 27.8
Bench: B

Starting Pitching: Barring trades that are supposedly brewing in early January (when this is being written) Doug Drabek, Greg Swindell, Pete Harnisch and Darryl Kile will have rotation spots. The remaining slot will be fought over by a ton of qualified kiddies, namely: Kevin Gallaher, Mike Hampton, Chris Holt, Mark Huisman, Domingo Jean, Shane Reynolds, Dave Veres, Billy Wagner, Donnie Wall and Brian Williams.

The best candidates for immediate insertion into rotation are Jean, Reynolds, Williams, Holt, Huisman and Hampton.

Starters: 97.6
Bench: A

Relief Pitching: Mitch Williams has the closing role to lose. Alvin Morman, Tom Edens, Todd Jones and Al Osuna should get serious looks for long-relief (look at Morman and Jones to get shots at closing should Williams self-destruct). Jim Daugherty, John Hudek (3.79 ERA, 18/11 K/W in 19 AAA innings) and Terry Mathews (3.55 ERA, 34/11 K/W in 33 AAA IP) are other options the Astros can choose to pursue.

Front-Line: 21.0
Second-Echelon:

Player Value: 216.6

Farm System: The Astros look well-stocked. Awfully well-stocked. In the infield, they have super-bat Roberto Petagine; James Mouton and Orlando Miller at second and short, respectively; and potential superstar Phil Nevin at third. In the outfield, the Astros have three possible stars in Bob Abreu, Richard Hidalgo and Brian Hunter (plus other possibilities in Horne, Montgomery, Mota and McNabb). With Mike Hampton, Kevin Gallaher, Chris Holt, Mark Huisman, Domingo Jean and Billy Wagner, the Astros are loaded at starter. They are reasonably thin at reliever with Al Morman and Dougherty, but you can't have everything.

Infield: A
Outfield: B+
Starters: A
Relievers: C
Overall: B+

Ownership and Management: *"Baseball Weekly"* and the Advocate staff are in agreement here: Drayton McLane has the potential to be the Steinbrenner of the NL Central. It is quite easy to see that the reason the Astros didn't win 90 games last year was because of a slightly inconsistent offense and the sub-par work of Drabek and Swindell. In essence, McLane blamed the diaper for being dirty (one can't fire the baby, after all) and got rid of Art Howe and Bill Wood. Howe and Wood had as much control over Swindell and Drabek's poor seasons, as we did.

Obviously the jury is out on Terry Collins and Bob Watson. Collins, a former Pirate coach, is a more aggressive, go-get-'em guy than Howe, but Howe and his staff coaxed some pretty solid seasons out of Bagwell, Kile, Portugal and Harnisch, can the pepper-pot Collins move the Astros up a notch? Watson's trades are neither here nor there. Hampton and Felder for Anthony is a wash. Jean and Stanky for Hernandez is probably a good move for Houston in the long-run, but how about now? The trade for Mitch Williams is something we'd rather not discuss. There's no one writing this book that has anything nice to say about Mitch's ability (we think he's a helluva guy – a great personality – but we don't want him closing *our* games).

1994 Outlook: This is the chance for Collins and Watson to shine. The Astros could win 90 games if Swindell and Drabek just come back to normal. If one of the kids were to become a solid 12-game winner, the Astros could win 95 games and the new guys could look like geniuses. Can it happen? Yes, it most certainly could. Chances are, however, one of last year's surprises (most probably Kile), will fall to earth; the rookie in the No. 5 hole will pitch poorly; and one of the hitters will drop down a big notch (Biggio?). This would probably put the 'Stros at the 85-88 win mark. In this division, that makes them strong contenders. With the new playoff system and the ability for teams to play exceptional ball for moderate amounts of time, the 1994 Astros could be world champs (just don't expect to see us at the betting window, laying $500 on Houston).

PITTSBURGH PIRATES

1994 Outlook: The Pittsburgh Pirates were expected to do one thing: Finish ahead of Florida. With Bonds, Drabek, Smiley and Bonilla gone, there were about 20-22 wins missing from the team that dominated the NL East during the early 90s. The Pirates had no proven starters that were healthy, their bullpen was riddled with question marks and the only proven hitters on their team were Van Slyke and Jay Bell. 75+ wins would have been a major moral victory.

April 11-11 (11-11, 6 games back)
It didn't take long for Philadelphia to build a sizable lead; of course the Phils played .773 ball in the first month.

The Bucs got a good start out of the blocks. Benefitting from six wins (two sweeps) over San Diego, Pittsburgh was 7-2 and one game out on April 15.

But five straight losses to L.A. and Cinci quickly dumped them down to a tie for fifth place. By the end of the month, they were an even .500, 6 games out and in fourth.

Orlando Merced got off to a fast start, hitting .343. The pitching staff was looking shaky, though. The starters were getting bounced around a bit, and Alejandro Pena and John Candelaria had missed the beginning of the season due to injury.

May 12-14 (23-25, 10.5 games back)
But the Pirates continued to hold their own against the league's best. They started the month with tough series' against Atlanta, Houston, and Philadelphia and managed to stay at .500 through the 12th. Of course, the Phils were managing to stay at .742 and were still gaining ground.

They booted a couple tough games in the remainder of the month, including a ninth-inning loss to the Marlins on the 25th, to wind up 10.5 out in fifth.

They weren't getting much done at the plate; the team hit .259 for May. Kevin Young hit .194 and Jeff King hit .216 (although he somehow knocked in 18 runs). Merced, on the other hand, continued his tear, hitting .380 with 15 RBI.

Youngster Steve Cooke made his presence felt, going 3-1 with a 3.12 ERA and Bob Walk had his best, and last decent, month, grabbing four wins and keeping his ERA at 3.47. Randy Tomlin was sidelined with a inflammation in his elbow, however, and he wouldn't return until July.

June 14-14 (37-39, 14.5 games back)
It was getting pretty clear that the Bucs were an average team and .500 wasn't going to keep them anywhere near the pack. Philadelphia had cooled down to a mere .642 by the end of the month, but Pittsburgh had lost another four games on them.

They played well at times, but a crucial road trip through Florida and St. Louis left them on the short end of back-to-back sweeps. The Mets proved to be medicinal, however, and the Bucs swept them, split with the Cubs and won a series in Philly. In a nutshell, Pittsburgh was inconsistent.

The loss of one of their most consistent players, Andy Van Slyke, didn't help. He went on the DL on the 15th with a fractured collarbone he received chasing a fly ball and would be out for the next 2.5 months.

July 10-18 (47-57, 18.5 games back)
The month of July firmly shut the door on whatever hopes the Bucs may have had.

After the All-Star break, they lost three of four to the Braves and were shut out twice by Avery and Glavine. This started a 4-10 skid against Montreal, Houston and Atlanta (1-3, again) that left them 18.5 out.

They just didn't have the firepower or the pitching to compete with the better teams. A month of nothing but top-flight ballclubs left them reeling.

August 15-13 (62-70, 20 games back)

The month began with a therapeutic trip through fourth-place Chicago and last Place New York. The Pirates won five of seven and looked to be on the road to recovery.

As proof, they split a hard-fought series with the Cardinals, but then lost a wild one in Florida. Tough to figure.

But they had definitely rebounded form their dismal July. The offense came to life, knocking in 133 runs and hitting .292, their best performance all year. Jay Bell led the charge, hitting .386 and slugging .526.

The pitching had deteriorated, however, and they posted a 5.39 ERA, largely due to the whopping 40 taters they'd served up.

Sept./Oct. 13-17 (75-87, 22 games back)

The home stretch was fairly rough. The Bucs had the luck of finishing the season with division contenders, either still in it or, like the Phils, warming up for the playoffs.

Fortunately, they had a couple series with teams like the Mets and Cubs to keep their record respectable, but the big guys basically beat them up.

Basically, who's more motivated, they guys looking at a twenty game deficit, or the guys who can still see imagine the champagne?

Pittsburgh coasted into a fifth-place finish, 22 games behind Philadelphia.

Park Effect. Three Rivers Stadium doesn't have much effect on hits and batting averages, but it does limit run production by three percent. This is largely due to the fact that it reduces homers by 12 percent; righties alone face a 18 percent reduction.

The stadium does yield extra base hits, however, as doubles are increased six percent and triples 18 percent.

You don't usually see a higher rate of errors on turf, but Three Rivers is an exception. Infielders have committed six percent more errors in Pittsburgh over the last three years.

Offense. Pittsburgh doesn't have much trouble getting on base, but they just don't have any power. Their 110 homers were the second lowest in the NL and they slugged only .393. Not surprisingly, they scored only 707 runs, 21 below the league average.

That's the way Pittsburgh has built its offense. They traditionally rely on a high OBP and good speed, but their running game was pitiful last year. They stole only 92 bases in 147 attempts and grounded into 129 double plays (two less than the league-leading Cubs).

They clearly need more power to round out their attack. The injury to Van Slyke hurt in that department, as well as their team speed, but everyone else was healthy. Their lineup this year should be much the same, so unless there is mass improvement, their production should also be the same.

Total Offense: 5.3

Pitching. If you adjust for park effects (i.e. Colorado's), Pittsburgh's starters were by far the worst staff in the NL. The main culprits were Walk and Wakefield, who combined for a 19-25 record and 5.65 ERA. The remainder of the staff, however, were either promising youngsters or veterans struggling with injuries so you might see much improvement.

The outlook for the bullpen is not so promising, however. The Belinda trade left Pittsburgh without an established closer and not much in the long-relief stable. The Pirates have some prospects to look at, but its doubtful they'll be ready to be effective this year.

Total Pitching: -0.4

Defense:

Infield: In a nutshell, Young and King are exceptional corner defenders and Jay Bell is roughly average. Bell's numbers are exceptional because last year an incredible number of balls were hit to shortstop – 651 – Cal Ripken had 571 hit to his zone and he played every inning of his team's games. Bell didn't turn a high percentage of those balls into outs, so his defense wasn't that great. The real problem is Garcia, though. He stank and because of this, he negated the fine defense from Y&K.

Pts: 1.0

Outfield: Andy Van Slyke's injuries really hurt the Pirates' center field defense. In left Al Martin was neither here nor there, so it was up to Orlando Merced to carry the flag for good outfield defense.

Pts: 0.5

Catcher: Don Slaught is not much on defense. In the glory days of the Pitt catching corps, "Sluggo" was the bat and "Spanky" LaValliere was the glove. Sluggo is sure-handed and not awful with his throwing, but the team's cruddy pitching hurt his rating.
Pts: 0.4
Total Defense: 1.9

1994 Personnel
Catcher:
Starters: Don Slaught will provide the catching onslaught.
Bench: Backups will include Tom Prince and Jerry Goff and possibly Osik.
Starter:12.8
Bench: C

Infield:
1B: Kevin Young, Brian Hunter and Rich Aude will fight all-day.
2B: Carlos "rotten 'd'" Garcia will start.
3B: Jeff King should retain dibs on third.
SS: Jay Bell and his over-rated glove will continue to provide solid play at short.
IF Bench: John Wehner, Brown and Morman, Ken Bonifay, Jose Sandoval, David Rohde are among the scrubs and kids who could get bench time.
Starters: 9.7
Bench: D

Outfield:
LF: Al Martin will play right.
CF: Look for Van Slyke here.
RF: Unless he's sold for scrap metal, look for Orlando Merced.
Bench: Look for Midre Cummings, Scott Bullett, Willie Pennyfeather, Ben Shelton, Andy Tomberlin, Glenn Wilson, Dave Clark, Lloyd McClendon. Prospects include Trey Beamon, Shon Walker, Danny Clyburn and Stanton Cameron.
Starters: 44.1
Bench: B

Starting Pitching: Let's hope Bob Walk has been put to sleep. Tim Wakefield, Paul Wagner, Brett Backlund, Randy Tomlin, Zane Smith, Steve Cooke, Jon Lieber, Dave Otto and Denny Neagle and John Hope are possibilities.
Front-Line: 20.9

Second-Echelon: D

Relief Pitching: Mark Dewey, Menendez, Joel Johnston, Toliver, Blas Minor and Denny Neagle look to get jobs. Down the road, look for Danny Miceli to get a shot at closing. Mark Petkovsek, Dennis Moeller, Alejandro Pena, Delosantos look like they could all have ERAs under 15.00
Front-Line: -5.0
Second-Echelon: E

Player Value: 82.5

Farm System: The system has a decent number of players. In the infield, the 'Rats have Rich Aude at first and Ken Bonifay at third. The outfield is much richer with Stanton Cameron and Midre Cummings at the top and young pups like Trey Beamon, Shon Walker and Danny Clyburn in the system's nether regions. Right now, all the OF kids are long on potential, short on production, but still, they might be giants (actually, Pirates). They have two nice relief prospects in Miceli and Lieber (thanks to the trade w/KC for Stan Belinda). Starting pitching is pretty thin. The only decent prospect they have is Backlund. All the other kids are in the rotation already.
Infield: C-
Outfield: B+
Starters: D
Relievers: B-
Farm Ranking: C

Management and Ownership: Vincent Sarni and Douglas Danforth are the two powers in charge of this team's future. These guys are like Pohlad and the group in Minnesota, only not so well-run. They claim they don't have $$$ (and let's face it, fan support in Pittsburgh isn't the greatest, even when they were winning), so they don't spend it. The front-office is really kind of a question mark, now GM Cam Bonifay hasn't really been able to do much except watch Doug Drabek leave. Free-agent signings have been comprised of "super-talents" like Lonnie Smith. As for the player development end, Bonifay's regime hasn't been in power long enough for one to really see how effective they are.

Manager Jim Leyland is pretty much a miracle worker. His reputation is that of a Kreskin or a David Copperfield. With the injuries and the ineffectiveness of his pitching staff, 75 wins last year was a pretty good performance. Leyland's current team is young and inexperienced, so they don't bunt, hit-and-run and do other fundamentals too well. Jimmy's used to having the horses on the staff, so he was a little inclined to let Cooke and Wagner pitch deep into games. These are two pretty good kids, so it's understandable why he did it. Leyland's primary strengths are that he's a good motivator who's excellent at communication; plus, he's a stern disciplinarian. With a young team, this'll keep the kids from getting too unruly.

Ownership: C-
Front Office: C-
Field Management: B+
Overall: C

1994 Outlook: The Pirates could improve to .500 or maybe even a bit over .500, but asking much more would be taxing. Right now, they need to solidify their pitching in three spots and get their bullpen in order, too. Until Miceli and Lieber are ready, they don't have viable closing at the big-league level. In addition, they need more offense (especially at first). If they can work Aude in and hide his glove, plus the kids keep pitching well, then the Pirates can be spoilers.

ST. LOUIS CARDINALS

1993 Outlook: There was reason for optimism when the Cardinals broke camp in the spring. Their rotation wasn't exactly stacked, but it didn't suffer from comparison in the league. St. Louis was fortunate to have two or three decent prospects at AAA that could step in if a starter faltered. Their offense was greatly improved with both the addition of Gregg Jefferies and the subtraction of Felix Jose. But St. Louis was far from being a flawless team. There were questions about the hitting of Geronimo Pena at second base and Todd Zeile at third. Pagnozzi was a guaranteed waste of plate appearances and the bullpen didn't look promising. Because of these blemishes, the Cardinals were considered a second or third place team in their division.

April 13-10 (13-10, 4.5 games back)
The Cardinals rotation had an 8-7 record for the month, but with a combined ERA of 3.41 it was evident that they suffered from a lack of support. The St. Louis offense could only muster a .245 batting average, and was little help to the pitching staff. Though Gilkey hit .339 in April, the lineup had difficulty scoring runs because no one else was hitting. Rene Arocha managed a 3-0, 1.66 start and was well on his way to a solid season when he broke his finger and was forced to spend a month on the DL. However, their troubles were academic. The Phillies had gotten off to a 17-5 start, leaving the Cardinals and the rest of the NL East in the dust.

May 12-14 (25-24, 9 games back)
Again, an inability to score runs kept the Cardinals from capitalize on some nice starts. Arocha and Cormier were the main victims. They each turned in a couple of quality starts in May, yet they walked away with a combined 1-1 record. Osborne had reason to gripe as well, being saddled with a 1-2 record despite a 2.87 ERA. The Cards had difficulty waking their bats up, hitting just .253 with a puny .320 slugging. The Phillies were showing no signs of relinquishing their grip on the league lead, and because of their anemic offense, St. Louis could do nothing to stop them.

June 20-7 (45-31, 6.5 games back)
The Cardinals broke their scoring drought in June, putting up a .297 average and a .358 on-base. Jefferies was the hot hitter, and his .444 batting average and .685 slugging helped to bring his season totals up to respectable levels again. Gilkey (.336 BA, .589 SLG) continued to swing the bat well and Ozzie Smith checked in with a .309 average as well. Even Pagnozzi hit .353 in limited duty. Everyone seemed to be getting in on the act. In the rotation, Joe Magrane was beautiful, winning five straight and posting a 2.47 ERA for the month. He led the starters to an 18-6 record with only three no-decisions. With the improved run-support, Osborne and Tewksbury had a combined total of eight wins. The Cardinals were clawing their way back into contention, but the Phillies weren't giving them any opportunities to catch up.

July 14-13 (59-44, 6 games back)

The St. Louis offense continued to surge, maintaining its .298 batting average, .358 on-base and .448 slugging. Gilkey (.333 average .530 slugging) and Jefferies (.367, .425 on-base) paced the Cardinal hitters. But their contributions would go largely unappreciated. Tewksbury had a 3.43 ERA for the month but he could only manage two wins due to sloppy work from the bullpen. The problem affected the other starters as well. The rotation was responsible for an 11-7 record in July while the bullpen struggled with a 3-6 mark. The Cardinals also decided to promote top pitching prospect Allen Watson to get some fresh blood in the rotation. He began his major league career by holding the Braves to one run in six innings July 8. But no matter how well the staff pitched, the bullpen sabotaged their efforts more often than not.

August 13-16 (72-60, 10 games back)

It was evident early on that the Cardinals had little chance to catch the Phillies in the NL East. Tewksbury was pitching in rare form and young Watson, with his six-game winning streak, was turning heads in the rotation. But Cormier had inflammation in his shoulder shut him down mid-month, and Osborne's arm trouble was just beginning to manifest itself. The St. Louis bullpen remained ineffective. Guetterman and Olivares were especially disappointing, and Joe Magrane had a 4.97 ERA for St. Louis when they up and released him. Jefferies (.350 average, .443 on-base.) continued to look like an MVP at the plate, but the rest of the Cards' lineup was stagnant, and they fell four games further off the pace.

Sept./Oct. 15-15 (87-75, 10 games back)

The season did not end on a promising note for the Cardinals. Brian Jordan underwent shoulder surgery and missed the remainder of the season. And though he didn't go on the disabled list, lefty Donovan Osborne didn't start a game after August 23 because of stiffness in his shoulder.

Tewksbury polished off a 17-win season and Jefferies finished third in the batting race with a .342 average. But in the end, it was a string of nagging injuries to key players, an inability to score runs, and a less-than-intimidating bullpen that did in the Cardinals' pennant hopes.

Park Effects. Busch Stadium favors the pitcher to a small degree. It's a symmetrical facility that has a 402 ft. center field wall and is 330 down the lines. There are no cheap home runs hit here. The largest effect the park has on a team's offense is in the home run category, where it is responsible for a 12 percent reduction in round-trippers. Over the past two years, runs have been reduced by at seven percent. While not a drastic reduction, the fact that scoring was generally hindered in St. Louis during an expansion season explains why Cardinal starters went 61-49 with an ERA of 4.03.

Offense: St. Louis scored 758 runs last year, putting their offense in the same class as the Colorado Rockies. It was a surprising amount of runs considering the lack of power in their lineup. St. Louis out-homered only Pittsburgh and Florida last year. But the Cardinals manufactured runs by getting on base well and having enough team speed to advance runners effectively. Their .341 on-base average and 153 stolen bases last year were good for second-place finishes in the National League. The lineup also hit well with runners in scoring position. But the reason why the Cardinals couldn't compete in their division last season was their inability to score runs when they needed them. They were one of the hottest lineups in the league in June and July, but the bottom dropped out when they hit just .259 for the month of August. By that time, the Phillies had a hammer-lock on the pennant.

Total Offense: 53.6

Pitching: The Cardinals didn't have a power-house pitching staff last year. In fact, they finished last in the league in strikeouts and allowed a .276 opposition batting average. The rotation turned in just five complete games and lasted only about six innings per start. But the Cardinals considered themselves fortunate to have a fairly stable, young starter corps throughout most of the season. By the time injuries started to hit, they were out of the race anyway.

The relief staff was your standard-issue bullpen, stocked to the brim with aging veterans who pitched like aging veterans. Mike Perez was the only pitcher under 30. Lee Smith performed capably as the closer, but was shipped off to the Yankees late in the season for a prospect and the search started for his replacement.

Total Pitching: 60.9

Defense:
Infield: The question at the beginning of the season was whether or not Jefferies could handle the move to first. By the end of April, all questions were answered as Jefferies turned in solid work around the bag. Luis Alicea emerged as the starting second baseman last year and displayed excellent range. Though he was a bit error-prone, his work at the plate was enough to distinguish himself from Geronimo Pena.

Ozzie Smith may have missed a few games here and there, but its hard to imagine a steadier glove at shortstop in the NL whose name isn't Barry Larkin. Ozzie's range factor last year was a nifty 5.54, reminiscent of his automatic Gold Glove glory years. Todd Zeile is not a natural third baseman. Consequently, he committed 33 errors in the field last year.

Pts: 37.6

Outfield: Gilkey slipped a bit in left field, but he battled a leg injury which might explain why his range factor fell off the table. He led NL left fielders in assists, indicating his arm is still intact. Ray Lankford and Mark Whiten (whose greatest defensive asset is his Smith and Wesson arm) were adequate in center and right, giving the Cardinals an average defensive outfield.

Pts: 4.5

Catcher: Nothing special here. Both Pagnozzi and Pappas could put the gear on and catch, but neither one of them had an arm. Between the two, they caught only 34 percent of opposing runners trying to steal against them. At least Pagnozzi had an excuse for his poor defensive showing-- he was hobbled by a knee injury that robbed him of some mobility behind the plate.

Pts: 7.8

Total: 49.9

1994 Personnel:
Catcher: Pagnozzi will be the starter again, and if his surgically repaired knee is healthy he should hit in the .250 range and drive in 40-50 runs in the bottom of the batting order. It's not what champions are made of, but the Cardinals can't afford to sign a free-agent catcher that can hit well, like Brian Harper.

Bench: Erik Pappas is the main backup to Pagnozzi. His hitting was a pleasant surprise to the Cardinals last year and he could find some extra at-bats filling in for the outfield. There isn't much depth in the minors at this position, but Marc Ronan stands out as a fine defensive prospect that could find a job with the parent club by mid-season.

Starter: 2.6
Bench: C-B

Infield:
1B: There's a good chance that Gregg Jefferies, barring injury, can repeat his fine performance of last year. His power, ability to hit for average and his speed make him one of the most versatile hitters in the league.

2B: Alicea may have won the starting job, but Geronimo Pena isn't going to go away unless he's traded. The two of them will fight for playing time if Pena isn't traded first. Neither has fulfilled his potential as a hitter.

3B: Todd Zeile took a huge step towards establishing himself as a major league hitter last year with 14 homers after the all-star break. The Cardinals are looking for him to improve upon his gains in '94, and so are we.

SS: The Wizard might be slipping a bit defensively, but he is still stealing bases and scoring runs like a 29 year-old. Unless he's beset with injuries, there's no reason why Ozzie can't pile another 70 or 80 runs scored onto his career total.

IF Bench: The Cardinals have nice depth here. Rod Brewer can fill in at first base. The presence of Jose Oquendo on the bench and Darrel Deak in the minors could allow GM Dal Maxvill to deal Geronimo Pena for some pitching depth. Stan Royer, who has proven to be a contact hitter with a little power, will fill in at first and third and be one of the first pinch-hitters called upon. And don't forget about Dmitri Young. Even though he struggled at the plate and had trouble finding a position, he is still an excellent hitting prospect and the Cards will find a way to get his bat in the lineup if he gets his bat untracked.

Starters: 86.6
Bench: B+

Outfield:

LF: Gilkey is just entering his prime and should be the leadoff hitter in St. Louis this summer. As long as he doesn't screw himself up trying to reproduce his 16 homers of last year, he should be able to get on base an awful lot and score in excess of 100 runs.

CF: Ray Lankford suffered from a wrist injury and a separated shoulder last year and his numbers went right down the toilet. He should bounce back to the 15 homer, 40 stolen base plateau he established in '92.

RF: Mark Whiten became a hero in September last year with his 4 home run, 12 RBI game. But expectations for him skyrocketed in St. Louis that night and he might have trouble living up to them.

OF Bench: Brian Jordan performed admirably in place of Ray Lankford last year. He'll be the first outfielder off the bench. Rod Brewer and Erik Pappas will probably see some playing time in the outfield if needed. Anthony Lewis (.482 slugging in AA) and John Mabry (.290 average and 16 homers in AA) will both be looked at closely in the spring, but will probably report to AAA Louisville along with Allen Battle. Any one of them could be called upon in case of injury.

Starters: 42.7
Bench: C-

Starting Pitching: The reconstructive surgery that was performed on Donovan Osborne's left shoulder effectively puts a crimp in the rotation plans. Tewksbury remains the ace of the staff, but extra pressure will be placed on Cormier, Watson, and Arocha to step up and deliver. The Cardinals would like to see more experienced arms leading the way, but they have no choice. Olivares could be called back into the rotation for the fifth spot. Tom Urbani could get another shot at a starting job. The Cardinals could also opt to call up 21-year-old Brian Barber if he performs well in the spring. He's their most advanced pitcher in the minors and has adapted to every challenge so far.

Front-Line: 35.5
Second-Echelon: B

Relief Pitching: The search will be on in the spring for the new closer. Joe Torre would like to see Mike Perez step up and take the job. But he has also talked about moving Arocha into the pen and giving him the closer's job. Rich Batchelor, acquired from the Yankees for Lee Smith last year, will probably make the staff in the spring. Rob Murphy and Paul Kilgus will be back for another year to round out the bullpen. Gabe Ozuna, who maintained a 2.93 ERA in Louisville last year has a chance to make the club in the spring. John Habyan, who signed during the winter as a free agent, will also get a shot.

Front-Line: 6.2
Second-Echelon: B

Player Value: 171

Farm System: The Cardinals have a well-stocked system, featuring plenty of live arms. Brian Barber, ranked as the number-one prospect in the organization by Baseball America, heads the list of pitchers. He might be in the majors by mid-season. Then there's number-one draft pick Alan Benes. Andy's baby brother might make the jump to AA this year and could make it to the show by '95. Jay Witasick, John Frascatore and Clint Davis may not be household words, but they all have talent and will be moving up into the higher levels this season. Jeff Alkire, Doug Creek, and Steve Montgomery all look pretty good too, so keep an eye on them.

Dmitri Young is an excellent hitter and the best infield prospect the Cardinals have. Shortstop Aaron Holbert has impressed the organization and could make the jump to AAA by the end of the season. John Mabry is the outfielder closest to the show right now. But Terry Bradshaw (43 SB) and Basil Shabazz (.297 and 29 SB) had nice seasons in Class-A in '93 and will be promoted to higher levels this year.

Infield:
Outfield:
Starters:
Relievers:
Farm Ranking:

Management and Ownership: We present August A. Busch III, chairman of Anheuser-Busch Co. Inc. and owner of the St. Louis Cardinals, in that order. We give you an owner that thinks nothing more of his baseball team than another way to advertise his beer. We're talking about an organization that plays the Budweiser theme during the seventh-inning stretch, for goodness sakes. It's an organization that worries more about the beer concession receipts than player development. We can only hope the players get better lodging on the road than the Clydesdales.

Dal Maxvill has done quite a bit for the Cardinals. His top draft picks the past few years (especially the '91 draft) have panned out pretty well. Most of them are poised to win some major-league playing time within a few seasons. He took a chance and signed cuban defector Rene Arocha, who ended up winning 11 games for the Cardinals last year. And finally, he pulled off the Jose-Jefferies trade last winter, improving his offense exponentially. Maxvill has been criticized in the past for not signing premium free-agents. Critics say that he isn't interested in putting a winner on the field. What they don't realize is that the Cardinals have put the draft picks they would have lost in compensation to good use. It's always better to build an organization from the ground up, and that's just what Maxvill has done.

Joe Torre has a tendency to pull his starters a bit early which will put a strain on the bullpen. However, that is about the only negative aspect about Torre's style. He got the most out of the Cardinal offense last year by using his player's talents wisely. The Cardinals attempted 225 stolen bases, the third highest total in the league, and were pretty successful with the hit-and-run. St. Louis pinch-hitters had a .278 batting average as will, indicating that the dude calling the shots has a clue what he's doing.

Ownership:
Front Office:
Field Management:
Overall:

1994 Outlook: The Cardinals haven't done a lot over the winter to change the look of their offense. They will depend instead on their young players developing and their everyday talent staying healthy. The loss of Osborne brings the rotation into question and the bullpen will be looking for a leader in the spring. There are plenty of youngsters waiting for jobs in the minors so things aren't as bad as they seem. But the Cardinals are probably another year away from contention.

Team Essays – NL West

Colorado Rockies

1993 Outlook: Realistic expectations for the newly-formed Rockies weren't running high coming out of spring training. Bob Gebhard had used the expansion draft to build an everyday lineup with experienced major-leaguers who could hit for decent average, figuring the power would be supplied by the park. They also looked solid defensively. But it was the general consensus that no amount of defense or offense could help the starting rotation. David Nied was to be the ace of the staff that featured such power-house pitchers as Bryn Smith and Bruce Ruffin. With a weak starting five and the atmospheric advantages of Colorado, 1993 promised to be a year of fireworks in Mile High stadium, with the Rockies coming out on the short end of the stick more often than not.

April 8-14 (8-14, 6 games back)
The offense didn't get off to a blistering start, but the hitting was a darn-sight better than the pitching. On April 11, the Rockies played the Expos in a game that would sum up their short-comings eloquently. In that game, Montreal and Colorado combined for 28 runs, but Montreal scored 19 of them. Colorado pitchers surrendered 22 of the 38 hits allowed that day.

Galarraga led the way with a .412 average and 25 RBI. Charlie Hayes and Dante Bichette both hit over .300 for the month to help push the overall team average to .272. But the rotation stunk to high heaven, recording only 10 quality appearances in 22 starts, and Darren Holmes proved he wasn't ready to start the season, let alone be the closer. He earned his first save of the season April 23 and a demotion to the minors May 5.

May 7-22 (15-36, 18 games back)
Not much can be said for the Rockies in May. Put simply, their hitters let off a bit and the rotation sunk even further into the septic tank. As a whole, the pitching staff allowed 343 hits in 258.2 innings and compiled a 7.03 ERA. David Nied, who was supposed to anchor the rotation, was beaten up on a regular basis, allowing five or more runs in four of his six starts. Butch Henry rattled off four straight losses and Andy Ashby recorded an 11.19 ERA in his three starts. Armando Reynoso, who won two games with a 3.32 ERA in May, was the only starter that could keep teams from scoring at will. And by the end of May, the Rockies had dropped 18 games off the pace, effectively ending their season.

June 11-14 (26-50, 24.5 games back)
The Rockies had one thing left to play for in 1993, respect. The hitters came alive in June, hitting almost .300 with 51 doubles and 23 homers. Galarraga's quest for .400 continued on track and he was joined by Dante Bichette as the main contributors of runs.

It was the same old story for the pitching staff, though, as David Nied went on the DL with a torn ligament in his elbow and there was no one capable of taking his place. The rotation limped to a 7-9 record with nine no-decisions and turned in only seven quality starts. Colorado won only four of those seven no-decisions, an indication that the bullpen was falling apart as well. And like a man trapped in quick sand, the harder the hitters struggled for respectability, the further the Rockies sank in the standings.

July 10-17 (36-67, 33 games back)
Colorado's lineup started feeling the burn in July. Galarraga went on the DL late in the month with a sprained knee and Girardi spent all of July on the DL with a hand injury. Meanwhile, the Rockies were auditioning minor league talent, most notably second baseman Roberto Mejia who got the call after hitting .299 with 14 HR in Colorado Springs.

The hitting was there, but yet again, the pitching staff was an embarrassment, creeping along at a 5.19 ERA pace and letting the league to run rough-shod over them. But Bob Geghard imported some pitching help, taking the contracts of Greg Harris and Bruce Hurst off the hands of the Padres. Even though Hurst was on the DL at the time, the move was at least an attempt to patch up the rotation.

August 14-16 (50-83, 36 games back)
Hurst made one start for the Rockies in August, pitching three and two-thirds innings, and Greg Harris won one game and posted a 6.27 ERA for the month. So much for bolstering the rotation.

August brought a change of pace to the Rockies as the hitting failed to produce and the pitching looked marginally better. Galarraga missed almost half of the month to his knee injury and he hit only .231 when he came back. Charlie Hayes was the other stinkbomb, hitting only .226 for the month.

Sept./Oct. 17-12 (67-95, 37 games back)

Finishing with a flourish, the Rockies hit .300 for the month and won more games than they lost for the first time in the '93 season. But it was too late to salvage anything from the year, and the Rockies fell short of the expansion record 71 wins. Even though it was their inaugural season, 1993 had to be considered a disappointment for the Rockies. They battled injuries to key players most of the season and didn't see many encouraging signs from the pitching staff.

Park Effect: Wow! We knew that the thin atmosphere in Colorado would juice up an offense, but we never realized it would affect an offense as much as it actually did. Runs went up an incredible 52 percent last year in Denver. No other stadium in the major leagues affected scoring as much as Mile High. In addition, Colorado saw a 12 percent rise in doubles, a 27 percent hike in homers and triples were increased 191 percent. Know what to expect from a pitcher in Colorado. If he has a tendency to give up flyballs, he will get hurt-- and badly too.

Offense: The Rockies had one of the better hitting lineups in the National League, scoring 4.77 runs in support for their pitching staff. Their .272 batting average ranked right up near the top, and their .341 on-base average was good for second in the league. The Rockies weren't without their flaws though. They hit well in Colorado, but their .240 average away from home was by far the worst in the league. They really didn't have a legitimate leadoff hitter last year either. Eric Young proved himself to be a legitimate threat on the bases with his 42 thefts last year, but he was lacking in plate discipline and made too many outs for a leadoff hitter.

Total Offense: -137.3

Pitching: It's hard to describe how bad the Colorado pitching staff was last year. The starters registered league lows with just nine complete games and 53 quality starts. They were the only staff in the majors that failed to produce a shutout. The rotation also allowed 1072 hits in just 878.2 innings. To put it bluntly, the starters in Colorado were hit unmercifully last season, and the Rockies burned up the transaction wires shuffling pitchers back and forth to Colorado Springs all season long.

The situation was no brighter in the bullpen. Darren Holmes finally warmed up to the closer's job by August, and had blown just four of 29 save opportunities when the dust cleared. But the rest of the pen looked like prisoners in a Kafka novel being led out one by one and shot in the town square.

Total Pitching: -92.4

Defense:

Infield: Galarraga didn't show much in the way of glovework last year, but he was hampered by a hamstring pull and a strained knee. Besides, his offensive contributions far outweighed any deficiencies he might have had in the field. Eric Young at second base didn't light up the world with his glove.

Benavides and Castilla were both shaky in the field. The Rockies' one screaming need last year was a shortstop that could either hit or field. As defenders go, Charlie Hayes is about as middle-of-the-road as you can get.

Pts. 10.2

Outfield: Jerald Clark played a little better than your average left fielder last year, and a whole lot better than his backup, Daryl Boston. Alex Cole was pretty terrible in center field and he lost quite a bit of playing time because his bat stunk too. In right field, Bichette was error-prone, but he flashed good range and had an excellent arm.

Pts. -3.0

Catcher: Girardi didn't have much of a pitching staff to work with, so his 5.25 CERA is forgivable. But the rest of his game is mediocre at best. It was obvious that Jayhawk Owens needed some work with the glove last year as Girardi's backup, but he at least flashed a decent arm.

Pts. 0.4

Total Defense: 7.6

1994 Personnel:

Catcher: Girardi figures to return as the starter, but there's a good chance his bat will go dormant. If it does, Eric Wedge should step in and take the job away from Girardi because he's younger and offers a better package at the plate. But Wedge will have to prove that he has recovered from shoulder surgery that forced him to miss the '93 season.

Bench: Jayhawk Owens got some needed experience last year, so he could step up as the backup if something happens to Girardi. Danny Sheaffer will probably spend his 14th season in the minors this year unless injuries hit the starters.
Starters: -2.8
Bench: D

Infield:
1B: The Rockies re-signed Galarraga to a four-year, $12 million deal, so he will again man first base and count his blessings that he is playing in the best hitter's park in the bigs.

2B: It took about a half a year for Eric Young to play himself out of a job. Roberto Mejia, 22., will be handed the starting job in the spring. He will struggle at the plate until he develops his batting eye, but his glove is ready for the majors right now.

3B: Charlie Hayes returns to third base for the Rockies in '94, but he will be hard pressed to repeat his offensive surge.

SS: Walt Weiss became the first player in the majors to play for both the Rockies and the Marlins when he signed on with Colorado during the winter. They plan to put his improved defense to good use and bat him leadoff.

Bench: Jay Gainer played most of the season in the minors last year, but he has an opportunity to join the parent club this year as a left-handed pinch-hitter and fill-in for Galarraga at first. Nelson Liriano will come up if something happens to Mejia at second base, but if that doesn't happen, he'll probably spend the season in Colorado Springs. At third base, the Rockies have good-field/no-hit Pedro Castellano ready to step in for Charlie Hayes. Newly-acquired Howard Johnson can also move to the hot corner in a pinch. And if Weiss should get injured, Craig Counsell could come up to play shortstop.
Starters: 18.3
Bench: C+

Outfield:
LF: The Rockies declined to offer Jerald Clark a contract for '94, which leaves Howard Johnson as the logical choice to take over here. Colorado is about the best place in the world to go if you're trying to resurrect your hitting, and Johnson could have a very solid season if he stays healthy.

CF: Ellis Burks signed with the Rockies over the winter and will play center field. 1994 could be a big season for Burks, who figures to hit in either the four or five hole.

RF: Dante Bichette will be the only regular outfielder from last season to return to the team. His offensive numbers fall to earth if adjusted for his park, but he still has the potential to hit 20 home runs this season, in or out of Coors stadium.

Bench: Alex Cole, who played himself out of a job last year, can find some playing time as a backup and pinch-runner. And it looks like Daryl Boston will come back as well to backup all three outfield positions. In the minor leagues, there's Ed Alice, Jim Olander and Quinton McCracken.
Starters: 21.1
Bench: C-

Starting Pitching: David Nied will again serve as the ace of the staff, but his arm motion while pitching makes the Rockies worry about his health. One thing is for sure, he should feel less pressure to succeed now that the Rockies have elevated losing to an art form. Greg W. Harris will serve as the second starter and the Rockies are hoping that he doesn't pitch like number-two like he did last year. Mike Harkey, signed over the winter as a free agent, falls nicely into place here as the number-three starter. The final two spots in the rotation will be taken by Kent Bottenfield and Armando Reynoso. Other possibilities include Curt Leskanic, Lance Painter, John Burke, Mark Thompson and Ryan Hawblitzel. Burke and Thompson were ranked one and two respectively in Baseball America's top-ten list of prospects in the organization.
Front-Line: 0.0
Second-Echelon: C-

Relief Pitching: The relief corps is in a state of disarray, and the Rockies haven't done much over the winter to address the seemingly endless parade of arms that marched through the pen last year. Closer Darren Holmes is the only marquee name and is the only pitcher guaranteed a job. Mike Munoz, Steve Reed and Bruce Ruffin should all get jobs in the spring. Other pitchers who could appear in the Colorado bullpen include Mark Grant, Mark Knudson, Gary Wayne, Keith Sheppard and Scott Fredrickson.

Front-Line: 5.0
Second-Echelon: C

Player Value: 41.6

Farm System: The nice thing about being out of the pennant race is that it allows a team to audition its minor league talent. The Rockies wore out the shuttle between Denver and Colorado Springs last year with all of the young players getting called up. The system is heavy on pitching, presumably so that the Rockies will have plenty of arms to sift through. Burke, Thompson, Jamey Wright and Joel Moore head a pack of pitching prospects that should see major-league action within two or three years.

Position players are in somewhat shorter supply. Mejia will be in the majors this year as the starting second baseman. Jay Gainer is close to being ready for a major-league job, but is blocked by Galarraga at the present time. Shortstop Neifi Perez and third baseman Tom Schmidt are both a few years away, but they are promising hitters and could climb the ladder quickly.

Infield: C-
Outfield: E
Starters: C
Relievers: D
Farm Ranking: D+

Management and Ownership: It's too early to tell what kind of ownership is in charge of the Rockies. Jerry McMorris, president of NW Transport Service, should be credited for landing the expansion franchise in the first place, though. He is one of the few owners willing to shell out money to free agents, which is a rarity in these times, but the Rockies made that easier by breaking all kinds of attendance records last year. He is currently serving on two committees, so he could quickly become one of the movers and shakers in the owners' corner.

GM Bob Gebhard did a reasonably good job putting a team on the field in '93. He had to choose from talent left available in the expansion draft, so the present day Rockies aren't really his. The real test of his competence will come when his draft picks start reaching the show in two or three years. So far, he has been active during the offseason, filling some of the more gaping holes in the organization. He has recently signed SS Walt Weiss, OF Ellis Burks, OF Howard Johnson, and SP Mike Harkey to free-agent contracts. His trade for Greg Harris and Bruce Hurst was criticized roundly last season, but at least he did something to try and help out the rotation. A lot of general managers would have stood their ground. But Gebhard took a chance on a couple of experienced pitchers and it backfired.

Don Baylor is a capable manager and a quiet clubhouse leader that handled his erratic team well last year. He prefers a running offense and will call the hit-and-run play often. He must still have nightmares about his seemingly never-ending stroll out to the mound last year. He gave his starters the quick hook a lot, but they really didn't give him a choice. The danger is that the weakness of the starting pitchers will wear out the bullpen. But Baylor needs to get himself a bullpen before he worries about abusing it.

Ownership: B+
Front Office: C-
Field Management: C
Overall: C+

1994 Outlook: The Rockies have addressed some of the bigger holes on their roster over the winter. The addition of Mike Harkey will help solidify their rotation and Walt Weiss fills a need at shortstop. They have also turned over two-thirds of their outfield from last season, acquiring Burks and HoJo to play center and left fields respectively. While all of the moves will help the Rockies in one way or another this season, they didn't do enough to shore up their pitching staff. It is their shaky pitching that will guarantee them another second-division finish in '94.

LOS ANGELES DODGERS

1993 Outlook: The Dodgers were one of the tough calls coming out of Spring. Their pitching and bats were straddling the line somewhere between solid and shaky, and Lasorda seemed able to patch together squads and compete without seriously contending.

The enigma began with pitching. Would Ramon Martinez have his comeback year? Were rookie Pedros Martinez and Astacio ready for greatness? About the only sure things were that Kevin Gross would lose as many games as he won and that the Dodgers didn't have a real closer.

The mystery continued in the order. Would OF pals Darryl Strawberry and Eric Davis pull out of career tailspins? Could the patchwork infield of veterans Tim Wallach and Lenny Harris and pups Eric Karros and Jose Offerman function defensively, much less with the lumber? Then of course, there was the marginal gamble of catching the highly touted yet unproven Mike Piazza.

The Dodgers were a mystery that they themselves could not divine, and it was anyone's guess which way they would fall.

April 8-15 (8-15, 6.5 games back)
On April 11, the Dodger circus opened its tent flaps by pitching the Martinez brothers together in a 3-0 loss to Atlanta. This was a first in L.A. Dodgers history.

The Dodgers lost their home opener on April 13 despite amassing 14 hits, but it was for a good cause as Cardinal closer Lee Smith garnered his major league record 358th save.

In the next game the Dodgers could manage only four hits against Cardinal wunderkind Donovan Osborne, and wasted an extremely nice start by knuckleballer Tom Candiotti.

Lasorda decided to sit pals Strawberry and Davis against the Cardinals because they were both hitting well under .200. He termed it an early season slump, but it was more likely a late-season slump held over from '92

Strawberry then fueled early season criticism by missing an April 20 game with a stiff back, a throwback to his injuries of the previous year.

The Mets' luck for the season was apparent after a game against the Dodgers on the 27th. The day before, starter Doc Gooden was walloped with a golf club, jeopardizing his appearance. He made it nonetheless so he could give up two hits (one of which was Piazza's third homer) and lose to Hershiser.

May 18-8 (26-23, 6 games back)
Pedro and Ramon reiterated their brother gig on May 5, and this time Pedro got a win out of it.

Fellow back-pain sufferers Tim Wallach and Strawberry homered in consecutive at-bats on May 8. Wallach's line was, "bad-back to bad-back homers." The way he's been hitting it's a good thing he's got a career after baseball.

Davis began his comeback in earnest with a grand slam on May 18. He had few extra-base hits since the season began, and it didn't seem possible that he would end the season with 20 homers.

Lest fans forget how good Orel Hershiser once was, he tossed his 24th career shutout on May 21. Ramon Martinez followed Orel's example just two days later by hurling his first shutout in almost a year.

Lest fans forget Eric Karros was last year's Rookie of the Year, he decided to revive his flagging bat, belting two much-needed homers in a game against the Padres, doubling his season home run total in the process.

By May29, the Dodgers had surprised even themselves and won an amazing 11 games in a row. It was their longest streak since 1976 and it propelled them to fourth place and a mere 5.5 games in back of San Francisco.

June 14-13 (40-36, 10.5 games back)
Davis was quietly making his own mark in the history books, swiping his 34th consecutive stolen base before being nailed by Cardinal receiver Erik Pappas, the third best streak in major league history.

Dodger reliever Ricky Trlicek was yet another accessory to a Gary Sheffield ejection. Trlicek clocked him with a pitch and a brawl broke out. As Baseball Weekly pointed out, Trlicek had given up seven earned runs in 1.1 innings. Thank goodness the ump cared about his ERA, even if Lasorda didn't.

The catalytic Dodgers had another brawl-filled affair on their hands as they pounded the Rockies 12-4 on June 15. Piazza used the melee to go 4-5 with two HR and five RBI.

By June 20, he had numbers (.345 BA, 14 HR and 46 RBI) which were already enough to ensure an average rookie year-end honors.

July 14-13 (54-49, 15 games back)

The Dodgers played the Phillies for 20 innings (six hours and change) and ended up losing on a Lenny Dykstra double. 39 players were used in all.

Considering the degree to which Candiotti owned the Giants this season (two runs in 24.1 innings as of August) it prompts raised eyebrows as to why Kevin Gross was elected to play spoiler in the season finale.

August 12-15 (66-64, 18.5 games back)

The month of August got mixed reviews from Ramon. While he suffered through a prolonged win drought, he did see it end on the 22nd with his third shutout of the season. Ramon's problem this year was luck more than ability, which doesn't necessarily bode well for his future as a Dodger.

Sept./Oct. 15-17 (81-81, 23 games back)

Sept. 3 was Eric Davis's debut as a Tiger. He performed so well that the Tiges decided to re-sign him for '94. What must the Dodgers think?

Park Effects: Dodger Stadium is a pitcher's dream. While average and runs aren't altered significantly, there's definitely a power shortage.

Home runs are lowered 12 percent and doubles 15 percent, while triples are as rare as hens' teeth at a whopping 40 percent below league standard.

Errors are also significantly increased, especially in the infield where they're 17 percent higher (this helps explain the cyanide capsule issued to Dodger pitchers when Jose Offerman plays short).

Those who hit for average enjoy Chavez Ravine, with lefties being slightly more ecstatic. In terms of power, both sides of the plate are diminished, but lefties fare better at 6 percent lower than righties at 17 percent lower.

Offense: For the first half of the season, the Dodger offense stayed alive by scoring runs sporadically but often in copious amounts. However, they dropped off radically in the second half, which explains their finishing 23 games and 202 runs scored behind San Francisco.

The base-stealing was solid enough, but they would have needed a lot more to make a difference. Anything the Dodgers seemed to do well was no better than average by league standards.

Total Offense: -33.5

Pitching: The pitching was better than one might think, posting a 3.50 ERA despite a record of 81-81. While no one on the staff was overwhelming, a staff with Tom Candiotti, Orel Hershiser and Kevin Gross is always gonna win some games.

Less impressive was the relief corps. After Pedro Martinez, who won quite a few relief appearances, the bullpen was comprised of the usual suspects (Jim Gott and Roger McDowell) and newcomers like Omar Daal and the supposedly healthy Todd Worrell. Gott picked up the relief reins in impressive manner, but he's only a short-term solution until Darren Dreifort appears on the scene.

Total Pitching: 136.0

Defense:

Catcher: Mike Piazza coupled his golden bat with a surprisingly good glove. He doesn't have the world's best arm, but he seems to handle the pitching well.

Pts: 5.0

Infield: Karros was solid at first base without turning any heads while Jody Reed was great as he always is.

Third base was handles by the uncharismatic duo of Dave Hansen and Tim Wallach, Wallach being the more reliable of the two.

The big shock was the play of Jose Offerman, who showed excellent range and glove skills. His performance was marred by a lack of focus and his tendency to muff the routine double play or force-out caused him to lead the NL in errors this year.

Pts: 17.7

Outfield: The outfield was good. LF Eric Davis was king and CF Brett Butler seemed to have recovered from last year's slight defensive slump to regain his old form. RF Cory Snyder was average, but that was good enough to give the Dodgers a better outfield than they deserved.

Pts: 19.2

Total Defense: 41.9

1994 Personnel:

Catcher: If you don't know who the Dodger's catcher is, then let your baseball education begin with the name Mike Piazza.

Bench: The moderately talented Carlos Hernandez will catch a lot more bullpen warm-up than he will Dodger starters.

Starter: 21.4
Bench: C

Infield:

1B: Eric Karros has something to prove now that teammate Piazza has shown how Rookie of the Year ought to be won.

2B: Delino DeShields brings wheels to the position which Jody Reed had saved with his glove alone. The Dodgers have really begun to put some stock into building a defense behind their pitchers.

3B: Tim Wallach and Dave Hansen should battle for control. Wallach's got the glove, but L.A. must like Hansen's bat better.

SS: Jose will be back, with his head screwed on, presumably. His defense should improve with Delino's aid.

IF Bench: The same four guys back up all four infield positions: Mike Sharperson, Lenny Harris, Cory Snyder and Rafael Bournigal. They're the best bets for P.T.

Starters: 25.1
IF Bench: C

Outfield:

LF: Left field has been vacated by Davis, so a prospect like Billy Ashley or Raul Mondesi will be given a chance to Make or break himself on the major league level.

CF: Brett Butler will roam center, bringing a sense of continuity rare to the line-up.

RF: Cory Snyder's probably as good as anyone else they could get, but he may give up some time to the youngsters.

Bench: Whoever loses the Ashley/Mondesi duel will be a big bench factor. Mitch Webster is a valuable backup and could start in either left or right, while 26-year-old Henry Rodriguez has looked strong in three years of Triple-A. Now he needs to translate it to the bigs. Look for Todd Hollandsworth and Roger Cedeno.

Starters: 27.0
Bench: B+

Starting Pitching: The rotation is pretty much set with Pedro Astacio, Orel Hershiser, Tom Candiotti, Ramon Martinez and Kevin Gross. Considering the prospects, though, this configuration may not last long. Ben VanRyn has an excellent chance to crack the rotation and hurlers Jose Parra and Rick Gorecki aren't far behind.

Front-Line: 106.6
Second-Echelon: A

Relief Pitching: Relief was less of a problem as the always solid Jim Gott took over and closed out almost 30 games. The Dodgers have failed with roger McDowell and Todd Worrell, so Gott should be the man until Darren Dreifort emerges from the minors.

Middle relief has some solid practitioners in Omar Daal as well as McDowell, but trading for guys like John DeSilva doesn't make much sense. Ricky Trlicek is always an adventure on the mound, but he gets by on guts. Steve Wilson should be back, but he's not much. As with most teams who are thriving with pitching prospects, the bullpen is an excellent training ground to hone their skills.

Front-Line: 15.6
Second-Echelon: B+

Player Value: 195.7

Farm System: Start with pitching. Parra, VanRyn and Gorecki have been mentioned. Other quality starters include Greg Hansell and 24-year-old Javier Delahoya (8-10 3.66 107 K's in 125.1 Double-A innings). Mark Mimbs has the stuff to overcome the problems that sent him to Double-A in '93 while Bill Bene has the stuff but can't get it near the plate.

L.A. has also developed some remarkable talent away from the mound. Roger Cedeno, Todd Hollandsworth and Karin Garcia are blue-chip OF prospects all. Mike Busch is the latest 3B prospect to be lauded by the Dodgers while Miguel Cairo looks like he'll have a shot at 2B in the next couple of years. 23-year-old C prospect Chris Abbe has the hardest job of any Dodger farmhand. At this rate he'd have better luck as a White Sox 1B phenom.

Infield: B-
Outfield: A
Starters: A
Relievers: A
Farm Ranking: A

Management and Ownership: The O'Malley family has always run their organization with distinction. For the O'Malley's baseball is not just business, but life. The team has been too willing to spend to improve the team with free-agent pickups and the O'Malleys have been perfectly willing to shell out the money they're making from the sushi stands in Chavez Ravine.

GM Fred Claire does things in grand style and there's no reason to not question on his moves: They either shine like the sun, or they smell like a dung heap. Moves like the Eric Davis trade and the Strawberry signing make him look like a fool. The DeShields trade, however, could almost singlehandedly redeem him. The team has done a good job of drafting talent, however, so his front-office gets a decent mark.

As for field-management, we don't think anyone out there thinks of Tommy LaSorda as some kind of managerial genius. He's an affable guy (to a lot of people, that is) and he's a great salesman for the Dodgers organization. Other than that, he's not really much of anything.

Ownership: B
Front Office: C+
Field Management: C
Overall: C+/B-

1994 Outlook: The 1994 Dodgers have a lot of questions that need answering, but they're now in a much weaker division. The Giants are the only real competition this year and they've not really done much to improve themselves. If the Giants staff slumps (and the Dodger offense can improve), then we could see the first NL West title for the Dodgers since 1988.

SAN DIEGO PADRES

1993 Outlook: The Padres walked into 1993 with heads high. They seemed to have built a nice little franchise around bats like Tony Gwynn, Fred McGriff and young Triple Crown contender Gary Sheffield. Who suspected that 2/3 of this trio would be gone by the middle of the season.

Admittedly, the rest of the order wasn't exceptionally strong, but a core like the triumvirate above was enough to win a lot of games.

Pitching was less impressive. After ace Andy Benes, the rotation could have rocked the NL as the American version of The Who. Doug Brocail and Frank Seminara were aging prospects, Seminara being solid and Brocail not looking to be very effective. Beyond them was former Mets reliever Wally Whitehurst, and no, that's not a joke.

Relief looked stinky. Gene Harris and Mark Davis were the only guys with a clue concerning the closer role, and it was only the late-season call-up of PA Martinez which garnered the Padres long relief a scrap of respect.

The Pads didn't look great, but were they worse than the Dodgers and the Rockies? They had to at least finish above them...didn't they? Nobody expected them to contend against the powerhouse Braves, so it was extraordinarily thoughtful of them to trade their best power hitter to Atlanta and thus ensure that one team would finish last and one would end up in first. The prediction business really stinks because of teams like the Padres. just when you pick 'em they dismantle the team right out from under ya.

April 10-12 (10-12, 4 games back)
Tim Teufel had the day of his life, as he had five hits in a game for the first time since he was a Twins rookie. You've gotta figure that those five hits accounted for about half his season's production.

Teufel also brightened his early season by becoming the first Padre to hit a home run with a man on base in '93.

Derek Bell began to earn his keep immediately. He had his first two-homer game by mid-April and he ended up looking a helluva lot better than Darrin Jackson did on Toronto's end.

3B Gary Sheffield was ejected after a scuffle with Mets C Todd Hundley on April 25. Although Sheffield was the more valuable of the two players, it was Hundley's replacement who committed a throwing error and kept Mets hurler Anthony Young's losing streak alive at 16 games.

May 10-18 (20-30, 12.5 games back)

Gwynn lined a shot off of Reds pitcher Tim Belcher's forearm on May 11, raising a welt large enough to cause Belcher to compare favorably to Popeye the Sailor.

Andy Benes was proving his ace-hood by the third week of May, amassing a 6-3 record with a 2.44 ERA. To be frank, he was the only starter who could win more than once or twice a month.

Bell had more to prove. He managed an eleven game hitting streak until May 29, hitting five homers in that span.

June 9-19 (29-49, 22.5 games back)

A Padre no more, Sheffield went 2-4 in his first game after being traded to the Marlins for Trevor Hoffman.

Craig Shipley was dubbed Roto God after he played three positions in an extra-inning game versus Cincinnati.

July 11-16 (40-65, 30 games back)

Andy Benes, who made the All-Star team, didn't get to play. While it was an honor just to make it (I'd like to thank the Academy...) it would have been nice to see him throw to Ken Griffey Jr. just once.

As of July 20th, Fred McGriff was officially a Brave, following the exodus of talent out of San Diego. He had three HR in his first two games as a Brave. You can see why the Padres wouldn't want to pay a bum like that.

Tony Gwynn added RBI to his list of club records (e.g. BA, runs, stolen bases...) on July 27 with his 627th.

August 12-15 (52-80, 33.5 games back)

Gwynn's record-breaking continued as he notched his fourth five+ hit game of the season on Aug. 4, putting him in the company of Willie Keeler , Stan Musial and Ty Cobb. He then followed by collecting his 2,000 hit two nights later versus the Rockies.

Sept./Oct. 9-21 (61-101, 43 games back)

San Diego finally dropped past Colorado into last on Sept. 11. They briefly passed them again on Sept. 13 but fell back down for good the next day.

43 games out was the widest margin between first and last in the majors since 1986. this had something to do with the Braves winning 104 games rather than 94 like the White Sox did, but the fact remains that the Padres auctioned their team away over the course of the season.

While there is hope remaining in the youthful they have begun to build, modern baseball cannot be won unless the owner is willing to tighten the built and break open the piggy bank. Maybe Tom Werner should practice in a Rotisse-league before he attempts the big time.

Park Effects: Jack Murphy was made for pure slugging. Speedy guys with slashing power need not apply.

Batting average is standard and run scoring is helped by 4 percent. As we said before, Bip Roberts types can take a hike since doubles and triples are cut by 13 and 16 percent respectively. Homers are where it's at, a whopping 27 percent above the league (Now Padre fans can lament the loss of Sheffield and McGriff in earnest).

Errors are also standard, which is good due to the mediocrity of the Padre infield.

There's about a 6 percent swing in batting average, with lefties losing 3 percent and righties gaining 3. In case you didn't catch it the first time, Jack Murphy spells P-O-W-E-R, to the tune of a 26 percent upgrade for lefties and a 28 percent raise for righties. This in mind, prospects like Dave Staton, Mel Nieves and Vince Moore should be pursued vigorously in fantasy drafts. Look what the change of venue did for Derek bell and Phil Plantier. 'Nuff said.

Offense: The Padre offense stank because they traded most of their talent away. They had three strong positions by season's end: left field, center field and right field. The infield and catcher were cancers. The team finished fourth from the bottom in runs despite playing in a basically neutral park. They had good power, but didn't hit for average and drew the second-fewest walks in the National League. There not much speed here, but you can't steal first: You gotta have people on base to steal bases.

Total Offense: -85.8

Pitching: The pitching staff will disintegrate if any of the rumored trades featuring Andy Benes go through. The Pads need an anchor to teach the kids to succeed. Last year, the rotation was a complete mess, while the bullpen was pretty good. The Padres' rotation ERA was 4.53, while the pen had a 3.65 ERA. Basically, Gene Harris, Hoffman and the boys kept the other team in check once the game was lost.
Total Pitching: 61.7

Defense:
Catcher: The Padres simply didn't have a catcher who stood out enough to be handed the job. Kevin Higgins and Brad Ausmus were the usual suspects, with Ausmus being the better of the two defensively.
Pts: 0.0

Infield: McGriff was average at first, and he soon departed to make way for a faceless platoon. Tim Teufel was the best that could be mustered at second, and he wasn't half bad with the glove (of course he was double bad with the bat).
Archi Cianfrocco was a liability at third, and was often spelled by the more reliable Craig Shipley. Ricky Gutierrez rounded out the sad-sack convention by bringing no talent to short.
Pts: 3.7

Outfield: The outfield was as tremendously good as the infield was nightmarishly bad. LF Phil Plantier kicked butt, and was the best in the NL by a mile.
CF Derek Bell showed that he had brought a lot more than a bat to his new home while RF Gwynn continued to be the best combination of glove and bat that RF has seen in awhile.
Pts: 31.6

Total Defense: 35.3

1994 Outlook:
Catcher: Brad Ausmus will start at catcher. The Padres are absolutely in love with this guy, so it will take an anvil to the cranium to displace him.
Bench: Brian Johnson, Kevin Higgins and Phil Clark and Dan Walters are possibilities.
Starter: 0.0
Bench: C

Infield:
1B: Phil Clark, Dave Staton, Mel Nieves and about 15 others will battle at first.
2B: Jeff Gardner and Tim Teufel look like they'll battle for the most PT at second..
3B: Archi Cianfrocco and Craig Shipley will probably play the most at third.
SS: Ricky Gutierrez is the answer here.
IF Bench: Freddy Velasquez, Billy Bean could also play first. Other infield possibilities include prospect Julio Bruno and Luis Lopez.
Starters: 13.1
IF Bench: D

Outfield:
LF: Phil Plantier is the man in left.
CF: Realistically, the Padres don't have many options. They need to keep Bell's bat active and he's a decent defensive CF.
RF: Look for some guy named Gwynn. They say he can hit for average.
Bench: Possibilities include Mel Nieves, Dave Staton, D.J. Dozier, Jim Vatcher and Ray McDavid.
Starters: 60.6
Bench: B-

Starting Pitching: Andy Benes is the starter, Wally Whitehurst is a warm body. The rest of the starters are going to come from the kiddie corps. Andy Ashby, Doug Brocail, Tim Worrell, Scott Sanders and Pedro A. Martinez are among the possibilities for the Grade Z rotation. All these kids have potential, but they'll probably get killed before the succeed.
Front-Line: 32.7
Second-Echelon: C-

Relief Pitching: Gene Harris and Trevor Hoffman are the best candidates to nail down the saves. Tim Scott, Jeremy Hernandez, Roger Mason, Tim Mauser and Rudy Seanez are also possibilities (if Seanez can stay healthy).
Front-Line: 24.0
Second-Echelon: C-

Player Value: 130.4

Farm System: The farm system is getting fat via the star-dump tradeline. OFs Mel Nieves, Vince Moore and pitcher Andres Berumen are among the dividends the

McGriff and Sheffield trades paid. OF Ray McDavid, 3B Julio Bruno, 2B Jason Hardtke and SS Sean Drinkwater are also good young players.

Infield: B
Outfield: B-
Starters: C
Relievers: D
Farm Ranking: C+

Management and Ownership: Tom Werner is the cheapest, worst owner in the game of baseball. Basically his saving grace is that he's not as much of a jerk as guys like Marge and George (did I call Marge Schott a "guy?" Whoops. ... She oughta stop rolling a pack of Luckies in the sleeve of her T-shirt, then). To comment further on this team's management is folly.

Ownership: F
Front Office: F
Field Management: Who cares?!
Overall: Guess. ...

1994 Outlook: Let's see, the team stinks and there's no real solution on the horizon. We think they may break the 100,000 barrier in attendence, but then again it is a spectacle to see a good Rookie Ball team take on the National League. Anything over 40 wins and we'll nominate Riggleman for Double-A manager of the year.

SAN FRANCISCO GIANTS

1993 Outlook: The Giants went into the season with their heads up, despite the many reports which said they would finish low in their division.

They had acquired the best player in the game in Barry Bonds and they had a veteran corps of players. Ironically, it was starting pitching which looked like their Achilles' heel. Swift had a good, if shortened year in '92, but after that it was the solid Burkett and question marks like Trevor Wilson.

Their relief was solid as usual. There were high hopes for Rod Beck (which he ultimately lived up to) and the long relievers were experienced. While they were a stable contender, nobody imagined they would seriously push Atlanta for the championship.

April 15-9 (15-9, tied for lead with Houston)

Like the Dodgers, the Giants opened with a circus of their own. On Opening Day, The Grateful Dead and crooner Tony Bennett showed up to sing (separately, thank God) and singer Michael Bolton showed up to receive a souvenir jersey and not sing (thank God Part II). The fireworks began when Bonds homered in his first at-bat. Everyone immediately agreed that he had earned his salary for the year.

Burkett and Atlanta's John Smoltz were one of the season's first pitching duels, which Burkett ultimately won. Burkett recorded seven strikeouts, but of course Smoltzie was two of them which tends to dim their luster.

On April 22, 2b Robby Thompson had a big game with four hits and four RBI. Nobody suspected it would turn out to be the beginning of such a huge season for him.

Bonds and Matt Williams ended April in style, tied for the NL home run lead with seven apiece.

May 18-9 (33-18, 0 games back)

On May 13, the Giants joined the fraternity of NL teams which were outhit by the Rockies (13-14) yet still whipped them (13-8)

By May 29, nobody was surprised by Thompson anymore. He had a 19-game hitting streak and was tearing up opposing batters.

Will Clark was not faring as well, having managed only two homers by the end of May.

June 19-9 (52-27, 0 games back)

June 5 saw the return of Trevor Wilson from the DL, and while pitching 5.1 scoreless innings was welcome, it was his solo shot off Pirate pitcher Tim Wakefield that won the game for him 3-2.

July 18-8 (70-35, 0 games back)

July 16 was witness to CF Darren Lewis's record-breaking 267th consecutive errorless game. More impressively, that streak stems from his very first chance as a major league outfielder.

That game was also a hair away from perfection for Bill Swift, who lost the perfecto in the eighth and had to settle for a one-hitter.

On July 26, the dodgers beat the Giants 15-1 in their worst defeat since 1975. A bit of foreshadowing, perhaps?

August 15-11 (85-46, 0 games back)

After losing 10 games in a row, jinxed starter Scott Sanderson began a three-game winning streak to key the Giants' stretch run.

Aug. 25 was the scene of the Bill Swift debacle at the hands of Giant fans. Billed as a pitchers' duel, Swift was to start against Atlanta's Greg Maddux, frontrunner for the Cy Young.

As you may recall, Swift was manhandled by McGriff and Justice in the first and was subsequently booed off the field by the home fans, classless dorks that they are. At least Bill has 21 wins to keep him warm this winter.

Sept./Oct. 18-13 (103-59, 1 game back)

The big story happened at the end of the month. The Giants had beens fending off the Braves only to find themselves locked in a tie heading into the final game of the season.

In a fit of perversity, Dusty Baker gave the ball to young Salomon Torres, a talented pitcher who had been ignored in the minors despite gargantuan numbers.

The game was against the Dodgers, and while five of Torres' eight starts in '93 were quality, this wasn't one of 'em. He pitched well to start and then got rocked, giving up the homer as is his wont.

The Giants were stunned. Meanwhile, the Braves were completing a season sweep of the Rockies, the first time an NL team had swept a regular season series from another team.

You've gotta wonder how much difference an earlier call-up of Torres would have made. He was erratic in his starts as a Giant, but he's proved he'll be among the best NL starters within the next few years.

In a way it was a fitting end. San Francisco had suffered through the injury of Matt Williams, but had also gotten unexpected and exceptional years from Robby Thompson and pitchers Burkett and Swift. They couldn't have expected to do as well as they did and they have the satisfaction of having built themselves a contender for years to come.

Park Effects: Candlestick is an imbalanced park which greatly favors pitching.

Batting average drops 5 percent and runs drops 11 percent (even lower than the Astrodome!). Triples are right at league standard with doubles close behind, but HR power is decreased by 7 percent.

The error factor is virtually nil. While it doesn't help bad fielders and the pitchers who despise them, neither does it hurt if the fielding ability is average.

Average is diminished a tad for both types of batters, but lefties get a definite edge in power as theirs is decreased by 2 percent and righthanders are shorn of 10 percent.

Offense: If you adjust for park effects, the Giants had the best offense in the league. Candlestick park is extreme in its suppression of scoring. The Giants had by far the best power in the league (taking the league slugging crown with a .427 mark over Philly's .426 and out-homering every team in the league except Atlanta [a team that plays in a bandbox]) and with their good B.A. and decent walks, they could have expected to score 840 runs in a neutral park. The team has roughly average speed and their 65 percent stealing rate was a bit below average (as was their GIDP rate). There are no real weaknesses offensively.

Total Offense: 124.1

Pitching: In all honesty, the pitching was league average if you adjusted for the park (as evidenced by their 4.00 road ERA). The rotation was solid, as was the bullpen. The rotation's major problem was stamina. The starters only completed four of 162 starts. The pitchers often went deep into the night, but were unable to finish what they started. In addition, most of the starters were unaccustomed to the workload they received in 1993. The team's ERA after the All-Star break was 3.87 (3.42 before), you can attribute most of that to the breakdown of Swift et al.

To put it briefly, the bullpen was very good. The long-relief situation was well handled by pitchers like Hickerson and short relief was in the good hands of Messrs. Jackson and Beck.

Total Pitching: 123.7

Defense:

Catcher: Kirt Manwaring proved once again to be the best of a motley NL lot. His arm was phenomenal, and the Cubs' Rick Wilkins was the only one who could push him defensively.

Pts: 17.3

Infield: 1B Will Clark's performance continued its decline. He's gone from Gold Glove to doghouse in a few short years. 2B Robby

Thompson was just the opposite, flashing the best glove in the majors after Ryne Sandberg and Craig Biggio.

Third was a lock with Matt Williams finally showing that his glove is as powerful as his bat. Short was the biggest weakness, as Royce Clayton turned out to be worthless defensively. This is not good, considering rotation anchor Bill Swift is an extreme groundball pitcher.

Pts: 20.3

Outfield: The outfield was one of the best in the game. LF Barry Bonds and RF Willie McGee were good without being spectacular, while CF Darren Lewis stole the show as the best at his position. Lewis has yet to make an error on the major league level.

Pts: 30.0

Total Defense: 67.5

1994 Personnel:

Catcher: Kirt Manwaring is pretty much a lock for right now.

Bench: Darren Reed is the most viable backup. The really nice looking long-term solution, Marcus Jensen is probably 18 months away, but he's a beauty.

Starter: 16.4
Bench: C+

Infield:
1B: J.R. Phillips and Todd Benzinger are the primary challengers for the position. Phillips could hit .220 and lose the job with his inability to hit for average and his strikeouts. We all know Benzinger is a Grade D 1B at best.

2B: Robby Thompson is back to do damage with his bat.

3B: Matt Williams will cover third and there's little anyone can do about it.

SS: Ditto here for Clayton. He really needs to get his glove in gear, though.

IF Bench: Mark Carreon is another option at first base. Around the infield, Mike Benjamin, Paul Faries or Steve Scarsone could spell Thompson.

Starters: 45.7
IF Bench: C-

Outfield:
LF: Bonds is single-handedly more valuable than most outfields!

CF: Darren Lewis is a flawless glove with a mighty speckled bat. He'll continue to play, though.

RF: In right, the usual gang of suspects: McGee, Carreon, Faneyte, etc. will vy for time.

Bench: Other possibilities include Dwayne Hosey, Dave Martinez and Luis Mercedes. Mega prospect Calvin Murray could explode and force his way onto the team.

Starters: 101.0
Bench: C-

Starting Pitching: The rotation will be Swift, Burkett, Portugal and Torres for sure. Kevin Rogers, Bud Black, Trevor Wilson, Hickerson and a pack of long-relief wannabes look like viable No. 5 hole candidates.

Front-Line: 87.0
Second-Echelon: C+

Relief Pitching:
Front-Line: 45.0
Second-Echelon: C+

Player Value: 295.1

Farm System: OF Calvin Murray and SP Salomon Torres are the cream of this team's crop. Other gems include starter Steve Soderstrom, OF Chris Singleton, C Marcus Jensen and SP Joe Rosselli. Other than that, there's nothing really to write home about.

Infield: D
Outfield: C+
Starters: C+
Relievers: D
Farm Ranking: C

Management and Ownership: Peter Magowan has flair. He signed Barry Bonds to an incredible contract and has shown further proof that he will pick and choose battles (choosing to retain Thompson and shore up the pitching with Portugal at the expense of Will Clark). Still, we haven't seen how dedicated he is to building a farm system.

GM Bob Quinn is a gem. He engineered excellent moves with the Reds and was unfairly fired after the Reds finished behind the Braves in 1992. The next two years will show us if he can work his magic in San Fran. Dusty Baker is in the same shoes as the other management types. He looks awful good, but we need to see him more to pass final judgment. He's a lot like Roger Craig in handling his offense: His teams execute the fundamentals well, but can also stomp you with the dinger. The only thing is, they don't have much speed (apart from Bonds and Lewis) and are terrible base-runners. When it comes to pitching, Baker handled his pitchers with exceeding care. No Giant starter threw a 120+ pitch start last year!

Ownership: C+
Front Office: B
Field Management: B
Overall: B

1994 Outlook: The 1994 Giants are a pretty imposing team. They have a potent offense, a solid rotation and a good bullpen. They have added a fine starter in Portugal, but he's coming off a career year, so expect him to decline. They lost a fine first baseman and will replace him with either reserves or a whiff-prone kid. Expect them to challenge for the West, heck, make them favorites to win the division, but they're probably not going to garner more than 95 wins this year.

Player Essay Index

A

Abbott, Jim 133
Abbott, Kurt 71
Abbott, Paul 133
Abreu, Bob 91
Aguilera, Rick 185
Alexander, Manny 71
Alicea, Luis 41
Alkire, Jeff 133
Alomar, Roberto 41
Alomar, Sandy 9
Alou, Moises 91
Alvarez, Tavo 133
Alvarez, Wilson 133
Amaral, Rich 41
Amaro, Ruben 91
Andersen, Larry 185
Anderson, Brady 91
Anderson, Garret 91
Andrews, Shane 57
Ansley, Willie 91
Anthony, Eric 91
Appier, Kevin 134
Aquino, Luis 134
Arias, Alex 41
Armas, Marcos 23
Armstrong, Jack 134
Arnold, Jamie 134
Arocha, Rene 134
Ashby, Andy 135
Ashley, Billy 92
Asmus, Brad 9
Assenmacher, Paul 185
Astacio, Pedro 135
Aude, Rich 23
Avery, Steve 135
Ayala, Bobby 185

B

Baerga, Carlos 41
Baez, Kevin 71
Bagwell, Jeff 23
Bailey, Cory 185
Bankhead, Scott 185
Banks, Willie 135
Barbara, Don 23
Barber, Brian 135
Barberie, Bret 42
Barker, Tim 71
Barnes, Brian 136
Barnes, Skeeter 24
Bass, Kevin 92
Batchelor, Rich 186
Bates, Jason 71
Batiste, Kim 57
Battle, Howard 57
Bautista, Danny 92
Bautista, Jose 186
Beamon, Trey 92
Beck, Rod 186
Becker, Rich 92
Bedrosian, Steve 186
Belcher, Tim 136
Belinda, Stan 186
Bell, David 57
Bell, Derek 92
Bell, George 93
Bell, Jay 71
Bell, Juan 72
Belle, Albert 93
Belliard, Rafael 72
Beltran, Alonso 136
Benavides, Freddie 72
Bene, Bill 187
Benes, Alan 136
Benes, Andy 136
Benitez, Yamil 93
Benjamin, Mike 72
Bennett, Joel 137
Benzinger, Todd 24
Bere, Jason 137
Berroa, Geronimo 93
Berry, Sean 57
Berryhill, Damon 9
Berumen, Andres 137
Bevil, Brian 137
Bichette, Dante 93
Biggio, Craig 42
Black, Bud 137
Blair, Donnie 137
Blankenship, Lance 94
Blauser, Jeff 72
Blazier, Ron 137
Blomdahl, Ben 138
Blosser, Greg 94

Blowers, Mike 57
Boever, Joe 187
Bogar, Tim 72
Boggs, Wade 58
Bolick, Frank 24
Bolton, Rod 138
Bonds, Barry 94
Bones, Ricky 138
Bonifay, Ken 58
Bonilla, Bobby 94
Bonnici, James 9
Boone, Bret 42
Borbon, Pedro 187
Borders, Pat 9
Bordick, Mike 73
Borland, Toby 187
Bosio, Chris 138
Boskie, Shawn 187
Boston, D.J. 24
Boston, Daryl 94
Bottalico, Ricky 187
Boucher, Denis 138
Bournigal, Rafael 42
Bowen, Ryan 138
Boze, Marshall 139
Bragg, Darren 95
Branson, Jeff 42
Brantley, Jeff 187
Bream, Sid 24
Brewer, Billy 187
Brewer, Rod 24
Briley, Greg 95
Brink, Brad 188
Brito, Bernardo 95
Brocail, Doug 139
Brock, Chris 139
Brogna, Rico 25
Bronkey, Jeff 188
Brooks, Hubie 95
Brosius, Scott 95
Brown, Jarvis 95
Brown, Kevin 139
Browne, Jerry 95
Browning, Tom 139
Brumley, Duff 139
Brumley, Mike 58
Brummett, Greg 140
Brunansky, Tom 95
Bruno, Julio 58

Buechele, Steve 58
Buford, Damon 96
Buhner, Jay 96
Bullett, Scott 96
Bullinger, Jim 188
Bunch, Melvin 140
Burba, Dave 188
Burgos, Enrique 188
Burguillos, Carlos 96
Burke, Alan 25
Burke, John 140
Burkett, John 140
Burks, Ellis 96
Burnitz, Jeromy 96
Busch, Mike 58
Bushing, Chris 188
Butcher, Mike 188
Butler, Brett 97
Butler, Rob 97
Byrd, Anthony 97
Byrd, Paul 140

C
Cabrera, Francisco 25
Cadaret, Greg 189
Cairo, Miguel 42
Calderon, Ivan 97
Cameron, Stanton 97
Caminiti, Kevin 58
Canate, Willie 97
Candaele, Casey 42
Candiotti, Tom 140
Canseco, Jose 98
Caraballo, Ramon 42
Carey, Paul 25
Caridad, Ron 141
Carlson, Dan 141
Carpenter, Cris 189
Carr, Chuck 98
Carreon, Mark 98
Carter, Joe 98
Carter, John 141
Caruso, Joe 189
Casian, Larry 189
Castellano, Pedro 59
Castilla, Vinny 73
Castillo, Frank 141
Castillo, Tony 189
Castro, Juan 73

Cedeno, Andujar 73
Cedeno, Domingo 73
Cedeno, Roger 98
Chamberlain, Wes 99
Charlton, Norm 189
Chavez, Tony 189
Christman, Scott 141
Christopher, Mike 190
Cianfrocco, Archi 59
Ciccarella, Joe 190
Cirillo, Jeff 59
Clark, Jerald 99
Clark, Mark 141
Clark, Phil 25
Clark, Tim 99
Clark, Tony 99
Clark, Will 25
Clayton, Craig 141
Clayton, Royce 73
Clemens, Roger 141
Colbrunn, Greg 26
Cole, Alex 99
Coleman, Paul 190
Coleman, Vince 99
Cone, David 142
Conine, Jeff 100
Conroy, Brian 142
Converse, Jim 142
Cook, Dennis 190
Cooke, Steve 142
Cooper, Scott 59
Cora, Joey 43
Cordero, Wilfred 73
Cordova, Martin 100
Correa, Jose 190
Correia, Rod 73
Costo, Tim 26
Cotto, Henry 100
Counsell, Craig 74
Cox, Danny 190
Crabtree, Tim 143
Cromer, Tripp 74
Crowley, Jim 43
Cruz, Fausto 74
Cummings, John 143
Cummings, Midre 100
Curtis, Chad 100
Cuyler, Milt 100

D

D'Amico, Jeff 143
D'Andrea, Mike 143
Daal, Omar 190
Darensbourg, Vic 190
Darling, Ron 143
Darwin, Danny 143
Darwin, Jeff 191
Daugherty, Jack 101
Daugherty, Jim 191
Daulton, Darren 9
Davenport, Adell 59
Davis, Chili 101
Davis, Clint 191
Davis, Eric 101
Davis, Mark 191
Davis, Russ 59
Davis, Storm 191
Davis, Tim 191
Dawson, Andre 101
Deak, Darrel 43
Deaks, Brian 9
Dedrick, Jim 192
Deer, Rob 101
Delahoya, Javier 144
DeLeon, Jose 192
Delgado, Carlos 9
Denson, Drew 26
Deshaies, Jim 144
DeShields, Delino 43
DeSilva, John 192
Destrade, Orestes 26
Dettmer, John 144
Devereaux, Mike 102
Diaz, Alex 102
Diaz, Mario 74
Dibble, Rob 192
Dickson, Lance 144
DiPino, Frank 192
DiPoto, Jerry 192
DiSarcina, Gary 74
DiSarcina, Glenn 74
Dishman, Glenn 144
Dismuke, Jamie 26
Dixon, Steve 192
Doherty, John 144
Donnels, Chris 59
Dopson, John 144
Doran, Bill 43

Downs, Kelly 193
Dozier, D.J. 102
Drabek, Doug 144
Drahman, Brian 193
Draper, Mike 193
Dreifort, Darren 193
Drews, Matt 145
Dreyer, Steve 145
Drinkwater, Sean 74
DuBose, Brian 27
Ducey, Rob 102
Duncan, Mariano 43
Dunston, Shawon 74
Durant, Mike 10
Durham, Ray 44
Dykstra, Lenny 102

E
Easley, Damion 44
Eckersley, Dennis 193
Edens, tom 193
Edmonds, Jim 102
Eichhorn, Mark 193
Eischen, Joey 145
Eisenreich, Jim 103
Eldred, Cal 145
Elliot, Donnie 145
Ellis, Robert 145
Embree, Alan 146
Erickson, Scott 146
Espinoza, Alvaro 60
Everett, Carl 103
Eyre, Scott 146

F
Fabregas, Jorge 10
Fajardo, Hector 146
Faneyte, Rikkert 103
Faries, Paul 44
Fariss, Monty 103
Farr, Steve 194
Fassero, Jeff 146
Felders, Mike 103
Fermin, Felix 74
Fernandez, Alex 147
Fernandez, Sid 147
Fernandez, Tony 75
Fetters, Mike 194
Fielder, Cecil 27
Finley, Chuck 147

Finley, Steve 103
Finnvold, Gar 147
Flaherty, John 10
Fleming, Carlton 44
Fleming, Dave 147
Flener, Huck 194
Fletcher, Scott 44
Flora, Kevin 44
Flores, Miguel 44
Floyd, Clifford 27
Foley, Tom 44
Fonville, Chad 75
Forkner, Tim 60
Forney, Rick 148
Foster, Kevin 194
Foster, Steve 194
Franco, John 194
Franco, Matt 27
Frascatore, John 148
Frazier, Lou 103
Fredrickson, Scott 194
Freeman, Marvin 194
Frey, Steve 195
Fritz, John 148
Frohwirth, Todd 195
Frye, Jeff 45
Fryman, Travis 60
Fullmer, Brad 60

G
Gaetti, Gary 60
Gagne, Greg 75
Galarraga, Andres 28
Gallaher, Kevin 148
Gallego, Mike 45
Gant, Ron 104
Garcia, Carlos 45
Garcia, Karim 104
Garcia, Omar 28
Gardner, Jeff 45
Gardner, Mark 148
Geisler, Phil 104
Giambi, Jason 61
Gibralter, Steve 104
Gibson, Kirk 104
Gibson, Paul 195
Gil, Benji 75
Gilkey, Bernard 104
Girardi, Joe 10

Gladden, Dan 105
Glavine, Tom 148
Goff, Jerry 10
Gomes, Wayne 195
Gomez, Chris 75
Gomez, Leo 61
Gonzales, Juan 105
Gonzales, Rene 61
Gonzalez, Alex 75
Gonzalez, Luis 105
Gooden, Dwight 148
Goodwin, Curt 105
Gordon, Tom 149
Gossage, Goose 195
Gott, Jim 195
Grable, Rob 61
Grace, Mark 28
Graffagnino, Anthony 45
Grahe, Joe 195
Granger, Jeff 149
Grebeck, Craig 76
Grebek, Brian 75
Green, Tyler 149
Greene, Rick 196
Greene, Tommy 149
Greene, Willie 61
Greenwell, Mike 105
Greer, Rusty 105
Griffey Jr., Ken 106
Griffin, Alfredo 76
Grimm, John 196
Grimsley, Jason 149
Grissom, Marquis 106
Gross, Kevin 150
Gruber, Kelly 61
Guardado, Eddie 150
Gubicza, Mark 196
Guetterman, Lee 196
Guillen, Ozzie 76
Gullickson, Bill 150
Guthrie, Mark 196
Gutierrez, Ricky 76
Guzman, Jose 150
Guzman, Juan 150
Gwynn, Chris 106
Gwynn, Tony 106

H
Habyan, John 196

Hale, Chip 61
Hall, Billy 46
Hamelin, Bob 28
Hamilton, Darryl 106
Hamilton, Joey 150
Hamilton, Mike 151
Hammonds, Chris 151
Hammonds, Jeffrey 107
Haney, Chris 151
Hansell, Greg 151
Hansen, Dave 61
Hanson, Erik 151
Hardge, Mike 46
Hardtke, Jason 46
Hare, Shawn 107
Harkey, Mike 151
Harnisch, Pete 152
Harper, Brian 10
Harris, Gene 196
Harris, Greg W. 152
Harris, James 152
Harris, Lenny 46
Hartley, Mike 196
Harvey, Bryan 196
Haselman, Bill 11
Hatcher, Billy 107
Hathaway, Hilly 152
Hatteberg, Scott 11
Haught, Gary 152
Hawblitzel, Ryan 152
Hawkins, LaTroy 153
Hayes, Charlie 62
Haynes, Heath 197
Haynes, Jimmy 153
Heberling, Keith 153
Heble, Kurt 197
Helfand, Eric 11
Helling, Rick 153
Hemond, Scott 11
Henderson, Daryl 153
Henderson, Dave 107
Henderson, Rickey 107
Henderson, Rod 153
Henke, Tom 197
Henkel, Rob 153
Henneman, Mike 197
Henry, Doug 198
Hentgen, Pat 154
Heredia, Gil 154

Heredia, Julian 198
Hernandez, Carlos 11
Hernandez, Fernando 154
Hernandez, Jeremy 197
Hernandez, Jose 76
Hernandez, Roberto 198
Hernandez, Xavier 197
Herrera, Jose 108
Hershiser, Orel 154
Hiatt, Phil 62
Hibbard, Greg 154
Hickerson, Bryan 198
Hidalgo, Richard 108
Higgins, Kevin 11
Higginson, Bob 108
Higuera, Ted 154
Hill, Glenallen 108
Hill, Ken 154
Hill, Milt 198
Hill, Shawn 198
Hill, Ty 155
Hillman, Eric 155
Hitchcock, Sterling 155
Hocking, Denny 76
Hoeme, Steve 198
Hoffman, Trevor 199
Hoiles, Chris 11
Holbert, Ray 76
Hollandsworth, Todd 108
Hollins, Damon 108
Hollins, Dave 62
Hollins, Jesse 199
Holman, Brad 199
Holmes, Darren 199
Holt, Chris 155
Holzemer, Mark 155
Honeycutt, Rick 199
Hope, John 155
Horn, Sam 28
Horne, Tyrone 109
Hosey, Dwayne 109
Howard, Dave 46
Howard, Thomas 109
Howe, Steve 199
Howitt, Dann 109
Hrbek, Kent 29
Hughes, Keith 109
Hughes, Troy 109
Huisman, Rich 155

Hulett, Tim 62
Hulse, David 109
Hundley, Todd 11
Hunter, Brian 29, 109
Huskey, Butch 62
Hutton, Mark 156
Hyers, Tim 29

I

Ignasiak, Mike 199
Ilsley, Blaise 156
Incavaglia, Pete 110
Innis, Jeff 199
Isringhausen, Jason 156

J

Jackson, Bo 110
Jackson, Danny 156
Jackson, Darrin 110
Jackson, Mike 200
Jaha, John 29
James, Dion 110
Jarvis, Kevin 156
Javier, Stan 110
Jean, Domingo 156
Jefferies, Gregg 29
Jensen, Marcus 12
Jeter, Derek 76
Jiminez, Miguel 156
Johnson, Brian 12
Johnson, Charles 12
Johnson, Howard 62
Johnson, Lance 110
Johnson, Randy 157
Johnstone, John 200
Jones, Bobby 157
Jones, Calvin 200
Jones, Chipper 77
Jones, Chris 111
Jones, Doug 200
Jones, Motor-Boat 111
Jones, Tim 77
Jones, Todd 200
Jordan, Brian 111
Jordan, Kevin 46
Jordan, Ricky 30
Jorgensen, Terry 63
Jose, Felix 111
Joyner, Wally 29
Juday, Bob 46

Juden, Jeff 157
Justice, David 111

K

Kamieniecki, Scott 157
Kapano, Corey 63
Karkovice, Ron 12
Karl, Scott 157
Karp, Ryan 158
Karros, Eric 30
Karsay, Steve 158
Keling, Korey 158
Kelly, Mike 111
Kelly, Pat 46
Kelly, Roberto 111
Kent, Jeff 47
Kessinger, Keith 77
Key, Jimmy 158
Kile, Darryl 158
Kilgus, Paul 200
King, Andre 112
King, Jeff 63
King, Kevin 201
Kirby, Wayne 112
Kirkreit, Daron 158
Klesko, Ryan 30
Knoblauch, Chuck 47
Knorr, Randy 12
Knudsen, Kurt 201
Koelling, Brian 47
Kotes, Chris 201
Kreuter, Chad 12
Krivda, Rick 159
Krueger, Bill 201
Kruk, John 30

L

Laker, Tim 12
Lampkin, Tom 13
Lancaster, Les 201
Langston, Mark 159
Lankford, Ray 112
Lansing, Mike 63
Larkin, Andy 159
Larkin, Barry 77
Larkin, Gene 112
LaValliere, Mike 13
Lawton, Matt 112
Leary, Tim 159
Lee, Derek 112

Lee, Manuel 77
Leftwich, Phil 160
Leiber, Jon 160
Leibrandt, Charlie 159
Leiter, Mark 160
Lemke, Mark 47
Leskanic, Curt 160
Lewis, Darren 112
Lewis, Mark 77
Lewis, Richie 201
Lewis, Scott 201
Lewis, T.R. 30
Lieberthal, Mike 13
Lilliquist, Derek 201
Lima, Jose 160
Limbach, Chris 202
Lind, Jose 47
Lindeman, John 31
Lindsey, Doug 13
Lira, Felipe 160
Liriano. Nelson 78
Listach, Pat 78
Lister, Marty 202
Litton, Greg 113
Livingstone, Scott 63
Lloyd, Graeme 202
Lockhart, Keith 63
Lofton, Kenny 113
Longmire, Tony 113
Looney, Brian 161
Lopez, Albie 161
Lopez, Javy 13
Lopez, Luis 47
Lovullo, torey 47
Lowery, Terrell 113
Luebbers, Larry 161
Luke, Matt 113
Luzinski, Ryan 13
Lydy, Scott 113

M

Maas, Kevin 31
Macfarlane, Mike 13
Mack, Shane 113
Maddux, Greg 161
Maddux, Mike 202
Magadan, Dave 63
Magnante, Mike 161
Magrane, Joe 161

Mahomes, Pat 161
Maksudian, Mike 31
Malave, Jose 114
Maldonado, Candy 114
Manahan, Anthony 47
Manto, Jeff 64
Manwaring, Kirt 14
Marrero, Oreste 31
Martin, Al 114
Martin, Chris 78
Martin, Norberto 48
Martinez, Carlos 64
Martinez, Dave 114
Martinez, Denny 162
Martinez, Domingo 31
Martinez, Edgar 64
Martinez, Pedro 162, 202
Martinez, Pedro A. 202
Martinez, Ramon 78, 162
Martinez, Tino 31
Masse, Billy 114
Mattingly, Don 31
Mauser, Tim 202
May, Darryl 162
May, Derrick 114
Mayne, Brent 14
McCarty, Dave 32
McCaskill, Kirk 162
McConnell, Chad 114
McDavid, Ray 114
McDonald, Ben 163
McDowell, Jack 163
McElroy, Chuck 202
McFarlin, Jason 115
McGee, Willie 115
McGehee, Kevin 203
McGinnis, Russ 64
McGriff, Fred 32
McGuire, Ryan 32
McGwire, Mark 32
McIntosh, Tim 14
McKnight, Jeff 48
McLemore, Mark 115
McMichael, Greg 203
McNabb, Buck 115
McNeely, Jeff 115
McRae, Brian 115
McReynolds, Kevin 116
Meacham, Rusty 203

Meares, Pat 78
Mejia, Roberto 48
Melendez, Jose 203
Mendoza, Rey 164
Merced, Orlando 116
Mercedes, Luis 116
Merchant, Mark 116
Mercker, Kent 203
Mesa, Jose 164
Miceli, Danny 204
Mieske, Matt 116
Milchin, Mike 204
Miller, Brent 33
Miller, Keith 64
Miller, Kurt 164
Miller, Orlando 78
Milligan, Randy 33
Mills, Alan 204
Mimbs, Mark 204
Minchey, Nate 164
Minor, Blas 204
Miranda, Angel 164
Mitchell, Kevin 116
Mitchell, Larry 165
Mitello, Sam 164
Mlicki, Dave 165
Moler, Jason 14
Mondesi, Raul 116
Monteleone, Rick 204
Montgomery, Jeff 204
Montgomery, Ray 117
Montgomery, Steve 205
Montoyo, Charlie 48
Moody, Richie 205
Moore, Kerwin 117
Moore, Marcus 205
Moore, Mike 117, 165
Moore, Vince 117
Morandini, Mickey 48
Mordecai, Mike 78
Morgan, Mike 165
Morman, Alvin 165
Morris, Hal 33
Morris, Jack 165
Mota, Gary 117
Mottola, Chad 117
Mouton, James 48
Moyer, Jamie 166
Mulholland, Terry 166

Munoz, Bobby 205
Munoz, Mike 205
Munoz, Orlando 48
Munoz, Oscar 166
Munoz, Pedro 117
Murphy, Rob 205
Murray, Calvin 118
Murray, Eddie 33
Murray, Glenn 118
Murray, Matt 166
Musset, Jose 205
Mussina, Mike 166
Mutis, Jeff 167
Myers, Greg 14
Myers, Randy 205
Mysel, Dave 167

N

Nabholz, Chris 167
Naehring, Tim 48
Nagy, Charles 167
Natal, Bob 14
Navarro, Jaime 167
Navarro, Tito 78
Neagle, Denny 206
Neal, Mike 79
Neel, Troy 33
Nelson, Gene 206
Nelson, Jeff 206
Nen, Robb 167
Nevin, Phil 64
Newfield, Marc 118
Newson, Warren 118
Nied, David 168
Nielsen, Jerry 206
Nieves, Melvin 118
Nilsson, Dave 14
Nixon, Otis 118
Nokes, Matt 14
Novoa, Rafael 168
Nunez, Edwin 206

O

O'Brien, Charlie 15
O'Donoghue, Orioles 207
O'Leary, Troy 119
O'Neill, Paul 119
Obando, Sherman 119
Ochoa, Alex 119
Offerman, Jose 79

Ogea, Chad 168
Ojeda, Bobby 168
Olerud, John 33
Oliva, Jose 64
Olivares, Omar 207
Oliver, Darren 207
Oliver, Joe 15
Olson, Greg 15
Olson, Gregg 207
Oquendo, Jose 79
Oquist, Mike 207
Orie, Kevin 79
Orosco, Jesse 207
Orsulak, Joe 119
Ortiz, Junior 15
Ortiz, Luis 65
Orton, John 15
Osborne, Donovan 168
Osteen, Gavin 168
Osuna, Al 208
Owen, Spike 79
Owens, Jayhawk 15

P

Pagliarulo, Mike 65
Pagnozzi, Tom 15
Palmeiro, Orlando 119
Palmeiro, Rafael 34
Palmer, Dean 65
Pappas, Erik 15
Paquette, Craig 65
Parks, Derek 15
Parra, Jose 169
Parrett, Jeff 208
Pasqua, Dan 119
Patterson, Jeff 208
Patterson, John 49
Pavlik, Roger 169
Peltier, Dan 119
Pemberton, Rudy 120
Pena, Geronimo 49
Pena, Tony 16
Pendleton, Terry 65
Pennington, Brad 208
Pennyfeather, William 120
Percival, Troy 208
Perez, Cesar 208
Perez, Eduardo 65
Perez, Melido 169

Perez, Mike 208
Perry, Gerald 34
Petagine, Roberto 34
Petralli, Geno 16
Phillips, J.R. 34
Phillips, Tony 49, 209
Piazza, Mike 16
Pichardo, Hipolito 169
Pierce, Jeff 209
Pirkl, Greg 34
Pittsley, Jim 169
Plantenberg, Eric 209
Plantier, Phil 120
Plesac, Dan 209
Plough, Clyde 35
Plunk, Eric 209
Polonia, Luis 120
Poole, Jim 209
Portugal, Mark 169
Posada, Jorge 16
Pose, Scott 120
Powell, Dennis 209
Powell, Jay 170
Powell, Ross 170
Pozo, Arquimedez 49
Prager, Howard 35
Pratt, Todd 16
Pricher, John 209
Pride, Curtis 120
Prince, Tom 16
Pritchett, Chris 35
Puckett, Kirby 120
Pugh, Tim 170
Pulsipher, Bill 170

Q
Quantrill, Paul 209
Quintana, Carlos 121

R
Radinsky, Scott 210
Raines, Tim 121
Ramirez, Manny 121
Randa, Joe 66
Rapp, Pat 170
Ready, Randy 49
Reardon, Jeff 210
Reboulet, Jeff 79
Reed, Jeff 16
Reed, Jody 49

Reed, Steve 210
Reese, Calvin 79
Reimer, Kevin 121
Renteria, Edgar 80
Renteria, Rich 49
Reyes, Carlos 210
Reynolds, Harold 49
Reynolds, Shane 171
Rhodes, Arthur 171
Rhodes, Karl 121
Ricci, Chuck 210
Richey, Jeff 210
Ridenour, Dana 171
Rijo, Jose 171
Ripken, Billy 50
Ripken, Cal 80
Risley, Bill 211
Rivera, Ben 171
Rivera, Luis 80
Rivera, Ruben 122
Roberson, Kevin 122
Roberts, Bip 50
Roberts, Chris 172
Rodriguez, Felix 172
Rodriguez, Frankie 172
Rodriguez, Henry 122
Rodriguez, Ivan 17
Rodriguez, Rich 211
Rogers, Kenny 172
Rogers, Kevin 211
Rojas, Mel 211
Roper, John 172
Rossy, Rico 50
Rowland, Rich 17
Royer, Stan 66
Rueter, Kirk 172
Ruffcorn, Scott 172
Ruffin, Bruce 211
Ruffin, Johnny 211
Rupp, Brian 80
Russell, Jeff 211
Ryan, Ken 212

S
Sabo, Chris 66
Salkeld, Roger 173
Salmon, Tim 122
Sampen, Bill 212
Samuel, Juan 50

Sanchez, Rey 80
Sandberg, Ryne 50
Sanders, Deion 122
Sanders, Reggie 122
Sanders, Scott 173
Sanders, Tracy 123
Sanderson, Scott 173
Santana, Julio 212
Santana, Ruben 50
Santiago, Benito 17
Sasser, Mackey 123
Satre, Jason 173
Saunders, Tony 212
Sax, Steve 123
Scanlan, Bob 212
Scarsone, Steve 50
Schall, Gene 35
Schilling, Curt 173
Schofield, Duckie 80
Schullstrom, Erik 174
Schutz, Carl 212
Schwab, Chris 123
Schwartz, Jeff 212
Scott, Tim 212
Seanez, Rudy 213
Sefcik, Kevin 50
Segui, David 35
Seitzer, Kevin 66
Sele, Aaron 174
Seminara, Frank 174
Servais, Scott 17
Service, Scott 213
Sharperson, Mike 51
Shaw, Jeff 213
Sheffield, Gary 66
Shepherd, Keith 213
Shields, Tommy 81
Shifflett, Steve 213
Shipley, Craig 81
Shuey, Paul 213
Shumpert, Terry 51
Sierra, Ruben 123
Silva, Jose 174
Simms, Mike 123
Simonton, Benji 123
Skeels, Mark 17
Slocumb, Heathcliff 213
Smiley, John 175
Smith, Bubba 35

Smith, Dan 175
Smith, Dwight 123
Smith, Lee 213
Smith, Ozzie 81
Smith, Pete 175
Smith, Zane 175
Smoltz, John 175
Snow, J.T. 35
Snyder, Cory 124
Soderstrom, Steve 175
Sojo, Luis 51
Sorrento, Paul 36
Sosa, Sammy 124
Spehr, Tim 17
Spencer, Shane 124
Spiers, Bill 51
Spoljaric, Paul 176
Spradlin, Jerry 214
Sprague, Ed 67
Springer, Russ 176
Stahoviak, Scott 67
Stankiewicz, Andy 51
Stanley, Mike 17
Stanton, Mike 214
Staton, Dave 36
Steinbach, Terry 18
Stewart, Dave 176
Stillwell, Kurt 81
Stocker, Kevin 81
Stottlemyre, Todd 176
Strange, Doug 51
Strawberry, Darryl 124
Strickland, Erick 124
Suppan, Jeff 176
Surhoff, B.J. 67
Sutcliffe, Rick 176
Suzuki, Makato 214
Sweeney, Mark 124
Swift, Billy 176
Swindell, Greg 177

T
Talemaco, Amaury 177
Tanana, Frank 177
Tapani, Kevin 177
Tarasco, Tony 125
Tartabull, Danny 125
Taubensee, Eddie 18
Tavarez, Jesus 125

Tavarez, Julian 177
Taylor, Billy 214
Taylor, Brien 178
Taylor, Sam 125
Taylor, Scott 214
Tettleton, Mickey 18
Teufel, Tim 51
Tewksbury, Bob 178
Therrien, Dominic 67
Thigpen, Bobby 214
Thobe, J.J. 178
Thomas, Frank 36
Thome, Jim 67
Thompson, Justin 178
Thompson, Mark 178
Thompson, Milt 125
Thompson, Robby 51
Thompson, Ryan 125
Thon, Dickie 81
Timlin, Mike 214
Tingley, Ron 18
Tinsley, Lee 126
Toale, John 36
Tomlin, Randy 178
Torres, Paul 36
Torres, Salomon 179
Trachsel, Steve 179
Trammell, Alan 81
Tranberg, Mark 179
Treadway, Jeff 67
Trinidad, Hector 179
Trlicek, Rick 215
Trombley, Mike 215
Tucker, Mike 52
Turang, Brian 126
Turner, Chris 18
Turner, Matt 215
Tyler, Brad 52

U
Urbina, Ugueth 179

V
Valdes, Marc 180
Valdez, Sergio 215
Valentin, John 82
Valentin, Jose 82
Valle, Dave 18
Van Poppel, Todd 180
Van Slyke, Andy 126

VanderWal, John 37
VanRyn, Ben 180
Vaughn, Greg 126
Vaughn, Mo 36
Velarde, Randy 82
Velasquez, Guillermo 37
Ventura, Robin 67
Veras, Quilvio 52
Vidros, Jose 52
Villone, Ron 180
Viola, Frank 180
Vitiello, Joe 37
Vizcaino, Jose 82
Vizquel, Omar 82
Vosberg, Ed 215

W
Wade, Terrell 181
Wagner, Billy 181
Wagner, Paul 181
Wakefield, Tim 181
Walbeck, Matt 18
Walk, Bob 181
Walker, Chico 52
Walker, Larry 126
Walker, Pete 215
Wallace, B.J. 182
Wallach, Tim 68
Walton, Bruce 215
Ward, Duane 216
Ward, Turner 126
Warner, Mike 127
Wasdin, Jason 182
Watson, Allen 182
Watson, Ron 215
Weathers, David 182
Wedge, Eric 19
Wegman, Bill 182
Wegmann, Tom 216
Weinke, Chris 37
Weiss, Walt 82
Welch, Bob 182
Wells, David 183
Wendell, Turk 183
Wertz, Bill 216
West, David 216
Wetteland, John 216
Whisenant, Matt 183
Whitaker, Lou 52

White, Derrick 37
White, Devon 127
White, Gabe 183
White, Jimmy 127
White, Rondell 127
Whitehurst, Wally 183
Whiten, Mike 127
Whiteside, Matt 216
Whitmore, Darrell 127
Whitten, Casey 183
Wickander, Kevin 217
Wickman, Bob 183
Wilkins, Rick 19
Williams, Bernie 128
Williams, George 68
Williams, Glenn 82
Williams, Matt 68
Williams, Mike 184, 217
Williams, Mitch 217
Williamson, Mark 217
Willie, Wilson 128
Willis, Carl 217
Wilson, Brandon 83
Wilson, Dan 19
Wilson, Nigel 128
Wilson, Preston 68
Wilson, Steve 217
Wilson, Tom 19
Wilson, Trevor 184
Wimmer, Chris 52
Winfield, Dave 128
Witasick, Gerald 184
Witt, Bobby 184
Witt, Mike 184
Wohlers, Mark 218
Wolak, Jerry 128
Wolff, Mike 128
Womack, Tony 83
Wood, Ted 129
Woodson, Tracy 68
Worrell, Tim 184
Worrell, Todd 218
Wunsch, Kelly 184

Y
Yaughn, Kip 184
Yelding, Eric 53
Young, Anthony 218
Young, Dmitri 37
Young, Eric 53
Young, Kevin 38
Young, Pete 218
Yount, Robin 129

Z
Zeile, Todd 68
Zinter, Alan 38
Zosky, Eddie 83
Zupcic, Bob 129